NEW!

 Achieve

for *Clinical Psychology*

Engaging Every Student.	Supporting Every Instructor.	Setting the New Standard for Teaching and Learning.

Achieve for *Clinical Psychology* sets a whole new standard for integrating **assessments**, **activities**, and **analytics** into your teaching. It brings together features that instructors and students loved about our previous platform, LaunchPad — interactive e-book, practice quizzing, and other assessments, interactive learning activities, extensive instructor resources — in a powerful new platform that offers:

- A clean, intuitive, mobile-friendly interface.
- Powerful analytics.
- Self-regulated learning and goal-setting surveys.
- iClicker classroom questions are available for each unit or the option to integrate your own.
- A video collection for *Clinical Psychology*!

Our resources were **co-designed with instructors and students,** on a foundation of *years* of **learning research**, and rigorous testing over multiple semesters. The result is superior content, organization, and functionality. Achieve's pre-built assignments engage students both *inside* and *outside of class*. And Achieve is effective for students of *all levels* of motivation and preparedness, whether they are high achievers or need extra support.

Macmillan Learning offers **deep platform integration** of Achieve with all LMS providers, including Blackboard, Brightspace, Canvas, and Moodle. With integration, students can access course content and their grades through one sign-in. And you can pair Achieve with course tools from your LMS, such as discussion boards and chat and Gradebook functionality. LMS integration is also available with Inclusive Access. For more information, visit MacmillanLearning.com/College/US/Solutions/LMS-Integration or talk to your local sales representative.

Achieve was built with accessibility in mind. Macmillan Learning strives to create products that are usable by all learners and meet universally applied accessibility standards. In addition to addressing product compatibility with assistive technologies such as screen reader software, alternative keyboard devices, and voice recognition products, we are working to ensure that the content and platforms we provide are fully accessible. For more information visit https://www.macmillanlearning.com/college/us/our-story/accessibility

Mobile: Based on user data, we know that lots of students use parts of Achieve on a **mobile** device. As such, activities such as e-book readings and videos are easily used across devices with different screen sizes.

Achieve for *Clinical Psychology*:   Assessments

Practice Quizzes

Practice Quizzes mirror the experience of a quiz or test, with questions that are similar but distinct from those in the test bank. Instructors can use the quizzes as is or create their own.

E-book

Macmillan Learning's e-book is an interactive version of the textbook that offers highlighting, bookmarking, and note-taking. Built-in, low-stakes self-assessments allow students to test their level of understanding along the way, and learn even more in the process thanks to the *testing effect*. Students can download the e-book to read offline, or to have it read aloud to them. Achieve allows instructors to assign chapter sections as homework.

Test Bank

The test bank for *Clinical Psychology* offers over 1600 questions, all meticulously reviewed. Instructors can assign out-of-the-box exams or create their own by:

- Choosing from hundreds of questions in our database.
- Filtering questions by type, topic, difficulty, and Bloom's level.
- Customizing multiple-choice questions.
- Integrating their own questions into the exam.

Exam/Quiz results report to a Gradebook that lets instructors monitor student progress individually and classwide.

Achieve for *Clinical Psychology*:   Activities

Achieve is designed to support and encourage active learning by connecting familiar activities and practices out of class with some of the most effective and approachable in-class activities, curated from a variety of active learning sources.

Video Collection for *Clinical Psychology*

This collection offers classic as well as contemporary clips from high-quality sources, with original content to support *Clinical Psychology*, Ninth Edition.

Accompanying assessment makes these videos assignable, with results reporting to the Achieve Gradebook. Our faculty and student consultants were instrumental in helping us create this diverse and engaging set of clips. All videos are closed-captioned and found only in **Achieve**.

Immersive Learning Activities

Focusing on student engagement, these immersive learning activities invite students to apply what they are learning, consider various clinical perspectives, or think critically about what they have read.

Clinical Perspectives A collection of podcasts by a diverse group of clinical psychologists asks students to evaluate and apply what they learned from the text and the podcasts.

Achieve for *Clinical Psychology*: Analytics

Achieve's **Innovation Lab** offers surveys that help students self-direct, and develop confidence in, their own learning:

- The **Intro Survey** asks students to consider their goals for the class and how they plan to manage their time and learning strategies.
- **Checkpoint surveys** ask students to reflect on what's been working and where they need to make changes.
- **Each completed survey generates a report** that reveals how each student is doing, beyond the course grade.

These tools help instructors engage their students in a discussion on soft skills, such as metacognition, effective learning and time management strategies, and other non-cognitive skills that impact student success.

Additional Instructor Resources in Achieve: All Within One Place

Image Slides and Tables

Presentation slides feature chapter photos, illustrations, and tables and can be used as is or customized to fit an instructor's needs. Alt text for images is available upon request via WebAccessibility@Macmillan.com

Instructor's Resource Manuals

Downloadable PDF manuals include a range of resources, such as chapter outlines or summaries, teaching tips, discussion starters, sample syllabi, assignment suggestions, and classroom activities.

Lecture Slides

Accessible, downloadable presentation slides provide support for key concepts and themes from the text and can be used as is or customized to fit an instructor's needs.

Customer Support

Our Achieve Client Success Team—dedicated platform experts—provides collaboration, software expertise, and consulting to tailor each course to fit your instructional goals and student needs. Start with a demo at a time that works for you to learn more about how to set up your customized course. Talk to your sales representative or visit https://www.macmillanlearning.com/college/us/contact-us /training-and-demos for more information.

Pricing and bundling options are available at the Macmillan student store: store.macmillanlearning.com/

CLINICAL PSYCHOLOGY

A Scientific, Multicultural, and Life Span Perspective

NINTH EDITION

CLINICAL PSYCHOLOGY

A Scientific, Multicultural, and Life Span Perspective

NINTH EDITION

JONATHAN S. ABRAMOWITZ

University of North Carolina at Chapel Hill

MITCHELL J. PRINSTEIN

University of North Carolina at Chapel Hill and Chief Science Officer of the
American Psychological Association

TIMOTHY J. TRULL

University of Missouri-Columbia

worth publishers

Macmillan Learning

New York

Executive Vice President, General Manager: Charles Linsmeier
Vice President, Social Sciences and High School: Shani Fisher
Senior Executive Program Manager: Christine M. Cardone
Senior Developmental Editor: Valerie Raymond
Editorial Assistant: Olivia Madigan
Executive Marketing Manager: Katherine Nurre
Marketing Assistant: Claudia Cruz
Senior Media Editor: Lauren Samuelson
Media Project Manager: Brian Nobile
Senior Director, Content Management Enhancement: Tracey Kuehn
Senior Managing Editor: Lisa Kinne
Lead Content Project Manager: Won McIntosh
Copyeditor: Sarah Wales-McGrath
Senior Project Manager: Aravinda Doss, Lumina Datamatics, Inc.
Executive Permissions Editor: Cecilia Varas
Photo Researcher: Krystyna Borgen, Lumina Datamatics, Inc.
Text Permissions Editor: Michael McCarty
Director of Design, Content Management: Diana Blume
Senior Design Services Manager: Natasha A. S. Wolfe
Senior Design Manager, Cover Design: John Callahan
Interior Designer: Tamara Newnam
Senior Workflow Project Manager: Paul Rohloff
Production Supervisor: Robert Cherry
Art Manager: Matthew McAdams
Composition: Lumina Datamatics, Inc.
Printing and Binding: Transcontinental
Rock Design Elements: Garsya/Shutterstock; DSBfoto/Shutterstock
Chapter Opening Image: Peter Cade/Getty Images

Library of Congress Control Number: 2022934124

ISBN-13: 978-1-319-24572-6 (Paperback)
ISBN-10: 1-319-24572-2 (Paperback)
ISBN-13: 978-1-319-42977-5 (Loose-leaf Edition)
ISBN-10: 1-319-42977-7 (Loose-leaf Edition)
ISBN-13: 978-1-319-44288-0 (International Edition)
ISBN-10: 1-319-44288-9 (International Edition)

Printed in Canada

1 2 3 4 5 6   27 26 25 24 23 22

Worth Publishers
120 Broadway
New York, NY 10271
www.macmillanlearning.com

Dedication

We dedicate this book to our students, who challenge us to be the best we can be.

About the Authors

Jonathan S. Abramowitz is Professor of Psychology and Neuroscience, and Director of Clinical Training at the University of North Carolina at Chapel Hill (UNC-CH). He also serves as Director of the UNC-CH Anxiety Clinic. Jon earned his PhD in clinical psychology at the University of Memphis in 1998 and has been at UNC-CH since 2006. His research and clinical interests focus on anxiety and related disorders, including obsessive-compulsive disorder (OCD), and he has received international recognition, honors, and awards for his scientific, clinical, and professional contributions in these areas. Most recently, he was awarded the University of North Carolina Faculty Award for Excellence in Doctoral Mentoring. Working with many students and collaborators, he has published over 300 research articles, book chapters, encyclopedia entries, and books. Jon served as President of the Association for Behavioral and Cognitive Therapy (ABCT) from 2015 to 2016 and founded (and served as the first Editor-in-Chief of) the *Journal of Obsessive-Compulsive and Related Disorders*. His previous positions include Assistant/Associate Professor at the Mayo Clinic and Mayo School of Medicine (2000-2006), and Postdoctoral Fellow and Instructor at the University of Pennsylvania (1999–2000).

Dr. Mitchell J. Prinstein is the Chief Science Officer of the American Psychological Association and John Van Seters Distinguished Professor of Psychology and Neuroscience at the University of North Carolina at Chapel Hill. For over 25 years, Mitch's research has examined interpersonal models of internalizing symptoms and health risk behaviors among adolescents, with a specific focus on the unique role of on- and off-line peer relationships in the developmental psychopathology of depression and self-injury. He has published over 150 peer-reviewed papers and 9 books, including graduate volumes on assessment and treatment in clinical child and adolescent psychology, a set of encyclopedias on adolescent development, and the acclaimed trade book, *Popular: Finding Happiness and Success in a World That Cares Too Much About the Wrong Kinds of Relationships*. He is a past Editor for the *Journal of Clinical Child and Adolescent Psychology*, a past-president of the Society for the Science of Clinical Psychology and the Society of Clinical Child and Adolescent Psychology, and served on the Board of Directors of the American Psychological Association. Mitch has received several national and university-based awards recognizing his contributions to research, classroom instruction, for professional development training, as a mentor, and for his national contributions to education and training at the local, state, and national level. Mitch and his work have been featured in over 200 pieces in The *New York Times*, The *Wall Street Journal*, National Public Radio, the *Los Angeles Times*, CNN, *U.S. News & World Report*, *Time* magazine, *New York* magazine, *Newsweek*, Reuters, *Family Circle*, *Real Simple*, All Things Considered, and in two TEDx talks.

Dr. Timothy J. Trull is the Curator's Professor of Psychological Sciences and Byler Distinguished Professor at the University of Missouri–Columbia. He enjoys teaching a variety of courses in clinical psychology, particularly Introduction to Psychopathology and Introduction to Clinical Psychology, as well as supervising clinical psychology graduate students in their research, assessment, and clinical work. Tim earned his MA and PhD in clinical psychology at the University of Kentucky. Tim publishes much of his research in the *Journal of Abnormal Psychology* (now called *Journal of Psychopathology and Clinical Science*), *Psychological Assessment*, and the *Journal of Personality Disorders*. Sponsored through grants from the National Institute of Health, the National Institute on Alcohol Abuse and Alcoholism, and the Borderline Personality Disorder Research Foundation, his research projects include evaluating etiological models of borderline personality disorder, exploring the relations between personality disorders and substance use disorders, assessing genetic and environmental influences on personality and psychopathology, and using ambulatory assessment in clinical psychology. In addition to his work at the university, Tim is a member of the scientific faculty at the Missouri Center for Addiction Research and Engagement (MOCARE) and is a practicing clinical psychologist. He has won a number of awards that include Outstanding Alumnus, University of Kentucky; the Graduate Faculty Mentoring Award, University of Missouri; the Robert S. Daniels Junior Faculty Teaching Award; and the Psi Chi Professor of the Year. Tim is a Fellow of the American Psychological Association and the Association for Psychological Science.

Brief Contents

Contents

Preface

We're thrilled that you've picked up the ninth edition of *Clinical Psychology*! It's been about a decade since the eighth edition was published, and to put it mildly, the world is a different place than it was in 2013—and so is the field of clinical psychology! For one thing, the COVID-19 pandemic has affected the daily routines; social and family lives; and work, school, and leisure activities of practically everyone on Earth. It's also led to increases in psychological distress and created unprecedented demands for mental health services. As clinical psychologists, we've been challenged to develop new and creative methods of remotely providing assessment and treatment; conducting research; and performing teaching, training, and supervision activities. Sadly, the pandemic has also amplified disparities in risk, resilience, and resources among people of different backgrounds. These realities compel us to integrate the impacts of COVID-19 within our new edition of the textbook.

Extraordinary world events and social movements have also unfolded in recent years that remind us of something we already knew, but not profoundly enough—substantial inequalities exist when it comes to psychological wellness because of race and ethnicity, gender and gender identity, sexual orientation, socioeconomic standing, geographical location, victimization, and the like. Accordingly, clinical psychological practitioners and researchers must gain a firmer grasp of multicultural issues and how we can reduce these inequities on both an individual and a systemic level. To be sure, previous editions of *Clinical Psychology* have reckoned with these topics. Yet in this new edition, you will find that we have substantially increased our attention to research-supported societal, multicultural, and economic factors and how they impact all areas of the field.

Given these major happenings, along with a decade's worth of advances all across our field, it is safe to say that the ninth edition of *Clinical Psychology* is more of an "overhaul" than a simple "update" of past editions. Of course, as in the past, a bedrock of the new edition is a clinical science perspective. In representing the full scope of the field, for example, we highlight the strengths and limitations of different points of view based on empirical evidence. The book also reflects a life-span approach and includes a broad focus both on youth and adult populations.

So, what *specifically* is new and improved about the ninth edition? One major change you'll notice is that Jonathan Abramowitz, PhD, has joined the author team. Recognized for his accomplishments and contributions as a clinician, researcher, and educator, Jon brings additional experience, expertise, and perspectives to this edition. As the lead author, Jon has helped us approach the coverage and presentation of subject matter as if writing a completely new book. For example, we've reduced the number of chapters (and realigned them) to make the text more suitable to a semester course. We've also reduced the length of each chapter to make the content more manageable and accessible for students. And you will notice the addition of colorful photos, flashy tables and figures, as well as abundant active learning features to engage students and help them apply key concepts. We also cover the DSM-5-TR.

Let us specifically call your attention to these novel features that we've added within each chapter:

Integrated case material. Readers follow two clients—Shane (a child) and Kiara (an adult)—across chapters, and often highlighted in *In Practice* boxes, as they (and their families) initiate clinical services, progress through evidence-based assessment, diagnosis, and case formulation, and receive empirically supported treatment. Their cases, as well as many other examples, are used to help the reader more deeply understand the work of clinical psychologists and the experiences of clients at each of these stages.

Embedded history highlights. In response to feedback and suggestions, we have eliminated the less popular *Historical Overview of Clinical Psychology* chapter (formerly Chapter 2). In its place, we have added concise *In Historical Perspective* boxes within the chapters that highlight key chronological events and provide a historical context in which to consider the present state of each area of the field.

End of chapter exercises. The end of each chapter includes suggested activities called *Applying What You've Learned* (e.g., use Beck's ABC model to conceptualize a case of depression in a 29-year-old man who has just had a relationship break-up [from Chapter 12, *Cognitive-Behavioral Interventions*]). These give students the opportunity to put into practice what they've just been reading about. We hope instructors will incorporate these exercises into classroom lectures or demonstrations (some involve group work) or assign them for completion outside of class.

Think Like a Clinical Psychologist questions. At multiple points within each chapter, we have included thought questions to spark critical thinking about portions of the text (e.g., How do you define a psychological problem, and how is your definition shaped by your values and cultural background? [from Chapter 9, *Diagnosis, Case Formulation, and Treatment Planning*]). There are over 50 such questions throughout the textbook to stimulate classroom discussion or to serve as essay questions for completion outside of class.

Focus questions, chapter outlines, and key words. Each chapter is preceded by a set of *Focus Questions* and a concise *Chapter Outline* to give the reader a sense of what to keep in mind as they move forward. Notable *Key Terms* appear in **boldface** type within the text and are listed, along with their definitions, at the end of each chapter.

Of course, with our efforts to re-envision the book's organization and presentation, we have not overlooked its content! The following are highlights of the book's up-to-date coverage of the field:

New edition, new material. For the ninth edition, we have added new chapters on professional issues (Chapter 2, *Who Is a Clinical Psychologist?*), ethics (e.g., confidentiality, ethical dilemmas; Chapter 3, *Ethics in Clinical Psychology*), as well as the science of assessment (Chapter 4, *Psychological Assessment: Science and Practice*) and the science of psychological treatment (Chapter 10, *Psychological Treatment: Science and Practice*). Within every chapter there is updated content to reflect cutting-edge research findings and other developments, as well as *A Closer Look* boxes to highlight current controversies and hot topics in the field. Among the many areas covered are new sections of material on licensing laws and telehealth; the use of technology and telehealth in assessment and treatment; updated versions of personality and intelligence tests; new perspectives on the concept of abnormality; coverage of the new DSM-5-TR (published in March 2022); critical thinking about the DSM classification system, psychiatric diagnosis, and NIMH's RDoC initiative; coverage of APA's clinical practice guidelines and evidence-based practice; enhanced material on mindfulness and "third-wave" (e.g., acceptance and dialectical) treatments; the latest advances in behavioral medicine; and clinical psychology's interface with the law.

Enhanced and integrated coverage of multicultural issues. Consistent with the field's accelerating appreciation of the impact of ethnicity, race, poverty, gender, gender identity, sexual orientation, immigration status, and other cultural factors on psychological functioning, this edition further expands its coverage of the multicultural perspective, integrating multicultural material and research, and highlighting topics such as biases in psychological tests, the underrepresentation of racial and ethnic groups in clinical research, disparities in access to mental health care, discrimination and prejudice, and the disproportionate impact of the COVID-19 pandemic on marginalized groups. We hope this edition challenges readers to think about diversity in every chapter and to consider how our field can better reflect the entire population we hope to help. In addition, to ensure that the book is accessible to a wide range of students and presents an inclusive and sensitive picture of mental health, we performed an assessment of the images and examples and reviewed the chapters with experts who advised us on a range of issues. Even a quick look through the pages of this textbook will reveal that it truly reflects the diversity of our society and of the field of clinical psychology.

Emphasis on critical thinking. There is no shortage of debates and disagreements over various professional issues and perspectives on the conceptualization, assessment, and treatment of mental and behavioral problems. How should clinical psychologists be trained and should they prescribe medications? What is the value of personality and intelligence tests? Is there validity to the concept of mental illness? How much weight should be given to the results of neuroimaging or heritability studies? Should we consider clinical judgment over statistical prediction? We cover these and many other debates throughout the book, challenging readers to understand different perspectives and use research data to draw conclusions.

Life-span focus. Rather than reifying the misperception that clinical child and adolescent psychology is simply a subspecialty of clinical (adult) psychology, we have integrated our discussion of clinical practice with youth throughout the book, thus adopting a life-span perspective. We do so not only to recapture the manner in which our field was first conceptualized over a century ago, but also to better reflect the growing interest in clinical child and adolescent psychology among students over the past several decades. Thus, we have enhanced the coverage of how clinical psychology can be applied to both the very young and the very old. Case examples from across the life span abound in this edition to illustrate how the field has much to offer individuals at every stage of the life cycle.

When you're as passionate about a discipline as we feel about clinical psychology, writing and teaching about it (and, of course, working in it) become enjoyable and rewarding pursuits. We hope our enthusiasm is evident in the pages of this text. Our field has never played as crucial a role in society as it does today, and this role will only grow in the years to come. We believe the ninth edition of *Clinical Psychology* is the ideal textbook for introducing undergraduates to our field's professional issues and ethics, research methods, and evidence-based approaches to assessment and intervention — all with the critical backdrop of cultural sensitivity and a life-span perspective. We hope you will agree.

Resources for Teaching and Learning

We are delighted to have a full suite of resources to accompany *Clinical Psychology, Ninth Edition*.

For Professors

Video Collection for *Clinical Psychology*

This video series offers contemporary clips on various clinical interventions, psychopathologies, research and treatments, including videos on current topics such as: the psychological impact of COVID-19; pandemic-related telemental health approaches; mental health apps and wearables; relationships between race, mental health, and treatment; mindfulness-based interventions; acceptance and commitment, and more. These cutting-edge videos are available in **Achieve**.

Instructor's Resource Manual This comprehensive guide includes detailed chapter outlines, focus questions, ideas for lectures, classroom activities, rubric for open-ended Applying What You Know questions from the book and grading rubrics. Finally, it includes a comprehensive set of valuable materials that can be obtained from outside sources — items such as relevant feature films, documentaries, teaching references, and Internet sites related to clinical psychology.

Lecture Slides Each chapter comes with a ready-to-use set of lecture slides for easy lecture preparation. These slides focus on key concepts and themes from the text as well as in-class discussion questions. They can be used as is or customized to fit a professor's needs. Also included are image slides for all of the chapter photos, illustrations, and tables.

iClicker Questions

iClicker allows you to ask questions, engage students, and gauge students' understanding and opinions. A set of iClicker questions for each chapter is available in Achieve.

Assessment Tools

The **Macmillan Learning Test Bank** includes a full assortment of test items. Each chapter features over 100 questions to test students at several levels of Bloom's taxonomy. All the questions are tagged to the outcomes recommended in the *APA Guidelines for the Undergraduate Psychology Major*, Bloom's level, the book page, the chapter section, and the Focus Questions from the book.

For Students

Achieve for *Clinical Psychology*, Ninth Edition, includes the following resources:

- **Clinical Perspectives** A collection of podcasts featuring interviews with a diverse group of clinical psychologists discussing their practice and therapies. Each podcast is followed by questions for students to answer in Achieve.

- **Clinical Psychology in Practice** author-created videos provide short demonstrations of various psychological treatments and approaches.
- **Clinical Psychology Video Activities** These video activities address various topics in the text. Students first view a video and then answer a series of thought-provoking questions.
- A global certified accessible **interactive e-book** allows students to highlight, bookmark, and make their own notes, just as they would with a printed textbook.
- **Applying What You Learned questions** that students can answer and submit to their instructor are included at the end of each chapter.
- **Practice Quizzes** mirror the experience of a quiz or test, with questions that are similar but distinct from those in the test bank. Instructors can use the quizzes as is or create their own.
- **Deep integration** is available between Achieve products and Blackboard Learn, Brightspace, Canvas, Moodle, and Joule by Moodlerooms. These deep integrations offer single sign-on and Gradebook sync, and enable you to customize and manage your course.

Acknowledgments

I am grateful to Tim and Mitch for inviting me to join them in working on this exciting new edition of the book! I also thank my lucky stars for my wife and best friend, Stacy, and two wonderful daughters, Emily and Miriam. Their love and support inspire me every day, and I cannot imagine a better family with whom to share the many months "stuck" inside as COVID-19 raged! I am also thankful to my wonderful mentors who have shared with me their wisdom and enthusiasm, shaping me into the clinician and scientist I am today: Kathleen Harring, Joel Wade, Art Houts, Edna Foa, and Marty Franklin. Finally, I thank my colleagues and students at the University of North Carolina at Chapel Hill for making my work as a clinical psychologist such a fantastic journey! **(JSA)**

I am grateful every day that I was trained by Dr. Annette La Greca in graduate school and Dr. Tony Spirito on internship/postdoc; terrific mentors are hard to find, and I feel lucky that I was guided, encouraged, and inspired by two selfless leaders in the field. My work on this textbook reflects my commitment to give back to the field, and help educate a new generation of psychologists as much as I was inspired by them. I love and appreciate my wife, Tina, and my kids, Samara and Max, every day. I am grateful to Tim for inviting me to join him on the eighth edition of this textbook and to Jon for leading us so energetically through this new edition. I am especially thankful for my students who give me an opportunity to talk about the field I love every day and educate me more than I help them. **(MJP)**

First, I want to thank my co-authors Jon and Mitch who are both brilliant, energetic, and dedicated clinical psychologists. They have contributed great insights to this new edition! Second, I am truly blessed to have such a loving and supportive family (Meg, Molly, and Janey). It turns out, they are all extremely funny too! They help me achieve the kind of life-work balance that has enriched my own life. Third, my mentors and colleagues over the years have helped shape my own career and my own perspective on the field of clinical psychology. In particular, thanks go out to Kenny Sher and Tom Widiger, who both greatly influenced me. Finally, my dear friend Ray Ronci has been such an inspiration to me over the last few decades. Thank you Ray! **(TJT)**

Readers seldom appreciate that editors are the real workhorses of the publishing business. Some read manuscripts line by line, word by word, and get almost as involved in the subjects as the writers. Our Senior Executive Program Manager, Christine Cardone and development editor, Valerie Raymond cared so much about their work and this topic that they became our conscience as we wrote this book. They honed our language and presentation with the perfect blend of constructive feedback and positive reinforcement. But, Chris and Valerie are only a part of a much larger team that helped to bring this book to life. Natasha Wolfe managed creation of the text's lively and readable design. Won McIntosh and Aravinda Doss coordinated building the text from manuscript to pages, a task that's harder than it sounds. Cecilia Varas and Krystyna Borgen supplied an array of interesting photos for us to choose for the text's interior, and John Callahan designed the beautiful cover. Paul Rohloff managed the production end of the print text while Lauren Samuelson curated and launched the impressive elements of the online platform, Achieve. Matt McAdams managed the illustrations and Dorothy Tomasini, Allison Curley, and Olivia Madigan supported all aspects of the development. We give thanks to them all.

The feedback and comments from the reviewers of the chapters of this book were also extremely helpful:

Chammie Austin, *Maryville University*
Usha Barahmand, *CUNY Queens College*
Shanna Cooper, *Temple University*
Janna A. Dickenson, *PhD, LP, University of California-San Diego*
Ernestine Duncan, *Norfolk State University*
Erin Fekete, *University of Indianapolis*
Sherecce Fields, *Texas A&M University*
Allyson A. Gilles, *PhD, University of Hawaii-West Oahu*
Joseph P. Green, *Ohio State University*
Benjamin Hankin, *University of South Carolina*
Stephen N. Haynes, *California State University-Los Angeles*
Mallory Klaunig, *University of Hawaii at Manoa*
Christian D. Klein, *University of Michigan-Dearborn*
David H. Krauss, *The College of New Jersey*
John E. Kurtz, *Villanova University*
Christopher McNally, *John Carroll University*
Larry L. Mullins, *Oklahoma State University*
Stephanie Poplock, *PhD, LCSW, SUNY Oneonta*
Dr. Michael Poulakis, *University of Indianapolis*
Lisa B. Smith, *Sacred Heart University*
Kyle Stephenson, *Willamette University*
James Sullivan, *Florida State University*
Christopher Trentacosta, *Wayne State University*

We want to especially thank the following reviewers for their reviews of the chapters for diversity, equity, and inclusion:

Scott M. Debb, *Norfolk State University*
Milton A. Fuentes, *Montclair State University*

Lorenzo Lorenzo-Luaces, *Indiana University–Bloomington*
April Miley, *Alcorn State University*
Emily Kroska Thomas, *University of Iowa*
Mikhila Wildey, *Grand Valley State University*

In addition, we want to thank Barinder Bhavra for developing the Instructor's Manual and Lecture Slides and Emily Thomas and Diana Joy for developing the Test and Practice Quiz Questions. Finally, we want to thank all of the instructors that continue to use this textbook, as well as the students who take their courses. As always, we welcome your comments and suggestions regarding the book.

CHAPTER 1

Clinical Psychology in Context

FOCUS QUESTIONS

1. What are the three major themes of the textbook?
2. What distinguishes a clinical psychologist from other mental health professionals?
3. How is clinical psychology different from other fields in psychology?
4. What are the major activities of clinical psychologists?
5. How do clinical psychologists seek to integrate a diversity or multicultural perspective?

CHAPTER OUTLINE

Imagine you had a runny nose. Perhaps also a long-standing cough, with considerable wheezing, and recently you spiked a fever. If you experienced symptoms like these, you would probably schedule a trip to see a health professional, perhaps at a local urgent care center.

When you arrive for your appointment, there are a few experiences you might expect to occur. For instance, you would probably not be surprised when a trained medical professional enters the room and asks you questions about your symptoms, such as when they started and if you've had any illnesses in the past. You would also expect that person to use various instruments to measure your body temperature, heart rate, and blood pressure; and you would anticipate that someone would use a stethoscope to listen to the sound of your heartbeat and your lungs as you breathed deeply in and out.

If after such an assessment your doctor told you that you had a bacterial infection, you might expect to receive a prescription for an antibiotic medication because your doctor understands how these types of drugs fight such infections. If you were diagnosed with the flu, you may expect some antiviral medicines because your doctor knows that it is important to decrease the flu virus's ability to reproduce. Depending on your diagnosis, your doctor would also likely give you a prognosis that is based on extensive research on the effectiveness of the medication; for example, that you would likely start to see significant improvements in 24–48 hours, and if not, a second course of treatment would be recommended as a follow-up.

This all feels rather routine, right? For most of us, a bad cough, a respiratory infection, or even the flu feels somewhat unremarkable because we usually have somewhat accurate expectations of what will happen in our interactions with a health care professional, and a reasonably good idea about the approaches likely to be used to treat us. Whereas the procedures for recognition, diagnosis, assessment, and treatment are fairly uniform across the various fields of medicine, there is a great deal more inconsistency (and no shortage of disagreement and debate) when it comes to the identification of, measurement of, and interventions for mental health concerns. For one thing, as you will learn about in Chapter 9, *Diagnosis, Case Formulation, and Treatment Planning*, the very concept of mental illness, and how best to define it, is hotly debated. This being the case, *how do you know* when you're even experiencing mental health symptoms that require the help of a mental health professional? And with the dizzying array of different types of mental health workers, *who should you call on* when seeking such services for yourself or a loved one — a psychiatrist? Clinical psychologist (i.e., the focus of this text!)? Social worker? Counselor? Psychotherapist? Although these professionals (and many others not listed here) are all trained to assess and treat mental health problems, their educational backgrounds differ, as do the approaches and methods they use to identify, measure, and treat mental health problems. Therefore, another set of questions pertain to *what kinds of methods and procedures* will most accurately identify your problem and what approach to treatment will be most effective. *Have these diagnostic and treatment approaches been carefully researched* with others who have your same problem? If so, *how well do they work*, and *do we understand why* they work? If so, *what is your prognosis*, and are there any factors that might interfere with successful treatment?

In many ways, it is remarkable to consider that over the course of a 12-month period, about one in five adults and one in six children experience **mental illness** — defined as a pattern of behavior, thinking, or feeling that causes significant personal distress or interference in daily functioning (Whitney & Peterson, 2019). Yet at the same time, most people have a poor understanding of the mental health professions, including the science and practice of assessment, diagnosis, and treatment approaches. Perhaps for this reason, the U.S. surgeon general estimates that only about 41% of those needing mental health services actually get professional help over the course of a year (Satcher, 2000); and the rates are far lower in many other nations. This is a tragic outcome — a dilemma that we imagine would prompt dramatic reaction if the suffering were due to a physical ailment.

In this book, you will learn about **clinical psychology**, the psychological specialty that provides assessment and continuing comprehensive mental and behavioral health care for individuals and families; consults with agencies and communities; provides training, education, and supervision; and conducts research to inform these practices. We begin here in Chapter 1 discussing a wide range of types of mental health professionals, with a focus on what sets **clinical psychologists**' training, expertise, and approaches apart from those in related fields.

In the chapters that follow, we delve into the education that clinical psychologists receive; the diverse settings in which they work; the importance of maintaining competency throughout one's career; and the role of ethics and science within this profession. We focus on how clinical psychologists assess different aspects of their clients — including mental health symptoms and behavior, intelligence, and personality — and how they put to use the information obtained during assessments to better understand their clients and develop a treatment plan. For treatment, the emphasis is on contemporary, research-based approaches to intervention. Lastly, we cover the key subspecialties within the diverse landscape of clinical psychology.

As you read this textbook, we hope you will note a number of themes woven throughout its pages. One theme is the importance of scientific principles in the assessment and treatment of mental health concerns. Yet even as clinical psychology continues to develop as a scientific field, unscientific concepts and methods abound. Throughout this book, we will help you differentiate between theoretical and practical approaches that are supported by research and those that are not. Another theme is multiculturalism and diversity, as consideration of these aspects of human experience are integral to the assessment, prevention, and treatment of mental health problems, as well as to conducting research in clinical psychology. A third theme of this book is its life span approach since, as we discuss later in this chapter, clinical psychologists assess, treat, and study individuals ranging from the very young to the very old.

Clinical psychologists assess, treat, and study individuals of all age ranges.

To get a sense of how clinical psychology overlaps and stands apart from other mental health fields, let's begin with an overview of the landscape of mental health professions.

▌▌▌ Professionals Working in the Fields of Mental Health

Numerous professionals provide mental health services, train individuals to become professionals, and conduct research on psychological problems. What differentiates the various types of professionals is their focus or specialization and their educational background. Most of these professions are *regulated*, meaning that they require one to be licensed in order to practice as a member of the profession. The requirements for licensure vary from field to field, but all include an educational requirement (such as a masters or doctorate degree in a related field); supervised practice; an examination to test knowledge of the field, state laws pertaining to each field, and professional ethics; and an evaluation of the person's character or reputation (such as a criminal background check). Regulation and licensing, as you will learn in Chapter 2, *Who Is a Clinical Psychologist?*, ensure that the public can feel secure knowing that professionals in a given field are properly trained and have demonstrated a certain level of expertise and professionalism.

Clinical psychology is unique among mental health fields in its enormous breadth; its training approach; and its scope of activities that include research, clinical practice, teaching, consultation, and administrative roles. It is safe to say that within the domain of mental health practitioners and scientists, doctoral-level clinical psychologists are often regarded as the most knowledgeable and best critical thinkers due to an emphasis on both scientific and practical training. In other words, it is assumed that a doctoral degree (such as a PhD) in clinical psychology qualifies people to be experts in their particular area of the field. But before we dive too deeply into the frameworks and practices that characterize this unique and critical profession, let's learn about the other major mental health professions, summarized in **Table 1.1**, and see how they differ from clinical psychology.

Psychiatrists

Psychiatrists represent about 9% of the mental health workforce in the United States. Psychiatrists are licensed physicians who engage in the diagnosis, assessment, treatment, and study of mental health problems and disorders. Consistent with the medical tradition, they generally regard these problems as biologically based illnesses (e.g., brain diseases) with specific causes that are best treated using medical approaches, such as medication and electrical or magnetic stimulation of particular brain regions. It is important to note that this is a fundamentally different approach than that of clinical psychologists. While clinical psychologists acknowledge the contributions of biology to their clients' problems, psychiatrists view these problems as resulting primarily from brain abnormalities and therefore requiring medical intervention. This is not to say that psychiatrists ignore the role of the environment or eschew nonmedical treatments (such as psychological therapy), only that these approaches are typically viewed as secondary. Clinical psychologists, on the other hand, are trained to appreciate cognitive, behavioral, and sociocultural aspects of clients' problems — and the use of psychological interventions — along with biological factors and treatments.

Training in psychiatry involves the completion of medical school to earn an MD or DO degree. Following this, and a general medical internship required of all physicians, psychiatrists receive specialty training during a four-year residency. This apprenticeship period

Table 1.1   Primary Fields of Mental Health

Field	Degrees Required	Brief Summary of the Field	Major Organizations and Websites Associated with the Field
Clinical psychology	Doctorate (PhD or PsyD)	Many roles and settings involved with the assessment, prevention, treatment, research, and teaching of psychological disorders	www.div12.org
Psychiatry	Doctorate (MD or DO)	Assessment and treatment of psychological disorders in various populations using a medical model (i.e., medications); less emphasis on research	www.psych.org
Social work	Masters (MSW), doctorate (PhD or DSW)	Many roles and settings involved with individual and group psychotherapy to enhance social functioning	www.helpstartshere.org www.naswdc.org
Licensed professional counselor (LPC)	Masters or doctorate (PhD) in counseling	Treatment and consultation in a variety of setting for emotional and behavioral problems; often specializing in substance use problems	www.counseling.org
Psychiatric nursing	Registered nurse (RN) plus masters (MA) or doctorate (PhD)	Assessment and treatment of psychological disorders; offer primary care services to those with mental health problems	www.apna.org
Marriage and family therapy	Masters (MA) or doctorate (PhD)	Individual and family psychotherapy from a family systems perspective focusing on relationship conflict, and parent and child conflict	www.aamft.org
Psychotherapist, life coach, and other unregulated terms		As these are unregulated titles, anyone can offer services using these titles	
Psychology		Includes the subdisciplines developmental, social, cognitive, behavioral neuroscience, and quantitative	
Counseling psychology	Doctorate (PhD or PsyD)	Assessment and treatment of a variety of populations with life stress and psychological disorders in private practice and counseling centers; less emphasis on severe disorders and research	www.div17.org
School psychology	Masters or doctorate (PhD or PsyD)	Assessment and intervention for children with emotional and academic difficulties in school settings	www.nasponline.org

involves supervised work with patients in an outpatient or hospital setting, accompanied by seminars, reading, discussion, and related activities. The amount of formal psychiatric course-work varies, but the core training experience is the treatment of patients under the supervision of a more experienced psychiatrist. There tends to be relatively little training in the psychological principles that govern human behavior (e.g., operant and classical conditioning), in formal assessment of psychological functioning, or in the use of research-supported psychological interventions. Indeed, only a small percentage of psychiatrists in training ever receive exposure to or more in-depth training in scientific methods and approaches to conducting psychiatric research.

Consequently, most psychiatrists do not implement psychological treatments with their patients, but rather tend to schedule brief (i.e., quarter-hour) "medication management" appointments with each patient (e.g., see Harris, 2011). Opportunities to work in depth with individuals experiencing psychological symptoms or to help teach behavioral skills that may reduce and prevent symptoms are more limited in psychiatry than in clinical psychology. Psychiatrists may work in one or more settings, including private practice clinics, general and psychiatric hospitals (including emergency departments), university medical centers, community mental health agencies, courts and prisons, nursing homes and hospice programs, industry, military settings, and rehabilitation programs. Most psychiatrists in the United States work in private practice.

Social Workers

The professional activities of **social workers** often seem similar to those of clinical psychologists and psychiatrists. Many social workers provide psychological treatment on an individual or group basis. They may also assist individuals, groups, or communities to restore or enhance their capacity for social functioning, by helping facilitate an environment favorable for their goals. The practice of social work requires knowledge of human development and behavior; of social, economic, and cultural institutions; and of the interaction of all these factors. In fact, one difference between social workers and clinical psychologists and psychiatrists is that social workers tend to place a greater focus on the familial and sociocultural factors underlying psychopathology.

Social workers attend graduate school and earn a master's degree, which typically requires two years. Compared to the training of clinical psychologists and psychiatrists, social work training is rather brief. As a result, the responsibilities of the social worker are generally not as broad as those of the psychiatrist or clinical psychologist. Characteristic of social workers is their intense involvement with the everyday lives and stresses of their patients. They are more likely to visit the home, the workplace, or other environments where their patients spend the bulk of their lives. Their role tends to be active, and they are less concerned with the abstract, theoretical generalizations that can be drawn from a particular case than they are with the practical matters of living.

Many social workers are employed by public agencies of one sort or another. Some find their way into private practice, where their work in individual or family therapy is often indistinguishable from that of psychiatrists or clinical psychologists. Other social workers function as part of a mental health team (including psychiatrists and clinical psychologists) in hospitals, social service agencies, or mental health clinics.

The field of social work has grown tremendously in recent decades. About a third of all mental health professionals are social workers, and they provide more than half of all the United

States' mental health services. Social workers are likely to gain an even greater foothold in the mental health market in the future because they are a low-cost alternative to psychiatrists and psychologists. Enrollment in social work programs continues to increase, and the number of social workers is predicted to continue rising.

Licensed Professional Counselor

Licensed professional counselors (LPCs) are mental health providers who are trained to work with individuals, families, and groups to treat mental, behavioral, and emotional problems and disorders, including substance use disorders. These professionals typically work in private practice or community mental health centers and clinics, but may also be employed in hospitals; rehab facilities; correctional facilities; or school, college, or university counseling centers. Many members of the clergy (e.g., rabbis, priests, pastors) are trained as LPCs as well. The approach of LPCs may vary, but typically involves psychoeducational techniques with individuals, families, and groups, as well as consultations with individuals, couples, families, groups, and larger organizations. Most LPCs have a masters degree (although a doctoral degree is available), and there are a wide range of both accredited (i.e., following a standard set of educational requirements) and unaccredited programs that train counselors. To the public, a "counselor" may sound indistinguishable from a "therapist" or perhaps even a "psychologist"; however, counseling programs are unique in their emphasis on listening and decision-making skills more than the use of scientifically supported treatments to reduce significant symptoms of mental illness. Within the U.S. mental health workforce, there are more LPCs than any other type of professional.

Psychiatric Nurses

Psychiatric nursing is a specialty within the field of nursing in which registered nurses work with individuals, families, groups, and communities to assess their mental health needs. A psychiatric nurse might make diagnoses, create and implement treatment plans, and then evaluate the treatment's effectiveness. In some settings, **psychiatric nurses** offer primary care services to individuals with psychiatric diagnoses and other mental health problems. Their skills overlap greatly with those of clinical psychologists and psychiatrists.

Psychiatric nurses have a masters or doctoral degree in psychiatric–mental health nursing. In some instances, they work as professors, researchers, or administrators. Because they spend many hours in close contact with patients, they are not only in a position to provide information about patients' hospital adjustment but also can play a crucial and sensitive role in fostering an appropriate therapeutic environment. Working in close collaboration with the psychiatrist or the clinical psychologist, they (along with those they supervise — attendants, nurse's aides, volunteers, etc.) implement treatment recommendations. Certified nurse practitioners now have prescription privileges in all but a few U.S. states. Therefore, nurses may be increasingly employed on the front lines of mental health services.

Marriage and Family Therapists

Marriage and family therapists (MFTs) are mental health professionals trained in psychotherapy and family systems. They are licensed to diagnose and treat mental, behavioral, and emotional problems within the context of marriage, relationships, and family systems. Their work

NoSystem images/Getty Images

Marriage and family therapists receive specialized training to understand and provide services from within a family systems perspective.

generally encompasses the treatment of marital and couples conflict, parent and child conflict, alcohol and drug abuse, sexual dysfunction, grief, children's behavior problems, and issues with eldercare, such as coping with a spouse's, parent's, or grandparent's dementia. MFTs might also work with families in which one member has problems that impact the rest of the family, such as chronic depression, anxiety, dementia, or schizophrenia.

While traditional psychological treatment tends to focus on the individual, MFTs focus on the individual's behavior in relationship to a couple or a family as a whole. Underlying this approach is the idea that regardless of whether a mental health problem appears uniquely to an individual or within a family system, getting other family members involved in the intervention process will result in more effective solutions. Treatment from this perspective tends to be goal-oriented and works toward an established end result.

Licensed MFTs have graduate training (a masters or doctoral degree) in marriage and family therapy that includes at least two years of specialized training and supervised clinical experience. About 7% of the mental health workforce are licensed marriage and family therapists. At any given time they are treating more than 1.8 million people.

"Psychotherapist," "Life Coach," and Other Unregulated Terms

Most of the professionals and paraprofessionals listed to this point have fulfilled specific educational requirements and licensing requirements regulated by state and provincial governments. In other words, these mental health workers must (1) document that they have obtained appropriate professional training; (2) pass a licensing exam indicating familiarity with current practice parameters, ethical regulations, and state laws; and (3) maintain their current knowledge of the field through ongoing educational requirements (i.e., continuing professional education). However, some titles are not regulated by the government (e.g., "therapist," "psychotherapist," "life coach"), and virtually anyone can offer services using these titles. Unfortunately, some members of the public are not aware of this distinction and may confuse the services offered by a professional with other unregulated services.

Psychologists

The term "psychologist" can be confusing. Indeed, many undergraduate students get a bachelors degree in psychology; however, a very small percentage go on to get graduate training in this field, and only a subset of those who do will eventually become a "psychologist." For most people, the term evokes an image of someone practicing as a clinician; thus, it might be assumed that every psychologist is a clinical psychologist. In fact, there are many different types of doctoral programs in psychology, which means that there may be many different types of psychologists. Importantly, some of these "subdisciplines" include training to practice psychology and some do not.

For instance, there are at least five different fields of psychology that offer doctoral training but do not prepare students to work in practice (see **Table 1.2**). Each of these subdisciplines focuses on a particular domain of psychological research. *Developmental psychologists* examine how psychological processes change as we mature, seeking an understanding of how our cognitive, social, moral, emotional, or intellectual abilities, for instance, may evolve as we progress through life stages and interact with our environment in more sophisticated ways. *Social psychologists* examine how individuals interact within groups, exploring how our attitudes and behaviors may be shaped by larger social and group processes, such as conformity, prejudice, attraction, and organizational behavior, just to name a few. *Cognitive psychologists* examine mental processes that help us navigate the world around us, with a focus on memory, language, perception, and decision making, for instance. *Behavioral neuroscientists* study connections between our thoughts, feelings, and behaviors and biological processes in our brain and peripheral nervous systems. *Quantitative psychologists* develop and examine new statistical procedures that can be used to study psychological phenomena.

Table 1.2 Subfields of Clinical Psychology with Doctoral Training, but No Work in Practice		
Subfield	**Brief Description**	**Major Organizations and Websites Associated with the Field**
Developmental psychologists	Study of how the psychological processes change over the life span	American Psychological Association, Division 7 www.apadivisions.org /division-7
Social psychologists	Study of how individuals interact within groups	American Psychological Association, Division 8 http://www.spsp.org/
Cognitive psychologists	Study of mental processes, for example, memory, language, perception, and decision making	Psychonomic Society http://www.psychonomic.org/ Cognitive Neuroscience Society http://www.cogneurosociety.org/
Behavioral neuroscientists	Study of the biology of behavior, including how the brain regulates behavior	American Psychological Association, Division 6 http://www.apadivisions.org /division-6/index.aspx
Quantitative psychologists	Study of statistical procedures used in psychological procedures	American Psychological Association, Division 5 www.apadivisions.org /division-5

Each of these areas of psychology offers a critical contribution to psychological science, and the application of work in each of these psychology subdisciplines has been valued in a variety of industries both in and outside of academia. For instance, behavioral neuroscientists often are employed at large pharmaceutical industries, cognitive and quantitative psychologists often are hired within tech and big data firms, social psychologists often make contributions within corporations and business schools, and developmental psychologists may have an impact on education and policy. Note, however, that none of these subdisciplines (sometimes together referred to as "experimental psychology") involve the provision of clinical services to ameliorate behavioral and physical health conditions.

Counseling and School Psychologists

Clinical, counseling, and school psychology come under the umbrella of health service psychology. Students who graduate with a doctoral degree in these three subdisciplines are the only types of psychologists who are eligible for a professional license to practice independently. Because the focus of this book is on clinical psychology, which we will discuss in great depth, a brief description of counseling and school psychology is presented below.

Counseling Psychology

Many **counseling psychologists** engage in activities that are pretty similar to the activities of clinical psychologists. However, the two fields were borne from different traditions, and there still remain some differences in the training and emphases of counseling and clinical psychology (Norcross, Sayette, & Mayne, 2008). Perhaps the biggest distinction between counseling and clinical psychology is evident in the types of presenting issues and research topics that may be addressed by each type of mental health professional. Clinical psychologists study and treat the entire range of adjustment difficulties, including people who may experience severe mental illness (bipolar disorder, pervasive developmental disorders, schizophrenia, suicidal depression, etc.) or who may be significantly impaired in their daily lives by mental health issues. In contrast, most counseling psychologists work only with generally healthy individuals, or those with mild to moderate adjustment problems. For instance, counseling psychologists, many of whom work in counseling centers on university campuses or within the community, may often address individuals' social relationships, career decisions, mild or moderate experiences with depression or anxiety, and perhaps risks for eating disorders. Like clinical psychologists, counseling psychologists also may be involved in assessing mental health issues. But while clinical psychologists may routinely conduct diagnostic assessments, counseling psychologists may work to measure academic abilities, personality, interests, and vocational aptitude. Although most counseling psychologists work within educational settings (e.g., colleges and universities), they also may work in hospitals, rehabilitation centers, mental health clinics, and industry.

Counseling psychologists have training at the doctoral level (usually PhD, but also PsyD or EdD) in programs that typically require at least four to five years of graduate study that involves coursework and integrated training experiences in a variety of topical areas and professional skills. Practicing counseling psychologists must have a state-issued license, which requires completion of a doctoral degree, postdoctoral training, and a passing score on tests of ethics and general knowledge within psychology.

The field of counseling psychology is much smaller than that of clinical psychology in terms of the number of professionals as well as the number of training programs. About 4000 health service psychology doctoral students complete their training in the United States each year; 3000 of these have been trained in clinical psychology, and the remainder are in counseling (about 500 each year); school psychology (about 350); or programs that combine clinical, counseling, and school psychology (about 150). Counseling psychology also differs in the types of departments where training takes place. Most clinical psychology programs are housed in departments of psychology and neuroscience, whereas many counseling psychology programs are based in education departments or schools of education.

School psychologists work with students, parents, faculty, and administrators to facilitate the intellectual, social, and emotional growth of school-age youth.

School Psychologists

In many ways, **school psychologists** serve as ambassadors for the field of psychology within primary and educational school settings. They are likely to be the first person the school comes to when issues come up that involve mental health, such as crises that may affect children's school performance, classroom behavior management, children's need for special services, or consultation with parents and administrators about mental health issues. Unfortunately, there are remarkably few school psychologists compared to the need for their services.

School psychologists' work involves students, educators, parents, and school administrators to promote the intellectual, social, and emotional growth of school-age children and adolescents. Toward this end, school psychologists may conduct psychological and educational assessments (often to diagnose giftedness, intellectual or learning disabilities, or ADHD); develop learning programs and evaluate their effectiveness; and consult with teachers, parents, and school officials. For instance, a school psychologist may develop a program to assist children with special intellectual, emotional, or social needs. This might begin with an evaluation of the child in question, followed by recommendations concerning special programs, treatment, or placement if necessary. In addition, the school psychologist might consult with teachers and school officials on the implementation of the programs as well as issues of school policy or classroom management. School psychologists also might work directly with teachers to help construct behavioral modification programs with the goal of helping some students manage behavioral or emotional issues that are impeding academic performance. School psychologists usually have training at the doctoral level (usually PhD, but also EdD) through programs that require four to five years of graduate study involving coursework and supervised training experiences.

As mentioned above, school psychologists are in high demand, as U.S. laws require that children who require special educational resources receive a thorough educational assessment. School psychologists conduct the majority of these assessments; thus, there is a great need for school psychologists to evaluate the intellectual ability and academic achievement of youth, many of whom remain on waiting lists for months or years until someone is available to conduct an evaluation. The majority of school psychologists work in schools, but some also work in nurseries, day-care centers, hospitals, clinics, and even penal institutions. A few are in private practice.

Think Like a Clinical Psychologist Why do people know so much less about mental health treatment than treatment for physical health ailments?

▉ Clinical Psychology

The field of clinical psychology encompasses research, teaching, and services relevant to the applications of principles, methods, and procedures for understanding, predicting, and alleviating intellectual, emotional, medical, psychological, social, and behavioral maladjustment, disability, and discomfort applied to a wide range of client populations. Thus, professionals in this field work with a range of persons, from infants to elderly persons. Their work can involve individuals, families/partners, school personnel, other health care workers, and communities across the range of socioeconomic status. Clinical psychologists also work in a large range of settings, including universities, hospitals, private practice offices, or group medical practices. Indeed, of all the possible mental health degrees and fields available, a doctoral degree in clinical psychology is considered the most versatile because it can lead to such a wide range of job opportunities.

It would be impossible to list all the issues and symptoms that are relevant to the field of clinical psychology. The number and kinds of problems are so extensive as to boggle the mind: depression, anxiety, psychosis, personality disorders, developmental disabilities, addictions, learning disabilities, conduct disorder, attention deficit–hyperactivity disorder, pervasive developmental disorders, suicide, vocational problems, and sexual difficulties — to name but a few. Further, this list does not cover those individuals who seek out assessment or intervention not because of current dysfunctional symptoms but as a way to better understand themselves or their family members.

However, what may be the most unique aspect about clinical psychologists is the breadth in perspective that guides both research and practice on psychopathology and adaptive functioning. As will be discussed in more detail in Chapter 2, clinical psychologists receive extensive training to understand human emotions and behavior from multiple perspectives, including the affective, biological, cognitive, behavioral, developmental, and sociocultural foundations of all human behavior, as well as a focus on the assessment and treatment of all forms of psychopathology. In clinical psychology, behavior is understood to be a product of biology and the environment, individual context, and one's context embedded within the larger cultural climate in which all human interactions take place. It is this holistic perspective cultivated throughout four to six years of graduate training in research and practice, followed by an additional year of internship/residency, and (in many states) another one to two years of supervised clinical practice that allows clinical psychologists to understand and treat human behavior with remarkable depth, knowledge, and experience.

Incorporating a Multicultural Perspective

In the last twenty years, clinical psychologists have increasingly recognized the need for far greater understanding of diversity (see IN HISTORICAL PERSPECTIVE: A Brief History at the end of this section for more details about how the science has evolved). Today, multicultural awareness, knowledge, and skills have been incorporated into our understanding of physical and mental health throughout the life span. Focusing on differences in gender experience, culture, ethnicity, race, sexual orientation, ability, religion, socioeconomic status, and other dimensions of diversity, great strides have been made toward building a multicultural framework for the field. Culturally informed resources have been created to sensitively assist members of all diverse groups, and also increase the number of clinical psychologists in training and leadership positions who represent diverse perspectives and backgrounds. Diversity factors are incorporated into decisions about how individuals are assessed and treated, and whether medical or mental health treatment is equally accessible to all.

That's a good start, but more action is needed. In 2021, the American Psychological Association issued a formal apology to the people of color for "APA's role in promoting, perpetuating, and failing to challenge racism, racial discrimination, and

The field of clinical psychology recognizes the importance of a workforce that represents diverse backgrounds and perspectives.

human hierarchy in US" (https://www.apa.org/about/policy/racism-apology). In its apology, APA notes that "The American Psychological Association failed in its role leading the discipline of psychology, was complicit in contributing to systemic inequities, and hurt many through racism, racial discrimination, and denigration of people of color, thereby falling short on its mission to benefit society and improve lives. APA is profoundly sorry, accepts responsibility for, and owns the actions and inactions of APA itself, the discipline of psychology, and individual psychologists who stood as leaders for the organization and field." The APA apology is then followed by a detailed plan of action steps that will begin to dismantle systemic racism, and several additional apology documents are planned to address others who have experienced systems of oppression, including those based on religion, sex, class, sexual orientation and gender diversity, and disability identity.

Clinical psychology is tragically a part of this shameful history, with numerous ways that its foundations in intelligence testing, its research suggesting a human biological hierarchy, and the use of its work to introduce eugenics, reify discrimination, and support exclusionary practices hurt people of color and created systemic barriers that persist to this day. Because this history is essential for the study of psychology, and extends beyond clinical psychology, we have included the entire historical chronology published by APA in this textbook (see Appendix). As you will see from this history, and from data below from APA (see **Figure 1.1**), there is much work is needed to eliminate systemic barriers in clinical psychology.

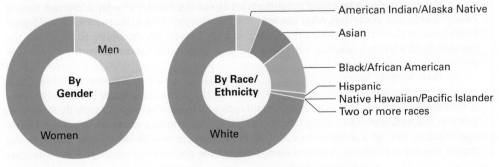

Figure 1.1 Who Are the Clinical Psychologists?

◐ ◑ ◔ ◕ 🌑 In Historical Perspective

A Brief History

The earliest example of any activity resembling today's clinical psychology appeared in the early 19th century when you could literally have your head examined using *phrenology* — the study of character traits by observing the size, shape, and bumps of one's skull. Franz Mesmer's treatment of emotional and behavioral problems using magnets was also popular during this time. While these methods were eventually rejected as unscientific, academic psychologists of the time were not concerned with mental disorders. Rather, it was the developing fields of psychiatry and neurology that focused on such problems, as exemplified by Sigmund Freud, a neurologist, who developed psychoanalysis in Vienna, Austria, in the late 18th century.

Lightner Witmer (1867–1956) is considered the father of modern clinical psychology. In 1896, at the University of Pennsylvania, he opened the first psychological clinic, which was dedicated to helping children with learning disabilities. Witmer also started the first

Lightner Witmer is considered the father of clinical psychology.

clinical psychology journal (*The Psychological Clinic*), where he coined the term "clinical psychology," defined as "the study of individuals, by observation or experimentation, with the intention of promoting change." By 1914, there were 26 psychological clinics in the United States.

During the early 20th century, clinical psychologists made further inroads into the mental health arena when the U.S. army commissioned psychologists to develop instruments for testing the intelligence of military recruits during World War I. The results were *Army Alpha* and *Army Beta*, which assessed verbal and nonverbal skills, respectively. Due to the success of these tests, assessment became the primary activity of clinical psychologists for the next 25 years. When World War II broke out, the military again called on clinical psychologists, this time to address the symptoms of psychological trauma (then labeled shell shock and eventually to be called posttraumatic stress disorder) that were observed among veterans engaged in combat. After the war, the Veterans Administration in the United States helped set up doctoral degree training programs for clinical psychologists to help treat the thousands of veterans needing care. This led to a tremendous increase in the number of professionals going into the field.

In 1949, leading academic clinical psychologists convened in Boulder, Colorado, and developed the scientist–practitioner (or Boulder) model of graduate study in which PhD programs emphasized training in both psychotherapy and in conducting research. By the 1960s, some in the field wanted training programs that focused more exclusively on clinical practice. Thus, in 1973 at a meeting in Vail, Colorado, the practitioner–scholar (or Vail) training model was born, resulting in formal recognition of the doctor of psychology (PsyD) degree.

This type of training would include a scientific *understanding* of psychology but emphasize clinical training similar to that obtained in medical school. Today, about half of all American graduate students in clinical psychology are enrolled in PsyD programs.

Over the past 50 years, the scope of clinical psychology has continued to expand. One important development has been the emphasis on evidence-based practice which integrates the best available research with clinical expertise in the context of patient characteristics, culture, and preferences. Another area of growth has been in the subfield of health psychology, which is concerned with understanding how psychological, behavioral, neurological, and cultural factors contribute to physical health and illness. Finally, within the past few decades, a third training model — the clinical science model — has emerged. This approach emphasizes training in the science of psychology and while students receive some clinical training (exclusively in evidence-based treatments), they spend the majority of their time conducting research with faculty mentors. Clinical science programs award the PhD and prepare students for academic careers, although some students do pursue positions in clinical settings.

Thomas Barwick/Getty Images

Within the clinical science training model, students not only receive clinical training, they also conduct research with their faculty mentors.

Other recent developments include the proliferation of multicultural training within doctoral programs, the emergence of multicultural perspectives on psychological problems, and the appearance of prescription privileges for clinical psychologists in some jurisdictions. In England an ambitious accomplishment of clinical psychology is the Improving Access to Psychological Therapies (IAPT) program, which began in 2008. IAPT has transformed the treatment of anxiety disorders and depression in that country by implementing training and supervision in evidence-based psychological therapies on a national level to optimize outcomes. Back in the United States, there is currently fierce competition for admission into PhD programs in clinical psychology, with an average acceptance rate of 8%. ■

Activities of Clinical Psychologists

We've seen how clinical psychologists are unique within the mental health workforce, but what do they actually do? We will discuss activities that many clinical psychologists engage in, but keep in mind that few clinical psychologists engage only in any single activity described below. Some work primarily as researchers/investigators and university professors, perhaps offering treatment one afternoon each week. Others offer psychological services within a hospital setting, while consulting on ongoing research or teaching a psychology class at a local university. Still others may incorporate consulting opportunities, or academic or corporate administration into their weekly schedule. Given the range of skills and multiple areas of expertise involved in clinical psychology training, many elect to engage in multiple activities that continually challenge and enrich their work lives, wearing different professional hats within any given week.

Intervention. Most clinical psychologists provide psychological treatment. Many people have an image of "therapy" (we use the term "psychological treatment" in this book) as an activity during which the client lies on a couch while the therapist sits with a notepad and furrowed brow. Actually, psychological treatment comes in many different sizes and shapes. Only a few therapists still use a couch; more often, the client sits face-to-face across from the therapist, or even side-by-side at a table. In some interventions — such as exposure therapy for social anxiety — field trips are taken so that clients can practice facing their fears by speaking to strangers. In most cases, treatment involves a one-to-one relationship, but couples or family treatment, parent training, and group treatment are also very common (see Chapter 15 *Family, Couples, and Group-based Interventions*. For example, a group of six or eight clients, all having trouble with alcohol use, may meet with a clinical psychologist to discuss adaptive behaviors and coping skills to work on their problems. Or a psychologist may meet with a child's parents to discuss ways that reinforcements in the home may reduce the child's disruptive behavior.

Historically, psychological treatments involved a search for insight into the origins of one's problems or the purposes an undesirable behavior served. Treatment consisted primarily of a relationship between client and therapist designed to produce an atmosphere of trust that would help dissolve the client's problems. Contemporary psychological interventions, however, are guided by research suggesting that learning and practicing specific skills is more beneficial for reducing emotional and behavioral problems. For instance, cognitive-behavioral treatments involve a structured format to help the client learn new and more healthy ways of thinking and behaving. Sometimes the goals of treatment are broad and involve major changes in behavior. Other times, patients desire help only with a single type of symptom (e.g., a very specific fear) that prevents them from achieving certain goals. In Chapters 10–15 you will learn more about the different approaches to psychological treatment in greater detail.

Diagnosis/Assessment. As we will cover in Chapters 4–9, assessment is also a crucial activity of clinical psychologists. Indeed, before one can implement an effective treatment, the problem must be thoroughly understood. Assessment can also help the clinician determine the degree to which a treatment is successful. Whether through direct observation, testing, or interviewing, assessment is a way of gathering information. Intelligence testing, for example, involves measuring a child's IQ and how much they've learned in school. This information can be used to determine whether the child has a learning disability that requires a plan to help them receive necessary resources. Personality tests can shed light on psychological factors that might contribute to depression or problems with substance abuse. Behavioral assessment can be used to understand factors that influence specific problems, such as arguments in relationships or compulsive checking rituals in an adolescent with obsessive-compulsive disorder (OCD). This information helps guide the implementation of cognitive or behavioral treatments. Finally, a diagnostic assessment may be necessary when conducting treatment or grouping individuals for the purposes of research. While most clinical psychologists engage in both assessment and treatment, some specialize exclusively in psychological testing and assessment.

Research. As noted above, clinical psychologists are unique among mental health professionals in that they are trained as both practitioners and scientists. This means that all clinical psychologists take courses in research methods and statistics so they are comfortable reading and understanding scientific research in the field. Many also receive training in conducting research so that they are able to contribute knowledge to advance the field. Many practicing clinical psychologists thus are in the unique position of being able to apply research findings to their work with clients. They are also able to carry out research projects on the prevalence and causes of mental disorders, the effectiveness of treatment interventions, and the accuracy of assessment instruments.

Sometimes research is done in the context of large investigations involving multiple teams of scientists at different sites using the same methods to study the same phenomenon or treatment approach. Clinical psychologists who direct these types of studies may apply for grant funding to be able to coordinate these different groups and hire staff (research assistants, graduate students, or postdocs) to help recruit study participants, collect data, and analyze the results. Then the study findings are presented and/or written up in a format (such as a journal article) that allows other researchers to learn from one another, and together, better understand how to reduce the burden of mental illness.

Other times research may be part of a clinical psychologist's daily practice. For instance, a clinical psychologist may collect anonymous data from their patients to learn what factors are most likely to lead to recovery. Or a clinician may look for weekly trends in their patient's severity of symptoms as treatment is conducted. This too makes clinical psychologists unique in their ability to seamlessly combine research and clinical practice in the same activity.

Teaching. Some clinical psychologists hold full- or part-time academic positions teaching in colleges and universities. Those whose responsibilities are primarily in graduate training programs teach doctoral students how to conduct assessment and treatment using various research methods. Some also teach undergraduate courses (it is likely that your instructor in this class is a clinical psychologist or graduate student). Even those who work in clinics and hospitals, or who operate a private practice, sometimes teach formal or informal classes to students; other mental health personnel such as social workers; and people in the community such as police officers, clergy, and business owners.

Clinical Supervision. Clinical supervision is a form of teaching that involves close one-on-one work with an individual or small group of trainees. Whether in a training program or other clinical or professional setting, many clinical psychologists spend time helping students or other professionals develop greater expertise in psychological assessment and treatment. Becoming skilled in the intricacies of therapy and assessment techniques requires more than just reading textbooks. It also involves seeing clients and then discussing their cases with a more experienced supervisor. Supervisors often watch their supervisees' live or recorded treatment sessions to provide detailed feedback on how best to create an environment that makes clients feel comfortable and how to apply specific techniques and procedures known to help clients' symptoms improve.

Consultation. Consultation takes many different forms and occurs in varied settings. A clinical psychologist with expertise in addiction, for example, might consult with a colleague who is having difficulty with a therapy case that involves substance use. Clinical psychologists also serve as consultants to companies such as advertising agencies or corporations interested in developing programs or products to improve the mental health of their workers or customers. They also offer consultation services within the legal system, either by assisting attorneys in the selection of jurors for a case or consulting with police departments in hostage negotiations. Finally, a growing number of clinical psychologists serve as consultants to physicians who deliver primary care services.

Administration. While most clinical psychologists spend some time on administrative tasks — for example, managing client records or serving on university or departmental committees — some become full-time administrators. Indeed, because of their training in understanding human behavior and skills in human relations, many clinical psychologists make good administrators who keep their organization running smoothly and efficiently. Being sensitive to the needs and problems of people in the organization and having the patience to sometimes suffer in silence are useful attributes in this regard. The ability to communicate well with those under supervision is also important, as is a knack for selecting the right people for the right jobs.

It would be difficult to list all the administrative posts held by clinical psychologists. However, common examples include chair of a university psychology department or director of clinical training, university dean or provost, director of a Veterans Administration clinic, vice president of a consulting firm, and director of a crisis center.

In Practice

To help you get a sense of how clinical psychologists function in practice, we'll follow two individuals introduced below — Kiara and Shane (composites of actual clients) — throughout this book. Their stories, along with anecdotes about other individuals we present throughout the book, will show you how clients interact with the field of clinical psychology. We also will include sections with information about the history of psychology and bios about actual psychologists and how they have developed their careers.

We introduce Shane and Kiara with just about the same amount of information a clinical psychologist might initially receive when they first get a referral to meet with a new client. In the chapters that follow, we will parallel the practices of clinical psychologists as they conduct and share the results of assessment with each individual, consider treatment options, and then apply psychological interventions.

In Practice Introductions to Shane and Kiara

Shane

Over the past six months, Shane has been having some difficulties. He shouts at his parents when they ask him to get ready for bed or finish his dinner. When he is very upset, he sometimes curses at his parents and hits other children. Last week, the principal at his school called his parents in for a conference. His teacher reports that his grades have dropped and he will not sit still in class. Yesterday, he threw a rock at a girl in his class and she got a black eye. The school recommends that Shane get professional help or they may have him expelled. Shane frequently complains of headaches.

Kiara

Kiara had just completed her RN degree and was a few months into her new job as a nurse at a prestigious local hospital. But her productivity was suffering because she was spending excessive amounts of time washing her hands before and after seeing each patient. She also found herself frequently getting stuck checking patient charts over and over, and sometimes came in to work on her days off to recheck that she hadn't made any mistakes in her record keeping. Kiara wasn't sleeping well and frequently complained of feeling run down and fatigued. Her colleagues were becoming concerned, and they urged her to seek help. ▰▰▰

Think Like a Clinical Psychologist Diverse perspectives are important in any health science and service delivery profession. What are some reasons this is especially true in the field of clinical psychology?

▍▌▎ Chapter Summary

Unlike the fields of medicine, in which all physicians complete rigorous doctoral training programs and use standardized methods of assessment and treatment, mental health domains are characterized by great diversity in their educational requirements and in the tools used for assessing and treating psychological and behavioral problems. This chapter provided an overview of the major professions within the field of mental health, including the scope and foundation, educational requirements, and settings where members of each field may be found. Clinical psychologists are unique among mental health professionals in that they receive training not only as clinicians but also as researchers. Accordingly, they consume scientific findings, contribute to the knowledge base of their field, and use scientific knowledge to inform their work with clients. We consider this among the greatest strengths of the profession, and one that qualifies clinical psychologists as the most knowledgeable and most skilled critical thinkers across the mental health landscape.

Because of their wealth of knowledge in working with people and studying behavior, clinical psychologists assume a wide range of roles in diverse settings, including private practice, hospitals and community clinics, colleges and universities, and various industries. In this textbook we will explore in depth the various roles of clinical psychologists as practitioners, scientists, and consultants.

Applying What You've Learned

Pick a Mental Health Care Provider

1. Keanu is about to graduate from college. He has been feeling pretty confused and stressed about what to do with his life. He is not sure what kind of career he may want, and he seems to start a lot of new romantic relationships, but they always end within about a month. He is really frustrated about what he may want to do after he graduates, and he has been mopey lately.

2. Sigourney has had a diagnosis of schizophrenia since she was about 18 years old. She has periods during which she hears things that others do not seem to notice. Occasionally, these sounds are voices that tell her to do something that scares her. A couple of weeks ago, she was very close to driving her car into a group of pedestrians because the voices said that if she didn't do so, she would be considered a coward and everyone would hate her.

3. Macauley is a 7-year-old boy who used to love school. He would be excited to leave the house every day when the bus came, and when he got home he would talk very excitedly about what he had learned. In the past several months, his grades have started to go down, especially in math. He is generally a happy boy with several friends. He also is really good at sports, and he works very hard at soccer practice. His parents are concerned about his grades and can't understand what may have changed so suddenly.

4. Sheldon has been given a diagnosis of autistic disorder. He is very intelligent and a talented mathematician. He has difficulty relating to his peers, however. Recently, he has been the target of victimization from peers, and he has started to avoid other children. Sometimes he skips lunch just to avoid entering the cafeteria. He also has walked home on each day over the past three months, despite very cold weather, just to avoid the kids on the bus.

5. Joe used to love spending time with his children and watching football. But lately he can't get out of bed. When his kids ask him to come play, he says they will annoy him, and he'd rather stay by himself. He has missed work at least once a week over the past month. He has thought about how he would end his life and began writing a suicide note.

6. Dave and Buster met when they were in college and quickly fell in love. Twenty years later, they are a happy married couple with a 14-year-old daughter. Their family was the picture of happiness until last year, when three life events occurred spontaneously. First, Buster got a promotion and began spending more time at work. Dave has been very upset about how little time they spend together. Second, their daughter entered high school. Third, Dave inherited a large sum from his aunt who passed away. Last week, Dave and Buster got a call from a schoolteacher with concerns that their daughter may be anorexic.

7. Wanda is married and has two children and a terrific family. She can't seem to find time to do the things she loves, however. She wants to spend more time doing yoga, reading novels, and traveling. But she also would love to advance further in her career and be the "perfect" mom. How will she fit it all in? Wanda would love to examine her life priorities and manage her time more effectively.

Key Terms

Clinical psychologist: A mental health professional devoted to understanding and treating individuals affected by a variety of emotional, behavioral, and/or cognitive difficulties. Clinical psychologists may be involved in numerous activities, including psychotherapy, assessment and diagnosis, teaching, supervision, research, consultation, and administration.

Clinical psychology: Field of psychology devoted to research, teaching, and services relevant to the applications of principles, methods, and procedures for understanding, predicting, and alleviating intellectual, emotional, medical, psychological, social, and behavioral maladjustment, disability, and discomfort applied to a wide range of client populations.

Counseling psychologists: Psychologists whose interests and activities overlap significantly with those of clinical psychologists. Traditionally, counseling psychologists have provided individual and group psychotherapy for normal or moderately maladjusted individuals and have offered educational and occupational counseling.

Licensed professional counselors (LPCs): Mental health providers who are trained to work with individuals, families, and groups in treating mental, behavioral, and emotional problems and disorders, including substance use disorders. These professionals work in a wide variety of settings, and the approach of LPCs may vary but typically involves psychoeducational techniques with individuals, families, and groups, along with consultations with individuals, couples, families, groups, and larger organizations.

Marriage and family therapists (MFTs): Mental health professionals trained in psychotherapy and family systems. They are licensed to diagnose and treat mental, behavioral, and emotional problems within the context of marriage, relationships, and family systems. MFTs focus on the individual's behavior in relationship to a couple or a family as a whole. Licensed MFTs have graduate training (a masters or doctoral degree) in marriage and family therapy that includes at least two years of specialized training and supervised clinical experience.

Mental illness: A pattern of behavior, thinking, or feeling that causes significant personal distress or interference in daily functioning.

Psychiatric nurses: Registered nurses who work with individuals, families, groups, and communities assessing their mental health needs. A psychiatric nurse might make diagnoses, create and implement treatment plans, and then evaluate the treatment's effectiveness. Psychiatric nurses have a masters or doctoral degree in psychiatric–mental health nursing, and certified nurse practitioners now have prescription privileges in all but a few U.S. states.

Psychiatrists: Physicians with intensive training in the diagnosis and treatment of a variety of mental disorders. Because of their medical backgrounds, psychiatrists may prescribe medications for the alleviation of problematic behavior or psychological distress.

School psychologists: Psychologists who work with educators to promote the intellectual, social, and emotional growth of school-age children. Activities of school psychologists may include evaluating children with special needs, developing interventions or programs to address these needs, and consulting with teachers and administrators about issues of school policy.

Social workers: Mental health professionals trained in psychiatric diagnosis and in individual and group psychotherapy. Compared to psychologists and psychiatrists, social workers' training is relatively brief, limited to a two-year masters degree. Social workers are intensely involved in the day-to-day lives of their patients and focus more on the social and environmental factors contributing to their patients' difficulties.

CONNECT ONLINE:

 | Check out our videos and additional resources located at: www.macmillanlearning.com

Who Is a Clinical Psychologist?

FOCUS QUESTIONS

1. What is the basis for the scientist-practitioner model?
2. Explain the origin and evolution of the PsyD degree.
3. What factors led to the formation of the Academy of Psychological Clinical Science?
4. Outline the path to obtaining a doctoral degree in clinical psychology.
5. Why is licensing and credentialing important in the field?
6. What are the primary specialties in clinical psychology?

CHAPTER OUTLINE

In Chapter 1, *Clinical Psychology in Context*, we discussed the ways that clinical psychologists are distinct from other mental health care providers and researchers. Within our discipline, however, there are also different types of clinical psychologists. It is important to learn about these types for several reasons. First, the types of mental and behavioral health problems that people may face are extremely diverse, and no single psychologist could ever be trained to address them all. Specialists, therefore, are needed in different areas of the field. Second, the discussion of differences among clinical psychologists offers a lot of information about the field itself, and informs debates that still ensue regarding its future. This chapter will help you understand these issues and allow you to become an expert when people ask you, "Do you know how I can pick a clinical psychologist to get help?" To understand how to answer that question, however, we need to go back to World War II for just a bit.

As we briefly noted in Chapter 1, the field of clinical psychology indeed existed prior to World War II — and schools or philosophies of psychological treatment have existed since the mid-1800s — but a major emphasis of the field in those days was intelligence testing for children and adolescents. Tragically, as we will call attention to in Chapter 8, *The Assessment of Intelligence*, some of this early work led to racist and misleading biases in the field of clinical psychology that should be acknowledged and confronted. The early emphasis on intelligence, along with other types of testing, also spearheaded an awareness of the importance of science in clinical psychology, which quickly established the field as unique in relying on measurable constructs, outcomes, and research findings to guide the discipline. Indeed, it was the emphasis on science that allowed clinical psychology to ultimately assert that perceived differences in intelligence test scores across racial and ethnic groups were not due to racial and ethnic differences at all, but rather to differences in socioeconomic status and educational opportunities that were inequitably distributed across racial and ethnic groups over centuries of systemic oppression.

Figure 2.1 A Timeline of Notable Events in Clinical Psychology

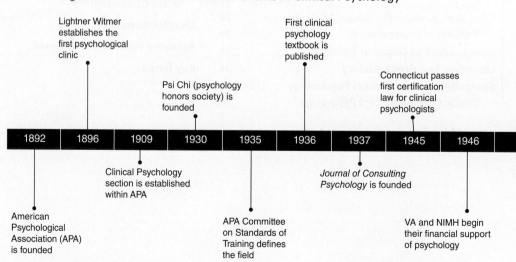

Following World War II, the U.S. government began to see enormous needs for clinical psychological practice to address combat stress reaction (the diagnostic term for posttraumatic stress disorder [PTSD] in those days) among war veterans. Within the next few decades, substantial funds were invested in the development of a diagnostic system for psychiatry (as we will discuss in Chapter 9, *Diagnosis, Case Formulation, and Treatment Planning*), in psychological research funded by the newly formed National Institute for Mental Health, and in the training of clinical psychologists at universities across the country (see **Figure 2.1**). The effects of this major cultural shift toward mental health are still evident. For instance, the building that houses the psychology department on your college campus may be one of many across the country that was initially

Many university psychology departments are housed in buildings that look like this one at The University of North Carolina at Chapel Hill. The distinctive architecture is that of the 1960s, a time when universities began putting resources into undergraduate and graduate psychology programs.

built in the 1950s or 1960s when heavy financial investments were made in this discipline. In addition, to this day, clinical psychology training programs in most departments are sizably larger than graduate programs in other areas of psychology.

In this chapter, we cover the path to achieving a doctoral degree in clinical psychology, as well as licensing and certification requirements, before we describe the primary specialties in the field. There are three different types of training models with differing perspectives on the balance between research and clinical practice, which is where we will begin.

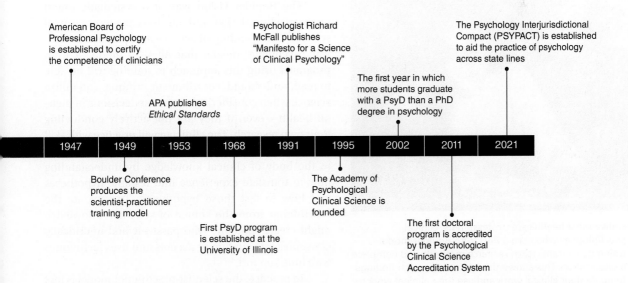

American Board of Professional Psychology is established to certify the competence of clinicians

Psychologist Richard McFall publishes "Manifesto for a Science of Clinical Psychology"

The Psychology Interjurisdictional Compact (PSYPACT) is established to aid the practice of psychology across state lines

APA publishes *Ethical Standards*

The first year in which more students graduate with a PsyD than a PhD degree in psychology

| 1947 | 1949 | 1953 | 1968 | 1991 | 1995 | 2002 | 2011 | 2021 |

Boulder Conference produces the scientist-practitioner training model

First PsyD program is established at the University of Illinois

The Academy of Psychological Clinical Science is founded

The first doctoral program is accredited by the Psychological Clinical Science Accreditation System

📚 Clinical Psychology Training Models

The Scientist-Practitioner Model (The Boulder Model)

As the field of clinical psychology expanded, professors and other leaders in the field gathered to discuss optimal approaches for training clinical psychologists, and to ensure that the field would always be represented by a reciprocal relationship between competencies in science and in practice. In 1949, a conference on graduate education in clinical psychology was held in Boulder, Colorado (Berenbaum et al., 2021). The **Boulder Conference** was a significant event in clinical psychology because it explicated the **scientist-practitioner model** (also known as the *Boulder model*) for training clinical psychologists, and it has served as *the* principal guideline for training ever since (Benjamin & Baker, 2000). In succinct terms, this model asserts that (a) clinical psychologists shall pursue their training in university departments; (b) they shall achieve competence in psychological assessment and treatment; (c) they shall receive training as researchers; (d) they shall be required to complete a clinical internship; and (e) the culmination of their training shall be the **doctor of philosophy (PhD) degree**, which involves an original research contribution to the field in the form of a doctoral dissertation.

Today, the focus on both science and practice may seem obvious, but it's kind of a big deal. Unlike other health care disciplines, clinical psychology began in universities as a branch of experimental psychology, the psychology subfield with doctoral training, but no work in practice (see Table 1.2). It arose within the structure of colleges of arts and sciences, where teaching, research, and other scholarly efforts were prominent. Note that physicians do not write a dissertation, nor do most other health care professionals, including those in mental health care.

The Boulder vision was of a systematic union between clinical skill and the logical empiricism of science. The blending of science and practice in clinical psychology means that all who graduate from programs using this approach to training will be able to read, understand, contribute to, critique, and utilize science when considering treatment decisions in mental health — even if they are not actively conducting their own research. The clinician will practice with skill and sensitivity, but will also be prepared to contribute to the body of clinical knowledge by understanding how to translate experience into testable hypotheses and how to test those hypotheses. To separate the practitioner from the source of scientific knowledge might create someone who passively and uncritically consumes information or accepts and uses techniques with little support.

In practice, the scientist-practitioner model is less a quantitative breakdown of one's daily activities than

recep-bg/E+/Getty Images

Unlike most health care professionals, clinical psychologists who earn a PhD from Boulder-model training programs learn research methods and complete a dissertation. This allows them to use research findings to guide their clinical work and use their clinical work to generate research ideas.

it is a state of mind. No one ever intended to have all clinicians devote exactly 50% of their time to their clinical practice and 50% to formal research. Some will be primarily practicing clinicians and others primarily researchers. Rather, it was intended that practicing clinicians be qualified to evaluate their clients' progress scientifically and select treatments using empirical evidence. Although many do not do much in the way of research, this may be because their work settings do not permit it; not because they do not wish to do so. Likewise, clinical researchers can produce solid, meaningful research only if they keep their clinical sensitivity and skills honed by continuing to work with clients. Just as practitioners must not forsake their research training and interests, neither must researchers ignore their clinical foundation.

For about the first 30 years after the scientist-practitioner model was developed, clinical psychologists were predominantly trained from this perspective. However, critiques emerged. Some felt that training in the *practice* of clinical psychology should receive greater priority over research training in graduate school (Benjamin & Baker, 2000). By modern standards, preinternship training in the 1960s and 1970s was often less available. Today, scientist-practitioner training affords between 550 and 1000 hours of preinternship training, followed by a requirement for 2000 additional hours of practice training during a year-long full-time clinical internship. Critics also complained that much of the research they conducted in graduate school seemed trivial, or that there was too much time dedicated to training in statistics, theories of conditioning, or principles of biological neuroscience and too little related to diagnosis, assessment, and psychotherapy. Last, some practitioners simply rejected the notion that clinical psychology was a scientific discipline, and saw it instead as an "art" captured within the therapeutic relationship.

The Practitioner-Scholar Model (The Vail Model)

In 1973, critics met to create an alternative approach to the scientist-practitioner model. This meeting was also held in Colorado (but this time in the city of Vail), and the **practitioner-scholar model** (also called the Vail model) was developed to place a primary emphasis on practice and less emphasis on science. The Vail model articulated a need for people's personal attributes to be emphasized rather than their potential to conduct scientific research when they were being considered as candidates for admission, and for research projects to be conducted to meet student interests, but only as pursuits secondary to many hours of practice experience.

The Vail model was largely rejected by academic clinical psychologists who worked in training programs that had adopted the scientist-practitioner approach. Few doctoral programs offering the PhD were interested in shifting to a model that de-emphasized the scientific basis of clinical psychology. Indeed, many universities similarly eschewed the notion that a PhD could be granted without a substantial amount of training in research and scientific methods.

A new doctoral degree was thus created: the **doctor of psychology (PsyD) degree**. The PsyD was developed with an emphasis on building clinical skills and a relative de-emphasis on research competence. A master's thesis is not required, and the dissertation is usually a report on a professional subject rather than an original research contribution. The first of the PsyD programs was established at the University of Illinois in 1968 (Peterson, 1971), although that school has since closed its program. Subsequently, similar programs were developed at Rutgers, Baylor, and elsewhere. As Peterson (1968) initially envisioned them,

PsyD programs are not substantially different from PhD programs during the first two years of training. The real divergence begins in the third year. At that point, increasing experience in therapeutic practice and assessment becomes the rule. The fourth year continues the clinical emphasis with a series of internship assignments. More recently, PsyD programs have moved toward compressing formal coursework into the first year and expanding clinical experience by requirements such as five-year practica.

Emergence of Professional Schools

The PsyD degree has evolved over the years. Noting a tremendous discrepancy between the number of students interested in education to become a clinical psychologist as compared to the number of slots available at traditional PhD programs (i.e., in the last 20 years, admissions rates have varied between 8% and 15% nationally in the United States) — so much so that students have even been willing to pay out of pocket for their education (i.e., in contrast to PhD programs, which traditionally offer tuition waivers for students in clinical psychology) — investors began to offer the PsyD degree at new for-profit institutions, or **professional schools of psychology**. Despite high tuition charges, and few tuition waivers offered at these new for-profit schools (many of which have now been renamed to include the word "University" in the institution name), these programs became extremely popular, contributing to very large faculty–student ratios (e.g., 1 faculty member for every 100–200 students enrolled). Today, more PsyD degrees are awarded than PhD degrees in the United States.

Various studies (Mayne et al., 1994; Norcross et al., 1998; 2010) indicate important differences between the PhD and PsyD paths to training in clinical psychology. First, there is a higher acceptance rate of applicants to PsyD programs as compared to PhD programs (41% versus 15%). Second, compared to PhD program faculty, a lower percentage of PsyD program faculty have expertise in evidence-based psychological interventions such as the behavioral and cognitive-behavioral treatments covered in Chapter 11, *Behavioral Interventions* and Chapter 12, *Cognitive-Behavioral Interventions*. Third, compared to students in PhD programs, a lower percentage of PsyD students receive full financial assistance (20%), and thus PsyD students accrue substantially more student loan debt than students in PhD programs (American Psychological Association, 2010). Fourth, data from the national matching system for clinical internship placements suggest that students from accredited PsyD programs are substantially less likely than students from accredited PhD programs to successfully match to an accredited clinical internship (81% versus 48%; Association of Psychology Postdoctoral and Internship Centers, 2019). Last, data from licensing boards reveal that students from accredited PsyD programs are substantially less likely than students from accredited PhD programs to successfully pass the national licensing exam to practice psychology (72% versus 90%; Association of State and Provincial Psychology Boards, 2016). Notably, data also suggest that discrepancies between the PhD and PsyD degrees are driven by students in free-standing for-profit "universities." Discrepancies in admission rates as well as student financial support between PsyD and PhD programs are evident, but are diminished when examining only PsyD programs that are housed within traditional nonprofit universities (i.e., that offer both under-graduate and graduate training across a variety of disciplines and majors). In contrast, there are far greater discrepancies on these same metrics when comparing PhD programs to PsyD programs that are housed within for-profit institutions. As described in A CLOSER LOOK: *The Argosy Disaster and Professional Schools of Psychology*, in 2019, one large for-profit institution collecting tuition from hundreds of clinical psychology graduate students across the country abruptly shut down, leaving many students on the path to their PsyD without a school to grant one.

The Argosy Disaster and Professional Schools of Psychology

Imagine that you've graduated from college and begun a training program to pursue your dream of becoming a clinical psychologist — but then your program suddenly closes, putting your whole future on uncertain footing. That's exactly what happened to thousands of professional psychology (PsyD) students at Argosy University in early 2019.

Argosy was a system of 22 for-profit career colleges that housed one of the largest PsyD programs in the United States. Established in 2001, its website boasted "convenient locations" and "flexible class formats." Indeed, there were Argosy campuses in all corners of the country (including Hawaii), with classes held in person and online to serve its roughly 8800 students. But in March 2019 — in the middle of the semester — Argosy was abruptly forced to announce its closing when its parent company went into "receivership" (a form of bankruptcy) and the U.S. government disqualified the school from receiving any further federal and state financial aid for its students. As if that wasn't bad enough, Argosy withheld millions of dollars in financial aid it *did* still have, and was supposed to give to its students. Instead, the school used this money to cover its own operating expenses and pay its faculty and staff.

The sudden closing of Argosy sent thousands of PsyD students scrambling to find other programs that would take them in and allow them to transfer their credits and complete their degree. Some schools willingly opened their doors to former Argosy students. But many students were unable to find spaces to continue their education. Not only that, since Argosy used its student financial aid money to pay its faculty and staff and to cover its own legal fees, many students who had already paid the high tuition costs (between $10,000 and $20,000 per semester) never received the financial aid they were promised — and were depending on — from the school. As a result, a number could not afford basic necessities like food, rent, and childcare. Some students turned to online fundraising to help their peers who unexpectedly faced eviction and other hardships.

The collapse of Argosy exposes a number of flaws of for-profit professional schools of psychology. For one thing, these schools lack the endowments and government funding afforded to most major public and private (nonprofit) universities. Therefore, professional schools are entirely tuition dependent, which means tuition is often expensive and many students graduate with large amounts of debt. It also means professional schools must admit large class sizes in order to operate and meet their profit margin. Moreover, tuition dollars go to support corporate investors rather than being invested back into opportunities to further enhance education. For-profit institutions also tend to engage in aggressive recruiting, leading to the admission of graduate students who may not be suitable for the profession. Although most PsyD programs are accredited by the APA and conform to the same standards as traditional PhD programs, some are not and do not. Such programs may therefore produce graduates with an uncertain education, high levels of debt, and limited career prospects.

SOURCE: https://www.washingtonpost.com/education/2019/03/09/argosy-university-closes-its-doors-students-scramble-transfer/; https://www.nationalregister.org/eo-desk-mar-2019/ ▬

The Clinical Scientist Model

As the Vail model and PsyD degree began proliferating, many science-minded clinical psychologists became quite upset. These scholars feared that the scientific basis for the field appeared to be eroding and there were many clinical psychologists graduating each year who lacked the ability to understand, contribute to, and clinically apply psychological science. In 1991, a prominent clinical psychologist named Richard (Dick) McFall wrote a call to action to reclaim the science of clinical psychology, based on the belief that clinical psychology, as currently practiced, was no longer well-grounded in science (Baker et al., 2009; McFall, 1991, 2006). According to this view, several methods that many practitioners now employ in their treatment have not been demonstrated to be effective in controlled clinical studies. In some cases, empirical studies of these techniques have not been completed; in other cases, research that has been completed does not support continued use of the technique. Similarly, the use of assessment techniques that have not been shown to be reliable and valid and to lead to positive treatment outcomes has been called into question. McFall's "call to action" for clinical scientists appeared in 1991, in his **"Manifesto for a Science of Clinical Psychology"** (McFall, 1991). In this document, he argued:

1. Scientific clinical psychology is the only legitimate and acceptable form of clinical psychology (p. 76).

2. Psychological services should not be administered to the public (except under strict experimental control) until they have satisfied these four minimal criteria:
    a. The exact nature of the service must be described clearly.
    b. The claimed benefits of the service must be stated explicitly.
    c. These claimed benefits must be validated scientifically.
    d. Possible negative side effects that outweigh any benefits must be ruled out empirically. (p. 80)

3. The primary and overriding objectives of doctoral training programs in clinical psychology must be to produce the most competent clinical scientists possible (p. 84).

In his 1991 "Manifesto for a Science of Clinical Psychology," Richard (Dick) McFall spearheaded the clinical scientist model of doctoral training.

Like-minded clinical psychologists were urged to help build a *science* of clinical psychology by integrating scientific principles into their own clinical work, differentiating between scientifically valid techniques and pseudoscientific ones and focusing graduate training on methods that produce clinical scientists — individuals who "think and function as scientists in every respect and setting in their professional lives" (McFall, 1991, p. 85).

This document, which proved to be quite provocative, led to the formation of the **Academy of Psychological Clinical Science**, in 1995. The academy consists of graduate programs and internships that are committed to this **clinical scientist model** of training, which involves instruction in empirical methods of research and the integration of research with clinical work (Baker et al., 2009). The academy is affiliated with the **Association for Psychological Science (APS)**, an international organization dedicated to advancing scientific psychology, and is comprised of over 60 member programs (including both doctoral and internship programs). The primary goals of the academy are listed in **Table 2.1**.

Table 2.1 Primary Goals of the Academy of Psychological Clinical Science	
Training	To foster the training of students for careers as clinical psychological scientists who will produce and apply scientific knowledge
Research and theory	To advance the full range of clinical science research and theory and their integration with other relevant sciences
Resources and opportunities	To foster the development of and access to resources and opportunities for training, research, funding, and careers in clinical science
Application	To foster the broad application of clinical science to human problems in responsible and innovative ways
Dissemination	To foster the timely dissemination of clinical science to policy-making groups, psychologists, and other scientists, practitioners, and consumers

Information from http://acadpsychclinicalscience.org/

In sum, today's clinical psychologists may have come from a variety of training programs that have embraced a variety of training models, and that offer different types of doctoral degrees. In the future, there may be more options as well, including licensed clinical psychology associates who are trained at a master's degree level, thus leading to even more changes in the field. National data in the United States suggest that at least 25% of the U.S. population have a mental health disorder, yet only 5% are engaged in any treatment from a qualified mental health professional. Clearly more clinical psychologists are needed, and more education is needed to help people find a professional that fits their needs.

Think Like a Clinical Psychologist Discuss the advantages and limitations of the three doctoral training models. If you were to pick a program to attend for your own training, which model would you choose and why?

▮▮▮ Components of Doctoral Training

You now know that there are two doctoral degrees that may allow someone to become eligible to be a licensed clinical psychologist. In this section, we discuss the steps to obtaining a doctoral degree.

First, it is important to note that unlike many other health care disciplines, the path to graduate training in clinical psychology does not include any undergraduate requirements per se. In other words, unlike a "premed" curriculum that is necessary to enter medical school, there is no "pre-clinical psychology" curriculum that precedes entry into a doctoral program in clinical psychology. Extensive knowledge regarding clinical psychology theories and research methods, however, does improve the chances of admission into these highly competitive programs. In fact, you may be reading this textbook for a class that is offered as part of a major in psychology. That major in psychology likely is based upon a set of competencies that have been articulated by the American Psychological Association (APA) to ensure that you are prepared to enter graduate school in psychology, including for clinical psychology. These competencies include (a) a knowledge base in psychological theories and scientific underpinnings; (b) a capacity to engage in scientific inquiry and critical thinking; (c) an understanding of psychologists' ethical and social responsibilities in a diverse world; and (d) communication skills (in oral and written formats) and professional development skills.

Doctoral programs in clinical psychology typically follow undergraduate education and sometimes relevant work (i.e., research) experience. This is confusing for many, because most assume that one must obtain a master's degree before pursuing doctoral studies. However, in most doctoral programs in clinical psychology, students obtain their master's degree as part of the doctoral program; thus, it is most common for those ready to commit to the field of clinical psychology to pursue doctoral training programs.

Clinical psychologists conduct work that has the potential to significantly benefit humans' lives, but also could inadvertently cause harm. Thus, clinical psychology doctoral programs are federally regulated to ensure that each curriculum meets a standard of accreditation. The APA and Psychological Clinical Science Accreditation System (PCSAS, through the Academy of Psychological Clinical Sciences) both are approved by the Council of Higher Education of Accreditation to offer accreditation to doctoral programs in clinical psychology; the APA also is approved by the U.S. Department of Education to do so. To obtain APA or PCSAS accreditation, a program must rigorously demonstrate that it is appropriately situated within an accredited institution of higher learning, and that it has appropriate resources, policies, rules, and guidelines to manage a competitive doctoral educational curriculum. APA accreditation evaluates whether programs have in place a curriculum that can ensure the program trains students to at least a minimal level in a wide array of competencies (see **Table 2.2**); PCSAS

Table 2.2	APA Competency Standards for Accreditation of Clinical Psychology Doctoral Programs
Discipline-Specific Knowledge	
Category 1: History and Systems	
Category 2: Basic Content Areas	
Affective Aspects of Behavior	
Biological Aspects of Behavior	
Cognitive Aspects of Behavior	
Developmental Aspects of Behavior	
Social Aspects of Behavior	
Category 3: Advanced Integrative Knowledge	
Category 4: Methods of Inquiry/Research	
Research Methods	
Statistical Analysis	
Psychometrics	
Profession-Wide Competencies	
Research	
Ethical and Legal Standards	
Individual and Cultural Diversity	
Professional Values/Attitudes/Behavior	
Communication/Interpersonal Skills	
Assessment	
Intervention	
Supervision	
Consultation and Interdisciplinary Skills	

accreditation is based on an evaluation of a program's ability to demonstrate training practices that are consistent with its own values, as well as excellence in science, the application of clinical science, ethics, and diversity (see **Table 2.3**).

Table 2.3   Summary of PCSAS Criteria for Clinical Psychology Training Program Accreditation
1. Conceptual foundations: A program must endorse the overall mission and goals that define PCSAS, but is given leeway to develop its own distinctive and innovative approaches to translating these core concepts into practical, effective, real-world doctoral programs because PCSAS believes that the field and the public benefit from diversity in how clinical science training is accomplished.
2. Design, operation, and resources: The Review Committee examines: (a) the quality, logic, soundness, and coherence of each program's overall operation; (b) its stability, educational plan, and pedagogical approach; (c) its content, curriculum, and administration; and (d) the availability and use of resources. The Review Committee also evaluates how effectively the program's design and resources are channeled toward achieving the program's goals.
3. Quality of the science training: The Review Committee evaluates the overall quality of the scientific content, methods, and products of the program's doctoral training and education (i.e., how well the program embodies the very best cutting-edge science of the discipline).
4. Quality of the application training: The Review Committee evaluates the extent to which clinical training is based on science and prepares graduates to function as independent providers of clinical services and assume responsibility for clients by making clinical decisions based on the best available scientific evidence.
5. Curriculum and related program responsibilities: Training programs must demonstrate that their students have the necessary breadth and depth of knowledge and training experiences to engage in high-quality clinical science scholarship, research, and clinical applications. Programs must clearly articulate their training goals; present a coherent training plan by which students will obtain the necessary breadth and depth of knowledge and experience (e.g., courses, workshops, practica, laboratory rotations); and describe the ways that they will ensure that students have achieved these goals. In addition, programs must ensure that ethical standards and concern for diversity are reflected in training for scholarship, research, and clinical applications as well as in program characteristics and policies.
6. Quality improvement: Programs must be invested in continuous quality improvement, including ongoing critical self-examination; openness to feedback; flexibility and innovation; monitoring of program results; and engagement in strategic planning as the field changes in response to the dynamic mental health care environment.
7. Outcomes: The Review Committee evaluates to what extent the activities and accomplishments of a program's faculty, students, and graduates exemplify the kinds of outcomes one expects of programs that successfully educate high-quality, productive clinical psychological scientists (e.g., ongoing contributions to research, dissemination of science-based practice).

Students in doctoral programs in psychology reach training competencies through numerous types of training activities, including coursework, independent research (i.e., a master's thesis, comprehensive or qualifying exam, and dissertation), and practical training in which they engage in the activities of a clinical psychologist (e.g., providing assessment, treatment, and consultation) with actual clients under close supervision. Doctoral training is not complete until students complete a full-time year-long **predoctoral internship**,

Every February, clinical psychology doctoral students who have completed their training program's coursework and clinical requirements take part in a computerized national match that determines where they will complete their year-long predoctoral internship.

which can occur at a variety of training sites all over the country (e.g., Veterans Administration [VA] centers, medical schools, private psychiatric facilities, community mental health centers, campus mental health centers). Admission to predoctoral internships is highly competitive and culminates in a computerized national match. Most internship sites also require accreditation, and there are fewer accredited internship slots available than the number of students being admitted to accredited doctoral programs in clinical, counseling, and school psychology. This has been an issue that has led to calls for more funding of mental health training programs in the United States. Currently, approximately $12 to $15 *billion* is appropriated by the federal government to subsidize the training of physicians, whereas only approximately $60 *million* is budgeted for training clinical psychologists.

Think Like a Clinical Psychologist Because there is a shortage of clinical psychologists in many parts of the country, some states allow psychologists to become licensed even if they participated in an unaccredited doctoral program and unaccredited predoctoral internship. What are the pros and cons of this approach?

Licensing and Credentialing

Once students complete their doctoral degree in clinical psychology (including their predoctoral internship), they are ready to call themselves a clinical psychologist and start seeing clients independently, right? Not quite. Clinical psychologists may not see clients without supervision until they are licensed within a particular state, province, or territory. In most locales, a license requires an additional 2000 hours of supervised clinical experience during a **postdoctoral fellowship** (i.e., a postdoc). In addition, licensure requires a passing score on two national licensing exams that are components of the **Examination for Professional Practice in Psychology (EPPP)**. Part 1 is designed to assess knowledge in broad bases of human behavior, and Part 2 is designed to assess competencies needed to ethically and appropriately work with clients. **Table 2.4** lists the content domains for each of these exams.

In addition to the completion of postdoctoral training (in most states), and a passing score on EPPP Parts 1 and 2, a license to practice psychology also requires a passing score on a jurisprudence exam specific to the state, province, or territory in which the individual wishes to practice. This exam may include information specific to state laws regarding ethics, regulations, and rules relevant to the practice of psychology that may vary across different locations.

Table 2.4 Content Covered on the Examination for Professional Practice in Psychology Exams, Parts 1 and 2
Part 1: General Knowledge
1. Biological bases of behavior
2. Cognitive-affective bases of behavior
3. Social and cultural bases of behavior
4. Growth and life span development
5. Assessment and diagnosis
6. Treatment, intervention, prevention, and supervision
7. Research methods and statistics
8. Ethical, legal, and professional issues
Part 2: Competencies
1. Scientific orientation
2. Assessment and intervention
3. Relational competence
4. Professionalism
5. Ethical practice
6. Collaboration, consultation, and supervision

Each state or province has a **state or provincial board of psychology** that determines the requirements for licensure in that jurisdiction and approves each individual license. Licensing requirements vary from place to place, but some consistency was introduced by the APA in the late 1980s and then again in 2010 with a model licensing act that can be used as a template for all state boards to adopt, or they can review and revise it based on their own specific requirements for licensure in their jurisdictions (e.g., see DiLillo et al., 2006). Common requirements for licensure are listed in **Table 2.5**.

Table 2.5 Summary of Typical Requirements for Licensure as a Psychologist	
Education	A doctoral degree from an American Psychological Association–accredited program in professional psychology (e.g., clinical) is required.
Experience	One to two years of supervised postdoctoral clinical experience is required.
Examinations	A candidate for licensure must pass (i.e., score at or above a certain threshold score) the Examination for Professional Practice in Psychology, Parts 1 and 2. In addition, some states and provinces require an oral or essay examination.
Administrative requirements	Additional requirements include citizenship or residency, age, evidence of good moral character, and so on.
Specialties	Licensure to practice psychology is generic. However, psychologists are ethically obligated to practice only within the scope of their demonstrated competence, as indicated by their educational background and training.

Clinical psychologists may get licensed in as many locations as they wish. In most U.S. states, keeping one's license active requires ongoing continuation and an annual fee. Generally, psychologists are only permitted to practice in states where they hold an active license.

The Psychology Interjurisdictional Compact (PSYPACT) allows licensed psychologists to work with clients living (or traveling in) other states.

During the COVID-19 pandemic, however, many state psychology boards banded together to form the **Psychology Interjurisdictional Compact (PSYPACT)**, an interstate agreement designed to facilitate the practice of telepsychology and the temporary in-person, face-to-face practice of psychology across state boundaries. This became necessary when the pandemic restricted travel, and clients who had difficulty finding qualified professionals in their home state realized they could use platforms such as Zoom and FaceTime to connect with clinicians across state lines. As of 2021, there were 26 states that had either joined or enacted legislation to participate in PSYPACT, and licensed psychologists in those states can apply for interstate practice privileges under this agreement. It remains to be seen whether this initiative will lead to longer-term changes in the transportability of licenses to locations more broadly. You can read more about PSYPACT at https://psypact.site-ym.com/

Think Like a Clinical Psychologist Why do you think it's necessary for states and provinces to regulate the practice of psychology by licensing psychologists within their jurisdiction? How does this protect the field of psychology? How does it protect the public?

Specialties within Clinical Psychology

Okay, so you completed your doctoral training coursework, clinical training, and predoctoral internship, and now you have completed your postdoctoral training, passed your EPPP Parts 1 and 2, and a state exam—whew! Now you can see any clients you want, right?

Sorry. No. As mentioned in Table 2.5, ethical guidelines for clinical psychologists (which we will cover in detail in Chapter 3, *Ethics in Clinical Psychology*, specify that one may only practice within the "bounds of one's competence," and most training programs offer expertise in some, but not all, areas of clinical psychology. Many of these areas (including the field of clinical psychology itself) are considered "specialties" by APA's Commission for the Recognition of Specialties and Subspecialties in Professional Psychology (CRSSPP). A list of all recognized specialties in the practice of psychology appears in **Table 2.6**, and we describe the most common specialty areas in detail next.

Table 2.6 Recognized Specialties within the Practice of Psychology	
Specialty Area	**Brief Overview**
Clinical neuropsychology	Focuses on understanding the relationships between brain and behavior as applied to diagnosis, assessment, and treatment
Clinical health psychology	Focuses on promoting health and well-being, and preventing, treating, and managing medical illness and physical disability
Psychoanalysis	Aims to modify personality by promoting awareness of unconscious, maladaptive, and habitually recurrent patterns of emotion and behavior
School psychology	Concerned with children, youth, families, and the schooling process, including developing and evaluating programs to promote positive learning
Clinical psychology	Provides continuing and comprehensive mental and behavioral health care for individuals and families; consultation to agencies and communities; training, education, and supervision; and research-based practice
Clinical child/adolescent psychology	Develops and applies scientific knowledge to the delivery of psychological services to infants, toddlers, children, and adolescents within their social context
Counseling psychology	Focuses on how people function both personally and in their relationships at all ages, and addresses the emotional, social, work, school, and physical health concerns people may have at different stages in their lives
Industrial and organizational psychology	Focuses on deriving principles of individual, group, and organizational behavior, and applying this knowledge to the solution of problems at work
Behavioral and cognitive psychology	Uses principles of learning, development, and cognitive processing to help people overcome behavioral and emotional problems
Forensic psychology	Provides professional psychological expertise within the judicial and legal systems
Couple and family psychology	Focuses on couples and families in relationships and in the broader environment in which they function
Geropsychology	Applies the knowledge and methods of psychology to understanding and helping older persons and their families to maintain well-being, overcome problems, and achieve maximum potential during later life
Police and public safety psychology	Concerned with assisting law enforcement and other public safety personnel and agencies in carrying out their missions and societal functions
Sleep psychology	Studies sleep, and evaluates and treats sleep-related problems
Rehabilitation psychology	The study and application of psychological principles on behalf of persons who have disability due to injury or illness

(Table 2.6 continued)

Specialty Area	Brief Overview
Group psychology and group psychotherapy	Focuses on identifying and capitalizing on developmental and healing possibilities embedded in the interpersonal/intrapersonal functioning of individuals in groups as well as collectively
Serious mental illness psychology	Applies specialized assessment and intervention to assist those who have serious mental illnesses or who are at risk of developing these problems
Clinical psychopharmacology	Focuses on the study and use of psychotropic medication

SOURCE: https://www.apa.org/ed/graduate/specialize/recognized

By far the most common specialties within clinical psychology (recall from Chapter 1 that counseling and school psychology are separate fields) are clinical child/adolescent psychology, health psychology, and adult clinical psychology (i.e., these are listed as "clinical psychology" among specialties). In this book, we provide examples related to clinical child/adolescent and adult clinical psychology throughout each chapter. Brief descriptions are provided below.

Clinical Child/Adolescent Psychology

Clinical child/adolescent psychology generally is concerned with psychological problems and psychiatric disorders among youth. Although many refer to this field using the term "clinical child psychology," research and clinical work usually involves exposure to youth at all developmental levels, including infants, toddlers, school-aged youth, and adolescents. Clinical child/adolescent psychologists may work as practitioners; as professors in academia; or in a variety of other settings such as medical centers and counseling centers in which research, teaching, and clinical work is possible.

Much of the work done by clinical child/adolescent psychologists can be organized into general themes of psychological problems, including externalizing disorders (e.g., conduct disorder, oppositional defiant disorder, attention deficit–hyperactivity disorder [ADHD]), internalizing disorders (e.g., anxiety, depression), developmental and intellectual disorders (e.g., autism), and serious mental illness (e.g., schizophrenia, bipolar disorder). Within each area, there are bodies of literature that examine (a) causes and consequences of symptoms, (b) efficacious and effective modes of treatment and the factors that may modify treatment efficacy, (c) prevention strategies, and (d) co-occurring problems and disorders. Increasingly, research in this area has integrated findings on biological, neurological, and genetic factors that may interact with psychosocial factors in the course of each problem or disorder.

Clinical Health Psychology and Pediatric Psychology

Clinical health psychology also is concerned with psychological problems and disorders, but with a particular emphasis on symptoms or adjustment that is related to some aspect of physical health. Clinical health psychologists interested in working with youth are referred to as **pediatric psychologists**. Clinical health and pediatric psychologists tend to work in general hospital settings more often than other clinical psychologists do. However, clinical health and pediatric psychologists also may open a private practice or work in academia as professors, and both options offer a wide range of areas for research and clinical work.

Much of the work done in clinical health and pediatric psychology is associated with one of the following questions:

- Do individuals with a physical illness (e.g., cancer, HIV) or physiological irregularity (e.g., chromosomal abnormality) experience psychological adjustment difficulties?

- Can psychological interventions be used to help increase individuals' adherence to medical regimens (e.g., for diabetes, asthma)?

- Can psychological interventions be used to help reduce health symptoms (e.g., bedwetting, pain associated with medical procedures)?

Pediatric psychologists conduct assessment and treatment of youth with medical diagnoses, often in hospital settings.

- What factors are associated with individuals' engagement in health risk or injurious behaviors (e.g., substance use, sexual risk behaviors, weight-related behaviors)?

- What is the association between psychological and physical health (e.g., stress, immunity)?

Clinical Adult Psychology

Much like clinical child/adolescent psychology, **clinical adult psychology** generally is concerned with psychopathology; however, the population of interest typically is older than 18 years of age. Psychologists interested in working specifically with the elderly may focus on **geropsychology**. Clinical adult psychologists represent the majority of all clinical psychologists (although interest in the three subfields described in this section is becoming more evenly distributed). Like clinical child/adolescent psychologists, clinical adult psychologists may work in a variety of settings (e.g., universities, medical centers, counseling centers) in which research, teaching, and/or clinical work is possible.

Clinical adult psychologists' work also is often divided by disorder and diagnosis. Perhaps the most common themes of research and clinical work include mood and anxiety (e.g., obsessive-compulsive disorder [OCD], phobias, depression), personality and personality disorders (e.g., borderline, narcissistic, antisocial personality disorders), substance use problems, eating disorders, and serious mental illness (e.g., schizophrenia, bipolar disorder). For each of these topic areas, there are bodies of literature that examine the causes and consequences of symptoms, different modalities of treatment, and co-occurring problems and disorders.

The field of geropsychology focuses on mental health treatment for elderly clients.

Board Certification

Most clinical psychologists ensure that they are practicing "within the bounds of their competence" by selecting clients and workplaces that will allow them to draw upon expertise that is consistent with their training. For instance, someone trained in clinical adult psychology would likely not accept a client who is a child or an adolescent without appropriate supervision. It also is possible to obtain **board certification** to document expertise within a specific specialty area in psychology. The **American Board of Professional Psychology (ABPP)** offers certification of professional competence in most of the specialty areas listed in Table 2.6. Much like board certification in medicine, this credential signals to the public that a clinical psychologist has an advanced level of training expertise in a particular specialty area. Board certification can be earned through verification of one's credentials (e.g., doctoral degree and clinical internship from accredited institutions, licensure). In addition, candidates are required to submit recorded samples of interactions with clients, provide a written statement regarding professional expertise and handling of clinical cases, and successfully complete an oral examination conducted by three expert peers. As you can see, these requirements are more rigorous than those involved in licensing. In essence, the public can be assured that such a clinician is someone who has submitted to the scrutiny of a panel of peers. Benefits to the clinical psychologist include reduced liability insurance, increased status as a clinician or expert witness, and increased ease of mobility if they choose to move to another state (Finch et al., 2006).

Think Like a Clinical Psychologist Imagine you are a psychologist who specializes in adults, but your graduate program offered no formal training in geropsychology. Now, you are beginning to receive referrals from many elderly individuals seeking assessment and treatment, but you don't believe you have the necessary expertise to work with such individuals. What might you do to extend your expertise so that you can ethically expand your practice to include geropsychology?

▋▋ Chapter Summary

This chapter has helped elucidate the great variability in clinical psychologists, their training, and areas of practice. It also suggests several different factors that clients would want to assess before making an appointment to see a clinical psychologist for treatment. What type of degree did the clinical psychologist obtain, and what was the training model or philosophy that guided their training? Did the clinical psychologist go to an accredited doctoral training program, and which type of accreditation did it have? Did the clinical psychologist go to an accredited predoctoral internship? What kind of postdoctoral training did the clinical psychologist obtain, and are they licensed to practice in your state, province, or territory? What was the focus of the clinical psychologist's training, and do they have specialty experience? Are they board certified in any area of practice? If you are interested in becoming a clinical psychologist, this chapter also gives you information and options to consider regarding graduate training and the various steps one must take to become a full-fledged independent professional. Anyone wanting to become a clinical psychologist or receive psychological treatment from one should be aware of the issues and differences related to each of the questions posed above. Now you are.

Interested in stories about training, practice, and research experience from professionals in the field? Read Clinical Psychologist Perspectives at www.macmillanlearning.com to learn more.

Applying What You've Learned

Exercise 1: Construct a detailed timeline that indicates the various requirements for becoming a licensed clinical psychologist and then board certified in child/adolescent psychology.
Exercise 2: What do you see as the major limitations of the existing training models for clinical psychologists?

Key Terms

Academy of Psychological Clinical Science: An organization of clinical psychology programs and clinical psychology internship sites committed to the clinical scientist model of training. The academy is affiliated with the Association for Psychological Science (APS).

American Board of Professional Psychology (ABPP): An organization that offers certification of professional competence in many psychology specialties. ABPP certification may be sought after five years of postdoctoral experience and is granted on the basis of an oral examination, the observed handling of a case, and records from past cases.

Association for Psychological Science (APS): The professional psychological organization formed in 1988 when an academic-scientific contingent broke off from the American Psychological Association. Goals of the APS include advancing the discipline of psychology, preserving its scientific base, and promoting public understanding of the field and its applications.

Board certification: Awarded by the American Board of Professional Psychology to document expertise within a specific specialty area in psychology.

Boulder Conference: A professional conference (held in Boulder, Colorado) that spelled out the scientist-practitioner model (also known as the Boulder model) of doctoral training in clinical psychology.

Clinical adult psychology: Specialty focusing on psychological problems and psychiatric disorders among those 18 years of age and older.

Clinical child/adolescent psychology: Specialty focusing on psychological problems and psychiatric disorders among children and youth.

Clinical health psychology: A psychological specialty that focuses on the prevention of illness, the promotion and maintenance of good health, and the psychological treatment of individuals with diagnosed medical conditions.

Clinical scientist model: A training model that encourages rigorous training in empirical research methods and the integration of scientific principles into clinical practice.

Doctor of philosophy (PhD) degree: An advanced degree in psychology which involves an original research contribution to the field in the form of a doctoral dissertation.

Doctor of psychology (PsyD) degree: An advanced degree in psychology with a relative emphasis on clinical and assessment skills, and less emphasis on research competence.

Examination for Professional Practice in Psychology (EPPP): Exam required for licensure. Part 1 is designed to assess knowledge in broad bases of human behavior, and Part 2 is designed to assess competencies needed to ethically and appropriately work with clients.

Geropsychology: Specialty of psychologists interested in working with the elderly.

Manifesto for a Science of Clinical Psychology: Richard McFall's "call to action" for scientifically oriented clinical psychologist in which he spelled out the goals of clinical psychology and objectives of graduate training from the clinical scientist perspective.

Pediatric psychologist: Clinical health psychologist interested in working with youth. Pediatric psychologists tend to work in general hospital settings more often than other clinical psychologists do.

Postdoctoral fellowship: Time after graduation during which additional supervised clinical experience (usually an additional 2000 hours) can be obtained to apply for licensure.

Practitioner-scholar model (also called the Vail model): Training model developed to place a primary emphasis on practice and less emphasis on science.

Predoctoral internship: A full-time year-long training required to complete doctoral training in clinical psychology. Internships are offered at a variety of training sites all over the country (e.g., Veterans Affairs hospitals and clinics, medical schools, private psychiatric facilities, community mental health centers, campus mental health centers).

Professional schools of psychology: Schools offering advanced training in psychology that differs from training offered by traditional doctoral programs. In general, professional schools offer relatively little training in research, emphasizing instead training in assessment and psychotherapy.

Psychology Interjurisdictional Compact (PSYPACT): An interstate agreement developed during the COVID-19 pandemic to facilitate the practice of telepsychology and the temporary in-person, face-to-face practice of psychology across state lines.

Scientist-practitioner model: The predominant training model for clinical psychologists (also known as the Boulder model). This model strives to produce professionals who integrate the roles of scientist and practitioner (i.e., who practice psychotherapy with skill and sensitivity, and conduct research on the hypotheses they have generated from their clinical observations).

State or provincial board of psychology: Board for each state or province that determines the requirements for licensure in that jurisdiction and approves each individual license.

CONNECT ONLINE:

 | Check out our videos and additional resources located at: www.macmillanlearning.com

Ethics in Clinical Psychology

FOCUS QUESTIONS

1. What are the five general principles that guide the practice of clinical psychology?
2. How do clinical psychologists ensure privacy and confidentiality in their work?
3. What events or situations require clinical psychologists to breach confidentiality?
4. How might clinical psychologists respond to clients who say they are thinking of harming themselves?
5. How do clinical psychologists adhere to ethical principles when conducting research?

CHAPTER OUTLINE

So far, we have discussed the numerous mental health professionals that are available to help children, adults, and families who receive psychological services. We also have talked about differences among clinical psychologists (how they are trained, what degree they have received, etc.) that may be important to understand when individuals are choosing a provider. In this chapter, we are ready to begin discussing what actually happens when clinical psychologists begin their work with a client. And the first step in every interaction with a clinical psychologist typically involves a discussion of ethics and the solicitation of informed consent from a client to begin treatment.

But wait, don't fall asleep yet! The discussion of professional ethics is not as mundane as it seems! Psychologists are faced with several remarkable ethical dilemmas on a routine basis and as the field has matured, so has the practice of professional ethics to keep up to date with the complexities of psychological services.

Imagine you are a clinical psychologist meeting with a distressed adult who tells you that he has been hitting his wife. He is extremely apologetic, but reports that he can't stop himself from doing it. He reports that neither he nor his wife have discussed his abuse with others, and he doesn't know how he will stop from doing it again tonight. As a psychologist, what is your responsibility to maintain confidentiality with your client when you know someone may be in serious harm's way?

Or imagine you have an adolescent research participant who tells you that she recently posted a suicide note on her Instagram account. She is in your lab participating in a study right now, but is scared that once she gets back to her dorm room she will get stressed out, and she suspects no one else will be there to help her calm down. You suggest that she call her parent about her suicidal thoughts and then go the emergency department at the nearest medical center, but she refuses. Are you permitted to tell your client's parent what you learned as part of this confidential study appointment?

Or imagine you are a psychologist in a very small rural area with only 500 people in town — the only community within 100 miles. Your car breaks down on the side of the road on a very cold, snowy evening, and the only tow-truck operator is one of your clients. You know from your work with this person that he is struggling financially, but he is so happy to do you a favor that he suggests he will tow your truck for free. Do you accept his offer, or risk offending him?

These are only a few of many different ethical dilemmas psychologists may encounter in their line of work. In this chapter, we will discuss the *ethical code* that psychologists must adhere to, and also several common issues that may require psychologists to engage in extreme measures to remain ethical. In addition, we will discuss how these same ethical standards are applied to research endeavors that form the basis of clinical psychology. Scientific investigations have helped us understand what psychological symptoms look like, who is at risk to experience them, how we can assess symptoms, and how best to treat psychological distress. Hundreds of thousands of research studies conducted to guide clinical practice each followed a strict code of ethical standards discussed below.

▥ General Principles and Ethical Standards

As a discipline, psychology became a pioneer in the mental health field by establishing a formal **code of ethics**. The APA published a tentative code as early as 1951; in 1953, it formally published the *Ethical Standards of Psychologists* (American Psychological Association, 1953). Revisions of these standards appeared in 1958, 1963, 1968, 1977, 1979, 1981, 1990, 1992, and 2002; and the 2002 revision was amended in 2010. The most current *Ethical Principles of Psychologists and Code of Conduct* presents five general principles as well as specific ethical standards relevant to various activities of clinical psychologists—assessment, intervention, treatment, research, forensic activities, and so on (American Psychological Association, 2002).

The five general principles are aspirational in nature, which means their intent is to guide and inspire clinical psychologists toward the highest ethical ideals of the profession. They are not enforceable rules or obligations and therefore can't be used as the basis for punishing psychologists for unethical practice. The general principles include the following:

- *Beneficence and nonmaleficence:* Psychologists strive to benefit those they serve and to do no harm.
- *Fidelity and responsibility:* Psychologists have professional and scientific responsibilities to society and to establish relationships characterized by trust.
- *Integrity:* In all their activities, psychologists strive to be accurate, honest, and truthful.
- *Justice:* All persons are entitled to access to and benefit from the profession of psychology; psychologists should recognize their biases and boundaries of competence.
- *Respect for people's rights and dignity:* Psychologists respect the rights and dignity of all people and enact safeguards to ensure protection of these rights.

In contrast to the general principles, the specific ethical standards are enforceable rules of conduct. Acceptance of membership in the APA commits psychologists to adhere to these standards, several of which are discussed in the following sections. Violation of these standards may result in receiving a reprimand or censure from the APA, termination of APA membership, or referral of the matter to a state or provincial licensing board which has the authority to suspend a psychologist's license to practice. Of course, actual clinical practice and its day-to-day demands can generate ethical decisions and dilemmas that would tax the judgment of the wisest in the field. Also, changes in our culture over time can provide a shifting ground that challenges a clinical psychologist's judgment.

Below, we discuss several key areas of the ethical standards.

Competence

Clinical psychologists must practice within the bounds of their **competence**. This has a few implications. First, clinicians must always represent their training accurately. Thus, master's-level clinicians must never lead anyone to believe they possess a PhD. Simply ignoring the fact that someone keeps referring to such a person as "Doctor" will not suffice. Similarly, a clinician trained as a counseling psychologist must be presented as such—not as a clinical psychologist. Clinicians have an obligation to "actively" present themselves correctly with regard to training and all other aspects of competence. This also means that clinicians should not attempt to use treatment or assessment procedures for which they lack specific training or supervised experience. When there is any doubt about specific competencies, it is wise to seek out supervision from more experienced clinicians. It is equally important that clinicians be sensitive to treatment or assessment issues that could be influenced by a client's gender, ethnic or racial background, age, sexual orientation, religion, disability, or socioeconomic status. Finally, to the extent that clinicians have personal problems or sensitive spots in their own personality that could affect performance, they must guard against the adverse influence of these problems on their encounters with clients.

Although these guidelines seem straightforward, many ambiguities may arise. For instance, what if there are no other mental health care providers available? Is it better to offer no mental health care than care that may be a bit outside one's formal training? Psychologists have wrestled with questions such as these for decades and solutions are available. For instance, psychologists who clearly state the bounds of their competence, and receive **informed consent** (discussed in detail later in this chapter) from a client who agrees to treatment, may offer services when other providers are unavailable. In these cases, psychologists are expected to engage in peer supervision from colleagues who have competence in the areas they lack.

Questions of competence have arisen in response to numerous new avenues that allow psychologists to offer professional advice, such as Twitter chats, Zoom-based treatment, and Internet-based groups. In 1953, the *Ethical Standards of Psychologists* (American Psychological Association, 1953) stated:

> Principle 2.64-1. It is unethical to offer psychological services for the purpose of individual diagnosis, treatment, or advisement, either directly or indirectly, by means of public lectures or demonstrations, newspaper or magazine articles, radio or television programs, or similar media.

This idea, in 1953, was pretty clear and seemed to make good sense. Professional advice is an individual thing. It must be tailored to the individual, and there is no way a clinician can do this on the basis of a three-minute conversation with a radio caller. But in 1953, there were relatively few radio call-in shows (or TV shows!) hosted by clinicians. Now, as we all know, there are many more. As in all professions, some hosts are flip, comedic, and in general poor clinicians, while others are skilled, concerned, and sincere in strongly advising the caller or viewer to seek professional help. Aside from strong media ratings, there are probably valid reasons now for having these shows. For many distressed or disadvantaged people, these programs may be their only route to help or support. The shows can also sensitize and educate other viewers and listeners, helping to prevent problems from developing or getting worse. For still others, these shows may provide the caller or viewer with that extra courage or understanding necessary to seek out professional services.

The 2002 APA revision of the ethical standards reflects these points by permitting "advice or comment" — as opposed to treatment — via radio or television programs, or via the Internet, as long as they take reasonable precautions to ensure that (a) statements are based on appropriate psychological literature and practice, (b) the statements are consistent with the Ethics Code, and (c) the statements do not cause the recipient to infer that a professional relationship (i.e., therapist–client) has been established

verbaska/Shutterstock

Telehealth is now a common method of delivering psychological services

● ● ● ● ● In Historical Perspective

Ethical Standards Reflect the Times

"These rules should do much more than help the unethical psychologist keep out of trouble; they should be of palpable aid to the ethical psychologist in making daily decisions."

This statement by psychologist Nicholas Hobbs (1948, p. 81) served as a mission statement for the first ethics code for psychologists. The field was becoming more involved in professional activities during and following World War II and therefore needed to begin policing itself to ensure that the public could maintain a trust in psychologists.

To gain insight on what to include in the first ethics code, a committee was formed to discuss situations in which ethical dilemmas were encountered. Hobbs himself chaired the group that ultimately created the first ethics document. His committee sought examples of ethical dilemmas from over 2000 psychologists and organized them into themes reflecting many of the political and social issues of the time including racial segregation, postwar politics, and the testing industry. The first version of the *Ethical Standards of Psychologists* was published in 1953 by the APA. The document was over 170 pages in length and contained descriptions of many ethical dilemmas that psychologists had written about and submitted to the first committee.

Revisions to the initial edition continued over the decades until the most recent version, which was published in 2002 and amended in 2010. Each revision has been guided by the objectives (set by Hobbs in 1948) to express the best ethical practices in the field as judged by a large representative sample of members of the APA; to reflect an explicit value system as well as clearly articulated decisional and behavioral rules; to be applicable to the full range of activities and role relationships encountered in the work of psychologists; to have the broadest possible participation among psychologists in its development and revisions; and to influence the ethical conduct of psychologists by meriting widespread identification and acceptance among members of the discipline.

Changes in culture, politics, the legal system, the economy, and the health care system have all influenced changes to the ethics code. For example, when it emerged that psychologists served as advisors to interrogators at Guantánamo Bay and other U.S. military facilities on improving the effectiveness of "enhanced interrogation techniques," the APA called on the U.S. government to prohibit the use of unethical interrogation techniques and labeled specific techniques as torture. In February 2010, the APA's Council of Representatives voted to amend the ethics code to make clear that its standards can never be interpreted to justify or defend violating human rights. Following this change, the APA officially banned psychologists from participating in military interrogations and from being involved in operations at military facilities operating in violation of international law. ■

with them personally. (For more on the establishment and evolution of the *Ethical Standards* guidelines, see IN HISTORICAL PERSPECTIVE: *Ethical Standards Reflect the Times*.)

Privacy and Confidentiality

Clinicians have a clear ethical duty to respect and protect the **confidentiality** of client information. Confidentiality is central to the client–psychologist relationship. When information is released without the client's consent, the trusting relationship can be irreparably harmed.

Clinicians should be clear and open about matters of confidentiality and the conditions under which it could be breached. In today's climate, not all information is deemed "privileged." For example, third parties (e.g., insurance companies) may be paying for a client's treatment. They may demand periodic access to records for purposes of review. Sometimes school records that involve assessment data may be accessible to others outside the school system under certain conditions (e.g., if they are subpoenaed by a court). More and more, clinicians cannot promise absolute confidentiality.

Yet, there are limits to confidentiality that require clinical psychologists to act, even against the client's wishes if need be. These include instances when someone may be at imminent risk of serious harm; when a client has been harmed (e.g., physical, emotionally, via sexual maltreatment); when a client may soon attempt to fatally harm themselves; or when a client is a minor. Let's look at each of these.

Harm to Others

Tarasoff v. Regents of the University of California is a famous and relevant legal case from 1976 (Bersoff, 1976). The events leading up to this case began when a client at a university counseling center told his therapist that he planned to kill his girlfriend. The therapist informed the campus police of the client's intentions. The police promptly took the client into custody, but because the girlfriend was away on vacation, they decided to release him. Subsequently, the client did indeed kill his girlfriend. Later, the woman's parents sued the therapist, the police, and the university, arguing that these three parties were negligent in not informing them of the threat. The California Supreme Court eventually ruled in favor of the parents, holding that the therapist was legally remiss in not informing all appropriate persons so that violence could have been avoided.

Today, clinical psychologists routinely explain to clients at the time of informed consent (usually during the initial session) that they plan to abide by the precedent set through the **Tarasoff case**, and will break confidentiality if they learn from their client that there is an imminent risk to a specific victim. As straightforward as this seems, it is still remarkably ambiguous for several reasons. First, legal precedents differ in various states. The APA *Ethical Standards* clearly state that psychologists must disclose confidential information to protect the client, psychologist, or others from harm *"as mandated or permitted by law,"* suggesting that some jurisdictions may use different standards to determine when reporting is required.

Second, it often is unclear what time frame may qualify as "imminent" when considering potential harm to others. A client's admission of a plan to attempt to kill their partner "next week" likely requires immediate reporting. But how about a statement indicating that the client plans to kill someone "one of these days" or "sometime soon" or "the next time he leaves the toilet seat up"?

Last, it often is unclear whether information communicated regarding one's intended victim is sufficient to necessitate reporting. A client may mention an intended victim by name, or a specific location where they intend to pursue mass violence (e.g., the name of a specific movie theater); however, it also is possible that a client's homicidal ideation is more vague (e.g., "One of these days, I'm going to start shooting people in a shopping center somewhere") and of course, without knowing any date or location of where violence may occur, it can be difficult to protect the public, and illegal to hold a potential perpetrator indefinitely.

Others Harming a Client

If a clinical psychologist learns that someone is harming their client, or that they have a "reasonable assumption" that their client — or someone the client knows — is at risk for future harm, reporting is required within many jurisdictions. Most commonly, this refers to instances when a minor reports neglect or physical, emotional, or sexual abuse and remains in contact with a potential perpetrator. In addition, domestic battery warrants similar reporting. In most cases, the state department of social services — or child, youth, and family services — is contacted, and psychologists are compelled to provide information regarding the identity of a suspected perpetrator and what is known regarding the history of prior abuse or neglect. Government employees, often social workers, review each report and determine when to dispatch resources to ensure the safety of potential victims. In many cases, services and resources are offered to ensure the safety of all involved; in severe cases, a child or battered spouse may be taken to a safe haven to protect them from further harm.

Psychologists are required by law to report instances of abuse or neglect; however, state laws vary, as do scenarios in which psychologists learn of harm. Thus, decisions to report suspected harm to others can be difficult. For instance, in some states, reporting suspected child abuse is not required unless the perpetrator is a "caregiver." When perpetrators are noncaregiving adults (e.g., an uncle who lives afar, a schoolteacher), psychologists are only required to report prior abuse to a child's primary caregiver (who then is obliged to take proper precautions). Similarly in some states, reporting is required only in instances in which the perpetrator and victim differ in age by more than three years (e.g., an 8-year-old hitting a 5-year-old would not require an abuse report). Many psychologists debate differences in reporting requirements such as these, but are nevertheless required to act in accordance with the law and may enter murky territory when the law and psychologists' ethical guidelines appear to suggest different courses of action.

Reporting suspected abuse can be made more challenging when clients do not want their experiences reported. Moreover, a perpetrator (e.g., a parent, a spouse) may be sitting near the psychologist's office when a client's disclosure is made. For these reasons, psychologists attempt to be as transparent as possible when making reports regarding abuse, which may include (1) a reminder of the signed informed consent that allows psychologists to break confidentiality following disclosures of abuse or neglect, (2) an opportunity for clients and/or perpetrators to participate in the call to the department of social services, and (3) a discussion regarding the steps that are likely to follow after a mandated report is made. Nevertheless, some clients or their family members may feel betrayed when their psychologist reports their behavior to a government agency, and often little can be done to repair the psychologist–client relationship.

Clients' Self-Harm

In 1971, Maxine Baker, a state legislator from Miami, Florida, introduced a bill granting the authority to judges, law enforcement officials, physicians, and mental health professionals to involuntarily admit individuals who are suicidal for an emergency psychiatric evaluation. The law passed in the state of Florida, and similar laws since have been applied throughout the United States based on what is now known as the **Baker Act**. Although laws vary slightly across jurisdictions, most indicate that individuals who are deemed to be at imminent risk for suicide can be held between 48 and 72 hours against their will to ensure that they are safe and to create a plan for care and monitoring that will maintain their safety following release.

Noel, Pappy(Frank E.). 1905-1966. Representative Maxine Baker smiles as holding a telegram and letters protesting her mental bill - Tallahassee, Florida. 1965-05-02: State Archives of Florida, Florida Memory.

Maxine Baker (1898–1994)

Clinical psychologists are among the professionals that must deliberate whether to "Baker Act" their clients. And it is not advisable to do so capriciously. Many individuals may feel depressed at times, or exhibit other suicide risk factors, but are unlikely to attempt to kill themselves. Even among the number of people who seriously consider suicide, only a small number will actually engage in suicidal behavior, and little is known regarding the factors that may make such an attempt "imminent." Psychologists thus must continually monitor their clients' suicidality, discuss safety plans, monitor periods of abrupt changes in mood or stress, and even create "contracts" with clients to help reduce the likelihood of suicidal behavior. Psychologists also work with clients to encourage voluntary admission to a psychiatric facility (e.g., a floor of a clinic or hospital) to receive an evaluation. Only when a psychologist determines that their client is in serious danger, and after exhausting all alternative efforts to ensure their client's safety, will they consider invoking the Baker Act. In doing so, clinical psychologists may divulge to the client's mental health evaluator only the information necessary to assist in the evaluation of the immediate crisis and determination of the client's safety.

This decision to break confidentiality is fraught with ambiguities. Is a suicide attempt imminent (i.e., within a few hours) or merely more likely than during prior sessions? Will an involuntary admission create additional stress to a client who is already vulnerable, or is it the only means necessary to save a life? Can a psychologist trust that an adolescent who is suicidal will be safe at home (rather than at a psychiatric facility) when it appears that the teen's parent also is experiencing severe stress or psychological symptoms? Will Baker Acting a suicidal client today make that client less trusting of mental health professionals in the future, and thus less likely to disclose suicide ideation in the future? These are among the very difficult ethical issues that psychologists must consider, suggesting a remarkable level of responsibility for many clinical psychologists.

Working with Youth

So far, we have discussed issues of confidentiality with the assumption that any information shared by the person a psychologist is treating (i.e., the client) will be kept secret. However, that is technically not correct when the client is a minor. Although laws vary among states, the majority do not offer confidentiality to youth below the age of 16 years, meaning that parents may request any and all details regarding their child's therapy, including the specific information that youth convey in session about sensitive matters.

As one might imagine, this can make therapy with youth especially challenging, as many are deeply concerned or troubled by their interactions with parents, and very strongly desire that their parents do not learn what they have disclosed to their psychologist. In other cases, youth may discuss their engagement in risk-taking behaviors, or illegal behaviors, that are highly relevant to discuss in the context of psychosocial treatment, but may elicit strong punitive reactions from parents.

Thus, clinical child and adolescent psychologists typically discuss the limits of confidentiality with youth clients, and their parents, in a different way. Specifically, it is common for psychologists to explain to parents how the promise of confidentiality will establish the trust and security that is needed for treatment to be successful, and ask parents to agree, in front of their child, that they will allow information shared in the context of therapy to remain confidential. Psychologists typically assure parents that they will indeed disclose life-threatening issues or risk of harm (as discussed above) to parents immediately. Parents occasionally specify additional topics that they wish to be notified about immediately. However, most psychologists

Various confidentiality issues may arise when children and adolescents enter therapy.

agree that the number of these exceptions should be kept to a minimum and that youth should be allowed the same rights to confidentiality as adult clients receive.

Relating with Clients

Psychologists are guided by what is in their client's best interests, and sometimes what is best is that the psychologist must decline to work with a client. This may happen for several reasons. First, psychologists are required to avoid **dual relationships**, which are defined as instances when a psychologist has any type of affiliation with the client outside the therapeutic context. In Hollywood, this is often depicted as a sexual relationship between psychologists and their clients, but this is actually quite rare, and (of course) ethically prohibited. In actuality, dual relationships can include a wide range of interactions that would be considered inappropriate. Employing a client, selling a product to a client, becoming friends with a client, having familial connections, having mutual social acquaintances with a client, dually serving as a client's teacher and therapist, or even asking a client to provide professional services in return for therapy are all examples of dual relationships. In each case, it is understood that the relationship between a psychologist and a client requires trust, integrity, confidentiality, honesty, and the psychologist's complete and unadulterated commitment to the well-being of a client; a "second" relationship or role with a client inherently introduces motives, knowledge, or social goals that are inconsistent with the foundation of an adaptive psychologist–client relationship, and thus must be avoided.

Another reason a psychologist would decline to provide services is if therapy is no longer helping the client. For example, in one case referred for review to an ethics committee, a clinical psychologist had been treating a child continuously for more than two years and had informed the parent that two more years of therapy would be necessary. The review committee decided that the treatment was not consistent with the diagnosis and that there was no evidence of reasonable progress. Cases such as these have communicated clearly that psychologists must work with clients to help them decide when they have improved and no longer require treatment. Continuing to charge clients for services that are not necessary is a clear violation of ethical guidelines.

Consenting

In this chapter, we have reviewed just a few of the ethical principles that guide the work of psychologists. There are many, many rules and guidelines that offer remarkable specificity in how psychologists must make decisions to ensure the protection of clients, and few of these are depicted accurately in pop culture.

For this reason, psychologists almost always begin every new professional relationship with an opportunity to review, understand, and inquire about the rights afforded to clients. This process is typically part of the usual process of obtaining informed consent. Of course, you have likely been asked to offer your consent before, so you have some sense of what this process is like. But unlike the quick exchange of papers and signatures that may characterize your experience at the entrance to an amusement park, psychologists often use the consent process as an opportunity to begin building a therapeutic relationship. For instance, among those new to psychological treatment, which includes most youth, psychologists may spend considerable time asking clients what they know about the treatment process, what they fear, what myths they may harbor, and what would make them most comfortable as they begin their professional relationship. Psychologists often will provide consent documents to a client and read through them together, answering questions along the way and addressing any fears or misconceptions that clients may have. The sample consent form in **Figure 3.1** is from a psychological services clinic based at a university where doctoral students in psychology are trained to become clinical psychologists.

T**hink Like a Clinical Psychologist** Imagine that a graduate student in a mental health training program cited her strong religious beliefs as a basis for her refusal to provide affirming treatment of LGBTQ+ clients. The student was dismissed from her graduate program due to discriminatory behavior. However, she believed her dismissal was a violation of her right to exercise her freedom of religion.[1] Discuss this issue from the perspective of the APA ethical code and the general principles listed above.

▮▮▮ Ethics and Clinical Psychology Research

Clinical psychologists must adhere to these same ethical standards when conducting research with study participants, whether human or other types of animals. The importance of ethics in conducting research is unfortunately highlighted by historical episodes of gross misconduct in biomedical and psychological studies, none more egregious than the Tuskegee Syphilis Study in which 399 Black men infected with this disease were promised free medical care in 1932 (e.g., readily available antibiotics) if they agreed to be observed for six months as part of this study on untreated syphilis. None of the men ever received treatment, however, and the study was extended to 40 years (until 1972) despite the syphilis-related deaths of 128 participants. The Tuskegee study not only raises concerns about racism (and plays a role in the mistrust of research that continues to this day among members of underrepresented groups), but it highlights how a number of ethical principles are directly relevant to psychological research.

---

[1]You can read more about the actual case on which this question is based at https://www.apa.org/monitor/jan02/exemption.html.

Figure 3.1 Sample Consent Form

CONSENT FOR TREATMENT, PAYMENT, AND HEALTH CARE OPERTIONS AND ACKNOWLEDGEMENT OF RECEIPT OF UNIVERSITY'S NOTICE OF PRIVACY PRACTICES

Welcome to the Psychological Services Clinic (the "Clinic"). This consent and acknowledgement document contains important information about our professional services and business practices, our outcome assessment system, and information about the Health Insurance Portability and Accountability Act (HIPAA). We encourage you to read it carefully and to ask any questions you may have. We will give you a copy to take home.

Clinic services are primarily provided by graduate student therapists and postdoctoral fellows, who are under the direct supervision of a Licensed Psychologist. The supervisor's name and contact information is listed below. Some services are also provided directly by Licensed Psychologists. It is standard procedure for sessions to be videotaped for supervision and educational purposes. Student therapists are supervised either on an individual basis or in a student therapist group. In addition, student therapists present clinical cases at the Clinic's weekly training seminar. One of the main purposes of supervision and training is to assist our therapists in providing the best possible services to their clients. Clients will be asked to complete various clinical assessment measures during treatment.

FEES AND INSURANCE REIMBURSEMENT: We are committed to providing high quality clinical assessment and treatment services. Since the Clinic's primary purpose is clinical training, our fees are modest and adjustable. The full fee is generally set at about 50% of community rates. Clients with specific financial difficulties are encouraged to discuss the matter with their therapist. Clients are expected to pay for each therapy session at the time of the appointment. Assessments are paid 50% at the first session and 50% at the second session (gifted and Early Kindergarten assessments are paid at the first session). Although the Clinic will not file an insurance claim for you, we will provide you with a comprehensive statement that you can send to your insurance company for reimbursement. We cannot ensure payment by third party payers and it is your responsibility to verify coverage if you plan to seek reimbursement. In the event of failure to pay fees, your name, address, and phone number may be forwarded to a collection agency in accordance with State policies and procedures.

MISSED APPOINTMENT POLICY: Therapy: Missed sessions are problematic for both clients and therapists. Therefore, we ask clients to make a commitment to attend sessions regularly. If you must cancel a session, call the clinic and leave a message for your therapist as soon as possible. You may be charged for missed sessions if you have not notified your therapist at least 24 hours in advance. Frequent cancellations or missed sessions may result in termination of therapy. If you wish to terminate therapy, we encourage you to discuss this decision with your therapist.

Assessment: Assessments take several meetings to gather the data necessary to answer the specific clinical question for which an assessment is sought. They require therapists to devote a significant amount of time and, because of their timesensitive nature, typically must be completed within a matter of weeks. Therefore, if you cancel, reschedule or miss more than one appointment or if there is more than one month between any of the assessment sessions, we may determine that we have to complete the assessment with the data collected up to that point.

(continued)

IN CASE OF EMERGENCY: The Clinic does not have 24-hour emergency coverage. In the event of an emergency, you may contact any of the following resources **if you are in need of urgent care: call 911 or the Emergency Department of the hospital nearest to you and ask to speak to the crisis worker on call.**

HIPAA—THE HEALTH INSURANCE PORTABILITY AND ACCOUNTABILITY ACT: The Health Insurance Portability and Accountability Act (HIPAA) is a federal law that provides privacy protections for treatment records and establishes client rights with regard to the use and disclosure of your Protected Health Information (PHI). PHI is your medical, billing and demographic information collected and created or received by the Clinic for the purposes of treatment, payment, and health care operations. HIPAA also permits use of PHI for teaching purposes. HIPAA requires that the Clinic provide you with a Notice of Privacy Practices. Our Notice, which is included with this document, explains HIPAA and its application to your PHI in greater detail. The law requires that we obtain your signature acknowledging that the Clinic has provided you with this information.

LIMITS ON CONFIDENTIALITY: Both state and federal law generally protect the privacy of communications between a client and a psychologist. In most situations, the Clinic cannot release information about your treatment to others unless you sign a specific written authorization or consent. However, there are certain situations in which the Clinic is mandated or permitted to disclose confidential information without your consent or authorization. These situations are outlined in the attached Notice of Privacy Practices. For instance, we may use and/or disclose protected health information (PHI) about you when necessary to prevent or lessen a serious threat to your health or safety, or to the health or safety of the public or another person. Also, we must disclose PHI about you to government authorities that are authorized by law to receive reports of suspected abuse, neglect or domestic violence. We must disclose PHI about you when required by federal, state or local law. We also must make disclosures of PHI when required by the Secretary of the Department of Health and Human Services to investigate or determine our compliance with the requirements of the HIPAA Privacy Regulations. If such a situation arises, your therapist will try to contact you before taking any action and will limit disclosure only to the information minimally necessary in the situation.

CONSENT AND ACKNOWLEDGEMENT: I understand I have the right to review the Notice of Privacy Practices prior to signing this document. This Notice describes the types of uses and disclosures of my PHI that may occur in my treatment, payment of my bills or in the performance of health care operations of the Clinic. The Notice also describes my rights and the Clinic's obligations with respect to my PHI. You may obtain a revised Notice by requesting a revised copy be sent in the mail, or asking for one at the time of your next appointment.

I consent to the use and disclosure of my Protected Health Information by the Clinic for the purpose of diagnosing or providing treatment to me, obtaining payment for my treatment, and/or conducting health care operations of the Clinic. I understand that diagnosis or treatment of me by the Clinic is conditioned upon my consent as evidenced by my signature on this document.

I may revoke my consent in writing at any time. That revocation will be binding when received by the Clinic except to the extent a) the Clinic has already taken action in reliance on my consent, b) the Clinic has legal obligations imposed by a court of law or by my health insurer that makes continued use and/or disclosure of my PHI necessary in order to process claims made under my policy, or c) I have not satisfied financial obligations to the Clinic that I have incurred.

My signature on this document is my consent for treatment, payment and health care operations and my acknowledgement that I have been informed about and received a copy of the Notice of Privacy Practices. ■

In this section, we offer a brief discussion of these research ethics, knowing that a more in-depth treatment likely will be offered in your research methods class.

Several sections of the ethical code refer directly to research activities. Note that several of these reflect the same general principals discussed above:

1. Plan and conduct research according to recognized standards of scientific competence and ethical principles. Psychologists must gain approval, if required by institutions, before conducting research.

2. Obtain informed consent from participants in research. Inform them of the research procedures, their right to withdraw, potential risks or discomforts, possible benefits, limits to confidentiality, incentives for participation, and whom to contact for questions about participation and participants' rights.

3. Use experimental deception as part of study procedures only when it is not possible to use alternative methods.

4. Take great care, in offering inducements for research participation, that the nature of the compensation (such as professional services) is made clear, and that financial or other types of inducements are not so excessive as to coerce participation.

5. Do not fabricate data and give proper credit to others for their contributions. Discuss publication authorship early in the research process, and base authorship on the relative contributions of the individuals involved.

6. Inform research participants of the anticipated use of the data and of the possibility of sharing the data with other investigators or any unanticipated future uses.

7. Provide participants with information at the close of the research to erase any misconceptions that may have arisen.

8. Treat animal subjects humanely and in accordance with federal, state, and local laws as well as with professional standards.

Several of these points warrant further comment.

Informed Consent

Good ethical practice and legal requirements demand that participants give their formal informed consent (usually in writing) prior to their participation in research. Researchers inform the participants of any risks, discomforts, or limitations on confidentiality. Further, researchers inform the participants of any compensation for their participation. In the process, the researcher agrees to guarantee the participants' privacy, safety, and freedom to withdraw. Unless participants know the general purpose of the research and the procedures that will be used, they cannot fully exercise their rights.

Confidentiality

Participants' individual data and responses should be confidential and guarded from public scrutiny. Instead of names, code numbers are typically used to protect anonymity. While the results of the research findings characterizing the entire study sample as a group are usually open to the public, they are presented in such a way that no one can identify a specific participant's data. Finally, clinical psychologists must obtain consent before disclosing any confidential or personally identifiable information in their writings, lectures, or presentations in any other public media (e.g., a television interview).

Deception

Sometimes the purpose of the research or the meaning of a participant's responses is withheld. Such **deception** should be used only when the research is important and there is no alternative to the deception (i.e., when study information beforehand might compromise participants' data). Deception should never be used lightly. When it is used, extreme care must be taken that participants do not leave the research setting feeling exploited or disillusioned. It is important that careful debriefing be undertaken so that participants are told exactly why the deception was necessary. We do not want participants' levels of interpersonal trust to be shaken. Clearly, how we obtain informed consent is very important when deception is involved.

In the famous Stanford Prison Experiment (Haney, Banks, & Zimbardo, 1973) college students became prisoners or guards in a simulated prison environment. The aim was to examine the effects of these roles, but some participants became aggressive toward others, while other participants had extreme negative psychological reactions. This study has received many ethical criticisms, including the lack of fully informed consent, as even the researchers did not know what was going to happen during the study.

An example of the need for deception in a study might be an experiment in which it is predicted that the viewing of gun magazines (or other materials associated with potential violence) will lead to increased scores on a questionnaire measuring hostility. All participants are told that the experiment is one focusing on short-term memory, and they will be completing a memory task on two occasions separated by a 15-minute waiting period during which they will be reading magazine articles. All participants first complete baseline measures (including the hostility questionnaire). Next, all participants complete a computer-administered memory task. During the waiting period, the experimental group is told to read selections from a gun magazine that is made available in the lab; the control group is told to read selections from a nature magazine (neutral with regard to violent imagery). All participants later complete the computer-administered memory task again. Finally, all participants complete the battery of self-report instruments a second time.

We are not so much interested in the viability of this hypothesis as we are in the need for some deception in the experiment. As you can see, to tell the participants the real purpose of the experiment would likely influence their responses to the questionnaires (especially to the one measuring hostility). Therefore, the investigator might need to introduce the experiment as one that is focusing on short-term memory.

Debriefing

Because participants have a right to know why researchers are interested in studying their behavior, a **debriefing** at the end of the research is mandatory. It should be explained to participants why the research is being carried out, why it is important, and what the results have been. In some cases, it is not possible to discuss results because the research is still in progress.

But subjects can be told what kinds of results are expected and that they may return at a later date for a complete briefing if they wish.

Fraudulent Data

It hardly seems necessary to mention that investigators are under the strictest standards of honesty in reporting their data. Under no circumstances may they alter obtained data in any way. To do so can bring charges of fraud and create enormous legal, professional, and ethical problems for the investigator. Although the frequency of fraud in psychological research has so far been minimal, we must be on guard. There is no quicker way to lose the trust of the public than through fraudulent practices.

The debriefing is an important part of research ethics. At the conclusion of a participant's study visit, the researcher clearly explains to the participant the actual purpose of the study and what the research team is hoping to learn.

Of course, these are only a few of the many ethical guidelines that are relevant to clinical psychologists' research activities. Note that as with clinical practice, ethical considerations adhere to the guiding principles discussed at the start of the chapter (*Beneficence and nonmaleficence, Fidelity and responsibility, Integrity, Justice, Respect for people's rights and dignity*) to ensure that clinical psychologists are always guided by ways to protect the public and engage in efforts that have the greatest chance of helping the human condition.

Think **Like a Clinical Psychologist** Why is it just as important for researchers to maintain the confidentiality of their participants as it is for therapists to maintain the confidentiality of their clients?

▥ Ethics and Diversity

The ethics code also addresses diversity, inclusion, and multiculturalism through its principles and standards. For example, the principle of respect for peoples' rights and dignity includes the need for awareness of and respect for cultural, individual, and role differences — including those based on age, gender, gender identity, race, ethnicity, culture, national origins, religion, sexual orientation, language, and socioeconomic status. In addition, the ethical standards state that psychologists must neither discriminate unfairly nor harass based on any of the above considerations. Psychologists are further obliged to ensure that they are competent when working with diverse populations; ensure that they use tests whose validity and reliability have been established for use with members of the population tested; interpret tests with consideration of linguistic and cultural differences; and ensure that consent is obtained when using interpreters.

These principles and standards help ensure more equal access to quality psychological services for individuals from traditionally marginalized groups who otherwise might not find them as readily available. They also serve to optimize the help (and minimize any harm) that psychologists can provide to clients from diverse backgrounds. Indeed, research suggests that interventions targeted to specific cultural groups are more effective than generic interventions provided to heterogeneous groups (Griner & Smith, 2006). In other words, psychologists should be able to upgrade the quality of their services to multicultural patients by adhering to these ethical principles and standards and accommodating multicultural perspectives into their practice.

▮▮ Chapter Summary

Ethics are of paramount importance in clinical psychology because clients — many of whom are vulnerable due to their mental illness — often place a high degree of trust in their psychologist and may reveal sensitive information about themselves that they have never before told anyone else. With this trust comes the responsibility to make sure that clients are protected, including being protected from improper influence by the psychologist. In this chapter, we discussed the ethical code that psychologists must adhere to for the protection of their clients. Several common issues may require psychologists to engage in extreme measures to remain ethical. For example, we presented an overview of the ethical standards to which clinical psychologists are held accountable, including issues of competence, confidentiality, and termination. In some instances, it is unclear how best to resolve ethical dilemmas. In such cases, clinical psychologists seek out consultation from other psychologists before deciding on a course of action.

We also highlighted how these same ethical standards are applied to clinical research. Just as with treatment providers, researchers are held accountable for their actions. Ethics in research uphold the values required for mutual respect, fairness, and accuracy in data collection and reporting. Participants in psychological research often reveal sensitive information about themselves that, if made public, could harm them socially, emotionally, financially, or in other ways. Some psychological experiments necessitate temporary deception in order to obtain the most accurate data. Accordingly, ethics support important social and moral values, such as the principle of doing no harm to others. Within the text, you will see references to several of the ethical guidelines discussed in this chapter.

Applying What You've Learned

Ethical Dilemmas

1. Dr. A is a licensed psychologist in private practice. He is approached by his ex-wife's friend who wants to see him for psychotherapy. Under what conditions, if any, would be ethical for Dr. A to accept this person as a client?
2. Dr. B lives in a rural area of North Carolina. One of her adult clients has a child who is experiencing debilitating symptoms of anxiety. Her client pleads with her to offer therapy to the child. However, Dr. B has never had any training in child psychotherapy. She begins to read books on child psychology, and watches a five-hour workshop on how to treat child anxiety. She agrees to see the child in therapy. Is Dr. B acting ethically? Why or why not?
3. Dr. C's new adolescent client tells him she was referred by her school principal because of disruptive behavior at school. She adds that her principal told her she would be

expelled if she does not attend therapy. After his initial session with this client Dr. C decides it would be a good idea for him to talk to his client's principal to better understand why she was referred for treatment. Discuss whether it would be appropriate for Dr. C to contact his client's principal.

4. Dr. D has been treating a child diagnosed with major depressive disorder. After the fifth session Dr. D discovers the client's parents' insurance company has authorized only six sessions for therapy. In order to behave ethically what should Dr. D do in this situation?

5. Dr. E has been treating a young man with relationship problems. Dr. E finds he identifies with his client's situation on a personal level and often thinks about his own relationship issues when in session with this client. It recently occurred to Dr. E he would enjoy being this client's friend. To ensure he behaves ethically what steps (if any) should Dr. E take?

6. Dr. F just received a friend request from her client on Facebook. For over six months, this client has been grieving a breakup with a former girlfriend and is very sensitive to rejection. What is Dr. F's ethical responsibility and how should she act?

7. Dr. G has a client in graduate school who reports that he often has fantasies about entering a movie theater with a semiautomatic weapon and shooting everyone who is watching a movie. Under what conditions, if any, does Dr. G have an ethical responsibility to tell the police?

8. Dr. H has an adolescent client who reports that her father sometimes touches her body in a way that makes her feel uncomfortable. Last week, her father told Dr. H that his daughter had gotten very upset with him for grounding her, and told a lie to the school principal. Specifically, she reported to the principal that her father made her stand outside alone in the snow for five hours overnight. She later recanted her story. The girl has no other parents at home. What should Dr. H do to act responsibly?

9. Dr. I's client is a 21-year-old male who has been clinically depressed for at least three months. A horrible rumor was spread about him in his college dorm yesterday, and he feels extremely embarrassed. He fears that everyone thinks he is "crazy." In session today, he says that he can't take it anymore and thinks everything would be better if he were no longer alive. Dr. I suggests that he may want to go to the hospital to stay safe, and the client becomes extremely agitated, saying that this will make the rumors about him get even worse. What is Dr. I's ethical responsibility?

10. Dr. J is asked to assess the IQ of a 10-year-old non–English speaking girl with academic difficulties. She administers only the nonverbal subtests of the WISC-IV (subtests from PRI and PSI) because she is concerned about the girl's limited verbal skills. The girl obtains results in the low average range. Dr. J uses these results as an index of her overall IQ, and bases her recommendations on these results. The child is then placed in remedial classes based on the test results and Dr. J's recommendations. Were Dr. J's test administration and interpretation ethical?

Key Terms

Baker Act: Bill granting the authority to judges, law enforcement officials, physicians, and mental health professionals to involuntarily admit suicidal individuals for an emergency psychiatric evaluation.

Beneficence and nonmaleficence: One of five general ethical principles stating that psychologists strive to benefit those they serve and to do no harm.

Code of ethics: As pertains to psychologists, enforceable rules of professional conduct identified by the American Psychological Association (APA).

Competence: An ethical principle that calls upon psychologists to recognize the boundaries of their professional expertise and to keep up-to-date on information relevant to the services they provide.

Confidentiality: An ethical principle that calls upon psychologists to respect and protect the information shared with them by clients, disclosing this information only when they have obtained the client's consent (except in extraordinary cases in which failing to disclose the information would place the client or others at clear risk for harm).

Debriefing: The legal requirement that researchers explain to participants the purpose, importance, and results of the research following their participation.

Deception: Instances when the purpose of the research or the meaning of a participant's responses is withheld so as to not influence the participant's response.

Dual relationships: Instances when a psychologist has any type of affiliation with the client outside the therapeutic context. A second relationship or role with a client inherently introduces motives, knowledge, or social goals that are inconsistent with the foundation of an adaptive psychologist–client relationship, and thus must be avoided.

Fidelity and responsibility: One of five general ethical principles stating that psychologists have professional and scientific responsibilities to society and to establish relationships characterized by trust.

Informed consent: In clinical practice, the legal requirement that researchers sufficiently inform clients about the proposed course of treatment such that the clients can make an informed decision about whether to enter treatment. In research, the requirement to inform potential participants about the general purpose of the study; the procedures that will be used; any risks, discomforts, or limitations on confidentiality; any compensation for participation; and their freedom to withdraw from the study at any point.

Integrity: One of five general ethical principles stating that, in all their activities, psychologists strive to be accurate, honest, and truthful.

Justice: One of five general ethical principles stating that all persons are entitled to access to and benefit from the profession of psychology; psychologists should recognize their biases and boundaries of competence.

Respect for people's rights and dignity: One of five general ethical principles stating that psychologists respect the rights and dignity of all people and enact safeguards to ensure protection of these rights.

Tarasoff case: A landmark 1976 case in which the California Supreme Court ruled that a therapist was legally remiss for not informing all appropriate parties of a client's intention to harm. This case legally established a therapist's "duty to protect."

CONNECT ONLINE:

 | Check out our videos and additional resources located at: www.macmillanlearning.com

CHAPTER

4

Psychological Assessment: Science and Practice

FOCUS QUESTIONS

1. What are the major steps in conducting a psychological assessment?
2. What are the major criteria for selecting an assessment instrument? Briefly describe each type.
3. What types of reliability and validity are relevant to psychological assessment? Describe each type.
4. What are the advantages and disadvantages of the clinical approach to prediction?
5. What are the advantages and disadvantages of the statistical approach to prediction?
6. How is psychological assessment used in research?
7. Compare and contrast epidemiological research, correlational research, and experimental research.

CHAPTER OUTLINE

In a way, we're all amateur psychologists. After all, it's human nature to try to understand other people. We continually gather information and use it to form impressions, infer what others are thinking and feeling, and predict their behavior. We also use this information—which may or may not be accurate—to make decisions about how to interact with others. Comparably, **psychological assessment** is the process of collecting and synthesizing information for the purposes of understanding a client's patterns of thinking and behavior, classifying the problems they have, developing a plan for intervention, measuring the effects of interventions, and conducting research to better understand psychological phenomena (Hunsley & Mash, 2020).

For many decades, assessment was the most common activity of clinical psychologists. Today, along with providing treatment, it remains a critical part of clinical practice. After all, without the ability to measure psychological phenomena, research on the nature and treatment of psychological problems would not be possible. An accurate understanding of an individual's difficulties also makes it possible to choose and implement an effective psychological intervention. Accordingly, before someone like Kiara or Shane (introduced in Chapter 1, *Clinical Psychology in Context*) can receive effective intervention, their psychological functioning must be thoroughly evaluated, and the results of this assessment carefully considered in light of factors such as their sociocultural background, their attitude toward being assessed, and even the nature and quality of the assessment instruments themselves.

Physicians have laboratory tests that have been carefully developed to measure biomarkers of health and illness and provide guidance for treatment. Medical professionals receive training in how to choose and administer the appropriate medical tests. Similarly, different types of psychological instruments have been developed to assess variables such as personality traits, intelligence, and various other indicators of psychological functioning. But assessing the extensive range of psychological phenomena in people with diverse backgrounds and experiences is fundamentally different from assessment in medicine. Whereas a one-size-fits-all blood test might be used to establish the presence of a medical illness, clinical psychologists must make many judgments about what to assess, which theoretical perspective should be used to approach the problem, and which assessment instruments will be most accurate.

Therefore, clinical psychologists also must undergo rigorous training to make sure they administer such tests properly. Indeed, the effectiveness of a psychological assessment depends on the skill and knowledge of the person administering and interpreting the test. When used improperly, psychological tests can lead to incorrect (and even harmful) conclusions and treatment decisions. Clinical psychologists are keenly aware of this and are highly conscientious when it comes to conducting assessments, interpreting test results, and communicating the results in careful and cautious language.

How do clinical psychologists decide what factors to assess in their clients? How do they choose which tests to use? How are tests and other assessment instruments developed—and how do we know that they're accurate and unbiased? This chapter provides an overview of the process of conducting a psychological assessment, the challenges of doing so, as well as the importance of

FatCamera/Getty Images

The results of psychological assessments must be considered in light of many factors, including one's cultural background.

clinical assessment for research in clinical psychology. Then, in the chapters to follow, you'll learn about the specific types of assessments that are available to clinical psychologists.

Psychological Assessment in Practice

Psychological assessment includes a sequence of steps that begins with the identification of a presenting problem and culminates in communicating the outcome of the assessment to the appropriate individual(s) as shown in **Figure 4.1**. In this section, we'll walk through these steps and learn about the various procedures and decisions that need to be made within each.

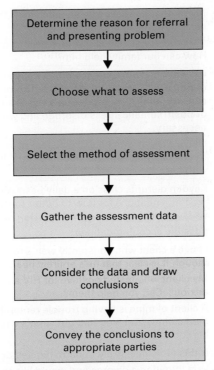

Figure 4.1 The Process of Clinical Psychological Assessment

The Referral and Presenting Problem

Generally, the first interaction between a clinical psychologist and client involves the client providing a **reason for referral** — that is, a description of why the psychologist's services are being sought. This **presenting problem** is what initiates an assessment. It helps the psychologist begin to think about what needs to be evaluated, what assessment instruments might be useful, and what the goals of the assessment will be. In many instances, such a referral is made over the telephone or via email. Clinical psychologists receive referrals from diverse sources and for a wide range of presenting problems. Some examples are included in **Table 4.1**.

Table 4.1 Common Referral Sources and Typical Presenting Problems	
Referral Source	**Reason for Referral/Presenting Problem**
Client	• I recently lost my father to cancer and I'm having trouble coping. • I'm tired all the time and my supervisor at work is telling me that my productivity is decreasing. • I'm worried that my family will disapprove of me if I tell them I'm gay. I don't know what to do. • My husband and I argue all the time and we think we need help to save our marriage.
Relative	• I can't get my 9-year-old son to go to school in the morning and I'm looking for help. • My mother has saved up so much stuff that she can't even get into certain rooms of her house. • My brother has relapsed and is back to using hard drugs every day. How can our family help him?
Another psychologist	• I'm working with a client who recently sustained a head injury during a car accident and has been complaining of trouble concentrating. I'm wondering if this is a neurological problem or posttraumatic stress disorder, and what treatment would be necessary. • I have a client with an extreme fear of vomiting but I've never treated anyone with this phobia before. Would you be able to work with her?
School	• Kayden disrupts class on a daily basis. We are interested in your recommendations for how to better manage her behavior. • We would like to have Garrison tested for a learning disability and possible accommodations.
Physician	• I have a client who constantly wants to be tested for leukemia even though it is clear that he's entirely healthy. Can you help? • My client who tested positive for HIV and his partner are very anxious. Can you help them? • A client of mine is having trouble remembering to take his medications. Can you find out what's wrong and help him improve his compliance?
Lawyer or court order	• Is this individual likely to harm himself or hurt others? • I am litigating a divorce and would like to have a psychologist's opinion of whether the child would be better off living with her mother or father.
Employer	• Is Eduardo well-suited for a job as a manager? • Is Tamira's psychological disorder severe enough that she should be missing work?

Clinical psychologists are not trained to be "all things to all people" so, once the presenting problem and goal of assessment are identified, psychologists must determine whether they match their expertise. For example, if Dr. Swanson has not been trained to perform custody evaluations, she would not agree to provide an assessment for a divorce lawyer looking to determine whether the children of a couple would be better off living with one parent or the other.

In Shane's case, his mother contacted the psychologist following a conference at school during which she learned of his disruptive behavior. The school principal gave Shane's mother a list of reputable child psychologists and informed her that Shane would be expelled from school unless he received professional help. Kiara, on the other hand, referred herself for help by looking up names of psychologists in her area who specialized in anxiety and compulsive behavior. She explained that she had diagnosed herself with OCD and was looking for help to stop her washing and checking rituals because they were interfering with her work productivity.

Choosing What to Assess

Once the psychologist's expertise is determined to match the presenting problem, the focus shifts to choosing what needs to be assessed. This decision is guided by a number of factors, including the goals stated in the referral and a conceptual understanding of the presenting problem. But people are highly complex, and as shown in **Table 4.2**, the range of characteristics that a psychologist might decide to assess is immense. This is one reason that clinical psychology training programs involve years of rigorous study and supervised practical experience. Professional psychologists must be able to make accurate judgments of what needs to be assessed.

Table 4.2 Client Characteristics a Psychologist Might Choose to Assess	
Characteristic	**Examples**
Demographics	Age, race, sex, gender identification, marital status, place of birth, cultural identity, religion, income/poverty, occupation
Mental status	Appearance and behavior in the session, orientation to time and place, ability to concentrate, short-term memory, speech and language
History of the problem	Duration and course of the problem, possible causal factors, treatment history
Social history and functioning	Social network, social support, dating/intimate relationships, social stressors, ethnic/cultural factors
Medical history	General health, pain, history of medical problems, surgeries, medications or other treatments, coping skills
Developmental history	Birth complications, developmental milestones, significant childhood events, relationship with parents and siblings
Family history	Family of origin, interactions with family members, cultural influences, psychological problems among relatives
Intellectual functioning	IQ, school achievement, years of education, degrees earned
Occupational functioning	Employment history, problems at work, career goals, recognition at work
Hobbies and interests	Leisure time, reading, interpersonal and independent functioning
Substance use	Frequency and amounts of use, types of substances used, problems because of substances

(Table 4.2 continued)

Characteristic	Examples
Sexual functioning	Libido (sex drive), attitudes toward sex, problems with sexual functioning, sexual preference, gender identity
Personality	Extraversion, introversion, openness to experiences, neuroticism, dependency
Behavioral/psychological symptoms (criteria for psychiatric diagnoses)	Anxiety, depression, stress, cognitive distortions, eating behavior, sleeping, hallucinations and delusions, impulsivity, posttraumatic stress, insight, impairment in functioning, destructive or oppositional behavior, autism spectrum symptoms
History of trauma or other environmental stressors	Experiences with abuse, experiences with racism or discrimination, death of family members
Self-assessment	Client's self-confidence, view of their own strengths and weaknesses, values
Legal history and history of violence	Police/arrest record, past violent behavior, previous suicide attempts, current suicidal or homicidal thoughts, time in prison

Shane's psychologist, for example, might use his knowledge of childhood disruptive behavior to decide that it's important to learn about the immediate antecedents and consequences of Shane's aggressive actions at school or home, as well as aspects of his social and intellectual history and current functioning, relationships with family and friends, the presence of stressors in his life, and how Shane copes with stress. As an expert on anxiety and OCD, Kiara's psychologist might assess the cognitive and behavioral details of her compulsive rituals, the presence of obsessions and depression, as well as when these problems developed and how they impair her functioning, among other factors.

Selecting the Method of Assessment

Once it has been decided which characteristics are important to assess, the psychologist faces another set of decisions: which particular instruments and methods to use to assess these characteristics. There are literally thousands of tests, interviews, questionnaires, and behavioral observation procedures available (and more are being developed all the time) to measure the characteristics listed in Table 4.2, and these instruments all have their pros and cons. As an example, there are over 10 measures of obsessive-compulsive symptoms, including interviews and questionnaires developed for adults and children (Lewin, 2019). Each instrument assesses obsessions and compulsions slightly differently.

What factors do psychologists consider when deciding which instruments to use? First, the instrument must address the presenting problems raised in the referral. Second, logistical concerns such as the length of time it takes to complete the assessment must be considered. It is best to strike a balance between collecting enough information on the one hand, and not burdening the person (or people) being evaluated on the other. Third, instruments are not created equal, and psychologists must use those that can be trusted to consistently provide accurate results. When assessment instruments are developed, they undergo **psychometric evaluation** — a process in which the developer subjects them to rigorous statistical analyses to determine whether they meet certain standards. When psychologists choose instruments on the basis of these scientifically determined standards, we call it **evidence-based assessment**. Let's consider the particular credentials psychologists consider when choosing evidence-based assessments: reliability, validity, and standardization.

Reliability

One credential psychologists look for in assessment instruments is **reliability** — the consistency with which the test measures a particular variable, such as anxiety, intelligence, or extraversion. There are three different types of reliability that are especially important to consider as we survey the types of assessment instruments used by clinical psychologists, and these are summarized in **Table 4.3** and discussed next.

Table 4.3	Common Types of Reliability That Are Used to Evaluate Psychological Tests
Type of Reliability	**Definition**
Test–retest reliability	The consistency of test scores across some period of time
Interrater reliability	The degree of agreement between two or more interviewers or raters
Internal consistency	The degree to which the items in a test all measure the same characteristic

Test–retest reliability addresses the question of whether the same person would receive a similar result if they took the same test multiple times. For example, Kiara should receive a similar score on a scale measuring the severity of OCD symptoms tomorrow (and next week) that she received today (assuming she is not undergoing any treatment). This kind of reliability is important because it demonstrates that the test is stable, and if used to assess the effects of an intervention, can be trusted to provide an accurate assessment of change over time. Researchers can determine the test–retest reliability coefficient for a particular instrument by administering that test to the same group of people days, weeks, or even months apart and then calculating the correlation between the two sets of results. A more reliable instrument will have a stronger correlation, although the time interval between administrations can also affect the strength of the correlation.

Interrater reliability refers to the extent of agreement between different interviewers or observers. That is, would two people administering the same test or interview get similar results for the same client? For example, a reliable diagnostic interview should result in Shane receiving the same diagnosis — perhaps oppositional defiant disorder — regardless of who is giving the interview. Interrater reliability is an important piece in establishing the accuracy of an assessment instrument. That is, if different interviewers assessing the same person cannot come up with the same (or very similar) results, the instrument cannot possibly be measuring what it is intended to measure. That said, even instruments with strong interrater reliability are not necessarily accurate — it simply means that different raters can get the same result. Researchers establish interrater reliability by calculating the extent to which different interviewers (or observers) obtain the same result when using the same instrument to test the same group of people (a statistic known as *kappa*).

Finally, **internal consistency** refers to the degree to which a test's questions all measure the same characteristic or skill, such as depression, reading comprehension, or sociopathy. Measures with good internal consistency are desirable because they have items that all contribute in a meaningful way to assessing the characteristic of interest. Those with poor internal consistency are more likely to have items that are not well-written and therefore less likely to measure the behavior or characteristic of interest. Researchers establish the internal consistency of tests by administering the test to large groups of individuals and deriving a statistic called *alpha* (which ranges from 0 [poor] to 1 [excellent] from correlations among the test items).

Validity

A second credential that is important for evidence-based psychological assessments is **validity** — the extent to which a test measures what it intends to measure. For example, does a questionnaire designed to assess the symptoms of Tourette's disorder actually provide an assessment of the symptoms of this condition? As summarized in **Table 4.4** and discussed next, there are five forms of validity that clinical psychologists must consider when choosing assessment instruments.

Table 4.4 Common Types of Validity That Are Used to Evaluate Psychological Tests	
Type of Validity	**Definition**
Construct validity	The extent to which a test measures the construct it's supposed to measure
Convergent validity	The extent to which a test of one characteristic correlates with other tests of the same characteristic
Discriminant validity	The extent to which a test of one characteristic is not correlated with tests of unrelated characteristics
Predictive validity	The degree to which test scores can predict (correlate with) behavior or test scores that are obtained at some point in the future
Incremental validity	The extent to which a test provides information not available through other means

Construct validity refers to how well scores on a test actually predict the characteristic that you're interested in evaluating. A psychologist assessing a client for bulimia nervosa, for example, needs to know to what extent the client's score on a particular questionnaire relates to the symptoms of this problem, or whether it's being influenced by some other characteristic, such as poor self-esteem. Researchers can establish the construct validity of a particular test by correlating it with a number of other measures and examining whether the pattern of correlations means the test in question is associated with other variables in theoretically predictable ways.

Convergent and **discriminant validity** are both subcategories of (and requirements for) construct validity. If an IQ test, for example, has good convergent validity, it correlates with other tests that assess IQ. Conversely, if an IQ test has discriminant validity, then it does *not* correlate with tests of characteristics *other than* IQ (such as anxiety or attentional problems). Knowing about these forms of validity enables the psychologist to trust that the tests they're using measure only what they purport to measure. Researchers examine these types of validity by administering the test in question, as well as one or more tests of related and unrelated characteristics to large groups of individuals and then computing the appropriate correlations.

Another form of validity is **predictive validity** — the extent to which a test can be used to forecast future behavior. Often, psychologists need to make inferences about how likely someone is to behave a certain way (e.g., to harm themselves) or what they are capable of achieving (e.g., success in school), which is why it's useful to know about this type of validity for different assessment instruments. Higher scores on the Scholastic Aptitude Test (SAT), for example, predict better grades in college (Frey, 2019). Researchers establish predictive validity using longitudinal studies in which they administer a particular test at some point in time and then examine how well scores on that test are correlated with some characteristic in the future.

Finally, **incremental validity** is the extent to which a test adds to our understanding of a person over and above what's been uncovered through other sources. For example, some psychologists believe that certain projective personality tests, such as the Rorschach Ink Blot Test (which we will cover in Chapter 6, *Personality Assessment*) reveal certain hidden (unconscious) aspects of a person that cannot be assessed through interview, observation, or paper and pencil tests. This form of validity can be assessed statistically by examining how much scores on a particular test add explanatory value to an existing regression model predicting the characteristic of interest.

Both the reliability and validity of a test are a matter of degree. Assessment instruments are neither perfectly reliable nor perfectly valid. But the stronger the evidence for reliability and validity, the more confident psychologists can be in their conclusions.

Standardization

A third credential that evidence-based assessments must have is **standardization**. Standardized tests include precise directions for administering, scoring, and interpreting the test. As you will see, most personality and intelligence tests come with highly detailed instructions for how to prepare the testing environment, present test questions, and score the respondent's answers. Standardization ensures that anyone taking the test has the same experience and scoring criteria, which allows psychologists to compare scores (such as the IQ scores) across different people.

Standardized tests also have **norms**, which are data about the average scores that can be expected in a certain population. Norms are established by administering the test to a large sample of the type of individuals for whom it is designed. For example, if the Weschler Intelligence Scale for Children (WISC-5) is designed to assess IQ in children ages 6 to 16, it would be administered to large groups of children within this age range (the standardization sample) to determine the typical scores in this population. Clinical psychologists use this information to determine whether a given child's score is average, below average, or above average relative to the population at large. (For more on the Weschler Intelligence Scale for Children assessment and the development of other assessment tools, see IN HISTORICAL PERSPECTIVE: *Psychological Assessment*.)

⚬⚬⚬⚬ In Historical Perspective

Psychological Assessment

Scientific approaches to assessment can be traced back to the first intelligence tests developed in France by Alfred Binet in the early 20th century. Binet and his colleague Theodore Simon were interested in ensuring that children with cognitive limitations were properly educated, and created Binet-Simon Scale to objectively classify children with such disabilities. Later, Henry Goddard introduced the Binet tests to America, and Lewis Terman produced an American revision in 1916. Around the same time, progress was being made in personality testing. Carl Jung began using word-association methods around 1905 to understand the unconscious. In 1910, the Kent-Rosanoff Free Association Test was published.

When the United States entered World War I in 1917, the need arose to screen and classify military recruits being pressed into service and the Army asked the American Psychological Association (APA) to create a system for classifying recruits according to their ability levels. The result was the Army Alpha test in 1917. This verbal scale was quickly followed by a nonverbal version, the Army Beta test.

The period of time between the two world wars (1920–1939) saw substantial progress in psychological testing. A major milestone was David Wechsler's development of the Wechsler-Bellevue Intelligence Test, which became the premier test of adult intelligence. Projective personality tests also made their way onto the scene in 1921, when Hermann Rorschach, a Swiss psychiatrist, described his use of inkblots to diagnose psychiatric clients. Rorschach's work proposed that when people respond to an ambiguous test stimulus, they will reveal something about their responses to real-life experiences. Another landmark of the projective movement occurred in 1935 when Christiana Morgan and Henry Murray published the Thematic Apperception Test (TAT), which requires the person to look at ambiguous pictures and then make up a story to describe the activities, thoughts, and feelings of the people in those pictures.

Another milestone in the history of assessment occurred in 1943 with publication of the Minnesota Multiphasic Personality Inventory (MMPI; Hathaway & McKinley, 1943). In contrast to the Rorschach and TAT, the MMPI was an objective self-report test whose major function, initially, was attaching psychiatric labels to clients. Although other tests such as the

Frequency of hand washing can be a cultural issue.

When sizing up the credentials of standardized tests, clinical psychologists need also to be conscious of the extent to which the standardization sample includes people like the individual to whom they are giving the test. Suppose, for example, a psychologist is evaluating a recent immigrant from Iran who is also a devout Muslim. If this client is given a standardized test of OCD with norms from an American population, her score might appear elevated because she engages in frequent handwashing behavior as part of her Muslim religious observance. But while such handwashing might be typical in Iran, it will appear excessive relative to the American standardization sample and might lead to an inappropriate diagnosis of OCD. In this case, the psychologist would need to find Iranian norms (and, of course, consider additional information) before interpreting this client's score as suggesting a diagnosis of OCD.

Rorschach were often put to similar uses, the MMPI was unique in that no theoretical interpretation of scores or responses was necessary.

The 1940s and 1950s witnessed a growing sophistication in testing technology. In 1949, Wechsler published the Wechsler Intelligence Scale for Children, which rivaled the Stanford-Binet scale. This was followed, in 1955, by the Wechsler Adult Intelligence Scale (a revision of the Wechsler-Bellevue Scale). These tests marked the beginning of a series of subsequent revisions of child and adult forms of the Wechsler scales that continue to this day (as we discuss in Chapter 8, *The Assessment of Intelligence*).

Beginning in the late 1950s, the behavioral movement began to assert its influence. Those who adhered to this orientation held that only overt behavior can be measured and that it is neither useful nor desirable to infer the level or existence of personality traits from psychological test results; personality traits, according to the radical behaviorists, cannot be measured directly. Personality assessment came under attack, and clinical psychology programs in the 1960s took on much more of a behavioral bent. In 1968, Walter Mischel made a strong case that traits exist more in the minds of observers than in the behavior of the observed. Situations, and not some nebulous set of traits, were said to be responsible for the ways we behave. In tune with this view, the 1970s would witness the rise of *behavioral assessment*. Behaviors were understood within the context of the stimuli or situations that either preceded or followed them. Chapter 7, *Behavioral Assessment*, in this textbook is devoted to this influential approach to assessment.

A discussion of the history of assessment would be incomplete without mention of the American Psychiatric Association's *Diagnostic and Statistical Manual of Mental Disorders*. The first version of this manual (DSM-I) appeared in 1952, with revisions appearing periodically, the most recent one in 2022 (DSM-5-TR). This diagnostic system's influence has been far reaching, yet as we cover in Chapter 9, *Diagnosis, Case Formulation, and Treatment Planning*, it is not without limitations. The DSM system also spurred the growth of another line of assessment tools — *structured diagnostic interviews*. These interviews consist of a standard list of questions that are keyed to the diagnostic criteria for various disorders from the *DSM*. Clinicians (or researchers) who need to formulate a *DSM* diagnosis for a client (or research participant) can use these interviews. ■

Gathering Assessment Data

Once assessment instruments have been selected, the clinician obtains the client's (or parent or guardian's) informed consent and data gathering begins. There are three primary methods of collecting assessment data: interviews, observations, and tests (a fourth, historical records, is sometimes used but not covered in this book). Clinical psychologists often draw on these different modalities (as opposed to relying on a single method) when evaluating an individual — a technique known as **multimethod assessment** (Hopwood & Bornstein, 2014). For example, in assessing Shane's difficulties, his psychologist might (a) directly interview Shane himself, (b) interview his parents and teachers, (c) ask the parents to complete a questionnaire about Shane's behavior, and (d) conduct a direct observation of Shane's behavior while he's in school.

Notice that Shane's assessment involves multiple informants and multiple methods. The advantage of this is that it minimizes the impact of any problems with reliability and validity.

For example, when directly interviewed, Shane might under-report his aggressive and opposi-tional behavior because he knows it is socially inappropriate. His teachers, on the other hand, might over-report this behavior due to their frustration. Thus, interviewing both sources, as well as Shane's parents (who observe him at home, but not at school), in addition to conducting a direct observation of Shane in school, provides a more complete picture of Shane's behavior.

Drawing Conclusions

Once all assessments have been administered, the client's responses to test items must be scored and interpreted in light of the reason for referral. Scoring procedures might be as simple as counting up the number of symptoms of depression a client reports, or as complicated as going through pages of notes from an observation to pick out instances of aggressive behavior. Regardless, data scoring and interpretation are of great consequence because they involve tak-ing responses to an assessment instrument and drawing conclusions about the person being assessed. As a general rule, the larger the leap from test responses to conclusions, the more vulnerable to error the clinical inference becomes.

As an example, consider Isabella, a sixth-grade girl whose parents were getting divorced. To help resolve the custody dispute, the court appointed a psychologist to assess Isabella and her parents to help determine which of them she should live with. The psychologist admin-istered a battery of tests, including the Draw-a-Person Test (Goodenough, 1926) in which Isabella was asked to draw a picture of a man, a woman, and herself (for an example of this type of drawing, see **Figure 4.2**). When her drawing of the man included a highly detailed rendering

Westend61/Getty Images

Figure 4.2 The Draw-a-Person Test This test is a measure of childhood intelligence that has been widely criticized for being weakly correlated with other measures of intelligence (i.e., weak convergent validity) and for the tendency of conclusions to be improperly influenced by irrelevant aspects of children's drawings (Harris, 1963).

of male genitalia, the psychologist initially raised concerns that Isabella's father had been sexually abusing her. Later, however, an interview with Isabella (and verification with her school) clarified that she happened to be learning about the anatomy of sex organs in her science class, which provided a far more reasonable explanation for why she included details of the man's penis in her picture! This example illustrates how dramatic inferences, especially when based on minimal data, can be off base (and have potentially grave consequences).

Another challenge when synthesizing assessment data is that information from different sources must be integrated. Alas, there are few evidence-based rules for how best to draw together results from interviews, questionnaires, observations, and other assessment methods to reach valid conclusions. Therefore, in drawing conclusions, psychologists often end up relying heavily on their *judgment*, a contentious subject that we will return to later in this chapter.

Communicating the Results

After synthesizing the assessment data and drawing conclusions, the psychologist generates an **assessment report** that contains the test results, interpretations, and conclusions. The report usually begins with a discussion of the reason for referral along with background information and history to set the context for the assessment. Next, the assessment strategy is outlined and a rationale for the choice of tests is given. The body of the report contains a discussion of test scores and conclusions, including whether the assessor felt the assessment truly reflected what it was intended to assess. Sometimes problems arise, such as a child being ill, that can threaten the validity of assessments. Finally, the report contains recommendations for how to address the questions and concerns raised in the referral. As appropriate, a copy of this confidential report may then be provided to the client, a parent, the courts, or school personnel so that action can be taken based on the recommendations.

There is no standard format for an assessment report. The nature of the referral, audience to which the report is directed, kinds of assessment procedures used, and theoretical persuasion of the clinician may affect how the document is written. What one communicates to a referring psychiatrist, for example, is likely to be couched in different language than what would be communicated to a lawyer. In **Table 4.5** we present a sample outline of a psychological test report (Beutler, 1995) and in IN PRACTICE: *A Case Illustration of a Clinical Report*, which follows directly, we present an example.

Table 4.5   Contents of a Psychological Assessment Report

    I.   Identifying information
        A. Name of client
        B. Date of birth and age (years/months)
        C. Gender
        D. Date of evaluation
        E. Referring clinician
   II.   Reason for referral and presenting concerns
  III.   Assessment procedures
  IV.   Background
        A. Information relevant to clarifying the referral question
        B. A statement of the probable reliability/validity of conclusions

(Table 4.5 continued)

    V.   Summary of impressions and findings
         A. Cognitive functioning
         B. Affect and mood
         C. Interpersonal functioning
   VI.   Diagnostic impressions
         A. Impressions about cognitive and affective functioning, *or*
         B. The most probable diagnoses
  VII.   Recommendations
         A. Duration, modality, frequency of treatment
         B. Assessment of risk, need for confinement, medication

---

In Practice   **A Case Illustration of a Clinical Report**

To illustrate several of the points that this chapter has made regarding clinical judgment and communication, let us consider a specific clinical case report.

Identifying Information

Name: Antonio Ramirez

Date of birth: 7/4/82

Sex: Male

Dates of examination: 8/22/22, 8/23/22

Referral Question

Antonio Ramirez, a 40-year-old sergeant with the Detroit, Michigan, Police Department, currently works as a narcotics officer. In the past few weeks, he has exhibited signs of stress but has refused to take sick leave, claiming that there is nothing wrong. He was referred by his commanding officer for psychological assessment to determine the extent to which recent events in Mr. Ramirez's life may have affected his ability to continue with his present duties.

Assessment Procedures

Mr. Ramirez's personnel file and the referring physician's report were reviewed, and Mr. Ramirez reluctantly agreed to allow his wife, Donna, to be interviewed. On August 22, 2022, Mrs. Ramirez was interviewed for one hour while her husband took the Minnesota Multiphasic Personality Inventory-3 (MMPI-3). He complained of headache and blurred vision, which he claimed prevented further assessment that day. He returned the next day for a one-hour interview, after which he completed the Rorschach and the Wechsler Adult Intelligence Scale-Revised (WAIS-IV).

Background

Mr. Ramirez is currently living with his wife of eight years, a 6-year-old daughter, and a 4-year-old son. He has been employed by the Detroit Police Department since 2010 and has a satisfactory record. In general his health is good, and he expresses satisfaction with his job and marriage. His social life is limited, which he attributes to the fact that as a police officer he is viewed with unease by potential friends, and also to the unpredictable hours he must work.

He has good relationships with his siblings but sees them rarely, as they all live in distant parts of the country. He has no hobbies and spends his limited spare time at home, occasionally playing with his children, but primarily maintaining his house and yard. His relationship with his wife is, by his report, "close," but he says they rarely discuss feelings and he would not burden her with his worries. His wife describes him as a good husband, faithful, even-tempered, and a loving father, but she says he takes life too seriously, and would like him to learn to have more fun.

Mr. Ramirez was raised by his mother in considerable poverty, his father having died in an industrial accident when Antonio was 8 years old. He remembers his father as "stern, but you knew he loved you." He describes his mother as "always worn out, always sad." At the time of his father's death, there were three younger children, ages 5 years, 3 years, and 6 months. Mr. Ramirez early took on the role of family supporter, working after school and on weekends to add to the family income, and helping to discipline his younger siblings. He remembers his teenage years as "not much fun, a lot of struggling to survive."

At school he was socially isolated because of his work schedule and also because he was determined to complete his education, and thus had no time for "fooling around with the guys." He learned to fight in self-defense when necessary, to pursue his own course, and to persist at whatever he tried. His sexual development was unremarkable. Since his mother seemed already to be burdened and since he had no close friends, he learned to keep problems and feelings to himself. After two years of college he entered the police academy, attracted by the discipline and structure of the organization and the opportunity to defend the public. On the police force he acquired a reputation for being fair, even-tempered, tough, and completely dependable, but not an easy person to get close to — indeed, almost frightening in his self-sufficiency.

In the last three months, he has experienced a number of disturbing events. His partner was wounded during a raid; Mr. Ramirez himself was shot at, though not injured, while making a routine traffic check; his wife was attacked, though not raped or physically harmed, on the way home from work one evening; and he was first on the scene to discover two children under the age of 5 beaten to death in a "crack house."

This accumulation of violence appears to have affected Mr. Ramirez in several ways. He has had several uncharacteristic outbursts of temper at minor frustrations; on one occasion, to the distress of his fellow officers, he fired his police weapon with insufficient provocation. Somatic symptoms include a 15-pound weight loss over the past two months, and (according to his wife) restless sleep and nightmares several times a week. In addition, he has become irrationally overprotective of his family, refusing to let the children visit friends' houses, and angrily demanding that his wife stop working. At work he appears jumpy and distractible, to an extent that has become a concern to his fellow officers. When doing work requiring close attention, he has, on several occasions, developed a headache. Several of his written reports, usually meticulously completed, have contained careless errors and omissions. He has refused to discuss any of these incidents or their impact with his partner, his immediate supervisor, or the police-appointed physician.

When asked about these unusual behaviors, Mr. Ramirez denied that he had changed and claimed that people were exaggerating. On probing, he admitted that sometimes, when he is involved in unrelated daily activities, he gets flashbacks (especially to the scene with the dead children), but claimed that they neither upset him nor made him lose concentration. He attributed his weight loss and restless sleep to the hot summer weather, and insisted throughout the assessment process that he is "fine," that the events of the past months are just part of his job and of life, and that he is capable of continuing to work as before.

Reliability and Validity of Conclusions

At various points in the evaluation, Mr. Ramirez became agitated and appeared irritated; he jokingly accused the examiner of trying to make him remember "things best forgotten."

In unstructured situations (the Rorschach), he produced fewer responses as the test proceeded. It is likely that his high level of arousal affected the validity of his responses to unstructured materials. He had fewer complaints regarding structured materials (the MMPI-3), but indices of validity indicate an effort to present himself in a favorable light and to deny pathology. During intellectually challenging tasks (the WAIS-IV), he appeared to try hard and was minimally distracted.

All external evidence indicates that Mr. Ramirez's behavior over the past few weeks represents a considerable departure from premorbid levels of functioning, despite his denials. The results of procedures should therefore be interpreted in the light of objective information from external sources.

Summary of Impressions and Findings

On both days of assessment, Mr. Ramirez arrived punctually, in full uniform and meticulously groomed. Whether standing or sitting, he held himself rigidly and made little movement, as if at attention. He made eye contact infrequently and briefly, and spoke in a clear, quite loud monotone voice, often pausing before speaking, and rarely expanding upon his answers without prompting. Even when he spoke of his inner experiences, he gave the impression of a person making a formal report to a superior. Only while he was responding to unstructured material was there a sense that his responses were spontaneous.

Intellectually, this man is functioning within the "bright normal" range of intelligence, but at a considerably lower level than previous assessment has indicated. In normal circumstances, he thinks carefully and logically (though unimaginatively), and is capable of sustained intellectual efforts. At the present time, he is easily distracted by intense inner experiences. Strong affect and mental images of unpleasant recent events appear to intrude on his problem-solving efforts and reduce his cognitive efficiency. Thus, his concentration and memory are somewhat impaired; recognizing this, he makes halting and ineffective efforts to overcome and compensate. These efforts produce increased physical tension, which may account for his somatic symptoms. It is likely that his reality testing is somewhat impaired under conditions of high stress, especially the stress of perceived threats to his sense of competence or to the welfare of others; under these conditions, his cognitive controls may be insufficient to prevent his becoming overwhelmed by internal or external stimuli. There is no evidence of a thought disorder, and it is likely that he can return to premorbid levels of functioning if he receives appropriate treatment.

Mr. Ramirez's mood is normally bland, almost stoic, with mild expression of emotions appropriate to the situation. He rarely exhibits anger, and, indeed, generally manages his affective experiences so as to avoid arousing strong feelings in himself. He is, however, capable of great emotional intensity, the expression of which he views as weakness, both in himself and in others. His greatest fear is the loss of self-control, since he believes such control to be the prime means of attaining satisfaction in life. Typically, he maintains control over his emotions by avoidance, withdrawal, and denial — even at home, where he feels less need to protect himself. He attempts to prevent both his wife and his children from expressing intense or prolonged affect, both positive and negative. He is experienced by others as emotionally insulated, but not cold or threatening.

Currently, he is reacting with unusual intensity to mild stimuli, and there are indications that he is experiencing acute dysphoria, with barely suppressed rage and frustration. It is apparent that his normal controls over affect are becoming less effective, though he continues to deny both the existence of strong emotion and his own inability to contain it. Since, as a police officer, he must work in daily contact with situations that are bound to elicit unpleasant emotions, and since he will never be able to completely protect his family from all harm, it is likely that his emotions will intensify and that his control will weaken further. A breakdown of control may manifest itself in more severe somatic complaints or in hostile and aggressive action, or in both. It is clear that Mr. Ramirez's current method of dealing with recently encountered stresses is increasingly ineffective.

Mr. Ramirez is generally conforming and conventional, with a need for structure and a strong sense of morality, loyalty, and responsibility to others. He performs best, and experiences a strong sense of competence and self-confidence, in situations where both role and task are clear. He has a need to be — and to be seen as — strong, effective, and in control. To this end, he is planful, vigilant, persistent, and determined, setting goals for himself and pursuing them in an organized manner. When difficulties arise, he tackles them immediately, directly, and actively, and is impatient with ambiguous resolutions to problems. On the other hand, he demonstrates a lack of flexibility and a tendency to be dogmatic and domineering, especially with those he views as inferior or in need of his protection. Because of his confidence and competence, others tend to trust, rely on, and respect him, but they find him emotionally distant and hard to know. Because of these attitudes and behaviors, Mr. Ramirez is, in general, a highly competent police officer.

In his personal life, both his single-minded pursuit of goals and his refusal to acknowledge intense affect make for a rather joyless and dogged existence. His need to avoid appearing vulnerable and his tendency to enjoy solitary pursuits keep him from an active social life, and he experiences considerable discomfort in what appear to him to be purposeless social occasions. Only in his most intimate relationships is he able to relax to some degree — for example, when playing with his children. He has a strong sense of the importance of family, and generally adheres to a traditional view of the male's role as provider and protector. Thus, the recent attack on his wife was experienced by Mr. Ramirez as a severe and multifaceted threat, calling for immediate action. Because he had no control over the situation and has no way to control future, similar situations, Mr. Ramirez feels helpless and vulnerable to a degree that is extremely difficult for him to tolerate.

Diagnostic Impressions

This man's premorbid functioning is likely to have been characterized by mild social phobia, a tendency to restrict affective experiences and expression, and a somewhat rigid personality structure. However, it is likely that he was generally effective in daily living, with stable work and personal relationships. Recent changes in his affect, behavior, and cognitive functioning appear directly related to several severe psychosocial stressors. He re-experiences these events; avoids stimuli associated with the events; and suffers from loss of interest in significant activities, poor concentration, exaggerated startle response, and intense irritability. These symptoms have persisted for at least one month. A DSM-5-TR diagnosis of Posttraumatic Stress Disorder is warranted.

Recommendations

Mr. Ramirez's responses to his environment are increasingly atypical and therefore unpredictable. His current assignment requires self-discipline and cool judgment, which he may no longer be able to produce reliably at premorbid levels. Furthermore, he has apparently almost no insight into his condition, is experiencing anger, and is capable of acting aggressively. It is recommended, therefore, that he be relieved of those duties that involve direct confrontation with violence or danger to himself or to others, with return to active duty contingent upon psychological change.

It is further recommended that Mr. Ramirez seek cognitive-behavioral treatment — in a group, if possible — that takes a self-management approach. His defensiveness, self-sufficiency, assumption of a conventional male role, and resistance to psychological material indicate that he is unlikely to be a good candidate for insight-oriented psychotherapy, which he would be likely to see as evidence of personal failure. However, it is essential that he learn to modify his need to control every aspect of life, especially if he wishes to continue his present career path. The behavioral/self-management approach seems most likely to present the process of self-examination and change in an acceptable light. ▬▬

Think Like a Clinical Psychologist Imagine you are preparing an assessment report for a male child (under the age of 18) who was referred to you for testing after being arrested for committing a crime. What considerations would you give to the different forms of reliability and validity when choosing your assessment strategy? How would you present your results differently to the child's caregivers, teachers, lawyer, and the courts?

▥ Assessment and Diverse Populations

With the U.S. population becoming increasingly diverse, it is necessary that clinical psychologists take a multicultural approach to assessment. Indeed, psychologists routinely encounter clients of cultural, ethnic, gender identity, and ideological backgrounds and worldviews that are different from their own. One challenge when working with such clients is to establish expectations and basic lines of communication and trust. Members of underrepresented groups and those from diverse cultural backgrounds may differ from other clients in their beliefs and expectations about the process and goals of assessment, as well as how much they believe psychological interventions will help them. Accordingly, it is up to the clinical psychologist to ensure that the assessment process is not socially or culturally biased in a way that would make it less valid for underrepresented clients (Dinne et al., 2020).

Clinical psychologists often work with clients of backgrounds different from their own and therefore must be aware of how cultural factors can affect the results and interpretation of psychological test.

sturti/E+/Getty Images

There is an entire field of **multicultural assessment research** focused on studying the extent to which psychological tests are valid for different populations (Dinne et al., 2020). This work is important because, if they exist, differences in validity across groups are a form of bias, and many psychological tests have been developed and normed on U.S. and European samples. Using psychological tests that are not applicable to other groups — a finding that can only be established by careful cross-cultural research — may be inappropriate and lead to invalid results and conclusions. Indeed, in some cases, the courts have prohibited their use for educational placement. Therefore, when assessing clients from different cultures, it is important that clinical psychologists be knowledgeable about how sociocultural factors affect the results and conclusions of assessments, as well as the choice and outcomes of interventions (Dinne et al., 2020). In the chapters that follow, we will discuss the role of multicultural factors and competencies in specific types of assessments.

Think Like a Clinical Psychologist Imagine a young Black male is referred for treatment, and arrives at a clinic to meet his psychologist for the first time. He has some trepidation about seeing a psychologist because he is concerned that he may not be fully understood. When he enters the room to begin his initial assessment at the clinic, he is surprised to see that his psychologist is white/Caucasian and he states that he is unsure he feels comfortable proceeding. Considering the historical treatment of racial and ethnic minorities in the mental health field, do you feel this new client's apprehension is appropriate, and how should it be addressed? How would the situation be different if the race/ethnicity of the client and psychologist were reversed? How might this apply to other types of diversity?

▉ Clinical Judgment Versus Actuarial (Statistical) Prediction

Judgments and decisions made by clinical psychologists during the assessment process can have considerable consequences for peoples' lives. For example, all of the following may hinge on the results and conclusions of an assessment: psychiatric diagnoses and labels, outcomes of custody disputes, competency to stand trial, the testing accommodations afforded to a child in school, recommendations for inpatient or outpatient treatment, and the use of psychiatric medications. It is therefore important to consider the methods by which psychologists make judgments and reach conclusions. Judgment is a cognitive process that we use to carefully assess a situation, draw conclusions, and make decisions. When psychologists are in the position to decide on important outcomes, they have two different methods of decision making at their disposal: *clinical judgment* and *actuarial prediction*.

Clinical Judgment

A psychologist draws conclusions and makes decisions on the basis of **clinical judgment**, using expert knowledge, personal experience, client perspectives, and other insights to do so. Proponents of this subjective form of decision making argue that the trained psychologist has specific experience, knowledge, and skills in a given area, including knowledge of rare events that may not be reflected in research findings. This knowledge and experience are thought to foster more accurate conclusions about individual cases and more informed judgments than would be possible using only statistical or research-based criteria.

Actuarial Prediction

Actuarial prediction, on the other hand, involves basing judgments and decisions on statistically determined probabilities. For example, the probability that an individual will respond to a particular treatment, reoffend when released from prison, develop a certain psychiatric disorder, or commit suicide. The actuarial (or statistical) method is therefore more objective than the clinical judgment approach. It eliminates the human factor so that conclusions and decisions rest solely on data from research findings relevant to the problem or event of interest (Dawes et al., 1989).

Which Approach Is Better (and Why)?

The superiority of clinical judgment versus actuarial prediction is often debated, yet research findings generally suggest that actuarial prediction provides the most accurate (although by no means *perfect*) information upon which to base clinical decisions (Heilbrun, 1997). Indeed, it is difficult for even the most experienced and knowledgeable psychologist to synthesize and weigh the wealth of knowledge needed to make many complex clinical decisions. Moreover, clinical judgment is subject to error because of a variety of cognitive biases and other human factors (**Table 4.6**) that can lead to mistakes (Kahneman, 2011) and therefore lower confidence in the outcomes of clinical decision making. Because actuarial prediction removes the human element and is therefore not affected by these cognitive biases, it will always lead to the same conclusion for a given set of information (Redelmeier et al., 2001).

Table 4.6 Factors That May Influence Clinical Judgments	
Factor	**Definition**
Knowledge deficits	Gaps in knowledge may interfere with making accurate decisions and recommendations, such as the clinician who is unaware of the latest research on the efficacy of certain treatments.
Confirmation bias	Weighing evidence that supports your hunch very strongly, but explaining away evidence that doesn't support your hunch. For example, discounting test results that go against your diagnosis of schizophrenia simply because some people with this disorder have delusional thinking that interferes with test-taking.
Availability bias	When a decision is made based on what's in the forefront of one's mind. For example, a psychologist recently read a book about bipolar disorder and became more likely to assign this diagnosis to clients.
Primacy bias	When a psychologist considers the first pieces of information collected as more important than information obtained later.
Recency bias	When a psychologist considers the last pieces of information collected as more important than information obtained earlier.
Overconfidence	An over-reliance on one's own ability, intuition, and judgment. For example, a psychologist believes she has made the correct decision *simply because it's the decision she made.*
Fatigue	A variety of factors can influence a psychologist's judgment, such as a lack of sleep, hunger, irritability, and stress.

Think Like a Clinical Psychologist Statistical prediction and clinical judgment are not mutually exclusive processes for making clinical decisions. If you were the psychologist charged with recommending the best form of treatment for a client with anorexia nervosa, how might you incorporate both into your decision?

📖 Psychological Assessment in Research

Assessment is not only vital to clinical practice, it is also the backbone of research in clinical psychology. Once researchers identify a particular hypothesis to test (e.g., that negative beliefs about oneself lead to depression), they must decide how to assess the study's independent (negative beliefs about oneself) and dependent (depression) variables. As we described earlier, the results of research also inform clinicians about which key client characteristics to assess (e.g., negative beliefs about oneself in clients with depression). Finally (as you'll learn about in Chapter 10, *Psychological Treatment: Science and Practice*), research evaluating the effects of treatment relies heavily on the assessment of indicators of outcome (e.g., symptoms of psychiatric diagnoses) that may be administered at the beginning of treatment, during treatment, or immediately after treatment, and at some point following the end of treatment to examine long-term effects. Depending on the research question and the study's design, clinical researchers must carefully choose reliable and valid instruments to measure study participants' thoughts, emotions, behaviors, abilities, physiology, and the environment.

Next, we cover research that helps us learn about the rates of mental health problems, as well as the features and possible causes of these problems. Such studies may contribute to conceptual models that psychologists use to guide assessment and treatment, as we will see in later chapters, for example, research showing that people who are afraid of the body sensations related to feeling anxious (e.g., racing heart, breathlessness) are at an increased risk of developing panic attacks (e.g., Schmidt et al., 1997), which has helped shape cognitive-behavioral models and treatments for panic attacks (e.g., Behenck et al., 2021).

Epidemiology Research

Epidemiology is the study of the incidence and prevalence of a phenomenon—such as a psychiatric disorder—in a given population. **Incidence** refers to the rate of new cases of the disorder that develop within a given period of time and can tell us whether a disorder is on the increase (e.g., is the rate of PTSD increasing this year compared to last year?). **Prevalence** tells us what percentage of the population is affected by the disorder. For example, the lifetime prevalence rate of schizophrenia is 4 to 7 people per 1000, suggesting that a member of the general population has a less than 0.01% chance of developing this disorder over the course of their life (Saha et al., 2005). Epidemiological research can also help identify groups of individuals who are at risk. For example, studies have shown higher rates of schizophrenia among individuals in lower socioeconomic classes than among those in higher socioeconomic classes (Hollingshead & Redlich, 1958). Armed with this information, clinicians can use assessments to identify people whose potential vulnerability to schizophrenia is high. They can then develop assessments to provide early evidence of its onset in such people, and develop treatments that will be readily available to those at risk.

As you can see, epidemiological research aims merely to describe a particular phenomenon without trying to explain or predict why it occurs. It is often the first step in research to understand a particular phenomenon or disorder, and relies heavily on surveys and clinical interviews. One limitation of this approach, however, is that study participants are often asked to remember things from their past, and such retrospective data can be subject to all sorts of distortions, omissions, or embellishments. The point here is that it is best to assess clients and research participants *at the time of interest* and not rely exclusively on retrospective reports.

Correlational Research

Correlational research enables us to determine the degree to which there is a relationship between two or more variables. For example, is a certain pattern of scores on an intelligence test related to specific psychiatric diagnostic categories? Is anorexia nervosa related to gender? A **correlation** is an index of the strength of association between two variables. Correlation coefficients range from +1.0 to –1.0. Positive correlations indicate that as one variable increases, the other increases as well. For example, higher outside temperatures are associated with higher rates of criminal behavior (Field, 1992). A correlation of zero indicates no association between the two variables. Negative correlations indicate that as one variable increases, the other decreases. For example, having more sex education is associated with fewer problems with sexual health and functioning (Afshar et al., 2012).

In correlational studies, researchers use assessment instruments to obtain data. For example, we might assess 100 study participants using a paper and pencil test of sexual knowledge as well as an interview to determine the presence and severity of any problems in sexual functioning (such as erectile dysfunction or anorgasmia). Using statistical procedures to correlate these data, one might find a correlation coefficient of –.76, indicating a strong negative relationship: as sexual knowledge scores increase, the severity of sexual problems decreases.

Importantly, correlational studies cannot answer the question of cause and effect (see A CLOSER LOOK: *False Causation Assumptions and the Dubious "Serotonin Imbalance" Theory*). They merely tell us how strongly two variables are related, not the direction of the relationship. No matter how logical it may seem, we cannot, on the basis of a correlation, say that one variable has caused another. Consider the example of socioeconomic status and schizophrenia. Just because an investigator discovers a correlation between being diagnosed with schizophrenia and lower socioeconomic status does not mean that schizophrenia is caused by having little wealth. For it could be the reverse — that having this disorder leads to a reduction in wealth. More likely, the real culprit is a third variable. For example, factors such as childhood abuse or neglect, extreme levels of stress, and poor self-care could affect both mental health and socioeconomic status. Therefore, because there is always the possibility that a third (unmeasured) variable is involved, the investigator must avoid assuming that one variable causes the other.

A Closer Look	**False Causation Assumptions and the Dubious "Serotonin Imbalance" Theory**

Researchers studying the biological aspects of psychiatric conditions often improperly infer causation from correlational studies. For example, a few studies that have found correlations between being depressed and levels of the neurotransmitter serotonin are frequently misunderstood as meaning that depression is caused by an "imbalance" of serotonin (Schatzberg & Nemeroff, 2009). But it is not possible to draw causal conclusions from correlational research. Indeed, the experience of an episode of depression might result in changes in serotonin levels. And there may also be third variables, such as the fact that many people with depression develop a sedentary lifestyle and have a long history of taking various psychoactive medications, both of which could conceivably affect neurotransmitter levels. Interestingly, pharmaceutical companies base their rationale for marketing antidepressant drugs on this highly dubious "serotonin imbalance" theory. ▬▬

Another reason that we cannot infer causation from correlational studies is that no variables are manipulated or controlled in such research. The investigators simply assess two (or more) variables and submit the data to statistical analysis. Interestingly, however, this fact often eludes us when we are faced with images of a living human brain, such as those presented in *neuroimaging studies* — a growing research trend in clinical psychology. Although such studies merely correlate psychological variables with brain-related variables, the fascination with, and perceived credibility of, images of the living brain with various regions "lit up" can be persuasive enough to lead to unjustified causal inferences (see A CLOSER LOOK: *Neuroimaging Research: Hope or Hype?*). Indeed, in a series of studies, McCabe and Castel (2008) found that participants were more likely to rate an article higher in scientific standing if it contained images from brain scans, as opposed to bar graphs or a topographic map of the brain. Experimental methods in which variables are manipulated (discussed later in this chapter), on the other hand, can help determine cause and effect. But sometimes we are forced to use correlational methods because we cannot either ethically or practically manipulate certain variables, such as age, sex, marital status, birth order, or biology. For example, we cannot ethically train someone to abuse a child in order to study the effects of maltreatment on PTSD! Certain things can only be studied by observing their occurrences; manipulating them is not an acceptable alternative.

A Closer Look   Neuroimaging Research: Hope or Hype?

"Brain Scans Reveal the Brain Region Responsible for PTSD"
"Democrats' Brains Function Differently than Republicans' Brains"
"Being in Love Changes the Brain"

Surely you've seen headlines like these. They are usually based on results from **neuroimaging studies** in which brain scanning techniques are used to reveal the living brain's structure and function. Neuroimaging can tell researchers about electrical and metabolic activity, and even show how different regions of the brain connect and communicate with one another in real-time, such as during tasks involving reading, remembering, and experiencing different emotions. One key promise of neuroimaging research is a clearer understanding of the biology of psychological problems and disorders leading to better, more specialized treatment. But have neuroimaging studies delivered on this promise? Let's take a closer look.

The Tools

Since the 1990s, clinical psychologists and psychiatrists have used a variety of neuroimaging methods to study the brain. Computed tomography (CT) scans are X-ray slices that show the density of brain structures. Positron emission tomography (PET) scans use radioactive tags to show which brain areas become active when someone performs a task. Magnetic resonance imaging (MRI) uses a magnetic field to form images of the brain's structure, and *functional* MRI (fMRI) tracks changes in blood flow and oxygen levels to indicate brain activity. When a particular brain area is more active, it consumes more oxygen and blood flow increases. Finally, diffusion tensor imaging (DTI) uses MRI to track how water molecules move in and around different parts of the brain and measure the density of the brain's connections. No doubt you've seen the fancy

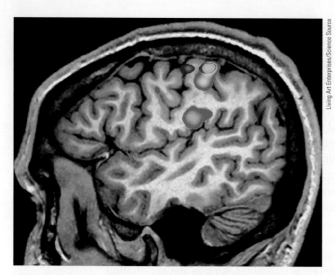

fMRI scans can vividly show which parts of the brain are experiencing increased activity (yellow) and decreased activity (blue) as study participants engage in experimental tasks.

looking colorful pictures of the brain that these tools produce. It's as if parts of the brain "light up" when they become active, whereas other areas are seemingly inactive. These images are very seductive because they appear to give physical qualities to abstract psychological experiences such as fear, sadness, love, or even a belief in God (McCabe & Castle, 2008).

With the goal of improving our understanding and treatment of psychological problems, clinical researchers use functional imaging to reveal the neural mechanisms involved in such disorders as PTSD, autism, and excessive substance use. For example, MRI scans suggest that narcissistic personality traits are associated with variations in prefrontal and insular brain structures (Nenadić et al., 2021). Scans can also help researchers assess whether treatments change the structure and functioning of the brain. This type of research is certainly flashy and exciting, yet despite three decades of neuroimaging research, its contributions to psychological theory and treatment are limited. Even with expensive technologies and tools, it turns out that understanding the brain isn't as clear cut as researchers might have hoped. Many critics of neuroimaging studies argue that the conclusions from such investigations — and therefore the flashy headlines — are often flawed and over-hyped. Specifically, they point to a number of reasons that it's difficult to make much sense out of brain scans (e.g., Satel & Lilienfeld, 2013).

What are the Limitations of Neuroimaging Studies?

Seeing isn't believing. Brain scans are not raw snapshots of the brain's real-time functioning (parts of the brain don't actually "light up" when they become active). Rather, they're highly processed statistical representations of the brain's activity that allow us to use magnetic signatures to infer where, for example, changes in blood flow are occurring (e.g., Roskies, 2007). Still the eye-grabbing images can make it easy for even careful researchers to overlook this fact and interpret scans as real-time photographic evidence of brain activity. This, however, can (and often does) lead to erroneous conclusions as demonstrated in a sobering study by Bennett, Baird, Miller, and Wolford (2010) that unmistakably reveals problems with the validity of brain scans. These neuroscientists placed a dead salmon in an fMRI machine and "presented it" with images of people expressing different emotions. But when the researchers "asked" the dead fish to judge what emotions were portrayed in the images, the fMRI seemed to pick up neural activity. In other words, parts of the dead salmon's brain "lit up"! The fact that an fMRI scan could show activity in a dead fish's brain demonstrates that brain scan methodology is subject to errors and can easily be misinterpreted and misleading. Indeed, researchers must be extremely careful when using brain scans to draw conclusions about the "biological basis" of psychological phenomena.

Oversimplification. The human brain is considered the most complex object in the known universe. So, even if part of it "lights up" on a brain scan, it doesn't mean the rest of the brain is inactive. Additionally, the way people think, feel, and act during psychological experiments — especially when placed in a brain scanning machine — is not necessarily identical to how they think, feel, and act in real life. This further clouds the interpretation of data from imaging studies. Finally, we haven't the faintest clue about the biggest mystery of all: how does a lump of grey matter produce the conscious experience you are having right now, reading this book? That is, exactly how does the brain give rise to the mind? No one knows.

Poor reliability. Because of the brain's complexity we cannot assume that activity levels in a particular brain region mean the same thing for different people, nor for the same person at different points in time. This raises concerns about the reliability of brain imaging for understanding the neural correlates of behavior and for predicting a person's behavior in the future. Confirming this problem, a recent study looked at fMRI data from 1008 people for whom they had two scans (Elliott et al., 2020). What the researchers found was surprising and unsettling: the test–retest correlations between the two scans ranged from .07 (very weak) to .49 (moderate). In discussing these findings, the study authors concluded that "A prominent goal of task-fMRI research has been to identify abnormal brain activity that could aid in the diagnosis, prognosis, and treatment of brain disorders. We find that commonly used task-fMRI measures lack the minimal reliability standards necessary for accomplishing this goal" (p. 803). The bottom line is that fMRI can't necessarily tell researchers what a person's brain activation will look like from one scan to the next.

Correlation is not causation. Finally, imaging studies are correlational. They might be able to show which regions of the brain are active when a person participates in a particular task, or which parts are larger or smaller depending on whether a person has a disorder like schizophrenia. But they can't tell which brain area *causes* a particular psychological experience or behavior. Perhaps alterations in the brain lead to schizophrenia; but it's also possible that having schizophrenia leads to alterations in the brain. People with this condition tend to develop multiple physical health problems (e.g., Smith et al., 2013), and it would not be surprising if the brain is impacted as well. Finally, it is possible that one or more unaccounted for factors influence both the development of schizophrenia and brain alterations.

Conclusions

Although it is difficult to point to any significant advances in understanding, categorizing, treating, or preventing psychological problems that are the direct result of neuroimaging research, some clinical psychologists believe that these methods hold great promise for the future. The challenge moving forward will be balancing the hopes of neuroimaging against the limitations of the technology and our own knowledge. ■■■

Cross-Sectional Versus Longitudinal Approaches

Another way of classifying research is by considering whether studies are cross-sectional or longitudinal. **Cross-sectional designs** assess individuals at a single time point. This might involve determining correlations between variables in a single group of participants, or comparing individuals with different psychological conditions on a particular variable; for example, comparing the levels of self-esteem in 50 clients with depression to those in 50 clients with schizophrenia. In such a study it also would be important to include a *control group* to test for the possibility that scores on the instrument assessing self-esteem in the two study groups are indeed different from those of individuals with no psychiatric diagnoses at all. Therefore, the study just described might include a third group of individuals who do not meet criteria for any psychiatric disorder.

Longitudinal studies follow the same individuals across time. Such studies may last months, years, or even generations to learn how family-related variables predict long-term psychological functioning.

In **longitudinal designs** the same research participants are assessed repeatedly at different points over time. Such studies allow us to understand how behavior or mental processes change with time, and enable investigators to better speculate about time-order relationships. For example, a researcher could identify 100 new mothers with postpartum depression and assess their children for developmental or behavioral problems longitudinally over the course of 10 years. Still, one cannot draw definitive conclusions about cause and effect because third variables (e.g., low socioeconomic status, high level of stress) might be present that influence both maternal depression and childhood functioning. Longitudinal research is also costly to carry out and requires great patience. In addition, participants sometimes drop out of long-term studies.

Experimental Research

Experimental studies involve the manipulation of one or more **independent variables** to determine their effect on one or more **dependent variables**. In addition, all other extraneous variables are controlled so that it is possible to determine if changes in the independent variable cause changes in the dependent variable. These studies usually involve the **random assignment** of participants to experimental or control groups. Random assignment helps ensure that any differences between and within the participant groups are not systematic at the outset of the experiment. Thus, any differences between groups assessed at the end of the experiment can be more confidently attributed to the manipulation of the independent variable. Accordingly, one may deduce causal relationships from well-conducted controlled experimental studies.

Individuals with body dysmorphic disorder may spend excessive time looking in the mirror examining perceived (or very minor) flaws in their appearance.

For example, a researcher studying body dysmorphia (in which someone excessively worries about an aspect of their physical appearance and spends a great deal of time checking their appearance in the mirror) might be interested in the effects of mirror gazing. The researcher might randomly assign 60 teens with a diagnosis of body dysmorphic disorder (BDD) to two groups: one that is instructed to look at themselves up close in a full-length mirror for 10 minutes (the experimental group), and the other that is simply asked to look at pictures of other people (the control group). Before and after the 10-minute exercise, both groups would complete an assessment of their appearance-related anxiety. When the data show that anxiety about appearance increased over time for the group that gazed at themselves in the mirror, but not for the group that looked at pictures, this effect can be attributed to the mirror gazing since that was the only variable that differed between the two groups in the experiment.

Experimental research has two main uses in clinical psychology. First, as we will cover in Chapter 10, we use this method to evaluate the effects of treatment. Second, controlled experiments like the one just described provide data that help us understand the nature of psychological problems and the factors that contribute to them. The experiment on BDD, for example, helps us understand this problem as a vicious cycle in which a person experiences appearance-related anxiety along with the urge to check their appearance in the mirror; but when they look at themselves in the mirror, it leads to more anxiety and more urges to check. This model provides the basis for cognitive-behavioral therapy for BDD, which involves exposure to appearance-related fear along with response prevention — the prevention of checking behaviors (e.g., Hartmann & Lyons, 2017). Critically, research-based conceptual models such as this provide information psychologists rely on when making evidence-based decisions about what to assess when evaluating clients. For example, when a client presents with body dysmorphic concerns, it is necessary to assess (among other factors) appearance-related anxiety, the frequency and intensity of mirror-checking behavior, as well as the effects (or *consequences*) of mirror checking.

Most experimental studies are conducted in the laboratory, as opposed to in naturalistic settings. Indeed, it is easier to manipulate independent variables, measure dependent variables, and control extraneous factors in the lab. In the BDD study, for example, the investigators needed to be sure participants looked in the same mirror (or at the same pictures of other people) under the same conditions (e.g., from the same distance) and for the same amount of time. If one of these conditions had varied, it could provide an explanation for the results other than the manipulation of the independent variable. But the issue here is that the researchers can only presume that the experimental conditions in the lab create a phenomenon that is analogous to naturalistic settings. There is no assurance, for example, that the experience of mirror gazing in a laboratory is the same as "real" mirror gazing in the everyday life of a person with BDD. Therefore, confidence in the results of experimental studies (sometimes called *analogue studies*) often hinges on the ability to make such an assumption.

Finally, it is sometimes difficult to recruit a sufficient number of individuals with a particular clinical diagnosis to participate in experimental studies. BDD, for example, is a relatively rare problem, and people with this disorder may be embarrassed to disclose their anxieties and volunteer to participate in research. Therefore, investigations on psychiatric disorders sometimes use samples of individuals who score highly on assessments of cardinal symptoms of the disorder under study, but do not necessarily meet the full diagnostic criteria for the disorder — what researchers call a *preclinical sample*. The use of preclinical samples is based on the idea that psychological problems occur on a continuum of severity from mild to severe, and that preclinical individuals therefore think and behave much like those who meet diagnostic criteria. While it turns out that this is a proper assumption in many instances (Abramowitz et al., 2014), the validity of conclusions from studies using preclinical samples rests on the extent to which these participants are really the same as participants professionally diagnosed.

Think Like a Clinical Psychologist *Vaccinations cause autism! A full moon causes increased crime rates! Strep infections cause mental illnesses!* It is very tempting to infer causation from correlational research. You've probably seen it in the media and heard it from your friends, family, doctor, or even your professor! What are some examples you have come across, and what are some alternative explanations (or third variables) that might account for the observed correlation?

▥ Chapter Summary

With so many variations in psychological and behavioral problems and concerns, and so many approaches to the assessment of each, it would be impossible for a single psychologist to become an expert on all tests and measures. That said, clinical psychologists do need to have certain skills and competencies when it comes to assessment. Many of these are laid out in the APA Ethics Code's guidelines for assessment. For example, they need to understand the theoretical, empirical, and contextual bases of assessment, including the concepts of reliability, validity, and standardization. They should be competent to administer, score, and interpret clinical interviews; behavioral observations; as well as tests of intelligence, personality, and cognitive functioning. Consistent with the principles of evidence-based assessment, they should also be able to identify the strengths and limitations of the tests they use, including the degree to which they are appropriate for members of special populations and underrepresented groups, and be able to integrate data from multiple assessments to draw evidence-based assessments. Finally, psychologists should be able to effectively communicate the results of assessments to others, whether orally or in writing. Research on the nature of psychological phenomena not only requires careful assessment but also provides the basis for what to assess when clients come through the door. In the chapters that follow, you will learn how clinical psychologists approach the assessment of personality, intelligence, and behavior.

Applying What You've Learned

Evaluating Reliability and Validity

Consider each of the following hypothetical scenarios and discuss each in terms of the following concepts:

Test–retest reliability	Construct validity	Incremental validity
Interrater reliability	Convergent validity	Multicultural sensitivity
Internal consistency	Discriminant validity	

1. A psychologist uses tea leaves to diagnose depression. She asks her clients to look at and then report what shapes and textures the client sees at the bottom of teacup immediately after finishing her drink. The psychologist decides to prove to her colleagues that this is a fool-proof new diagnostic assessment. However, her colleagues critique her by saying that she sometimes reaches different conclusions when revising the same client's responses more than once.

2. A researcher develops a new scale to assess mania and conducts a study in which she gives the new scale, along with an existing scale that is well-known as an assessment of mania, to a group of people with bipolar disorder. When this researcher computes the correlation between the new scale and the older scale, it is an indicator of which concept from the list above?

3. The researcher in the previous question also includes a measure of anxiety in her study. She expects the correlation between her new measure of mania and the measure of anxiety to be fairly weak. This correlation is an index of which concept from the list above?

4. A psychologist has conducted an assessment with a 12-year-old boy and is baffled by the results. The young boy seemed to have high intellectual ability and adaptive social relationships. However, when the psychologist asked the boy to draw a picture of his family at Christmastime, the psychologist was surprised that the drawing revealed no holiday tree, it had no iconic symbols of the holiday, and the boy was unable to discuss even the most fundamental pieces of the Christmas story. Rather, the picture depicted a series of spinning tops with Hebrew letters, candles, and gold coins. The psychologist concluded that the boy may have experienced a trauma at church and was repressing his memories related to his religious experiences.

5. A clinician finishes an interview with a client, but is not sure of what diagnosis to give. So, he administers another self-report measure that helps determine the best diagnosis. Since this measure provides additional valuable information, it is said to possess which concept from the list above?

Key Terms

Actuarial prediction: Judgments and decisions based on statistically determined probabilities.

Assessment report: Contains test results, interpretations, and conclusions. It includes the reason for referral along with background information and history to set the context for the assessment, a discussion of test scores and conclusions, and recommendations for how to address the questions and concerns raised in the referral.

Clinical judgment: An approach to clinical interpretation that is largely intuitive and experiential. Subjective or clinical interpretation requires that the clinician be sensitive to information from a wide range of sources and make a series of inductive or deductive generalizations to link the observations and predict the outcome.

Construct validity: The extent to which interview scores predict the characteristic being evaluated and correlate with other measures or behaviors in a logical and theoretically consistent way. To be construct valid, an interview must demonstrate both convergent and discriminate validity.

Convergent validity: The extent to which scores correlate with scores on other relevant measures administered at the same time.

Correlation: A statistic (usually symbolized by r) that describes the relationship between two variables. r ranges between -1.0 and $+1.0$; its sign indicates the direction of the association, and its absolute value indicates the strength.

Correlational research: Research methods that allow us to determine whether one variable is related to another. In general, correlational methods do not allow us to draw inferences about cause and effect.

Cross-sectional design: A research design that compares different individuals or groups of individuals at one point in time.

Dependent variable: The variable in an experimental design that is measured by the investigator (i.e., the outcome of interest).

Discriminant validity: The extent to which interview scores do not correlate with measures other than those related to the construct being measured.

Epidemiology: The study of the incidence, prevalence, and distribution of illness or disease in a given population.

Evidence-based assessment: When psychologists choose assessment instruments on the basis of demonstrated reliability, validity, and standardization.

Experimental study: Research study that allows the researcher to determine cause-and-effect relationships between variables or events.

Incidence: The rate of new cases of a disease or disorder that develop within a given period of time. Incidence figures allow us to determine whether the rate of new cases is stable or changing from one time period to the next.

Incremental validity: The extent to which a test adds to our understanding of a person over and above what's been uncovered through other sources or means.

Independent variable: The variable in an experimental design that is manipulated by the investigator.

Internal consistency: The degree to which the items in a test all measure the same characteristic.

Interrater reliability: The level of agreement between at least two interviewers who have evaluated the same client independently. Agreement can refer to consensus on symptoms assigned, diagnoses assigned, and so on.

Longitudinal design: A research design that compares the same group of individuals at two or more points in time.

Multicultural assessment research: The study of the extent to which psychological tests are valid for different populations.

Multimethod assessment: The use of more than a single method when evaluating an individual.

Neuroimaging studies: Studies in which brain scanning techniques are used to examine the brain's structure or function.

Norms: Data about the average scores that can be expected in a certain population. Norms are established by administering the test to a large sample of the type of individuals for whom it is designed.

Predictive validity: The extent to which a test can be used to forecast future behavior.

Prevalence: The overall rate of cases (new or old) within a given period of time. Prevalence figures allow us to estimate what percentage of the target population is affected by the illness or disorder.

Presenting problem: The concerns and problems that lead a client to treatment.

Psychological assessment: The process of collecting and synthesizing information for the purposes of understanding a client's patterns of thinking and behavior, classifying the problems they have, developing a plan for intervention, measuring the effects of interventions, and conducting research to better understand psychological phenomena.

Psychometric evaluation: A process in which the developer subjects assessment instruments to rigorous statistical analyses to determine whether they meet certain standards.

Random assignment: The random placement of participants into experimental or control groups to help ensure that any differences between and within the participant groups are not systematic at the outset of the experiment.

Reason for referral: A description in the psychological assessment of why the psychologist's services are being sought (e.g., Why is a particular child earning poor grades?).

Reliability: The consistency with which the test measures a particular variable, such as anxiety, intelligence, or extraversion.

Standardization: The precise directions for administering, scoring, and interpreting the test. It ensures that anyone taking the test has the same experience and scoring criteria, which allows psychologists to compare scores (such as IQ scores) across different people.

Test–retest reliability: The consistency of assessment test scores over time. Generally, we expect individuals to receive similar diagnoses from one administration to the next if the interval between administrations is short.

Validity: The extent to which a test measures what it intends to measure.

CONNECT ONLINE:

 | Check out our videos and additional resources located at: www.macmillanlearning.com

CHAPTER 5

The Clinical Interview

FOCUS QUESTIONS

1. What are major issues to consider when conducting a clinical interview?
2. What are the most common types of clinical interviews? Briefly describe each type.
3. What are the similarities and differences between structured and unstructured interviews?
4. What are the advantages and disadvantages of the different types of interviews?
5. What is cultural humility and why is it important?

CHAPTER OUTLINE

As noted in the prior chapter, clinical psychologists dedicate a considerable amount of their time to conducting assessments to understand their clients' psychological functioning. What are their clients' symptoms? When are those symptoms the worst? What are clients' strengths, and what is their life like on a day-to-day or even an hour-to-hour basis? What are some skills or deficiencies clients have that they may not even realize? What are clients' short-term goals for treatment and long-term goals for the future?

There are many ways that psychologists can conduct assessments, and a thorough assessment will of course rely on multiple approaches, maybe even collecting information from multiple people to get the most complete information. One of the most common of these approaches involves interviewing a client directly. This often is referred to as a **clinical interview**.

But what exactly is involved in this interview? Is it simply asking questions and jotting down the answers? Is there something different about the type of interview a clinical psychologist might conduct as compared to, let's say, what an automated computer could do?

In fact, there are many different types of clinical interviews, and each varies in its purpose, its method, and the types of conclusions that psychologists are able to draw from its results. In this chapter, we first discuss some commonalities related to clinical interviewing in general — the who, where, and how. Then we discuss different types of clinical interviews and their purposes. A clinical interview is not quite the same as a simple conversation with friends, and takes a little practice to get used to, so the chapter concludes with a role-play exercise.

▮▮ General Characteristics of Clinical Interviews

As you probably already know, an interview is an interaction between at least two people. This interaction is "dynamic," however, meaning that each participant is contributing to — and perhaps unwittingly changing the behavior and reactions of — the other. This is what happens in most conversations — when one person laughs, for instance, it may lead the other to smile and think of similarly humorous things. Or sometimes someone's sad mood evokes quiet, the use of a softer voice, or a feeling of gloom in their conversation partner. This is common, and happens almost automatically in most conversations. However, in clinical interviewing psychologists can use the dynamic nature of this interaction to better understand the client. In other words, a clinical psychologist uses their interaction skills to create moments and opportunities that will allow the client to feel comfortable, open, and safe so a psychologist can learn as much as possible to help them. Almost all clinical interviews are initiated with a goal or set of goals in mind. The interviewer approaches the interaction purposefully, bearing the responsibility for keeping the interview on track and moving toward the goal. Thus, the easy informality that often characterizes ordinary conversation is less evident. A good interview is one that is carefully planned, deliberately and skillfully executed, and goal-oriented throughout.

Interviewing takes many forms — from fact finding to emotional release to cross-examination. However, all forms of psychological interviews are devoid of one feature that characterizes normal conversation: interviewers are not using the interchange to achieve their own personal satisfaction or enhanced prestige. They are using it to elicit clinical data, information, beliefs, or attitudes in the most skilled fashion possible. It is an interaction focused solely on one person, the client. Throughout the interaction, the psychologist's job is to redirect attention back to the client's thoughts, feelings, and other experiences.

Clinical psychologists conduct clinical interviews with consideration for a variety of factors that typically are taken for granted within our social interactions, but are thoughtfully considered by psychologists. Specifically, as part of graduate training, psychologists learn to consider *where* to conduct an interview, how to quickly develop *rapport*, and how to use various verbal and nonverbal techniques. They also learn how to superimpose a multicultural perspective to minimize the impact of their own biases when conducting interviews. Each of these points is discussed next.

Where to Conduct a Clinical Interview

Certain physical arrangements are especially desirable for a clinical interview. Two of the most important considerations are privacy and protection from interruptions. Nothing is more damaging to the continuity of an interview than a phone that rings or vibrates relentlessly, an administrative assistant's query, or a disruptive knock on the door. Not only are such interruptions distracting, they can subtly convey the message that the client and their problems are of secondary importance. After all, in businesses, administrative assistants do not knock on the door or put through a call if they have been instructed otherwise.

Because a lack of privacy can lead to many negative outcomes, soundproofing is also very important. If noise from a hallway or an adjacent office intrudes, clients will probably assume that their own voices can also be heard outside. Few clients are likely to be open and responsive under such conditions.

The office or its furnishings can be as distracting as loud noises and external clamor, which is why most clinicians prefer to keep their spaces fairly neutral, yet tasteful. Office furnishings that demand attention or seem to cry out for comment are not ideal. Imagine walking into a psychologist's office that is home to three cats. Maybe you'd feel right at home, but become preoccupied with the furry friends to the point that you're unable to focus on the clinician's questions. This is why psychologists avoid decorations associated with, for example, specific musical artists or genres. And just as some people are put off by cats (or are allergic to them), decorations that could be divisive — such as anything that makes a political, social, or religious statement — are also avoided. Even when well-meaning, for clients with conflicting values or beliefs, such ornamentation can provoke discomfort, interfere with building rapport (discussed next), and hamper the interview process.

Of course, it may be that a psychologist's office is, by definition, an uncomfortable setting for clients. Note that among some racially and ethnically minoritized groups, for instance, a doctor's office has historically been a place where discrimination, exploitation, and even persecution have taken place.

Glasshouse Images/The Image Bank/Getty Images

Clinical psychologists put a great deal of thought into how they furnish their office space.

Sladic/E+/Getty Images

Psychologists often use toys or games to help children feel more comfortable during clinical interviews.

Thus, psychologists need to be flexible and culturally sensitive when considering the best location to conduct a clinical interview. It may be that some clients feel most comfortable and safe in a community center, a church basement, or a local park, in the midst of surroundings that help them feel that their psychologist will be able to understand their culture and community. In turn, it is essential that psychologists do not try to force all clients to adapt to their own context (e.g., within a fancy medical building where they must pay for parking, or travel through hallways of predominantly white professionals), but rather demonstrate that it is the psychologist who is most interested in adapting to, and experiencing the life experiences of, their client.

When working with youth, of course, it is also essential that clients have an opportunity to feel comfortable and unintimidated. For that reason, clinical interviews with youth often take place in the context of toys, games, or playgrounds. Many clinical child and adolescent psychologists conduct clinical interviews while their client draws pictures, or while they play a board game together. Adolescent clients might participate in a clinical interview while playing basketball with their psychologist, or while both surf the Internet. Although this may seem unorthodox to adults who imagine doctor–client interactions as formal, professional interactions within an office setting, it is important to consider how foreign and intimidating this interaction would seem to a child or teen; instead the psychologist attempts to "meet clients where they are" to help communicate that we are interested in their experiences and are willing to get to know them on their own terms.

How to Develop Rapport

Perhaps the most essential ingredient of a good clinical interview (and the therapeutic relationship in general) is the alliance between the clinician and the client—which is referred to as **rapport**. Thus, cultivating this alliance is a psychologist's first task when interacting with a new or prospective client. Good rapport is usually achieved through an attitude of acceptance, understanding, and respect for the integrity of the client. This does not require that the clinician like every client, but it *does* require that clients not be prejudged based on the problems they seek help for or their individual circumstances and backgrounds.

Should psychologists use their status as an "expert" to build rapport? Often, rapport is founded on mutual respect, confidence, and trust. But cultural issues can play a role here as well (Flaskas et al., 2018). For example, people from traditional Chinese backgrounds may expect their clinician to behave as an authority figure and might be less likely to open up if the interaction is too informal. In other instances, psychologists can feel that their credentials are being challenged—for example, some female clinicians (especially younger ones) and those who are members of ethnic or racial minoritized groups. As upsetting as this sounds, in such cases gaining rapport might involve earning the "benefit of the doubt" by "proving oneself." Thus, finding a way to both establish one's training and qualifications while not responding with frustration is a key skill in building rapport for many clinicians. There are also clients whose past experiences or psychological symptoms prevent them from accepting even genuine overtures for a professional relationship. But in most cases, if the clinician perseveres in the proper role and maintains an attitude of respect while searching for understanding, good rapport will develop naturally.

The process of building rapport can be more complex when engaged in family or group therapy, given that there are multiple relationships to establish simultaneously, and sometimes with individuals who have conflictual relationships with one another. Moreover, within many families or groups, there may be varying enthusiasm among clients for attending the session. Interviewing child and adolescent clients similarly requires the psychologist to establish rapport with both the parent(s), who most often has initiated contact with the psychologist, and the child, who may feel blamed by this parent. Rapport building also can be challenging when the client

To put their clients at ease and help facilitate rapport, psychologists sometimes conduct clinical interviews in less formal environments.

is aware that the information collected during the interview likely will be used to determine a school placement; meet employment criteria; or formulate a legal disposition regarding child custody, legal sanctions, or maltreatment allegations. In each of these cases, it is essential to remain cognizant of these challenges and consider how this may affect the validity of the interview data that are being collected.

How to Use Verbal and Nonverbal Language

Psychologists talk funny. But the ways psychologists speak can make a lot more sense when you are familiar with a few simple techniques used to help build rapport and extract useful information within the context of a clinical interview.

It may go without saying that psychologists must be mindful of the age and educational level of their clients. In most cases, the use of technical or grandiose jargon is not helpful, nor is it necessary to infantilize people seeking help; asking for help does not imply that one has a diminished capacity to understand. Similarly, clinicians who try to use "teenage" language in order to seem "cool" when interviewing a 15-year-old may wind up not only alienating the client but looking foolish in the process.

Instead, psychologists use a variety of communication techniques when conducting clinical interviews, including the use of questions, active listening, silence, consideration of client strengths, and one's own stimulus value. Each is discussed briefly below.

The Use of Questions

As one might expect, a clinical interview typically requires psychologists to ask their clients questions. Several different types of questions may be asked to elicit different types of information, however. These include **open-ended**, **facilitative**, **confronting**, **direct**, and **clarifying questions**. Each is designed in its own way to promote communication. And each is useful for a specific purpose or client. **Table 5.1** offers an example of each type of question.

Table 5.1	Five Types of Interview Questions	
Type	**Importance**	**Example**
Open-ended	Gives the client responsibility and latitude for responding	"Would you tell me about your experiences in the army?"
Facilitative	Encourages the client's flow of conversation	"Can you tell me a little more about that?"
Confronting	Challenges inconsistencies or contradictions	"Before, you said you felt depressed all day long, but now you're saying that you go out with friends and have fun every night. Can you help me understand?"
Direct	Challenges appropriately once rapport has been established and the client is taking responsibility	"What did you say to your father when he criticized your choice?"
Clarifying	Encourages clarity or amplification	"That sounds difficult. Can you tell me what it was like for you?"

SOURCE: Research from Maloney and Ward (1976).

Open-ended questions often are used to begin discussions of a new topic. Facilitative questions are used either to help clients clarify what they mean so the psychologist can better understand, or to guide clients to better understand themselves; indeed, clients often correct themselves as they elaborate in response to a facilitative question and achieve greater awareness of their own feelings or intent. Confronting and direct questions more forcefully guide the flow of a clinical interview, or may help a client who is experiencing a blind spot. Clarifying questions often are used as part of active listening, which is discussed next.

Active Listening

We often know someone is listening to us based on their nonverbal behaviors (e.g., eye contact, head nodding) while we talk. **Active listening** is a bit different, however. It is meant to demonstrate that we not only hear our conversation partner, but that we understand what they have said, perhaps even at a level beyond what they understand themselves. For that reason, active listening is quite commonly used by psychologists in all interactions, including clinical interviewing, and it is remarkably powerful. Active listening often involves a technique referred to as reflection or reflective listening in which a psychologist repeats back what they heard the client say. Occasionally, a psychologist may do so word for word, which is not nearly as awkward as it sounds and indeed can be effective. But more often, a psychologist will paraphrase what has been said, and reflect either the content or the affect expressed by their client. Doing so reliably guides the course of the interview toward warmth, openness, trust, and greater rapport.

For instance, if a client were to say, "Every time I see him, I feel scared that he'll leave," a psychologist may simply respond by saying "You feel scared he'll leave every time you see him," and the client often will immediately expound as the response sinks in, they hear themselves, feel understood, and have a chance to think about their feelings a bit more. Or a psychologist might engage in active listening by reflecting a client's feelings, by saying for instance, "You talk about feeling scared, but as you say that, you seem angry," to which a client might say,

"Yes! That's true, I guess I feel angry too. In fact, I end up arguing with him and I don't even know why sometimes." In each case, the use of active listening retains the focus on the client, helps guide the client to consider their thoughts and feelings more deeply, and helps the client feel close and supported by the psychologist conducting the interview.

Silence

Sometimes psychologists also sit with **silence** during a clinical interview (or a treatment session) for far longer than one might expect in a typical conversation. This too is a simple technique that makes use of conversation dynamics to help establish rapport and guide an interaction. Of course, it's pretty unnerving, for both clients and novice interviewers who are used to the social demand to fill silence with more

When conducting interviews, clinical psychologists may use silence to communicate different things.

speech. But silence paradoxically communicates that in some moments it is okay for the focus of the interaction to stay on what was just said and to let the client reflect on their own thoughts and feelings for a bit. For this reason, silence often is effective in communicating safety to a client. It conveys that the psychologist is present exclusively for their client's needs, will not rush the client, and is comfortable with anything that is said or needs to be contemplated by the client. Silence also often prompts the client to continue talking, and in doing so, to further elaborate on their own thoughts.

Consideration of Client Strengths

Clients initiate contact with psychologists because of problems; these are the legitimate first topics of the interview. Yet, it also is helpful to gain an understanding of the client's strengths, which are the foundation on which treatment will build. How has the client coped successfully with past and current distress? What are their accomplishments and sources of inner value? What do they get out of their friendships, work accomplishments, and family support? What hobbies and interests do they have? Questions such as "What are you proud of?" or "What do you like about yourself?" often reveal such information.

Too often this information becomes an afterthought in the course of conversation. For example, one client took great pride in her volunteer work through her church. She mentioned it only in passing as she discussed how she likes to spend her time. Yet, this volunteer work was her only current source of personal value. She turned to it when she became upset about her difficulties in other areas of life.

Psychologists' Stimulus Value

When we are engaged in a conversation, our behavior is often guided by the person we are speaking to. But not just by their verbal and nonverbal responses. We also are guided simply by what our conversation partner looks like, their behavior, their position of authority, and assumptions we make about them. Sometimes these assumptions are wrong of course, built on stereotypes, but humans are guided by them nevertheless, and this dynamic may have a strong effect on the direction and effectiveness of each of our conversations.

Psychologists thus need to be aware of their own **stimulus value** — what do we look like? What may people think of us based on our race, gender, educational background, professional status? What is the power differential and dynamic? What may we be eliciting, or suppressing, in each of our interactions and how can we overcome this when we conduct a clinical interview?

Consider two therapists working in the same clinic. One is a 50ish female psychologist wearing a big flowery dress. Another is a young male psychologist who is very fit, wearing a tight fashionable shirt. It is inevitable that these two clinicians would be perceived differently by their clients, yet these perceptual differences may vary based on each client. Who do you think would be most likely to understand you if you talked about your fears about your future? Who would you feel is best able to understand your struggles with feeling discriminated against? Would you be more likely to tell your most intimate insecurities to one of these psychologists as compared to the other? Who do you assume would understand you best if you talked about feeling body-conscious or concerned about aging? The answers are likely different for each client, but we all bring biases and assumptions into interactions that would change our behavior when talking to these two therapists.

In a perfect world, clients would all recognize that their assumptions may be incorrect, and all humans would enter into new interactions without any expectations or pre-judgments whatsoever. Yet in reality, people do change their behavior based on who (they assume) they are talking to. Importantly, this does not suggest that psychologists need to change their stimulus value, or who they are at all. The young psychologist does not need to make themselves look older; nor does any psychologist need to change a preferred style of dressing. Rather, it is the use of the techniques discussed above, including the use of questions, active listening, and silence, that will demonstrate the ability to establish rapport and create an environment where clients feel understood and cared for. Through our questioning and our understanding of our clients' emotions, we can demonstrate that we are open to hearing about anything the client wishes to discuss, and our own prior experiences (whether they are real or assumed) are not as important as our commitment to understanding how our clients feel, from their own perspective.

Finally, breaks in rapport can occur from time to time during the initial interview, such as if the therapist infers the wrong gender identity of a client based on appearance or inadvertently forgets an important historical detail that the client had previously disclosed. These things happen to all of us; and although they can feel extremely awkward and uncomfortable in the moment, they are not necessarily catastrophic to the therapeutic relationship if they are directly and compassionately addressed.

Psychologists' Own Multicultural Lenses

Of course, psychologists are human beings too, which means that we are just as subject to biases and misperceptions as are our clients. Thus, a critical component of training in clinical psychology is a recognition that our own past experiences have created biases, filters, or lenses through which we see the world. This is a difficult and potentially threatening realization for many psychology trainees. No one wants to consider that they may harbor prejudicial attitudes and many are reluctant to admit that they make knee-jerk assumptions about people based on others' demographic characteristics. Those from dominant groups (e.g., white, male, cisgender, heterosexual, upper-middle class, Protestant, physically able, nonimmigrant) may be especially sensitive to this type of self-awareness, as many work diligently to understand their privilege and avoid accusations of racism, sexism, and so on. Yet, even the most earnest efforts to be multiculturally aware do not fully erase our biases, they merely allow us to confront our cultural assumptions more honestly.

For this reason, many training programs assist clinical psychologists to develop **multicultural humility**, defined as an awareness that no matter how insightful or sensitive we may think we are, psychologists must never fully stop learning about our own filters and continually challenge ourselves to question our own assumptions. In some cases, this may mean that a psychologist has to rethink a clinical diagnosis based on a culturally based understanding of what appears to be a pathological symptom (as we discuss further in Chapter 9, *Diagnosis, Case Formulation, and Treatment Planning*). But in other cases, it may simply reflect a difference in understanding the salience, meaning, or significance of everyday experiences; for example, how news stories about changing immigration policies might affect members of certain ethnic and cultural groups more than others.

Within a clinical interview, psychologists may often ask, "What does that mean for you?" to help reflect that their own assumptions may differ from their clients'. Psychologists may use limited, brief personal disclosure to illustrate a difference in culture and ask for clarification (e.g., "When I grew up, my parents used to talk about becoming a doctor all the time. How does it feel within your family now that you have been accepted to medical school?"), or may even simply discuss a visible cultural difference to illustrate that the psychologist is interested and comfortable talking about a client's whole experience explicitly (e.g., "I am not familiar with how that would feel within the trans community — can you tell me more about whether that is a relevant piece of this for you?"). Psychologists' ability to act in accordance with their own multicultural humility is essential for any clinical interview and often for the work of psychological treatment that may follow.

Think Like a Clinical Psychologist Imagine interviewing a client who explains that they hold political ideologies, religious beliefs, or cultural values that are the polar opposite of your own. How, if at all, would this affect your work together? How would you establish rapport with this person?

Different Types of Clinical Interviews

Up to this point, we have reviewed various interviewing essentials and techniques that are relevant to the interviewing process, regardless of the type of interview. In this section, we discuss the types of interviews that clinical psychologists conduct. It is important to note, however, that more than one of these interviews may be administered to the same client. For example, the same client may complete an *intake-admission interview* when admitted to a hospital, a *mental status examination interview* once in the hospital unit, and later a *structured diagnostic interview* by the treating clinician. Each is discussed below.

The many varieties of interviews have two primary distinguishing features. First, interviews differ in their purpose. For example, the purpose of one interview may be to evaluate a client who is presenting to an outpatient clinic for the first time (i.e., *intake-admission interview*), whereas the purpose of another interview may be to arrive at a DSM diagnosis (**diagnostic interview**).

The second major distinguishing factor is the extent to which an interview is unstructured (often labeled a clinical interview) or structured. In **unstructured interviews**, clinicians ask any questions that come to mind in any order. In contrast, **structured interviews** require the clinician to ask, verbatim, a set of predetermined standardized questions in a specified sequence. The use of structured interviews allows for **standardization** in the administration and scoring of the interviews, meaning that questions are asked and scored the same way with every client every time. Standardization is especially important because it allows for scientific inferences regarding the responses. A structured interview is therefore especially important to consider when using clients' responses to determine clinical diagnoses. There are also **semi-structured interviews** that include standardized questions or "prompts," but also leave room for the psychologist to follow up with questions of their own. The three types of interviews all have their place in clinical practice and in research settings, but they each have advantages and disadvantages, as shown in **Table 5.2**.

Table 5.2	Major Advantages and Disadvantages of Structured Versus Unstructured Interviews	
	Advantages	**Disadvantages**
Structured	**Less interviewer bias** — the element of interviewer judgment is removed, leading to consistency in both methodology and information gathered **Greater reliability and validity** — due to the standardized questions and scoring rubric	**No flexibility** — the interviewer is restricted to predetermined closed-ended questions and cannot explore unanticipated or interesting topics that might surface **Less rapport** — more formal with no room for the interviewer to make small talk or delve into areas that the participant wants to talk more about
Unstructured	**No specified script** — interviewer is free to use open-ended questions and do what's needed to build rapport **Flexibility** — interviewer can explore what seems important and generate ideas and hypotheses	**Less reliability and validity** — each interviewer may ask different questions to different people, so replicability and validity are threatened **Risk of interviewer bias** — interviewer's choice of questions and interpretation of answers are completely based on judgment and therefore subject to bias
Semistructured	**Compromise** — interviewer is given guidance on what topics to assess (helping reliability and validity), *and* can more fully probe interesting or important areas (maximizing rapport)	**Interviewer bias** — although reduced, there is still some risk of bias because of open-ended follow-up questions

The same kinds of interview skills are required regardless of the purpose or type of interview. Rapport, good communication skills, appropriate follow-up questions, and good observational skills are all necessary, even when administering a structured interview. Also, as we have discussed, it is important for interviewers to maintain a healthy sense of multi-cultural humility. Although there may be a high degree of similarity across people, and one can tentatively apply the same concepts to diverse social groups, many of the instruments we describe in the remainder of this chapter have been applied primarily to white people in Western cultures (which reflects a shortcoming of clinical psychology that is shared by many other fields). We organize our presentation in this section according to the purpose of an interview. However, it is important to keep in mind that structured and unstructured (and in some cases, semistructured) versions of all these interviews exist.

Intake-Admission Interview

An **intake-admission interview** generally has two purposes: (a) to determine why the client has come to the clinic or hospital and (b) to judge whether the agency's facilities, policies, and services will meet the needs and expectations of the client. Often, these interviews occur face-to-face, although since the COVID-19 pandemic, there has been an increasing tendency to use teletherapy methods in which the interviewer and interviewee meet remotely (over the Internet) via webcam. Because of the convenience of remote interviewing, this practice is likely to continue to be the norm for some clinicians. IN PRACTICE: *Sample Intake Report, Kiara* presents an example of an intake report based on an interview with Kiara in a community-based outpatient clinic.

In Practice   Sample Intake Report, Kiara

Name: Kiara

Age: 29

Sex: Female

Occupation: Registered nurse

Date of Interview: June 1, 2020

Therapist: Luke Baldry, PhD (fictitious name)

Identifying Information: The client is a 29-year-old female who is presently working as a nurse in Luzerne County General Hospital. Currently, she lives alone in an apartment in Wilkes-Barre.

Chief Complaint: The client presents to the clinic today complaining of "OCD and depression" that reportedly has become worse over the past 2 months.

History of Presenting Problem: The client reports that she has experienced obsessional thoughts, compulsions, anxiety, and depression "off and on" for many years, but that these symptoms have worsened since graduating nursing school and starting her full-time job as a nurse. These symptoms include (a) unwanted thoughts and anxiety that she might mistakenly do something that harms one of her patients, such as contaminate them with germs or administer the wrong dose of medication; (b) excessive handwashing and checking behavior, such as repeatedly reading over medical charts to reassure herself that she didn't make mistakes; (c) depressed mood ("feeling sad and guilty"); (d) appetite disturbance but no significant weight loss; (e) sleep disturbance (early morning awakening); (f) fatigue; and (g) difficulty concentrating. All of these symptoms have been present nearly every day over the past 2 months.

   The client reports that she has always been a "worrier," a "perfectionist," and someone who tends to "jump to conclusions" but says that when she finished school and started her new job, the increased responsibility of caring for her own patients escalated her anxiety. She says that even when away from work, she thinks about mistakes that she could have made, and feels the urge to check and reassure herself that she hasn't harmed any patients. She recounted an episode, about a week ago, in which she went to work in the middle of the night just to make sure a certain patient on her floor hadn't died from an overdose of medication she feared she had mistakenly given him during her shift.

The client reports recognizing that her recurring fears are senseless, and that she probably does not need to check and wash her hands so much — she has never found an error when checking — but that she "can't stand the uncertainty" and "needs to know for sure" that she didn't make any mistakes. She also wonders why she thinks about harming patients so much, and worries that deep down, she might want to harm someone. The client reports no history of violence or harmful behavior and says this is the last thing she would ever do.

The client also reports having difficulty with productivity due to excessive time spent washing her hands to prevent contaminating patients, and checking over charts. According to her, this has led to receiving negative feedback from her superiors, as well as to feelings of guilt, depression, and hopelessness.

Past Treatment History: The client reports that she has not previously sought out psychological or psychiatric treatment.

Medical History: No significant medical history was reported.

Substance Use/Abuse: The client denies any current symptoms of substance abuse or dependence. She "tried" marijuana on three occasions in the past (while in college) but denies current use. She reports drinking, on average, three or four alcoholic drinks per week, and always in social situations (with work colleagues, family, or friends).

Medication: The client reports that she is not currently taking any medication.

Family History: Both of the client's biological parents are living, and she has one brother (age 32) and one sister (age 26). The client reports that her mother suffers from depression and has received outpatient treatment on numerous occasions. Further, she reports that her maternal grandfather was diagnosed with depression. No substance use problems among family members were noted.

Suicidal/Homicidal Ideation: The client denies any current or past suicidal or homicidal ideation, intent, or action.

Mental Status: The client was well-groomed, cooperative, and dressed appropriately. She was alert and oriented in all spheres. Her mood and affect were anxious and dysphoric. Her speech was clear, coherent, and goal-directed. Some attention and concentration difficulties were noted. There was no evidence of formal thought disorder, delusions, hallucinations, or suicidal/homicidal ideation. Her insight and judgment appear to be fair to good.

Diagnostic Impression: Obsessive-Compulsive Disorder; Major Depressive Disorder.

Recommendations: Individual psychotherapy. Cognitive-behavioral treatment for OCD. ▬

The Social History Interview

A **social history interview** offers an opportunity to document as much of a client's personal history as possible. The psychologist is interested in concrete facts, dates, events, and — perhaps more importantly — in the client's feelings about them. In essence, the purpose of the social history is to provide a broad background and context in which both the client and the problem can be placed. This historical-developmental context is critical to best understand how clients' diagnoses and therapeutic implications can be more reliably determined.

The range of material covered in social histories is quite broad. They may cover infancy, childhood/adolescence, and adulthood, and they often include educational, sexual, medical, parental-environmental, religious, and psychological matters. Although, as noted earlier, much of this material will be factual, it is extremely important to note how clients *present* the material—how they speak about it, their emotional reactions to the material, evasiveness or openness, and so on. Notice in Kiara's intake report how the interviewer notes what Kiara *reports*, rather than stating what she says as *facts*.

For most adults, particularly those whose cognitive abilities and reality testing are intact, social history interviews are conducted with the client themselves. Among youth, however, social history interviews more commonly are conducted with "external informants," including a parent, extended family members, and perhaps even schoolteachers. **Table 5.3** presents a typical social history outline.

Table 5.3 A Typical Social History Outline

1. Identifying data, including name, gender, occupation, address, date and place of birth, religion, and education.
2. Reason for coming to the agency and expectations for service.
3. Present situation, such as description of daily behavior and any recent or impending changes.
4. Family constellation (family of orientation), including descriptions of mother, father, and other family members and the respondent's role in the family growing up.
5. Early recollections, descriptions of earliest clear events and their surroundings.
6. Birth and development, including ages of walking and talking, problems compared with other children, and the person's view of his or her early experiences.
7. Health, including childhood and later diseases and injuries, problems with drugs or alcohol, and comparison of one's body with others.
8. Education and training, including subjects of special interest and achievement.
9. Work record, including reasons for changing jobs and attitudes toward work.
10. Recreation and interests, including volunteer work, reading, and the respondent's report of adequacy of self-expression and pleasures.
11. Sexual development, covering first awareness, kinds of sexual activities, and view of the adequacy of sexual expressions.
12. Marital and family data, covering major events and what led to them, and comparison of present family of birth and orientation.
13. Self-description, including strengths, weaknesses, and ideals.
14. Choices and turning points in life, a review of the respondent's most important decisions and changes, including the single most important happening.
15. View of the future, including what the subject would like to see happen next year and in five or ten years, and what is necessary for these events to happen.
16. Any further material the respondent may see as omitted from the history.

SOURCE: Norman D. Sundberg, *Assessment of Persons*, copyright © 1977, pp. 97–98. Reprinted by permission of Pearson Education, Upper Saddle River, NJ.

The Mental Status Examination

A **mental status examination** is typically conducted to assess the presence of in-the-moment cognitive, emotional, or behavioral problems. In other words, this type of interview is often conducted to provide a record of how a client presented and what it was like to "be in the room" with them at a given point in time. Information from mental status exams often are used to determine whether a client is experiencing acute psychosis (i.e., are they oriented to the present day, time, and place where they are?), to describe a client's general demeanor and presentation when arriving at a formal assessment session, and also within forensic settings.

The general areas covered in these interviews, along with excerpts from a sample report, are shown in **Table 5.4** and IN PRACTICE: *Excerpt from a Sample Mental Status Interview*, respectively.

Table 5.4 General Outline of Mental Status Examination
I.   General Presentation: Appearance, Behavior, Attitude
II.   State of Consciousness: Alert, Hyperalert, Lethargic
III.   Attention and Concentration
IV.   Speech: Clarity, Goal-directedness, Language Deficits
V.   Orientation: To Person, Place, Time
VI.   Mood and Affect
VII.   Form of Thought; Formal Thought Disorder
VIII.   Thought Content: Preoccupations, Obsessions, Delusions
IX.   Ability to Think Abstractly
X.   Perceptions: Hallucinations
XI.   Memory: Immediate, Recent, Remote
XII.   Intellectual Functioning
XIII.   Insight and Judgment

In Practice   **Excerpt from a Sample Mental Status Interview**

The client appeared disheveled and exhibited "odd" behavior throughout the interview. Although he appeared alert, some impairment in his attention and concentration was noted. Specifically, he experienced difficulty repeating a series of digits and performing simple calculations without the aid of pencil and paper. No language deficits were noted, although the client's speech was at times difficult to understand and did not appear to be goal-directed (not a response to the question posed). He was oriented to person and place, but was not oriented to time. Specifically, he was unsure of the month and day. He reported his mood as "fine"; his affect appeared to be blunted. He demonstrated some signs of formal thought disorder, including tangentiality and loose associations. He denied suicidal ideation but did report his belief that he was being "framed by the FBI" for a crime he did not commit. When confronted with the fact that he was in a psychiatric hospital, not a prison, he stated that this was all part of an FBI "cover-up," so that he could be made to look "crazy." Although he denied hallucinations, his behavior suggested that, on occasion, he was responding to auditory hallucinations. For example, he stared off into space and began whispering on several occasions. His ability to think abstractly appeared to be impaired. For example, when asked how a baseball and an orange are alike, he responded, "They both are alive." The client's immediate and recent memories were slightly impaired, although his remote memory was intact. It is estimated that he is of average intelligence. Currently, his insight and judgment appear to be poor. ▄▄▄

The Diagnostic Interview

As mentioned above, some clinical psychologists evaluate clients according to DSM criteria. Insurance companies, research protocols, or even court proceedings may require a diagnostic evaluation. How clinicians arrive at their diagnosis, however, is for the most part left up to the psychologist. Historically, psychologists use a clinical interview—a free-form unstructured interview with content that varies greatly from clinician to clinician. As might be expected, this interviewing method often results in unreliable ratings because two clinicians evaluating the same client may arrive at different diagnostic formulations. Research on the reliability of diagnoses using unstructured clinical interviews indicates it is not an effective approach (e.g., Mueller & Segal, 2014).

Fortunately, things have changed. Researchers have developed **structured diagnostic interviews** that can be used by clinical psychologists in their research or clinical work. A structured diagnostic interview consists of a standard set of questions and follow-up probes that are asked in a specified sequence. The use of structured diagnostic interviews ensures that all clients or research subjects are asked the same questions. This makes it more likely that two clinicians who evaluate the same client will arrive at the same diagnostic formulation (high interrater reliability).

Structured interviews sometimes are critiqued as too rigid or culturally insensitive, however. When administered by a computer, for instance, it is not possible to (a) determine whether clients understand each question, (b) clarify questions based on clients' backgrounds, or (c) probe responses to be sure that responses are accurate and consistent based on clients' responses. More common, therefore, is the use of semistructured interviews that offer psychologists an opportunity to ask standardized questions and a set of standardized clarification, follow-up, and probing questions. Moreover, semistructured interviews offer a standardized scoring system that allow interviewers to offer quantitative judgments regarding the presence of past or current psychological symptoms.

For example, the Schedule for Affective Disorders and Schizophrenia for School-Age Children, Present and Lifetime Version (sometimes referred to as the Kiddie-SADS, or KSADS-PL; Kaufman et al., 2016) is a semistructured diagnostic interview. Each

PeopleImages/Getty Images

Clinical psychologists use structured diagnostic interviews that contain standardized questions both in research and with therapy clients.

diagnosis includes separate items (with standardized probes and follow-up questions) for each specific symptom within the DSM. For depressed mood, clients are first asked:

Have you ever felt sad, blue, down, or empty? Did you feel like crying?

And then follow-up questions include:

When was that?

Do you feel _____ (sad, blue, down, or empty) now?

Was there ever another time you felt _____?

Did you have any other bad feelings?

Did you have a bad feeling all the time that you couldn't get rid of?

Did you cry or were you tearful? Did you feel _____ all the time, some of the time? (Percent of awake time: summation of % of all labels if they do not occur simultaneously.)

Did it come and go? How often? Every day? How long did it last?

What do you think brought it on?

Could other people tell that you were sad?

Based on responses to these items psychologists may assign a score to indicate whether their client has this single symptom of depression. A standardized scoring system includes:

0: No information

1: Not present; not at all or less than once a week

2: Subthreshold; depressed mood at least 2–3 days/week, for much of the day

3: Threshold: depressed mood more days than not (4–7 days/week), most of the day (at least 50% of awake time)

A similar procedure is then used for each additional symptom of a major depressive disorder, including irritability/anger, anhedonia, thoughts of death, and so on. Notice that this approach can remove much of the subjectivity of the diagnostic interview process, increasing its reliability and validity, and thus increasing the accuracy of diagnosis. Several additional structured diagnostic interviews are available to clinical psychologists to help evaluate both adults and youth. For example, among adults, the Structured Clinical Interview for DSM-5 (SCID-5; First et al., 2016) and the Mini International Neuropsychiatric Interview (MINI; Sheehan, 2016) are often used for this purpose.

Despite the availability of a wide range of structured and semistructured interviews for diagnosis, it appears that few clinicians use these in everyday practice. For example, one study estimated that clinicians used structured diagnostic interviews with only about 15% of their clients (Bruchmüller et al., 2011). Interestingly, clinicians markedly underestimated their clients' acceptance of structured interviews, and this appeared to be at least partially responsible for the clinicians' reluctance to use these in routine clinical practice. A previous study of clients that had undergone structured interviewing indicated that clients on average were highly satisfied with the interview, almost all clients rated their relationship to the interviewer as positive, and only a small proportion felt "questioned out" after the procedure (Suppiger et al., 2009). These studies, therefore, suggest that clinicians should not assume that structured diagnostic interviews will be viewed as onerous or unhelpful to our clients. Rather, if used routinely, these interviews can help us arrive at reliable and valid diagnoses that can inform treatment and intervention.

> **Think Like a Clinical Psychologist** Imagine you are a client visiting a clinical psychologist for the first time. What would you expect to be asked during your initial appointment? How would you feel about opening up and revealing sensitive aspects of yourself? How would the race and gender of the psychologist affect your level of comfort and willingness to self-disclose?

▥ Chapter Summary

The clinical interview is the most basic and most serviceable assessment technique used by clinical psychologists. There are two primary distinguishing factors among interviews. First, interviews are unstructured, structured, or semistructured. In contrast to unstructured interviews, structured and semistructured interviews require the clinician to ask verbatim a set of standardized questions in a specified sequence. Second, interviews differ with regard to their purpose. In this chapter, we discussed the intake-admission interview, the social history interview, the mental status examination interview, and the diagnostic interview. Regardless of the type of interview or its purpose, certain skills are required, including rapport, good communication skills, asking the right types of questions, active listening, and multicultural humility.

Applying What You've Learned

Find a classmate or friend for a role-play exercise. One person plays the therapist and one plays the client. The "client" should read through Table 5.4 and IN PRACTICE: *Excerpt from a Sample Mental Status Interview*. The "therapist" will now conduct a clinical interview with the client. Keep in mind the skills described in the first part of the chapter (active listening, acknowledging strengths, open-ended questions, etc.). After the interview, ask yourselves the following:

For the therapist: (1) What kinds of questions did you use in your interview, and how successful were they? (2) Do you feel like you understand the client? Why or why not? (3) What was the hardest part in conducting the interview? (4) How would you characterize the level of rapport you had with the client?

For the client: (1) What was it liked to be interviewed? Did you feel the therapist asked the right questions? If no, why not? (2) Which types of questions did you feel helped the interview the most? (3) How would you rate the level of rapport and active listening?

Imagine you are a clinical psychologist about to meet with a new client for the first time. What could you do beforehand to make sure your client feels at ease? How would you introduce yourself? How would you start your initial interview? How would you ask about private or sensitive information (e.g., about their sexual behavior)? What would you do if they aren't willing to answer some of your questions? How would your answers to these questions be different if the client was of a different gender, racial/ethnic, cultural, socioeconomic, or educational background than your own?

Key Terms

Active listening: Not only hearing what the client is saying but also understanding what has been said; the therapist will often use reflection to demonstrate understanding.

Clarifying questions: Questions used by therapists to make sure they understand what the client is expressing.

Clinical interview: One of the most basic techniques employed by the clinical psychologist for the purpose of answering a referral question. If administered skilfully, the assessment interview can provide insight into the problem and inform clinical decision making.

Confronting questions: Questions used by therapists to challenge inconsistencies or contradictions.

Diagnostic interview: An interview conducted for the purpose of arriving at a DSM-5-TR diagnostic formulation.

Direct questions: Questions used by therapists to gather information; best used once rapport has been established and the client is taking responsibility.

Facilitative questions: Questions used by therapists to encourage clients' flow of conversation.

Intake-admission interview: An interview conducted for the purposes of (a) determining why the client has come to an agency (e.g., clinic, hospital), (b) determining whether the agency can meet the client's needs and expectations, and (c) informing the client about the agency's policies and procedures.

Mental status examination: An interview conducted to evaluate the client for the presence of cognitive, emotional, or behavioral problems. In the MSE interview, the clinician assesses the client in a number of areas, including (but not limited to) general presentation, quality of speech, thought content, memory, and judgment.

Multicultural humility: An awareness that no matter how insightful or sensitive, psychologists have never fully stopped learning about their own filters, and must continually challenge themselves to question their own assumptions.

Open-ended questions: Questions used by therapists to give clients responsibility and latitude for responding; these questions require more than a yes or no answer.

Rapport: A word often used to characterize the relationship between client and clinician. In the context of the clinical interview, building good rapport involves establishing a comfortable atmosphere and sharing an understanding of the purpose of the interview.

Semistructured interview: Interview that includes standardized questions or "prompts," but also leaves room for the psychologist to follow up with questions of their own.

Silence: Effective in communicating safety to a client by conveying that the psychologist is present exclusively for their client's needs, will not rush the client, and is comfortable with anything that is said or needs to be contemplated by their client. Silence also often prompts the client to continue talking, and in doing so, to further elaborate on their own thoughts.

Social history interview: An interview conducted for the purpose of gaining a thorough understanding of the client's background and the historical-developmental context in which a problem emerged.

Standardization: In the context of interviews, questions are asked and scored the same way with every client every time.

Stimulus value: The way the therapist appears and behaves; may affect individual clients in different ways.

Structured diagnostic interview: A diagnostic interview that consists of a standard set of questions asked in a specified sequence. The questions may be keyed to the diagnostic criteria for a number of disorders.

Structured interview: An interview that requires the clinician to ask, verbatim, a set of pre-determined, standardized questions in a specified sequence.

Unstructured interview: An interview in which the clinician asks any questions that come to mind in any order.

CONNECT ONLINE:

 Check out our videos and additional resources located at: www.macmillanlearning.com

CHAPTER

6

Personality Assessment

FOCUS QUESTIONS

1. What are the advantages and disadvantages of projective tests?
2. Why are the reliability and validity of projective measures so difficult to assess?
3. What are the advantages and disadvantages of objective tests? What are the major strategies of test construction? Briefly describe each of these.
4. What are the similarities and differences between objective and projective measures?
5. What does and what does not constitute evidence for test bias?

CHAPTER OUTLINE

What is personality? It's a strange question. After all, isn't personality what we all use to form impressions of others? And don't we consider personality when predicting how someone will respond or interact with us in a given situation? Don't we look for people with certain personality traits to form relationships with? We can define **personality** as the continuity in a person's behavior and emotional style over time. And a **personality trait** is a stable and consistent way of perceiving the world and of behaving. Traits may be influenced by the environment (i.e., through conditioning), biology (i.e., through genetics), or a combination of these factors. Research shows that personality traits can have clinical significance. Some traits, for example, are correlated with substance use problems; others with anger issues, medical conditions, aggression, and violence.

But are people really consistent in their behavior, or is this merely a perception? Could our perception of someone's personality be based on observing a limited sample of their behavior in a limited number of circumstances? Can youth have a personality, or is it still developing? Consider that in the wake of some violent attacks, such as school shootings, the perpetrators may be described by their families and neighbors as "reserved," or "the last person" they'd ever expect to commit a violent rampage. Might our perception of consistency in behavior or emotional style be influenced by cognitive biases, such as the human brain's tendency to look for patterns in randomness? We hope you'll keep these questions in mind as you read this chapter, which covers the various viewpoints on the concept of personality, the major approaches to measuring personality traits, and issues related to fairness and bias in personality testing.

Perspectives on the Concept of Personality

When we talk about ourselves and others, we frequently refer to different characteristics of an individual's personality. Clinical psychologists who work with adults do much the same thing when they assess personality, but on a more systematic and scientific level. The goal of personality assessment is to help clinical psychologists clarify a clinical diagnosis, guide therapeutic interventions, and predict how people may respond in different situations. How to study personality has been a topic of interest throughout human history (see IN HISTORICAL PERSPECTIVE: *Personality and Personality Testing*).

The Five-Factor Model

The most well-studied model of personality is the **Five-Factor Model (FFM)**, which proposes that personality is comprised of five dimensions or "traits," known as the "Big Five." **Table 6.1** shows the facets that represent each dimension; a person can be low or high on any of these dimensions (Goldberg, 1993). One of the personality tests you will learn about in this chapter — the Neuroticism, Extraversion, Openness Personality Inventory (NEO-PI) — is based on this conceptual model. Proponents of this approach argue that it provides a comprehensive approach to understanding personality. Critics, however, maintain that the traits included in this approach are overly broad and therefore not particularly helpful in making useful

●●●●● In Historical Perspective

Personality and Personality Testing

Interest in personality dates as far back as Ancient Greece (circa 370 BCE), where Hippocrates proposed that temperament was influenced by imbalances of the body's humors. Aristotle was also interested in connections between behavior and physical aspects of the body. In the mid- to late 18th century, Franz Gall, a neuroanatomist (and father of phrenology, the practice of feeling for bumps on a person's skull to determine their intellectual and personality functioning), further advanced the hypothesis of a relationship between brain and behavior, but it was the iconic case of Phineas Gage in the 19th century that solidified this hypothesis. Gage was a railroad construction worker in 1848 when an accident caused a tamping iron to be driven through the side of his face, behind his left eye, and all the way through the top of his skull. Miraculously, Gage recovered. However, the brain injury from the accident seemingly resulted in changes in his demeanor: once a moralistic and calm person, he became irreverent, impatient, and profane after the accident. His case is one of the first to provide physical evidence that personality is linked to specific brain regions.

Phineas Gage's accident helped bring to light the relationship between the brain and personality.

At the dawn of the 20th century, and as a backlash against earlier biological models, psychiatrist Sigmund Freud proposed his psychoanalytic model of personality. This was followed shortly thereafter by Carl Jung, a student of Freud's, who claimed individuals fall into dichotomous personality categories, such as introverted or extraverted. The typology model of personality was further popularized by Katherine Cook Briggs and Isabel Briggs Myers, who developed the Myers-Briggs Type Indicator, which remains a widely used personality test to this day.

Trait theory, the idea that personality can be understood in terms of adjectives or descriptive phrases (e.g., self-confident, introverted), was advanced by psychologist Gordon Allport in the 1930s. In the 1940s, Raymond Cattell developed a 16-trait model of personality. Paul Costa and Robert McCrae (1992) later developed the Five-Factor Model of personality, which describes personality in terms of five broad factors (the "Big Five"), which could be assessed using a number of measures, including self-report questionnaires. The Five-Factor Model continues to dominate the field of personality to this day. ∎

predictions about people's behavior and emotion. Also note that psychological scientists rarely study personality among youth. Although historical perspectives once regarded childhood experiences as important determinants of personality, current work regards these concepts as less relevant to child development. Consequently, psychologists today who study personality consider these "traits" to have formed stably only after individuals reach adulthood, and our discussion of personality in this chapter thus remains focused only on adults.

Table 6.1 Dimensions and Facets of the Five-Factor Personality Model	
Dimension	**Facets**
Neuroticism	Anxiety, Hostility, Depression, Self-Consciousness, Impulsiveness, Vulnerability
Extraversion	Warmth, Gregariousness, Assertiveness, Activity, Excitement Seeking, Positive Emotions
Openness to Experience	Fantasy, Aesthetics, Feelings, Actions, Ideas, Values
Agreeableness	Trust, Straightforwardness, Altruism, Compliance, Modesty, Tender-Mindedness
Conscientiousness	Competence, Order, Dutifulness, Achievement Striving, Self-Discipline, Deliberation

The Situational Perspective

As alluded to in the introduction to this chapter, not all clinical psychologists agree with the concept of personality. Those who take a behaviorist view (which is covered in greater depth in Chapter 7, *Behavioral Assessment*), for example, are more likely to take a **situational perspective**. From this perspective, people's behavior is entirely a product of situational factors such as learning and conditioning from the environment, rather than resulting from personality traits (Mischel, 1973, 2013). For example, *assertiveness*, rather than being ascribed to the trait of extraversion, would be viewed as learned through positive reinforcement for speaking up for oneself. Similarly, emotions and behaviors are viewed as resulting from beliefs about situations and events. For example, fear would be seen as stemming from exaggerated estimates of danger (e.g., "The dog is likely to attack me"), rather than from the possession of a trait such as neuroticism. At a broader level, culture—with its shared beliefs, values, and norms—also shapes behavior. The very fact that you are reading this textbook likely means that your own culture encourages (and reinforces) the behavior of pursuing an education.

The Middle Ground

The concept of personality is a somewhat contentious issue within the field of clinical psychology. Although both of the aforementioned conceptualizations have ardent supporters (and opponents), most psychologists take a middle ground. These psychologists acknowledge that human behavior and emotion rely on an interaction between personality traits *and* situational factors. These different views are represented in the different approaches to assessing and measuring personality, as we will see in the remainder of this chapter.

Think Like a Clinical Psychologist Are personalities real or are they illusions? Do people possess traits that influence their feelings and behaviors, or is the appearance of traits the result of our human tendency to want to predict other people's (and our own) behavior?

Personality Tests

Thinking back on our discussion of the science of assessment in Chapter 4, *The Science of Assessment*, a useful personality test must be able to be administered and scored the same way each time, regardless of who is taking the test (*standardization*). Moreover, since personality is supposed to be a stable characteristic, the same individual should achieve a similar result if they take the test multiple times (*reliability*). Finally, the test should tell us something more about the individual being assessed than what can be gleaned through other sources such as via a clinical interview or by observing how they respond to the items on the test itself. That is, personality tests should have *incremental validity*. In particular, they should be predictive of the person's future behavior.

To give an example, discovering from a personality test that a 70-year-old widower "seems to be grappling with intense feelings of loneliness" hardly represents a breakthrough in incremental validity, even though the statement may be entirely true. Asserting that test scores of a person with schizophrenia reveal adjustment difficulties or that the responses of a client known to be depressed are suggestive of dysphoria and sadness adds little if anything to existing knowledge. Similarly, if Kiara scores highly on a measure of the trait neuroticism, this would hardly come as a surprise given that she has a diagnosis of OCD, which is associated with high levels of anxiety. If, however, a personality test can tell Kiara's clinician something *new* about her tendency to become anxious and how she will respond to treatment—something that cannot be identified through other means of assessment and that will assist in developing an effective treatment plan—then such a test has incremental validity. As you learn in this chapter about the most widely used personality tests, we invite you to consider the extent to which such assessments possess this type of validity.

An important challenge for personality tests is that personality itself cannot be directly observed or measured. That is, the phenomena linked to how personality is conceptualized—such as traits, drives, and ego defense mechanisms—are hypothetical constructs. Accordingly, it is difficult to establish clear criteria for validation. That is, how do we know when we are assessing the construct in question?

Types of Personality Tests

Two broad approaches — *projective* and *objective personality tests*—have been developed in an attempt to address the challenges just described. As we will see in the sections that follow, these types of tests are based on very different assumptions and use diverging methods to assess personality. The overall origins of personality testing, however, can be traced to Hermann Rorschach's use of inkblots as a method for psychiatric diagnosis in the early 1920s. Rorschach believed that a person's psychological characteristics could be ascertained by observing how they responded to an ambiguous situation. In the century that has followed, personality assessment and test interpretation has become a major part of training in psychology, and one of the chief activities of psychologists in both clinical and forensic settings. In the next section, you will learn about the nature of projective and objective personality tests, popular examples of each flavor of test, their pros and cons, and how they are typically used in practice.

Heritage Images/Hulton Archive/Getty Images

Hermann Rorschach (1884–1922)

Think Like a Clinical Psychologist The issue of incremental validity is important. What would you want to know about a client you are working with that would not be accessible through the other forms of assessment you have read about in this textbook?

▥ Projective Tests

Broadly speaking, **projective personality tests** consist of presenting the test taker with ambiguous (e.g., vague, abstract, incomplete) stimuli and then assessing how the individual responds to such stimuli. This method is based on the **projective hypothesis**, which proposes that test takers will unconsciously reveal critical aspects of their personality when trying to make sense of ambiguous material. The properly trained psychologist, according to this view, is then able to work backward from the test taker's responses to gain insight into the person's needs, wishes, conflicts, and other personality dynamics. This idea is derived from Freud's concept of *projection*, an ego defense mechanism in which people unconsciously project their own negative impulses and traits onto others around them. Thus, projective tests are thought to bypass conscious awareness and to allow psychologists access to personality features of which the test-taker is not consciously aware. Proponents argue that in doing so, such tests provide incremental validity over and above other forms of assessment. Accordingly, projective tests typically have the following characteristics:

- **Ambiguous test stimuli.** Examinees are asked to respond to unstructured stimuli, such as describing what they see when they look at an inkblot, or how they complete an incomplete sentence (e.g., When I wake up in the morning, the first thing I like to do is _____).

- **Indirectness.** Because it is important that examinees do not censor the data they provide on projective tests, they are kept unaware of what the test is intended to measure. Although it may be possible to figure out that psychological functioning is being assessed in general, there are no direct questions about thoughts, feelings, or other problems. The hope is that keeping respondents unaware of the purpose of the tests and significance of their responses will foster a more honest and open (less biased) response.

- **Freedom of response.** This refers to the use of open-ended test items that permit a nearly infinite range of responses, as opposed to many questionnaires that restrict responses to a range of numbers on a rating scale.

- **Qualitative response interpretation.** Objective personality tests, as we will see later in this chapter, are focused, quantitative, and usually provide a single score that gets interpreted by the clinician. Projective tests, however, are interpreted qualitatively and along multiple dimensions (e.g., needs, adjustment, diagnostic category).

- **Lack of standardization.** Although proponents of projective tests often describe such tests as if they have norms, there are no attempts at standardization. It is often argued that interpretations of projective tests cannot be standardized because every person is unique, and interpretation is therefore an "art."

Owing to these characteristics, the determination of the reliability and validity of projective tests is difficult. For example, it is surely too much to expect an individual to produce, word for word, exactly the same description of inkblots on different occasions. Yet to what extent are such differences permissible? And what about the consistency of the interpretations made by clinicians? The reliability of the test is therefore confounded by the reliability of the clinician administering and interpreting it. Similarly, because projective tests are used for such a wide range of purposes, there is little point in asking questions such as "Is the Rorschach a good personality test?" Such questions must be more specific: "Does the Rorschach predict aggression in situation A?" or "Does such a response to inkblot 5 correlate with anxiety?" With these issues in mind, we turn now to a discussion of some of the more popular projective tests.

The Rorschach Inkblot Test

Although the **Rorschach** originated in Europe, its subsequent development and elaboration occurred in the United States with the general rise of the psychodynamic, psychoanalytic movement and the emigration of many of its adherents from Europe to the United States in the 1930s (Butcher, 2010). What has confused many and perhaps impeded efforts to demonstrate reliability and validity is the fact that there are several different general Rorschach approaches (Exner, 1993). These approaches differ in the manner in which they administer, score, and interpret the results of the test and in the instructions they provide to examinees. This has created many problems in interpreting the results of research studies and in generalizing from one study to another. In addition, Exner and Exner (1972) discovered that 22% of the clinicians they surveyed did not formally score the Rorschach at all, and 75% reported that when they did use a scoring system, it was a highly idiosyncratic one.

Description

The Rorschach consists of 10 cards (numbered 1 to 10) on which are printed inkblots that are symmetrical from right to left. Five of the 10 cards are black and white (with shades of gray), and the other 5 include colors. A simulated Rorschach card is shown in **Figure 6.1**.

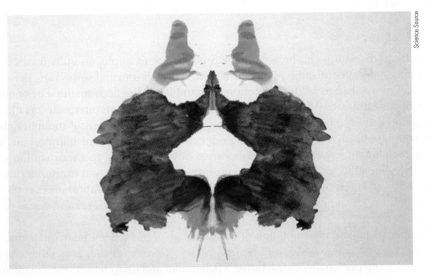

Science Source

Figure 6.1 A Simulated Card   This inkblot is similar to those administered in a Rorschach test.

Administration

There are various techniques for administering the Rorschach; however, the process usually goes something like this: the clinician hands the respondent the first card and says, "Tell me what you see — what it might be for you. There are no right or wrong answers. Just tell me what it looks like to you." All of the subsequent cards are administered in the same way and in order. The clinician writes down verbatim everything the respondent says. Some respondents produce many responses per card, and others produce very few. All spontaneous remarks or exclamations are also recorded.

Following this phase, the clinician moves to what is called the *Inquiry*. Here, the respondent is reminded of all previous responses, one by one, and asked what it was that prompted each response. The respondent is also asked to indicate for each card the exact location of the various responses. The respondent is given the opportunity to elaborate or clarify their responses.

Scoring

Although Rorschach scoring techniques vary, most employ three major determinants. *Location* refers to the area of the card to which the individual responded — the whole blot, a large detail, a small detail, white space, and so on. *Content* refers to the nature of the object perceived in the inkblot (an animal, a person, a rock, fog, clothing, etc.). *Determinants* refer to those aspects of the card that prompted the individual's response (the form of the blot, its color, texture, apparent movement, shading, etc.). Currently, the Exner (1993) Comprehensive System for scoring the Rorschach is the most frequently used formal scoring system. Although the specifics of this system are beyond the scope of this chapter, many people are surprised to learn that more weight is supposed to be given to the *determinants* than to the actual *content* of the responses. However, many clinicians do not bother with formal scoring, preferring to rely on the informal notation of determinants. Furthermore, these clinicians tend to make heavy use of content in their interpretations.

Interpretation

Rorschach interpretation can be a complex process. For example, an individual's overuse of form may suggest conformity. Poor form, coupled with unusual responses, may hint at psychosis. Color is said to relate to emotionality, and if it is not accompanied by good form, it may indicate impulsivity. Extensive use of white spaces has been interpreted as indicative of oppositional or even psychopathic qualities. Extensive use of details is thought to be correlated with compulsivity or obsessional tendencies. But content is also important. Seeing small animals might mean passivity. Responses of blood, claws, teeth, or similar images could suggest hostility and aggression. Even turning a card over and examining the back might lead to an interpretation of suspiciousness. However, it is important that the interpreter treat these as examples of potential interpretations or hypotheses and not as successfully validated facts!

Another issue with interpretation of the Rorschach (and indeed many projective tests) is the clinician's tendency to rely on intuitive, *yet scientifically invalid*, associations between test responses and personality characteristics (Chapman and Chapman, 1969). For example, a person who sees eyes in the inkblots would be characterized as suspicious or paranoid. Similarly, someone who describes guns might be described as violent. There is no evidence of any actual links here, but it can be difficult to avoid making interpretations based on these kinds of **illusory correlations** even when instructed not to.

Reliability and Validity

At the most basic level, Rorschach responses should be able to be scored and interpreted reliably across raters. If the same responses cannot be scored similarly by different raters using the same scoring system, then it is hard to imagine that the instrument would have much clinical utility. Unfortunately, the extent to which Rorschach scoring systems meet acceptable standards for this most basic and straightforward form of reliability remains a contentious issue (e.g., Bender, 2020). It is probable that two clinicians trained together over several years can achieve reliability in their interpretations of Rorschach responses. However, the tendency of many clinicians to use freewheeling interpretive approaches makes the calculation of this type of reliability difficult.

Despite many questions raised about the validity of the Rorschach, several studies have placed the test in a favorable light. For example, Parker and colleagues (1988), in a broad survey of Rorschach studies, found the average validity coefficient to be moderate. Still, many remain critical of the quality of the individual studies that have been cited as supporting the validity of Rorschach scores. Perhaps most important, a reanalysis of the studies included in Parker and colleagues' (1988) meta-analysis arrived at a different conclusion. Garb and colleagues (1998), using data from the same studies reviewed by Parker and colleagues, reported significantly lower validity estimates. These findings, in addition to findings that fail to support the incremental validity of Rorschach scores, led the authors to recommend that less emphasis be placed on training in the use of the Rorschach. Indeed, in recent years, clinical psychology programs have progressively offered less training in projective techniques.

The debate over the utility of the Rorschach in clinical assessment continues (e.g., Bender, 2020). Advocates argue that the test is useful when the focus is on the unconscious functioning and problem-solving styles of individuals. However, critics remain skeptical of the clinical utility of Rorschach scores as well as their incremental validity (Hunsley & Mash, 2007).

The Thematic Apperception Test

The **Thematic Apperception Test (TAT)** was introduced by Morgan and Murray in 1935 (Morgan & Murray, 1935). It purports to reveal a person's basic personality characteristics through the interpretation of their imaginative productions in response to a series of pictures. Although the test is designed to reveal central conflicts, attitudes, goals, and repressed material, it actually produces material that is a collage of these plus situational influences, cultural stereotypes, trivia, and so on. The clinician's job is to distinguish the valuable pieces of information from the worthless ones.

Most clinicians who use the TAT use it as a method of inferring psychological needs (for achievement, affiliation, dependence, power, sex, etc.) and of disclosing how an individual interacts with the environment. In contrast to the Rorschach, the TAT is used to infer the content of personality and the mode of social interactions. With the TAT, clinicians are likely to make specific judgments, such as "This person is hostile toward authority figures, yet seeks their affection and approval." The TAT is less likely to be used to assess the degree of maladjustment than to reveal the locus of problems, the type of treatment that might be most helpful, or the quality of interpersonal relationships.

Example of a card from the Thematic
Apperception Test

Description

The TAT consists of 31 cards, most of which depict people in a variety of situations, though a few contain only objects (one is an entirely blank card). Murray suggested that 20 of the 31 cards be selected for a given examinee. As a test, the TAT does not appear to be as ambiguous or unstructured as the Rorschach. However, though the figures in the pictures may clearly be people, it is not always clear what their gender is, exactly who the figures are, what they are doing, or what they are thinking.

Several additional instruments based on the TAT have been developed for administration to youth. The Roberts Apperception Test includes cards with animated drawings of adults and children. These cards typically do not portray gender in an ambiguous fashion, and often the drawing clearly depicts a specific activity (e.g., a conflict). The Children's Apperception Test is similar to the Roberts Apperception Test; however, all cards depict animals engaged in anthropomorphic activities. Since children often enjoy telling stories, and often are asked to make up stories based on pictures in school assignments, these tests are usually enjoyed by youth. However, many clinicians use them to develop rapport with children and perhaps generate initial hypotheses about the child's thinking processes. Formal scoring of the Roberts Apperception Test or Children's Apperception Test is rarely conducted, and these instruments often are used to facilitate a clinical interview rather than as a measure of children's personality.

Administration

In practice, clinicians typically select somewhere between 6 and 12 TAT cards for administration to a given client. Although the exact instructions used vary from clinician to clinician, they go something like this: "Now, I want you to make up a story about each of these pictures. Tell me who the people are, what they are doing, what they are thinking or feeling, what led up to the scene, and how it will turn out. Okay?" The respondent's stories are transcribed verbatim by the clinician (or sometimes tape-recorded).

Scoring and Interpretation

Although many scoring techniques have been proposed over the years, most clinicians accept that quantified scoring systems cause clinically useful evidence to be distorted or lost, and use such systems only for research purposes. On the other hand, the sheer volume of possible TAT interpretations from the various story cues is tremendous, which highlights the difficulty of assessing the test's validity. Here are a few of the interpretations provided by Lindzey and Silverman (1959):

- Paranoia is indicated by stereotyped phrases used throughout the respondent's stories.

- Anxiety is indicated by an emphasis on sudden physical accidents and emotional trauma, such as loss of a loved one, losing a job, a house burning down, or a stock market crash.

- Dependency is indicated by three or more references to one or more members of the family.

- Sexual problems are indicated by avoiding mentioning certain cues to sex or gender in some of the pictures (e.g., a nude female on one of the cards).

Unfortunately, these interpretations have received little research attention. Further, there is no research suggesting that information obtained from the TAT is related to treatment outcome. Given the TAT's purported ability to identify interpersonal styles that might influence choices regarding the therapist's treatment approach, this is somewhat surprising.

Reliability and Validity

It is difficult to evaluate the reliability and validity of the TAT in any formal sense because there are so many variations in instructions, methods of administration, number of cards used, and type of scoring/interpretation system (if any). In a review of research on the TAT, Lilienfeld and colleagues (2000) concluded that although there is preliminary modest support for the ability of certain TAT scores to assess need for achievement and for relationships, it is not clear that the routine use of the TAT is warranted. Adequate norms for TAT scores are lacking, and more importantly, clinicians typically do not compute scores but rather rely on qualitative impressions of the stories provided by respondents (Hunsley & Mash, 2007).

Think Like a Clinical Psychologist What do you think of the *projective hypothesis*, the idea that people unconsciously reveal critical aspects of their personality when responding to ambiguous material? How can the validity of such tests be established?

▥ Objective Tests

Objective personality tests involve the administration of a standard set of questions or statements to which the test taker responds using a fixed set of options. Many objective tests use a true/false or yes/no response format; others provide a dimensional scale (e.g., 0 = strongly disagree; 1 = disagree; 2 = neutral; 3 = agree; 4 = strongly agree). Such tests grew out of a dissatisfaction with the subjectivity of projective personality tests and the lack of clear evidence for their reliability or validity. Thus, with objective tests, there is no representation or interpretation. The test taker's response to each test item is considered an intrinsically valuable piece of information itself, as opposed to serving as the "royal road to the unconscious." Put another way, if Kiara answers that she experiences a great deal of anxiety, this response is taken at face value as a piece of assessment data.

Since the 1940s, objective tests have played a central role in the development of clinical psychology (Butcher, 2010) due in large part to their clear advantages. First of all, they are economical. After only brief instructions, large groups can be tested simultaneously, or a single individual can complete an inventory alone. Even remote/online administration along with computer scoring and interpretation of these tests are possible. Second, scoring and administration are relatively simple, making interpretation easier and requiring less interpretive skill on the part of the clinician. Yet while this simplicity is attractive, it does not necessarily result in the validity claimed for it. In fact, it can lead to widespread misuse by ill-trained testers. A final advantage of objective tests, particularly for clinicians who are disenchanted with the problems inherent in projective tests, is their apparent objectivity and reliability.

On the other hand, the items on many objective personality tests concern behaviors that may (or may not) characterize the respondent. As proponents of projective tests often point out, those interested in identifying motives or personality dynamics can glean little understanding through objective tests. For example, although two individuals may endorse the same behavioral item ("I have trouble getting to sleep"), they may do so for entirely different reasons.

Some objective tests contain a mixture of items dealing with behaviors, cognitions (i.e., thoughts and beliefs), and emotions (i.e., feelings). Yet inventories often provide a single overall score, which may reflect various combinations of these behaviors, cognitions, and emotions. Therefore, two individuals who achieve the same score may actually be quite different, even in reference to the personality trait or construct in question. Thus, the same score on a measure may have several alternative interpretations.

Other difficulties involve the transparent meaning of some inventories' questions, which can obviously facilitate faking on the part of some test takers. Some tests tend to depend heavily on the individual's self-knowledge. In addition, items on which respondents must choose their answer from a set of possible answers (sometimes called *forced-choice* items; e.g., true/false questions) prevent individuals from qualifying or elaborating their responses so that some additional information may be lost or distorted. One's experience, culture, and context can also influence how well test items are understood. For example, the context for test questions that ask about abstract concepts, such as *morality* or *achievement,* is more likely to be understood by individuals in mostly white, academically educated, industrialized, rich, and democratic societies than by those in more rural and less academically educated societies (Laajaj et al., 2019). The limited understanding or even limited reading ability of some individuals may lead them to misinterpret questions (a misinterpretation not necessarily attributable to personality determinants) or to answer questions in a random fashion.

Constructing Objective Tests

Now that we have some appreciation of the advantages and limitations of objective tests, let's turn to the methods involved in constructing these instruments. Over the years, a variety of strategies for developing objective personality tests have been proposed.

PeopleImages/E+/Getty Images

Content Validation

The most straightforward approach is for the psychologist to decide what they wish to assess and then to simply ask the client for that information. Ensuring content validity, however, involves more than deciding what you want to assess and then making up items that seem to do the job. Thus, sophisticated **content validation** methods involve (a) carefully defining all relevant aspects of the personality variable you want to measure; (b) writing test items and asking independent judges ("experts") to assess each potential item's relevance to the variable of interest; and (c) using psychometric analyses to statistically evaluate each item's performance before deciding to include it in the test (Nunnally & Bernstein, 1994).

Have you ever been tripped up by a poorly written test question? Writing good test items is more difficult than you might think.

There are, however, limitations of the content validity approach. First, it can't be assumed that every test taker will interpret a given item in exactly the same way. Second, some individuals are not good at reporting on their own behavior. Third, it is easy for respondents to answer questions in socially desirable ways or in patterns that they think will place them in a good light (or even a bad light). Fourth, the "experts" might not correctly define the essence of the concept they are trying to measure.

Empirical Criterion Keying

In an attempt to remedy the foregoing difficulties, the **empirical criterion keying** approach was developed. The most prominent example of this method is the original Minnesota Multiphasic Personality Inventory (MMPI), which we will discuss in depth later in this chapter. Here, no assumptions are made as to whether a test taker is telling the truth or whether the response really corresponds to behavior or feelings. Rather, what is important is that certain groups of people (e.g., those with a particular personality profile or psychiatric diagnosis) will respond to the test questions in the same way.

From this perspective, it is not necessary to select test items in a rational, theoretical fashion. All that is required is to show an empirical basis that the members of a given diagnostic group respond to a given item in a similar way. As a hypothetical example, in contrast to people who do not self-injure, if most individuals who do deliberately harm themselves agree with the item "I like to read fashion magazines" (and most who do not self-injure do not agree with that item), then that item is a good one because it is endorsed by members of the self-injury group. Thus, independent of an item's surface content, the test response becomes a "sign" of this behavior or personality characteristic. Importantly, the utility of an item is thus determined solely by the extent to which it discriminates among groups, even if the item's content is not directly associated with the behaviors that characterize members of that group.

Criterion keying also has its limitations, such as the difficulty of interpreting the meaning of a score. As another hypothetical example, if individuals with schizophrenia also happen to come from less educated backgrounds, when such people endorse the item "I almost never read books," that endorsement may reflect a poor educational background rather than their personality. Although demonstrating that a test can discriminate among various groups is one aspect of establishing the validity of the test, the sole use of the empirical criterion keying method to select items for a test is not recommended (Strauss & Smith, 2009).

Factor Analysis

The majority of test developers use a **factor analytic approach** to test construction. Here, the idea is to develop a universe of test items and then use *factor analysis*, a statistical procedure for determining which items "hang together," to reduce the number of items to those measuring basic elements — personality, adjustment, diagnostic affiliation, or whatever — in an attempt to arrive at the core traits and dimensions of personality. Although a detailed explanation of factor analysis procedures is beyond the scope of this textbook, the strength of this approach is the emphasis on an empirical demonstration that items purporting to measure a variable or dimension of personality are highly related to one another. On the other hand, a limitation is that it does not in and of itself demonstrate that these items are actually measuring the variable of interest; we only know that the items tend to be measuring the same "thing."

Construct Validity Approach

The **construct validity approach** combines many aspects of the content validity, empirical criterion keying, and factor analytic approaches. Here, scales are developed to measure specific concepts from a given theory of personality. Validation is achieved when it can be said that a given scale measures the theoretical construct in question. For example, a construct valid measure of extraversion must actually measure *extraversion*, and not some other personality trait. The selection of items is based on the extent to which they reflect the theoretical construct under study. Test developers also conduct **item analysis**, in which responses to individual test items are carefully examined to assess whether the item is unclear or misleading. Then factor analysis and other procedures are used to ensure that the scale is homogeneous — meaning that the items all assess the same construct. Construct validity for the scale is then determined by demonstrating, through a series of studies, that those who achieve certain scores on the scale behave in nontest situations in a fashion that could be predicted from their scale score. For example, a researcher might assess individuals on a scale of extraversion and then later observe the extent to which these respondents demonstrate extraversion in other settings. Because of its comprehensiveness, the construct validity approach to test construction is both the most desirable and the most labor-intensive. In fact, establishing the construct validity of a test is a never-ending process, with empirical feedback used to refine both the theory and the personality measure.

The MMPI

Eighty years after its publication by Hathaway and McKinley in 1943, the **Minnesota Multiphasic Personality Inventory (MMPI)** is still considered the preeminent objective personality test (Barbian-Schimberg, 2020). It has been used in clinical and research settings for virtually every predictive purpose imaginable, ranging from determining marriage suitability to forecasting the likelihood of psychotic episodes. The test has been updated and restandardized three times since its initial publication, including the MMPI-2 released in 1989, the MMPI-Restructured Form in 2008, and the MMPI-3 in 2020 (Ben-Porath & Tellegen, 2020).

Description, Scoring, and Interpretation

Hathaway and McKinley developed the MMPI to identify psychiatric diagnoses. The original test included 550 items to which the respondent answered "true," "false," or "cannot say" to questions such as "I have a great deal of stress at work" and "I don't worry about my health." From these items, 10 subscales were derived that corresponded to common psychiatric complaints with labels and conceptualizations that we would now consider outdated (e.g., hysteria, psychasthenia, hypochondriasis). With each revision of the test, however, the test items and subscales have been restructured and updated so as to be more meaningful and useful. The contemporary MMPI-3 contains 335 true/false items and takes from 15 to 35 minutes to complete. It includes 52 scales addressing virtually all domains of individual and interpersonal psychopathology, as is shown in **Table 6.2**. Although paper and pencil can be used, most clinicians ask respondents to complete the test using computer software which scores the test and provides a report for the clinician. This report includes a thorough interpretation of the individual's responses corresponding to the 52 clinical and validity scales. This MMPI profile may then be used by the clinician as a piece of data along with other assessment information.

Table 6.2   Clinical and Validity Scales of the MMPI-3

Higher-Order Scales

Emotional/Internalizing Dysfunction — Problems associated with mood and affect
Thought Dysfunction — Problems associated with disordered thinking
Behavioral/Externalizing Dysfunction — Problems associated with undercontrolled behavior

Restructured Clinical Scales

Demoralization — General unhappiness and dissatisfaction
Somatic Complaints — Diffuse physical health complaints
Low Positive Emotions — Lack of positive emotional responsiveness
Antisocial Behavior — Rule breaking and irresponsible behavior
Ideas of Persecution — Self-referential beliefs that others pose a threat
Dysfunctional Negative Emotions — Maladaptive anxiety, anger, irritability
Aberrant Experiences — Unusual perceptions or thoughts associated with thought dysfunction
Hypomanic Activation — Overactivation, aggression, impulsivity, and grandiosity

Somatic/Cognitive Scales

Malaise — Overall sense of physical debilitation, poor health
Neurological Complaints — Dizziness, weakness, paralysis, loss of balance, and so on
Eating Concerns — Problematic eating behaviors
Cognitive Complaints — Memory problems, difficulties concentrating

Internalizing Scales

Suicidal/Death Ideation — Direct reports of suicidal ideation and recent attempts
Helplessness/Hopelessness — Belief that goals cannot be reached or problems solved
Self-Doubt — Lack of self-confidence, feelings of uselessness
Inefficacy — Belief that one is indecisive and inefficacious
Stress — Problems involving stress and nervousness
Worry — Excessive worry and preoccupation
Compulsivity — Engaging in compulsive behaviors
Anxiety-Related Experiences — Multiple anxiety-related experiences such as catastrophizing, panic, dread, and intrusive ideation
Anger Proneness — Becoming easily angered, impatient with others
Behavior-Restricting Fears — Fears that significantly inhibit normal behavior

Externalizing Scales

Family Problems — Conflictual family relationships
Juvenile Conduct Problems — Difficulties at school and at home, stealing
Substance Abuse — Current and past misuse of alcohol and drugs
Impulsivity — Poor impulse control and nonplanful behavior
Activation — Heightened excitation and energy level
Aggression — Physically aggressive, violent behavior
Cynicism — Non-self-referential beliefs that others are bad and not to be trusted

Interpersonal Scales

Self-Importance — Beliefs related to having special talents and abilities
Dominance — Being domineering in relationships with others
Disaffiliativeness — Disliking people and being around them
Social Avoidance — Not enjoying and avoiding social events
Shyness — Feeling uncomfortable and anxious in the presence of others

PSY-5 (Personality Psychopathology Five) Scales

Aggressiveness — Instrumental, goal-directed aggression
Psychoticism — Disconnection from reality
Disconstraint — Undercontrolled behavior
Negative Emotionality/Neuroticism — Anxiety, insecurity, worry, and fear
Introversion/Low Positive Emotionality-Revised — Social disengagement and anhedonia

(Table 6.2 continued)

Validity Scales

Combined Response Inconsistency — Combination of random and fixed inconsistent responding
Variable Response Inconsistency — Random responding
True Response Inconsistency — Fixed responding
Infrequent Responses — Responses infrequent in the general population
Infrequent Psychopathology Responses — Responses infrequent in psychiatric populations
Infrequent Somatic Responses — Somatic complaints infrequent in medical patient populations
Symptom Validity Scale — Noncredible somatic and cognitive complaints
Response Bias Scale — Exaggerated memory complaints
Uncommon Virtues — Rarely claimed moral attributes or activities
Adjustment Validity — Uncommonly high level of psychological adjustment

SOURCE: Excerpted from the Minnesota Multiphasic Personality Inventory®-3 (MMPI®-3) Manual for Administration, Scoring, and Interpretation by Yossef S. Ben-Porath and Auke Tellegen. Copyright © 2020 by the Regents of the University of Minnesota. All rights reserved. Used by permission of the University of Minnesota Press. "MMPI" and "Minnesota Multiphasic Personality Inventory" are registered trademarks owned by the Regents of the University of Minnesota.

The MMPI updates have also incorporated more and more representative and diverse standardization samples. Whereas the original test was normed using a largely white, married, and educated sample from Minnesota, the standardization sample for the MMPI-3 is nationally representative (based on 2020 U.S. census projections for race and ethnicity, education, and age) and thus includes individuals from much more diverse racial, ethnic, educational, and socioeconomic backgrounds. Spanish translations and norms are also now available. The MMPI-3 requires a minimum fifth-grade reading level and can be used with individuals who are at least 18 years old. A version of the MMPI specifically developed for adolescents (MMPI-A) is also available.

Validity Scales

As we have mentioned, a potential problem with objective personality tests, including the MMPI-3, is that some respondents may wish to place themselves in a favorable light; others may "fake bad" to increase the likelihood of receiving help, sympathy, or perhaps a discharge from military service; still others have a seeming need to agree with almost any item regardless of its content. Obviously, if the clinician is not aware of these response styles in a given test taker, interpretation of the results can be in gross error.

To help detect malingering (faking bad), other test-taking attitudes, and carelessness or misunderstanding, all versions of the MMPI have incorporated **validity scales**. The 10 validity scales in the MMPI-3 are shown at the bottom of Table 6.2. These scales take into account factors such as the number of items left unanswered, the tendency to answer many items in a way suggestive of defensiveness (e.g., "Criticism from others never bothers me"), whether the test taker endorsed behaviors seldomly endorsed by the standardization group (which might suggest attempts to exaggerate one's problems), and whether the test taker indicated virtues that are unlikely to be true of most people and which might suggest one is trying to make themselves appear in a very socially desirable light (e.g., "I like everyone I meet"). Considered together, these validity scales provide a means for understanding the individual's motivations and test-taking attitudes.

Reliability and Validity

The MMPI-3 clinical scale scores have been carefully evaluated for internal consistency as well as test–retest reliability (Whitman et al., 2020). Data suggest that these are adequate to good.

Recall that MMPI items were selected primarily for their ability to discriminate between groups, and not as a function of their ability to measure a unitary dimension or construct. In contrast, the clinical scale scores have traditionally shown good test–retest reliability over time (Whitman et al., 2020).

With respect to validity, correlations between scores on MMPI-3 scales and other tests of the constructs that these scales measure suggest that the MMPI-3 scales have good convergent and discriminant validity when it comes to assessing most psychological problems in clinical and neuropsychological settings. A separate question, however, is whether the MMPI-3 shows **incremental validity** and provides information about a person's behavior, personality features, or psychopathology that is not provided by other measures. This issue of incremental validity tends to be neglected for all psychological tests, including the MMPI (Hunsley & Mash, 2007).

The Revised NEO-Personality Inventory

The **Revised NEO-Personality Inventory** (**NEO-PI-R**; Costa & McCrae, 1992) is another popular measure of personality and personality pathology, and the standard test of the Five-Factor Model of personality described at the beginning of this chapter. It provides a systematic assessment of emotional, interpersonal, experiential, attitudinal, and motivational styles, and a detailed picture of one's personality based on this model. The original version of the instrument assessed only three of the five personality factors (Neuroticism, Extraversion, and Openness), whereas the revised version measures all five (Neuroticism, Extraversion, Openness, Conscientiousness, and Agreeableness).

Description and Administration

The NEO-PI-R is a self-report measure that consists of 240 items and takes about 30 to 40 minutes to complete. Individuals rate each of the 240 statements on a 5-point scale (strongly disagree, disagree, neutral, agree, strongly agree). Approximately half of the items are reverse scored; that is, *lower* scores are more indicative of the trait in question. This was done to address a potential acquiescence (or nay-saying) bias that may present problems for inventories in which all or most items are presented in the same direction. To this end, the NEO-PI-R does not include validity scales (as the MMPI does) to evaluate respondents' test-taking approaches. Instead, it includes three individual items that assess the validity of responses. One item asks respondents to indicate if they have responded to the items in an honest and accurate manner, another asks if they have answered all items, and the last assesses whether responses have been placed in the correct spaces.

Scoring and Interpretation

The NEO-PI-R can be scored by hand or by a computer program. Respondents receive five domain scores (one for each of the five personality factors), which provide a broad overview of the test takers' personality characteristics. Next, within each domain, there are six subscales that correspond to "facets" of that particular domain (there are 30 facets across all five domains). For example, within the Extraversion domain, the six facets are: (a) warmth, (b) gregariousness, (c) assertiveness, (d) activity, (e) excitement-seeking, and (f) positive emotions. These facet scales provide an even more detailed and fine-grained understanding of personality within each domain. IN PRACTICE: *The NEO-PI-R, Kiara* describes how the measure is interpreted in a clinical setting.

Reliability and Validity

NEO-PI-R scores show excellent internal consistency and test–retest reliability. Scores from the instrument also relate in predictable ways to personality trait scores from a variety of other personality measures, peer reports, and adjective checklists. Several studies have supported the utility of NEO-PI-R in assessing personality characteristics of individuals with mood, anxiety, and substance use disorders (e.g., Trull & Sher, 1994). Taken together, these studies suggest that the NEO-PI-R is useful as a clinical assessment tool.

Limitations

The NEO-PI-R has been criticized for its relative lack of validity items. Indeed, the test does not assess response styles that may influence interpretations of the obtained scores. Second, the NEO-PI-R may not be especially well suited for the general purpose of clinical diagnosis because its development was guided by a model of "normal" personality. Third, too little research has been conducted on the use of the NEO-PI-R in treatment planning to warrant the routine use of this measure in clinical settings at this time.

> **In Practice** **The NEO-PI-R, Kiara**
>
> The use of personality tests varies across settings. In more intensive treatment centers (e.g., psychiatric hospitalization or partial hospitalization programs) where individuals with complex psychopathology are often found, personality testing tends to be a routine part of the assessment process. In school settings, and in legal and forensic cases, such testing may also be used to inform educational, treatment, or remediation plans. Yet, such tests are used with less regularity in routine outpatient service or community mental health clinics unless specific questions arise about conceptualization and treatment that cannot be answered using other forms of assessment. As part of Kiara's initial clinical assessment, she completed the NEO-PI-R. The results of her testing appear in **Table 6.3**. As can be seen, Kiara produced elevations on many Neuroticism facets and scored in the low range on several Extraversion facets. Several interpretive statements regarding these NEO-PI-R scores illustrate how the test could be useful in understanding Kiara's clinical difficulties and in treatment planning. As you read these statements and review Table 6.3, consider the question we asked at the beginning of the chapter:
>
> . . . Kiara's elevated Neuroticism and low Openness scores are consistent with her diagnosis of OCD.
>
> . . . Kiara is experiencing a great deal of personal distress, as indicated by her high scores on Depression, which is perhaps a result of the functional interference associated with OCD.
>
> . . . Kiara's high score on Self-Consciousness suggests she might feel especially embarrassed by her OCD symptoms. This is a common observation among people with this disorder.
>
> . . . Kiara's low scores on Assertiveness, Extraversion, and Gregariousness suggest she might not be willing to speak up for herself if she has concerns about how treatment is going. The therapist should be sure to check in with Kiara about her perceptions of treatment.
>
> . . . Kiara's low scores on Impulsiveness and Fantasy, combined with her high Competence score, suggest that she might be a good fit for a skills-based treatment, such as the approach that has been found to be consistently effective for individuals with OCD: cognitive-behavioral therapy using exposure and response prevention.
>
> . . . Kiara's high levels of Compliance and Conscientiousness suggest she is likely to work hard in treatment. While this might be a predictor of positive outcome, her high

Dutifulness score might indicate a tendency to want to please the therapist, which is not ideal for getting the most out of treatment. Individuals do best in treatment for OCD when they are working for themselves, rather than to please their clinician. ▬

Table 6.3   Revised NEO-Personality Inventory Personality Profile for Kiara

Scale	Range	Clinical Implications
Neuroticism	Very high	Fearful/avoidant
Anxiety	Very high	Nervous/ruminative
Angry Hostility	Average	
Depression	High	Hopelessness
Self-Consciousness	High	Insecure/ashamed
Impulsiveness	Very low	Deliberate/measured
Vulnerability	Average	
Extraversion	Low	Shy/quiet
Warmth	Average	
Gregariousness	Low	Shy/withdrawn
Assertiveness	Low	Tentative/reticent
Activity	Average	
Excitement Seeking	Low	Avoidant
Positive Emotions	Average	
Openness	Average	
Fantasy	Low	Predictable
Aesthetics	Average	
Feelings	Average	
Actions	Average	
Ideas	Average	
Values	Average	
Agreeableness	Average	
Trust	Average	
Straightforwardness	Average	
Altruism	Average	
Compliance	High	Adherent
Modesty	Average	
Tender-Mindedness	Average	
Conscientiousness	High	Meticulous/diligent
Competence	High	Perfectionistic
Order	Average	
Dutifulness	High	Responsible/reliable
Achievement Striving	Average	
Self-Discipline	Average	
Deliberation	High	Thoughtful/measured

> **Think Like a Clinical Psychologist** If you were the psychologist in charge of developing an assessment protocol for your clinic, would you include projective tests, objective tests, or both? Explain why.

▥ Discrimination and Bias in Personality Testing

Since the rise of the civil rights movement, most people have become increasingly aware of systemic discrimination and bias against members of underrepresented groups. Unfortunately, personality testing is deserving of similar criticism (e.g., Colella et al., 2017). The original standardization samples of many such tests, for example, contained an overrepresentation of (if not exclusively) white, middle-class, academically educated, cis-gendered, heterosexual individuals. Accordingly, it is often charged that personality tests are really designed for white middle-class populations and that other groups are being tested with devices that are inappropriate for them (e.g., Benuto et al., 2020). This, in turn, could lead to unfair systematic discrimination against underrepresented groups who respond differently to such stimuli.

Sometimes underrepresented group members' lack of exposure to the way certain tests are worded or handled may be a major source of the problem. Such is the case when the presence of an examiner from another race or culture may affect test performance. There is a lot of history behind some individuals potentially fearing that certain examiners are looking down on them, and quite honestly, that could be the reality of the given situation. Often, too, test materials are prepared or embedded in a racially biased context. For example, the TAT cards all depict white characters and many aspects that are more commonly present in white cultures than nonwhite cultures, which advantages those who are especially familiar with them. Similarly, scoring criteria and interpretation manuals often have a European, white, middle-class, and heterosexist bias. The problem here is that the test items themselves, the manner in which they are presented, the circumstances surrounding the test, and the way that results are interpreted may all work to the disadvantage of underrepresented groups.

It is important to remember that significant differences between mean scores on a test for different groups do not in and of themselves indicate **test bias** or discrimination. Rather, test bias or discrimination is a validity issue. That is, if it can be demonstrated that the validity of a test (e.g., in predicting criterion characteristics or performance) varies significantly across groups, then a case can be made that the test is "biased" for that purpose. In other words, a test is biased to the extent that it predicts more accurately for one group than for another group.

An example can illustrate these considerations. Let us assume that the authors developed a personality inventory measuring the trait "hostility." As part of the standardization process for this test, the authors discovered that men scored significantly higher than women on this test. Does this indicate that the test is biased? Not necessarily. The authors found, in a series of validity studies, that the relationship (correlation) between hostility inventory scores and the number of *verbal* fights over the succeeding 2 months was quite similar for both men and women. In other words, the predictive validity coefficients for the two groups were comparable; similar hostility scores "meant" the same thing (predicted a comparable number of verbal fights) for men and women. On the other hand, it is quite possible that the strength of the correlation between hostility scores and *physical* fights over the next 2 months is significantly greater for men than for women. In this case, the use of the test to predict physical aggression in women would be biased if these predictions were based on the known association between hostility scores and physical fights found in men.

Several general points should be clear. First, differences in mean scores do not necessarily indicate test bias. In the previous example, there may be good reasons men score higher on average than women on a measure of hostility (e.g., hormonal differences or other biological factors may lead to higher levels of hostility for men). In fact, to find no difference in mean scores might call into question the validity of the test in this case. Second, the pronouncement of a test as "valid," although frequently seen in the clinical psychology literature, is incorrect. Tests may be valid (and not biased) for some purposes but not for others. Finally, one can "overcome" test bias by using different (and more appropriate) interpretations and equations for the different groups. In other words, bias comes into play when the clinical psychologist makes predictions based on empirical associations that are characteristic of another group (e.g., men) but not of the group of interest (e.g., women). The goal is to investigate the possibility of differential validity and, if found, to use the appropriate prediction equation for that group (e.g., Reynolds & Suzuki, 2013).

Think Like a Clinical Psychologist Why is it important to consider cultural influences on personality and personality tests? What are the implications for not considering cultural influences?

▥ Chapter Summary

There are different perspectives on the concept of personality and how it should be measured. Whereas some focus on the presence of relatively stable traits that give way to predictable behavioral and emotional responses, others view personality as an illusion created by the human tendency to want to predict others' (and our own) behavior. Supporters of the latter point of view also view behavior as mediated by conditioning experiences, as opposed to personality traits. Studies and clinical practice with youth rarely consider personality, as it is assumed that children and adolescents do not yet have stable personality traits.

Instruments for assessing personality can be divided into projective and objective tests. Projective tests, which are based on Freud's psychoanalytic theory, use test takers' responses to ambiguous stimuli to provide information about unconscious personality features such as needs, drives, and defense mechanisms. Proponents believe such tests provide key information about which the test taker is not aware and cannot therefore describe consciously. Objective tests take a very different approach, and include a carefully constructed and empirically evaluated pool of items, answers to which have been shown to correspond to certain behavioral and emotional tendencies. The MMPI (and its various forms) is the most extensively studied personality inventory and is known to be predictive of a plethora of abnormal and normal behavioral and emotional tendencies.

Importantly, the most widely used personality tests have been revised to stay relevant in a changing world. They have also been updated to account for the fact that different cultures have their own perception of what is normal and what is abnormal. While there is evidence that widespread bias does not exist within personality tests, if these instruments are used without knowledge or sensitivity to issues of diversity, it can lead to labeling as "abnormal" that which is actually part of the cultural norm. In other words, it is important for clinical psychologists to recognize the meaning of clients' behavior and emotion — including results on personality tests — within the context of each client's culture.

Applying What You've Learned

Doodle Personality Inventory

Each member of a group of three to five students takes a plain sheet of paper and is asked simply to "doodle for five minutes." After the five minutes have passed, the group members independently score and interpret each page of doodles (one at a time) using the following scoring system:

Small doodles = depression
Large doodles = mania
Dark shading = self-confidence
Light shading = tentativeness
Symmetrical doodles = perfectionism
Half-completed doodles = distractibility

Circles = femininity
Squares = masculinity
Arrows or points = aggressiveness
Eyes = paranoia
Houses = need for security

After using the scoring system, group members can discuss the following:

- How easy was it to score the doodles? What issues came up that caused problems?
- To what extent did different group members agree on their scoring and interpretations (reliability)? What factors influenced the degree of agreement?
- To what extent does the scoring system seem accurate in measuring someone's personality characteristics (validity)? What are its strengths and limitations?
- Which approach to personality testing does this "Doodle Personality Inventory" illustrate? What are the limitations of this approach?

Key Terms

Construct validity approach: An approach to test construction in which scales are developed based on a specific theory, refined using factor analysis and other procedures, and validated by showing (through empirical study) that individuals who achieve certain scores behave in ways that could be predicted by their scores.

Content validation: The process by which one ensures that a test will adequately measure all aspects of the construct of interest. Methods of content validation include carefully defining all relevant aspects of the construct, consulting experts, having judges assess the relevance of each potential item, and evaluating the psychometric properties of each potential item.

Empirical criterion keying: An approach to test development that emphasizes the selection of items by members of different diagnostic groups, regardless of whether the items appear theoretically relevant to the diagnoses of interest.

Factor analytic approach: A statistical method often used in test construction to determine whether potential items are or are not highly related to each other.

Five-Factor Model (FFM): A comprehensive model of personality that comprises the dimensions of Neuroticism, Extraversion, Openness, Agreeableness, and Conscientiousness as well as six facets belonging to each dimension.

Illusory correlation: In the context of projective testing, the phenomenon by which certain test responses become associated with specific personality characteristics. These responses come to be viewed as signs of the trait in question and may be given undue weight when interpreting the test.

Incremental validity: The extent to which a scale score provides information about a person's behavior, personality features, or psychopathology features that is not provided by other measures.

Item analysis: A process for examining responses to an individual test item to determine whether the item might be unclear or misleading.

Minnesota Multiphasic Personality Inventory (MMPI): A measure of psychopathology that was originally developed using the empirical criterion keying approach. The current version (MMPI-3) contains 335 true/false items and includes 52 scales addressing virtually all domains of individual and interpersonal psychopathology. Most clinicians ask respondents to complete the test using computer software which scores the test and provides a report for the clinician. This report includes a thorough interpretation of each individual's responses corresponding to the 52 clinical and validity scales. This MMPI-3 profile may then be used by the clinician as a piece of data along with other assessment information.

Objective personality test: Personality assessment tool in which the examinee responds to a standard set of questions or statements using a fixed set of options (e.g., true or false, dimensional ratings).

Personality: The continuity in a person's behavior and emotional style over time.

Personality trait: A stable and consistent way of perceiving the world and of behaving. Traits may be influenced by the environment, biology, or a combination of these factors.

Projective hypothesis: Proposes that people unconsciously reveal critical aspects of their personality when trying to make sense of ambiguous material.

Projective personality test: Psychological testing technique that uses people's responses to ambiguous test stimuli to make judgments about their adjustment–maladjustment. Proponents believe that examinees "project" themselves onto the stimuli, thus revealing unconscious aspects of themselves.

Revised NEO-Personality Inventory (NEO-PI-R): A self-report measure of the FFM that consists of 240 statements, each of which is rated on a 5-point scale. This test yields scores on all five domains of the FFM (Neuroticism, Extraversion, Openness, Agreeableness, and Conscientiousness) as well as the six facets corresponding to each domain.

Rorschach: A projective technique that interprets people's responses to a series of 10 inkblots.

Situational perspective: The perspective that people's behavior is entirely a product of the environment and factors such as operant and classical conditioning.

Test bias: The situation in which different decisions or predictions are made for members of two groups, even when they obtain the same score on an instrument.

Thematic Apperception Test (TAT): A projective technique that purports to reveal clients' personality characteristics by interpreting the stories they produce in response to a series of pictures.

Validity scale: Test scale that attempts to shed light on the respondent's test-taking attitudes and motivations (e.g., to present themselves in an overly favorable light, to exaggerate their problems or symptoms, to engage in random responding).

CONNECT ONLINE:

 | Check out our videos and additional resources located at: www.macmillanlearning.com

Behavioral Assessment

FOCUS QUESTIONS

1. What are the factors of functional analysis?
2. Why is behavioral assessment an ongoing process?
3. What factors affect the reliability and validity of observations?
4. What are the pros and cons of self-monitoring?
5. How does technology facilitate self-monitoring?
6. How is the evaluation of cognitive factors integrated into behavioral assessment?

CHAPTER OUTLINE

Behavioral assessment is an approach to measuring and understanding a person's behavior that is based on learning theory—primarily operant and classical conditioning. As such, behaviorally oriented psychologists make no assumptions about the existence of personality traits, unconscious processes, or clinical diagnoses. Rather, the focus is on defining a specific problem (or "target") behavior or response, and then directly observing that response and understanding it in the context of the client's previous experiences (their learning history) as well as the environmental conditions immediately before and after the behavior.

For example, the assessment of a child who throws tantrums might reveal that the tantrums usually occur at bedtime when her parent is tucking her in for the night. It might also show that to soothe the child, her parent gets in bed and goes to sleep with her. From an operant conditioning perspective, this assessment data could be used to explain the child's tantrums as being positively reinforced by their ability to get her parent's attention. As we will see in Chapter 9, *Diagnosis, Case Formulation, and Treatment Planning*, this has direct implications for developing an intervention to stop the child's tantrums (e.g., by changing how her parent responds to them).

This chapter begins with a discussion of the factors that make behavioral assessment different from the other types of assessment covered in this book. We then turn to the major types of behavioral assessment that are used in clinical and research settings. In recent years, technology has been used to improve behavioral assessment as mobile devices can be turned into powerful tools for collecting data on moment-by-moment behavior and other areas of functioning. Finally, although this chapter is titled "Behavioral Assessment," behaviorally oriented clinicians and researchers also pay a great deal of attention to the role of cognitive factors (e.g., beliefs and perceptions) in influencing behavior and emotion—one reason that the term "cognitive-behavioral" has largely replaced "behavioral" when describing methods of assessment, conceptualization, and treatment. Accordingly, we include the assessment of cognitions in this chapter.

How Does Behavioral Assessment Differ from Other Forms of Assessment?

There are important differences between behavioral assessment and the other forms of assessment covered in this book. So, before we delve into the specific methods of behavioral assessment, let's consider what makes behavioral assessment unique.

Sample Versus Sign

Behavioral assessment views a person's behavior during a test, an interview, or an observation as a **sample**—that is, an *example*—of how they generally respond under similar conditions. If, for instance, Shane frequently responds aggressively to classmates while he is being observed at school, we would assume that this aggression is typical of his behavior at school. A behavioral assessment, therefore, should provide a representative sample of the person's behavior—especially the behavior of interest, which we call the **target behavior**. It should also allow for a careful examination of the details of the target behavior, in Shane's case, aggression, including where and when it occurs, its frequency, intensity, and duration. For example, assessment would outline the specific behaviors Shane displays when he becomes aggressive (e.g., rock throwing, making threats), the situations in which such episodes occur, as well how often they occur and how long they last.

This emphasis on individual behaviors and their context stands in stark contrast to personality, diagnostic, and intellectual assessments, which seek to identify **signs** or *symptoms* of internal processes such as personality traits, psychiatric disorders, or intelligence. From a diagnostic perspective, for example, Shane's aggressive behavior would be viewed as a symptom of a psychiatric disorder, such as oppositional defiant disorder or conduct disorder. Similarly, Kiara's compulsive handwashing behavior would be considered a symptom of obsessive-compulsive disorder (OCD).

Functional Analysis

Another unique feature of behavioral assessment is the **functional analysis** (also called *behavioral analysis*), which refers to the process of understanding the relationship between the target behavior and the situational factors that, according to learning theory, exert control over that behavior (Sturmey, 2020). (To understand more about the influence of situational factors and the birth of the behavioral assessment movement, see IN HISTORICAL PERSPECTIVE: *Behavioral Assessment.*) Using knowledge of operant conditioning—the principle that behaviors are learned and maintained by their consequences—the clinician identifies the **antecedents**, the stimuli or conditions that precipitate the target behavior, as well as the **consequences**, the circumstances that follow the behavior. Once these two sets of conditions are assessed, the clinician is in a position to hypothesize how the target behavior is influenced, as well as how it can be modified. In contrast to diagnostic assessment, in which the overall goal is to establish a clinical diagnosis, the aim of functional analysis is to understand a person's particular problem behavior in context so that an intervention can be devised to reduce it. In this way, behavioral assessment represents an **idiographic** (person-specific) approach to assessment, whereas diagnostic assessment is **nomothetic** (general) in that it largely overlooks the role of contextual factors.

It might be discovered, for example, that Shane usually takes objects (e.g., a pencil) from another child when the teacher is paying attention to others in the classroom. When this aggressiveness occurs, the teacher almost invariably gives Shane attention, which results in the entire class giving him attention. A functional analysis, then, reveals that lack of attention (antecedent) is followed by taking a pencil from another child (target behavior), which in turn is followed by attention (consequence). Getting attention (even negative attention) can be reinforcing for some children—as is apparently the case with Shane. As we will see in later chapters, once this pattern of relationships is established, steps can be taken to modify the undesirable behavior.

As we will see later in this chapter, contemporary *cognitive*-behavioral therapists have broadened the functional analysis to include *cognitive* antecedents and consequences (e.g., Zayfert & Becker, 2020). For example, it's important to assess attitudes and beliefs that are characteristic of individuals prone to anxiety or depressive episodes. Kiara's compulsive washing rituals, for instance, occurred when she experienced specific cognitive antecedents—intrusive thoughts that she might spread contamination and sicken one of the patients she was responsible for. The consequences of her washing behavior were also cognitive-affective: an immediate reduction in doubt and anxiety. Therefore, we would say that Kiara's compulsive checking behavior is negatively reinforced by the reduction in distress it engenders.

Behavioral Assessment

Behavioral assessment grew in popularity in the 1950s and 1960s when behaviorally oriented psychologists became dissatisfied with projective and self-report personality assessment. Consistent with learning models of behavior, the behaviorists felt it was important to focus on directly observable responses and pointed out that personality assessment relied on the presumption of *traits* that were not directly observable. Spearheading this movement was Walter Mischel (1968, 1973), who argued that personality traits are illusions which arise from biases in the language we use to describe people. For example, when we refer to someone as "introverted" (a personality trait) what we really mean is that they often behave in a shy and reticent manner. Mischel also argued that the apparent consistency in a person's behavior is not due to the existence of personality traits, but rather to consistency in features of the environment. For example, people who display shy and reticent behavior might do so because it has been reinforced in the past (perhaps by helping them control social anxiety). Finally, Mischel argued that because we have a strong need as humans to predict peoples' behavior, we're fooled into perceiving person-

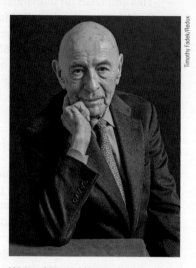

Walter Mischel (1930–2018), an Austrian-born psychologist, argued that the situation is more important than a person's traits in understanding behavior.

ality traits where these do not in fact exist. He might, for example, point to common inconsistencies in most peoples' behavior as evidence that the appearance of stable personality traits is merely an artifact of human cognitive biases.

Walter Mischel would have considered being "bookish" or "introverted" the wrong interpretation of a behavior as a personality trait. Rather, he would argue that this observation merely suggests the individual finds reading and spending time alone to be rewarding.

Behavioral Assessment as an Ongoing Process

A behavioral assessment is not a one-time evaluation performed at the beginning of treatment. Rather, it is an ongoing process that occurs before, during, and after treatment (Sturmey, 2020). Before and during the initial stages of treatment, behavioral assessment helps identify the target behaviors for change as well as the goals of treatment. The functional assessment then informs how the target problem is conceptualized, as well as the selection of treatment strategies (Persons, 2012). Once treatment is begun, continual behavioral assessment provides feedback regarding how well the intervention is working. If a reduction in undesirable behavior (or an increase in desirable responses) is observed, it is assumed that the selected intervention is appropriate and should continue. If, however, no improvement is noted, it is assumed that something was overlooked in either the functional assessment or treatment selection. In this case, rather than viewing the client as "treatment resistant," the clinician goes "back to the drawing board" and the assessment and conceptualization process begins anew. This process is repeated until success is achieved. Finally, at the conclusion of treatment, behavioral assessment helps determine its effectiveness.

With these notions in mind, we now turn to an examination of the most widely used behavioral assessment methods: behavioral interviews, behavioral observation, and self-monitoring.

Think Like a Clinical Psychologist Some psychologists believe that behavioral assessment is "superficial" because it doesn't account for internal factors (e.g., needs, drives, incentives, personality dynamics) that influence the behavior being observed. Do you agree? How would you respond to this claim?

▥ Behavioral Interviews

The usual first step in a behavioral assessment is an interview to identify the target problem(s) as well as the goals for behavior change. One focus of **behavioral interviews** is to obtain a careful and precise description of the problem behavior. This behavior must be described in observable terms so that it can easily be measured. For adult clients, the interview usually occurs with the client themselves. With child clients, however, this is most typically conducted with the child's caregiver and/or perhaps a teacher.

The second step is to identify the conditions that control the problem behavior — both the antecedent conditions and consequent events. Such events as time, place, and people present when the behavior occurs are noted, along with the specific outcomes that follow the behavior of concern. As such, behavioral interviews are directive and goal-oriented interactions. IN PRACTICE: *Excerpt from a Behavioral Interview with Kiara* shows an excerpt from a behavioral interview.

In Practice   **Excerpt from a Behavioral Interview with Kiara**

Interviewer: Kiara, when we spoke over the phone, you mentioned that your problems with handwashing and checking rituals were starting to get in the way of working as a nurse. To begin with, what can you tell me about these difficulties?

Kiara: Well, it's the OCD that makes me have a compulsive personality, so I just can't stop checking my patients' charts and washing my hands over and over. The need to do these compulsions is just irresistible.

Interviewer: I see. Let's try to be as specific as possible. Maybe we can start with the washing. Can you walk me through the last time you got stuck washing your hands at work?

Kiara: Sure, it happens every day. Like yesterday, before I went to check in with the first patient on my list, I went into the bathroom to wash, but I got stuck and was in there for 20 minutes washing over and over. It was like I couldn't get clean enough. Then, I was finally able to go and see the patient. But my supervisor was asking where I was and got really concerned. This happens several times each day.

Interviewer: Okay, that's very helpful. When you wash, do you have any particular method of washing, or do you just scrub your hands?

Kiara: Yes, I have a certain way it has to be done — otherwise it's not good enough. I have to scrub with soap in between my fingers and up to my elbows five times. And if I lose count, I have to start all over again. Then, I have to make sure all the soap is off of my hands, so I do the whole thing again without soap. And I have to use very hot water.

Interviewer: Got it, and I can see why it takes so long then. And is it always right before you see a patient that you get stuck washing your hands like that?

Kiara: Yeah. Every time. And that's pretty much the only time I do it, too.

Interviewer: Ok, that's very helpful. So, I wonder what's going through your mind before you see your patients that might be making you want to wash. Can you tell me?

Kiara: Well, I'm always thinking, "What if I spread germs to the patients and it's my fault that they get sicker or die?" After all, these people are susceptible to germs, so I worry that I could spread my own germs to them.

Interviewer: I see. So, it's the fear of making them sick that makes you want to wash?

Kiara: Yes, that's exactly right.

Interviewer: Okay. And after you wash your hands, what happens to that fear?

Kiara: Well, I feel cleaner, so I stop worrying. I guess the washing makes me feel like I won't contaminate anyone.

Interviewer: Yeah, that makes sense. So you wash everything off and then you're set.

Kiara: Well, it only works for a short time. Once I touch other things around me — like a patient's bed, the computers on the floor, or use the bathroom, I feel dirty again and I'll need to do the washing ritual again.

Interviewer: Okay, so it seems the washing ritual makes you feel better in the short-term, but it only works temporarily. Do I have that right?

Kiara: Yes. That's right. ■■■

A behavioral interviewer focuses on understanding the antecedents and consequences of behaviors, rather than viewing them as symptoms of a psychiatric disorder or personality trait.

Notice that the interviewer asks very specific questions about Kiara's washing rituals and tries to focus her attention on the observable details of this problem, rather than on possible causal explanations. A common obstacle in behavioral interviews is that people often describe their behavior in terms of a disorder or personality trait, such as the way Kiara explains her compulsive washing as resulting from her OCD and her "compulsive personality." In this behavioral interview, however, the clinician focuses on collecting information for a functional analysis of Kiara's washing, namely the situations and thoughts that cue such behavior, and the consequences of the washing. These data reveal what was noted above, that her washing rituals are precipitated by recurring thoughts about being responsible for harming her clients (i.e., "obsessional thoughts"), as well as feelings of fear and anxiety. The washing behavior also provides an escape from this distress. Indeed, this is a hallmark of OCD; but rather than understanding it as a disease process, the behavioral interview approach focuses on understanding it at the level of individual behaviors, their antecedents, and their consequences.

We can then apply learning theory (i.e., operant conditioning) to further understand why Kiara's washing rituals occur so frequently; namely, they appear to be negatively reinforced by the reduction in distress that they engender. In other words, Kiara has learned that when she becomes fearful of making her patients sick, handwashing rituals remove this fear and make her feel better. Therefore, she'll perform the rituals whenever she's in a situation that provokes this fear, such as getting ready to interact with a patient. But doing the rituals also prevents the natural extinction of her fear. That is, by compulsively washing, Kiara never has the chance to learn that her fear is far-fetched. Therefore, she'll remain afraid of contaminating her patients, and the OCD problem will persist. This functional analysis has clear treatment implications. For example, Kiara could touch items that provoke her fear — such as a computer keyboard — and then interact with patients without performing her handwashing rituals. This would help her learn that her fear will naturally subside even without the washing behavior. That is, the washing behavior isn't necessary to prevent disaster. As we will cover in Chapter 11, *Behavioral Interventions*, this approach, called *exposure and response prevention*, is an effective behavioral treatment for OCD.

Although behavioral interviews can provide a wealth of valuable information for understanding and treating specific behaviors, they focus narrowly on one target behavior (or set of related behaviors) at a time. For example, after focusing on her washing rituals, Kiara's therapist would next conduct an in-depth interview about her checking rituals, and so on, until all of her rituals have been discussed. As a result, this approach can be time-consuming, especially when the client's clinical presentation is complex. In addition, because they rely on the client's ability to recall information about antecedents, behaviors, and consequences that occur outside the treatment session (and the interview), behavioral interviews can be unreliable. For this reason, they're often complemented by interviews with other people familiar with the client and the client's target behavior, such as parents, teachers, and the like. Another strategy for obtaining additional behavioral data is to use direct observational methods, as we describe next.

Think Like a Clinical Psychologist Imagine that you are conducting a behavioral interview with someone from a different culture or racial/ethnic background than your own. How (if at all) might this affect the questions you ask? How might it influence how you interpret the information you collect from the interview?

▐▌ Behavioral Observation

The direct observation of behavior is a foundation of scientific inquiry and clinical psychology. **Behavioral observation** generally refers to a clinician or researcher directly monitoring (e.g., seeing, hearing) and then systematically documenting an individual's (or group's) behavior as it occurs in a natural setting, such as at home, in the classroom, within the peer group, on the playground, or under contrived conditions in a laboratory or clinic. If practical, observations are conducted "live" and "on the scene," yet if more convenient, a video or audio recording of the behavior can be made (and sometimes transcribed into written form), and the clinician or researcher can later observe and document the behavior from the recording.

During the assessment, the observer notes important aspects of the target behavior including its frequency, intensity, duration, and pervasiveness. The situations in which the behavior is provoked and the consequences of the behavior are also recorded. As with behavioral interviewing, the aim of behavioral observation is to establish the possible antecedents and consequences that drive the behavior in question so that an intervention can be derived. An advantage of behavioral observation, however, is that rather than relying on the client's retrospective descriptions of behavior (which can be subject to error), the clinician directly observes the behavior occurring. When practical, others who are routinely part of the person's environment (e.g., a parent, teacher, or nurse) may also be trained to monitor the target behavior.

Observation Methods

To maximize the reliability and validity of observational data, it is important to carefully define the target behavior being observed. That is, whoever is monitoring the response in question must be able to precisely identify it and differentiate it from other similar behaviors. Accordingly, the target behavior must be an *active* or *observable* response, as opposed to a *passive* or *covert* one. Examples of active behaviors include handwashing, threatening someone, speaking out of turn, eating, and thumb-sucking. Examples of passive behaviors, on the other hand, include thinking, feeling, daydreaming, gratitude, and forgetfulness. Avoidance, such as resisting an urge to wash your hands, is also passive and not directly observable. In instances where one wishes to assess passive or covert reactions, the clinical psychologist must find behavioral manifestations of them that can be directly observed. Gratitude, for example, could be behaviorally defined as smiling or saying "Thank you." Similarly, depression could be defined as crying or social isolation. Finally, yelling or physical aggression could be used as a behavioral indicator of anger.

Reliability and validity are also optimized when target behaviors are defined as *specifically* as possible. Hyperactivity, for example, is an abstract construct that could refer to many responses, such as fidgeting, speaking out of turn, getting out of one's seat, and the like. But this leaves too much guesswork. Two different raters, for example, might disagree over whether a behavior qualifies as "hyperactive." Therefore, it's important that the target behavior (or behaviors) be a clear-cut response. Someone observing a fifth-grade student might, for example, choose to monitor particular behaviors such as getting out of one's seat or speaking out of turn, rather than "hyperactivity." This ensures that the observer knows specifically what to look for and record during the observation.

For these reasons, it is important to note that culture can play an important role in influencing observations. For instance, behaviors that may appear to be hostile or demeaning within one culture (e.g., teasing, challenging) may be considered playful and fun within others. Similarly, behaviors that are unusual within an observer's culture (e.g., speaking to the deceased) may be common and accepted within the culture of the client that is being observed. It is therefore essential that, in order to be objective, a psychologist who may be unfamiliar with the client's typical behavior collaborate with clients and/or their family members, solicit input on exactly what types of behaviors are relevant to the client, and get the client's input on how to interpret the data that come from observational assessments.

In South Korea, university students rarely (if ever) ask questions in class because of a socio-cultural reverence for authority as well as a collective, versus individualistic, orientation. In the United States (and many other Western countries), asking questions is a routine part of the classroom experience that might even help boost a student's participation grade.

Once specific behaviors have been identified and described in clear and objective terms, there are numerous approaches for how observational coding may be conducted. Interval and event coding approaches are discussed briefly below.

Interval Coding

Interval coding is a procedure in which the observer records whether the target behavior occurs within a specific period of time (i.e., the interval). This procedure is preferred when the target behavior is lengthy, when the target behavior occurs less frequently, or the starting or ending point of the behavior is less apparent. An example might be monitoring a student's participation during different classes while at school. In such an instance, the observer might record whether or not (and how often) the student engaged in any of the following behaviors during each 50-minute class (interval): raising a hand, speaking to the teacher, or participating in a group discussion. This would provide information regarding the student's pattern of class participation and whether it occurs in certain classes or at certain times of the day more than others.

Event Recording

Event recording is a procedure in which the observer records each discreet occurrence of the target behavior during the entire observation period. Event recording is optimal when the target behavior has a distinct beginning and end, such as smoking a cigarette, binging, purging, hitting, and handwashing. Someone with Tourette's disorder, for example, might display frequent tics, such as throat clearing, eye-blinking, or the unintentional uttering of inappropriate words (i.e., coprolalia). In such a case, event recording could be used to keep track of how many times the person engages in such tics during a typical day (or a portion of it). Additional information about the context of the tics could also be collected, such as whether they are more likely to occur when the person is alone, around others, or in a stressful situation (e.g., at work or school).

Observation Settings

Behavioral observations can be conducted in almost any setting. Naturalistic observations have the benefit of occurring in the client's everyday environment. More contrived settings have the advantage of greater control over certain parameters of the behavior, but they also sacrifice the "real world" element.

Naturalistic Observation

The **naturalistic observation** method refers to carrying out observations in the person's own environment. No attempt is made to intervene or manipulate the situation — the goal is merely to observe and document behavior as it naturally occurs. The environment chosen for observation is usually one in which the person spends a great deal of time, or in which the target behavior is likely to occur. The greatest advantage of naturalistic observation is it provides a first-hand look at a client's or research participant's behavior in the person's true environment. It therefore maximizes **ecological validity**, the extent to which the observations represent how a person generally acts when not being observed. On the other hand, because there is no manipulation involved in this approach, it cannot be guaranteed that the subject of the observation will engage in the target behavior one hopes to observe. In addition, because there is no control over the environment, there is no way to determine the precise causes of the behavior being observed.

Naturalistic observation may take place in various settings, such as home environments, classrooms, playgrounds, psychiatric hospitals, institutions for those with developmental disabilities, and treatment sessions. Because experiences in the family or home have such pervasive effects on

Clinical psychologists working with children who have behavioral problems often conduct naturalistic observations in classrooms since that's where children spend much of their time.

Spencer Grant/Science Source

adjustment, a number of assessment procedures have been developed for observing behaviors occurring in this setting. A good example of this is the *Mealtime Family Interaction Coding System* (MICS; Dickstein et al., 1994), which involves the use of a videotaped interaction of the entire family eating at mealtime, without the presence of a clinician or researcher. Trained observers then watch the videotape and rate the family on several domains, including how parents manage feelings expressed by family members, the degree to which family members show concern for each other, the use of discipline, the appropriateness of verbal and nonverbal communication, and how family members divide tasks and responsibilities (Fiese, 2021).

Naturalistic observations are also made during testing or interview sessions. That is, the psychologist is interested not only in the client's responses to their clinical questions but also in the client's general behavior. IN PRACTICE: *Naturalistic Observation, Shane* is an excerpt from a report that Shane's psychologist wrote reflecting a naturalistic observation that occurred as the psychologist interviewed Shane.

In Practice Naturalistic Observation, Shane

Shane is a 10-year-old boy of above average height and average weight for his current age. His hygiene, grooming, and attire were appropriate for his gender, age, and social background. There were no observable physical disabilities.

Overall, Shane appeared somewhat timid and uncomfortable throughout the testing session. He had a withdrawn and quiet style and often appeared to be distracted. On several occasions, Shane responded using only one- or two-word utterances, which was atypical given his age and the nature of question prompts.

At times, sometimes suddenly, Shane exhibited very different behavior. When asked to discuss his relationship with his father, for instance, Shane became very loud and he began to move around the room excitedly and rapidly. During these times, Shane would appear to be happy, and also more animated in his movements. On some of these occasions, Shane would appear to be less aware of how his body was moving (e.g., his arms would wave or flap so excitedly that he banged into furniture loudly).

Shane alternated between this happy, excited affect and a more subdued, quiet, and at times sad affect. His speech was often slow, and occasionally he used words that were imperceptible, and may have been gibberish. ▬▬

Clinical psychologists often deal with behavior problems that take place in the school setting; some children are disruptive in class, are overly aggressive on the playground, are generally fearful, cling to the teacher, will not concentrate, and so on. Although the verbal reports of parents and teachers are useful, the most direct assessment procedure is to observe the problem behavior in its natural habitat. Several methods have been developed for use in *school observation*. One example is Achenbach's *Direct Observation Form* (DOF; McConaughy & Achenbach, 2009) of the Child Behavior Checklist. This consists of a checklist of 88 problem items that observers are instructed to rate according to their frequency, duration, and intensity within 10-minute observation periods conducted over the course of several days at different times of the day. **Table 7.1** provides sample items from the DOF.

Table 7.1	Sample Items from the Direct Observation Form (DOF) of the Child Behavior Checklist

1. Argues
2. Defiant or talks back to staff
3. Cruel, bullies, or mean to others
4. Disturbs other children
5. Physically attacks people
6. Disrupts group activities
7. Nervous, high-strung, or tense
8. Apathetic, unmotivated, or won't try
9. Shy or timid behavior
10. Stares blankly
11. Unhappy, sad, or depressed
12. Withdrawn, doesn't get involved with others

NOTE: All items are rated on a scale of 0 to 3 for the specified observation period. 0: no occurrence; 1: very slight or ambiguous occurrence; 2: definite occurrence with mild to moderate intensity/frequency and less than 3 minutes total duration; 3: definite occurrence with severe intensity, high frequency, or greater than 3 minutes total duration.

Naturalistic observation techniques are also used in psychiatric hospitals and institutions for those with chronic mental illness (such as severe psychosis) and neurocognitive disorders such as developmental disability (intellectual disability) and Alzheimer's disease. The confines of these settings have made careful observation of behavior much more feasible than in more open, uncontrolled environments. An example of a hospital observation measure is the *Time Sample Behavior Checklist* (TSBC; Power, 1979), which involves making brief observations of different areas of a patient's functioning at regular intervals, such as every hour. Specifically, at each observation, the observer first notes the activity the person is engaged in (e.g., free time, eating a meal) as well as the time and location (e.g., social hall, dining room). Next, the observer watches the patient for precisely 2 seconds and records the following parameters of behavior: position (e.g., sitting, standing, walking), awake–asleep (eyes open or closed), facial expression (e.g., smiling, grimacing, neutral), social orientation (alone, with other residents, with staff), appropriate activity (e.g., eating, grooming, playing a game), and inappropriate activity (e.g., crying, staring, rocking).

Controlled Observation

Sometimes the specific behavior a clinical psychologist wants to observe does not occur very often in the natural environment. Arguments among siblings, for example, may occur rarely if the siblings are separated or happen to be getting along well for a period of time. Therefore, time and resources can be wasted waiting for such arguments if a naturalistic observation approach is used (and just when an argument is about to break out, a parent might step in and intervene). As a way of handling these problems, clinicians often use **controlled observation** (sometimes called *analogue observation*), in which the environment is "designed" to elicit the targeted behavior—for example, having siblings play a game that is known to have provoked arguments in the past, or asking a couple to discuss topics about which they disagree (e.g., finances, child rearing) in the laboratory, so that these relatively rare interaction patterns can be observed (Balderrama-Durbin et al., 2020).

Behavioral approach tasks (BATs) for specific phobias are an excellent example of controlled observations. BATs are used in clinical and research settings to get a realistic idea of the severity of a person's fear and avoidance behavior when faced with their feared situation. Blakey and colleagues (2019), for instance, developed a BAT to measure the severity of spider phobia before and after treatment. This task includes 13 progressively more challenging steps (shown in **Table 7.2**) ranging from standing at the opposite end of a room from a tarantula in a covered terrarium to allowing the tarantula to crawl up one's bare arm. Clients are asked to engage in each step for at least 10 seconds before moving on to the next step, and a "point" is given for each step successfully completed. Clients also rate their level of anxiety and disgust at each step of the BAT. In this way, BATs allow clinicians and researchers to quantify avoidance behavior (number of steps completed) and distress (total distress ratings) in a controlled setting.

Table 7.2 Steps in a Behavioral Approach Task (BAT) to Measure Fear and Avoidance in People with Spider Phobia			
BAT Step	**Completed? (Y/N)**	**Anxiety (0–10)**	**Disgust (0–10)**
1. Stand at opposite side of room from covered terrarium	_____	_____	_____
2. Stand at opposite side of room from exposed terrarium	_____	_____	_____
3. Stand halfway across from exposed, closed terrarium	_____	_____	_____
4. Stand 1 meter across from exposed, closed terrarium	_____	_____	_____
5. Stand 1 foot from exposed, closed terrarium	_____	_____	_____
6. Allow assessor to remove terrarium lid	_____	_____	_____
7. Stand directly over exposed and open terrarium and look down at tarantula	_____	_____	_____
8. Touch outside walls of the exposed, open terrarium (entire palm touching glass, placed vertically)	_____	_____	_____
9. Place hands on inside walls of exposed, open terrarium (entire palm touching glass, placed vertically)	_____	_____	_____
10. Touch tarantula inside the open terrarium	_____	_____	_____
11. Stand right next (within arm's distance) to assessor, who is holding the tarantula	_____	_____	_____
12. Hold tarantula in own hands	_____	_____	_____
13. Allow tarantula to crawl up arm	_____	_____	_____

Advantages of controlled observations include the ability to systematically vary aspects of the situation to observe their effects on behavior. This increases the accuracy of observations, as well as the ability to draw conclusions about the causes and consequences of the observed behavior. Despite these advantages, a drawback of controlled observation is **reactivity** — the fact that people often behave in more socially desirable ways when they know they are being observed. The talkative person suddenly becomes quiet. The oppositional child suddenly becomes compliant. Reactivity threatens the ecological validity of observations because it makes the observed behavior unrepresentative of what normally occurs, which affects the extent to which one can generalize from the controlled setting to the natural environment.

Think Like a Clinical Psychologist Do you believe it is ethical to conduct behavioral (e.g., naturalistic) observations without getting consent from the person being observed? Why or why not? What could you do to reduce the effects of reactivity when the person being observed knows that an observation is taking place?

Self-Monitoring

Behavioral observations can be expensive in terms of both time and money. It is, for example, impractical to follow clients around and observe them as they engage in their daily lives. Another limitation of observational methods, as mentioned, is that they cannot directly assess private experiences such as thoughts, feelings, and internal physiological sensations. Therefore, clinicians and researchers often rely on **self-monitoring**, in which individuals are taught to observe and record their own behaviors, thoughts, emotions, and other internal experiences (e.g., body sensations) as they occur.

With self-monitoring, clients are asked to maintain systematic and organized logs or diaries over some predetermined time period such as a day or week. Such a log can provide a running record of the frequency, intensity, and duration of one or more target behaviors or private experiences, along with the conditions that accompanied these behaviors and the consequences that followed. Data from such logs are especially useful in telling both the clinician and client how often the behavior in question occurs and under what conditions it is most likely to occur. In addition, they can provide a way of measuring change as a result of treatment (e.g., by comparing the daily amount of time Kiara spends washing her hands *before* treatment to the amount of time washing takes up *after* treatment). Self-monitoring also helps focus the client's attention on the target behavior and thus can help in reducing it. Finally, clients can come to realize the connections between environmental stimuli, the consequences of their behavior, and the behavior itself.

Self-monitoring is widely used in cognitive and behavioral therapies to track target behaviors and assess treatment outcome. Common uses include measuring the number of hours of sleep one gets per night, food choices, frequency of drug or alcohol use, the occurrence and triggers of panic attacks, binge–purge episodes, intensity of pain, and the number of hairs pulled during an episode of trichotillomania. As is common in the treatment of OCD (e.g., Abramowitz & Jacoby, 2014), Kiara's therapist instructed her to use the form in **Table 7.3** to self-monitor the time of day, situational and internal triggers, and the frequency and duration of compulsive washing and checking rituals. A form such as this provides a great deal of information for a treatment provider. For example, it can be seen that at 10 p.m., Kiara got out of bed and went back to work to check medical charts (that she had already checked earlier that day) when she experienced obsessional doubts that she might have made a mistake.

Table 7.3	Partial List from Kiara's Self-Monitoring of Her Own Washing and Checking Rituals

Ritual A: Handwashing
Ritual B: Checking patient medical charts

Date	Time	Activity or Obsessional Thought That Evoked the Ritual	Anxiety Level (0–100)	Minutes Spent on Rituals	
				A	B
6/11	4:30 p.m.	Before seeing patient: "What if I contaminate him?"	85	25	
6/11	5:00 p.m.	Before seeing patient: "What if I make her sick?"	75	15	
6/11	5:35 p.m.	About to leave work: "What if I give the patient the wrong medicine?"	90		20
6/11	10 p.m.	At home in bed: "What if I messed up at work and gave someone the wrong dose of their medicine?"	95		2 hrs

Of course, there are limitations of self-monitoring. Some people, for example, may be inaccurate or may purposely distort their observations or recordings to give the impression that they are either better off or worse off than they actually are. Others may simply resist the whole procedure because it involves a good deal of time and effort. Self-monitoring also requires that the person pay attention to an undesirable behavior or emotional state, which can be upsetting. Some types of self-monitoring may also be difficult for younger children who are less self-aware. Despite these difficulties, self-monitoring has become a useful and efficient assessment technique in clinical and research settings. When used properly, it can provide a great deal of information at a low cost.

There are numerous ways to collect self-monitoring data. Clients can be given counters or stopwatches, depending on what is to be monitored. Paper and pencil forms are routine, and small wallet-sized cards have been developed to allow for quick and discreet recording of information. Smartphones can also be used for self-monitoring and provide higher-quality data than paper and pencil diaries because time stamps indicate exactly when the experience was logged, and, as we turn to next, it is possible to portray the sequence of moods, behaviors, and cognitions across time (Melbye et al., 2020).

Think Like a Clinical Psychologist Think of a behavior you would like to change about yourself. What factors might get in the way of successfully self-monitoring this behavior over the course of a week (i.e., between treatment visits)? Now, imagine you are a clinical psychologist asking your client to self-monitor that same behavior. What would you say to increase the likelihood that your client completes the self-monitoring fully and accurately?

▌▌▌ The Use of Technology: Ecological Momentary Assessment

Any mobile device can be turned into a behavioral assessment tool using apps for ecological momentary assessment.

The availability of specially designed applications can turn mobile computers, tablets, and smartphones into powerful instruments for collecting behavioral assessment data in real time. For example, mobile technologies are increasingly being used to gather data on individuals in their natural environment using biosensors (e.g., Wang et al., 2021), audio and video recorders (e.g., Simonazzi et al., 2020), and GPS or activity monitors (Yim et al., 2020)—a procedure known as **ecological momentary assessment (EMA)** or *experience sampling*. In some forms of EMA, an application is installed on a client's or research participant's mobile device that is programmed to give a prompt (e.g., a beep or vibration) at specific times or intervals of time throughout the course of the day (or night). These prompts signal participants to complete self-monitoring of one form or another using the application. Assessment items might ask about one's thoughts, emotional state, or behaviors at that particular point in time (e.g., "What is your mood right now?"). The person can enter their responses into the application, which can be either saved on the mobile device and downloaded later or transmitted in real time to the clinician or researcher.

EMA offers important advantages over traditional behavioral assessment methods. For one thing, it is much less laborious and therefore less costly than traditional behavioral observation in which one or more observers are paid for their time and efforts. Second, because it allows target behaviors to be assessed in real time, the effects of memory biases are reduced. Third, EMA provides uniquely high ecological validity since behaviors, thoughts, and feelings are reported as they're experienced in their "natural habitat." Because research indicates the value of EMA for examining the behavioral mechanisms of various mental health concerns (e.g., Yim et al., 2020), this behavioral assessment method is rapidly gaining popularity among clinicians and scientists.

Research also suggests that EMA improves compliance with self-monitoring over traditional paper and pencil methods. In a creative study (Stone et al., 2002), researchers asked participants to self-monitor their levels of pain on a daily basis, and time-stamped their paper pain diaries with a photocell to record when the diaries were actually opened. They found that only 11% of the scheduled paper diary recordings were completed at the appropriate times. However, participants *reported* complying with scheduled recording 95% of the time (i.e., they backdated their ratings to create the impression of compliance). In contrast, a comparison group of participants using EMA completed 94% of scheduled assessments at the time of the scheduled prompt. Thus, real-time computerized monitoring is clearly advantageous.

Think **Like a Clinical Psychologist** The use of mobile phones and other remote monitoring devices to assess psychological and behavioral problems raises potential ethical issues. Discuss the challenges that might arise regarding (a) informed consent, (b) storage and transmission of personal assessment data, and (c) maintaining privacy and confidentiality.

▥ Checklists and Inventories

Clinicians and researchers also use **rating scales** to identify and assess the severity of behaviors, emotional responses, and perceptions of the environment. This method involves the client's (or perhaps the client's caregivers') completion of one or more standardized questionnaires either online or using paper and pencil forms. For example, the Saving Inventory (Frost et al., 2004) is widely used to assess behaviors associated with hoarding disorder. The most updated version of this scale consists of 23 questions that address the following aspects of hoarding: excessive saving of unnecessary items, difficulty with discarding unneeded items, and the presence of clutter (Kellman-McFarlane et al., 2019). **Table 7.4** provides examples of items on this scale. The client indicates which response is most appropriate for them, and the scores across all 23 questions are summed to produce an overall total score that gives the clinician an idea of the severity of the hoarding problem.

Table 7.4 Sample Items from the Saving Inventory (revised version; Frost et al., 2004)

3. To what extent do you have so many things that your room(s) are cluttered?
   0 = Not at all
   1 = To a mild extent
   2 = To a moderate extent
   3 = To a considerable extent
   4 = Very much so

4. How often do you avoid trying to discard possessions because it is too stressful or time-consuming?
   0 = Never avoid, easily able to discard items
   1 = Rarely avoid, can discard with a little difficulty
   2 = Sometimes avoid
   3 = Frequently avoid, can discard items occasionally
   4 = Almost always avoid, rarely able to discard items

5. How distressed or uncomfortable would you feel if you could not acquire something you wanted?
   0 = Not at all
   1 = Mild, only slightly anxious
   2 = Moderate, distress would mount but remain manageable
   3 = Severe, prominent and very disturbing increase in distress
   4 = Extreme, incapacitating discomfort from any such effort

---

Kiara's psychologist sent Kiara an email containing a link to complete three self-report rating scales online that assess obsessive-compulsive symptoms and other relevant behaviors and emotions: (a) the Obsessive-Compulsive Inventory (Abramovitch et al., 2021), which is a 12-item measure of the severity of different types of obsessions and compulsive rituals over the past week; (b) the Depression Anxiety and Stress Scale (Lovibond & Lovibond, 1995), a 20-item instrument that measures the severity of both anxiety and depression over the past week; and (c) the Sheehan Disability Scale (Sheehan, 1983), a 3-item questionnaire that assesses the extent to which her problems currently interfere with her social life, home life, and work functioning. Once Kiara completed these questionnaires, her scores were sent to her psychologist, who was able to interpret the results to see that not only were her symptoms quite severe relative to most people with OCD but also that her obsessions and compulsions were causing a substantial degree of interference in her overall functioning.

A dizzying array of questionnaires have been created to measure virtually all types of behavioral and psychological problems and their manifestations in children and adults. The development process for these instruments involves carefully writing questions and then rigorously testing them to ensure they are reliable and valid measures of what they intend to assess (Rosellini & Brown, 2021). Because of their convenience and ability to provide information about a wide range of behaviors over a longer period of time than is possible with other behavioral assessment methods, rating scales are widely used in clinical practice and in research to assess the severity of target problems, as well as changes in these problems as a result of treatment. The main limitation of self-report inventories, however, is that because they typically contain transparent questions, respondents who are motivated to make themselves look especially well or unwell can answer the items in misleading ways.

However, given the ease with which they are administered, and the large number of people who have completed them, questionnaires also can offer valuable norms that can be used to better understand the typicality of clients' behaviors. For instance, the Achenbach (2009) Child Behavior Checklist, Teacher Report Form, and Youth Self-Report Forms (all included within the Achenbach System of Empirically Based Assessment [ASEBA]) each have been administered to thousands of youth within each age group, gender, and race/ethnicity, as well as across broad geographic regions, yielding a database that can be used to determine whether a client's responses are common or are observed only among a small subset of youth. Moreover, scores from inventories such as the ASEBA have been compared across individuals with and without clinically determined diagnoses to help demonstrate the validity of these checklists, allowing psychologists to feel reasonably confident that scores above a "clinical threshold" on checklist measures increase the risk for a diagnosis or may predict future behavior. For instance, from the use of a simple parent-reported questionnaire regarding depressive behaviors (e.g., loss of interest in activities that were previously pleasurable, changes in appetite or sleep), a psychologist can consider the possibility that their client may be experiencing a depressive disorder or may be at increased risk for self-injurious behavior. **Figure 7.1** is a sample inventory for Shane.

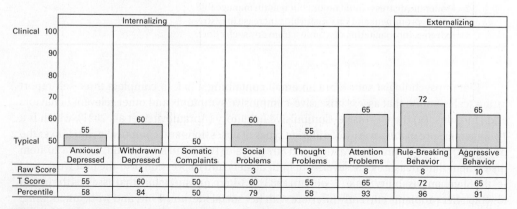

Figure 7.1 Adaptation of a Child Behavior Checklist profile for Shane indicating elevated scores on attention problems, rule-breaking behavior, and aggression.

▥ Cognitive-Behavioral Assessment

Cognitive-behavioral assessment derives from the notion that a person's thoughts — their self-images and self-statements — play an important role in their behavior (Brewin, 1989). Accordingly, assessment and functional analysis of a target problem or behavior must include measuring thinking processes. To this end, the evaluation of cognitive factors is easily woven into some of the behavioral assessment methods described in this chapter. For example, during behavioral interviews, clients can be instructed to "think aloud," or verbalize the thoughts they had in a particular situation that triggered a problem behavior. Kiara's therapist, for example, asked her what was "going through her mind" that made her want to wash her hands before interacting with clients (see IN PRACTICE: *Excerpt from a Behavioral Interview with Kiara*). Self-monitoring forms have also been developed to measure cognitive aspects of target problems, including the Cognitive Monitoring Form in **Figure 7.2**. A client might be instructed to complete this form, which is based on the cognitive model of emotion (Beck, 1979), when they experience negative moods in a particular situation. Most importantly, the form allows the client to record the automatic thoughts and beliefs (i.e., the cognitions) that are thought to *lead to* the negative emotions. As we will see in Chapter 12, *Cognitive-Behavioral Interventions*, such information helps with targeting and modifying dysfunctional thoughts during cognitive-behavioral treatment. Sometimes, the "situations" that clients have maladaptive thoughts and beliefs about are private, *internal* experiences such as arousal-related body sensations (e.g., a racing heart, feelings of dizziness). A CLOSER LOOK: *Assessing Cognitions about Private Experiences* describes methods used to assess such cognitions in the context of panic attacks.

A (Activating event or situation)	B (Beliefs or interpretation)	C (Emotional/behavioral consequences)
Going to a party	No one will want to talk to me. I'm not fun or interesting.	Depressed, anxious, want to stay home

Figure 7.2 **Cognitive Monitoring Form** Using this form, a client would record activating events and situations (A) and cognitions or beliefs (B) that lead to unwanted emotional or behavioral consequences (C).

Finally, a great many self-report inventories have been developed to assess cognitive aspects of most psychiatric disorders and problem behaviors. For example, as a companion measure to the Saving Inventory (see Table 7.4) Steketee and colleagues developed the Saving Cognitions Inventory (SCI; Steketee et al., 2003) to assess dysfunctional cognitions that have been found to be associated with hoarding behavior. This scale includes a list of 24 ideas that people might have when deciding whether or not to discard something. Respondents are asked to indicate (from 1 [not at all] to 7 [very much]) the extent to which they had each thought during the previous week. Examples include "Losing this possession is like losing a friend" and "Throwing some things away would feel like part of me is dying." Cognitive-behavioral therapists use cognitive measures to assist with case conceptualization and intervention, whereas researchers use them to study the cognitive aspects of psychological problems.

As part of her assessment, Kiara completed the Acceptance and Action Questionnaire for Obsessions and Compulsions (AAQ-OC; Jacoby et al., 2018), which contains items assessing cognitions associated with OCD, such as "I am afraid of my intrusive thoughts." From Kiara's responses to this 13-item self-report instrument, her therapist was able to understand that Kiara interpreted (and responded to) as literal truths her thoughts about contamination and about needing to make sure that she hadn't made a mistake—rather than simply as thoughts or ideas. Extensive research indicates that these types of cognitive and behavioral responses to intrusive thoughts play an important role in maintaining OCD. The therapist was able to use this information to explain the cognitive-behavioral model of OCD to Kiara and also to track changes in these cognitions and behavioral responses over the course of treatment.

A Closer Look   Assessing Cognitions about Private Experiences

We often think of the cognitive model of emotion as applied to how clients interpret situations and events in the *environment*. For example, someone with anorexia nervosa sees a reflection of herself and thinks, "I'm overweight." Someone with depression gets a flat tire and thinks, "This always happens to me. I'm such a loser." But for people with panic attacks, it's catastrophic interpretations of benign *internal* events (sometimes called interoceptive cues) associated with feeling anxious (i.e., the fight-or-flight response) that lead to heightened anxiety and panic. For example, a racing heart is misinterpreted as a *heart attack*, and shortness of breath as *suffocation*. These catastrophic misinterpretations lead to increased fear and anxiety, which intensifies the internal sensations and sets in motion a vicious cycle leading to a panic attack (and often the urge to seek medical assistance).

For such individuals, cognitive-behavioral assessment is focused on measuring the client's responses to various interoceptive cues. These body sensations are provoked by a series of exercises performed in a controlled manner in the office, such as spinning in a swivel chair (dizziness), hyperventilating (tingling, heart racing, sweating), and breathing through a straw (breathlessness, choking). The psychologist helps the client provoke each set of sensations and then records the client's response using the Interoceptive Assessment Form shown in **Figure 7.3**. Sensations that provoke strong fear (and misinterpretations) can then be incorporated into exposure-based

Anthony Harvie/Photodisc/Getty Images

Interoceptive assessment for individuals with panic attacks involves a controlled observation procedure in which various arousal-related body sensations (e.g., dizziness) are deliberately provoked (e.g., by spinning in a chair) to assess the client's responses.

therapy for panic disorder, which aims to change how the client thinks about and responds to arousal-related internal sensations (e.g., Abramowitz et al., 2019).

Figure 7.3 Interoceptive Assessment Form

NAME: _____   DATE: _____

Interoceptive Exposure Assessment Form

Exercise	Sensations	Interpretations	Intensity of Fear (0–10)	Intensity of Sensation (0–10)
Spin (60 seconds)				
Breathe through straw (60 seconds)				
Hyperventilate (60 seconds)				

Think Like a Clinical Psychologist Is there a difference between *cognitions* (i.e., thoughts and interpretations of situations around you) and *talking to oneself*? How are they similar? How are they different? Many psychologists who ascribe to the behavioral tradition consider cognitions a form of behavior. Do you agree? Explain why or why not.

Chapter Summary

Behavioral assessment is unique from other types of assessment in fundamental ways as it emphasizes direct assessments (naturalistic observations) of problematic behavior, antecedent (situational) conditions, and consequences (reinforcement). By conducting such a functional analysis, clinicians can obtain a more precise understanding of the context and causes of behavior. It is also important to note that behavioral assessment is an ongoing process, occurring at all points throughout treatment.

We have surveyed some of the more common behavioral assessment methods. Behavioral interviews are used to obtain a general picture of the presenting problem and of the variables that seem to be maintaining the problematic behavior. Observation methods provide the clinician with an actual sample (rather than a self-report) of the problematic behavior. Observations can be made in naturalistic conditions (as behavior typically and spontaneously occurs) or under more controlled conditions (in simulated or contrived situations or conditions).

Behavioral assessors may also have clients self-monitor ("self-observe") their own behaviors, thoughts, and emotions. Finally, we have discussed the use of technology, and of checklists and inventories, as well as cognitively focused assessments. The future of cognitive-behavioral assessment is likely to take even greater advantage of technological advances to make evaluation more precise, valid, and efficient.

Applying What You've Learned

To demonstrate self-monitoring as an assessment tool, try to monitor one of your own behaviors (e.g., vegetables eaten, hours of sleep, hours studying, positive thoughts) over the course of a week. Develop your own self-monitoring form based on the examples shown in this chapter. You might decide that a paper and pencil format is best, or perhaps you could use an electronic device.

Once you've completed your week of self-monitoring, think about how easy (or difficult) it was to remember to complete the monitoring form. How accurate do you think you were, and what might have affected your degree of accuracy? Finally, what challenges did you face in recording the information?

Discuss, based on your experiences, the pros and cons of the assessment method you developed.

Key Terms

Antecedent: Stimulus condition, or condition that leads up to the behavior of interest.

Behavioral approach task (BAT): An assessment technique used to measure levels of fear and avoidance in which an individual approaches a feared situation until unable to proceed further.

Behavioral assessment: An assessment approach that focuses on the interactions between situations and behaviors for the purpose of effecting behavioral change; based on learning theory.

Behavioral interview: Interview conducted for the purpose of identifying a problem behavior, the situational factors that maintain the behavior, and the consequences that result from the behavior.

Behavioral observation: A primary technique of behavioral assessment that typically involves a clinician or researcher directly monitoring (e.g., seeing, hearing) and then systematically documenting an individual's (or group's) behavior as it occurs in a natural setting, such as at home, in the classroom, within the peer group, on the playground, or under contrived conditions in a laboratory or clinic. Observation is often used to gain

a better understanding of the frequency, strength, and pervasiveness of the problem behavior as well as the factors that are maintaining it.

Cognitive-behavioral assessment: An assessment approach recognizing that the person's thoughts or cognitions play an important role in behavior.

Consequence: Outcome, or event that follows from the behavior of interest.

Controlled observation: An observational method in which the clinician exerts a certain amount of purposeful control over the events being observed; also known as *analogue behavioral observation*. Controlled observation may be preferred in situations where a behavior does not occur very often on its own or where normal events are likely to draw the patient outside the observer's range.

Ecological momentary assessment (EMA): A method of behavioral assessment in which participants record their thoughts, feelings, or behaviors as they occur in the natural environment; also known as experience sampling. This is typically accomplished through the use of electronic diaries or smartphones.

Ecological validity: In the context of behavioral assessment, the extent to which the behaviors analyzed or observed are representative of a person's typical behavior.

Event recording: A procedure in which the observer records each discreet occurrence of the target behavior during the entire observation period.

Functional analysis: A central feature of behavioral assessment. In a functional analysis, careful analyses are made of the stimuli preceding a target behavior and the consequences following from it to gain a precise understanding of the relationship between the target behavior and the situational factors that, according to learning theory, exert control over that behavior.

Idiographic: Consistent with behavioral assessment, this approach emphasizes target behaviors and influences that are specific to the individual person.

Interval coding: Procedure in which the observer records whether the target behavior occurs within a specific period of time (i.e., the interval). This procedure is preferred when the target behavior is lengthy or occurs less frequently, or the starting or ending point of the behavior is less apparent.

Naturalistic observation: Carrying out observations in the person's own environment, such as in their home, at school, or in the hospital. No attempt is made to intervene or manipulate the situation — the goal is merely to observe and document behavior as it naturally occurs. The environment chosen for observation is usually one in which the person spends a great deal of time, or in which the target behavior is likely to occur.

Nomothetic: In contrast to behavioral assessment, this diagnostic approach emphasizes target behaviors and influences that apply to the general population, not to a specific individual.

Rating scale: In behavioral assessment, the use of checklists or inventories to identify and assess the severity of behaviors, emotional responses, and perceptions of the environment. This method involves the patient's, or the patient's caregivers', completion of one or more standardized questionnaires either online or using paper and pencil forms.

Reactivity: In the context of observation, the phenomenon in which individuals respond to the fact that they are being observed by changing their behavior.

Sample: Behavioral assessment uses a "sample" orientation to assessment — that is, the goal is to gather examples that are representative of the situations and behaviors of interest.

Self-monitoring: An observational technique in which individuals observe and record their own behaviors, thoughts, or emotions (including information on timing, frequency, intensity, and duration).

Sign: Traditional assessment uses a "sign" approach to testing — that is, the goal is to identify markers of underlying characteristics.

Target behavior: The behavior of interest; once identified and defined precisely, the clinician conducts a functional analysis of behavior to understand the relationship between the target behavior and the situational factors that, according to learning theory, exert control over that behavior.

CONNECT ONLINE:

 | Check out our videos and additional resources located at: www.macmillanlearning.com

The Assessment of Intelligence

FOCUS QUESTIONS

1. What is intelligence, and what are some of the problems we face in measuring this construct?
2. What is the relationship between intelligence and school success, as well as between intelligence and occupational status and success?
3. What do studies suggest regarding the genetic versus environmental influence on intelligence?
4. How are the Stanford-Binet Fifth Edition (SB-5) and Wechsler scales (WAIS-IV, WISC-V) similar? How are they different?
5. How are intelligence tests used in clinical situations? What are some of the limitations regarding their use in these situations?

CHAPTER OUTLINE

The field of clinical psychology got its start with a focus on assessment, in particular, the assessment of intelligence in children to determine what we now call intellectual developmental disorder. The laudable goal of intelligence assessment originally was to ensure that children with cognitive limitations were properly educated (Thorndike, 1997). However, there is little question that over the years these tests have been misused at times (e.g., in ways that have penalized underrepresented groups), and as we will cover in this chapter, have long been the subject of debate.

So what, then, is the value of intelligence tests to clinical psychologists today? Clinical psychologists (as well as school psychologists) still frequently conduct intelligence tests to help understand the broader picture of an individual's symptoms and development. Before a clinical psychologist can understand whether a client's behaviors are typical or atypical, it is important to know whether they are functioning at an intellectual ability commensurate with their age or far older than their chronological age, or perhaps are experiencing broad intellectual disabilities. Intelligence tests also are commonly used within the subfield of neuropsychology to learn how the effects of head trauma or other biological injuries may have broadly affected cognitive functioning. We conclude the chapter on this topic.

Intelligence is a hypothetical construct, which means it exists only in how we define it and measure it. Intelligence tests are our attempt to operationally define the concept of intelligence. But the tests we have are imperfect and there is no shortage of unresolved questions and controversies in this area of the field. Can the true nature of intelligence ever be accurately defined? Can it ever be measured in ways that reflect a fair representation of all cultural groups? To what extent is intelligence genetic or environmentally determined?

In this chapter, we talk about intelligence testing with a focus on how intelligence is defined and measured, and how assessments are incorporated into clinical practice. We explore the concepts and theories of intelligence, as well as the most popular ways of estimating this characteristic. We will also delve into some of the controversies over intellectual assessment, and discuss the appropriate interpretation of intelligence test scores.

▥ The Concept of Intelligence

Definitions of Intelligence

It might surprise you to know that there is no universally accepted definition of **intelligence** (Sternberg, 2018). In fact, the very concept of intelligence — how to define and measure it — is one of the most controversial issues in the field of clinical psychology. Most attempts to define intelligence fall into one of three classes:

1. Definitions that emphasize adjustment or adaptation to the environment — adaptability to new situations, the capacity to deal with a range of situations

2. Definitions that focus on the ability to learn — on educability in the broad sense of the term

3. Definitions that emphasize abstract thinking — the ability to use a wide range of symbols and concepts; the ability to use both verbal and numerical symbols

   To illustrate, consider the following examples that have appeared over the last century:

   • [Intelligence is] the aggregate or global capacity of the individual to act purposefully, to think rationally, and to deal effectively with his environment. (Wechsler, 1939, p. 3)

- As a concept, intelligence refers to the whole class of cognitive behaviors which reflect an individual's capacity to solve problems with insight, to adapt himself to new situations, to think abstractly, and to profit from his experience. (Robinson & Robinson, 1965, p. 15)

- Intelligence is a very general mental capability that, among other things, involves the ability to reason, plan, solve problems, think abstractly, comprehend complex ideas, learn quickly and learn from experience. It is not merely book learning, a narrow academic skill, or test-taking smarts. Rather, it reflects a broader and deeper capability for comprehending our surroundings — "catching on," "making sense" of things, or "figuring out" what to do. (Arvey et al., 1994)

- Intelligence is defined in terms of the ability to achieve success in life in terms of one's personal standards, within one's socio-cultural context. (Sternberg, 2003, p. 141)

These definitions are not mutually exclusive. Furthermore, some of them contain overtones of both social values and motivational elements. Beyond this, most are quite general, which calls into question whether definitions make all that much difference, or whether intelligence tests are simply a collection of questions and items that we hope will correlate with some external criterion (e.g., school grades).

Theories of Intelligence

There have also been many different theoretical approaches to understanding intelligence (Sternberg, 2018). We present an overview of several influential theories here.

Spearman (1927) hypothesized the existence of a **general intelligence factor (g)** that governs all mental abilities and operations. That is, he thought that having more or less *g* determined one's overall level of intelligence. Later, he proposed *specific factors of intelligence (s)* (e.g., arithmetic, spatial, logical, and mechanical) which vary from person to person and explain why different people are more or less proficient in different sorts of intellectual tasks.

Thurstone (1938) later proposed that intelligence was comprised of seven **primary mental abilities** that work together in combination, including numerical facility, word fluency, verbal comprehension, perceptual speed, spatial visualization, reasoning, and memory.

After a few decades, Cattell (1965) partitioned Spearman's *g* into two components: **fluid ability** and **crystalized ability**. Fluid abilities are nonverbal culture-free mental skills such as the capacity to adapt to new situations. Crystallized abilities, on the other hand, are reflected in skills and knowledge acquired through interactions that are specific to one's culture and indicated by intellectual achievements such as writing a paper, receiving a good grade in school, or solving a problem.

More recent approaches to understanding intelligence focus on information-processing and take a more dynamic view than the older theories of mental components. For example, some theories emphasize the speed of processing, speed in making choices in response to stimuli, and speed with which individuals can extract various aspects of language from their long-term memory. But many problems and questions remain, such as whether there are general problem-solving skills or merely skills specific to certain ability areas.

Gardner (1999) described a **theory of multiple intelligences**. Human intellectual competence involves a set of problem-solving skills that enable the person to resolve problems or difficulties. Sometimes this results in the potential for acquiring new information. To date,

Camille Tokerud/Stone/Getty Images

Child prodigies possess extreme talents that some psychologists view as a form of intelligence.

Gardner has described a family of eight intelligences: linguistic, musical, logical-mathematical, spatial, bodily-kinesthetic, naturalistic, interpersonal, and intrapersonal (Chen & Gardner, 2005). For example, the interpersonal refers to the ability to notice, appreciate, and make distinctions among other individuals in terms of feelings, beliefs, and intentions. A criticism of Gardner's theory, however, is that some of his proposed intelligences may be better conceptualized as "talents" (Neisser et al., 1996). Nevertheless, Gardner's views have attracted a great deal of attention from psychologists and educators alike and emphasize areas of potential and ability that are not tapped by traditional psychological tests.

Sternberg (2005) also proposed a theory of multiple forms of intelligence. He maintains that people function on the basis of three aspects of intelligence: componential, experiential, and contextual. This approach deemphasizes speed and accuracy of performance and instead focuses on planning responses and monitoring them. The componential aspect refers to analytical thinking; high scores would characterize someone who is a good test taker. The experiential aspect relates to creative thinking and characterizes people who can take separate elements of experience and combine them insightfully. Finally, the contextual aspect is seen in people who are practical, know how to "play the game," and can successfully manipulate the environment (i.e., those who are "street smart"). According to Sternberg, a person's performance is governed by these three aspects of intelligence.

Although Spearman, Thurstone, and others may seem to have given way to Cattell, Gardner, or Sternberg, clinicians' day-to-day use of intelligence tests suggests that they have not really outgrown the *g* factor of Spearman or the group factors of Thurstone. Indeed, the notion of a single *intelligence quotient (IQ)* score that represents an individual's overall intelligence implies that we're still trying to discover how much *g* the person has. As we will see, however, most current intelligence tests are composed of subtests so that the total *IQ* represents a composite of subtest scores. This implies that, to some extent, we have also accepted Thurstone's group factors. We seem to want to quantify how much intelligence the person has, yet cannot escape the belief that intelligence is patterned — that two people may have the same overall *IQ* score and still differ in specific abilities. Thus, it would appear that practicing clinicians think more in line with Spearman or Thurstone and are less affected by the recent information-processing and multiple intelligence perspectives.

Think Like a Clinical Psychologist As you have read, there are different types of intelligence. When you meet someone who strikes you as being "intelligent," what is it about them that makes you feel this way? What factors do you believe are the most important in deciding how intelligent a person is? How might your answers to these questions be influenced by your own cultural background?

▦ The IQ: Its Meaning and Its Correlates

The Intelligence Quotient (IQ)

Ratio IQ

Alfred Binet, who invented the first intelligence test in 1905, coined the term **mental age** (MA) to describe a person's mental performance. This idea was based on the notion that individuals of a certain age should have mastered certain abilities. At the conclusion of the test, the number of items answered correctly determined the person's MA. Subsequently, Stern (1938) developed the concept of **intelligence quotient** (IQ) to be able to express intelligence as a ratio of a person's MA relative to their **chronological age** (CA) using the following formula:

$$IQ = MA/CA \times 100$$

A person's IQ score thus provides an estimate of intelligence relative to the general population. IQ scores have a mean of 100 and a standard deviation of 15, so approximately two-thirds of the population have an IQ between 85 and 115. About 2.5% score above 130 or below 70.

Deviation IQ

Although appealing, the ratio IQ is limited in its application to older age groups because an MA score (even if very high) accompanied by an increasing chronological age (CA) will result in a lower IQ. Thus, it may appear that IQ has decreased over time when in fact one's intellectual ability has been maintained. To deal with this problem, Wechsler introduced the **deviation IQ**, which involves a comparison of individuals' performance on an IQ test with that of their age peers. Thus, the same IQ score has a similar meaning, even if two individuals are markedly different in age (e.g., a 22-year-old versus an 80-year-old). In both cases, an IQ of 100 indicates an average level of intellectual ability for that age group.

Jupiterimages/Stockbyte/Getty Images

Research indicates that intellectual abilities such as critical thinking and problem-solving skills often remain stable as we age.

Correlates of IQ

Does the concept of IQ have **validity**? In other words, is it a good measure of a person's intelligence? That depends on how we define intelligence. If we're looking for a global aptitude above and beyond school-related achievements, the answer is probably no. But if we define intelligence mainly as a predictor of success in school, then the answer is likely to be yes. Regardless of how we define intelligence, society ultimately decides which abilities are valued, rewarded, and nurtured. Perhaps this is why all intelligence tests seem so much alike — they are designed to predict what society values. As you read this section, keep in mind that IQ tests (and indeed the very concept of IQ itself) were primarily developed using average white/European American standards, values, opportunities, and motivations. So, are IQ tests really objective, equal, or innate measures

Success in school is associated with many factors, but research shows that across different cultures, IQ scores are strongly predictive of grades.

of intelligence for everyone? What about people with fewer resources and opportunities for learning, and cultures that place less of an emphasis on verbal ability, analytical skills, logical reasoning, and reading? Is IQ really a valid indicator of intelligence?

School Success

In general, and cross-culturally, IQ relates substantially both to success in school and to achievement tests that measure what has been learned (e.g., He et al., 2021; Hunt, 2011; Jalili et al., 2018). The correlation between IQ scores and grades is about .56 (Strenze, 2007). It seems apparent that success in school is related to a host of variables, including motivation, teacher expectations, cultural background, attitudes of parents, and differences in opportunities and resources. We are then confronted with the very difficult clinical task of sorting out these variables. When success or failure in school occurs, is it because of intelligence, motivation, cultural background, opportunities, or what? Any behavior is complexly determined by many variables other than just general or specific intelligence.

Occupational Status and Success

Because amount of education would seem to be, in general, a strong determinant of the kind of job one can obtain, it should come as no surprise that IQ and occupational status are related. This relationship seems to be true whether occupational status is defined in terms of income or prestige, regardless of gender or ethnicity (Strenze, 2007). Interestingly, however, intelligence scores are also good predictors of job performance (e.g., Murtza et al., 2020); IQ scores outperform predictors such as biographical data, reference checks, education, and college grades. However, once entry to a profession has been gained, the degree of intelligence may not separate the more outstanding from the less eminent. Apparently, some minimum level of ability is necessary to achieve entry into (or minimal performance within) a given occupation or elected office (though even this is debatable). Yet once an individual gains entry, the degree of subsequent success may be more a function of nonintellectual factors such as the ability to communicate clearly, build rapport and trust with others, and increase the perception that you have credibility and expertise.

Many high-achieving adults earned only average grades in school. Research shows that success as a professional is often related to nonintellectual factors, rather than to IQ.

Demographic Group Differences

Although most studies find few if any significant differences between males and females in overall IQ scores, significant differences between the genders have been obtained for specific abilities (Hunt, 2011). Males tend to score significantly higher on measures of spatial ability and, after puberty, on measures of quantitative ability. Females tend to score significantly higher on measures of verbal ability (Neisser et al., 1996). Presently, there is no research addressing IQ among nonbinary gender groups.

Among racial/ethnic groups, Latinx and Black Americans in North America tend to obtain significantly lower IQ scores than do European Americans in North America (e.g., Kamphaus, 2019). We will return to this topic in the section *IQ, Intelligence Tests, and Cultural Bias*. These findings, although consistent, have been the source of much controversy. Neisser and colleagues (1996) point out that although we do not know what causes these ethnic/racial differences, the size of the differences is within a range that could be accounted for by environmental factors, such as the aforementioned differences in regard to the opportunities and resources available to youth from different ethnic backgrounds in North America. More research is needed in this area to provide insight into the nature of these ethnic/racial differences. Despite the differences, however, among Latinx and Black Americans, IQ scores are good predictors of school, college, and work achievement (Lo, 2017).

Heredity and Stability of IQ Scores

Is Intelligence Inherited?

Almost all psychologists now acknowledge that intelligence is influenced, at least in part, by genetic factors (e.g., Kamphaus, 2019). The reasons for this agreement are consistent findings from a large body of **behavioral genetics** studies over the past several decades (e.g., Plomin et al., 2008; Sauce & Matzel, 2018). A CLOSER LOOK: *Behavioral Genetics* presents a brief overview of the methods of behavioral genetics.

A Closer Look   Behavioral Genetics

Behavioral genetics is a research specialty in which both genetic and environmental influences on a particular behavior are evaluated. One research design used in this field is the twin method, which involves comparing **monozygotic (MZ) twins**, who are genetically identical, with **dizygotic (DZ) twins**, who share only about 50% of their genetic material. The similarity among twin pairs is typically presented in the form of a **concordance rate** or *similarity index*. In its simplest form, a concordance rate is the percentage of instances across all twin pairs in which both twins exhibit similar behaviors or characteristics. A concordance rate or similarity index for the MZ twin sample that is significantly greater than that for the DZ twin sample suggests that genetic influences play an important role in the development of that set of behaviors or features.

However, because MZ twins are identical and, if reared together, may be treated more similarly than DZ twins, one could argue that higher concordance rates for MZ twins than for DZ twins may have as much to do with environmental influences as genetic influences. An even more informative method used in behavioral genetic studies involves sampling MZ twins reared together (MZT), MZ twins reared apart (MZA), DZ twins reared together (DZT), and DZ twins reared apart (DZA). In this way, it is easier to separate genetic and environmental influences.

The twin method compares similarity of characteristics or features among monozygotic twins (like Rami and Sami Malek) to that of dizygotic twins.

For example, the following findings would suggest genetic influences in the manifestation of the behaviors or features under study: (a) the concordance rates for MZT and MZA twins are significantly greater than those for DZT and DZA twins, respectively; (b) the concordance rate for MZA twins approaches that of MZT twins; and (c) the concordance rate of DZA twins approaches that of DZT twins. These findings would suggest that genetics plays an important role because similarity/concordance is a function of the amount of genetic material shared, and being raised in different environments does not have an appreciable effect on similarity.

This is a brief and simplistic overview of behavioral genetics. Interest in this field has waxed and waned over the years, and at times the field has been the target of attacks for a variety of reasons (Plomin et al., 2008). For example, concordance rates or similarity indices less than 100% (or 1.00) *necessarily* implicate environmental influences. Therefore, behavioral genetics methods are tools for identifying and quantifying environmental as well as genetic factors in behavior. In addition, findings from behavioral genetics studies are often interpreted in overly simplistic ways that overlook the complex interplay between genes and the environment. Finally, finding that a behavior or characteristic is genetically influenced does not mean that it is immutable or unchangeable. Indeed, environmental factors such as diet, oxygen levels, and light cycles are known to influence how genes are expressed (Harden, 2021). ▬

Is Intelligence Fixed or Changeable?

In general, estimates of the percentage of IQ associated with genetic factors range from 30% to 80% (Deary et al., 2010; Sauce & Matzel, 2018). But does this mean that IQ is not malleable? No, and this is the source of much confusion and controversy. Heritability estimates are not 100%, and biological relatives who were reared together are more similar than biological relatives who were reared apart. There is also a significant correlation between the IQs of nonbiologically related but reared-together relatives. Thus, the environment clearly plays some role in the development of intelligence.

Even if heritability estimates were 100%, this does not rule out the possibility that IQ scores may change. Some "genetically determined" traits, such as height, can be influenced by environmental circumstances, and some genetic disorders can be controlled or even cured by environmental intervention. In fact, the heritability of intelligence does not appear to be stable across the life span; it ranges from about 20% in infancy, to 60% in young adulthood, to 80% in old age (Deary et al., 2010). In summary, then, it's not a matter of *either* genetic *or* environmental influences. Clearly, both play some role in the development and expression of intelligence.

Think Like a Clinical Psychologist What factors do you think influence a person's intelligence or IQ? Can people develop an IQ higher than their parents? Explain why or why not.

Paul Archuleta/FilmMagic/Getty Images

📚 Intelligence Tests

There are dozens of intelligence tests available today, and clinical psychologists must be familiar with the capabilities of each so they can choose a test (or tests) to match the needs of an individual client. Shane's psychologist, for example, might want to determine whether Shane's difficulties in school could be attributed to particular areas of intellectual weakness. She would also want to choose an intelligence test that would not be affected by Shane's behavioral difficulties apparent from the referral.

The overall goal of intelligence testing is to compare the performance of the person being tested (i.e., the person's MA) with the performance of a representative sample of others at the same CA—the standardization sample. To do this requires that the test be administered to each client in the exact same manner that it was administered to the standardization sample. Accordingly, intelligence tests come with detailed manuals that contain specific instructions for how to instruct the test taker, and administer and score test items. Training as a clinical psychologist involves becoming proficient at giving and scoring such tests. Indeed, deviating from the standard procedures can influence how a client appears relative to the standardization sample, which can have implications for school placement and other accommodations.

In this section, we briefly describe several of the most frequently used tests for determining overall intelligence (i.e., IQ) for children and adults. These tests are, for example, able to identify individuals as intellectually gifted or as having intellectual developmental disorder. Later in this chapter, we'll return to the topic of how psychologists use these tests in clinical settings.

The Stanford-Binet Scales

For many years, the Binet scales were the preferred tests. They have undergone various revisions after Binet's initial work in 1905 (see IN HISTORICAL PERSPECTIVE: *Intelligence Testing: Yesterday and Today*), with the most recent revision appearing in 2003—the **Stanford-Binet Fifth Edition**, or **SB-5** (Roid, 2003). This version includes 10 individual sets of tasks ("subtests") that assess verbal and nonverbal aspects of the following five general cognitive abilities (one verbal and one nonverbal subtest per ability):

1. *Fluid reasoning* refers to the ability to solve new problems.

2. *Quantitative reasoning* involves solving numerical and word problems, as well as understanding fundamental number concepts.

3. *Visual-spatial processing* involves seeing relationships among objects, recognizing spatial orientation, and conducting pattern analysis.

4. *Working memory* involves the ability to process and hold both verbal and nonverbal information and then to interpret it.

5. *Knowledge* involves the ability to absorb general information that is accumulated over time through experience at home, school, work, or the environment in general.

The SB-5 can be administered to individuals age 2 years through adulthood. You may wonder how the same test can be used for both young children and adults. The SB-5 is an "adaptive" test, which means that it begins with two "routing tests" designed to determine the starting point for each of the other subtests. A person who does better on the routing tests

●●●●● **In Historical Perspective**

Intelligence Testing: Yesterday and Today

Several historical developments in the latter half of the 19th century influenced the introduction of measures of intelligence (Wasserman, 2018). First, laws requiring education for children in the United States and elsewhere resulted in a more diverse student body, with many students coming from previously uneducated families. As a result, the failure rate in schools dramatically increased and there was pressure to identify those students most likely to have difficulty. Second, psychological scientists demonstrated that mental abilities could be measured. In France, Alfred Binet and Theodore Simon devised the Binet-Simon test in 1905 to identify individual differences in mental functioning, and institutions such as schools, industries, military forces, and governments became interested in identifying people who were most likely to perform well in these settings. Their work was quickly picked up by Lewis Terman, a psychologist at Stanford University, who in 1916 developed an American version of the test called the Stanford-Binet Intelligence Scale. Intelligence testing prospered through the first half of the 20th century.

Alfred Binet (1857–1911)

By the end of the 1960s, however, the validity of these tests was challenged — the argument being that they discriminate through the inclusion of unfair items. As a result of a civil rights suit (*Larry P. v. Wilson Riles*) begun in 1971, the California Board of Education in 1975 suspended the use of intelligence tests to assess disabilities in Black Americans. The court held that IQ testing is biased against Black American children and tends to unjustly place them in stigmatizing programs for cognitively impaired individuals (others disputed the court's judgment, however, claiming it assumed Black Americans would do poorly on the tests). This touched off a debate that led to the publication of noteworthy books. One of these, Stephen Gould's (1981) *The Mismeasure of Man*, critiqued the very concept of intelligence and

Theodore Simon (1872–1961)

its measurement, pointing out that many studies on intelligence have been heavily biased by the faulty belief that the behavior of different races is best explained by genetic factors. A second book, *The Bell Curve* (Herrnstein & Murray, 1994), was a largely political and highly controversial response to Gould's critiques that drew connections between race and intelligence, suggesting policy implications based on these unsubstantiated connections. Indeed, intelligence tests have been misused at times in ways that have penalized underrepresented groups. There is also little doubt that some tests contain items that have adversely affected the performance of various groups. We should therefore do everything we can to develop better tests and to administer and interpret them in a sensitive fashion. However, banning tests seems an inappropriate cure that may ultimately harm the very people who need help. ■

starts with more difficult questions than one who does poorly. As testing proceeds within each subtest, the questions get progressively more difficult. Questioning continues as long as the individual is able to answer correctly—the further they get, the higher the score. Scores are also adjusted for age so that if you consider children of different ages with the same score, the older child will have answered more questions correctly.

The SB-5's verbal subtests require proficiency with words and printed material (reading or speaking). Examples include tests of vocabulary (used for routing), memory for words, the ability to identify things such as body parts and tools, objects, and number concepts. The nonverbal subtests consist of making movement responses such as pointing and assembling or manipulating objects. These subtests are included to reduce the use of language in assessing IQ so that non-English speakers are not put at a disadvantage. Examples include making designs, following patterns, and identifying absurdities in pictures. Depending on the age and ability of the individual being assessed, administration of the SB-5 can last from 15 to 75 minutes.

Example of a practice item from the Stanford-Binet Fifth Edition. The test taker must correctly identify what is silly or impossible about what they see.

Research indicates that the SB-5 has excellent reliability and validity (Roid & Pomplun, 2005). **Internal consistency**, the extent to which items on the scale correlate with one another, ranged from .95 to .98 for IQ scores, and from .90 to .92 for scores on the five abilities. **Test–retest reliabilities** across all age groups were also generally high, in the .80s for factor scores and in the .90s for IQ scores. As for validity, the relationships between IQ scores as measured by the SB-5 and scores on other accepted tests of intelligence are consistently strong. For example, the correlation between SB-5 IQ scores and those on the 1986 Stanford-Binet Fourth Edition (SB-4) was .90, and those between the SB-5 and scores on another IQ test (the Wechsler scale described next) were .84 for children and .82 for adults. Finally, participants with learning disabilities, developmental disabilities, or attention deficit–hyperactivity disorder could be reliably classified and distinguished from their peers based on SB-5 scores.

The Wechsler Scales

Early versions of the Stanford-Binet test had a number of disadvantages that led David Wechsler in 1939 to develop the Wechsler-Bellevue Intelligence Scale. This was a test designed for adults—one that would offer items whose content was more appropriate for and more motivating to adults than the school-oriented Binet. In contrast to the Stanford-Binet, whose items were arranged in age levels, the Wechsler-Bellevue Intelligence Scale grouped its items into subtests. For example, all arithmetic items were put into one subtest and arranged in order of increasing difficulty. In addition, there was a Performance Scale and a Verbal Scale (consisting of five and six subtests, respectively). A separate IQ for each scale could be calculated, along with a Full Scale IQ. Today, there exists a suite of three Wechsler intelligence scales covering various age groups across the life span. We describe these next.

David Wechsler (1896–1981) published the Wechsler-Bellevue Intelligence Scale in 1939. Subsequent revisions of this test have become the most widely used techniques to assess intellectual functioning.

The Wechsler Adult Intelligence Scale-IV

A new version of the Wechsler-Bellevue, known as the **Wechsler Adult Intelligence Scale (WAIS)**, first appeared in 1955. A revised edition (WAIS-R) was published in 1981. The *Wechsler Adult Intelligence Scale Third Edition (WAIS-III)* was introduced in 1997, and the most recent version, the WAIS-IV, was published in 2008.

The WAIS-IV, which is used for individuals 16 years and older, includes 15 subtests (described below), which can be combined to provide the Full Scale IQ score as well as **Index scores** for Verbal Comprehension, Perceptual Reasoning, Working Memory, and Processing Speed. These Index scores provide a more detailed evaluation of the examinee's strengths and weaknesses than does the Full Scale IQ score. Following are brief descriptions of the 15 WAIS-IV subtests, with the corresponding Index scale (in parentheses) to which the subtest belongs.

1. *Vocabulary (Verbal Comprehension).* Here, the examinee must define words that increase in difficulty. This subtest correlates highly with Full Scale IQ scores, and some feel that it comes close to measuring what is usually termed *g*.

2. *Similarities (Verbal Comprehension).* This subtest consists of a series of items, and for each one, the examinee must explain how two objects are alike. The subtest requires the basic ability to form abstractions and develop concepts.

3. *Arithmetic (Working Memory).* These items are similar to arithmetic problems that appear in most school textbooks. The items are administered orally, and the examinee is not allowed to use paper and pencil.

4. *Digit Span (Working Memory).* This subtest is a measure of short-term memory and attention. Three sets of digits are read aloud by the examiner. For the first list, the examinee must repeat the digits in the order that they were read. For the second list, the digits must be repeated backward. Finally, for the third list, the digits must be repeated back to the examiner in ascending order.

5. *Information (Verbal Comprehension).* These short questions tap knowledge that one would be expected to have acquired as a result of everyday living and cultural interactions.

6. *Comprehension (Verbal Comprehension, supplemental subtest).* The items of this subtest require the examinee to explain why certain procedures are followed, to interpret proverbs, and to determine what should be done in a given situation. The items measure common sense and practical judgment in solving a problem. This is a supplemental subtest for IQ scores.

7. *Letter-Number Sequencing (Working Memory, supplemental subtest).* This subtest consists of items that assess working memory and attention. A combination of numbers and letters is read, and the examinee must recall first the numbers in ascending order and then the letters in alphabetical order. Each item consists of three trials of different combinations of numbers and letters. This is a supplemental subtest for IQ scores.

8. *Picture Completion (Perceptual Reasoning, supplemental subtest).* This subtest consists of colored cards, each showing a picture with a part missing. The examinee must identify the missing part. This requires concentration and the ability to note details and incongruities. This is a supplemental subtest for IQ scores.

9. *Coding (Processing Speed).* This code-substitution task requires the examinee to fill in the appropriate code in the blanks under a long series of numbers, using a key. The subtest requires the examinee to work in a direct, single-minded fashion.

10. *Block Design (Perceptual Reasoning).* The examinee must assemble up to nine blocks to match the designs on a set of cards. The task involves visual-motor coordination and analytic synthesizing ability.

11. *Matrix Reasoning (Perceptual Reasoning).* This subtest consists of items that measure visual information processing and abstract reasoning skills.

12. *Symbol Search (Processing Speed).* This subtest consists of items that ask the respondent to indicate whether a stimulus symbol appears in the array that is present.

13. *Visual Puzzles (Perceptual Reasoning).* This new subtest requires the examinee to choose from a list correct pieces of a puzzle that when placed together reconstruct the puzzle picture that is presented.

14. *Figure Weights (Perceptual Reasoning, supplemental subtest).* This new subtest asks the examinee to look at a two-dimensional representation of a scale with missing weights and then select the weights necessary to keep the scale balanced. This is a supplemental subtest for IQ scores.

15. *Cancellation (Processing Speed, supplemental subtest).* This new subtest requires the examinee to go through a list of colored shapes and mark the targeted shapes. This is a supplemental subtest for IQ scores.

Simulated item from the WAIS-IV Picture Completion subtest. The test taker is asked to identify what is missing from the picture (i.e., the back left wheel).

Data support both the reliability and validity of Full Scale IQ scores derived from the WAIS-IV. For example, test–retest reliabilities over an average of three weeks range from .74 to .90 across age groups for the various subtests. Relevant subtest scores from other tests of cognitive ability are also strongly correlated with corresponding subscale scores derived from the WAIS-IV. For example, the WAIS-IV Working Memory Index is highly correlated with scales from other measures tapping attention and concentration, and the WAIS-IV Verbal Comprehension Index correlates significantly with scores on other tests of language fluency and language comprehension.

The Wechsler Intelligence Scale for Children-V

The *Wechsler Intelligence Scale for Children (WISC)* was first developed in 1949, revised in 1974 (WISC-R), again in 1991 (WISC-III), and again in 2003 (WISC-IV). The latest version, the **Wechsler Intelligence Scale for**

A Wechsler Intelligence Scale for Children (WISC) kit includes manuals for administering and scoring the test, all the necessary stimuli needed to administer the 15 subtests, and a set of forms for recording the examinee's responses and scores.

Children Fifth Edition (WISC-V), was published in 2014 (Wechsler, 2014). It is considered an age-downward extension of the WAIS-IV and appropriate for children ages 6 through 17 years. The WISC-V involves administration of 10 primary subtests to yield five primary Index scores. The Full Scale IQ score is derived from 7 of the 10 primary subtests: both Verbal Comprehension subtests, one Visual Spatial subtest, two Fluid Reasoning subtests, one Working Memory subtest, and one Processing Speed subtest (Wechsler, 2014). **Table 8.1** shows the various subtests that align with the five primary indices.

Table 8.1	Subtests and Indices of the Fifth Version of the Wechsler Intelligence Scale for Children	
Index	**Subtest**	**Description**
Verbal Comprehension (a measure of the child's ability to reason through reading or speaking)	Similarities*	Child indicates how two items are alike
	Vocabulary*	Child must define a provided word
	Information	General knowledge questions
	Comprehension	Questions about social situations or common concepts
Visual Spatial (a measure of the ability to tell where objects are in space)	Block Design*	Child puts together red-and-white blocks in a pattern according to a model while being timed
	Visual Puzzles*	Child views a puzzle in a stimulus book and chooses from among pieces of which three could construct the puzzle
Fluid Reasoning (is a measure of inductive and quantitative reasoning)	Matrix Reasoning*	Child is shown an array of pictures with one missing square, and must select the picture that fits the array from five options
	Figure Weights*	Child views a stimulus book that pictures shapes on a scale with one empty side and must select the choice that keeps the scale balanced
	Picture Concepts	Child sees a series of pictures in rows and must determine which pictures go together
	Arithmetic	Child solves orally administered timed arithmetic word problems
Working Memory (a measure of the ability to temporarily hold and process information)	Digit Span*	Child listens to sequences of numbers and must repeat them (a) as heard, (b) in reverse order, and (c) in ascending order
	Picture Span*	Child views pictures and then indicates those they remember seeing
	Letter-Number Sequencing	Child is given a series of numbers and letters and asked to provide them to the examiner in a predetermined order
Processing Speed (a measure of the time it takes to do mental tasks)	Coding*	Child under age 8 years marks rows of shapes with different lines according to a code; child over age 8 years transcribes a digit-symbol code using a key (these tasks are time-limited)
	Symbol Search*	Child is given rows of symbols and target symbols and asked to mark whether or not the target symbols appear in each row
	Cancellation	Child scans random and structured arrangements of pictures and marks specific target pictures within a limited amount of time

*Indicates a primary subtest.

The **split-half reliability** (which involves correlations between two parts of the same test) of the Full Scale IQ was .96; the overall average reliability coefficients for WISC-V primary Index scores ranged from .88 to .93, and reliability of the individual subtests ranged from .80 to .94. With regard to validity, the WISC-V is significantly correlated with other measures of IQ and achievement, adaptive behavior, executive function, and behavior and emotion. IN PRACTICE: *Intelligence Tests, Shane* describes how a psychologist would interpret the results of a WISC-V administration and draw conclusions about a child's academic, intellectual, and psychological functioning. Such conclusions could be used to inform interventions, as we will see later in the chapter.

In Practice   Intelligence Tests, Shane

Recall that Shane's teacher reported that Shane was frequently "off-task" at school. She indicated that Shane's academic ability was "low" to "average" as compared to his peers, particularly in math and reading; however, he demonstrated strength in art and science. Results from the WISC-V revealed that Shane's Full Scale IQ score was within the average range; however, there was significant variation across each of the primary Index scales, suggesting that his overall (i.e., Full Scale) IQ score is not a valid measure of his ability. Consistent with his teacher's reports of distractible behavior, his Processing Speed index was at the lower end of the average range, suggesting some mild weaknesses for him, as compared to his own performance. However, his Verbal Comprehension index was in the above average range. When coupled with his teacher's reports regarding low performance in related skills (e.g., reading), results suggest that Shane may be performing below his intellectual abilities. Such a result would alert a clinical psychologist to the possibility of a learning disability, suggesting that someone's achievement is significantly lower than their intellectual capacity, perhaps due to difficulties processing stimuli (seeing letters, processing words) in the same way as others. In Shane's case, his scores on a subsequent achievement test (similar to a WISC, but with an emphasis on acquired knowledge rather than innate intellectual ability) revealed that he did not formally qualify for a learning disability diagnosis. Nevertheless, feedback to Shane, his parents, and his teacher regarding his advanced intellectual ability in verbal comprehension proved very important in helping everyone rethink why Shane may be experiencing difficulties in school. ▬

The Wechsler Preschool and Primary Scale for Intelligence-IV

The **Wechsler Preschool and Primary Scale of Intelligence (WPPSI)** was developed in 1967, followed by the WPPSI-II in 1989, the WPPSI-III in 2002, and the current WPPSI-IV in 2012. The focus of the most recent update was to improve measurement of working memory and processing speed. The scale is similar to the WISC-V but geared specifically toward the assessment of intellectual ability among much younger children. The age range of the WPPSI-IV is divided into two age bands: ages 2 years, 6 months to 3 years, 11 months; and ages 4 years to 7 years, 7 months.

The WPPSI-IV yields three indices: the Full Scale IQ, the Verbal Comprehension Index, and the Visual Spatial Index.

The Wechsler Preschool and Primary Scale for Intelligence (WPPSI) is an age-downward extension of the other Wechsler scales.

It contains developmentally appropriate versions of many of the same subscales used in the WISC (e.g., Information, Block Design, Object Assembly, Coding, Matrix Reasoning), but also includes several subscales designed specifically for younger children. These focus on vocabulary, reasoning, and picture concepts.

Research shows that the internal consistency, test–retest reliability, and **interrater reliability** — the level of agreement between different psychologists testing the same child — of the WPPSI-IV are good to excellent (Syeda & Climie, 2014). In addition, there is strong evidence for the scale's content validity, as well as convergent and discriminant validity. Accordingly, the WPPSI-IV has a number of positive attributes that make it an effective tool for assessing cognitive functioning in younger children (Syeda & Climie, 2014).

> **T**hink Like a Clinical Psychologist Think about each type of intelligence assessed on the various tests described in this chapter. On which type do you think you would score the highest? On which do you think you would score the lowest? Why?

▌▌▌ IQ, Intelligence Tests, and Cultural Bias

Research shows that for several decades, the average IQ score of Asian Americans has been higher than that of European Americans; and the average IQ of European Americans is higher than that of Black Americans and Latinx Americans (Marks, 2010). To explain these group differences, some have argued that intelligence tests (and indeed the enterprise of IQ testing more broadly) are unfairly biased against certain groups, resulting in IQ scores that do not accurately reflect their intellectual ability and that can lead to unfair decisions about educational or employment opportunities (Weiss & Saklofske, 2020).

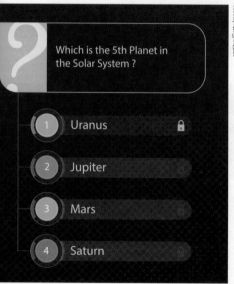

amitus/Getty Images

One observation to support this argument is that there are existing social factors that place groups with lower average IQs at a competitive disadvantage. For example, exposure to discrimination, lower-quality schooling, and poverty may result in children from certain ethnic groups being less well-prepared or motivated than children in other groups to succeed on intelligence tests (e.g., Duckworth et al., 2012). Members of disadvantaged racial groups might also feel less at ease in testing situations, or less trusting of adult testers (many of whom might be members of a majority group). Thus, the group differences in IQ scores may result (at least in part) from social, motivational, and emotional factors rather than actual intellectual ability (e.g., Claro et al., 2016; Rimfeld et al., 2016).

Can you identify the cultural bias in this question from an actual intelligence test?

Another observation is that IQ tests themselves appear to have inherent biases. For example, they include many test items that reflect middle-class culture in Europe and the United States. The problem is that the skills and vocabulary necessary to score highly on these items are more familiar to children from some cultural backgrounds than from others. As a result it's *familiarity*, not intelligence per se, that can partially explain why members of some groups systematically achieve higher scores than do members of other groups.

Despite these observations, clear scientific evidence for bias in IQ tests has been elusive. Test developers use standardization samples so as to be representative of people from all demographic groups, and during the norming process, they carefully analyze responses to each test item. If, due to unfamiliarity with an item's vocabulary or other content, members of one ethnic group respond incorrectly at least 20% more often than other groups, that item is eliminated from the final version of the test. Indeed, greater care in producing standardized tests is aiming to eliminate all culturally biased items from the widely used intelligence tests.

What about the factors that place some groups at a disadvantage? Indeed, IQ scores necessarily reflect the fact that some people have had greater opportunities than others to develop certain cognitive abilities. Accordingly, we might view intelligence tests as measures of the degree to which people have developed the cognitive abilities perceived as most valuable in a society that, unfortunately, contains inequality. In other words, IQ tests may be accurately detecting abilities and knowledge that are not represented equally in all groups. But does this mean the tests are unfairly culturally biased, or that IQ scores are influenced by the different educational and intellectual opportunities which may be unfairly afforded to different groups (Sackett et al., 2008)? And if the answer is the latter, an important question is "How can we increase these opportunities among members of traditionally disadvantaged groups?"

Although intelligence tests likely contain some cultural bias, the differences in average IQ scores across racial and ethnic groups probably have more to do with disparities in socioeconomic conditions. While we should continue to improve IQ tests in order to minimize any cultural bias, it is also important to see such tests as helping to *expose* systematic disadvantages so that we can take curative action.

Think Like a Clinical Psychologist Should psychologists be studying differences in intellectual ability between people of different races, ethnicities, cultures, and socioeconomic status? Why or why not? What are the risks and the benefits?

▥ Using Intelligence Tests in Clinical Practice

Estimating General Intelligence

The most obvious use of an intelligence test is as a means for estimating a client's general intellectual level (*g*). Often, during an initial interview or observation, the clinician recognizes something that suggests the person is not functioning as well as their potential would indicate. The potential can form a baseline against which to measure current achievements, thus providing information about the client's current level of functioning. This can be especially useful when attempting to determine whether a child's academic difficulties are due to cognitive or mental health difficulties, or whether a child's academic achievement is substantially lower than their cognitive ability (in extreme cases, this is referred to as a learning disability). In Shane's case, his academic achievement was lower than what would be expected given his above average verbal IQ score, yet he did not meet criteria for a learning disability diagnosis.

Accordingly, a clinical psychologist might next try to better understand how Shane's disruptive behavior and episodes of depressed mood could play a role in his academic performance.

Intellectual ability test results, when available, also can be used to help determine how well an individual may be able to recover cognitive abilities following a head trauma or illness that compromises intellectual performance. Simply obtaining an IQ score, however, is not the end of a clinician's task — it is only the beginning. The IQ score must be interpreted. Only through knowledge of the client's learning history and by observations made during the testing situation can that score be placed in an appropriate context and adequately understood.

Predicting Academic Success

As mentioned previously, there is a relationship between intelligence test scores and school success. To the extent that intelligence reflects the capacity to do well in school, we can expect IQ tests to predict school success. Not everyone would equate intelligence with scholastic aptitude, but a major function of intelligence tests is to predict school performance. One must remember, however, that intelligence and academic success are not the same thing.

The Appraisal of Style

As we have noted, what is important is not only whether the client succeeds or fails on particular test items but also how that success or failure occurs. Thus, another value of intelligence tests is that they permit us to observe the client at work, which helps in interpreting an IQ score. For example, was Shane sufficiently motivated to try as hard as possible on his achievement test? Was there anxiety during the testing session that could have detracted from his performance? On a broader level, contextual factors need to also be considered, such as the test-taking setting, whether the client got a good night's sleep, remembered to take their medication, or were under pressure from family to perform well. Finally, there can be incentives for clients to deliberately perform *poorly* on intelligence and achievement tests, such qualifying for accommodations in school (e.g., extra time on exams). Such questions and factors, and the ensuing interpretations, breathe life into an otherwise inert IQ score.

Think Like a Clinical Psychologist Intelligence tests such as the Wechsler intelligence tests should be administered, scored, and interpreted only by trained psychologists. Furthermore, only summaries of the results (rather than the actual IQ scores themselves) are usually released to clients or their families. Why do you think such strict regulations exist for these tests? What consequences, if any, might result from their misuse?

▐ Chapter Summary

The assessment of intelligence has a long history in clinical psychology. Compulsory education and psychologists' ability to measure mental abilities contributed to the development and success of the field of intelligence testing. However, by the end of the 1960s, the validity of these tests was being challenged. To this day, there are many controversies about how intelligence is defined and how it is measured. Clinical psychologists tend to believe in both a general factor of intelligence (*g*) and specific abilities that underlie the general intelligence factor. Intelligence scores are correlated with school success, occupational status, and job performance. IQ scores are more stable for adults than they are for children. In addition, there are group differences in intelligence test scores between ethnic/racial groups. Although intelligence test scores are influenced by genetic factors, environment does play a major role in the development and testing of intelligence.

We have discussed four major intelligence tests in use today. The Stanford-Binet Fifth Edition assesses children, adolescents, and adults; the Wechsler Adult Intelligence Scale Fourth Edition assesses adolescents and adults; the Wechsler Intelligence Scale for Children Fifth Edition assesses children; and the Wechsler Preschool and Primary Scale of Intelligence Fourth Edition assesses preschool children. Intelligence test results are used to quantify overall levels of general intelligence as well as specific cognitive abilities. This versatility allows clinical psychologists to use intelligence test scores for a variety of prediction tasks (e.g., school achievement).

Applying What You've Learned

On your own, or with a small group of students, create your own theory of intelligence. Consider what constitutes intelligence: what domains should be included? What domains should be excluded? Why? Propose how you would measure intelligence according to your theory. Discuss your theory and test ideas with other students or groups. What commonalities and differences emerge across the different theories of intelligence?

Key Terms

Behavioral genetics: A research specialty that evaluates both genetic and environmental influences on the development of behavior.

Chronological age: What we commonly refer to as age; years of life.

Concordance rate (or similarity index): An index of similarity between individuals. The simplest form of concordance rate is the percentage of instances in which two individuals exhibit similar behaviors or characteristics.

Crystallized ability: One of two higher-order factors of intelligence conceived by Cattell. Crystallized ability refers to the intellectual capacities obtained through culture-based learning.

Deviation IQ: A concept introduced by Wechsler to address problems observed when applying the ratio IQ to older individuals. Individual performances on an IQ test are compared to those of their age peers.

Dizygotic (DZ) twins: Fraternal twins, or twins that share about 50% of their genetic material.

Fluid ability: One of two higher-order factors of intelligence conceived by Cattell. Fluid ability refers to a person's genetically based intellectual capacity, culture-free mental skills.

General intelligence factor (*g*): The term introduced by Charles Spearman to describe his concept of a general intelligence.

Index score: Score that corresponds to one of the major ability factors that underlie the WAIS-IV subtest scores (i.e., Verbal Comprehension, Perceptual Reasoning, Working Memory, and Processing Speed).

Intelligence: There is no universally accepted definition of intelligence. However, many definitions of intelligence emphasize the ability to think abstractly, the ability to learn, and the ability to adapt to the environment.

Intelligence quotient: A term developed by Stern in 1938 to address problems with using the difference between chronological age and mental age to represent deviance. Typically, a deviation IQ score is used.

Internal consistency: The extent to which the items on a scale correlate with one another.

Interrater reliability: The level of agreement between two or more raters who have evaluated the same individual independently. Agreement can refer to consensus on behaviors, attributes, and so on.

Mental age: A term introduced by Binet as an index of mental performance. This idea was based on the notion that individuals of a certain age should have mastered certain abilities.

Monozygotic (MZ) twins: Identical twins, or twins that share 100% of their genetic material.

Primary mental abilities: Seven factors of intelligence derived by Thurstone on the basis of his factor analytic work: numerical facility, word fluency, verbal comprehension, perceptual speed, special visualization, reasoning, and memory.

Split-half reliability: The extent to which an individual's scores on one half of a test (e.g., the even-numbered items) are similar to scores on the other half (e.g., the odd-numbered items).

Stanford-Binet Fifth Edition (SB-5): An intelligence test that measures five general cognitive factors (fluid reasoning, quantitative reasoning, visual-spatial

processing, working memory, and knowledge), each of which includes both verbal and nonverbal subtest activities.

Test–retest reliability: The consistency of assessment test scores over time. Generally, we expect individuals to receive similar diagnoses from one administration to the next if the interval between administrations is short.

Theory of multiple intelligences: A theory forwarded by Gardner that posits the existence of eight intelligences: linguistic, musical, logical-mathematical, spatial, bodily-kinesthetic, naturalistic, interpersonal, and intrapersonal.

Validity: The extent to which a test measures what it is supposed to measure.

Wechsler Adult Intelligence Scale (WAIS): An adult intelligence test that is now in its fourth edition. The WAIS-IV is comprised of 15 subtests and yields a Full Scale IQ score, in addition to Index scores for Verbal Comprehension, Perceptual Reasoning, Working Memory, and Processing Speed.

Wechsler Intelligence Scale for Children Fifth Edition (WISC-V): An intelligence test designed for children between the ages of 6 and 17 years.

Wechsler Preschool and Primary Scale of Intelligence: An intelligence test divided into two age groups: 2 years, 6 months to 3 years, 11 months; 4 years to 7 years, 7 months. The test is currently in its fourth edition.

CONNECT ONLINE:

 Check out our videos and additional resources located at: www.macmillanlearning.com

Diagnosis, Case Formulation, and Treatment Planning

FOCUS QUESTIONS

1. Why have clinical psychologists virtually abandoned the terms "normal" and "abnormal"?
2. How was *Diagnostic and Statistical Manual of Mental Disorders*, known in its latest version as the *DSM-5-TR*, developed?
3. In what ways do the *Research Domain Criteria* (*RDoC*) differ from the *DSM-5-TR*?
4. What are the primary elements of a case formulation?
5. How do clinical psychologists form treatment plans and communicate them to their clients?

CHAPTER OUTLINE

Once assessment is complete, the process turns to making sense of the data that have been gathered. Psychologists might use assessment information to diagnose their clients with one or more mental disorders. They might also (or instead) use a case formulation approach to specify the key psychological factors involved in the presenting problem and decide on a treatment plan. In this chapter, you will learn how these methods work, as well as how clinical psychologists communicate a diagnosis, case formulation, and treatment plan to their clients and monitor the progress of treatment.

But how do we know when someone has a psychological problem in the first place? And when are such problems serious enough to deserve treatment? Moreover, who makes these decisions—the client? A close family member (e.g., a parent)? A psychologist? It was once commonplace to use the term "abnormal" to label behaviors, thoughts, and emotions (and even *people*) that seem to require intervention of one sort or another. Yet, clinical psychology has evolved to recognize that human diversity and cultural diversity are too broad to be contained—or constrained—by the metaphor of abnormality. Because this issue sits at the heart of diagnosis, formulation, and treatment planning, that is where we will begin.

▥ Beyond Normal and Abnormal

The concept of *abnormality* has always been imprecise and difficult to define. But it is also pejorative and stigmatizing toward people and phenomena that deserve thoughtful study and careful treatment. As a result, clinical psychologists have all but abandoned the terms "normal" and "abnormal" in their professional work. Many colleges and universities have even changed the name of their abnormal psychology courses to "psychopathology" or "psychological disorders" (perhaps yours has, too), and one of the oldest and most respected scientific journals in the field—the *Journal of Abnormal Psychology*—recently changed its title to *Journal of Psychopathology and Clinical Science* (MacDonald et al., 2021). Indeed, the multiplicity of human experience simply cannot be distilled down to *normal* versus *abnormal*. Let's explore why.

Russell Monk/The Image Bank/Getty Images

Halloween? Clinical psychologists are careful to not distill things down to normal versus abnormal.

Abnormal as Socially or Statistically Deviant

"Abnormal" is sometimes synonymous with terms like "atypical," "rare," "unusual," "nonconformist," and "outrageous." Take Shane and Kiara, for example. Shane's oppositional and aggressive behaviors depart considerably from those of the average child. Kiara's scores on measures of OCD symptom severity are elevated compared to the general population. This aspect of deviance from the norm is very clear in her case because it can be described with numbers.

But when we define abnormality based on social or statistical deviance, we overlook the reasons behind the so-called deviant behavior. If you learned that Shane had been relentlessly bullied by the girl he hit with a rock, would you consider his behavior outrageous? What if his parents were harsh and abusive at home? Would it change how you think about his tendency to shout at them? What is deviant for one person (or group) is not necessarily so for another. And some behaviors that seem appropriate at one developmental stage may appear inappropriate at another.

Defining abnormality as "atypical" is inherently stigmatizing. It relies on a faulty assumption that the behaviors or characteristics of the majority are "right," and those in the minority are wrong. For instance, for years the *Diagnostic and Statistical Manual of Mental Disorders* (DSM; which we discuss in detail later in this chapter) classified sexual and gender diversity as abnormal, leading to prejudice and discrimination — some of which continue to be hotly debated today. But sexual and gender identities and behaviors that are *different* from the majority are not *wrong*, and the lifetime prevalence of diagnosable mental illness overall in the United States is close to 50% (Kessler et al., 2005), further demonstrating the limitations of the deviance approach to defining abnormality.

Abnormal as Distressing

From this perspective, whether a person feels happy or sad, tranquil or troubled, and fulfilled or barren are the crucial considerations for abnormality. It is people who feel depressed, by this definition, who are labeled *abnormal*. But not everyone we consider to have a psychological problem reports subjective distress. Clinicians sometimes encounter individuals who have little contact with reality and yet profess inner tranquility. Another problem with this definition concerns the amount of subjective distress necessary to be considered abnormal. All of us become aware of our own anxieties from time to time, so how much is allowed, and for how long, before it is considered abnormal?

Abnormal as Dysfunctional

From this angle, behavior is abnormal when it creates social (interpersonal) or occupational (or educational) problems. For example, Shane's behavior at school kept him from making friends and interfered with his grades. Kiara's obsessing and compulsive behavior were interfering with her productivity at work. But who is best suited to determine when an area of functioning becomes impaired? The client? The psychologist? Parents, teachers, or friends? An employer? Judgments of both social and occupational functioning are value-based. Although most of us may agree that having relationships and contributing to society as an employee or a student are valuable characteristics, it is harder to agree on what specifically constitutes an adequate (or *normal*) level of functioning in these spheres.

Where Does This Leave Us?

The discussion above highlights how human and cultural diversity simply do not accommodate terms like "abnormal" or "normal." Thus, clinical psychologists have various options when trying to understand their clients' presenting complaints. One of these is psychiatric diagnosis, in which clients are classified as having one or more mental disorders based on their behavior, cognition, or emotion. Another option involves an investigational approach focusing on largely biological processes. A third option is case formulation, in which the focus is on understanding client behavior, cognition, and emotion in context using research-supported conceptual models. These options are not mutually exclusive, and they can even be complementary, but they do have very different implications for how we understand clients and their problems. We now turn to considering each approach in detail.

Think Like a Clinical Psychologist How do you define a psychological problem, and how is your definition shaped by your cultural background and your values? What, if anything, should you do about this?

▌ Psychiatric Diagnosis and Classification of Mental Disorders

The fifth edition, text revision, of the *Diagnostic and Statistical Manual of Mental Disorders* (American Psychiatric Association, 2022), known as the **DSM-5-TR**, is the current official diagnostic and classification system for mental disorders. Although it was developed and published by the American Psychiatric Association, it is widely used around the world in both clinical and research settings. What is a **mental disorder**? The DSM-5-TR states that a mental disorder is

> . . . a syndrome characterized by clinically significant disturbance in an individual's cognition, emotion regulation, or behavior that reflects a dysfunction in the psychological, biological, or developmental processes underlying mental functioning. Mental disorders are usually associated with significant distress or disability in social, occupational or other important activities. An expectable or culturally approved response to a common stressor or loss, such as the death of a loved one, is not a mental disorder. Socially deviant behavior (e.g., political, religious, or sexual) and conflicts that are primarily between the individual and society are not mental disorders unless the deviance or conflict results from a dysfunction in the individual, as described above (American Psychiatric Association, 2022, p. 14).

Perhaps you noticed that this definition incorporates deviance, distress, and dysfunction—the three perspectives we discussed earlier in regard to trying to define abnormality. Yet, it also acknowledges that culture-bound behaviors meeting these criteria are not necessarily mental disorders. The evolution of psychiatric diagnosis and the DSM is a rich and interesting story as described in IN HISTORICAL PERSPECTIVE: *The DSM and Psychiatric Diagnosis.* Because clinical psychologists often use the DSM-5-TR to make diagnoses, let's take a closer look at its main features, uses, and limitations.

DSM-5-TR

The DSM-5-TR provides a catalogue of mental disorders, classified by type, along with descriptions and sets of diagnostic criteria that clinicians use when deciding which disorder best characterizes a client. In general, disorders thought to be more influenced by biological and developmental factors appear toward the beginning of the manual, and those with similar features are listed adjacent to each other. **Table 9.1** provides a broad overview of how the DSM-5-TR is organized.

Table 9.1 Overview of the DSM-5-TR's Organization

Section I: DSM-5-TR Basics

Introduction

Use of the manual

Information for forensic use

Section II: Diagnostic Criteria and Codes

Neurodevelopmental disorders

Schizophrenia spectrum and other psychotic disorders

Bipolar and related disorders

Depressive disorders

Anxiety disorders

Obsessive-compulsive and related disorders

Trauma- and stressor-related disorders

Dissociative disorders

Somatic symptom and related disorders

Feeding and eating disorders

Elimination disorders

Sleep-wake disorders

Sexual dysfunctions

Gender dysphoria

Disruptive, impulse-control, and conduct disorders

Substance-related and addictive disorders

Neurocognitive disorders

Personality disorders

Paraphilic disorders

Other mental disorders

Medication-induced movement disorders and other adverse effects of medication

Other conditions that may be a focus of clinical attention

Section III: Emerging Measures and Models

Assessment measures

Culture and Psychiatric Diagnosis

Alternative DSM-5 model for personality disorders

Conditions for further study

Appendix

Alphabetical Listing of DSM-5-TR Diagnoses

Numerical Listing of DSM-5-TR Diagnoses

DSM-5-TR Advisors and Other Contributors

> ● ● ● ● ● **In Historical Perspective**
>
> ## The DSM and Psychiatric Diagnosis
>
> The 1800s saw a movement to develop treatments for individuals who had been filling up mental hospitals in the United States and Europe. This led to the first attempt to classify mental health problems by French psychiatrist Jean-Etienne-Dominique Esquirol in 1845. Some years later, in 1883, German psychiatrist Emil Kraepelin developed a classification system that distinguished between two forms of mental illness: dementia praecox (which would later become known as schizophrenia) and manic-depressive disorder (which would form the basis for depression and bipolar disorder).
>
> In the late 1800s, the U.S. government sought to determine the prevalence of different types of mental illness, leading to the creation of the *Statistical Manual for the Use of Institutions for the Insane* in 1917 by the American Medico-Psychological Association (which later became the American Psychiatric Association). This manual, which identified 22 broad categories of mental illness using a psychoanalytic framework, was continually updated until 1942 and represented the precursor to the first edition of the DSM.
>
> ### DSM-I and DSM-II
>
> By the late 1940s numerous classification systems were in use, which led to confusion among mental health professionals. Accordingly, the American Psychiatric Association developed a new system that would be used nationwide to provide a common diagnostic scheme. The result was the first edition of the DSM in 1952. The manual was a thin spiral-bound book that contained 102 broad diagnostic categories that were based on Freudian psychoanalytic principles and divided into (a) conditions that were assumed to be caused by some type of brain dysfunction and (b) conditions that were assumed to be the result of a stressful environment. This second group was subdivided into (a) *psychoses:* severe conditions, such as schizophrenia and manic-depressive disorder, and (b) *psychoneuroses,* which included personality disorders, depression, and anxiety-related conditions. Although better organized than its predecessors, the first DSM had very little diagnostic utility and exhibited little influence on the diagnostic process.
>
> A second edition of the DSM appeared in 1968 and was also heavily influenced by Freudian theory. It increased the number of mental illnesses to 182 in an attempt to broaden the client base of psychiatry. Descriptions of the various illnesses, however, were vague and difficult to interpret, which resulted in poor interrater reliability.
>
> ### DSM–III and the Remaking of Psychiatry
>
> The 1960s and 1970s were troubling times for psychiatry as a field. The lack of confidence in its diagnostic system, along with the fact that most psychiatrists remained wedded to unscientific (e.g., Freudian) theories, had reduced psychiatry's standing. Meanwhile clinical psychology, which had moved on to science-based treatment methods, was beginning to threaten psychiatry's long held monopoly on the care for those with mental illness. Popular books and movies, such as *One Flew Over the Cuckoo's Nest* (1962, 1975), propagated a negative view of psychiatry, as did harsh critics such as Thomas Szasz (a psychiatrist himself) who raised serious challenges to the idea that psychiatric disorders were real illnesses (Szasz, 1960). As a result, few medical students were entering the field, and its leaders recognized the need for rebranding.
>
> A major part of this rebranding, which occurred during the 1970s and 1980s, was the shift to a biomedical orientation in practice, research, and training. This included a new classification system, which was rolled out in the DSM-III, released in 1980. The DSM-III featured several modifications designed to increase reliability and depict the diagnostic categories as similar to medical illnesses. For example, the Freudian nomenclature of past DSMs was replaced with biomedical terminology (e.g., obsessive-compulsive *neurosis* became obsessive-compulsive *disorder*) along with sets of specific diagnostic criteria. Many new disorders

were also included in this edition, including posttraumatic stress disorder and attention deficit disorder — the DSM-III contained 256 disorders in all. Of note, homosexuality, which was included as a mental illness in the DSM-II, was finally excluded from the DSM-III. All of this ushered in a more biologically oriented view of mental illness, which continues within psychiatry to this day. It also set the stage for the wealth of funding psychiatry has attracted from granting agencies and the pharmaceutical industry as part of its revival.

Homosexuality was considered a psychiatric disorder until it was finally excluded from the DSM-III in 1980.

DSM-III-R

In 1987, the American Psychiatric Association published the DSM-III-R, a revised edition of the DSM-III that renamed and reorganized some disorders, while making changes in the diagnostic criteria of others. This update contained 292 diagnostic categories and further emphasized purely descriptive categories with the aim of increasing interrater reliability.

DSM-IV and DSM-IV-TR

In 1994, the DSM-IV was published, listing 297 different disorders. A major update was also the specification that a person must experience *clinically significant* distress or impairment in social, occupational, or other areas of functioning in order to meet the criteria for most diagnoses. The year 2000 saw the publication of a text revision of the DSM-IV, called DSM-IV-TR. While the diagnostic categories in this revision remained essentially the same, the sections describing various features of the disorders were updated.

DSM-5 and DSM-5-TR

As psychiatry's embrace of the biomedical model continued to grow, some of the field's leaders envisioned a diagnostic system based entirely on neurobiology (similar to how disorders in other areas of medicine are biologically based). Throughout the 2000s, the American Psychiatric Association convened numerous conferences to review the scientific data and establish biologically based categories and diagnoses that would provide better targets for biological treatments such as medication. At one point, for example, the anxiety disorders were to become "fear circuitry disorders." In the end, however, even the most fervent champions of this idea were forced to accept that there was insufficient evidence to establish a classification system based on biology. Accordingly, the DSM-5 and DSM-5-TR, published in 2013 and 2022 respectively with about 265 different disorders, retained their predecessors' descriptive diagnostic criteria.

That's not to say there weren't other significant changes. A number of disorders were added (e.g., hoarding disorder) and removed (e.g., Asperger's syndrome), the traditional five subtypes of schizophrenia were deleted, new categories of obsessive-compulsive-related disorders and trauma-related disorders were created, other categories were altered (e.g., intellectual developmental disorder), and greater consideration was given to issues of culture, gender, racism, and discrimination. Some of these changes were controversial, such as the creation of a prolonged grief disorder. Still, the lack of a biological foundation for psychiatric diagnosis was met with disappointment by the National Institute of Mental Health, which vowed to stop funding research based on DSM disorders and developed their own conceptually derived classification system, the Research Domain Criteria (which we describe later in this chapter). ■

Depending on how they are counted, there are approximately 265 disorders listed in the DSM-5-TR. These disorders are grouped under the various categories in Section II of the manual, and each disorder has specific diagnostic criteria. As shown in the example in **Table 9.2**, these criteria primarily refer to the presence and duration of specific **signs** (outwardly observable phenomena, such as avoidance behavior) and **symptoms** (subjective experiences, such as fear). The DSM-5-TR also includes a summary of each disorder's **associated features**, including prevalence, course, prognostic factors, and common co-occurring diagnoses. Finally, each disorder appears with a diagnosis code which clinicians, institutions, and agencies may use for data collection and billing purposes. These diagnostic codes are derived from the coding system used by all U.S. health care professionals, known as the *International Classification of Diseases* (or ICD).

Table 9.2   Condensed Diagnostic Criteria for Social Anxiety Disorder

A. Marked fear or anxiety about one or more social situations in which the individual is exposed to possible scrutiny by others (e.g., having conversations, meeting unfamiliar people, being observed eating or speaking, offending others). In children, the anxiety must occur with peers and not just during interactions with adults.

B. Fears of acting in ways, or showing anxiety symptoms, that will be negatively evaluated, embarrassing, or lead to rejection.

C. The social situations almost always provoke fear or anxiety. In children, this may be expressed by crying, clinging, or failing to speak.

D. The feared social situations are avoided or endured with intense fear or anxiety.

E. The fear or anxiety is out of proportion to the actual threat posed by the situation and to the sociocultural context.

F. The fear or avoidance behavior has persisted for 6 months or more.

G. The fear or avoidance causes clinically significant distress or impairment in social, occupational, or other important areas of functioning.

H. The fear or avoidance is not attributable to the physiological effects of a substance (e.g., a drug of abuse or medication) or a medical condition.

I. The fear or avoidance is not better explained by another mental disorder, such as panic disorder, body dysmorphic disorder, or autism spectrum disorder.

J. If a medical condition (e.g., obesity, disfigurement from burns) is present, the anxiety or avoidance is unrelated or excessive.

Note that Section III of the DSM-5-TR contains tools and techniques to enhance the diagnostic decision-making process, understand the cultural context of mental disorders, and recognize proposed diagnoses that are currently undergoing research (e.g., internet gaming disorder). It also includes a novel model for the diagnosis of personality disorders as an alternative to the types of diagnostic criteria shown in Table 9.2.

Developing and updating a diagnostic manual such as the DSM-5-TR takes years of work by hundreds of experts organized into committees on each set of disorders. These committees conduct literature reviews, commission field studies, and entertain comments and suggestions by individuals and stakeholders both within and outside the various fields of mental health. Each committee then comes to a consensus regarding which disorders to add or exclude, and what the various diagnostic criteria should be. Whereas previous DSMs were considered static documents, the DSM-5-TR will be continually updated as new information becomes available.

With all of its diagnostic information, the DSM-5-TR has become the "bible" of mental health (indeed, you will find a copy on the bookshelf of virtually every mental health practitioner and clinical scientist). But not everyone is a true believer! In fact, its integrity and authority are matters of great controversy, which we will explore next.

Advantages of the DSM-5-TR

It is easy to take for granted the utility of diagnosing individuals because that's what we expect to occur in health care settings. But why should we use mental disorder diagnoses in the first place? There are at least three advantages of a diagnostic system such as the DSM-5-TR.

A sign of social anxiety disorder is avoidance, and a symptom is the belief that others will judge or treat you harshly.

Communication

Suppose a colleague refers to you a client with a diagnosis of bulimia nervosa. Immediately, without knowing anything else about the client, a symptom pattern comes to mind: body image concerns, binging and purging behavior. Diagnosis can therefore be thought of as a "shorthand" for representing features of a particular problem. Using standard diagnostic criteria ensures some degree of comparability with regard to mental disorder features among clients diagnosed by any mental health professional.

Research

The use of diagnoses also enables research by guaranteeing that any study conducted on, say, borderline personality disorder (BPD), involves clients with similar patterns of psychological distress and dysfunction. For example, consider the

Because it contains diagnostic information and insurance codes for all types of mental disorders, most mental health clinicians and researchers own a copy of the DSM-5-TR.

hypothesis that childhood sexual abuse predisposes individuals to developing BPD. The first empirical attempts to test this hypothesis involved assessing the prevalence of childhood sexual abuse in groups of participants defined by their diagnosis of BPD, some other psychiatric disorder, or no disorder at all. Indeed, these studies indicated that childhood sexual abuse occurs frequently in individuals with BPD, and that these rates are significantly higher than those in clients with other (non-BPD) mental disorders and without any psychiatric disorders.

Treatment

Finally, diagnoses are important because, at least in theory, they suggest which mode of treatment is most likely to be effective for a particular disorder. This is a general goal of a classification system for mental disorders (Blashfield & Draguns, 1976). For example, a diagnosis of schizophrenia suggests that the administration of an antipsychotic medication is more likely to be effective than is a course of psychoanalysis.

Limitations of the DSM-5-TR

On the other hand, there are a number of difficulties with the DSM-5-TR system, and indeed the very concept of psychiatric diagnosis. These primarily relate to issues with reliability and validity, as we will see next.

Reliability Issues

If psychologist A and psychologist B both observe the same client but cannot agree (i.e., achieve interrater reliability) on the diagnosis, whose diagnosis should we accept? Prior to the DSM-III, the reliability of psychiatric diagnoses was unacceptably low. In one study by Beck, Ward, Mendelson, Mock, and Erbaugh (1962), for example, different psychiatrists who interviewed the same 153 clients agreed on a client's diagnosis only 54% of the time (which is not much better than chance). As a result, efforts were made to improve interrater agreement by replacing the often hazy descriptions of disorders that appeared in the DSM-I and DSM-II with more specific diagnostic criteria in the DSM-III and beyond. Yet, as **Figure 9.1** shows, even with these detailed criteria, the interrater reliability of many prevalent DSM-5-TR disorders (e.g., generalized anxiety disorder, major depressive disorder, OCD, alcohol use disorder) remains fair at best. The data in the figure come from a series of *field trials* conducted to examine the degree to which two clinicians could agree on DSM-5 diagnoses (which are largely

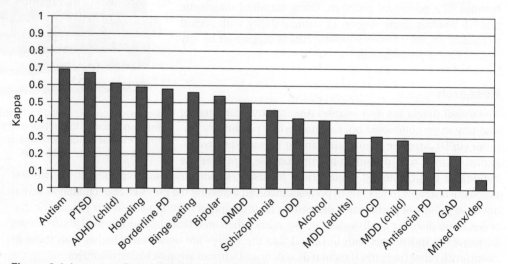

Figure 9.1 Interrater Reliability (Kappa) of DSM-5 Diagnoses in the DSM-5 Field Trials

SOURCE: Regier, D. A., Narrow, W. E., Clarke, D. E., Kraemer, H. C., Kuramoto, S. J., Kuhl, E. A., & Kupfer, D. J. (2013). DSM-5 field trials in the United States and Canada: Part II. Test-retest reliability of selected categorical diagnoses. *American Journal of Psychiatry, 170*(1), 59–70.

PTSD = posttraumatic stress disorder; ADHD = attention deficit–hyperactivity disorder; PD = personality disorder; DMDD = disruptive mood dysregulation disorder; ODD = oppositional defiant disorder; MDD = major depressive disorder; OCD = obsessive-compulsive disorder; GAD = generalized anxiety disorder.
Kappa values of 0.00–0.20 = no to slight agreement; 0.21–0.40 = fair agreement; 0.41–0.60 = moderate agreement; 0.61–0.80 = substantial agreement; 0.81–1.0 = near perfect agreement.

unchanged in DSM-5-TR) when the same client was interviewed on separate occasions. *Kappa* represents the percent agreement between two independent raters (after correcting for chance agreement).

These reliability data raise serious concerns about the *validity* of some of the most common psychiatric disorders. Indeed, if diagnosticians cannot agree on who has which disorder (or a disorder at all), how can we be sure that such disorders are present at all (i.e., that they have construct validity)? We now consider several problems with psychiatric diagnosis that raise questions about the validity of the disorders in the DSM-5-TR.

Use of Descriptive Criteria

Flip back to Table 9.2 and look closely at the diagnostic criteria for social anxiety disorder. Notice that they are merely lists describing signs and symptoms. There is no criterion of a positive test for some sort of underlying medical pathology. The DSM-5-TR is constrained to such **descriptive diagnosis** because there are no objective tests for psychiatric disorders, and the causes of these disorders are not well understood. But descriptive criteria by themselves can't tell us what is really wrong or pathological — if anything at all.

The following scenario illustrates the problem: imagine going to your doctor because you have a sore throat. The doctor listens to you describe when it started and how much it hurts, and then gives you a diagnosis of "sore throat disorder." So you then ask, "Doctor, how do you know it's sore throat disorder?" To which your doctor replies, "Because you have a sore throat." The trouble is that a physician is supposed to gather objective information about your complaint — such as by physical examination, throat culture, x-ray, or blood test — to provide an underlying explanation such as a bacterial (strep) or viral infection, allergic reaction, dryness, or cancer. That is what makes the diagnosis a valid one.

A DSM-5-TR diagnosis, however, is the equivalent of sore throat disorder. In the absence of any objective tests, we are left with "You have social anxiety disorder because you are anxious in social situations; and you are anxious in social situations because you have social anxiety disorder." But simply naming and describing a phenomenon does not make it a valid disorder; if so, then *any* behavior could become a psychiatric illness (e.g., internet gaming disorder). Recall that the DSM-5-TR was crafted by committees, the members of which represent varying scientific, theoretical, professional, and even economic constituencies. Consequently, which phenomena become classified as psychiatric disorders (and which do not) may reflect compromises that make the DSM acceptable to these stakeholders (as opposed to scientific advances). For example, although it was the correct decision, the demise of homosexuality as a psychiatric disorder occurred because of a vote by the American Psychiatric Association, rather than careful consideration of research findings.

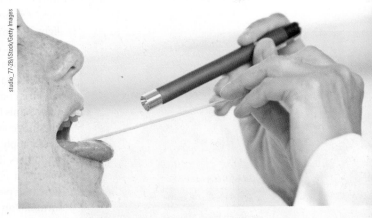

studio_77-28/iStock/Getty Images

Unlike diagnosing a sore throat, there are no reliable or valid medical tests to diagnose any of the disorders in the DSM-5-TR. Therefore, psychiatric diagnoses are based merely on descriptions of signs and symptoms.

Ambiguous Criteria

What if the Internal Revenue Service (the federal agency that oversees the collection of taxes) suddenly decided that taxpayers should just pay their "fair share," without giving any further guidance? Individuals, accountants, and tax collectors would have different interpretations of "fair share" and how to determine this, leading to chaos. The DSM-5-TR diagnostic criteria are often similarly ambiguous in that they fail to specify under what conditions the criteria are met, leaving clinicians to provide their own interpretations.

As an example, let's again consider social anxiety disorder. In criterion A, how do you know when fear or anxiety is "marked"? How are we to determine if it is "intense" enough to meet criterion D? And what constitutes "clinically significant" distress or impairment in criterion G? Recall the issues with relying on subjective accounts of distress and impairment when deciding whether a psychological phenomenon is abnormal. What one clinician considers "marked" or "intense" another might not. This poses a further threat to validity: how can social anxiety disorder be a valid construct if its very recognition depends on so much subjectivity?

Sociocultural Context

Although the DSM-5-TR has improved upon its predecessors' consideration of multicultural factors, its descriptive approach still implies that thoughts, feelings, and behaviors can be signs and symptoms of mental illness regardless of (a) the sociocultural context in which they occur and (b) how they are interpreted by a clinician. But is it a sign of schizophrenia if a devoutly religious person has conversations with an invisible deity? Consider a young Black man who has an extreme fear of police officers — does he have a phobia? And what if a fashion model, struggling to make ends meet, uses amphetamines to stay as slim as the modeling agency requires so she can keep her job — does she have a substance use disorder? Of course, culture, race, ethnicity, gender, sexual preference, and socioeconomic status affect behaviors, belief systems, and coping strategies. And just as your own personal history likely affects your impression of these three cases, the background and lived experiences of clinicians also affect their diagnostic impressions. Indeed, a diagnostic system that neglects the importance of social context in this way is of questionable validity.

FatCamera/E+/Getty Images

As mentioned, the DSM-5-TR does attempt to highlight the impact of culture on psychiatric diagnosis. First, it includes *cultural concepts of distress*, including **cultural syndromes**—collections of signs and symptoms that are restricted to a limited number of cultures. Koro, for example, which is common in Southeast Asia and China, is the fear that one's penis has retracted inside the body (Teodoro & Afonso, 2020). Second, some diagnostic criteria have been updated to better apply across cultures. An example is the fear of offending others in the criteria for social anxiety disorder, which reflects a common manifestation of this disorder among Japanese people. Finally, the DSM-5-TR contains a cultural formulation interview to allow clients to define their distress in their own words and help others, who may not share their culture, understand their problems. These important features give interested clinicians a more comprehensive foundation on which to base diagnosis and treatment.

The DSM-5-TR is designed to take social and cultural factors into account.

Categories Versus Dimensions

The DSM-5 -TR's approach of placing clients into diagnostic categories based on their thoughts, emotions, and behaviors is also a threat to its validity. This is because, as noted earlier in this chapter, "atypical" behavior is not qualitatively different from so-called typical behavior. Rather, these are endpoints of a continuous *dimension.* The difference, for example, between strange cognitive experiences (e.g., hearing the voice of a loved one who has died) that occur in the general population and clinical hallucinations that are part of schizophrenia is one of *degree* (i.e., frequency, intensity, and duration) rather than *kind* (Stip & Letourneau, 2009). Yet, categorical diagnoses imply that individuals either have the disorder (and the characteristic thoughts, emotions, and behaviors) in question or they do not.

To illustrate this further, consider **Table 9.3**, which shows thoughts, emotions, and behaviors related to going on a job interview on a continuum from nonanxious to extremely anxious. Notice that the anticipatory thoughts range from those associated with confidence to those of fear and dread. Likewise, emotional experiences may range from mild physical arousal to those which are maladaptive and disruptive. Finally, behavioral responses to this situation range from attending the interview to various degrees of avoidance. It is only when our thinking patterns, emotions, and behaviors cause great distress or problems in functioning that we consider them indicative of a diagnosable mental disorder.

Table 9.3	Continuum of Worry, Anxiety, or Fear Related to the Prospect of a Job Interview		
Anxiety Level	**Thoughts**	**Emotion**	**Behaviors**
Nonanxious	"I'm going on a job interview today. I hope they like me. I'm going to show them what I've got!"	Slight physical arousal but good alertness	Going to the job interview and performing well
Mild	"I'm going on a job interview today. I wonder if they will think badly of me. I hope my voice doesn't shake."	Mild physical arousal, perhaps feeling a bit tingly, but with good alertness	Going to the job interview but fidgeting a bit
Moderate	"Wow, I feel so nervous about that interview today. I bet I don't get the job. I wonder if I should just forget about it?"	Moderate physical arousal, including shaking and trembling, with a little more difficulty concentrating	Drafting two emails to cancel the interview but not sending them. Going to the interview but appearing physically nervous
Severe	"My God, that interview is today. I feel sick. I just don't think I can do this. They will think I'm an idiot!"	Severe physical arousal, including shaking, dizziness, and restlessness, with trouble concentrating	Postponing the interview twice before finally going; appearing quite agitated during the interview and unable to maintain eye contact
Extreme (anxiety disorder)	"No way can I do this. I'm a total loser. I can't get that job. Why even bother? I'll make a fool of myself and be embarrassed to show my face in public!"	Extreme physical arousal with dizziness, heart palpitations, shaking, and sweating, with great trouble concentrating	Canceling the interview and staying home all day

Overinclusiveness

With over 250 possible diagnoses, the DSM-5-TR cannot be faulted for being too limited! However, some feel that its scope is unnecessarily broad. For example, a host of difficulties that occasionally arise in childhood are included as mental disorders: the child who has dyslexia, speech problems such as stuttering, or great difficulties with arithmetic is given a DSM-5-TR diagnosis. But are these problems really mental *disorders*? Many question the appropriateness or benefit of labeling them as such. Another example is the inclusion of "premenstrual dysphoric disorder" as a diagnostic category. Many women objected to this diagnosis when it was first proposed in the DSM-IV, arguing that such a category could be used to discriminate against women and did not adequately capture those who have unusual sensitivity to physiological changes that occur during certain phases of the menstrual cycle.

Additional Concerns

The use of the DSM-5-TR raises a number of additional issues, such as how terms like "disorder" and "symptom" suggest the presence of a medical disease which is so far unsubstantiated. In addition, the DSM-5-TR caters to the public's desire to regard psychological problems as conditions that can be relieved simply with a pill, scalpel, or other medical device. Although such a view may be practical in dealing with medical problems, solving psychological problems usually requires hard work.

A final issue is that diagnosis can be harmful or even stigmatizing to the person who is labeled. Although antistigma campaigns to promote mental illnesses as "diseases like any other" have reduced society's tendency to blame individuals for their psychological problems, this has come at a high cost. For example, studies (see Lebowitz & Appelbaum [2019] for a review) show that the DSM-5-TR's biomedical model promotes **essentialism**—the view that those with psychiatric disorders are intrinsically different from everyone else. One effect of this is the general impression that mental illnesses are relatively untreatable. Another is reduced confidence in one's own ability to overcome such problems. Yet another is the desire for greater social distance from people with mental illness (Schomerus et al., 2012). Indeed, diagnosis seems to obscure the real person; observers see labels, not the people behind them (Deacon, 2013). Such labels can damage relationships; prevent people from being hired or promoted; keep them from seeking treatment; and in extreme cases, result in a loss of civil rights.

John Stillwell - PA Images/Getty Images

The Head Above Water sculpture created by British designer Steuart Padwick is part of London's mental health antistigma campaign. Despite such movements, research shows that people diagnosed with psychiatric disorders are viewed as inherently different than everyone else.

Think Like a Clinical Psychologist The stated aims of the modern DSM classification system (beginning with the DSM-III in 1980) were to improve the recognition, understanding, and treatment of mental illness. Do you believe these goals are being met? Are we winning the war on mental illness?

⦀ Research Domain Criteria (RDoC)

Various difficulties with the latest editions of the DSM, most notably their failure to base psychiatric diagnoses on objective measures (see IN HISTORICAL PERSPECTIVE: *The DSM and Psychiatric Diagnosis*), led to an initiative at the National Institute of Mental Health (NIMH) called the **Research Domain Criteria (RDoC)** (Insel et al., 2010). The goal of RDoC (pronounced "R-doc") is to promote research integrating genetics, neuroscience, and behavioral science, leading eventually to an objective diagnostic system of "biotypes" that align with effective (mainly biologically based) treatments (Cuthbert, 2020). As **Table 9.4** shows, the RDoC include six domains, each containing a set of constructs (which appear in **boldface** in the Description column of Table 9.4). Scientists seeking grant funding from the NIMH (which is by far the largest supporter of mental health research in the United States, if not the world) must explain how their research will help further the understanding of the genes, molecules, cells, brain circuits, physiology, behavior, and self-reported experiences associated with one or more RDoC domains and related constructs (rather than how it is relevant to DSM-5 disorders).

Table 9.4 **Summary of the RDoC Structure**	
Domain Name	**Description (and Constructs)**
Negative valence systems	Brain systems that control responses to adverse situations such as fear (**acute threat**), anxiety (**vague threat**), prolonged exposure to threat (**sustained threat**), grief and sad events (**loss**), and losing out on a potential reward (**frustrative nonreward**)
Positive valence systems	How the brain responds to receiving rewards (**reward responsiveness**), learns to adapt to reward contingencies (**reward learning**), and places values on rewards (**reward valuation**)
Cognitive systems	Brain processes that control awareness (**attention**), representations of the environment (**perception**), memory for facts (**declarative memory**), how we represent the world through verbal communication (**language**), decision-making processes (**cognitive control**), and short-term memory storage (**working memory**)
Social processes	The brain's regulation of how we relate to others, including developing social connections (**affiliation and attachment**), production and reception of verbal and nonverbal communication (**social communication**), self-awareness (**perception and understanding of oneself**), and awareness/understanding of others (**perception and understanding of others**)
Arousal and regulatory systems	The body's regulation of hunger, thirst, sleep, and sex (**arousal**); energy; physical/mental health (**circadian rhythms**); and sleep (**sleep/wakefulness**)
Sensorimotor systems	Processes responsible for learning to control and execute motor behaviors (**motor actions**)

To illustrate how the RDoC are intended to function differently than psychiatric diagnosis, imagine that you are experiencing extreme sadness most of the day nearly every day accompanied by a reduction in pleasurable activities, social interactions, appetite, and sleep. A clinician using the DSM-5-TR would diagnose you with depression, which would imply the presence of an illness requiring some form of psychological or medication treatment. The aim of RDoC, however, is to translate each of the signs and symptoms just mentioned to the framework in Table 9.4 (e.g., loss, motor actions, affiliation and attachment, arousal, sleep/wakefulness) so that these problems could be understood in terms of their corresponding neurobiological processes to determine the best treatment approach. Of course, such a system is only at the preliminary research phase at this point. The use of any framework resembling RDoC on a routine basis in clinical practice is still a long way off.

Compared to the DSM-5-TR's approach to diagnosis and classification, the RDoC structure has some advantages. For one thing, it is dimensional rather than categorical. That is, RDoC acknowledges that emotion and behavior occur along a continuum of severity, rather than categorizing individuals as either having a disorder or not (**Figure 9.2**). The RDoC approach also works from the ground up, starting with brain–behavior relationships and linking these to clinical signs and symptoms. On the other hand, the DSM-5-TR works from the top down, starting with categories and determining what fits into those categories. Finally, as an alternative to the DSM-5-TR's descriptive diagnostic system, the RDoC is clearly grounded in biological theory.

Figure 9.2 A Continuum Whereas the DSM-5-TR groups people into categories based on whether or not they meet certain diagnostic criteria, the Research Domain Criteria (RDoC) framework views clinical problems as existing on a continuum of severity. The latter approach is most consistent with research on psychopathology.

Yet there are also drawbacks of the RDoC project (Lilienfeld, 2014). First, it conceptualizes psychological signs and symptoms primarily as dysfunctions in brain systems even though specific biological causes of these problems have not been identified (e.g., Deacon, 2013). As such, it undervalues the role of empirically supported psychosocial, personality, and developmental processes, for example, by leaving little room for understanding the multicultural context of mental illness. Second, the RDoC initiative privileges biological methodology, such as neuroimaging (see A CLOSER LOOK: *Neuroimaging Research: Hope or Hype?* in Chapter 4, *The Science of Assessment*), and assumes that such tests and measures possess strong reliability and validity. Yet, research demonstrates that, for example, the test–retest reliability of functional magnetic resonance imaging (fMRI) measures — a major source of brain imaging data — is quite modest (.50 on average; e.g., Bennett & Miller, 2010).

A third limitation of the RDoC approach is that it assumes the identified domains and constructs are exclusively markers of psychological distress and dysfunction. But they are not. Indeed, people sometimes develop healthy manifestations of the domains and constructs in Table 9.4. Someone with high levels of negative emotionality (negative valence), for example, *may* manifest this predisposition in an anxiety disorder, yet may also express it in artistic productivity (Sheldon, 1994). Similarly, sensation seeking (arousal and reward valuation) can be manifested in destructive (e.g., crime, substance abuse) or constructive (e.g., firefighting, law enforcement) outlets depending on talents, interests, and other psychosocial and cultural factors (Harkness & Lilienfeld, 1997). Indeed, many prisoners and firefighters have the same levels of sensation-seeking (Zuckerman, 1994).

In conclusion, RDoC is presently a framework for research on psychological distress and dysfunction, rather than an alternative diagnostic system. It proposes variables for experimental studies organized around domains and constructs of functioning rather than traditional diagnostic categories. The value in this approach is that it brings together clinical and basic sciences to identify aspects of mental illness that span different areas including executive functioning, perception, and emotion. Its proponents hope that at some point, a critical mass of study findings guided by this agenda will be able to inform a new psychiatric diagnostic system based on objective biological factors.

Think Like a Clinical Psychologist The existing domains and constructs in the RDoC framework prioritize biological factors. If you were to add psychosocial domains and constructs, what would they be? How would cultural differences and experiences be reflected in the RDoC framework?

▥ Case Formulation

Suppose Shane meets the criteria for oppositional defiant disorder. This diagnosis tells us what signs and symptoms we can expect him to display. An RDoC approach might someday be able to identify biological correlates of these signs and symptoms. But neither of these approaches tells us much about the unique factors that drive this problem *for Shane in particular*. Although biological factors undoubtedly play some role, psychological problems develop and persist (and are treated) within personal, interpersonal, and cultural contexts. Therefore, clinical psychologists desire a richer understanding of the **mechanisms** at play within a particular person's problems. For example, understanding the various ways that Shane's parents reinforce his aggressive behavior (e.g., by yelling at him) helps with choosing an appropriate intervention (e.g., training his parents to intervene in more effective ways).

Accordingly, in place of (or along with) giving a DSM-5-TR diagnosis, clinical psychologists apply a **case formulation** approach when making sense of assessment data and deciding on appropriate treatment strategies for their clients. A case formulation is a hypothesis about the particular psychological mechanisms (e.g., cognitive styles, reinforcement contingencies, skill deficits) that give rise to and maintain an individual's psychological distress and dysfunction (Persons, 2012). Unlike the DSM-5-TR's descriptive and atheoretical diagnostic criteria, case formulation is principle-driven in

How a parent intervenes when a child misbehaves can shape the child's future behavior. Yelling, for example, can reinforce aggression.

that it is grounded in research-based psychological theories, such as classical and operant conditioning, and cognitive theory. As described next, such theories are used as "templates" for understanding client-specific assessment data.

Components of Case Formulation

Case formulation includes four elements: a problem list, mechanisms, predisposing factors, and precipitants. Within each element, psychologists make use of information collected using one or more of the assessment methods described in the preceding chapters.

Problem List

First, the psychologist and client (including the client's caretakers, if applicable) develop a **problem list**, outlining the presenting problems. These might include issues related to the client's own emotional or behavioral health (e.g., body image concerns, tantrums, feeling depressed), social or interpersonal functioning (e.g., frequent arguments with one's partner), or academic and occupational difficulties (e.g., poor grades or inadequate job performance). The problem list is usually kept to a maximum of five to eight items and is often developed using data from a clinical interview. The clinician might also select a relevant DSM-5-TR diagnosis at this point. Self-report questionnaires, testing data, and observational methods might be used to further assess the severity of the problem.

Hypotheses about Mechanisms

The clinician then chooses a conceptual model of the presenting problems (or diagnosis) to serve as a template for a working hypothesis about the factors that contribute to the cause and mainte-nance of each problem. For example, the cognitive model of emotion (e.g., Dobson et al., 2018) would lead to the hypothesis that a client's extreme sadness and loss of interest in fun activities (i.e., depression) is caused by overly general negative beliefs about herself, the world, and the future, such as "I'll always be a nobody." A behavioral model applied to the same individual would lead to the hypothesis that her depression is maintained by a lack of positive reinforcement, since she avoids enjoyable activities (Blakey et al., 2019). These hypotheses also inform decisions about how to address each problem in treatment. For example, negative interpretations could be addressed using cognitive therapy, and the lack of positive reinforcement, using behavioral activation.

Predisposing Factors

It may also be useful to generate hypotheses about the **predisposing factors** that may lead clients to develop their psychological problems. For example, perhaps the client's parents also suffered from depression, and she modeled their thinking and behavior patterns. Maybe she experienced an abusive childhood. Or, possibly there was a traumatic brain injury leading to neuropsychological changes. A careful assessment of the client's social and family history, including key events in upbringing or development, can help inform such hypotheses.

Precipitants

Precipitants are events that trigger or worsen the client's problem in the moment. They can be situational, such as being discriminated against, receiving bad news, or encountering a fear stimulus (e.g., a thunderstorm). They can also be internal, such as a sad memory, a distressing mental image, or uncomfortable body sensations. Clinicians use functional analysis (as described in Chapter 7, *Behavioral Assessment*) to assess precipitants and the sequence of events that leads to the presenting problem. As the client explains how the problem unfolds, the clinician considers how the process is tied to the hypothesized mechanisms.

Applying Case Formulation

Table 9.5 summarizes the four components, as well as how they apply to Shane and Kiara. Sample case formulations (a synthesis of the four elements) for these two individuals are shown in IN PRACTICE: *Sample Case Formulation* that follows.

Table 9.5	Components of a Case Formulation		
Component	**Definition**	**Shane**	**Kiara**
Problem list	Psychological signs and symptoms, and difficulties with various areas of life (e.g., social, academic)	• Aggressive behavior • Self-injury • Attention difficulties	• Obsessional fears of harm, mistakes, and contamination • Washing and checking compulsions • Depressed mood, sleep and appetite disturbance, tiredness and trouble concentrating at work
Mechanisms	Empirically supported factors that maintain the problem (e.g., cognitive distortions, classical conditioning)	• Behavioral reinforcement (i.e., attention) follows each act of aggression • Poor emotional understanding and inconsistent emotional expression • Family disruption	• Dysfunctional cognitions about intrusive thoughts, need for certainty, and responsibility lead to obsessional fear • Compulsions are maintained by negative reinforcement • Depressive symptoms result from negative cognitions about self and future • Trouble at work results from compulsive behaviors, fatigue
Predisposing factors	Factors that predispose the client to developing problems (e.g., traumatic brain injury, sexual abuse)	• Social withdrawal • Poor verbal skills	• Perfectionist and worry tendencies • New job • Family history of depression
Precipitants	Factors that trigger or worsen the client's problems (e.g., being turned down for a date)	• Aggressive behavior occurs when lonely or isolated	• Working with clients • Recording information in charts • Thoughts/reminders of germs and mistakes

> **In Practice** **Sample Case Formulation**
>
> **Shane**
>
> Shane exhibits symptoms of oppositional defiant disorder as well as attention deficit–hyperactivity disorder. There are several theoretical models available to help develop hypotheses regarding causal and maintaining mechanisms. Research most clearly supports mechanisms that involve Shane's social environment and cognitive biases that have led to his behaviors, consistent with a behavioral and cognitive-behavioral framework. Operant conditioning principles would help explain how Shane's disruptive behavior is positively reinforced by attention from his mother, and his mother's attention (i.e., yelling) is negatively reinforced by the cessation of his disruptive behavior. Cognitive models may be used to hypothesize that Shane's difficulties with his peers are explained and maintained by a hostile attribution bias, or a tendency to assume that others are being mean to him even when they are not. This bias may lead Shane to act aggressively toward his peers in ways that others feel is unprovoked. Ongoing negative feedback from peers and from teachers following moments when he is unable to sustain attention may lead Shane to develop negative feelings about himself, which could increase his risk for depression.
>
> **Kiara**
>
> Kiara's difficulties fit squarely within the DSM-5-TR categories of OCD and major depressive disorder. Accordingly, her psychologist chose well-researched cognitive-behavioral models of these problems (e.g., Abramowitz, 2006; Dobson et al., 2018) as conceptual templates for understanding the causal and maintaining mechanisms. From this perspective, Kiara's obsessional fear arises when various situational triggers provoke unpleasant intrusive thoughts (e.g., about harm, mistakes, and germs) that she had learned to interpret as danger signals. Such misinterpretations arise from core dysfunctional beliefs about the need for certainty, overestimates of threat and responsibility, and the importance of thoughts. Indeed, Kiara had always been a "worrier" and "perfectionist," which suggests a long-standing tendency toward catastrophic thinking and intolerance of uncertainty. Starting a new job as a nurse in a demanding environment likely further activated her inflated sense of responsibility and need for certainty. According to this model, Kiara's compulsive rituals were negatively reinforced by the reduction in distress they engendered and thus developed into strong behavioral tendencies. Yet, the more Kiara performed these rituals, the more she (mistakenly) associated them with the non-occurrence of disasters. Thus, her rituals prevented her from learning that (a) her obsessional thoughts are not predictors of danger and (b) she can manage anxiety without the rituals. The result was a vicious cycle of obsessional thoughts and rituals that led to functional interference and overly negative beliefs about herself and her future (e.g., hopelessness), resulting in depression and the associated symptoms of fatigue, loss of appetite, and loss of interest. ■■■

Multicultural Considerations

As we have discussed, cultural factors can play a role in the origins of hypothesized mechanisms and predisposing factors, such as cognitive schemas and dysfunctional beliefs. Thus, it is critical that the case formulation reflect sociocultural variables such as racial and ethnic identity, religious beliefs, gender identity, sexual preference, socioeconomic status, sociocultural values (e.g., historical experience of client's cultural group), and the degree of assimilation or acculturation. Psychologists therefore make sure to assess these variables, and their effects on the elements of the case formulation, during the clinical interview. Psychologists also consider the context in which behavior occurs, recognizing that opportunities, privileges, and experiences vary based on systemic factors that can change experiences in meaningful and impactful ways for different people. Behaviors that might be considered atypical in one community (e.g., running away from police, even in the absence of illegal behavior) may be considered adaptive in another community; thus, assessment and conceptualization of behavior must be considered within a broad context.

An Iterative Approach

Recall that the case formulation is a *hypothesis*. Thus, once it is complete, the psychologist puts it to the test by gathering additional assessment data. For example, a college student with severe stuttering might be asked to keep track of certain situations, thoughts, behaviors, and emotions to test out the hypothesis that his stuttering is exacerbated in situations where he is anxious and thinking that others are judging him harshly. If the information gathered reveals that this formulation is correct, then it is appropriate to move forward with the suggested intervention (e.g., cognitive therapy to address dysfunctional thinking patterns). On the other hand, if the client's self-monitoring reveals that his stuttering is precipitated by other factors, such as feeling exhausted as a result of poor sleep, the psychologist would revise the formulation and treatment plan accordingly (e.g., improving sleep hygiene to address insomnia). We refer to this process of testing and revising the formulation as *iterative* in that it is repeated throughout the course of treatment, especially if the client's problems do not seem to respond to the chosen intervention. Sometimes the process needs to recur multiple times (iterations) until the client and clinician are satisfied with the treatment response.

Evaluation of the Case Formulation Approach

As with psychiatric diagnosis and RDoC, the case formulation approach has its strengths and limitations. On the plus side, it is rooted in cognitive and behavioral theory, which is strongly supported by a large body of clinical research. Case formulation is also tailored to the individual client, rather than assuming that all clients with a particular problem are identical. Related to this, case formulation takes into account the role of sociocultural factors in the development, maintenance, and treatment of psychological problems. Another advantage of the case formulation approach is that (like RDoC) it assumes psychological "typicality" and "atypicality" exist on a continuum, rather than having a natural boundary. That is, it accepts that the psychological mechanisms governing extreme thoughts, emotions, and behaviors (as in Table 9.3) are the same as those governing mild levels of these phenomena. A final advantage is the iterative approach. If the client does not respond to the indicated treatment, the clinician can "go back to the drawing board" to see whether something was missed in the initial formulation, collect additional data, modify the working hypotheses, and adjust the treatment plan as needed.

That said, there is relatively little research evaluating case formulation in and of itself (Bieling & Kuyken, 2003). For example, its reliability is largely unknown: can different clinicians examining the same client derive the same case formulations and treatment plans? Similarly, although some studies have addressed its validity (e.g., Litt et al., 2019), important questions remain largely unanswered: how useful is case formulation in practice? What is the relationship between a formulation and treatment outcome? Although many clinical psychologists *assume* the reliability and validity of this conceptually and logically consistent approach, the strongest support for its treatment utility comes from the method's reliance on evidence-based theories that are used as templates for hypotheses about mechanisms and treatments. A related limitation is that in order to accurately formulate a client's problems, clinicians must keep up to date on the relevant psychological theories.

Think Like a Clinical Psychologist Choose one of your own behavior patterns (perhaps one that you would like to change) and use what you know about psychological theory to conduct a case formulation. What are the mechanisms, predisposing factors, and precipitants of the behavior? What cultural factors might be involved? If you wanted to change this behavior, how does your case formulation suggest you do so?

▥ Developing and Communicating the Treatment Plan

The ultimate function of assessment, diagnosis, and case formulation is to guide effective treatment. The DSM-5-TR addresses this by identifying a "disorder" to remedy, whereas RDoC aspires to isolate biological targets for biological treatments. Case formulation pinpoints causal and maintenance processes that become targets for indicated interventions, which might be psychological or biological. In this section, we cover how psychologists form treatment plans and communicate them to their clients.

Treatment Planning

Treatment planning is the process of using a case formulation to guide the selection of an intervention. In providing a best guess hypothesis about what causes and maintains the target problems, the formulation allows psychologists to devise a general "flight plan" for a course of treatment. This plan includes specific interventions known to address the hypothesized mechanisms identified in the case formulation. The examples of Shane and Kiara shown in IN PRACTICE: *Treatment Planning* illustrate this process.

In Practice   Treatment Planning

Shane

Shane's formulation pointed to contextual factors in his social environment (e.g., his mother's yelling) that are maintaining his behavior. Treatment therefore may involve educating Shane's mother about the reinforcing effects of even punitive behaviors, and helping her develop a plan for providing positive reinforcement in moments when Shane is exhibiting behavior she would like to see more of. Similarly, Shane's mother can be instructed how to interact in a nonreinforcing way (e.g., by ignoring or using a time out) when Shane exhibits undesirable behavior. To address the cognitive roots of Shane's behavior (e.g., his tendency to assume hostile intent among others), Shane's therapist would likely help Shane better encode or notice all social cues around him before jumping to a conclusion or interpretation of others' intent. His therapist also could help Shane consider a variety of alternative interpretations and use observable data (rather than his emotional "gut" assumptions) to confirm or disconfirm each of these possible interpretations. In treatment, Shane would eventually learn to use this process to think differently about his social interactions, generate and consider a wide variety of possible responses to social situations, and practice more appropriate ways of interacting with peers, either in role plays with his therapist, or in "real life" in the community during each session.

Kiara

Kiara's formulation suggested that the combination of exposure therapy and response prevention could be helpful in reducing her obsessional fear and compulsive ritualizing (as this is the recommended treatment for individuals with a diagnosis of OCD; e.g., Abramowitz & Buchholz, 2020). Specifically, this cognitive-behavioral intervention involves repeatedly confronting feared situations and intrusive thoughts (exposure) while resisting urges to perform compulsive rituals (response prevention). The goal of these procedures is to teach the client new information, in Kiara's case that (a) the likelihood of harm, mistakes, and contamination is lower than she predicts; (b) she can manage obsessional doubt and uncertainty without the need for rituals; and (c) feelings of anxiety are safe and manageable. The formulation also suggested that acceptance and commitment therapy (ACT) could be used to help Kiara change her relationship to her intrusive thoughts and anxiety so that when these private experiences show up for her, she can continue to "be in the moment" without having to spend extra time and effort trying to control or dismiss them. Given that Kiara's depression was hypothesized to result from the functional interference associated with OCD symptoms, it was predicted that reducing her obsessional fear and compulsive rituals would lead to a reduction in depressive symptoms as well. ▬▬

Communicating the Treatment Plan

Once the clinician has arrived at a treatment plan, the next step is to describe it for the client and provide a rationale for the chosen approach. This discussion begins with an explanation of the client's diagnosis (if applicable) and case formulation.

Next, the clinician describes the recommended treatment approach and provides a clear rationale with a description of the risks and benefits. This rationale helps increase the client's buy-in to the suggested treatment by giving them confidence that the therapist truly understands their difficulties and will provide an intervention that addresses them.

Lastly, the psychologist explains the logistics of treatment and obtains the client's (or a caregiver's) agreement and informed consent to proceed. It is also important to clarify that the treatment plan is tentative and may include alternatives that need further discussion. If medication is recommended, the psychologist provides a referral to a psychiatrist (if the client is not already in touch with a physician). Sometimes clients want to think over treatment suggestions, get more information, or talk with family members. Finally, it may be tempting to provide false reassurance at this point, such as "Everything is going to be okay." Yet, it is improper (and indeed unethical) to make such guarantees. A better approach is to let the client know that you have a sound plan for treatment and are looking forward to working together as a team to overcome the problem.

IN PRACTICE: *Communicating the Treatment Plan for Kiara* illustrates how Kiara's therapist relayed this information to Kiara.

In Practice   **Communicating the Treatment Plan for Kiara**

[Explanation of diagnosis and case formulation] *Now that I've had a chance to consider all of the assessment information you've given me, I'd like to give you my impressions and recommendations for moving forward. As you already know, you meet the criteria for a diagnosis of OCD, and your symptoms fall within the moderately severe range. You also* *meet criteria for a diagnosis of depression, which seems to be related to how much the OCD symptoms cause distress and get in the way of your functioning. But let's talk about what this all means. When a person has OCD, they take normal, benign unwanted thoughts — like the ones you have about mistakes, harm, and contamination — and misinterpret them as signaling a real threat. This leads to obsessional fear and doubt, which provoke the urge to do compulsive rituals like washing and checking to remove the perceived threat. Yet while these rituals temporarily reassure you and make you feel less afraid, they don't work in the long run because sooner or later the unwanted thoughts and anxiety return and you're back to doing more and more rituals. Plus, all the rituals keep you from learning two things: first, that the obsessional thoughts and fears are not as threatening as they seem — things would be okay even if you didn't do the rituals — and second, that you could manage the feelings of anxiety and doubt. As a result, you get caught in a vicious cycle of obsessing and ritualizing.*

[Recommended treatment with clear rationale] Although we don't understand all the factors that <u>cause</u> OCD, effective treatment relies more on understanding how OCD <u>works</u>; and this is something we understand very well. The most effective treatment for OCD is called <u>exposure and response prevention</u>. It involves practice with confronting situations and thoughts that provoke obsessional fear without doing rituals so that you can learn that these situations and thoughts are not threatening and that you don't need rituals for everything to be okay. In particular, you might practice entering data into a patient's chart without the extra checking for mistakes, and then going home and deliberately thinking about the mistakes you <u>could</u> have made. When this provokes the urge to go back to work and check, you would practice refraining from this ritual so you can learn not only that things with your patient are likely to turn out okay but that you can manage the anxiety and uncertainty of the situation without the wasteful checking rituals.

Now, as you can imagine, this treatment is hard work and you can expect to feel pretty anxious when you try these exercises. Of course, that's the goal. As your therapist, my job is to coach you through this anxiety; and with lots of practice you will see that it gets easier. In time, you'll feel less and less like you need to perform rituals, which will create less interference in your daily life and help you feel more hopeful about things. What questions do you have?

[Logistics of treatment and consent to proceed] If you decide you'd like to begin treatment, we will spend the first few sessions developing a list of situations to practice for exposure and a list of rituals to work on resisting. Then each week we'll practice with a different situation, and I will ask you to continue practicing between our appointments. Of course, I'll never force you to do any exposures or response prevention. But I will challenge you to do these things because I know how helpful they can be. In most cases, I meet with clients for anywhere between 12 and 20 weekly sessions. Treatment will end when we both agree that the OCD symptoms have decreased to the point that they are not interfering with your life or causing you distress. Finally, although research shows that this treatment can work really well, I can't guarantee what your outcome will be. I can, however, tell you that the more work you put into it, the more you're likely to get out of it. So, what do you think about this plan? What questions can I answer for you? How do you feel about proceeding? ▬

Monitoring Progress

As treatment proceeds, the therapist and client collect data to test the formulation and monitor the process and outcome of therapy. Some data are collected formally, using the assessment methods described in previous chapters (e.g., self-report questionnaires and behavioral approach tasks [BATs]). Other data may be collected informally using observations or client verbal report. Collecting these data allows the client and psychologist to track the extent to which the target problem is improving and whether the hypothesized maintenance processes are changing as expected. If the outcome is poor, the psychologist collects additional data to get information about what might be interfering with progress and evaluate whether the case formulation or treatment plan needs to be modified. Thus, as mentioned earlier in this chapter, treatment is part of an iterative process where each client is treated like a case study in which the formulation is the hypothesis being tested. Monitoring progress also strengthens the relationship between psychologist and client by building a shared evidence-based collaboration. It also helps the clinician identify any problems so they can be addressed before treatment is undermined. Kiara's psychologist, for example, asked Kiara to complete the Obsessive Compulsive Inventory and Beck Depression Inventory at every other appointment to assess her progress.

Think Like a Clinical Psychologist The example you read in the preceding section applies to an adult with a diagnosis of OCD. Discuss any modifications you would make to the treatment description and rationale if the client were a child, such as Shane. For example, what kind of language would you use? Would you include a parent in the discussion? If so, how would you handle confidentiality?

▥ Chapter Summary

Clinical psychologists have abandoned terms such as "normal" and "abnormal" when referring to behavior, cognition, emotion, and people. These terms elude clear definition, are disparaging, and overlook the diversity in human experience and culture that provides a context for psychological distress and dysfunction. The DSM is the most widely used system for diagnosing and classifying psychiatric disorders. Yet DSM-5-TR disorders are defined not by objective tests as in other areas of medicine but rather by descriptions of signs and symptoms. This descriptive approach opens the DSM-5-TR up to criticism from various angles. For example, its reliability is questionable, as different clinicians interviewing the same client often disagree over some of the most common diagnoses. Threats to validity include the descriptive and ambiguous diagnostic criteria, the undervaluation of multiculturalism, and the categorical nature of DSM-5-TR diagnoses.

Backlash against the DSM by some researchers led to the development of the RDoC as an alternative way of conceptualizing mental illness. This investigational agenda focuses on identifying the biological correlates of key domains of psychological functioning. Although the RDoC improves upon the DSM by assuming a dimensional perspective, its strong emphasis on neurobiology raises other concerns, including the lack of evidence for biological causes of mental illness and the lack of consideration for well-established psychosocial and multicultural influences on mental functioning.

The case formulation approach allows the clinician to understand clients' presenting problems within the context of their individual background, as well as within the framework of empirically supported psychological theories. Case formulations function as hypotheses about the causes and maintaining factors of target problems, and inform the selection of interventions with research supporting their efficacy in modifying these factors to achieve improvement. The process of treatment planning involves designing an intervention based on the case formulation, informing the client of the process and rationale for treatment, and choosing strategies for assessing progress.

Applying What You've Learned

Exercise 1: Describe how you might integrate data on the RDoC domains of psychopathology into the case formulation process. Which of these domains seem most relevant to a case formulation for an adult with an anxiety disorder, and why?

Exercise 2: What kinds of assessment data would you collect, and from whom, to monitor treatment progress for an adult suffering from depression? How often would you collect these data, and why?

Key Terms

Associated feature: Aspect of a psychiatric disorder such as its prevalence, course, prognostic factors, or common co-occurring diagnoses.

Case formulation: A hypothesis about the particular psychological mechanisms, grounded in research-based theories, that give rise to and maintain an individual's psychological distress and dysfunction.

Cultural syndrome: Signs and symptoms of psychopathology that are restricted to a limited number of cultures.

Descriptive diagnosis: The use of signs and symptoms to identify psychiatric disorders because there are no definitive causes or objective tests for these disorders.

DSM-5-TR: Official diagnostic and classification system for mental disorders.

Essentialism: The view that those with psychiatric disorders are intrinsically different from everyone else.

Mechanism: Empirically supported factor that maintains the problematic behavior, cognitions, and emotions of a client.

Mental disorder: According to the DSM-5-TR, a syndrome characterized by clinically significant disturbance in an individual's cognition, emotion

regulation, or behavior that reflects a dysfunction in the psychological, biological, or developmental processes underlying mental functioning. Usually associated with significant distress or disability in social, occupational, or other important activities.

Precipitant: Factor that triggers or worsens the client's problems.

Predisposing factor: Factor that makes the client more susceptible to developing problems.

Problem list: First step in a case formulation. The psychologist and client develop a list of presenting problems; the list is usually kept to five to eight items and is often developed using data from a clinical interview.

Research Domain Criteria (RDoC): System designed to promote research integrating genetics, neuroscience, and behavioral science leading eventually to an objective diagnostic system of "biotypes" that align with effective (mainly biologically based) treatments.

Sign: Outwardly observable phenomenon.

Symptom: Subjective experience reported by the client.

Treatment planning: Process of using a case formulation to guide the selection of an intervention.

CONNECT ONLINE:

 Check out our videos and additional resources located at: www.macmillanlearning.com

Psychological Treatment: Science and Practice

FOCUS QUESTIONS

1. What are different ways to assess whether a psychological treatment works?
2. What is the difference between the efficacy and effectiveness of a psychological treatment?
3. What are the specific factors in psychological treatments and how are they different from nonspecific factors?
4. Explain the concepts of evidence-based treatment and evidence-based practice.
5. What are the complications that arise with disseminating psychological treatments, and how are these complications overcome?

CHAPTER OUTLINE

As we have seen, the primary purpose of assessment, diagnosis, and case formulation is to guide **psychological treatment** — the most common professional activity of clinical psychologists. There are several approaches or "schools" of treatment, which we will cover closely in the chapters that follow. The present chapter, however, provides an overview of important questions relevant across the different interventions, including the following: how do we define psychotherapy and psychological treatment? How well does it work? How do we know that it works? For whom does it work? and Why does it work? You will learn the answers to these questions through the lens of treatment outcome research, which seeks scientific data on the efficacy and effectiveness of psychological interventions. You will also learn about the general process of treatment from the perspective of the client. Over the past century, psychological scientists have built an impressive empirical database to guide psychological practice, and although some clinicians do not heed its findings, others in the field are working hard to ensure that adults and children with psychological problems have access to the most effective interventions, including people from all racial, ethnic, and sociocultural backgrounds.

▥ Defining Psychotherapy and Psychological Treatment

Psychotherapy refers to methods of inducing changes in a person's behavior, thoughts, or feelings with the aim of improving their mental or physical health and related functioning. But, you might ask, how is this any different from talking with a family member, close friend, teacher, or even a bartender? Psychotherapy involves intervention in the context of a confidential professional relationship initiated by the client or the client's guardians. In some cases, it is undertaken to solve a specific problem or to improve the individual's capacity to deal with existing behaviors, feelings, or thoughts that impair functioning at work, at school, or in relationships. In other cases, the focus is on the prevention of problems. In still other instances, the focus is on increasing the person's ability to "get more out of life."

Over the years many definitions of psychotherapy have been offered. Perhaps the most widely used is that provided by Jerome Frank (1982):

> Psychotherapy is a planned, emotionally charged, confiding interaction between a trained, socially sanctioned healer and a sufferer. During this interaction the healer seeks to relieve the sufferer's distress and disability through symbolic communications, primarily words but also sometimes bodily activities. The healer may or may not involve the patient's relatives and others in the healing rituals. Psychotherapy also often includes helping the patient to accept and endure suffering as an inevitable aspect of life that can be used as an opportunity for personal growth. (p. 10)

SDI Productions/E+/Getty Images

Psychological treatment involves a client and clinician working together using scientifically supported interventions to understand and solve the client's particular problems.

As you probably noticed, Frank's definition is a very broad and general one. More recently, Barlow (2004) suggested that it is important to differentiate between therapeutic procedures and techniques that are supported by research and the more generic forms of psychotherapy that are less well studied. So, he proposed that clinical psychologists use the term "psychological treatment" when referring to interventions that are (a) derived from psychological science, (b) tailored to the psychological processes that cause and maintain particular problems and disorders, and (c) shown to work in controlled treatment outcome studies (see A CLOSER LOOK: *"Psychological Treatment" versus "Psychotherapy": What's in a Name?*).

A Closer Look — "Psychological Treatment" Versus "Psychotherapy": What's in a Name?

As you may have noticed, when we refer to the services that clinical psychologists provide we typically use the terms "psychological treatment" and "psychological intervention," as opposed to "psychotherapy" or "talk therapy." Sure, these names all sound alike — and people often use them interchangeably — but they actually mean different things. Let us explain.

"Psychological treatment" (or "psychological intervention") describes specific research-supported techniques and procedures that are grounded in psychological theory and derived from models of psychopathology to target particular causal or maintenance mechanisms and improve specific aspects of psychological, emotional, behavioral, or physical health and related functioning. An example is the use of cognitive interventions to correct dysfunctional beliefs that lead to disruptive emotions, such as depression, anxiety, and anger. Another is behavioral activation, which increases engagement with pleasurable activities, thereby improving one's mood. These two interventions have been rigorously studied, leading to an understanding of (a) *how well* they work and (b) the *mechanisms* by which they work. Clinical psychologists are trained not only in how to implement psychological treatments with clients but also to understand the conceptual basis for using such interventions and the degree of empirical support that they have.

"Psychotherapy" (or "talk therapy"), on the other hand, is a much broader term for a variety of tools and strategies that mental health (and sometimes medical) professionals and **paraprofessionals** might use when working with their clients. These therapies may or may not be derived from psychological theory and have generally not have been tested scientifically (or shown to be effective in rigorously conducted studies). Examples include giving advice about whether or not to stay in a relationship, providing support to someone who is grieving the loss of a loved one, and using descriptions of one's dreams to explain the roots of a particular problem. Rather than targeting particular psychological mechanisms, psychotherapy provides more general support and guidance to help clients solve problems, make decisions, understand themselves, or feel validated. ■■■

There are countless different "brands" of psychotherapy — perhaps as many as 600 specific types — many of which meet none of Barlow's (2004) criteria for consideration as "psychological treatments." Those that do satisfy these criteria can be distilled down to four major (yet overlapping) approaches: behavioral, cognitive-behavioral, dialectical, and mindfulness/acceptance-based. You will learn about the framework, goals, and specific procedures within each approach in Chapter 11, *Behavioral Interventions*; Chapter 12, *Cognitive-Behavioral Interventions*; and Chapter 13, *Acceptance, Mindfulness, and Dialectical Interventions*, respectively. In Chapter 15, *Group, Family, and Couple-Based Interventions*, we will see how these approaches can be delivered in groups and with couples, and adapted to address interpersonal problems. Two additional "schools" of therapy, psychodynamic and client-centered (also called humanistic), are of historical significance and only partially meet Barlow's criteria;

yet remain in use among some clinical psychologists today. We cover these approaches in Chapter 14, *Early Approaches to Psychotherapy: Psychodynamic and Client-Centered Perspectives*. **Table 10.1** briefly summarizes these major approaches.

Table 10.1 Major Approaches to Psychological Treatment	
Approach	**Description**
Behavioral	Uses techniques derived from learning theory to modify behaviors associated with target problems
Cognitive-behavioral	Focuses on identifying and modifying maladaptive thinking and behavior patterns that maintain target problems
Dialectical	Focuses on developing skills for coping with stress, regulating strong emotions, and improving relationships with others
Mindfulness/Acceptance	Uses metaphors and experiential exercises based on relational frame theory to promote a healthier relationship with unwanted thoughts and feelings
Psychodynamic	Focuses on gaining insight into unconscious psychological forces thought to underlie target problems
Client-centered (Humanistic)	Uses the client–therapist relationship and unconditional positive regard to promote full growth potential

As you can see in Table 10.1, the various approaches include more or less unique therapeutic techniques and procedures derived from different perspectives on psychological problems and disorders. To illustrate, behavioral approaches directly target the problem identified by the client (along with other difficulties that might contribute to the primary problem). So, a behavioral intervention for Shane might involve identifying the antecedents and consequences of his oppositional behavior and training his parents to use appropriate contingencies to reinforce more desirable conduct. In contrast, humanistic therapy looks to help clients achieve their full potential. So, a psychologist using this approach might explore factors thought to stifle Shane's social connections and sense of purpose, and address them with empathy, unconditional positive regard, and genuineness to promote personality and behavioral change (Sharf, 2012). Later in this chapter, we will study what a course of treatment entails. But first, let's examine the effects of *psychological interventions* and how researchers determine whether they work.

Think Like a Clinical Psychologist In some cultures, it's considered trendy to seek treatment for a mental health issue. In others, however, this is frowned upon. There are also generational differences in how psychological treatment is perceived. Why do you think this is? What is your own perspective, and how has that been shaped by your own background?

▥ Do Psychological Treatments Work?

Although this might seem like a straightforward question, the answer is not so simple. As with other areas of psychology, only carefully conducted research can inform us of whether, and how well, treatments for psychological problems work, or for whom they are most likely to work. It is not enough to treat a group of clients, determine that they seem to be getting better, and then conclude that treatment is effective. Is your assessment biased? Would the clients have improved on their own even without therapy? Was the improvement due to the techniques you employed, or was the crucial factor the mere presence of a warm, interested person who listened? The study of psychological treatments and their effects is a broad field with its own methodologies and controversies, as we will see next. The field also has a rich history, which places these methods and controversies in context (see IN HISTORICAL PERSPECTIVE: *The Study of Psychological Treatments*).

Whom Should We Ask?

Because of the inherent subjectivity in assessing psychological functioning, one methodological question concerns the source of the information; that is, *who is in the best position to say whether a treatment is working?* Hans Strupp, a renowned treatment researcher, suggested that three different parties, each with their own investment in the outcome of treatment, might have different perspectives (Strupp and Hadley, 1977). One party (of course) is the *client*. Indeed, the goal of treatment is to improve clients' functioning and so their opinion about their own progress is obviously important . . . but it is also biased. A client with social anxiety, for example, might shy away from giving any negative feedback and thus report doing well even when there's been little change. Someone with depression who experiences hopelessness and helplessness might vastly underestimate the benefits of treatment and report doing poorly despite making great strides. Conversely, clients with high hopes of improvement—perhaps due to their investment of time, effort, and money in the treatment process—might overestimate treatment gains.

So, why not just ask the *clinician*? Psychologists, as we have seen, have the necessary training and expertise to objectively assess mental health. Yet, a practitioner's perspective can also be misleading. Consider that psychologists observe only a sliver of their clients' lives and therefore depend on client reporting (which can be inaccurate, as we just noted) to estimate functioning outside of treatment sessions. Clinicians can also fall prey to unintentional self-serving biases, such as the tendency to overestimate or underestimate their own skills as a treatment provider.

Finally, we might consider the perspectives of "third parties" who have a stake in the client's progress, such a parent, a partner, a teacher, an employer, the legal system, or the insurance provider that is footing the bill for treatment. Yet while asking such individuals or groups about progress might circumvent some of the limitations mentioned above, it raises other concerns. For example, the insurance provider might be motivated to overestimate treatment effects so as to minimize their own costs. And overly concerned family members might underestimate how their loved ones are progressing. Because there are benefits and drawbacks to assessing progress by asking each of the three "parties" discussed above, researchers conducting studies and clinicians who desire the best estimate of a client's response often consider information obtained from multiple informants.

How Should We Ask?

As you read about in Chapters 4–8, a variety of standardized, reliable, and valid methods are available for assessing psychological and behavioral phenomena, and these instruments often

● € ℃ ◖ ◙ In Historical Perspective

The Study of Psychological Treatments

The history of research on psychotherapy can be divided into four phases (Braakmann, 2015), as we describe here.

1920–1954: The Birth of Psychotherapy Research

Although Freud (Breuer & Freud, 1895/1955) published a number of detailed individual case reports, it wasn't until the 1920s that systematic research on the outcome of psychotherapy appeared with any regularity in scientific journals. Data for these early studies were collected in psychiatric institutions (such as the Menninger Clinic) that had begun to document their clients' progress. But most of these early studies were very basic and focused solely on therapist-perceived improvement. Moreover, diagnoses were vague and the samples were small and heterogeneous, which prohibited strong conclusions about treatment effects.

During this period, Carl Rogers and his team (Rogers et al., 1942; Snyder, 1945) also began examining recordings of treatment sessions and found

Hans Eysenck's provocative 1952 article "The effects of psychotherapy: an evaluation" challenged the field of clinical psychology to more rigorously examine the outcomes of its interventions before assuming that they work.

(among other things) that acceptance and clarification of feelings led to a higher degree of client insight than did psychodynamic interpretations by the therapist. These contributions helped highlight the significance of research on psychotherapy, as well as the importance of understanding the factors that lead to successful outcomes.

The end of this period, however, was marked by a bombshell scientific article by Hans Eysenck (1952), who analyzed data from several existing studies and concluded that psychotherapy was of little benefit. He argued that any improvement observed was likely due to natural fluctuations in the severity of clients' problems — what's known as *spontaneous remission*. While some vigorously challenged Eysenck's provocative assertions, the field as a whole took them as a challenge to improve not only the effects of psychotherapies but also the methodology used to study them (Rosenzweig, 1954).

1955–1969: Advancing Process Research

Rising to Eysenck's challenge, the next period of time saw more sophisticated psychotherapy research. For example, simple case studies were replaced by controlled trials and rather than only considering the clinician's judgment of improvement, studies included self-report and observational measures. Specific primary outcomes (e.g., number of panic attacks) and secondary outcomes (e.g., depressive symptoms, functional interference) were also identified and carefully assessed as dependent variables in studies. Another advance was the emphasis on **process research**, which focuses on the mechanisms responsible for improvement (e.g., communication patterns between therapists and clients; Saslow and Matarazzo, 1962).

Finally, the collection of large datasets allowed treatment researchers to begin examining the factors that predict a good or poor outcome.

1970–1984: Expansion and Refinement

During this period, outcome and process research continued to grow, and methodology continued to improve. One specific advance was a more careful study of the client–therapist relationship (termed the "working alliance") and its influence on outcome (Bordin, 1979). Another direction was the increased precision of **outcome measures**, which became increasingly comprehensive, reliable, and valid (Waskow & Parloff, 1975). A significant milestone was the development of meta-analysis (as described in the *Treatment Efficacy* section of this chapter). The first psychotherapy meta-analysis included 475 studies (Smith et al., 1980) and clearly showed that treatment was superior to no treatment (and to control conditions), finally putting to rest Eysenck's earlier claims. Yet, this study (along with others; e.g., Luborsky et al., 1975) surprisingly found that the different types of treatment all seemed equally effective — a phenomenon which became known as the *Dodo bird verdict* (see the *Common Factors* section in this chapter) and touched off debates about the relative importance of specific and common factors in psychological treatment that continue to this day.

1984–Present: The Embrace (and Discard?) of The Medical Model

Publication of the DSM-III in 1980 paved the way for treatment researchers to develop and evaluate the efficacy of specific interventions for particular psychological problems and disorders. The *randomized controlled trial* (RCT; as described in the *Treatment Efficacy* section of this chapter) was adopted as the gold standard study design because it optimizes internal validity. This ever-growing body of literature differentiated between the effects of specific schools of therapy and became the foundation for lists of **empirically supported treatments (ESTs)** and disorder-based treatment guidelines (e.g., Chambless & Ollendick, 2001). Critics, however, questioned the applicability of RCTs (and therefore such guidelines) to "real-world" (nonresearch) settings (e.g., Persons & Silberschatz, 1998), which led to effectiveness studies that evaluate how treatments perform in the "real world."

Others have criticized the RCT approach on the grounds that it aligns with the DSM's dubious classification and diagnosis scheme (e.g., Deacon, 2013). This has motivated some researchers to focus on evaluating empirically supported principles of change (e.g., extinction, behavioral activation) that can be applied to maladaptive psychological processes (as opposed to disorders) (e.g., Hofmann, 2020). Indeed, one group of scientists has distilled the core ingredients of effective treatments into a unified protocol intended to address the core psychological processes underlying a broad range of emotional problems and disorders (Barlow & Farchione, 2017).

This most recent phase of treatment research has seen studies evaluating online and Internet-assisted versions of empirically supported treatment to help disseminate these interventions to individuals in rural communities and those not able to attend traditional office-based sessions. Researchers have also noted that the general lack of diversity in study participants limits the generalizability of existing psychological interventions. As a result, they have stepped up efforts not only to increase the diversity in study samples but also to develop and evaluate culturally sensitive versions of effective treatments. ∎

serve as dependent variables in treatment outcome studies. Yet, what would happen if we used an interview or self-report questionnaire to ask Shane about his aggressive behavior? If he is even aware of how often such behavior occurs, he might understate its frequency to avoid looking bad. Therefore, direct observations of his conduct at school would provide a more accurate picture of any changes occurring as a result of treatment. On the other hand, self-report and interview assessments would be absolutely necessary in assessing changes in Kiara's obsessional thinking and anxiety, since these private experiences cannot be directly observed. You can see how important it is for researchers to consider how they measure treatment response, as this will impact study results.

When Should We Ask?

Another consideration is the point at which a researcher or clinician measures treatment response. It's usually desirable to include a *pretreatment* assessment of client functioning to serve as a baseline for comparison after treatment. But at what point do we measure progress? One possibility is right when treatment ends, or what is called *posttreatment*. But wouldn't we also want to know whether (and for how long) the benefits of treatment last beyond the final therapy session? For this reason, studies often include *follow-up* assessments at some point weeks, months, or even years after treatment has ended (e.g., Lemmens et al., 2019). Still other studies are interested in the changes that take place *during* psychological treatment and may assess progress at each session (e.g., Buchholz et al., 2019). So, depending on the aims of the particular study (or a practicing clinician), psychologists need to think carefully about *when* they measure the effects of treatment.

Treatment *Efficacy*

The **efficacy** of a treatment refers to how well it performs in research studies. But different study designs can be used to answer different questions about the effects of therapy, and each design has its strengths and limitations. *Case studies*, in which a single client is measured repeatedly over the course of treatment, offer rich detail when investigating a new or experimental technique. Yet, we cannot assume that results from a single client will *generalize* to other individuals with similar problems. *Single group pre–post* studies, in which a larger group of clients with the same problem all receive the same treatment (i.e., the **treatment group**[1]), can address the issue of generalizability. But a problem with these studies (as well as with case studies) is that there is no **control group**. Thus, it's impossible to know whether improvement was caused by the treatment itself, or some other factor such as placebo effects.

So, to most clearly determine the efficacy of a particular psychological treatment for a particular problem, researchers conduct **randomized controlled trials (RCTs)**. RCTs are studies in which one or more groups of clients (all with the same problem) receive a particular treatment (the experimental treatment condition) and another group receives a control condition. The control group might be told they are on a **waiting list** for treatment, although to equate expectations of improvement across groups, researchers prefer to use credible placebo controls in which clients engage in a "therapy" that the investigators do not expect to have any

---

[1]Despite the term "group," clients in treatment studies do not necessarily all receive treatment at once.

effect on the target problem. As shown in **Table 10.2**, RCTs have a number of important design features that maximize **internal validity** — the ability to draw strong cause and effect conclusions about the relationship between treatment and outcome. These features make RCTs the gold standard efficacy study.

Table 10.2	Key Features of Randomized Controlled Trials
Feature	**Advantages**
Control group	Allows researchers to estimate the true effects of an active treatment over and above any placebo effects
Random assignment to treatment or control groups	Clients have an equal chance of being in any of the study conditions, which eliminates bias and improves generalizability of the results to the larger population
Manualized treatment and well-trained therapists	Ensures that the treatment(s) being studied is/are delivered optimally and in the same way to all clients
Carefully selected and homogeneous client groups	Ensures that the results speak to how well a treatment works for a particular target problem or disorder
Blinded assessment	To reduce potential bias, personnel who assess clients in the study are kept unaware of which treatment they are receiving

A countless number of RCTs have been conducted in research labs around the world to evaluate the various types of psychological treatments. Researchers have also used **meta-analysis**, a method in which one compiles all studies relevant to a topic and combines the results statistically to provide an empirically determined summary of the findings for different types of treatment and different problems. Individual studies and meta-analyses collectively indicate that psychological treatments generally work well, and that they are helpful in reducing a wide range of psychological and behavioral problems and disorders (e.g., Barkham et al., 2021; Munder et al., 2019; Tolin, 2010; Weisz et al., 2006). Yet while the overall effect of these interventions is medium to large, not everyone benefits.

Some experts argue that the same rigor and design features that make RCTs the best type of study for determining a treatment's efficacy also render the results of these studies irrelevant to "real-world" clinical practice (e.g., Persons & Silberschatz, 1998). And this is a point worth considering. Many RCTs, for example, exclude individuals with multiple problems and those who have failed previous rounds of treatment; yet, these are the people who typically show up for treatment in routine clinical settings. Similarly, in most clinical settings, treatment does not proceed using a manual, and most practitioners are not as closely supervised as they are in RCTs. But should these concerns disqualify the results from RCTs, or can psychological interventions that have been developed and tested in research labs be successfully used under "real-world" conditions? This important question is addressed by *effectiveness* studies.

Treatment *Effectiveness*

Treatment **effectiveness** refers to how well an intervention performs outside of research settings when implemented by "typical" therapists working with "typical" clients. Effectiveness studies therefore emphasize **external validity**, which is the ability to generalize study findings to people and settings outside the study. Fortunately, the results of effectiveness studies generally

Effectiveness studies generally show that psychological treatments perform just as well in "real world" clinical settings as they do under controlled conditions in research labs.

mirror what's been found in efficacy studies. For example, in meta-analyses of effectiveness studies on cognitive-behavioral treatment (CBT) for anxiety and depression, Hans and Hiller (2013a, 2013b) identified large effects that were nearly as strong as what is reported in efficacy studies of the same interventions for the same problems.

An exemplary effectiveness study is McAleavey and colleagues' (2019) large collaborative investigation of 9895 clients who received routine psychological treatment from 1454 clinicians at 108 university counseling centers. The number of treatment sessions per client ranged from 1 to 86, with a mean of 7.1, though 97% had fewer than 20 sessions. The types of treatment and presenting problems varied (e.g., there were no treatment manuals or highly selective study inclusion criteria), and at each appointment all clients completed a self-report measure that assessed depression, anxiety, hostility, academic-related distress, eating concerns, and substance use. The results of this study indicated that across most of these problem domains, clients underwent substantial improvement from pre- to posttreatment that was almost equivalent to what has been observed in RCT studies. However, the most highly distressed clients at pretreatment achieved somewhat less improvement as compared to those who started off only mildly or moderately distressed. This suggests that routine psychological treatment administered in counseling centers is effective, but could still be improved, especially for highly distressed clients.

Although very informative, these results need to be considered in light of limitations common to many effectiveness studies. Most notably, McAleavey and colleagues' study was uncontrolled, so it's not possible to tease out whether clients would have improved on their own without the help they received. It is also possible that other things the clients were doing along with their treatment (e.g., using medication, starting a new exercise regimen) might have caused changes in their mental health. The type and duration of treatment, as well as therapist expertise levels, were also not controlled, and the data were collected using a self-report questionnaire, which may introduce bias. Finally, although university counseling centers serve a diverse client base, it is not known how well the results generalize to other populations and settings. These limitations aside, the large number of effectiveness studies, in concert with efficacy studies, strongly support the benefits of psychological treatment for a wide range of problems and psychiatric diagnoses.

Multicultural Considerations

Although the rates of many psychiatric disorders among people of color are similar to those among white populations (e.g., Tobin et al., 2020), much of the information we have about the efficacy and effectiveness of psychological treatments is based on research that has traditionally suffered from a lack of diversity in participant samples (e.g., Polo et al., 2019). This raises the question of whether the findings from RCTs generalize to diverse cultural groups. Fortunately, over time, RCTs have increasingly included significant numbers of ethnically underrepresented and low-income participants (e.g., Polo et al., 2019). Still, studies are far more likely to exclude, rather than include, linguistic minorities, and have not enrolled a meaningful number of Asian American, Native Hawaiian/Pacific Islander, Native American/ Native Alaskan and multiethnic participants. Moreover, note that treatments typically have been developed by white psychologists and initially tested among predominantly white clients, then later "adapted" to nonwhite populations; substantial research is needed by people with lived experience to derive conceptual models and treatment approaches that begin from the perspective of people of color. Finally, treatment effects are almost never presented separately for different racial and ethnic groups. Accordingly, it is difficult to draw strong conclusions as to which treatments may be most beneficial for particular cultural groups; however, available data suggest comparable effectiveness across racial and ethnic groups when studied.

Think Like a Clinical Psychologist Suppose you are seeking psychological treatment and your psychologist tells you that although many studies have demonstrated the efficacy and effectiveness of the intervention you're about to begin, the clients in those studies differed from you in terms of race, ethnicity, gender, disability status, age, religion, or sexuality. Would this change your confidence in the treatment or in your clinician's ability to deliver it effectively for you? Why or why not?

▉▉ How Do Psychological Treatments Work?

If the psychological treatments listed in Table 10.1 work, then *how* do they work? Some experts believe these interventions work through the specific techniques and methods that are part of each approach. Others feel equally strongly that they work through factors common to all the approaches, such as the client–therapist relationship and an expectation (or hope) of improvement. Still others argue that the debate between specific and common factors is a false dichotomy — they must be integrated to achieve benefits (McAleavey & Castonguay, 2015). In other words, the specific techniques give the common factors a medium through which to operate. Let's explore these different viewpoints, and their scientific support, in more detail.

Common Factors

Advocates of the **common factors** view propose that the "active ingredients" in psychological treatments are a core set of therapeutic characteristics shared by all such interventions, such as empathy, a supportive client–clinician relationship, and the client's expectation of improvement (e.g., Wampold, 2015). This viewpoint has its roots in the unexpected finding that when different types of treatment — for example, behavioral and psychodynamic — are matched against one another in head-to-head comparison studies, the result is often a tie (e.g., Luborsky et al., 1975). But how could this be if the different schools of treatment include such diverse techniques and methods? One possibility is that the different strategies target different mechanisms but happen to lead to similar outcomes. Yet, a more reasonable explanation is that the different treatments are more alike than they present themselves to be, and that it is the therapeutic qualities they have in common, rather than their unique features, that are most crucial to promoting improvement and therefore responsible for the equivalent outcomes. This notion has been dubbed the *Dodo bird verdict*, referring to a scene from *Alice in Wonderland* in which the characters have a race and the Dodo bird declares that "everybody has won, and all must have prizes." So, what are these change-promoting common therapeutic factors?

Wampold (2015) proposed a contextual model of common factors in which, following the establishment of an initial bond between client and practitioner, psychological treatments are hypothesized to work through three pathways. The first is the genuine alliance between client and practitioner which is thought to provide the client with a connection to a caring and empathic person and thus be healing in and of itself (especially for clients with suboptimal social relationships). The second pathway is through the client's expectations or hope, which are also thought to be curative themselves. Psychological treatments all provide an explanation for how the client developed the problem or disorder and what can be done about it. Thus, they give clients reasons for optimism that they can do what's necessary to improve their lives. The third pathway involves the specific techniques within the intervention, but only to the extent that they stimulate healthy action in general. In other words, it is not assumed that specific treatment techniques exert their effects through reversal of particular causal or maintaining processes, but rather that they're a vehicle through which the first two pathways can have their effects.

Indeed, some studies suggest that factors common to all psychological treatments are associated with outcome (Laska et al., 2014; Norcross & Lambert, 2018). In particular, aspects of the client–therapist relationship such as goal consensus, collaboration, empathy, genuineness, and affirmation have been shown to account for up to 40% of clinical improvement (e.g., Norcross & Lambert, 2018). Data also show that clients with more positive attitudes about the treatment process are more likely to experience improvement, regardless of the therapist's actions (Wampold, 1997). These findings, however, are largely correlational and it is therefore not clear whether such a relationship is a cause or consequence of improvements in psychological functioning. It is indeed possible that the client–practitioner relationship and positive attitudes about treatment become stronger once the client has begun to demonstrate improvement. As we will see next, critics of the common factors approach and Dodo bird verdict also point out that when outcomes are examined for individual psychological processes and problems, some specific interventions are clearly superior to others.

Specific Factors

In contrast to the common factors view, the **specific factors perspective** holds that theories and procedures particular to a given approach to treatment *are* necessary for psychological or behavioral change. That is, guided by a particular conceptualization, the clinician says something or prompts the client to take some sort of action, which results in (a) changes to the psychological processes that cause or maintain the target problem, and (b) reductions in psychological distress and dysfunction (e.g., Abramowitz & Blakey, 2020). This might include confronting one's fears or changing reward contingencies (behavioral interventions), learning to think about situations in more adaptive ways (cognitive-behavioral treatments), expressing difficult emotions or improving interpersonal relations (dynamic therapies), being more accepting of one's private experiences (acceptance and commitment therapy), and so forth.

Results from many studies, including RCTs, support the specific factors view and suggest that certain psychological techniques and treatments are indeed superior to others, especially when applied to specific problems and disorders. In particular, there are clear first-line treatments for bulimia nervosa, binge eating disorder, chronic pain, phobias, social anxiety, obsessive-compulsive disorder (OCD), posttraumatic stress disorder (PTSD), insomnia, panic attacks, sexual dysfunction, disruptive behavior in children, some substance use problems, some types of psychosis, and borderline personality disorder (e.g., Westmacott & Hunsley, 2007). An increasing number of practice guidelines are now available that encourage attention to such findings. These include guidelines available from the American Psychological Association, American Psychiatric Association, and American Academy of Child and Adolescent Psychiatry. It is also important to recognize that there are some problems, such as depression and generalized anxiety disorder, for which multiple treatment options work relatively well (e.g., Barlow, 2021).

Compelling data in favor of the specific factors view also come from **dismantling studies**, which investigate treatments that have multiple components with the goal of identifying those techniques that are most strongly associated with treatment benefit. Different cognitive-behavioral treatment (CBT) programs for panic disorder, for example, include combinations of psychoeducation, breathing retraining, muscle relaxation, cognitive restruc-

Scott Lilienfeld (1960–2020) was a leader in the field of psychological science who helped raise awareness of effective and ineffective treatments for psychological problems and disorders.

turing, interoceptive exposure, and *in vivo* exposure. A review of 72 studies examining various combinations of these techniques suggested that interoceptive exposure to fear-provoking (but safe) bodily sensations is *most* critical for positive outcomes (i.e., fewer panic attacks), while muscle relaxation is *least* critical (Pompoli et al., 2018).

Finally, there are some psychological interventions that are of no help and can even *harm* clients. Likewise, deviations from, and misapplications of, otherwise helpful interventions can weaken treatment effects or cause harm (McKay & Jenson-Doss, 2021). These findings further point to the important role that specific techniques, processes, and mechanisms play in treatment outcome. Scott Lilienfeld (2007), who was a fierce advocate for science in clinical psychology, identified a list of interventions that, in multiple studies (including RCTs), were associated with harmful effects such as deterioration in functioning (for the client or relatives), the appearance of new problems, excessive dependency on the clinician, and premature dropout from treatment. In a meta-analysis by Williams and colleagues (2020) two interventions, Scared Straight for juveniles with conduct problems and Critical Incident Stress Debriefing for trauma-exposed individuals, emerged as being ineffective at best, and potentially harmful at worst (Williams et al., 2020).

The Interactional Perspective

Perhaps, however, the decades-old debate over specific versus common factors is a false dichotomy. Some have argued, for example, that these elements of treatment cannot really be disentangled (de Felice et al., 2019). In other words, a client's hope and expectations of improvement (common factors) may best be realized when working collaboratively with the clinician to implement particular treatment techniques (specific factors). It is also likely that specific theory-based techniques work in part *because of* the relationship between the client and clinician (Bordin, 1979). For example, as we will see in Chapter 11, the successful use of behavioral interventions for many anxiety-related problems involves systematic confrontation with feared stimuli to extinguish learned fear (i.e., exposure therapy). Research suggests that clients are more likely to fully engage in (and therefore benefit from) such challenging techniques to the extent that they trust the psychologist who suggests these procedures (Buchholz & Abramowitz, 2020). To this end, arguments over whether specific or common factors are more important make little sense. Regardless of their theoretical orientations, most psychologists agree that treatment goes more smoothly when the clinician and client perceive their *alliance* to be strong. Therefore, it is probably most valuable to understand that both of these fundamental components of treatment work together to promote change.

T**hink Like a Clinical Psychologist** Lilienfeld (2007) argued that clinical psychologists should prioritize efforts to pinpoint treatments that are actually *harmful* or *ineffective* over efforts to identify the *best* interventions for specific problems. Do you agree? Why or why not?

▓ The Course of Psychological Treatment

What is the experience like for a client who decides to seek the help of a psychologist? Given the sheer number of different problems and interventions (some of which we detail in subsequent chapters), there is no fixed sequence of procedures that applies equally well to every case. Add to this the fact that clinical psychologists provide services to people of diverse racial, ethnic, cultural, and socioeconomic backgrounds. Their clientele might have different religious beliefs and political ideologies than their own, or identify with a different sexual orientation or gender identity than they do. Finally, clients' life experiences are often different from those of their psychologist.

In this section, we walk through a *typical* course of psychological treatment using the examples of Kiara and Shane to illustrate the major phases of the process as they apply to adults and youth. The details of how treatment is implemented are omitted here, as you will read about these in later chapters. We do, however, highlight multicultural considerations as they are relevant to each phase of the process.

Initial Contact

Like many people, when Shane's parents first contacted Shane's psychologist, they didn't know exactly what to expect. His mother felt a mix of anxiety, embarrassment, and inadequacy for having to seek help for her child. Even though she was a nurse, Kiara felt these emotions as well; and like some people of color, she also felt suspicious. Would her psychologist genuinely care about her difficulties or be dismissive? Could she trust that she would be treated with respect and understanding? Shane's mother also had questions: would the clinician meet regularly with her or with only Shane, or would Shane's father be expected to participate? Anticipating such concerns, both Shane's and Kiara's respective psychologists began by establishing rapport and explaining the process of treatment. This important step can have a significant bearing on the client's trust, attitude toward treatment, and willingness to engage with the psychologist.

It is valuable for psychologists to have an awareness of their own cultural values and expectations with regard to help-seeking, as this will help them understand what this process is like for clients from diverse backgrounds. In addition, it is important for psychologists to provide opportunities for clients to talk about their experiences, questions, or assumptions regarding their identities. This is relevant for many different aspects of diversity, including racial, ethnic, gender, and sexual diversity, as well as differences in ability and disability, religion, socioeconomic status, and any other identity or experience that may be perceived by clients as relevant to their life experiences, or may be perceived as different from their psychologist's own identity and thus may lead clients to wonder whether their experiences will be fully understood. Note too that sometimes apparent similarities between psychologists and their clients also may require discussion at the outset of therapy to acknowledge and avoid the fallacy of homogeneity within identities; even people who share many socioeconomic characteristics nevertheless have many different experiences, and it is important not to assume a shared understanding or equivalent experiences between people who may seem to come from similar backgrounds.

For these reasons, psychologists are trained in **multicultural humility**, which includes an awareness, knowledge, and skills in addressing what psychologists don't know about their clients due to the unique life experiences that may shape psychologists' own perceptions and assumptions. As psychologists become aware of their own biases, assumptions, and expectations, rooted in their own cultural backgrounds, they are better able to adopt an inquisitive, curious, and open-minded approach to understand their clients with greater empathy.

Informed Consent

Once the client's reasons for seeking help have been discussed and it seems appropriate to begin treatment (as opposed to providing a referral for more appropriate services), the next step is to make sure clients are aware of certain information they are entitled to know before any treatment commences. Accordingly, both Kiara's and Shane's family were given a consent form similar to that shown in Chapter 3, *Ethics in Clinical Psychology*, which their respective psychologists carefully reviewed with them. The form described professional qualifications, matters related to fees, confidentiality and its limits, and other pertinent details. In addition to being an essential part of the ethical practice of psychology, reviewing this information enhanced both Kiara's and Shane's family's impressions of their clinician and the process of treatment (Handelsman, 1990).

Assessment, Conceptualization, and Treatment Planning

As we have already seen, a variety of assessment procedures may be used depending on the nature of the client's problem, the psychologist's theoretical orientation, and other factors. For some clients, consultations with other professionals may be desirable. A neurological workup may be necessary, or a medical examination may be scheduled to rule out nonpsychological factors. For clients whose problems are related to economics or unemployment, additional consultation with social workers or job counselors may be appropriate. As described in

Chapter 9, *Diagnosis, Case Formulation, and Treatment Planning*, a synthesis of assessment data and an initial conceptualization provided the guidelines and goals for the interventions used to help Kiara and Shane. As treatment proceeds, changes in these conceptualizations might occur, and goals and techniques may be modified accordingly.

It is important to guard against inaccurately labeling the behaviors of members of diverse groups as indicative of a clinical problem simply because such behaviors are unfamiliar or seem unusual. In such instances, the psychologist can gather additional information (either from the client or another source) as to the appropriateness of the behavior in the client's cultural context. If language barriers exist and a translator must be used, it is best if the translator shares the client's cultural background and has a background in mental health. Moreover, the interpreter should translate what has been said only after the speaker stops speaking (as opposed *while* the speaker is still talking), and the use of friends, relatives, and bilingual children as translators should be avoided in order to preserve confidentiality.

In many ways, what comes out of case conceptualization and goal-setting approximates a "contract" in which the psychologist agrees to help alleviate a specified set of problems and to do it in the most effective way possible. Naturally, no one can absolutely promise a perfect cure or resolution of all problems. Clients in turn will state their desires and intentions. In effect, this contract usually covers such matters as the goals of therapy, length of therapy, frequency of meetings, cost, general format of therapy, and the client's responsibilities.

When a child's behavior is the focus of treatment, these discussions may include the child in a variety of ways. Some children do not understand what therapy is or why they are attending, or they may not agree that treatment is needed to address their behavior. Many children attend treatment as a result of their parents' wishes, but not their own. In Shane's case, treatment was recommended by his school. Compounding these complexities further, parents legally have a right to learn anything that occurred between the psychologist and the child during treatment, although most clinicians discourage parents from intruding on the confidentiality of their work with a child. Consequently, Shane's psychologist began by meeting with Shane and his mother together to set goals and determine a course of treatment. This helped engage Shane in the process, establish trust, and teach his parent about the clinician's role as an advocate for both Shane and his parent simultaneously. Importantly, psychologists take clients only where they are psychologically prepared to go. Moving too fast or setting up grandiose objectives can frighten or alienate some individuals. It is usually desirable to proceed with enough subtlety and skill so that clients feel they are the ones establishing or modifying the goals.

Implementing Treatment

After the initial goals are established, the therapist decides on how interventions will be applied. As in Kiara's case, treatment may focus on a specific problem (i.e., her obsessions and compulsions); or, as with Shane, it may involve a broader approach to changing the client's parent–child interactions or behavioral repertoire. All of this must be carefully described to the client in terms of how it relates to the length of time involved, the anticipated outcome, and the challenges that may lie ahead. Exactly what is expected of the client must also be detailed — self-monitoring or "homework" assignments, for example. In the chapters to follow we will cover specifics of how the various forms of psychological treatment are implemented. In the remainder of this section, we discuss several key processes and techniques that effective clinicians employ regardless of which approach they are using.

Providing Psychoeducation

Whether directly or indirectly, most psychological treatments include an educational component that provides clients with new and helpful ways to understand themselves, their target problems, and treatment. Sometimes, misinformation plays a clear role in the development and maintenance of the client's problems, and psychologists can provide corrective information to help alleviate such difficulties. Examples include education about the physiology of anxiety and fear in the treatment of panic attacks and sex education to reduce relationship distress concerning matters of sexual functioning. Psychoeducation might involve presenting advice or information in a straightforward manner, or providing material for clients to read on their own. Indeed, *bibliotherapy*—sometimes with minimal clinician involvement—can be effective in reducing some psychological problems (Yuan et al., 2018).

Maskot Bildbyra/SuperStock

Many psychological treatments include an educational component to help clients understand their problems and get the most out of the intervention.

Managing Emotional Distress

Although the occasional experience of psychological discomfort is an inevitable part of life, and can even serve as an incentive for clients to work hard in treatment, extreme levels can be debilitating. Thus, an early aim in the therapeutic process is to use the client–practitioner relationship to promote a supportive atmosphere and help clients gain emotional footing and confidence. At first, this might involve providing direct reassurance (e.g., "I know things seem difficult right now, but we're going to work together to help you learn the skills to make things more manageable"). As treatment progresses, more specific techniques such as cognitive restructuring, acceptance and commitment therapy (ACT) metaphors, or progressive muscle relaxation may be introduced to diminish distress or change the client's response to such feelings.

Assigning Work and Practice between Sessions

Because clients like Kiara and Shane typically spend only about an hour per week with their psychologist (sometimes even less), it's often necessary for them to also set aside time between appointments to review key points discussed in treatment sessions; practice the skills taught in therapy sessions in real-world situations; and/or self-monitor various situations, thoughts, feelings, and behaviors. Clients, or clients' caregivers, such as Shane's mom, are often asked to keep track of their efforts between sessions (perhaps using specialized forms and worksheets), and it is important for clinicians to follow up and review this "homework" at the beginning of the subsequent appointment to reinforce its importance. Poorly explained assignments and the therapist's failure to follow up can result in noncompliance, which is associated with poorer short- and long-term outcomes irrespective of the treatment approach (Kazantzis et al., 2016; Kazantzis & Ronan, 2006). Finally, when there is a substantial difference between the socioeconomic status or the values of the client and those of the therapist, some researchers have found that the client's willingness to work hard in treatment may suffer (Hall et al., 2021).

This further highlights the need for cultural sensitivity on the part of the practitioner, as well as for culturally sensitive mental health services.

Fostering Optimism and Self-Efficacy

Once Kiara got to know and trust her clinician, she, like many clients, found herself with high hopes and expectations of improvement. Indeed, for some individuals who seek help, the prospect of a powerful experience guided by a highly trained expert with the mysterious ability to "analyze" and "heal" is difficult to disavow. While such expectations may not be entirely realistic, it is useful for psychologists to promote in their clients a healthy sense of optimism regarding positive change. This contributes to the nonspecific effects of treatment (Constantino et al., 2018), perhaps through increasing adherence to challenging within- and between-sessions skill-building work. The more optimistic Kiara felt, for example, the more she pushed herself to complete challenging exposure therapy practices. The more hopeful Shane and his mother felt, the harder they worked, as well.

One excellent way to facilitate such confidence is by providing reassurance that with hard work by both client (and family) and therapist, the desired changes are possible. Setting the client up for early successes and then drawing on such triumphs as the work becomes more challenging also raises trust in the prospect of meaningful improvement. An added advantage of these strategies is that they empower clients and enhance self-efficacy by drawing attention to their own efforts as the cause of their positive changes (Bandura, 1982). For example, the more Shane's mother practiced the tools she was learning to use, the more she began to notice how her own positive behavior resulted in quality interactions with Shane, along with subsequent changes in his behavior at home and at school.

Termination, Evaluation, and Follow-up

After about four months of weekly appointments with her psychologist — and lots of work and practice between sessions — Kiara found that she had learned the skills for managing her obsessions, compulsions, and anxiety independently. It was almost as if she were "her own therapist" now. This prompted a discussion about the end of treatment; and after one final appointment to assess Kiara's current level of distress and functioning, and discuss relapse-prevention strategies, her course of treatment was concluded. As is sometimes the case, Shane's termination was a more gradual process in which meetings were reduced from once a week to once every two weeks, and then to once a month for a few months. All told, Shane's course of treatment lasted six months; his mother had learned skills that she would continue to use to ensure that Shane maintained the improvement he had achieved while in treatment.

As termination approaches, it is important that it be discussed in detail and that the client's feelings and attitudes are thoroughly aired and dealt with. Clients do sometimes terminate suddenly, in some cases before the therapist feels it is appropriate. Whenever possible, however, it is important to find the time to discuss at least briefly the client's feelings about ending treatment and the possibility of returning later for additional sessions if necessary. Many therapists find that "booster sessions" scheduled months after termination — perhaps six months and then one year later — can be quite helpful. These booster sessions are used to review the client's progress, address new problems or issues that have arisen in the interim, and solidify the gains that have been made.

As we have seen, at the end of treatment, it is important to evaluate and discuss with clients the progress they have made. Clinicians should also compile data and make notes on progress in order to evaluate the quality of their own efforts or the agency's services and continue to improve services to clients. Indeed, clinicians and agencies owe it to themselves and their clients to evaluate the success of their own efforts using assessment instruments with known psychometric properties.

Think Like a Clinical Psychologist Consider your own unique personal experiences and cultural background. What values are most important to you? If you were seeking psychological treatment, which values would you want your clinician to be aware of, and why?

▮▮▮ Evidence-Based Treatment, Evidence-Based Practice, and Dissemination

What Are Evidence-Based Treatment and Evidence-Based Practice?

As we have seen, a great many studies support the efficacy and effectiveness of certain psychological interventions targeting particular psychological processes and problems. **Evidence-based treatment (EBT)** refers to those interventions or techniques that demonstrate beneficial effects in RCTs. **Evidence-based practice (EBP)** is a broader category that includes treatments informed by a number of sources, including scientific evidence about the intervention (i.e., EBT), clinical expertise, and client needs and preferences (Kazdin, 2008) (see **Figure 10.1**). EBP has always been a topic of interest to those in the medical field, but it became especially relevant for clinical psychologists in the 1980s and 1990s when health care reforms placed greater pressure on mental health service providers to demonstrate that their treatments worked. Particularly important for psychologists was whether the treatments that they provided were better or worse than the treatments that could be provided in the fields of psychiatry, social work, or other mental health disciplines (e.g., counseling, marriage and family therapy).

In 1995, psychologist Diane Chambless was appointed by the American Psychological Association to lead an effort to develop criteria for establishing whether specific interventions had enough scientific support to be classified as "empirically validated treatments" (this term was a precursor to the use of "EBT") for particular mental health difficulties (see **Table 10.3**). The criteria that Chambless's committee developed have been altered over the years, but the basic framework remains intact: treatments are categorized as "Well Established," "Probably Efficacious," and "Experimental" or "Possibly Efficacious." Over time,

Courtesy of the Department of Psychology, University of Pennsylvania.

In her role as Chair of the American Psychological Association's Promotion and Dissemination of Psychological Procedures task force, psychologist Diane Chambless helped develop criteria for empirically evaluating psychological treatments.

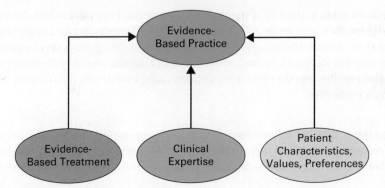

Figure 10.1 Evidence based practice (EBP) is informed by information about evidence-based treatments (EBTs), a clinician's own expertise, and a patient's own characteristics, values, and preferences.

Table 10.3 Criteria for Empirically Validated Treatments (now EBTs)

Well-Established Treatments

I. At least two good group design studies, conducted by different investigators, demonstrating efficacy in *one or more of the following ways*:
  A. Superior to pill or psychological placebo or to another treatment.
  B. Equivalent to an already established treatment in studies with adequate statistical power (about 30 clients per group).

OR

II. A large series of single case design studies demonstrating efficacy. These studies must have:
  A. Used good experimental designs and
  B. Compared the intervention to another treatment as in I.A.

FURTHER CRITERIA FOR BOTH I AND II:

III. Studies must be conducted with treatment manuals.
IV. Characteristics of the client samples must be clearly specified.

Probably Efficacious Treatments

I. Two studies showing the treatment is more effective than a waiting-list control group.

OR

II. Two studies otherwise meeting the well-established treatment criteria I, III, and IV, but both are conducted by the same investigator. Or one good study demonstrating effectiveness by these same criteria.

OR

III. At least two good studies demonstrating effectiveness but flawed by heterogeneity of the client samples.

OR

IV. A small series of single case design studies otherwise meeting the well-established treatment criteria II, III, and IV.

Experimental Treatments

Treatment not yet tested in trials meeting task force criteria for methodology.

SOURCE: Chambless, D. L., Baker, M., Baucom, D. H., Beutler, L. E., Calhoun, K. S., Crits-Christoph, P., Daiuto, A., DeRubeis, R., Detweiler, J., Haaga, D., Johnson, S., McCurry, S., Mueser, K., Pope, K., Sanderson, W., Shoham, V., Stickle, T., Williams D., & Woody, S. (1998). Update on empirically validated therapies. II. *Clinical Psychologist, 51*(1), 3–16.

less emphasis has been placed on the use of manuals to guide treatment, but the need for internal validity and consistency in how treatments are administered remains (see A CLOSER LOOK: *The Pros and Cons of Treatment Manuals*).

A Closer Look   The Pros and Cons of Treatment Manuals

Treatment manuals — session-by-session protocols for delivering psychological interventions for particular problems — are typically developed by treatment outcome researchers to ensure that all clients in a particular study receive the same intervention. When research indicates that the protocols in such manuals are effective in addressing a specific problem or DSM disorder, they are rapidly disseminated into nonresearch settings. Most manuals specify a clear theoretical basis, the number and sequencing of treatment sessions, the content and objectives of each session, and the procedures required to achieve the objective of each session.

There are a number of obvious advantages to manual-based treatments. Most importantly, the programs described within them have been demonstrated to work for a particular problem in the most rigorous types of studies. Manuals also standardize the delivery of treatments, making them easy to disseminate and teach to practitioners. Moreover, therapists who master manual-based treatments are attractive to managed care companies because these treatments are recognized as efficacious and efficient.

Yet, a number of critiques have also been leveled at the use of treatment manuals for specific problems and disorders. Abramowitz and Blakey (2020), for example, grant the importance of disseminating empirically supported psychological interventions via manuals, but lament that the rigid adherence to such manuals has resulted in a "cookbook approach" to treatment wherein practitioners have come to lean too heavily on following manuals instead of learning about the relevant psychological processes underlying the target problem and the mechanisms of change that effective interventions tap into. These authors therefore call for a "flexibility within fidelity" approach in which the focus is on empirically supported *mechanisms of change* that address relevant etiological and maintenance processes (instead of disorders per se). They provide two reasons that such an approach may be superior to diagnosis-specific treatment manuals.

First, in most clinical settings, clients present with complexity and co-occurring problems and diagnoses that are not addressed in most manuals. Clinicians using the cookbook approach often find themselves abandoning the treatment manual and perhaps empirically supported interventions altogether. Yet if a clinician understands the psychological processes that contribute to the clients' problems (sometimes called transdiagnostic processes), rather than simply assigning a diagnosis, and the empirically supported mechanisms of change that can address the presenting problems, evidence-based treatment may still proceed without the need for disorder-based treatment manuals.

Second, focusing on mechanisms of change affords advantages over a manual-driven approach when it comes to clinical training. Indeed, it is easier to teach practitioners how to operate from a single conceptual model than it is for trainees to learn the specifics of a multitude of different problem/diagnosis-based treatment manuals. Indeed, many manuals share core components, procedures, and mechanisms of change (e.g., exposure therapy for anxiety-related problems). In turn, trainees are able to begin working with a greater diversity of clients sooner than they would be if they had to be trained in several manual-driven treatments.

Others have criticized manuals for undermining the clinical judgment of practitioners and ignoring therapist effects on outcome (e.g., Truijens et al., 2019). Yet, the psychological testing and clinical judgment literature suggests that clinical judgment is limited and likely to be outperformed by empirically supported **manualized treatments** that prescribe for the therapist the methods of intervention for a given problem. There are also no data to support the position that manual-based treatments are inferior to treatment-as-usual with regard to comorbid psychological problems. ▬

EBT and EBP Effectiveness

Do EBTs and EBP improve the practice of clinical psychology? The answer is *yes*. In a classic meta-analysis, John Weisz and colleagues (2006) combined the results from 32 RCTs in which an EBT was compared to an alternate approach (i.e., "usual care") in the treatment of youth from varied ethnic backgrounds who experienced an array of psychological problems and disorders. This study allowed for an examination of whether EBP (a) offers advantages over other treatment approaches, (b) benefits youth who experience *severe* psychological distress and dysfunction, (c) is effective for youth from ethnically diverse groups, and (d) is effective in different types of settings. The results revealed that on average, youth who received EBT had better outcomes than 62% of those who received usual care. Moreover, the advantages for youth who had received EBT were maintained up to two years following treatment. Finally, the differences in effects between EBT and other approaches were unrelated to (a) therapist qualifications, (b) the severity and complexity (e.g., multiple diagnoses) of clients' problems, (c) whether treatment took place in a research or clinical setting, and (d) client ethnicity. Although such findings strengthen the argument that some psychological treatments work better than others, there is still work to be done to determine whether specific treatments are particularly effective for some individuals, for some diagnoses, or in certain contexts, more than others (Kazdin, 2008).

Resistance to EBTs and EBP

Despite RCTs and meta-analyses showing that some psychological treatments work better than others, some clinical psychologists reject the ideas of EBT and EBP, arguing that psychotherapy is an "art" and the changes it brings about are difficult to define and measure scientifically. This has resulted in a sizable *research–practice gap* in which the results of efficacy and effectiveness studies are ignored by some clinicians based on the assumption that one can rely on clinical judgment, rather than on research findings, to determine when a treatment works (e.g., "I see my clients get better with my own eyes. Why do I need research to tell me what to do in my practice?").

This type of reasoning, however, is misguided (Lilienfeld et al., 2013). As we have discussed at various points in this book, even the most experienced and skilled clinicians can fall prey to preconceptions, biases, and misinterpretations — often without realizing it. Thus, what psychologists appear to "see" in their practice is not always accurate. As we have also discussed, the specific techniques and methods clinicians use are not the only active ingredients in psychological treatment. **Table 10.4** lists several factors that may serve as competing explanations for a client's improvement. These factors are often invisible to practitioners observing their own clients and therefore can trick even the most observant professional into believing a treatment is having an effect when it is not. Finally, assumptions based on judgment violate a logical error known as *post hoc, ergo propter hoc* or "after this, therefore because of this." In other words, largely for the reasons listed in Table 10.4, just because a change is observed *following* treatment does not mean it was necessarily *caused by* the treatment. Of course, in some cases improvement is indeed caused by the intervention, so inferences regarding therapeutic effectiveness are by no means always inaccurate. Yet, as we discussed earlier in this chapter, because of how they are designed, RCTs are the only way to get around the biases and caveats in Table 10.4 and therefore the best (even if imperfect) way to determine whether a treatment is effective.

Table 10.4 Rival Explanations for Apparent Client Improvement in Psychological Treatment	
Rival Explanation	**Description**
Placebo effects	By instilling hope and belief that one can rise above life's challenges, most credible treatments can be at least somewhat helpful for combating demoralization, which is a central component of many psychological problems.
Spontaneous remission	The longer people remain in treatment, the greater the opportunity for factors such as natural healing processes, social support, and positive experiences in everyday life to foster change.
Regression to the mean and natural fluctuations in psychological problems	Many clients seek help when they have reached extreme levels of distress, which are naturally inclined to moderate over time, giving the illusion of treatment as the cause of improvement.
Effort justification	Clients invest a great deal of time, energy, effort, and money in treatment, and may feel a psychological need to justify this commitment and report improvement to their therapist.
Multiple treatment interference	When clients seek help, they often make multiple changes simultaneously, which makes it impossible to conclusively attribute improvement to a particular intervention.
Reporting bias	Clients might tell their clinicians they are doing better because this is socially desirable; and those who do not improve might drop out of treatment and never explain their lack of change to their therapist.

Dissemination of EBTs

Why is it critical to address the research–practice gap? Because about half the population of the United States (and indeed worldwide) can expect to experience clinically significant psychological distress and dysfunction (that meet the criteria for a DSM-5-TR disorder) at some point during their lives (Kessler et al., 2005) and it is important that they have access to effective treatment. As a result, researchers have begun studying ways to *disseminate* EBTs more effectively — that is, to ensure that these interventions are adopted and implemented into routine clinical practice by clinical psychologists, other mental health professionals, and even trained nonprofessionals, perhaps assisted by the use of technology (see A CLOSER LOOK: *Technology and Dissemination of Psychological Treatments*). The goal of such *dissemination science* is to bridge the gap between evidence-based interventions and their use in clinical practice.

| A Closer Look | **Technology and Dissemination of Psychological Treatments** |

"Telehealth," "telepsychology," "e-therapy" — whatever you call it, more and more clinical psychologists are successfully using mental health apps, online therapy programs, and videoconferencing platforms (such as Zoom) to conduct treatment sessions both synchronously and asynchronously with their clients (e.g., Carlbring et al., 2018). When much of health care went virtual at the start of the COVID-19 pandemic, these tools became standard practice and are likely here to stay in one form or another. Let's explore their benefits and limitations, as well as some recent research findings and ethical considerations.

Advantages

The use of technology can reduce costs and increase access to clinical services for those who are homebound, who live in remote areas, or who might not seek services in-person due to stigma. Technology also reduces missed appointments due to illness, lack of child-care, or travel. Videoconferencing might be particularly useful with certain skills-based (i.e., cognitive-behavioral) interventions. Examples include exposure therapy for fears and phobias in which clients practice confronting anxiety-provoking situations and stimuli in various contexts between appointments, and behavioral parent training in which parents practice using new skills when responding to their child's conduct at home (e.g., at mealtimes). The use of technology in such cases can allow clinicians to virtually coach their clients through these experiences in real time.

Disadvantages

Not all households have a computer or smartphone, however; and among those that do, not all have reliable (or any) Internet service. Some people, especially older adults, aren't familiar with technology, which can make telehealth confusing and intimidating. These barriers tend to impact already marginalized communities like low-income households, people in rural areas, and racially/ethnically minoritized groups. Virtual platforms can also reduce the ability to pick up on important nonverbal cues in treatment, such as body language and facial expression, which may make it difficult to communicate and discern emotions. This is especially relevant when working with clients from diverse backgrounds, where missing or misunderstanding such nuances can harm the client–practitioner relationship. Finally, not all clients or problems are adaptable for remote treatment, such as clients who are easily distracted or those at heightened risk of suicide.

Research Findings

Before the COVID-19 pandemic, research had already demonstrated the efficacy and effectiveness of digital therapy for many mental health problems (e.g., Lawes-Wickwar et al., 2018). But the number of studies grew exponentially in 2020 and 2021. Here are few of the interesting findings that have emerged:

- **Adolescents (ages 10–19) have a varied reaction to teletherapy.** For teens, "online" typically means social media; and while using the same space for treatment comes naturally to some, others find it uncomfortable. Some youth respond best to shorter, more frequent sessions (e.g., 30 minutes, multiple times per week; Burgoyne & Cohn, 2020).
- **Concerns that people with serious mental health problems are less likely than other groups to engage with teletherapy are unfounded.** Individuals diagnosed with schizophrenia, bipolar disorder, severe major depressive disorder, substance use disorders, borderline

personality disorder, suicidality, and PTSD had higher teletherapy attendance rates than the general population (Miu et al., 2020).

- **While teletherapy might be an important tool in desperate times (such as during the pandemic), it shouldn't permanently replace face-to-face treatment — at least not for everyone.** Although often effective, teletherapy removes important aspects of a trusted relationship, which plays a role in treatment. This may add to feelings of loneliness and isolation, which propel many people to seek treatment in the first place (Luiggi-Hernández & Rivera-Amador, 2020). Combining online and in-person treatment may be the best long-term solution (e.g., Hughes et al., 2019).
- **The disadvantages of teletherapy are especially pronounced when working with children who have been abused, neglected, or otherwise traumatized.** Many children do not yet have the attention and emotion regulation skills needed for virtual treatment. It is also difficult for practitioners to identify dissociative symptoms over a digital platform (e.g., Racine et al., 2020).

Ethical Considerations

The use of teletherapy can also present ethical challenges in addition to those covered in Chapter 3. Specifically, to guarantee client privacy and confidentiality over the Internet, psychologists must make sure data and emails are encrypted, computers and mobile devices are protected from viruses and malware, and videoconferencing software is secure. In addition, Informed consent should address issues such as (a) what clients should do in the event of an interruption in transmission during a session, (b) costs and payment policies for online services, (c) expectations for responsiveness to clients' communications, and (d) emergency in-person services that can be accessed in a timely manner. Finally, when working with clients out of one's own state, province, or territory, the psychologist must be in compliance with the local laws relevant to providing clinical services, including licensing regulations (many jurisdictions require licensure in both jurisdictions) and reporting requirements for the suspicion of abuse or neglect of minors, elderly persons, or vulnerable adults, along with mandatory reporting requirements when clients make threats to harm identifiable others (i.e., Tarasoff reporting requirements). ▄▄▄

Specifically, dissemination scientists study the processes and factors that lead to widespread use of an evidence-based intervention for a particular target population and then develop and evaluate clinical practice models that optimize both the availability and delivery of such EBTs. Consider the evidence-based treatment of oppositional behavior in youth, such as Shane; which includes techniques such as behavioral parent training, cognitive therapy, and problem-solving skills training. Although these interventions could be offered by a few highly specialized doctoral-level clinical psychologists at community mental health clinics, the wait to see these professionals is likely to be long, and the cost is likely to be high. Yet, treatment could be made more widely available and less expensive by training other mental health professionals (e.g., social workers, counselors) working in diverse settings where people often go (e.g., schools, libraries, places of worship) in urban, suburban, as well as rural areas. Technology-enhanced versions of these interventions (e.g., Jones et al., 2021) could even be disseminated to anyone with a computer or smartphone without the need for attending treatment sessions. Kazdin (2008) proposed that programs to successfully disseminate evidence-based psychological treatments would require these, along with other key features, as listed in **Table 10.5**.

Table 10.5 Essential Features of Successful Dissemination Programs for Evidence-Based Psychological Treatments
Accessible to large numbers of people
Make services available in settings where people already go (e.g., places of worship, shopping malls)
Reduce the cost of care relative to alternatives
Reach individuals who are often not traditionally served by mental health professionals (e.g., those in rural areas)
Capable of being adapted for individuals of diverse racial, ethnic, socioeconomic, and cultural backgrounds
Increase the availability of services by training individuals without advanced (e.g., doctoral or master's) degrees to deliver treatment
Acceptable to both clients and practitioners

SOURCE: Kazdin, A. E. (2018). *Innovations in psychosocial interventions and their delivery: Leveraging cutting-edge science to improve the world's mental health.* Oxford University Press.

Overcoming Complications with Dissemination

Although it might seem like an obvious way to fight the "war on mental illness," the dissemination of EBTs can be an uphill struggle. Imagine, for instance, that the clinicians at the center where Shane's parents took Shane for treatment attended a continuing education workshop during which it was recommended that all the clinic's staff receive intensive training and begin using the three evidence-based interventions mentioned above when working with children with oppositional behavior and their families. Even if the clinic's leaders believe this is a smart plan, several factors might complicate its implementation: clinicians might require intensive training to be able to properly use these techniques, training workshops might be expensive in terms of both time and money, and therapists might not even be interested in changing how they treat youth like Shane.

Thus, a first step in successful dissemination is often to educate therapists and administrators about the benefits of the new treatment approach as compared to treatment as usual. The costs of implementing such a plan also need to be considered as doing so would require expensive training and clinicians' time away from providing services. The center would also have to think through a quality assurance system to ensure that clinicians continue to deliver the treatment properly and tailor it for clients of different cultural backgrounds. Finally, to justify the time, effort, and expenses involved, the center would want to implement a system for evaluating the effectiveness of the new approach relative to previous outcomes.

Probably the most successful large-scale dissemination initiative within clinical psychology is England's Improving Access to Psychological Therapies (IAPT) program (Clark, 2018), which began in 2008 and incorporates many of the features in Table 10.5. Collaborating with economist Lord Richard Layard, British clinical psychologist David M. Clark persuaded that country's National Health Service (NHS) that the nationwide availability of evidence-based psychological treatments for adults and children with severe anxiety and depression (primarily behavioral and cognitive-behavioral interventions) would result in massive cost savings. IAPT uses a *stepped care model* in which the most effective, yet least resource intensive treatment, is first delivered by practitioners trained to treat mild to moderate anxiety and depression. Clients only "step up" to more intensive services (delivered by practitioners with more experience and expertise) when the initial level of care proves unsuccessful. Now, more than a decade into its implementation, IAPT has trained roughly 10,000 practitioners to serve the approximately 1 million people who access its services yearly. It also incorporates pre- and posttreatment assessment so that its effects can be measured (e.g., Wakefield et al., 2021). This program has transformed psychological treatment in England, and other countries have begun to follow suit.

British economist Lord Richard Layard (left) and clinical psychologist David M. Clark (right) developed and launched the Improving Access to Psychological Therapies (IAPT) dissemination program.

Think Like a Clinical Psychologist What do you think are the pros and cons of using technology in the treatment of psychological problems? How can clients and practitioners get the most out of technology? Should it replace face-to-face therapy appointments? Why or why not?

▥ Chapter Summary

Clinical psychologists use psychological interventions to induce changes in a person's behavior, thoughts, or feelings. Psychotherapy is a form of intervention that occurs in a professional context whose aim is to solve psychological problems, improve coping and functioning, prevent future problems, or increase life satisfaction. Psychological treatments are forms of psychotherapy that have a strong foundation in psychological science. Evidence from rigorously conducted studies suggests that psychotherapy is efficacious, especially for certain types of psychological problems. However, no one form of psychotherapy or intervention is superior for all problems.

Certain features or characteristics are common to all forms of treatment, including the expert role of the practitioner, the relationship between client and practitioner, and the client's hope and expectations of change. Although specific characteristics of particular interventions also appear to influence outcome, it is likely that a combination of these factors is necessary to bring about durable psychological change.

Psychotherapy research is aimed at assessing whether or not certain interventions are effective with specific client populations, what factors seem related to change, and how such change can be brought about. More recent studies examine whether a specific therapy is useful with clients with specific psychological problems (e.g., specific DSM-5-TR diagnoses). Finally, whereas some practitioners resist the idea that clinical research should inform the delivery of psychological treatment, research has helped shape the practice of psychology to incorporate treatments with empirical support.

Applying What You've Learned

Exercise 1: You are in charge of evaluating a new treatment for depression. Explain how you might design an efficacy study (RCT) for this new treatment. What features would you be sure to include? Now think about designing an effectiveness study. What features would you be sure to include?

Exercise 2: Why do you think there is a gap between what science tells us about the efficacy of treatments and what clinicians typically do with their clients? Discuss how you would go about bridging this gap. What kinds of dissemination practices might you use to make clinicians more aware of what treatments are efficacious?

Key Terms

Common factors: A set of features that characterize many therapy orientations and that may be the source of the positive changes effected by psychological treatment.

Control group: In psychotherapy research, the group that does not receive the treatment under investigation.

Dismantling study: Investigates treatment that has multiple components with the goal of identifying those techniques that are most strongly associated with treatment benefit.

Effectiveness: Refers to how well an intervention performs outside of the research setting. A treatment is considered effective to the extent that clients report clinically significant benefit from the treatment.

Efficacy: Refers to how well a treatment performs in research studies. A treatment is considered efficacious to the extent that the average person receiving the treatment in clinical trials is demonstrated to be significantly less dysfunctional than the average person not receiving any treatment (e.g., those on a waiting list for treatment).

Empirically supported treatment (EST): Treatment for various psychological conditions that has been shown through careful empirical study to be either "well established" or "probably efficacious." A list of ESTs is updated and published periodically by the APA's Division of Clinical Psychology.

Evidence-based practice (EBP): Treatments informed by a number of sources, including scientific evidence about the intervention, clinical expertise, and client needs and preferences.

Evidence-based treatment (EBT): An intervention or technique that has produced significant change in clients in controlled trials.

External validity: The ability to generalize study findings to people and settings outside the study; stronger in effectiveness studies.

Internal validity: In the context of psychotherapy research, the ability to draw strong cause and effect conclusions about the relationship between treatment and outcome; stronger in efficacy studies (RCTs).

Manualized treatment: Psychotherapeutic treatment that is presented and described in a standardized, manual format (i.e., outlining the rationales, goals, and techniques that correspond to each phase of the treatment).

Meta-analysis: A method of research in which one compiles all studies relevant to a topic or question and combines the results statistically.

Multicultural humility: Awareness, knowledge, and skills in addressing what psychologists don't know about their clients due to the unique life experiences that may shape psychologists' own perceptions and assumptions.

Outcome measure: In psychotherapy research, indicator of client functioning following treatment; used to gauge the treatment effectiveness.

Paraprofessional: Individual without advanced education in psychology who has been trained to assist professional mental health workers.

Process research: Research that investigates the specific events that occur in the course of the interaction between therapist and client. Some therapy processes have been shown to relate to treatment outcome.

Psychological treatment: Specific research-supported techniques and procedures that are grounded in psychological theory and derived from models of psychopathology to target particular causal or maintenance mechanisms and improve specific aspects of psychological, emotional, behavioral, or physical health and related functioning.

Psychotherapy: In the context of a professional relationship, refers to methods of inducing changes in a person's behavior, thoughts, or feelings with the aim of improving their mental or physical health and related functioning.

Randomized controlled trial (RCT): RCTs are studies in which one or more groups of clients (all with the same problem) receive a particular treatment (the experimental condition) and another group receives a control condition.

Specific factors perspective: Holds that theories and procedures particular to a given approach to treatment *are* necessary for psychological or behavioral change; specific interventions are necessary to prompt the client to take some sort of action, which results in (a) changes to the psychological processes that cause or maintain the target problem and (b) reductions in psychological distress and dysfunction.

Treatment group: In psychotherapy research, the group that receives the treatment under investigation. Despite the term "group," clients in treatment studies do not necessarily all receive treatment at once.

Waiting list: A control group whose members receive treatment only after the study is completed.

CONNECT ONLINE

Check out our videos and additional resources located at: www.macmillanlearning.com

Behavioral Interventions

FOCUS QUESTIONS

1. What is the theoretical basis of behavioral interventions?
2. Describe the stages of behavioral treatment.
3. What kinds of problems are behavioral treatments used for, and what techniques are specifically used?
4. What is aversion therapy, and what are some of the ethical issues with this technique?
5. Explain the strengths and limitations of behavioral treatments.

CHAPTER OUTLINE

I f ever you have seen psychotherapy depicted in Hollywood, you likely have seen someone lying on a couch, with a therapist sitting next to them holding a clipboard, perhaps smoking a pipe. We hope you are aware that this depiction is remarkably inaccurate. Although psychotherapy can involve a great deal of conversation between the therapist and client (with both sitting upright), behavioral interventions also include approaches that allow clients to address their concerns in real time, right there in the session. As you will read in this chapter, behavioral interventions for anxiety may require psychologists to drive across a bridge or ride in an elevator with their client. It could include spinning a client in a chair to induce symptoms similar to a panic attack. With children and adolescents, therapy might include walking with a client through a mall or coaching them while they interact with new peers, or use coping strategies while in the context of provocative stimuli. Behavioral interventions address problematic behavior by helping people to engage in new behaviors right there in the context of the session. This is not what therapy may look like on TV, but it is very much what clinical psychologists do.

Behavioral interventions (often grouped together with cognitive interventions, as we will cover in Chapter 12, *Cognitive-Behavioral Interventions*) have evolved into a major force in the practice of clinical psychology. They are used by clinicians from a wide range of theoretical orientations and professional backgrounds in the treatment of a vast array of problems in people of all ages. Because they have such strong scientific support, behavioral interventions form the backbone of many evidence-based psychological treatment programs. Behavioral treatment is active, and it involves learning and practicing skills to reduce problematic behavior and increase more adaptive behavior. We begin this chapter by defining behavioral interventions, including a brief presentation of their historical roots. Next, we cover the general course of treatment, before turning to a discussion of how this process is applied with specific techniques to a number of psychological problems. We conclude with a discussion of the strengths and criticisms of the behavioral approach.

█ What Is Behavioral Treatment?

Behavioral treatment is a broad approach to clinical practice that encompasses many different techniques and methods derived from the science of learning theory. As such, there is an emphasis on the role of operant and classical conditioning, modeling, and skills training; and a focus on observable, measurable behavior. The primary goals of behavioral techniques include helping the client reduce maladaptive behaviors, decrease negative emotions that accompany such behaviors, and modify the environment to support healthier and more adaptive alternatives.

On the whole, behavioral treatments reflect an empirical approach to understanding and modifying behavior (for a history of the "behavioral movement," see IN HISTORICAL PERSPECTIVE: *Behavioral Treatment* on pages 236 and 237). As such, behavior therapists tend to focus on the client's current circumstances and problems, rather than probing into early experiences or stages of development (as many psychodynamic approaches do). Similarly, the role of concepts that are not directly observable — such as the unconscious, dreams, personality traits, and even psychiatric disorders — is de-emphasized. Put another way, the behavioral approach focuses on measurable stimuli and responses, rather than on variables that are presumed to cause them.

The following five guiding principles form the foundation of behavioral treatment:

- All behavior observed in the clinical setting is best understood in terms of basic learning principles of operant and classical conditioning.

- It is not necessary to establish an underlying motive for maladaptive behaviors. These behaviors *are* the problem, rather than signs or symptoms of a disorder or disease process.

- It is typically not necessary to know how a problematic behavior was learned in the first place. The focus of treatment should be on the processes that *maintain* the behavior (e.g., reinforcement, classical conditioning).

- Most maladaptive behavior encountered in the clinical setting can be modified and replaced with new, more adaptive, learned behavior through the appropriate application of learning principles.

- Behavioral treatment methods are precisely specified and tailored to the needs, strengths, and situations of each client.

Think Like a Clinical Psychologist The five guiding principles of behavioral treatment are assumed to apply broadly to humans regardless of race, ethnicity, culture, religious background, gender, sexual orientation, socioeconomic status, and physical or intellectual ability. Do you agree? Why or why not?

▥ The Process of Behavioral Treatment

Stages of Behavioral Interventions

In line with its scientific orientation to clinical practice, behavioral interventions typically progress in a manner similar to a carefully conducted single case study. **Figure 11.1** (on page 238) outlines the stages of behavioral treatment, which are discussed in greater detail next.

Target Definition and Baseline Assessment

Before treatment can begin, an observable target problem (or problems) must be identified and defined in behavioral terms. What is the behavior that someone wants to reduce, or increase, and how can that be described in scientifically precise terms? Sometimes just asking this question is therapeutic in itself. For instance, when a parent takes her child for therapy saying that he "acts out all of the time," a psychologist engaging in behavioral treatment may ask, "What exactly does 'acting out' look like? How often does that happen? Is it the same intensity every time? When is it likely to happen?" Often this line of questioning itself helps a client, or their caregiver, start to look at the problem in a more systematic way.

In other words, a behavioral definition pinpoints precisely what the target problem looks like and includes only what can be directly observed — not what one *assumes* a client is doing or why they're doing it. A good example of a behavioral definition is: *Gabriella (age 20) spends all of her time in her room watching YouTube videos. She is afraid of social interactions, avoids people outside of her family, and refuses to attend school or work outside the home.*

In Historical Perspective

Behavioral Treatment

The groundbreaking work of John B. Watson and Rosalie Rayner (1920) is often credited with launching the behavior therapy movement. Their notorious (and ethically dubious) study of "Little Albert" demonstrated how a phobia (then known as "neurosis") can develop in a child. In the tradition of Pavlovian conditioning, Albert was given a laboratory rat to play with. But each time the rat was introduced, a loud noise was introduced simultaneously. After a few such trials, the rat (previously a neutral stimulus) elicited a fearful (conditioned) response in Albert that is reported to have also generalized to similar furry objects.

In another well-known study, Mary Cover Jones (1924) demonstrated how such learned fears can be removed. A 3-year-old boy, Peter, was afraid of rabbits, rats, and other such objects. To eliminate the fear, Jones brought a caged rabbit closer and closer as the boy was eating. The feared object thus became associated with food, and after a few months, Peter's fear of the rabbit disappeared. Watson's conditioning of fears and Jones's "reconditioning" of them paved the way for systematic desensitization and contemporary exposure therapy techniques, which would arrive on the scene some 30 years later.

B. F. Skinner pioneered and popularized the field of behavior therapy in the mid-1900s.

In the 1950s, Joseph Wolpe and Arnold Lazarus in South Africa, and Hans Eysenck at Maudsley Hospital in London, began to apply the results of earlier human and animal research to the elimination of clinically severe anxiety. Wolpe, for example, had clients, while in a state of relaxation, conjure up images of feared situations. This technique of **systematic desensitization**, like Jones's earlier work, provided a practical demonstration of how

When her parents urge her to be more sociable, Gabriella yells at them. A poor behavioral definition would be: *Gabriella never leaves the house because she's too lazy to find a job or go to school.*

The importance of behavioral definitions is that they allow the clinician to assess how often the **target behavior** occurs (its *frequency*), its severity (or *intensity*), and how long each instance lasts (its *duration*). Once the target is defined, it is assessed along these parameters to establish baseline (pretreatment) levels that will be compared with later assessments to gauge treatment response. Ideal targets for behavioral interventions are undesirable or maladaptive behaviors that are (a) under the client's voluntary control and (b) performed with unacceptably high or low frequency, intensity, and duration. For Gabriella, this might include avoidance of social situations and yelling at her parents. Additional examples include excessive gambling, problematic substance use, self-injury, avoidance behavior, compulsive rituals, aggressive principles of learning could be applied in the clinical setting. These behaviorists, however, argued that their techniques were not new, but rather derived from the framework of a systematic experimental science. In addition, they went to great lengths to point out that their demonstrations of the origins and treatment of "anxiety neuroses" proved that it was unnecessary to subscribe to the "mentalistic demonology" of Freudian psychoanalysis or to the "psychiatric labels" espoused by the *Diagnostic and Statistical Manual*.

At about the same time that Wolpe, Lazarus, and Eysenck were developing their conditioning procedures, the operant tradition was beginning to have an impact. B. F. Skinner and his colleagues (Lindsley & Skinner, 1954; Skinner, 1953) were demonstrating that the behavior of hospitalized individuals with psychosis could be modified by teaching certain skills and controlling the environment to ensure that appropriate (but not inappropriate) responses are followed by positive reinforcement (rewards).

When it was first introduced in the mid-1900s, behavior therapy was considered a radical approach and strongly resisted by the psychiatric establishment which dominated mental health practice at that time. Indeed, the notion that behavior constitutes a subject matter worthy of consideration in its own right was in complete contrast to the prevailing Freudian/psychoanalytic perspective. Moreover, the behavioral approach largely steered clear of psychiatric diagnoses and the medical model, which were becoming more popular during this period. Finally, the objective assessment of presenting problems, as opposed to the use of projective tests (as discussed in Chapter 6, *Personality Assessment*) to understand underlying personality structures, was unprecedented. For the first time, however, psychological assessment and intervention were tightly linked and conceived in terms of experimentally researched principles such as reinforcement, punishment, and extinction.

In the end, the ability to clearly define and measure clinical problems, understand them using scientifically established concepts, derive interventions from these concepts, and use rigorously conducted studies to show that these interventions lead to desirable outcomes turned out to be a formula for success. Through the latter half of the 20th century the behavioral movement (often in collaboration with cognitive approaches) grew in popularity among scientists and clinicians, and now finds itself very much at the forefront of mainstream psychological treatment. ■

behaviors (e.g., hitting, biting), habits (e.g., nail biting, hair pulling, pornography use), crying, oppositional behavior (e.g., failure to follow directions or complete schoolwork), binging, and purging (and many others).

Many approaches to psychotherapy would view behaviors like those listed above as signs of underlying problems rather than as problems in their own right. For example, some practitioners might attribute excessive alcohol consumption to an "addictive personality" or an "oral fixation." Gabriella's avoidance might be attributed to "having a mental illness" called social anxiety disorder. Behavior therapists, however, avoid speculations about such inner causes, and instead stick to what they can directly assess — the problem behavior itself. This includes a de-emphasis on psychiatric diagnoses since they imply that the target behavior stems from an underlying illness — one that can be neither directly observed nor measured apart from the target behavior.

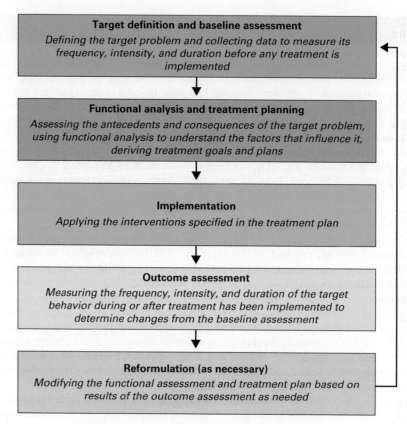

Figure 11.1 Stages of Behavioral Interventions

Functional Analysis and Treatment Planning

Next, the clinician conducts a functional assessment (as discussed in Chapter 7, *Behavioral Assessment*) to understand the relationship between the target behavior and the various factors that, according to learning principles, exert control over that behavior; namely its antecedents and consequences, as well as patterns of associative (classical) conditioning that might predict when it occurs. Understanding the target behavior in terms of learning theory puts the clinician in a position to develop a treatment plan for modifying the behavior's frequency, intensity, and duration.

Implementation

The behavior therapist's role is similar to that of a teacher or coach who helps the client (or those close to the client) learn and practice skills to foster behavior change. This is different from traditional psychotherapy in which the clinician primarily serves as an advice-giver. Behavioral treatment may also be conducted outside the office in the natural environment. For example, after teaching and role playing assertiveness skills with a client in the office, a clinician might plan a "field trip" to a store where the client can practice returning a previously purchased item and asking for her money back. "Homework assignments" also are commonplace, wherein this client would practice assertiveness skills on her own between sessions in different real-world situations. Importantly, field trips and homework assignments are carefully planned and discussed ahead of time so that the goals are clear and any concerns about confidentiality are addressed. Homework also is closely reviewed at the subsequent session.

Outcome Assessment

Is treatment working? It's remarkable how often clients remain in treatment without ever really asking, or receiving, an answer to this question. However, in behavioral therapy, consistent with the empirical approach to intervention, observation and assessment of the target behavior continue throughout behavioral treatment to monitor progress and determine whether the intervention is yielding the desired changes in the frequency, intensity, or duration of the problem. That is, behavior therapists frequently re-administer the same self-report, self-monitoring, observational, or interview methods that were used to establish baseline levels of the problem to assess outcome during and after an intervention. This objective method of assessing treatment response contrasts with more subjective methods such as asking the client, "How are you doing this week?" or the like. If assessment reveals that treatment goals are reached, the intervention is considered successful and the process is complete.

Research indicates that when psychologists continually monitor progress, clients do better in treatment than when outcome is assessed infrequently or not at all (Fortney et al., 2017). Moreover, measurement-based care is associated with decreased costs and a lower likelihood of relapse while in treatment (Lewis et al., 2019).

Reformulation (as necessary)

What if treatment is not working? If the ongoing assessment reveals that the target behavior is not changing, the behavior therapist assumes that the functional analysis and treatment plan need to be revised. Notably, this perspective differs from viewing a poor response as resulting from the client being "treatment resistant." It is neither demoralizing nor threatening to the behavior therapist when the initial formulation is inadequate and the process in Figure 11.1 needs to be restarted. Indeed, case formulations are fluid and it is common for them to become increasingly sophisticated as time goes by. Greater familiarity with the target behavior and the client's strengths and limitations in implementing the treatment plan usually increase the chances of success with each iteration. IN PRACTICE: *The Process of Behavioral Treatment, Shane* describes how a clinical psychologist would approach a trial of behavioral treatment for this youngster.

In Practice **The Process of Behavioral Treatment, Shane**

To give you an idea of how the process of behavioral treatment might play out, let us imagine that Shane's parents sought out a behavioral psychologist to help their son.

During the initial appointment, Shane's parents were asked to describe their son's difficulties, and they replied that Shane "has anger and attention issues because of his ADHD." But rather than focusing on emotions, cognitions, traits, and disorders, the psychologist helped Shane's parents identify concrete, observable behaviors that Shane performs either too frequently or too infrequently. These included excessive shouting, making verbal threats, and other antagonistic behavior (e.g., taunting other children or taking their belongings) as well as difficulty sitting still, following directions, and completing schoolwork on time. These problems are ideal targets for behavioral treatment because they can be directly observed and measured. Shane and his parents decided that Shane's oppositional behavior should be the initial focus of treatment since that was what got Shane in trouble at school. The therapist agreed and arranged for behavioral assessment (as described in Chapter 7) to establish baseline levels of the frequency, intensity, and duration of these behaviors.

At the next session, the psychologist examined the assessment data and interviewed Shane and his parents to clarify (a) the specific situations in which Shane engages in oppositional behavior, (b) the particular events that precede such behavior, and (c) what happens immediately thereafter (e.g., how do others respond to Shane?). Recall from Chapter 7 that such a functional analysis revealed that a lack of attention was often an antecedent of Shane's oppositional behavior, and gaining attention was a typical consequence. Aware of operant conditioning principles, and the reward value of attention — even negative attention — for a 10-year-old like Shane, his psychologist hypothesized that Shane's oppositional conduct is reinforced by the attention he receives. In other words, the function of Shane's oppositional behavior is to receive attention from others.

In thinking about Shane's treatment, the psychologist decided that it would be important to train Shane's parents and teachers to reinforce only desirable behaviors (to *increase* their frequency) while ignoring or punishing undesirable behaviors (to *reduce* their frequency). Specifically, since attention is rewarding to Shane, his parents and teachers should (a) enthusiastically offer praise and other forms of attention when he behaves appropriately, (b) simply ignore antagonistic behaviors that are not terribly disruptive, and (c) place Shane in time-out (i.e., removal from other people and pleasurable activities) for 10 minutes (i.e., time-out often is based on the age of the child — one minute per year) if his behavior becomes disruptive or harmful.

Over the course of the next few sessions, this treatment plan was designed and implemented with input from Shane, his parents, and some of his teachers (through videoconferences with the psychologist). Shane was made aware of the plan so that he knew how to earn attention and avoid being put in time-out. His parents received training in how to manage Shane's behavior and give rewards and consequences. Finally, his teachers were given similar instructions for responding to Shane's behavior at school (we discuss the application of such techniques in more detail later in this chapter). The effectiveness of this plan was continually assessed by asking Shane's parents and teachers to provide a daily rating of Shane's oppositional behavior from 0 (absent) to 5 (severe). These ratings were reviewed at each appointment.

But imagine that Shane's hostile behavior in school persisted following several weeks of implementing this plan. An interview with Shane's teachers might reveal that Shane gets attention from peers each time he misbehaves — a fact that was left out of the functional assessment. Taking this into consideration, the psychologist might hypothesize that Shane's oppositional behavior in school is principally reinforced by his peers' attention in particular. This would necessitate a modification to the treatment plan, such as introducing social skills training (also discussed later) to help him gain his peers' attention in more appropriate ways. The process would then circle back to the intervention stage and continual outcome monitoring. ▬

The Client–Practitioner Relationship

In Chapter 10, *Psychological Treatment: Science and Practice*, we discussed how the client-practitioner relationship is considered a key agent of change in some forms of psychological treatment. Yet although behavior therapists recognize the significance of this relationship, they tend to view it less as a vehicle of change per se, and more as a context in which behavioral interventions promote change. A good analogy is that of a coach or instructor. Imagine taking lessons to learn how to play a sport or musical instrument. Your coach or instructor would first assess your existing skill level to determine your strengths and weaknesses, and then help you build your talent through education (explaining the theory behind the methods being used so you can get the most out of them) and teaching you the right ways to practice the new skills. Naturally, you are likely to work harder for an empathic, supportive, trustworthy, and inspiring coach; but what's even more important is that the coach knows how to help you learn the skills to be able to play the sport or instrument proficiently. The same applies in behavioral treatment, where it is the clinician's job to teach the client skills to promote behavior change and the client's (or family's) job to practice these skills.

Multicultural Competence and Behavioral Interventions

Of course, behavioral therapy is most likely to work if a psychologist's understanding of the target behavior, and the systems that maintain it, are viewed through a cultural lens. Some behaviors may not carry the same meaning or function in different cultures. For instance, a child teasing a peer, or poking fun at them when they are down, may seem aggressive among some females, but a way of showing friendship and closeness among some males. Expressing anxiety to many others may be perfectly appropriate with a family from a western European background, but could be seen as dishonorable among those from other cultures. Similarly, a behavioral intervention may consider a grandparent's authority toward childrearing to be disrespectful to the parent in one culture, yet very much respected in another. Thus, it is critical for psychologists to consider behavior, and behavioral interventions, *within a cultural context.*

Of course, no psychologist can understand all of the possible cultural meanings that could underlie each behavior or each strategy used to address behaviors. Moreover, given the intersectionality between different areas of diversity (e.g., gender and race; sexual orientation and religion), there are far too many cultural contexts to be fully understand by any psychologist. Thus, it is crucial for psychologists to adopt *cultural humility,* wherein the therapist realizes that their own personal experiences have created a unique lens in which they view the world, yet that lens is inherently biased, making it difficult to understand how others may view the same experiences. With cultural humility, a therapist may ask, "Can you tell me what (that behavior) means to you? What would it be like in your experience to have your parent praise you in that way? What do you and others you interact with think about you engaging in (this behavior) in a different way?" Seeing differences in one's cultural context with open-ended, accepting, and empathic questions, such as these, communicates to clients that there is no "right" way for behaviors to be understood and the psychologist is most interested in understanding it the

The role of grandparents in childrearing differs across cultures, and behavioral therapists must keep this in mind when planning interventions.

way their client does, so they can work together on what will work for the client's own context, not a set of values or expectations imposed upon the client by the psychologist.

Think **Like a Clinical Psychologist** Shane's parents accepted their role in helping their son change his behavior. They worked hard and achieved the results they were hoping for. But some parents refuse to get involved in their child's treatment. In what situation might this seem more or less appropriate? How would you address this as a behavior therapist?

▌Applications of Behavioral Interventions

Behavioral interventions work very well in reducing a variety of behavioral and psychological problems, including skill deficits (e.g., social skills), anxiety and fear, depressed mood, problematic habit behaviors, and problems with sexual functioning. Let's look at each of these next.

Addressing Skill Deficits

Social Skills Training

Deficits in the ability to communicate effectively, display appropriate manners, use good hygiene, show empathy and consideration for others, and tactfully express one's own needs and opinions are often the result of a failure to learn social skills. Accordingly, **social skills training** (Goldfried and Davison, 1994) is a widely used behavioral intervention because having such skills is essential for healthy casual and intimate interpersonal relationships and successful employment. Poor social skills are also associated with increased depression, anxiety, and stress in both adults and children (e.g., Feldman et al., 2017). Depending on the strengths and limitations of the individual client, training might involve learning proper etiquette, appropriate verbal (e.g., how to express compassion) and nonverbal (e.g., smiling, making eye contact) communication skills, and skills for engaging in casual conversations and resolving conflicts.

Skills training begins with the clinician providing a rationale for the importance of learning new behaviors. Next, a list of the situations in which the client has difficulty is created. **Table 11.1** provides an example of such a list in order of increasing complexity of the skills required. In this example, the client is a 17-year-old boy who had difficulty making friends. An observation of the child, as well as interviews with his parents and teachers, revealed the five domains of social skill deficits listed in the table. It was hypothesized that improvement in these areas would eventually lead to developing stronger interpersonal relationships.

Table 11.1   List of Skills and Situations for Social Skills Training
1.   Speaking softly when indoors
2.   Refraining from talking out loud to myself at school and at home
3.   Getting peoples' attention with subtle verbal and nonverbal cues (rather than tapping them) at home and at school
4.   Waiting for my turn to speak instead of interrupting others at home and at school
5.   Asking questions to others instead of talking only about myself at home and school

Moving through the list one at a time until proficiency is reached, the clinician and client first practice in-session role plays in which the clinician provides instruction, coaching, and feedback. Sometimes videotaped replays are used as an aid. In other instances, the clinician trades roles with the client to provide an appropriate model. The clinician might also accompany the client on field trips (e.g., to a restaurant or store) to practice in real-world settings before the client is instructed to practice the newly acquired skills in real-life situations between sessions. Clients keep written records of their practices, including their thoughts and feelings about, and the consequences of, using their new skills. At the subsequent appointment, the between-session practice is discussed; successes are praised and difficulties are addressed. Numerous randomized controlled trials and meta-analyses indicate that social skills training (in-person, as well as using various technology platforms) is efficacious for improving such skills in individuals diagnosed with various psychiatric disorders, including autism, schizophrenia, developmental disability, and social anxiety disorder (e.g., Kapse & Nirmala, 2017; Soares et al., 2021).

Assertiveness Training

Some clients have trouble expressing their opinions and wishes to others. They may be *aware* of their thoughts, feelings, and needs, but refrain from speaking up because they believe they aren't entitled to stand up for themselves or fear that others will react negatively. As a result, they are often taken advantage of and manipulated into doing things they don't want to do. Not surprisingly, such unassertiveness is associated with anxiety, low self-worth, depression, and even anger (Speed et al., 2018).

The guiding principle in **assertiveness training** (which is often conducted in groups) is that everyone has a right to express their thoughts, feelings, and needs to others, as long as we do so in a respectful way without making demands. Treatment focuses on learning how to confidently ask for favors, give opinions and compliments, say "no" and refuse unreasonable requests, compromise and negotiate, and respond effectively to provocations (e.g., Speed et al., 2018). Importantly, assertiveness is not the same as teaching people to be *aggressive*. Rather, it is a method of learning how to express oneself without trampling on the rights of others in the process. Take the spectator at a basketball game

The basis of assertiveness training is the universal right to express one's own thoughts, feelings, and needs — including the right to respectfully say "no" and refuse requests.

who cannot see because the person in front of her is constantly standing up. To react by issuing a threat — "If you don't sit down, I'll knock you down" — is aggressive. But saying "Please, I wish you would sit down; I can't see when you're standing" is an assertive response.

Modifying Behavior with Rewards and Consequences

Behavioral Modification/Parent Training

Like Shane, many children and adolescents are brought to clinical psychologists by their parents or guardians seeking help for "bad behavior" such as "acting out," rule-breaking, or tantrums. Along with other forms of treatment that are implemented one-on-one with the child (e.g., skills training, cognitive interventions), many practitioners will devote time to training parents to use **contingency management** — a set of behavioral techniques based on operant conditioning to foster more appropriate behavior in youth. Specifically, these strategies all have the goal of controlling behavior by manipulating its consequences. Here are just a few examples.

- **Shaping:** A desired behavior is developed by first rewarding (reinforcing) any behavior that approximates it. Gradually, through rewarding actions more and more closely resembling the desired behavior, the final behavior is shaped.

- **Time-out:** Undesirable behavior is extinguished by removing the child temporarily from a situation in which that behavior is reinforced. A child who disrupts the class is removed so that the disruptive behavior cannot be reinforced by the attention of others.

- **Contracting:** A formal agreement or contract is struck between therapist, parents, and client, specifying the consequences of certain behaviors on the part of both. Specifically, the parents agree to consistently provide rewards for certain desirable behavior and punishment for undesirable behavior.

- **"Grandma's rule":** The basic idea here is akin to Grandma's exhortation "Work before play!" It means that a desired behavior is reinforced by allowing the child or adolescent the privilege of engaging in a more attractive behavior once the target behavior is complete. For example, the child is allowed to use electronic devices only after homework is finished. This method is sometimes referred to as the **Premack principle** (Premack, 1959).

Research demonstrates that instructing parents or guardians to implement contingency management can be very effective in reducing problem behaviors in youth. A meta-analysis of 15 studies on school-age children with autism-related disorders, for example, showed that such interventions lead to improved communication and adaptive functioning, as well as reduced problem behavior (Ratliff-Black & Therrien, 2020). Graziano and colleagues (2020) also found that brief intensive parent training (five sessions over 2 weeks) was as effective as a more routine schedule (one weekly session over 10 weeks) in reducing behavioral problems for children from highly stressed families. Finally, the results of a meta-analysis by Thongseiratch and colleagues (2020) suggest that parent training can also be successfully delivered online.

Token Economies

Techniques based on operant conditioning are also used with adults and youth in hospitals, residential care facilities (e.g., for individuals with developmental disabilities or chronic severe mental illness), and classroom settings. A common example is the **token economy** in which desired behavior is positively reinforced using "vouchers" that can be exchanged for sought-after rewards and privileges such as special treats or screen time (Ivy et al., 2017; Krasner, 1971). If you think about it, we all live in a token economy of sorts! The coins and paper money with which we are all familiar have no intrinsic value. But we work hard to earn such tokens so that we can exchange them for goods and services of necessity and luxury.

Implementing a *therapeutic* token economy program first requires specifying the desirable behaviors (hard work) that will be reinforced; for example, neatness, hygiene, exercise, greater social participation, and superior completion of chores or other work. Next, a clearly defined token (or medium of exchange) must be determined, such as poker chips. Third, a "menu" of backup reinforcers is established. These are the special privileges or other rewards desired by the client(s). Thus, two tokens, each worth 10 points, might be exchanged for permission to use the Internet for an hour, or one token worth 5 points might be exchanged for a piece of candy. It goes without saying that a token economy requires a fairly elaborate system of record keeping and a supervising adult that is very observant and committed to the importance of the program.

Token economies can be very effective with youth with various behavioral problems. But why use tokens at all? Why not reinforce good behavior directly? The reason is that the effect of reinforcement is greater if the reinforcement is provided immediately after the desired behavior occurs. If the reward of attending a movie occurs 10 hours after a client makes her own bed, it will not be as effective as a token given instantly. That token will come to signify the reward and will assume much of the effectiveness of the backup reward for which it may be exchanged.

Reducing Clinical Anxiety and Fear

Many anxiety- and fear-related problems can be understood from a classical (Pavlovian) fear conditioning perspective in which clinically elevated anxiety becomes associated with fear-relevant situations and stimuli (e.g., Sewart & Craske, 2020). As an example, imagine getting ready to climb into bed only to pull back the covers and see a large and very scary-looking spider waiting there for you! Shocked and startled (an unconditioned response; UR), you recoil and let out a bloodcurdling scream. Your heart pounds, you have trouble catching your breath, and you feel a wave of dread wash over you. Maybe you were previously unafraid of spiders, but after the terror of unexpectedly finding a spider in your bed (an unconditioned stimulus; US) you might begin to fear (a conditioned response; CR) all spiders (conditioned stimuli; CS) and avoid situations in which you may come across them. If this fear and its related avoidance cause significant distress and impairment, you might meet the diagnostic criteria for specific phobia.

Courtesy Jon Abramowitz

Exposure Therapy

The process of reducing or eliminating a conditioned fear response by weakening its association with the US is called fear **extinction**. This is best achieved using **exposure therapy**, a behavioral intervention in which clients repeatedly confront the CS in the absence of the US. In the previous example, your fear of spiders would be extinguished if you were repeatedly exposed to spiders in the absence of feeling surprised and terrified. That is, after repeated planned exposures, the notion of spiders being associated with extreme terror would be dampened by new learning that (a) spiders are generally safe and (b) feelings of anxiety and fear are themselves temporary and manageable (e.g., Abramowitz et al., 2019). As a result, spiders would lose their association with feelings of being terrified, and this new learning would extinguish your fear.

Clients can develop conditioned fears of different types of stimuli. Therefore, exposure must sometimes be conducted in different ways. **_In vivo_ exposure** (exposure in real life) entails direct confrontation with actual situations and objects, such as animals (e.g., spiders, dogs), social or evaluative situations (e.g., speaking up in class), and environments (e.g., shopping malls,

Using exposure _in vivo_, clients are helped to confront actual situations and stimuli that they fear, but that objectively pose an acceptably low risk of danger.

elevators). In **imaginal exposure**, clients confront unwanted thoughts, doubts, and memories that provoke elevated fear (such as by writing or talking about them). Finally, **interoceptive exposure** involves provoking benign bodily sensations that trigger inappropriate fear, such as a racing heart, breathlessness, and feeling lightheaded. Such sensations are activated using exercises such as hyperventilation, breathing through a straw, and spinning in a swivel chair.

A course of exposure therapy begins with a few sessions of treatment planning during which the client and therapist collaboratively develop a list or "menu" (often called an **exposure hierarchy**) of the feared situations, thoughts, body sensations, and other stimuli that will be confronted during exposure trials. Items on the list must be those that the client expects will lead to negative outcomes, but that objectively pose no more than acceptable (everyday) risks. These stimuli are then ranked from the least to the most challenging, and often (but not always) confronted in order from easiest to most difficult. At each session, the psychologist coaches the client through exposure to a different item and instructs the client to perform the same (or similar) exposure task(s) between appointments. You might think of exposure therapy as a set of experiments in which clients collect experiential data to disconfirm their expectations of danger.

Table 11.2 shows a sample exposure list for a client with social anxiety. This client was afraid that others would judge her harshly, they would become angry with her, and she would literally "die of embarrassment." As you can see, each exposure item is tied to a particular **danger-based expectation**, a prediction about what the client assumes will happen when exposed to the feared situation. The aim of each exposure task is to disconfirm the associated expectation. Thus, the exposure program in Table 11.2 was designed to help this client learn that others generally don't mind when she speaks to them; that people generally mind their own business rather than focus on her; and that although feeling embarrassed is *uncomfortable*, it is not permanently damaging. This new learning extinguished the client's extreme fear of social interactions. Traditionally, exposure therapists asked clients to also rate each exposure item on a scale of difficulty from 0 to 100, but this practice is no longer considered essential.

Table 11.2 Sample Exposure List for a Client with Social Anxiety	
Description of the Exposure Task	**Danger-based Expectation**
Make eye contact with people	They will be angry with me.
Eat lunch alone in a crowded cafeteria	Everyone will notice me and talk about me.
Ask someone for the time	The person will be angry with me.
Initiate a conversation with someone	I won't know what to say and it will be terrible.
Drop a handful of change in a store	Everyone will laugh at me.
Ask a foolish question to a someone	I'll die of embarrassment.

While exposure lists are highly individualized based on the client's particular fears, there are some general rules of thumb that psychologists use when implementing exposure, including:

- Each exposure session is typically of long rather than short duration.

- Exposure to each item is repeated in different settings until the client no longer expects danger.

- Exposure *can* be gradual, starting with less anxiety-provoking stimuli and progressing to more challenging stimuli; but it does not have to progress hierarchically.

- It is important for clients to attend to the feared stimulus and interact with it as much as possible.

- Clients must not try to fight the feelings of anxiety exposure provokes. Instead, these feelings must be allowed to persist until they subside on their own — a natural process known as **habituation**. Habituation helps the client learn that anxiety itself is safe, manageable, and temporary.

- Exposure ends when the client no longer expects the once-feared (and avoided) situations to produce danger or extreme fear.

Like many behavioral interventions, exposure can be used as a singular treatment or as one part of a multicomponent program. For example, Craske, Meadows, and Barlow (2000) describe a treatment program for clients diagnosed with panic disorder that includes exposure along with psychoeducation and cognitive therapy. Specifically, interoceptive exposure is used to help clients confront feared physiological sensations such as a racing heart, rapid breathing, and dizziness. Indeed, panic attacks result when such stimuli become associated with fears of medical or psychological catastrophes such as a heart attack, stroke, or "loss of control." When clients confront the exact internal sensations they expect will lead to disaster, and yet no tragedy befalls them, their fear of these sensations is extinguished. Of course, a therapist cannot always ensure that feared outcomes won't occur; see A CLOSER LOOK: *But What If the Feared Outcome Actually Happens?* to learn how exposure therapists handle the situation when things don't go as planned.

A Closer Look   But What If the Feared Outcome Actually Happens?

Although practitioners try to expose their clients to stimuli that are "objectively safe," this is not the same thing as "absolutely risk-free." Sometimes dogs bite, elevators get stuck, people are teased or humiliated, accidents happen, and so on. So, what's an exposure therapist to do if feared outcomes occur during treatment? Wouldn't this undermine fear extinction and the whole process of exposure therapy? Interestingly, research shows that extinction is actually *enhanced* when the conditioned and unconditioned stimuli are occasionally paired during exposure trials — that is, when "bad" things happen that seemingly confirm the client's fears (Craske et al., 2014; Krompinger et al., 2019).

Translating this to clinical applications, one of the authors once worked with a man who was afraid of elevators — specifically, he was afraid of being *stuck* in an elevator. As a result, he had avoided them for many years. After a few sessions spent convincing this client to try exposure to riding in the elevator within the clinic building, he finally agreed . . . as long as the therapist accompanied him. But after a few trips up and down to different floors, the elevator they were on got stuck between floors! The client became significantly distraught and experienced a full-blown panic attack. Since this happened before the advent of cell phones, all the therapist could do was remain calm, use the elevator telephone to call building maintenance, and then wait. After about 15 minutes, a maintenance worker pried open the elevator doors and helped the client and therapist climb out safely. But this exposure had reinforced the client's worst fear. How would treatment ever be able to move forward?

But when this client returned for his appointment a week later, his distress over being stuck in the elevator the previous week had remarkably lessened. Unprompted, he even remarked that getting stuck was "probably a good exposure for him" because it ended up not being as awful as he would have anticipated. After all, he had believed that getting stuck would result either in the elevator car plummeting to the bottom of the building or running out of air — neither of which happened. To the therapist's amazement, this client was now *more* willing to expose himself to riding in elevators. After several more weeks of practice with different elevators in different buildings (none of which ever became stuck), he completed treatment and had successfully extinguished his fear.

This example demonstrates that it is okay, and perhaps even preferable, if aversive outcomes are occasionally reinforced in the course of exposure therapy. Indeed, clients can benefit from learning that such occurrences will not be their undoing. Thus, exposure therapists are trained to occasionally plan for such occurrences, especially during the treatment of fears in which aversive outcomes tend to happen occasionally after treatment, such as social rejection, bee stings, anxiety-related body sensations, and becoming stuck in an elevator (among others; Sewart & Craske, 2020). It is also most advantageous to incorporate aversive outcomes during the later phases of treatment, rather at the beginning as in the present example.

Finally, incorporating aversive outcomes is not always appropriate — and certainly not when it may cause undue harm. For example, it would clearly not be ethical to re-expose an individual with a fear of snakes to an actual snake bite during an exposure. Similarly, exposing a trauma survivor to another traumatic event would be wholly unacceptable. ▄▄▄

Theo Wargo/Getty Images

Psychologist Edna Foa is a pioneer in the field of exposure therapy for obsessive-compulsive disorder and PTSD.

Psychologist Edna Foa and her colleagues have spent decades researching exposure therapy for trauma survivors (e.g., Gallagher et al., 2020). The program they developed involves psychoeducation, cognitive therapy, and imaginal exposure in which clients practice reliving the memories of their traumatic experience. The notion is that for people diagnosed with posttraumatic stress disorder (PTSD), such memories become associated with the trauma itself, and thus provoke unnecessarily intense anxiety and avoidance. Confronting such memories extinguishes fear by helping clients learn that (a) thinking about traumatic experiences is not dangerous, and (b) they are capable of managing the distress that such memories provoke. *In vivo* exposure to objectively safe reminders of the trauma (e.g., places, people, and objects) is also used to extinguish conditioned fears of such stimuli.

The treatment of obsessive-compulsive disorder (OCD) also involves both *in vivo* and imaginal exposure. But as explained in IN PRACTICE: *Exposure and Response Prevention, Kiara*, these techniques are used slightly differently than for PTSD. Moreover, the treatment of OCD includes another behavioral intervention, **response prevention**, which means refraining from compulsive rituals.

In Practice   Exposure and Response Prevention, Kiara

Recall from Chapter 9, *Diagnosis, Case Formulation, and Treatment Planning*, that Kiara's case formulation and treatment plan suggested the use of **exposure and response prevention (ERP)** — confrontation with feared obsessional thoughts and stimuli along with refraining from compulsive rituals — to reduce her problems with OCD. The first stage of this program involved a thorough functional analysis to assess all of the intrusive thoughts and external stimuli that Kiara associates with elevated anxiety, her danger-based expectations, and the rituals she uses to reduce her anxiety. Next, the therapist and Kiara discussed the process and rationale for

ERP: although it would be anxiety provoking, repeatedly confronting feared situations and obsessional thoughts without relying on rituals would help Kiara learn that the situations and thoughts she fears are not as threatening as she anticipates, and that anxiety and uncertainty are safe and manageable. The functional analysis was then used to develop the exposure list shown below. Exposure list items appearing in regular type refer to *in vivo* exposures, whereas those in italics were imaginal exposures.

Order	Exposure Item	Danger-based Expectation
1	Read about infections that doctors and nurses can pass along to patients	The uncertainty will be unbearable and I will need to check.
2	*Maybe I gave a patient an infection*	I can't stand not knowing if it's true. I'll be responsible and I'll get in trouble.
3	Wash hands for 10 seconds (per protocol) before working with a patient	I will give the patient an infection.
4	Read/watch stories about nurses who made mistakes	I can't tolerate the uncertainty.
5	*Maybe I made a mistake and a patient will die because of me*	I can't tolerate the uncertainty. I will really be responsible for making a terrible mistake.
6	Enter data into a patient's chart without checking	I will make a mistake.

Kiara's treatment sessions were structured using an expanding schedule wherein sessions 1–6 occurred twice weekly (for 3 weeks), sessions 7–12 were once weekly (for 6 weeks), and sessions 13–16 were every other week (for 8 weeks). During the first exposure session, Kiara's psychologist gave Kiara material to read about the various illnesses that doctors and nurses sometimes inadvertently spread to their patients. As expected, this provoked anxiety along with urges to check her patients' records and make sure that none had developed such illnesses. For response prevention between sessions, Kiara was instructed to resist engaging in any such checking (outside of what was required as part of her work), and record any compulsive checking she could not resist on a self-monitoring form supplied by her clinician. In addition, she was asked to practice reading similar anxiety-provoking material to increase the urge to check and make the exposures more challenging. Kiara was helped to "lean into" her anxiety and unwanted thoughts, rather than trying to ignore them or push them away.

During session 2, Kiara was introduced to imaginal exposure. In the treatment of OCD, imaginal exposure provides a systematic way of repeating and prolonging confrontation with intrusive obsessional thoughts, images, and doubts that are associated with elevated anxiety. Clients create written scripts of their obsessions that can be re-read or recorded (e.g., on a smartphone or computer) and played back to allow for new learning that such thoughts are safe, manageable, and not predictive of imminent danger. Imaginal exposure is often combined with *in vivo* exposure, as for a client with obsessions about causing fires. Such a client might leave an appliance plugged in while taking a walk outside (*in vivo* exposure) and imaginally exposing herself to thinking that she has caused a serious fire. Kiara and her psychologist created several scripts related to her obsessions about mistakenly harming the patients she was taking care of, such as the one shown below. Notice that the script incorporates Kiara's danger-based expectations associated with this obsession.

> *Mr. S is a patient of mine who is recovering from a bone marrow transplant. His immune system is in an extremely vulnerable state and it is my responsibility to make sure he does not get any viral or bacterial infections because it could make*

him very sick or even die. But these germs are invisible. What if I didn't fully disinfect myself or something in Mr. S's room and he catches an infection? It would be my fault if something happened. His family would blame me, I would be fired, and I could never live with myself. I want to double-check Mr. S's health status just to make sure he is okay; but I am working on not doing that. What if he has caught an infection that I mistakenly gave him?

Kiara first practiced imagining this script by itself to learn that she could manage these distressing ideas without turning to compulsive rituals. Then she moved on to the next item on her exposure list — washing her hands only as directed by hospital protocol (instead of excessively) — before working with patients. After each patient visit, she would expose herself to the imaginal script and refrain from any checking to further reinforce her new learning.

Kiara worked gradually through her exposure list and then began practicing the more challenging exposures in different situations. For example, at one point, she set an alarm to wake her up in the middle of the night so she could practice reading an imaginal exposure script about having mistakenly administered too much of a medication to a particular patient. But instead of going in to work to check the medication log, Kiara practiced going back to sleep while feeling uncertain. Over time, such exercises helped extinguish the anxiety associated with such thoughts and situations, which also led to her spending less time performing rituals. ▪▬

The beneficial effects of exposure therapy for clinical anxiety and fear are among the most consistent research findings in all of clinical psychological science. Indeed, behavioral and cognitive-behavioral treatment programs for individuals diagnosed with specific phobias, panic disorder, agoraphobia, social anxiety, PTSD, and OCD all include forms of exposure as a central component and are consistently found to be efficacious and effective in randomized controlled trials and in meta-analyses of the literature (e.g., Carpenter et al., 2018). Research also indicates that exposure-based treatment is, in many instances, as effective (if not more so) than psychotropic medication in the treatment of clinical anxiety (e.g., Foa et al., 2005). These findings apply to both adults and youth with such problems (e.g., Abramowitz et al., 2005).

Progressive Muscle Relaxation

For clients with chronic stress and anxiety, the prolonged muscle tension can manifest in physical problems such as chronic pain (e.g., headaches, joint pain), high blood pressure, and insomnia. Accordingly, psychologists working with such individuals often use **progressive muscle relaxation (PMR)**, a behavioral technique that involves tensing and then relaxing various muscle groups (e.g., facial muscles, arm muscles, leg muscles) one at a time while focusing on the sensations of relaxation that follow (Hazlett-Stevens & Bernstein, 2021). Often used in tandem with other cognitive-behavioral techniques, PMR follows a script with specific instructions for tensing and relaxing the various muscle groups (e.g., Jacobson, 1938; such scripts are widely available online if you are interested in trying it out). With practice, clients learn to use PMR more and more efficiently and in different situations to become relaxed without having to follow the script.

Because PMR is most effective for mild to moderate levels of anxiety and stress, it is not used in lieu of exposure therapy for conditioned fear responses as described in the previous section (e.g., Montero-Marin et al., 2018). In fact, because it is not expected to relieve severe anxiety, relaxation is often used as a control (placebo) intervention in RCTs examining the efficacy of exposure and other treatments for anxiety disorders (e.g., Clark et al., 1994). Rather, PMR is best employed to help with general anxiety and stress associated with medical conditions.

Improving Depressed Mood

From a behavioral perspective, depression results from a lack of positive reinforcement from social relationships and other aspects of the environment (Lewinsohn & Shaffer, 1971). That is, when a person fails to experience enjoyment and satisfaction from their daily activities, they may begin to feel sad, angry, lonely, or frustrated. But these negative feelings lead to reduced motivation, further social isolation, and continued inaction. The result is a vicious cycle in which the person is deprived of social rewards, leading to continued depression, further inactivity, and so on (e.g., Carvalho & Hopko, 2011). To break this cycle, behavior therapists implement **behavioral activation (BA)** in which clients are helped to (a) more routinely engage in pleasurable and rewarding activities that provide consistent positive reinforcement to improve their mood and (b) decrease engagement in activities that increase the risk of feel-

In behavioral activation, clients repeatedly engage in activities they enjoy (often with others) to help them experience positive feelings and improve their mood.

ing depressed. To put it simply, the notion behind BA is that it is difficult to feel depressed when engaged in enjoyable activities and positive social encounters that provide a sense of accomplishment.

BA is a structured and short-term intervention that can be used on its own or as one piece of a multicomponent cognitive-behavioral treatment program. As described by Lejuez and colleagues (2001), it begins with helping the client understand that the best way to reduce depression is to become aware of the relationship between behaviors and feelings and to make sure each day contains activities that bring a sense of enjoyment or fulfillment. Importantly, clients cannot afford to wait to feel motivated before engaging in pleasurable activities; they must be proactive and change their behavior first. Only then they will start to feel better.

Next, clients monitor their behavior for a week (using forms provided by the therapist), rating the level of importance and enjoyment of literally everything they do. These activity lists are reviewed with the aim of identifying patterns that maintain feeling depressed. The client and therapist then come up with ideas for where in the client's schedule changes could be made to add more meaningful and enjoyable activities and reduce those that evoke negative feelings. Such changes are then planned using detailed schedules, and goals are set to increase the likelihood that the client will make the changes. Clients continue to keep records of their daily activities, along with corresponding ratings of their mood. Research shows that BA is effective in promoting changes in mood in the context of depression as well as other clinical problems such as anxiety and problem substance use (e.g., Blakey et al., 2019; Cuijpers et al., 2007).

Modifying Habit Behaviors

A number of behavioral interventions are used to help clients reduce problematic habits such as excessive hair pulling, skin picking, nail biting, pornography use, shopping, smoking, alcohol or drug use, gambling, and excessive use of digital media/Internet. From a learning perspective, both positive and negative reinforcement, as well as classical conditioning, play roles in the development and persistence of such habits (e.g., Wetterneck et al., 2012). Excessive pornography use that persists despite being problematic provides an excellent example. Of course, the sexual behavior itself (e.g., arousal, masturbation, orgasm) is positively reinforced by the physiological pleasure it produces. But pornography use may also be preceded by negative feelings such as loneliness, anxiety, depression, or interpersonal stress (Rousseau et al., 2020), and may be negatively reinforced by the escape from distress that it engenders. Finally, the urge to use pornography can become a CR to previously neutral stimuli such as activities, locations, and objects that are repeatedly paired with using pornography (Snagowski et al., 2016). For example, after frequently using a smartphone to view pornography (US), merely seeing the phone (CS) can provoke sexual arousal and urges to view pornography (CR). Understanding these processes has led to the application of behavioral interventions, as we describe next.

Habit Reversal Training

The first stage in **habit reversal training** (HRT; e.g., Morris et al., 2013) is **awareness training** in which the client keeps a running log of each incident of the target behavior throughout the day. Details recorded in self-monitoring logs include the time and situation (e.g., alone, with drinking buddies); associated physical states (e.g., fatigued, sexually aroused); thoughts and emotions (e.g., anxious, bored); and aspects of the behavior itself, such as how much hair was pulled, how many drinks were consumed, and the amount of time spent gambling.

A second component of HRT is **stimulus control**, wherein the client and therapist use the data from awareness training logs to design strategies for reducing the influence of conditioned stimuli that trigger the target behavior. **Table 11.3** shows a sample stimulus control plan for an adult client seeking help for an embarrassing thumb sucking habit. The client tries using the various strategies one at a time to determine which one(s) work to reduce the target behavior.

Table 11.3 Sample Stimulus Control Plan for an Adult Client with Thumb Sucking		
Type of Trigger	**Example of Trigger**	**Stimulus Control Strategies**
Social	Mostly when alone, but sometimes with others when they are not looking	Stay within sight of others as much as possible
Tactile	Physical urge felt in mouth	Chew gum, use hard candy
Location	Could be anywhere, but often in bed	Wear gloves in bed, put lotion or bitter-tasting substance on thumb
Activity	While sedentary (e.g., reading, watching TV, lying in bed)	Wear gloves, put lotion or bitter-tasting substance on thumb
Emotional	Boredom, stress, tired	Wear gloves

The third component of HRT is **competing response practice**, which entails responding to the urge to perform the target behavior by instead engaging in a behavior that is incompatible with the target. For example, when the client just described experiences an urge to suck her thumb, she might sit on her hand or hold an object as a competing response. As another example, a client who engages in excessive gambling might instead spend his time socializing with friends who do not gamble. Of course, a limitation of both stimulus control and competing response practice is that it is up to clients to change their behavior patterns. When faced with the choice to engage in a pleasurable (albeit maladaptive) behavior versus abstaining, it can be challenging to choose the latter. Nevertheless, controlled studies and meta-analyses (e.g., Bate et al., 2011) indicate that HRT, often in combination with other cognitive-behavioral interventions, is associated with large and stable reductions in habit-related behaviors in both adults and children.

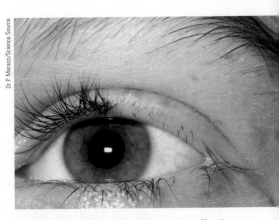

Dr P. Marazzi/Science Source

Cue Exposure

As we described earlier, some habits become conditioned responses after being paired with the same stimuli again and again. Take problematic drug use. Drugs are US that produce reliable biological and psychological URs. Yet through classical conditioning, things like syringes, friends, and locations that are present during drug use often become CS that can trigger

Habit reversal training can be highly effective in the treatment of maladaptive habits, such as excessive hair pulling (in this case, of eyelashes).

CRs in the form of drug cravings (Everitt and Robbins, 2016). This associative link, however, can be extinguished with repeated nonreinforced presentations of CSs so that they lose their capacity to produce the CR. This conceptualization has led to the use of **cue exposure** in the behavioral treatment of many problematic habits. Much like the treatment of fear, cue exposure subjects clients to CSs — such as the sight and smell of alcohol, walking through a casino, or using a smartphone — while resisting the usual behavioral response (e.g., drinking, gambling, and pornography use, respectively). The goal is to weaken the CS–US link via extinction and by extension attenuate cravings. But while some research supports the use of cue exposure, results have been inconsistent, and the overall effects are generally weak to moderate and not long-lasting (e.g., Mellentin et al., 2017). Accordingly, if it is used at all, cue exposure is usually part of a multicomponent cognitive-behavioral treatment package.

Aversive Conditioning

Based on the principle of **punishment** — the notion that when a behavior is followed by an unpleasant consequence (e.g., pain, loss), it will diminish — **aversive conditioning** involves pairing an unpleasant stimulus with the undesirable target behavior. An illustrative example is the use of Antabuse in the treatment of problem drinking. Antabuse is a medication that causes an intensely unpleasant reaction (e.g., nausea, vomiting, headache) if even small amounts of alcohol are consumed. In treatment, clients combine Antabuse (US) and alcohol (CS) until even the sight of a drink induces classically conditioned discomfort (CR). Wolpe (1973) described other aversive agents that could be paired with target behaviors, including stale cigarette smoke, loud noise, vile-smelling solutions, and shame. Although the range of potential punishments is limited only by the resourcefulness of the therapist, as we discuss later, there are obvious ethical considerations when using aversive conditioning.

Cautela (1967) developed a related procedure known as **covert sensitization** that works via the same principle but relies on imagery rather than the use of actual consequences. Here, clients *imagine* themselves engaging in the behaviors they wish to eliminate. Once they have a clear mental image of the undesired target behavior (CS), they are instructed to vividly imagine extremely aversive events (US) with the aim of establishing discomfort as a CR. A typical therapy session might, for example, involve the therapist instructing the client to imagine biting one's nails *and developing violent nausea and diarrhea*.

Aversive conditioning has many critics. The use of punishment, and what may be highly unpleasant stimuli, seems incompatible with the APA's ethics code. Moreover, positively reinforcing adaptive responses usually produces longer-lasting behavior change than does punishment. Others, however, maintain that aversive techniques, when used in a sensitive fashion with consenting clients, have merit. Even so, these interventions tend to see use only after other approaches have failed and with clients in the most serious and debilitating of circumstances (e.g., severe alcohol use, unlawful sexual activity). Finally, the aversive stimuli are kept to brief durations, and clients are never *required* to engage in treatment, but do so by choice (Spiegler & Guevremont, 2010).

Improving Sexual Functioning

Many problems with sexual functioning can be viewed from a behavioral perspective. For example, people with trouble maintaining erections during intercourse (i.e., erectile dysfunction) often experience arousal-inhibiting performance anxiety that is classically conditioned to the expectation of sexual activity (Kane et al., 2019). Difficulty reaching orgasm can be associated with a lack of practice (Marchand, 2020). Finally, communication deficits between partners often play a role in problems with sexual functioning (Jones et al., 2018).

Accordingly, a staple of treatment for virtually all manner of difficulties related to sexual functioning is a behavioral technique called **sensate focus**. Initially developed by Masters and Johnson (1970), sensate focus involves a series of structured touching and discovery exercises that a couple performs together to extinguish performance-related anxiety, enhance communication, and learn about one's own and their partner's sexual response (Weiner & Avery-Clark, 2017). Specifically, the exercises provide opportunities for experiencing one's own and one's partner's body and learning about preferences for stimulation and sexual communication in a nondemand, exploratory way. Sensate focus is an intervention for couples of all different ages, gender identities, and sexual orientations. It is practiced when the couple can be relaxed and uninterrupted for an hour.

During the first phase, each partner takes turns slowly and gently exploring the other's body (with hands and fingers only) while avoiding specific areas, such as the genitals and breasts. At first, this might be practiced dressed, and then undressed. The focus is simply on experiencing sensations such as temperature, pressure, and texture. The receiving partner is encouraged to provide nonverbal feedback, such as placing their hand over their partner's as a guide to location and pressure. In addition to fostering communication, this exercise helps extinguish anxiety associated with intimacy by learning to focus on the sensations (which one can directly control), as opposed to arousal (which is not always under voluntary control).

During the second phase, partners continue to explore the pleasurable areas identified previously, with the addition of genitals and breasts. Intercourse, however, is avoided, and although arousal and orgasm might occur, they are not the goal. The focus is to learn awareness of response to stimulation and increase personal pleasure associated with being touched. In the third stage, the couple begins progressing to intercourse, building on the exploration and communication of previous stages to maintain feelings of arousal and comfort.

Many studies show the efficacy and effectiveness of sensate focus (alone or in combination with other techniques) for improving sexual functioning (e.g., Avery-Clark et al., 2019).

The technique is also effective for sexual difficulties associated with medical conditions, such as breast cancer. Sensate focus is accepted well by clients, sex therapists, and physicians.

> **Think Like a Clinical Psychologist** As with any form of treatment, not all clients achieve benefits following behavioral interventions. Discuss the variables that you believe might predict which clients improve and which clients do not.

▥ Evaluating the Behavioral Approach

Proponents of behavioral treatments see their progress as tangible evidence of what can be accomplished with an objective and experimental approach to psychological treatment. In many ways, behavior therapy revolutionized clinical psychology. Critics, on the other hand, see behavioral interventions as superficial, pretentiously scientific, and even dehumanizing in their mechanistic attempts to change human behavior. We close with an examination of some of the strengths and criticisms of this approach.

Strengths

Efficacy

As mentioned throughout this chapter, there is ample evidence that a wide variety of behavioral interventions are efficacious, and in fact, the treatment of choice for many clinical problems. The majority of individual and meta-analytic studies that have compared the effectiveness of behavioral or cognitive-behavioral techniques with that of other psychological treatments (e.g., psychodynamic or humanistic therapy) have found a small but consistent superiority for behavioral and cognitive-behavioral methods (Tolin, 2010). Clearly, these are important treatment techniques for clinical psychologists to master.

Efficiency

The behavioral movement also brought with it a series of techniques that were shorter and more efficient than pre-existing psychotherapies. The interminable number of 50-minute psychotherapy hours was replaced by a much shorter series of consultations that focused on the client's specific complaints. A series of equally specific procedures was applied, and the entire process terminated when the client's complaints no longer existed. Gone was the lengthy "rooting out" of underlying psychic conflicts, the exhaustive sorting out of the client's history, and the protracted quest for insight. In their place came an emphasis on the present and a pragmatism that was signaled by the use of specific techniques for specific problems. Because of its efficiency, behavioral techniques are especially well suited for the managed care environment.

In fact, many behavioral interventions can be implemented by technicians who are trained to work under the supervision of a doctoral-level psychologist. Token economies, for example, should be designed by trained professionals, but their day-to-day execution can be put in the hands of technicians, paraprofessionals, nurses, and others. This constitutes a considerable savings in mental health personnel and enables a larger client population to be reached than can be treated by the in-depth, one-on-one procedures of an exclusively psycho-dynamic approach.

It is also worth repeating that behavior therapy is the undisputed leader in "manualizing" its treatments so that empirically supported techniques can be administered in a standardized fashion. Not only does this facilitate conducting research and providing effective treatment, but it also facilitates the training of future clinical psychologists to administer these effective treatments.

Breadth of Application

A major contribution has been the extension of the range of applicability of psychological treat-ment. Traditional psychotherapy had been reserved for the middle and upper classes who had the time and money to devote to their psychological woes and for articulate, relatively sophis-ticated college students with well-developed coping behaviors who were attending colleges or universities that made counseling services available to them at little, if any, cost. Behavioral treatments have changed all that.

Now, even those with more limited financial means, and those with limited verbal skills, severe cognitive disabilities, or chronic clinical conditions, can be helped by therapy. Some people may not reach a level of fully independent functioning, but with the advent of operant procedures and token economies, their adjustment can often be significantly improved. In cases where lengthy verbal psychotherapies that were highly dependent on insight, symbolism, or the release of some inner potential were likely to fail, a broad band of behavior therapies offers hope for a broader proportion of the population in need.

Criticisms

Although behavioral interventions are effective in the treatment of a multitude of mental and behavioral health problems, there are problems for which they are not effective, and there are numerous factors which impact the usefulness or functionality of these treatments. For exam-ple, by themselves, behavioral interventions have little long-term effectiveness in the treatment of psychosis, severe depression, bipolar disorder, and some personality disorders. Importantly, behavioral techniques might be included in multicomponent treatment programs that are helpful for these problems. Moreover, behavioral interventions are skill-based treatments that require a great deal of effort on the part of the client. Not all clients are willing and able to put in the time and effort that it takes to get desired results (especially since, as you read, some behavioral treatment techniques are challenging to implement).

Behavioral treatments also have a public relations problem. Indeed, terms such as "stim-ulus," "response," and "operant," for example, are not as comforting or dramatic as those from other schools of treatment (e.g., "unconditional positive regard" in humanistic therapy or "penis envy" in psychoanalysis). Yet, the systematic use of learning principles should not lead to the inference that behavior therapists are cold, manipulating robots whose interests lie more in their learning principles than in their clients. That said, the history of behavior therapy does include a few unfortunate episodes. The use of aversion techniques, for example, is regarded by some as immoral (Danaher, 2018). Behavior therapy has also been criticized as not fostering "inner growth." While it provides skills, it fails to offer fulfilling creative experiences. Although it may alter behavior, it falls short of promoting understanding or focusing on the "inner person."

Another problem is the perception that behavioral treatments represent an assault on the client's capacity to make decisions, assume responsibility, and maintain dignity and integrity. But clients typically seek help voluntarily, thereby acknowledging their need for guidance in altering their behavior. Clients also have the opportunity to accept or reject the procedures offered (though this defense may not apply as well in institutional settings). Further, many behavioral techniques are aimed at helping clients establish skills that lead to greater self-direction, self-control, and happiness.

Think Like a Clinical Psychologist One criticism often levied at behavioral interventions is that they reduce emotional experiences and social interactions down to scientific-sounding concepts such as antecedents, behaviors, and consequences. What do you think of this critique?

🏛 Chapter Summary

Behavioral treatment is based on the assumption that clinical problems should be addressed using assessments and interventions that have empirical support and are based on established principles from experimental psychology. Although procedures derived from classical and operant conditioning initially dominated this approach, behavior therapy has been broadened to include procedures that draw from learning theories based on skills training and observational learning. Traditional behavioral treatments include contingency management, exposure therapy, and aversion therapy. These treatments have documented efficacy, and several are the treatments of choice for certain clinical problems (e.g., exposure therapy for clinical fears, BA for depression). Still, multicultural competence is imperative for delivering effective behavioral treatment and reducing the known disparity of health care to individuals from diverse backgrounds.

With its wide range of effective and efficient treatments, behavioral approaches, along with cognitive techniques (which we will explore in the next chapter) have had the greatest impact on the field of clinical psychology over the last century when it comes to improving mental and behavioral health. Indeed, lists of evidence-based treatments are dominated by these techniques, and the behavioral approach has led the way with respect to manualizing its interventions and facilitating research, training, and practice. In many ways, it is the ideal therapeutic orientation choice for scientist-practitioners and clinical scientists. Still, there are myths about the behavioral approach that plague the field, including that behavior therapy is dehumanizing and overly controlling.

Applying What You've Learned

Exercise 1: You are in charge of developing and implementing a treatment for a 12-year-old girl with a fear heights (i.e., acrophobia). Explain how you might design an exposure-based treatment for this condition. What features would you be sure to include, and why? Now explain how you might design a treatment for generalized anxiety disorder (i.e., chronic anxiety) that incorporates progressive muscle relaxation (PMR). What features would you be sure to include, and why?

Exercise 2: Discuss how you might design a habit reversal training intervention for a 33-year-old man who is dependent on alcohol (i.e., has an alcohol use disorder). What are the steps in HRT that you would follow? Use the format of Table 11.3 to outline a stimulus control plan for this client's problems with alcohol use.

Key Terms

Assertiveness training: Using behavioral rehearsal and other techniques to train people to express their needs effectively without infringing on the rights of others.

Aversive conditioning: A treatment in which an undesired behavior is followed consistently by an unpleasant consequence (e.g., nausea, disgust), thus decreasing the strength of the behavior over time.

Awareness training: First stage of habit reversal training in which clients keep a running log of each incident of the target behavior throughout the day.

Behavioral activation (BA): Behavioral treatment in which clients are helped to (a) more routinely engage in pleasurable and rewarding activities that provide consistent positive reinforcement to improve their mood and (b) decrease engagement in activities that increase the risk of feeling depressed.

Behavioral treatment: A framework for treating disorders that is based on the principles of conditioning or learning. The behavioral approach is scientific in nature and deemphasizes the role of inferred (i.e., unobservable) variables on behavior.

Competing response practice: Responding to the urge to perform the target behavior by instead engaging in a behavior that is incompatible with the target.

Contracting: A contingency management technique in which the therapist and client draw up a contract that specifies the behaviors that are desired and undesired as well as the consequences of engaging or failing to engage in these behaviors.

Contingency management: Any one of a variety of operant conditioning techniques that attempts to control a behavior by manipulating its consequences.

Covert sensitization: A form of aversion therapy in which clients are directed to imagine themselves engaging in an undesired behavior and then are instructed to imagine extremely aversive events occurring once they have the undesired behavior clearly in mind.

Cue exposure: Repeated exposure to conditioned stimuli while resisting the usual behavioral response (e.g., drinking, gambling, and pornography use).

Danger-based expectations: Prediction about what the client assumes will happen when exposed to the feared situation.

Exposure and response prevention (ERP): A behavioral technique often used for the treatment of OCD. In this technique, clients are exposed to the situation that spurs their obsession (e.g., touching a doorknob) and are prevented from engaging in the compulsive behavior that relieves the obsession (e.g., repeated handwashing). Ultimately, clients will habituate to their obsession, and the compulsive behavior will be extinguished.

Exposure hierarchy: A list or "menu" of the feared situations, thoughts, body sensations, and other stimuli that will be confronted during exposure trials.

Exposure therapy: A behavioral technique for reducing anxiety in which clients expose themselves (in real life or in fantasy) to stimuli or situations that are feared or avoided. To be effective, the exposure must provoke anxiety, must be of sufficient duration, and must be repeated until all anxiety is eliminated.

Extinction: The elimination of an undesired response (e.g., behavioral, emotional).

Habit reversal training: Behavior change technique that involves a series of steps including awareness training, stimulus control, and competing response practice.

Habituation: The elimination of a response that comes about from the repeated and/or prolonged presentation of the provoking stimulus.

Imaginal exposure: Confronting oneself with unwanted thoughts, doubts, and memories that provoke elevated fear (such as by writing or talking about them).

Interoceptive exposure: Self-generating bodily sensations that trigger inappropriate fear, such as a racing heart, breathlessness, and feeling lightheaded. Such sensations are activated using exercises such as hyperventilation, breathing through a straw, and spinning in a swivel chair.

***In vivo* exposure:** Direct confrontation with actual situations and objects, such as animals (e.g., spiders, dogs), social or evaluative situations (e.g., speaking up in class), and environments (e.g., shopping malls, elevators).

Premack principle: Also known as "**Grandma's rule**," the contingency management technique in which a behavior is reinforced by allowing the individual to engage in a more attractive activity once the target behavior is completed.

Progressive muscle relaxation (PMR): A series of actions to produce a state of lowered anxiety, stress, and physiological arousal. Relaxation may be induced by tensing and then relaxing various muscle groups or via breathing exercises, imagery exercises, or hypnosis.

Punishment: The notion that when a behavior is followed by an unpleasant consequence, it will diminish.

Response prevention: A behavioral intervention in which clients are helped to refrain from performing compulsive rituals.

Sensate focus: Involves a series of structured touching and discovery exercises that a couple performs together to extinguish performance-related anxiety, enhance communication, and learn about one's own and their partner's sexual response.

Shaping: A contingency management technique in which a behavior is developed by first rewarding any behavior that approximates it and then by selectively reinforcing behaviors that more and more resemble the target behavior.

Social skills training: Behavioral intervention to improve social skills necessary for healthy interpersonal relationships and successful employment (e.g., communicate effectively, display appropriate manners, use good hygiene, show empathy and consideration for others, and tactfully express one's own needs and opinions).

Stimulus control: Stage in habit reversal training in which the client and therapist use the data from awareness training logs to design strategies for reducing the influence of conditioned stimuli that trigger the target behavior.

Systematic desensitization: A behavioral technique for reducing anxiety in which clients practice relaxation while visualizing anxiety-provoking situations of increasing intensity. In this way, the client becomes "desensitized" to the feared stimulus.

Target behavior: Initial focus of behavioral assessment in which the problematic behavior is defined and characterized by how often it occurs (its *frequency*), its severity (or *intensity*), and how long each instance lasts (its *duration*).

Time-out: A contingency management technique in which a person is removed temporarily from the situation that is reinforcing the undesired behavior.

Token economy: A system in which desired behaviors are promoted through the strict control of reinforcements. Establishing such a system requires specifying the immediate reinforcers for each behavior as well as the backup reinforcers for which clients can exchange their immediate reinforcers.

CONNECT ONLINE:

 Check out our videos and additional resources located at: www.macmillanlearning.com

Cognitive-Behavioral Interventions

FOCUS QUESTIONS

1. Explain the cognitive model of emotion and the relationship between events, beliefs, and emotions.
2. What are the implications of the cognitive model for psychological treatment?
3. Describe the process of cognitive-behavioral treatment and how it is influenced by cultural factors.
4. What is cognitive bias modification and how is it different from other forms of cognitive-behavioral treatment?
5. What are the strengths and limitations of the cognitive-behavioral approach to psychological treatment?

CHAPTER OUTLINE

I magine that it's the first day of a new semester and you're headed to your first class. On the way you run into two friends, Alex and Kendall, but you are in a rush so you just wave and say, "Hey, I'll text you later, bye." Alex thinks that you look really busy, smiles at you, and is excited to catch up that evening. But Kendall interprets this as a "brush-off," gets angry that you didn't bother to stop to chat longer, and ignores your text for a few hours after you send it. Both of your friends experienced the exact same event but how they *thought about* what happened changed the way they felt and also influenced their behavior. It's not a big deal if you only infrequently think the way Kendall did, but consider how it would affect your feelings and behaviors if you were to think this way about all of your interactions.

In the 1960s and 1970s, the idea that how we think influences our thoughts and our behavior was a break from behaviorism. Accordingly, this notion began the **cognitive revolution** — a paradigm shift during which psychological scientists began to recognize that operant and classical conditioning, even with their precision and objectivity, could not completely explain the entirety of human experience. Social, developmental, and personality psychologists turned their focus to studying processes such as perception, memory, thinking, and decision making. Clinical psychologists saw opportunities to apply this new cognitive science to understanding and helping people with behavioral and psychological problems. In this chapter, you'll learn about these cognitive approaches to treatment, which — as discussed in IN HISTORICAL PERSPECTIVE: *The Evolution of Cognitive-Behavioral Treatment* — have become integrated with behavioral approaches in recent decades. We'll begin by covering the conceptual and theoretical basis for cognitive interventions, before looking in-depth at how they're implemented.

▥ What Is Cognitive-Behavioral Treatment?

Simply put, **cognitive-behavioral treatment (CBT)** promotes improvement in psychological functioning by correcting maladaptive patterns of thinking and behaving. It helps people change how they think and feel about themselves, others, and unpleasant situations they can't easily control. It helps them act in ways that lead to more effective problem solving, communicating with others, and operating in their various life roles. Because we have covered behavioral interventions in Chapter 11, *Behavioral Interventions*, we will focus primarily on the cognitive aspects of CBT in the present chapter; but it is important to recognize that CBT generally employs a combination of behavioral and cognitive techniques.

The **cognitive perspective** emphasizes how our thinking — that is, our beliefs, interpretations, judgments, attributions, expectations, and other forms of "self-talk" — influence our emotions and behaviors. From this viewpoint, clinical problems are thought to arise from *maladaptive* thinking patterns; and in CBT the clinician and client work together to identify these patterns, evaluate whether they seem logical or useful, and then use verbal and behavioral techniques to change them into healthier and more useful ways of thinking. This approach has a great deal of research support (e.g., Hofmann et al., 2012), and in fact is seen as among the most efficacious of all psychological interventions. For example, CBT interventions appear in treatment guidelines as first-line therapies for many problems and DSM disorders (e.g., American Psychological Association, 2017; Koran & Simpson, 2013), and have been shown to be of equal or superior efficacy to alternative psychological and psychopharmacological options for many problems in adults (e.g., Foa et al., 2005; Hollon et al., 2005; Pan et al., 2019) and youth (e.g., Chorpita et al., 2011; McGuire et al., 2015; van Dis et al., 2020).

Theoretical Basis of CBT

The basic idea behind CBT is that although our environment, learning history, and biology all have some degree of influence over our emotional and behavioral tendencies, it is our **cognition** — the way we think about events and situations in our environment — that plays the greatest role. Healthy and accurate thinking leads to constructive emotions, appropriate behavior, and greater satisfaction with life. But as human beings, we sometimes make mistakes in our thinking and judgment; and when we develop persistent patterns of inaccurate or irrational cognitions (e.g., setting unreasonably high standards for oneself or focusing only on the negative side of situations) it can bias our thinking in many different circumstances and lead to emotional distress, unhealthy behavior, and poorer quality of life. These maladaptive patterns of self-talk often become so habitual that we call them **automatic thoughts**. Automatic thoughts can take different forms: **appraisals** are judgments we make, **interpretations** are meanings that we assign when there is uncertainty in a particular situation, and **attributions** are the explanations we come up with in our mind to explain why something happened.

The **ABC model** illustrated in **Figure 12.1** provides a useful way to think about all of this. In the model, "A" stands for *activating event, activity, or adversity* and represents a situation that actually happens (e.g., you walking quickly past your friends and saying hello); "B" stands for *beliefs* and signifies automatic thoughts, appraisals, perceptions, and interpretations of the situation at "A" (e.g., different interpretations from Alex and Kendall); and "C" stands for the emotional and behavioral *consequences* that occur as a result of "B" (e.g., Alex looks forward to hearing from you, while Kendall ghosts you when you text). To reiterate, it is "B" (beliefs) rather than "A" (activating events) that primarily leads to "C" (consequences).

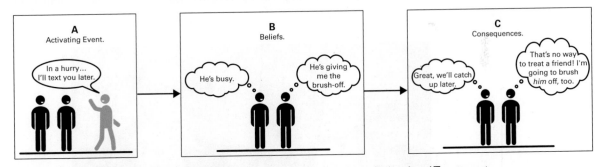

Figure 12.1 The ABC Model of Emotion That Guides Cognitive-Behavioral Treatment

But if our emotions and behaviors come largely from automatic thoughts, then where do our automatic thoughts come from? Why does Alex have a certain set of Bs that are different from Kendall's? According to the cognitive approach, the way we make sense of the world is driven by frameworks of knowledge and associations called **schemas**, which exist in our long-term memory. For instance, maybe Kendall has frequently been ignored by peers, or maybe Alex never has. Multiple experiences may create — a "peer schema" — that involves knowledge of how peers act, what different peer behaviors mean, and what to expect when around peers. We all build cognitive schemas around situations, people, activities, and objects, and they

In Historical Perspective

The Evolution of Cognitive-Behavioral Treatment

Aaron T. Beck and Albert Ellis are the undisputed originators of cognitive-behavioral treatment (CBT). Both were initially trained as psychoanalysts, yet ultimately found this approach unsatisfactory because of its lack of efficiency and nonscientific basis. Influenced by the cognitive revolution during the middle decades of the 20th century, Beck and Ellis also believed that behaviorism overlooked the role of thinking processes in emotions and behaviors. Specifically, they observed that their clients often described rigid, catastrophic, and otherwise exaggerated beliefs — such as the overly negative thoughts about oneself, the world, and the future that typify people with a chronically depressed mood. In their own way, Beck and Ellis each drew on the work of the Stoic philosopher Epictetus, who wrote that *people are not upset by things, but rather by their judgments about things*. From this notion sprang Ellis's "rational therapy" (which has undergone several name changes) and Beck's "cognitive therapy," which are discussed in detail later in this chapter.

But even as these cognitively focused interventions gained wider use through the 1970s, many behaviorally oriented psychologists were hesitant to embrace them. This reluctance was mostly based on the fact that, as mental events, cognitions are not directly observable. A number of developments, however, ultimately convinced many behaviorists to change their tune and eventually helped unite the behavioral and cognitive schools of thought. First, Albert Bandura's (1969; 1977a) and Julien Rotter's (1970) work from a social learning perspective empirically demonstrated the importance of vicarious learning (learning by observation) and the role of cognition in both mood and behavior. Bandura (1977b) advanced the idea that learning is an active, rather than a passive, process. That is, a host of personality characteristics and cognitive processes can influence behavior independently of classical and operant conditioning. Finally, research was showing that a number of

Photo by Michael Fenichel

Aaron T. Beck (L; 1921–2021) and Albert Ellis (R; 1913–2007) are considered the fathers of cognitive-behavior therapy.

frequently encountered clinical conditions (e.g., depression) were not so easily addressed by behavioral treatments based purely on classical or operant conditioning (e.g., Shaw, 1977).

Through the 1980s and 1990s, behavioral and cognitive psychologists continued to work together to understand and treat psychological problems. Clinicians and psychological scientists alike recognized how learning and cognitive processes operate in tandem to maintain clinical problems, and how the two schools of thought provide clients with complementary sets of skills for alleviating them. As a result, multicomponent cognitive-behavioral treatment (CBT) programs were developed, evaluated in numerous clinical trials, and disseminated in the form of published treatment manuals for many DSM disorders. Many clinical psychologists, and managed care and insurance companies, embraced these programs for obvious reasons: they are brief, usually 16 sessions or fewer, and therefore much more economical than alternative forms of treatment (e.g., psychodynamic therapy). CBT programs are also structured and protocol-driven, sticking to a plan without wandering all over the place for years at a time.

Courtesy of Beck Institute for Cognitive Behavior Therapy, www.beckinstitute.org.

Dr. Judith Beck is a clinical psychologist, daughter of Aaron T. Beck, and president of the Beck Institute for Cognitive Behavior Therapy — a leading organization in the dissemination of CBT worldwide.

During the 2010s, it became more fashionable for clinical psychologists to think transdiagnostically — that is, to focus on cognitive and behavioral *processes* and *mechanisms* of change rather than on DSM diagnostic categories per se. This has led to programs such as the Unified Protocol for Transdiagnostic Treatment of Emotional Disorders (UP) (Barlow et al., 2017), which presented an array of cognitive and behavioral interventions that could be selected and implemented depending on the client's unique presentation (rather than based on a single diagnosis).

What really prompted CBT's extraordinary rise is that it is far and away the most empirically supported psychological treatment available. Taught in almost every mental health training program in the United States, CBT dominates the field in North America; much of Europe; and increasingly, Asia and Latin America. The Beck Institute, led by Judith Beck (the daughter of Aaron Beck), is a major force in the dissemination of CBT, training thousands of health and mental health professionals in over 130 countries. CBT has also become the "official" psychological treatment of the health care arm of the U.S. Department of Veterans Affairs, which has in place a national training program for treating depression and PTSD — the largest such program in the country. CBT is has also been disseminated through the explosion of self-help books and smartphone apps based on CBT principles, some of which have been tested (and found to be effective) in well-designed treatment outcome studies. Finally, online CBT has become very popular in the last two decades, and especially during the COVID-19 pandemic. Some studies show that doing CBT online can be as effective as meeting face-to-face with a psychologist (e.g., Miller et al., 2021). ∎

generally help us navigate through life by telling us, for example, that rock concerts will be loud, electrical outlets can be dangerous, and you will find cakes and pies at a bakery. But when schemas lead to exaggerated or incorrect beliefs and assumptions about particular categories of people or things, they can cause problems. Kendall's "peer schema," for example, might include the notion that peers can be dismissive or unreliable, and that at a whim they may start distancing themselves. This could lead to Kendall's perception that your quick hello and wave were a "blow-off" (even if that was not your intention), and then to feelings of hurt or anger.

This scenario highlights another important facet of the ABC model that you might have already noticed: the same event can be associated with different emotional and behavioral reactions depending on what the person is thinking. Cognitive psychologists call this **cognitive specificity**. For example, overly general beliefs concerned with failure and loss (e.g., "I'm just a *loser* and *no one* likes me") lead to depressed mood and behavior. Rigid beliefs and demands about how others should behave (e.g., "Children *must* follow the rules") lead to feelings of anger and hostile behavior when others inevitably break such rules; and automatic thoughts focused on self-blame (e.g., "*I should* have been a better daughter") lead to guilt. Predictions related to the likelihood and severity of threat (e.g., "My neighbor's dog is *very dangerous* and will *probably* bite me") lead to anxiety, fear, and taking action to reduce the perceived threat (e.g., avoidance). Finally, optimistic thinking (e.g., "My friends appreciate me") leads to positive emotions.

Although clinicians who use CBT tend to think in terms of cognitions, behaviors, and emotions, rather than DSM-5-TR diagnoses, the ABC model predicts that clients diagnosed with different disorders would have different types of (maladaptive or *biased*) thinking patterns. Indeed, researchers have largely found that this is true. To illustrate, **Table 12.1** shows examples of cognitive biases typical of various common DSM-5-TR disorders. This research is useful for clinicians because it provides a roadmap for understanding what types of Bs will likely need to be addressed in CBT depending on which diagnosis the client has been given. As we will see in the next sections, the aim of CBT is to correct these cognitive biases and maladaptive thinking patterns.

Table 12.1 Examples of Typical Cognitive Biases and Maladaptive Beliefs in Some Common DSM-5-TR Disorders	
DSM-5-TR Disorder	**Cognitive Biases and Maladaptive Beliefs**
Major depressive disorder	The tendency to see oneself as a failure, the future as hopeless, and to focus on negative aspects of situations
Generalized anxiety disorder	The tendency to overestimate the probability and severity of a crisis (e.g., losing a job)
Social anxiety disorder	The belief that others are always very critical and that it's awful to be evaluated negatively
Obsessive-compulsive disorder	Overestimates of threat and responsibility, beliefs that intrusive thoughts are highly significant and need to be controlled, and the intolerance of uncertainty and imperfection
Panic disorder	The idea that experiencing anxiety is dangerous or harmful (e.g., when my heart beats fast, I worry I'm having a heart attack)
Illness anxiety disorder	Beliefs that one is medically ill (despite a lack of evidence) and that any pain or discomfort is a sign of a serious medical problem

Treatment Implications

The ABC model sets the stage for CBT in a number of ways. First, it suggests that since thinking is the most important determinant of emotions and behaviors, the best way for clients to conquer their psychological distress is to change their thinking—that is, to modify their Bs. This idea, however, may be foreign to many clients who enter treatment believing they need to change or "fix" A—their adverse circumstances—in order to feel better (e.g., "My partner broke up with me and you've got help us get back together!"). But focusing on A presents a problem: we simply can't control many situations. So, while it is not always easy, it is ultimately more empowering for clients to learn to think more adaptively and rationally so they can better master their emotions and behavior regardless of the circumstances (e.g., "It's painful when a relationship ends; maybe I can use this opportunity to make some changes so future relationships work out better").

A second implication is the distinction between thinking *positively* (e.g., "Everything will work out great!") and thinking *rationally* (e.g., "Things may or may not work out as I'd like, but I will get through it"). **Rational thinking**, which is the ability to objectively consider facts, opinions, judgments, and data to arrive at a sound conclusion, may realistically include both positive and negative ideas. Positive thinking, on the other hand is arbitrary and it often leads to overlooking important (yet disappointing) facts and failing to take appropriate action.

Third, the ABC model implies that one cannot feel happy (or even *good*) all the time. Negative emotions are universal experiences and many, such as sadness, regret, concern, and irritation, are appropriate responses in circumstances such as the death of a loved one, the loss of a job or close relationship, or following a traumatic event. In fact, these **constructive negative emotions** can be useful, motivating one to take action and problem-solve. In CBT, constructive negative emotions are distinguished from more intense and long-lasting destructive negative emotions, such as hopelessness, worry, and rage, that stifle healthy coping and lead to impulsive or self-defeating behavior. **Table 12.2** compares destructive and constructive negative emotions, the difference often being a matter of frequency, intensity, and duration.

Table 12.2 Comparison of Destructive and Constructive Negative Emotions	
Destructive, Self-Defeating, Physically Harmful Negative Emotions	**Constructive, Appropriate, Useful, Adaptive Negative Emotions**
Depression, hopelessness, helplessness, despair, misery, woe	Sadness, grief, sorrow, unhappiness, disappointment
Guilt, shame, remorse	Contrition, regret, disappointment
Anxiety, worry	Concern, appropriate short-term fear
Anger, frustration	Irritation, annoyed, disappointment

Finally, the ABC model implies the importance of **unconditional self-acceptance**, which means becoming comfortable viewing oneself as fallible and seeing one's own self-worth as separate from one's behaviors and circumstances. Clients might lose a job or relationship, fail out of school, commit immoral or illegal acts, or spend money unwisely; but this does not make them bad *people*, merely people who (like everyone else) have personal strengths and limitations. But do not confuse CBT for merely *rationalizing* undesirable behavior; rather, it is a tool for learning how to *think rationally* about it.

> **T**hink Like a Clinical Psychologist Some psychologists consider thinking to be another form of behavior — a *mental* behavior. Do you agree? Why or why not?

▐▐▌ The Process of CBT

Defining the Target Problem

As we have mentioned, it is common for some clients to pursue psychotherapy looking for help with solving *practical* problems, such as how to win more friends or make sure Aunt Ethel doesn't ruin the next family gathering by ranting about politics. Other clients pursue treatment for emotional *disorders*. In CBT, however, the emphasis is on addressing maladaptive cognitive and emotional *responses to* undesirable circumstances, rather than trying to directly change these circumstances per se. Thus, suitable target problems include the types of strong negative emotions shown on the left side of Table 12.2, especially when these occur with high frequency, intensity, and duration; lead to psychological suffering; or interfere with functioning. Clients might initially be asked to self-monitor episodes of negative emotions with a focus on the situations and thoughts associated with them.

Explaining the ABC Model

Next, the clinician provides a description and rationale for CBT, focusing on the ABC model and the importance of changing thinking patterns to improve feelings and behaviors. This gives clients an explanation for their problem in terms that they can readily understand. It also prepares them for getting the most out of treatment. For children, explanations of the cognitive model and idea of CBT must include simple and concrete language. Some clinicians use graphics and diagrams to help children visualize concepts such as how situations, thoughts, feelings, and actions are connected (**Figure 12.2**). For example, a worksheet may have drawings with blank thought bubbles that the child and psychologist discuss (e.g., "What do you think the person in the picture is thinking about?) and complete together.

Assessing A, B, and C

The ABC model (rather than a DSM diagnosis) guides the collection of information necessary for formulating and implementing a CBT plan. Many clinicians begin with assessing Cs — how the client feels and behaves in the context of A, the adverse circumstances. A simple method is to ask open-ended questions, such as "How did you feel when you went to the party?" Notably, CBT practitioners avoid implying a causal relationship between A and C. So, rather than "How did it *make you feel* when the other student sat in your seat?" a more suitable question would be "How were you feeling when you saw the other student sitting in your seat?" It is also important to assess the frequency, intensity, and duration of such consequences. Clients can be given self-monitoring forms (such as those discussed in previous chapters) on which to record situations in which negative emotions arise between treatment sessions. These forms can be reviewed at the subsequent appointment.

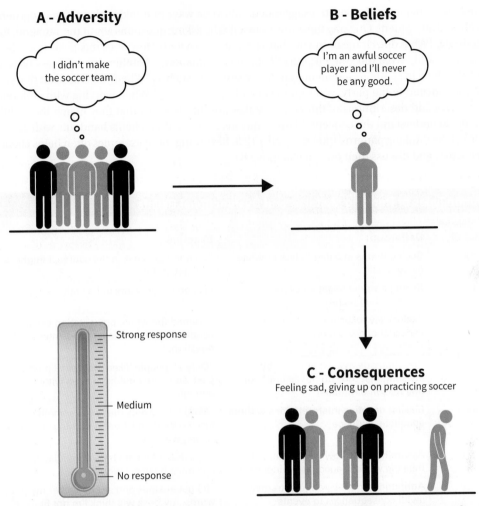

A - Adversity

I didn't make the soccer team.

B - Beliefs

I'm an awful soccer player and I'll never be any good.

Strong response

Medium

No response

C - Consequences

Feeling sad, giving up on practicing soccer

Figure 12.2 Use of Graphics and CBT Clinicians implementing CBT with children often use graphics and diagrams to help their clients visualize concepts such as the intensity of emotions and how situations, thoughts, feelings, and behaviors are connected.

Next, the specifics of the activating events (A) are assessed, which entails determining the facts of the situation that triggered the emotional episode (e.g., "She threw a party and I wasn't invited"). The self-monitoring strategy just described is useful for this purpose as well. Sometimes, clients report no specific As, and instead say things like, "I feel anxious about *everything*," or "I just feel angry — there's no trigger." In such instances, clinicians can use detailed interviewing questions (and client self-monitoring) to try to pin down individual events. Sometimes, ongoing stressors such as work, school, strained relationships, and finances are associated with such complaints.

Finally (and perhaps most importantly), the focus shifts to assessing B — the client's beliefs, assumptions, and perceptions about activating events. CBT therapists look for thinking mistakes and other sorts of **dysfunctional beliefs** (such as those listed in **Table 12.3**), which are inaccurate, logically flawed, exaggerated, inflexible ways of thinking that are incongruent with goal attainment. One way these are assessed is by asking questions about the situation; for example, "What does it mean to you that you weren't invited? How does this pose a problem for you?" and "What did you tell yourself about this situation?" Another way to assess Bs is to ask the client to complete a sentence about the situation, such as "When you found out that you weren't invited to the party, you said to yourself _____." When working with children, the terms and descriptions of thinking mistakes are simplified so that they match the child's ability to understand the concept. Many clinicians also give their clients handouts with examples of the thinking patterns shown in Table 12.3. Reviewing these examples often helps clients recognize and discuss their own maladaptive Bs.

Table 12.3 Common Types of Thinking Mistakes and Dysfunctional Beliefs

Type of Thinking Mistake or Dysfunctional Belief	Definition	Example
All-or-nothing thinking	Seeing things in either "black or white" categories	"If I don't get an A in the course, I might as well get an F."
Overgeneralization	Seeing a single negative event as a never-ending pattern	"No one ever wants to be with me."
Mental filter	Exclusively focusing on a negative aspect(s) of a situation	"I ruined the whole presentation because I couldn't answer one audience member's question."
Disqualifying the positive	Rejecting positive experiences by insisting that they do not "count," for one reason or another	"Only 25 people 'liked' my social media post, so it must not have been witty enough."
Jumping to conclusions	Making negative interpretations without adequate evidence	"My doctor wants me to have another test, so there must be something seriously wrong with me."
Mind reading	Assuming you know what others are thinking without adequate evidence	"She didn't text me back immediately, so she must be upset with me."
Catastrophizing	Attributing or anticipating extremely awful consequences to events	"If I get anxious and stumble over my words, my boss will think I'm not fit to work here and fire me; then I'll be unemployed for the rest of my life."
Emotional reasoning	Assuming that negative emotions necessarily reflect the situational reality	"I'm feeling depressed; therefore, I must be seriously flawed."
"Should" and "must" statements	Endorsing rigid yet arbitrary rules	"Professors *should* give students study guides before every exam."
Labeling and mislabeling	Taking one behavior or characteristic of oneself (or others) and applying it to the whole person	"He won't go on roller coasters, so he's just a big wuss."
Personalization	Entirely blaming oneself, or someone else, for a situation that involved many factors or was out of your control	"If I had been on time, she wouldn't have had to run down the stairs, so it's completely my fault that she fell and broke her leg."
Maladaptive thoughts	Endorsing thoughts that are not necessarily irrational or distorted, but are nevertheless unproductive or unhelpful	"It's not fair that social situations are so much harder for me than for other people."

The **downward arrow technique** is another strategy for assessing deeply held beliefs that influence emotions and behaviors. It involves (1) identifying a particular adverse event, (2) asking the client what this situation means, and (3) continuing to ask the same question until one or more dysfunctional thinking patterns (such as those in Table 12.3) is revealed. **Figure 12.3** illustrates the use of this strategy for a client with social anxiety. Many clinicians also use self-report instruments to assess cognitive distortions, such as those we described in Chapter 7, *Behavioral Assessment*.

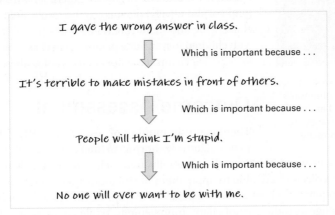

Figure 12.3 Illustration of the Downward Arrow Technique to Identify a Dysfunctional Belief

Implementation

CBT is a skills-based treatment, so clients learn and practice strategies for changing maladaptive cognitions and behaviors. We describe these strategies in detail later in this chapter, but in a general sense they focus on (a) identifying maladaptive patterns of thinking, (b) challenging (i.e., thinking critically about) these cognitions, and (c) modifying them into healthier and more adaptive cognitions. Thus, sessions are usually structured and characterized by goal-oriented exchanges between the clinician and client.

As mentioned, CBT places relatively little emphasis on changing the situation itself, so clinicians don't typically provide practical advice (although assertiveness skills may be taught in some instances). There is also little emphasis on trying to identify the root causes of maladaptive cognitions. Sometimes, however, the sources of dysfunctional thinking are unmistakable and cannot be overlooked. For example, some adult clients take valid ideas that were instilled in them as youth (e.g., "It's important to get good grades in school") and escalate them into maladaptive rigid rules and extreme expectations (e.g., "I must get all As in school; otherwise, I can't be successful in life"). In such cases it may be useful to have a more in-depth discussion about the origins of such ideas and the pros and cons of deciding to let them go.

Although most CBT skills can be learned and practiced in the context of a traditional clinic appointment, there are times when this work is also done outside of the session. Many CBT providers give clients worksheets (described later in this chapter) to self-monitor their As, Bs, and Cs, and record their progress with challenging and modifying dysfunctional thinking patterns. For youth, parents might be included in treatment sessions so that they are able to help with homework assignments between appointments.

In CBT, psychologists often provide worksheets for clients to complete between appointments. These worksheets are then reviewed at the subsequent session to ensure that clients are practicing and learning CBT skills correctly.

Clients might also be assigned **behavioral experiments** to "put their beliefs to the test." It might be suggested, for example, that the client referred to previously approach a handful of "successful" people between sessions, ask them about their grades in school (e.g., whether they got all As), and record the results of these interviews. Most likely, such an experiment would suggest that one need not achieve perfect grades to be successful (or happy) in life. Similar to exposure therapy, such experiments need to be carefully (and collaboratively) planned so the results are indeed useful in challenging and modifying unhelpful beliefs. Clinicians working with children may include planners, checklists, or a rewards chart to help their clients remember and complete these tasks.

Outcome Assessment

There is no set number of sessions in CBT, although it tends to be a relatively short-term intervention, with many treatment programs lasting between 8 to 20 weeks. Generally, treatment ends when clients have learned the appropriate skills and are able to apply them in situations that once provoked maladaptive negative thoughts and emotions. Like behavior therapists, CBT practitioners use objective measures of change as indicators of client improvement. While changes in behavior are certainly an important metric, so are changes in cognition. One way to measure cognitive change is to assess the frequency and intensity of the destructive emotions in Table 12.2 and dysfunctional thoughts and beliefs described in Table 12.3. Specifically, clinicians can ask clients to quantify (e.g., out of 100%) how strongly they hold such ideas before treatment begins and compare these pretreatment ratings to revised estimates during and after treatment. An advantage of such ratings is that they are client-specific. Reliable and valid self-report measures that assess the presence and strength of dysfunctional beliefs can also be administered before and after treatment to track changes in dysfunctional cognitions.

Client–Practitioner Relationship

A unique characteristic of CBT is that the client — regardless of age — and practitioner share responsibility for the direction of treatment. This kind of teamwork is called **collaborative empiricism** (Beck et al., 1985). Specifically, practitioners and clients discover together how the client's maladaptive thinking contributes to distress and how adopting healthier thinking patterns can reduce this distress. The client and clinician then work together to put automatic thoughts and schemas "on trial," explore evidence for against these cognitions, and collaboratively craft new and more useful ways of thinking.

Multicultural Considerations

CBT was predominantly developed by — and tested with — white, male, cis-gender, heterosexual, Protestant upper-middle class individuals from Western nations. Is CBT appropriate for everyone else? The answer is complicated. Data suggest that CBT works generally as well for people with all different types of identities and cultural experiences (Naeem, 2019), although this remains a topic that requires more research. However, it is crucial that psychologists recognize that a discussion about thoughts that may or may not be logical, rational, or "automatic" is inherently based in a specific point of view, which itself is very much related to our own unique and diverse experiences. Thus, multicultural considerations impact every aspect of the intervention process, including assessment, goal-setting, what is acceptable to think or talk about, and what acceptable methods of facilitating change may look like (Rosmarin, 2018). During assessment, CBT therapists consider ways in which clients' cultural background interacts with their thinking patterns and emotional responses. This might involve asking questions about parenting practices, gender roles, acculturation, family structure, discrimination experiences, spiritual beliefs and practices, and — of course — views about mental health concerns and treatment (Sue et al., 2009). Clients' attitudes toward their own thoughts and behaviors are especially important to understand.

Because CBT emphasizes clients' beliefs, psychologists must carefully consider cultural factors such as spirituality, gender roles, race, and ethnicity that can influence such cognitions.

Cultural differences also influence treatment goals and methods (Graham et al., 2013). For example, cognitive techniques that require clients to consider the validity of their negative thoughts may be especially challenging when such thoughts are about situations in which they have experienced oppression, discrimination, or racism. Behavioral experiments must also be carefully planned in partnership with clients to ensure such exercises are culturally appropriate and consistent with the clients' values.

Because CBT is very much aligned with Western ideas and values, clients from cultures influenced by different sets of values may find its goals less palatable (e.g., Hall & Ibaraki, 2016). For example, CBT emphasizes assertiveness, personal independence, behavior change, attention to thoughts, and rationality, which may clash with cultural beliefs that prioritize subtle communication, interdependence, acceptance, nonlinear types of cognitive processing, and a spiritually oriented worldview (Jackson et al., 2006). In such instances, **culturally responsive modifications** can be made that, for example, foster a less directive stance or include options to respond directly to experiences of oppression and minority stress (Bedoya et al., 2017).

Perhaps most important, psychologists must be aware that their own backgrounds and experiences are influencing therapy as well, and it is critical not to impose their own assumptions onto clients. In graduate school, psychologists learn to confront their own automatic thoughts and recognize that they are neither right nor wrong, and do not serve as a standard for comparison with their clients. Rather, psychologists are like curious scientists with their clients, asking questions in specific and precise ways to learn about their clients' experiences from their clients' points of view.

Think Like a Clinical Psychologist Discuss your own automatic thoughts and cognitive schemas, and how they are influenced by your own culture and values. If you were a clinical psychologist using CBT with a client, how might your culture and values influence your work as a clinician? What, if anything, should you do about this?

▐▌▐ Applications of CBT

CBT is routinely applied in the treatment of adults and youth with a wide range of psychological problems and mental health conditions, ranging from depression and anxiety to PTSD, panic attacks, eating and sleep dysfunctions, childhood attentional and conduct problems, anger and impulse control problems, and problems with addiction and substance use. It is also used as an intervention for psychotic, personality, and bipolar disorders and to reduce the distress associated with chronic pain. This section explains the practical aspects of three common (and overlapping) cognitive interventions, and then discusses how cognitive and behavioral interventions are used together in multicomponent treatment packages for common psychological problems.

Rational Emotive Behavior Therapy

Albert Ellis developed the pioneering form of CBT in the 1950s, which he initially called *rational therapy* (RT) (Ellis, 1957). RT was based on the ABC model described earlier and made use of a variety of emotive and metaphorical techniques to help clients change their feelings and behavior by altering the way they think about situations in their lives. Responding to criticism that RT ignored clients' feelings, Ellis changed the name to *rational emotive therapy* (RET) (Ellis, 1962) in the early 1960s to better highlight the emphasis on emotions. Some years later, amidst the uniting of cognitive and behavioral traditions, Ellis again updated the name to **rational emotive behavior therapy (REBT)** to underscore the fact that the intervention incorporates behavioral as well as cognitive techniques.

In its contemporary form, REBT distills the dysfunctional thinking patterns in Table 12.3 down to the four types of **irrational beliefs** shown in **Table 12.4**. Do *you* ever hold any of these beliefs? They're common among most people—with or without clinically significant psychological problems or DSM diagnoses. However, when a person stubbornly holds on to these sorts of beliefs and uses them dogmatically to make sense of adverse situations, they create emotional and behavioral problems. Therefore, the primary goal of REBT is to help clients confront their irrational thinking and view situations more flexibly and realistically so they can attain greater satisfaction in life.

Table 12.4	Common Irrational Beliefs Addressed in REBT	
Irrational Belief	**Definition**	**Example**
Demandingness	Absolutistic ideas such as *musts*, absolute *shoulds, have tos*, "I need," and "I ought"	"I want to graduate on time and therefore I *should* or *must*."
Awfulizing	Evaluating something as more than 100% bad	"If I make a mistake during the recital, it will be *absolutely awful!*"
Low frustration tolerance	The idea that a struggle (or other situation) is truly unbearable	*"I can't stand it"* when people are rude to me."
Conditional self-/other acceptance	Labeling oneself (or someone else) based only on a single characteristic or an aspect of behavior	"If I fail at something, then I am a *failure.*" "She is *inconsiderate* because she talks loudly."

In REBT, the clinician assumes the role of an active and directive teacher, disputing—sometimes in a challenging or confrontational way—clients' irrational thinking. Disputing irrational beliefs often involves the use of **Socratic dialogue** in which the therapist asks the client pointed, open-ended questions that encourage reflection and promote new and more logical perspectives. Clients are also taught that when they begin to feel upset in real situations, they should pause; ask themselves "What am I telling myself?"; and try using their new, more rational, beliefs. When working with children, REBT takes into account the child's level of cognitive development in selecting appropriate intervention procedures (e.g., DiGiuseppe & Bernard, 2006). This in-session work is reinforced with homework assignments in which clients try out activities to strengthen their new ways of thinking. IN PRACTICE: *Disputing Kiara's Irrational Beliefs* illustrates two methods of disputing maladaptive thoughts based on logic and empirical evidence.

In Practice Disputing Kiara's Irrational Beliefs

Along with her obsessions and compulsions, Kiara frequently experienced a depressed mood, feelings of hopelessness, and a loss of interest in things she typically enjoyed. Therefore, in addition to exposure and response prevention (ERP), Kiara's psychologist used REBT techniques to address these mood-related problems. Kiara identified a number of the thinking mistakes described in Table 12.4, including "I am a weak person because I have OCD" (an example of conditional self-acceptance) and "If one of my patients died it would be the most horrible thing possible" (awfulizing). Her therapist hypothesized that these irrational thoughts had a lot to do with Kiara's depression and anxiety, and used two different **disputation strategies** to help her challenge and change them: *logical disputes* and *empirical disputes*.

Logical Disputes

In **logical disputes**, the rules of reason and logic are used to challenge and modify the client's irrational beliefs. Here's an excerpt from a logical dispute that Kiara's psychologist used to address Kiara's belief about being a weak person:

Psychologist: Let's talk about your belief that you're a weak person because you have OCD. That sounds like a pretty harsh way to think of yourself. To begin with, what's your definition of a *weak* person. How would you know if you ran into one on the street?

Kiara: I guess a weak person is someone who is broken, like me. I'm not perfect . . . I have OCD. That's a weakness.

Psychologist: I see. So everyone with OCD is a weak person?

Kiara: Well . . . yeah. They have a weakness, so they're weak. Right?

Psychologist: I'm not so sure about that. OCD is certainly a *problem*, but are problems like mental illnesses really *weaknesses*? Millions of people have OCD and other psychological disorders. Are they all weak people?

Kiara: Hmmm. I never thought about it that way. I always thought of my mental illness as a personal weakness.

Psychologist: But there are lots of people who have psychiatric diagnoses and mental health problems. Are you writing them all off as weak? Did you know that both Abraham Lincoln and Beethoven had mental illnesses? Lincoln had debilitating depression and Beethoven had bipolar disorder. Does that make them weak *people*?

Kiara: No. I guess not.

Psychologist: So if they're not weak *people*, then what are they?

Kiara: Hmmm. I never thought about it like that. I guess they're just people with some strengths and some limitations.

Psychologist: And so what about you? And everyone else in the world?

Kiara: Hmmm. Good point. I guess it's the same for me, too. After all, I did make it through nursing school and got a good job.

Psychologist: Yep, that's all true. Look, having OCD really stinks — it's a problem for you; one that we're working hard to fix. But it's just one part of you, not *who you are.* You've got plenty of strengths as well. And it's the same for everyone else in the world. Everyone's got strengths and limits — but these don't make us strong, weak, good, or bad *people.* People are way too complicated to be reduced to one adjective! How do you feel when you think about it that way? What would happen if you told yourself something like that rather than beating up on yourself for having OCD?

Kiara: Well, that makes a lot of sense. I guess it makes me feel better about myself . . . more hopeful and worthwhile.

Empirical Disputes

Empirical disputes use objective, verifiable data and evidence (such as observations and research results) to challenge irrational thinking. Kiara's therapist used this technique to address Kiara's awfulizing thoughts about her patients dying:

Psychologist: When you awfulize about your patients dying there are two issues here. The first is the likelihood of patients dying on your floor. The second is how *awful* it is when this happens. Our exposure therapy work is addressing the first part, but let's talk about the second — the awfulness.

Kiara: I can't believe you're going to try to tell me that it's not completely *awful, terrible, horrible,* if a patient dies! Isn't that the absolute worst thing that could happen?

Psychologist: Well, I see where you're coming from, and I think we can agree that it's a *sad* thing when someone dies in the hospital. But, let's look at how *terrible* it really is. You must have had experiences when patients die, no? Can you tell me about them?

Kiara: Thank goodness it's never been one of *my* patients. But it's happened to some of my co-workers.

Psychologist: Okay, tell me about what happened.

Kiara: Well, the patients that I remember developed complications from their surgery — like infections and such. My co-workers all did what they could to try to save them, but sometimes the body just isn't strong enough to fight it off and they lose the battle.

Psychologist: And have you spoken with your co-workers when this happened?

Kiara: Yeah, we all talk about it together and support one another when that sort of thing happens.

Psychologist: Oh, I see. And what is *that* like?

Kiara: It's actually very nice. We have a very supportive team and helpful supervisors. Everyone understands that these kinds of things happen in a hospital. It's unavoidable. Surprisingly, no one blames each other.

Psychologist: Surprisingly? Did you expect finger-pointing?

Kiara: Yeah, I did. But everyone knows we're doing our best to help. Like I said, it's more about support than finger-pointing.

Psychologist: Hmmm. But you were just telling me that it's the most *awful, horrible* thing if someone dies. And now you're saying everyone shows support and there's no finger-pointing. How can it be both of those things?

Kiara: I see what you're getting at. But it hasn't happened to one of *my* patients. That would be different.

Psychologist: What's your basis for saying that? What evidence do you have that your co-workers would react any differently if one of *your* patients died?

Kiara: Hmmm. I guess I don't have any.

Psychologist: That's right. And what do your observations suggest about how *awful* it is to go through something like that?

Kiara: Okay, so it's probably not as awful as I'm thinking. Very sad, but not *awful.*

Psychologist: Yes, very *sad*, but not *awful.* What if you kept that in mind when you get to thinking about your patients dying?

Kiara: I'd be a lot less worried. Still careful, but less anxious. And I'd probably be able to concentrate better. ▄▄▄

Reviews of the empirical literature indicate that REBT is an effective psychological treatment for adults and youth. In a meta-analysis of 68 studies comparing REBT to other treatments, David and colleagues (2018) found medium to large effect sizes in favor of REBT on outcomes related to emotion (e.g., anger, anxiety, depression), behavior change, irrational beliefs, general health, quality of life, and school performance. The fact that REBT reduced irrational beliefs provides support for the theory underlying this treatment. Indeed, understanding why a psychological treatment works is just as important as knowing how effective it is. A meta-analysis of 19 outcome studies with youth showed that REBT produced improvements in anxiety, disruptive behaviors, irrational thoughts, self-concept, and grade point average (Gonzalez et al., 2004).

Beck's Cognitive Therapy

From a conceptual standpoint, Aaron Beck's cognitive therapy is like REBT in that it also aims to modify dysfunctional thinking patterns. Yet Beck's approach diverges somewhat in terms of its technique and style. Specifically, it is less directive and uses a form of collaborative empiricism called **guided discovery** in which clients are helped to notice and challenge their own thinking mistakes. Clients learn that they can change maladaptive automatic thoughts (and therefore improve their feelings and behaviors) by "slowing down" the ABC process, which involves recognizing maladaptive automatic thoughts (sometimes called *cognitive distortions*), treating them as hypotheses, testing them out empirically, and considering alternative thoughts based on the evidence. Although developed for adults, cognitive therapy is easily adapted for children by translating abstract, holistic concepts into concrete examples and by relating them to day-to-day events which children can use, relate to, and understand. Clients, including children for whom it is developmentally appropriate, are often given worksheets, like the one shown in **Figure 12.4**, to help guide them through this process. This worksheet was completed by Shane to address negative thoughts and feelings he had about himself.

Situation
- I got in trouble at school again.

Negative Automatic Thoughts
- This always happens to me. (overgeneralization)
- No one at school likes me. (disqualifying the positive)

Thought Challenges
- I get in trouble sometimes, but it's not every day or even every week.
- Sometimes my teachers tell me that I'm doing a good job.
- I am getting help so that I don't get in trouble so much.
- I'm forgetting that Ben and Amir are my friends.
  We have been friends for a long time.

Alternate Thoughts
- Sometimes I get in trouble, but it's not as much as before,
  and I am getting help and learning to control my behavior better.
- There are some kids who don't like me, but I also have some
  friends. No one can be liked by everyone.

Figure 12.4 Shane's Cognitive Therapy Worksheet

Shane's feelings of depression were associated with negative automatic thoughts that came to mind when he got in trouble for misbehaving at school or at home. After reviewing a list of thinking errors similar to that in Table 12.3, Shane recognized his automatic thoughts as examples of *overgeneralization* and *disqualifying the positive*. Then Shane was taught how to "put his thinking mistakes on trial" by asking himself Socratic questions like those listed in **Table 12.5**. The point of these questions is to help clients gain a more objective perspective on their situations (not all of the questions are relevant to every situation or client). After considering evidence for and against his automatic thoughts, as well as some important facts that he had been overlooking (recorded in the Thought Challenges section of the worksheet in Figure 12.4), Shane came up with alternate ways of thinking that were based on facts, rather than thinking errors. Shane completed additional worksheets about other situations both at home and in session with his psychologist to help him become more skilled at generating alternatives. The eventual goal was for Shane to be able to do this exercise in his head, rather than having to write it down on paper.

Table 12.5   Examples of Socratic Questions Used in Beck's Cognitive Therapy to Challenge Automatic Thoughts

What evidence do I have for and against this thought?

Is there an alternative way of looking at the situation?

Am I forgetting relevant facts? Am I focusing too much on irrelevant facts?

How would someone else think about this situation?

What would I tell a friend who was in the same situation?

What are the real and probable consequences of the situation?

Am I confusing a low-probability event with a high-probability event?

Am I setting an unrealistically high standard for myself?

Am I overestimating how much responsibility I have in this situation?

Is this situation so important that my entire future hinges on the outcome?

How will things seem a week, a month, or a year from now?

What's the worst thing that could happen — and if that's true, what is so bad about that?

In addition to discussions and worksheets focused on restructuring automatic thoughts, Shane and his psychologist thought of behavioral experiments Shane could try to further test out the validity of his automatic thoughts. In one such experiment, he kept a log of each time he got in trouble for misbehaving at school. He found that, contrary to his automatic thoughts, this was not something that *always* happened, but rather an infrequent occurrence. A CLOSER LOOK: *The Pie Graph Technique* examines another type of behavioral experiment that cognitive therapists use when clients exaggerate how much they are to blame for unfortunate situations.

A Closer Look   The Pie Graph Technique

Clients with clinically severe anxiety or depression commonly engage in *personalization* — a thinking error in which they blame themselves (or someone else) for something that was actually caused by a complicated chain of events, or that was otherwise completely outside their control. For example, many survivors of traumatic events such as sexual assault or childhood abuse incorrectly blame themselves for what was done to them. The **pie graph technique** is a behavioral experiment cognitive therapists can use to help clients gain perspective on their own role (or lack thereof) in causing such negative events. This involves asking the client to identify all *possible* contributing factors, rating how much each factor contributes (what percent) to the overall responsibility for the negative event, and then using the ratings to create a pie chart to visually illustrate the logical error.

The pie chart on page 280 shows how this experiment was used in the case of a client, Yun, who was feeling depressed and blaming himself that one of his friends, Noah, had turned down an invitation to go to a basketball game on campus together. Specifically, Yun's automatic thought was "It's something terrible about me that made Noah not want to go to the game." First, the psychologist had Yun list factors (other than himself) that realistically could have contributed to such a situation:

1. Noah doesn't actually like basketball that much.

2. Noah has a big week of exams.

3. The game doesn't start until 9 p.m. and Noah has an 8:00 a.m. class every morning.

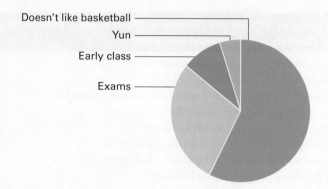

Doesn't like basketball

Yun

Early class

Exams

Next, Yun rated each factor based on what percent it likely influenced Noah's decision totaling up to 100%: he rated the factors 60%, 30%, and 10%, respectively. Then he created a pie graph (above) that he and his psychologist examined and discussed. After this discussion, Yun finally added an estimate of his own perceived level of responsibility. Given that Noah was a good friend and there seemed to be no personal reason for him to decline the invitation (e.g., they had done many other activities together recently), Yun labeled his own contribution as 5%. This helped him put the situation into perspective and change his automatic thoughts so that he wasn't blaming himself. ▬

Considerable research evidence supports Beck's cognitive therapy as a stand-alone intervention and as a component in broader CBT programs for a wide range of emotional and psychological problems for children and adults (e.g., Beck & Dozois, 2011; Hofmann et al., 2012). The available evidence also suggests not only that cognitive therapy is as effective as medication for depression (e.g., Strunk & DeRubeis, 2001) but also that the effects of cognitive therapy are longer-lasting (DeRubeis et al., 2008; Hollon et al., 2014). That said, it is not a panacea for all clients. For example, some individuals fare better with more purely behavioral interventions for depression and anxiety. Yet despite some question about its efficacy for more severely depressed clients, cognitive therapy appears to be as effective as medication in this group as well.

Cognitive Bias Modification

Imagine being able to sit at a computer — or launch a smartphone app — and alter maladaptive thinking habits simply by clicking or tapping on the screen. No need for therapy appointments or in-depth discussions and worksheets. **Cognitive bias modification (CBM)** is an experimental intervention in which clients complete game-like screen-based tasks that train them to change biased thinking processes such as the tendency to preferentially attend to negative aspects of situations (i.e., attention bias) and jump to negative conclusions (i.e., interpretation bias). In contrast

oatawa//iStock/Getty Images

Using cognitive bias modification, clients are trained by playing game-like tasks on a computer or smartphone to correct biased thinking patterns.

to the highly mindful and intellectual process that characterizes cognitive change in REBT and cognitive therapy, change in CBM is hypothesized to occur in an "online" and less conscious manner that more closely matches how people naturally think in the moment. The idea behind CBM derives from a large body of experimental research demonstrating that cognitive biases contribute to the cause and maintenance of many psychological problems (e.g., Azriel & Bar-Haim, 2020). Therefore, CBM represents the translation of experimental findings to clinical practice in the purest sense.

A typical example of a CBM program is **word-sentence association training**, which aims to teach users to make benign, rather than negative, interpretations of uncertain or ambiguous situations (Beard & Peckham, 2020). As depicted in **Figure 12.5**, in this task the client (or "user") is first presented with either a threat-related word (e.g., "hostile") or a benign (i.e., neutral or positive) word (e.g., "friendly") that remains on the screen briefly and is then replaced by a one-sentence description of an ambiguous situation (e.g., "You approach your professor and ask a question"). The user is then prompted to click (or tap) a button corresponding to "Yes or "No" to indicate whether or not the word and sentence are related. Positive feedback ("You are correct!") is given if the client selects YES for a benign (or NO for a negative) interpretation, and negative feedback ("You are incorrect!") is given if the client selects NO for a benign (or YES for a negative) interpretation. There are 100 such trials, and speed and accuracy are emphasized, which makes CMB like a competitive video game. The idea is that working toward receiving more positive feedback trains the user to more automatically interpret situations in a positive or neutral way.

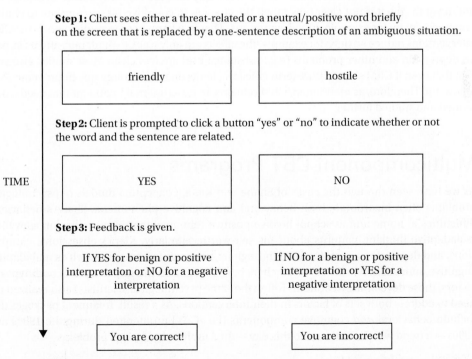

Step 1: Client sees either a threat-related or a neutral/positive word briefly on the screen that is replaced by a one-sentence description of an ambiguous situation.

| friendly | hostile |

Step 2: Client is prompted to click a button "yes" or "no" to indicate whether or not the word and the sentence are related.

TIME

| YES | NO |

Step 3: Feedback is given.

| If YES for benign or positive interpretation or NO for a negative interpretation | If NO for a benign or positive interpretation or YES for a negative interpretation |

| You are correct! | You are incorrect! |

Figure 12.5 The Progression of a Word-Sentence Association Task Trial

CBM interventions are considered experimental because their efficacy and effectiveness are still being studied (Fodor et al., 2020). Accordingly, they are not yet widely available for use in general clinical practice. Most studies testing CBM use experimental software programs installed on computers in research labs or clinics where researchers can observe sessions and provide supervision as needed. Part of CBM's appeal, however, is its potential as a self-help intervention that people can use in their own home. Accordingly, a few studies have examined CBM as an online (app-based) intervention with no psychologist involvement (e.g., Namaky et al., 2021). This method may be especially preferable for clients who do not have access to therapy, who are not interested in face-to-face therapy, or who have problems that do not require a higher intensity of treatment.

Other studies have examined CBM as a precursor to more traditional CBT (e.g., Brosan et al., 2011; Williams et al., 2013). It is possible that completing CBM leads to greater cognitive flexibility, making clients more responsive to interventions like REBT and more confident about engaging in behavioral interventions such as exposure therapy or assertiveness training. CBM may also benefit clients who are already engaged in CBT. For example, it could be used as a homework exercise to increase clients' awareness of how often they automatically jump to negative conclusions. Finally, CBM may be an ideal low-intensity intervention in primary care settings (Weisberg et al., 2021). Most individuals first seek treatment for psychological problems from their primary care physician (Verhaak et al., 2009). The integration of behavioral health and primary care is becoming more common, and interventions like CBM are appealing because they can be "prescribed" and easily monitored.

How effective is CBM? Results from a number of meta-analyses (e.g., Fodor et al., 2020; Jones & Sharpe, 2017) indicate that CBM consistently reduces cognitive biases in adults, but not in youth. Yet, it is not clear how much the changes in cognitive biases translate to clinical improvement in, for example, mood symptoms. That is, whereas some studies show that CBM interventions reduce anxiety, for example, the effects are only weak to moderate; and its impact on depression and other problems (e.g., substance use) are less clear. Most studies also suggest that even if CBM shows short-term efficacy, clients do not maintain any improvements at follow-up. Therefore, as mentioned, CBM remains an experimental treatment that needs to be refined and studied further.

Multicomponent CBT Programs

As we have seen through the cases of Shane and Kiara, conceptual models of psychological problems often incorporate both behavioral and cognitive phenomena. Shane's behavioral difficulties at home and at school involve positive reinforcement of his behavior, as well as maladaptive thinking patterns about his self-worth. Similarly, Kiara's obsessions, compulsions, and depression are maintained through negative reinforcement as well as maladaptive cognitive appraisals. As clinical researchers have recognized the importance of both types of factors, those developing treatments (often the same psychological scientists) also realized the need to address both sets of factors in their interventions. As a result, treatment packages that include behavioral *and* cognitive components (i.e., CBT) proliferated during the 1980s and 1990s — a trend which continues to this day — for a multitude of target problems.

In many (but not all) instances, these treatment programs were developed with particular DSM disorders in mind, and then manualized and rigorously tested in RCTs that included clients meeting criteria for the target disorder. This has helped make CBT easy to disseminate as the empirically supported "treatment of choice" for particular DSM disorders. To illustrate how contemporary CBT combines behavioral and cognitive interventions, **Table 12.6** describes a number of multicomponent evidence-based treatments (see Chapter 10, *Psychological Treatment: Science and Practice*) that include both behavioral and cognitive components targeting various problems and DSM diagnoses.

Table 12.6 Multicomponent Empirically Supported CBT Programs Used for Major Psychological Problems and Disorders			
Target Problem or Disorder	**Behavioral Component(s)**	**Cognitive Component(s)**	**Number of Sessions**
General anxiety (in adults and youth)	Imaginal exposure, muscle relaxation skills, problem solving	Cognitive therapy/REBT	16–20
Social anxiety	*In vivo* exposure	Cognitive therapy	16–20
Panic attacks	Interoceptive exposure	Education, cognitive therapy for catastrophic thinking	12–16
PTSD	*In vivo* and imaginal exposure	Education, cognitive therapy	8–15
Depression (in adults and children)	Behavioral activation	Cognitive therapy/REBT	8–16
Bulimia nervosa	Self-monitoring, response prevention, stimulus control	Education, cognitive therapy focused on body-related thoughts	20
Substance use problems	Contingency management, self-monitoring,	Cognitive therapy to reduce stress and negative beliefs	8–24
Insomnia	Modification of behaviors that disrupt sleep (i.e., improve sleep hygiene)	Cognitive therapy to modify thoughts that interfere with sleep	6
ADHD (in adults and youth)	Parent training, social skills training, coping skills training (e.g., organization, time management)	Cognitive therapy	12–15
Hair pulling/skin picking	Habit reversal training	Cognitive therapy	12–16

SOURCE: American Psychological Association Division 12 (https://div12.org/diagnoses/) and Society of Child and Adolescent Clinical Psychology (https://effectivechildtherapy.org/).

Think Like a Clinical Psychologist As with any form of treatment, not all clients achieve benefits following CBT. What variables (and why) do you think might predict which clients improve and which do not?

▌▌ Evaluating the Cognitive-Behavioral Approach

Effectiveness

The main advantage of CBT is that it works! In a review of 269 meta-analyses, Hofmann and colleagues (2012) found that for adults and children CBT was associated with higher response rates than control conditions, and at least an equivalent response in direct comparisons to other treatments (including, in some cases, psychiatric medication) for an extensive range of psychological problems and psychiatric diagnoses among adults and youth in outpatient, residential, and medical settings. CBT is shown to be effective when delivered individually, in groups, as well as remotely (i.e., online or in self-help books) with minimal (or no) clinician contact (e.g., Axelsson et al., 2020). Moreover, the effects of CBT translate well from highly controlled efficacy studies to effectiveness studies conducted in routine clinical settings with representative clients and clinicians (e.g., Samaan et al., 2021).

Efficiency

Like behavioral interventions, cognitive and CBT techniques are characterized by their practicality and pragmatism — they are meant to be learned, practiced, and mastered over a relatively brief period of time. The abundance of evidence-based CBT treatment manuals for a wide range of presenting problems also facilitates the integration of CBT within today's managed care environment. Indeed, mental health providers with relatively little experience can be trained to deliver effective CBT (Wilson, 2007). Not only does this facilitate the delivery of effective psychological treatment, it also aids research and enables the training of students within the various fields of mental health.

Scope of Use

Finally, as we have alluded to, CBT is known to be effective for a countless number of specific problems and populations (e.g., Hofmann et al., 2012). Studies, however, vary in their strength of support for CBT, with the largest and most consistent effect sizes among problems related to depressed mood and anxiety in both children and adults (e.g., Tolin, 2010). The efficacy of CBT for substance use problems has also been demonstrated consistently, although there is some evidence of greater effect sizes for behavioral approaches (McHugh et al., 2010). Among people with schizophrenia, CBT is associated with a moderate beneficial effect on positive symptoms (i.e., delusions and hallucinations) as well as general functioning, mood, and anxiety, particularly as an adjunct to pharmacotherapy (Jauhar et al., 2014). Although not as effective with anorexia nervosa, CBT is associated with reduced body dysmorphic disorder symptoms and body image disturbances, and medium effect sizes were found in meta-analyses comparing CBT to control treatments for bulimia nervosa and to pharmacotherapy for binge-eating disorder (Hofmann et al., 2012). Finally, CBT for problems related to sleep (e.g., insomnia) has consistently been shown to be more efficacious than control treatments (Trauer et al., 2015). Results of meta-analyses of CBT for personality disorders, however, are mixed (e.g., Cristea et al., 2017).

Criticisms

An important limitation of CBT is its cultural context. Indeed, as noted above, its developers (and their clients) were primarily of dominant cultural identities. Accordingly, its perspective and assumptions reflect a strong European American influence. Moreover, research on CBT has not traditionally been conducted with diverse samples, focusing principally on people of European American descent and cultural majority groups. For example, Stewart and Chambless (2009) conducted a meta-analysis of 57 studies of CBT and found that in only 6 (10.5%) studies did African American individuals or Caribbean American individuals of African descent make up at least 20% of the sample, and in only two (3.5%) did Latinx people make up at least 20% of the sample. A few studies explicitly explored the efficacy of CBT in historically underrepresented groups and tested culturally sensitive adaptations for gay, lesbian, and bisexual clients; recent immigrants to the United States; and others (e.g., Pachankis et al., 2015). Fortunately, efforts have been made more recently to conduct research and adapt CBT interventions across populations and contexts. A meta-analysis of cultural adaptations of psychological interventions included 24 studies of CBT adapted for various underrepresented groups, and found that these interventions produced better outcomes than comparison conditions (Hall et al., 2016). In addition, increasing recognition of the influence of multicultural factors has led to the development of work incorporating principles of multiculturalism into CBT.

Another limitation of CBT is that it requires a great deal of effort from the client. Indeed, it is the kind of intervention where one will only "get out of it what they put into it." Individuals who are unable or unwilling to practice skills or complete homework assignments are likely to experience little benefit. In fact, homework is arguably the most crucial element of CBT, as it involves rehearsing the skills that are first learned during treatment sessions. For many clients, the expectation is that they will spend an hour or more per day working on these therapeutic elements. For clients with poor motivation to change, those with severe depression, and those with extremely complex psychological problems, this can put limits on the utility of a cognitive-behavioral approach. Similarly, because of the highly verbal nature of the intervention, and the emphasis on logical thinking, it may not be appropriate for clients with severe learning difficulties or developmental disabilities.

Think Like a Clinical Psychologist One criticism of CBT is that it focuses too much on negative cognitions and overlooks the benefits of positive thinking and optimism. How would you respond to this critique?

Chapter Summary

During the second half of the 20th century, some clinical psychologists broke with the strict behaviorists and embraced the growing focus on the role of cognitive factors in emotion and behavior. Albert Ellis (a clinical psychologist) and Aaron Beck (a psychiatrist) were two noteworthy figures who adopted this position and developed interventions based on philosophical reflection and empirical data indicating that beliefs and interpretations are critical contributors to feelings and behavioral tendencies. Over time, the promise and empirical rigor of cognitive science began to appeal to increasing numbers of psychological scientists and clinicians who recognized the interplay between behavior and cognition. The result was a "merger" between the cognitive and behavioral traditions that strongly endures to this day.

The main cognitive components of CBT are Ellis's REBT and Beck's cognitive therapy. Although these interventions have much in common from a conceptual standpoint, in practice REBT tends to be a directive treatment in which the clinician takes an active role in disputing the client's irrational thinking. In cognitive therapy, the clinician takes on a more collaborative role, teaching the client skills for challenging negative automatic thoughts and replacing them with more realistic alternatives. Finally, CBM is a newer approach to changing thought processes via computer programs or smartphone applications that train clients at a more automatic level to choose positive or neutral responses over negative ones. Still an experimental intervention, CBM is not widely available in clinical settings.

Along with the behavioral perspective, CBT and its conceptual model have had (and continue to have) an enormous impact on the field of clinical psychology. In fact, over the past half-century, most of the breakthrough achievements in understanding and treating psychological and mental health problems have derived from this school of thought. Still, CBT is not a magic bullet. It is not effective for all clients and all problems. Moreover, it has a strong cultural (i.e., European American) influence that may mitigate its effects with clients from other cultural groups. It is crucial that researchers include more diversity in their study samples and that the field continue to develop multicultural modifications of CBT.

Applying What You've Learned

Exercise 1: Use the ABC model to conceptualize depression in a 29-year-old man who has just had a relationship break-up. Give examples of three possible dysfunctional beliefs that might contribute to his depression. How might the client and therapist "test" these beliefs (i.e., conduct behavioral experiments)?

Exercise 2: What are the major differences between Ellis's REBT and Beck's cognitive therapy? What behavioral components might be used to supplement the cognitive components of REBT and cognitive therapy?

Key Terms

ABC model: A way to conceptualize psychological problems. "A" stands for *activating event, activity, or adversity* and represents a situation that actually happens; "B" stands for *beliefs* and signifies automatic thoughts, appraisals, perceptions, and interpretations of the situation at "A"; and "C" stands for the emotional and behavioral *consequences* that occur as a result of "B" that primarily lead to "C" (consequences).

Appraisal: Judgment we make; type of automatic thought.

Attribution: Explanation we come up with in our mind to explain why something happened; type of automatic thought.

Automatic thought: Maladaptive pattern of self-talk that may become habitual.

Behavioral experiment: Method for clients to "put their beliefs to the test."

Cognition: The way we think about events and situations in our environment.

Cognitive-behavioral treatment (CBT): A psychological treatment modality that focuses on correcting maladaptive patterns of thinking and behaving.

Cognitive bias modification (CBM): An experimental intervention in which clients complete game-like screen-based tasks to change biased thinking processes such as the tendency to preferentially attend to negative aspects of situations and jump to negative conclusions.

Cognitive perspective: Emphasizes how our thinking — that is, our beliefs, interpretations, judgments, attributions, expectations, and other forms of "self-talk" — influence our emotions and behaviors.

Cognitive revolution: A paradigm shift during which psychological scientists began to recognize that operant and classical conditioning, even with their precision and objectivity, could not completely explain the entirety of human experience.

Cognitive specificity: The phenomena that the same event can be associated with different emotional and behavioral reactions depending on what the person is thinking.

Collaborative empiricism: Practitioners and clients discover together how the client's maladaptive thinking contributes to distress and how adopting healthier thinking patterns can reduce this distress.

Constructive negative emotion: Universal experience that may be an appropriate response in certain circumstances.

Culturally responsive modification: The notion that CBT methods can pivot in order to incorporate experiences of oppression and other stressors related to being a member of a historically underrepresented group in order to make the intervention more appropriate to the client.

Disputation strategy: Challenge to irrational thinking.

Downward arrow technique: Involves (1) identifying a particular activating event, (2) asking the client what this situation means, and (3) continuing to ask the same question until one or more dysfunctional beliefs are revealed.

Dysfunctional belief: Inaccurate, logically flawed, exaggerated, inflexible, way of thinking that is incongruent with goal attainment.

Empirical dispute: A disputation strategy that uses objective, verifiable data and evidence (such as observations and research results) to challenge irrational thinking.

Guided discovery: Used in cognitive therapy where clients are helped to notice and challenge their own thinking mistakes.

Interpretation: Meaning that we assign when there is uncertainty in a particular situation; type of automatic thought.

Irrational belief: Dysfunctional thinking pattern.

Logical dispute: A disputation strategy where rules of reason and logic are used to challenge and modify the client's irrational beliefs.

Pie graph technique: A behavioral experiment cognitive therapists can use to help clients gain perspective on their own role in causing negative events.

Rational emotive behavior therapy (REBT): A form of CBT developed by Albert Ellis that expanded the ABC model to place more emphasis on emotions and to recognize the integration of behavioral and cognitive therapy.

Rational thinking: The ability to objectively consider facts, opinions, judgments, and data to arrive at a sound conclusion; can include both positive and negative ideas.

Schema: The way we make sense of the world, driven by frameworks of knowledge and associations; exist in our long-term memory.

Socratic dialogue: A method in which the therapist asks the client pointed, open-ended questions that encourage reflection and promote new and more logical perspectives.

Unconditional self-acceptance: Becoming comfortable viewing oneself as fallible and seeing one's own self-worth as separate from one's behaviors and circumstances.

Word-sentence association training: A technique used to teach users to make benign, rather than negative, interpretations of uncertain or ambiguous situations.

CONNECT ONLINE:

 Check out our videos and additional resources located at: www.macmillanlearning.com

Acceptance and Dialectical Interventions

FOCUS QUESTIONS

1. How is mindfulness related to both acceptance and dialectical treatment approaches?
2. Explain the conceptual foundations for acceptance and commitment therapy (ACT) and the six core processes addressed in this treatment.
3. Describe the theoretical basis of dialectical behavior therapy (DBT) and the techniques used in this approach.
4. What are the similarities and differences between "third-wave" treatments and more traditional cognitive-behavioral treatment (CBT)?
5. How well do ACT and DBT work?

CHAPTER OUTLINE

cceptance and dialectical thinking are distinct but related concepts. Underscoring both of these is **mindfulness**, which refers to present moment awareness and which originated with the teachings of the Buddha, who lived around 2600 years ago in what is now India. In modern clinical psychology, mindfulness is defined as paying attention to the present moment in a purposeful way and nonjudgmentally (Kabat-Zinn, 1994). This description casts mindfulness as a skill involving thoughtful consideration of what is occurring without *evaluating* the experience, but rather by simply *noticing* it. **Acceptance** picks up where mindfulness leaves off and refers to the willingness to embrace internal experiences—such as thoughts, feelings, and physical sensations—even when they seem unpleasant. **Dialectical thinking**, which has its roots in the Chinese philosophy that all aspects of the universe contain seeds of their opposites (i.e., yin and yang), means being able to view issues from multiple perspectives, bring together seemingly contradictory positions, and accept that two opposing ideas can be true at the same time.

In recent decades, some clinical psychologists have woven mindfulness, acceptance, and dialectics into traditional cognitive and behavioral treatments, leading to the emergence of a group of so-called "third-wave" CBT interventions (see IN HISTORICAL PERSPECTIVE: *Acceptance and Dialectics in Psychological Treatment*). These treatments have in common the view that a life worth living has both positive and negative aspects, and as such it is important to

●●●◗● In Historical Perspective

Acceptance and Dialectics in Psychological Treatment

The "behavioral revolution" during the early to mid-1900s led, for the first time, to psychological interventions that were based on scientific principles (i.e., learning theory) and shown to be effective in rigorously conducted studies. Within a few decades, the cognitive revolution yielded a "second wave" of interventions — cognitive-behavioral treatments (CBT) — which were also based on scientific theory and empirically supported. These first two generations of CBT share the assumption that psychological problems arise from certain learning histories and maladaptive cognitions. Traditional CBT interventions are therefore aimed at changing reinforcement contingencies, conditioned responses, and thinking patterns with the goal of eliminating, or at least reducing, unwanted unpleasant emotional responses.

Beginning in the 1980s, cognitive-behavioral interventions began to emerge that extended these traditional CBT principles to include the concepts of mindfulness, acceptance, and dialectics. This "third wave" of CBT shifts the emphasis away from trying to *reduce* unwanted thoughts and emotions and instead helps clients show up to the present moment, step toward what matters in life, and accept themselves *despite* their unwanted thoughts, feelings, and other difficult experiences. Even with seriously distressed clients, third-wave CBT emphasizes empowerment through learning to observe and experience unwanted thoughts and feelings, think about situations from different perspectives, and balance acceptance with the need for change (e.g., Hayes et al., 2016).

The first of these interventions was dialectical behavior therapy (DBT), which emerged from attempts to apply standard behavior therapy to the treatment of suicidal individuals (Linehan et al., 1991). DBT began as a trial-and-error clinical effort based on the application of learning theory with clients who had strong emotional reactions and suicidal behaviors. Its developers, however, reported that some of these "difficult to treat" clients felt criticized, misunderstood, and attacked by the exclusive focus on behavior change. Thus, inspired by the idea be able to accept unpleasant thoughts and feelings as necessary (and even *valuable*) parts of the human condition. Such experiences can be barely noticeable; or they can be quite prominent, as in the case of anger, depression, anxiety, thoughts of self-harm, heart palpitations, and cravings for psychoactive substances. From this perspective, the primary goal of treatment is to help clients learn to stop judging themselves and their inner experiences as good/bad or right/wrong, and instead develop the ability to stay in the present moment regardless of what's happening around them (and within them) so they can lead a meaningful and value-driven life. In other words, rather than aiming to change the content of clients' thoughts and feelings, these interventions focus on the context, processes, and functions of how a person relates to thoughts, feelings, sensations, and other internal experiences. In this chapter, we will examine the two most well-known and well-studied third-wave CBT interventions: **acceptance and commitment therapy** (ACT; Hayes et al., 2016) and **dialectical behavior therapy** (DBT; Linehan, 2014).

Andrey Prokhorov/Getty Images

Dialectical thinking reflects the ancient Chinese philosophy of yin/yang, the idea that opposite forces can in fact be complementary.

of dialectics, an effort was made to create a more collaborative approach to treatment that might appeal to clients with firm worldviews. Dialectics are a way to bring opposing forces together: a therapist with certain ideas of healthy behavior and a client with ideas and behaviors that lead to distress, dysfunction, and even physical harm. Over time, the clinician guides the client to incorporate healthier ideas and behavior patterns into their ways of thinking and behaving.

Throughout the 1980s and 1990s, a number of other interventions emerged with roots in classical behavioral (and cognitive) theories and therapies, including ACT (which was initially called *comprehensive distancing*; Zettle, 2005). ACT focuses on helping clients change their agenda of struggling against unwanted thoughts and feelings, and instead mindfully notice them simply as experiences that do not have to stand in the way of a meaningful life.

Although this chapter focuses on ACT and DBT—the two most well-known and widely used third-wave interventions—there are numerous other products of this movement, including acceptance-based behavior therapy, functional analytic psychotherapy, mindfulness-based stress reduction, and mindfulness-based cognitive therapy. Many self-help resources and group training workshops inspired by third wave interventions have sprung up in recent decades as these concepts have caught on not only with mental health practitioners but also with the public at large. In fact, many organizations and businesses have embraced these interventions, seeking out professional seminars for their employees. Finally, the Association for Contextual Behavioral Science established itself in 2005 as the flagship professional organization for clinicians and researchers interested in third-wave treatments.

Generally speaking, third-wave treatments complement more traditional cognitive and behavioral interventions such as exposure therapy, cognitive therapy, and behavioral activation; and in fact, many clinical psychologists blend these strategies together. In fact, later in this chapter we discuss some of the issues concerning the extent to which the third wave of CBT represents something that is truly brand new or merely a rebranding of more traditional interventions. We invite you to keep this question in mind as you read the remainder of the chapter. ■

Historic Collection/Alamy

Acceptance and Commitment Therapy

Developed by psychologist Steven Hayes, ACT is an experiential, contextual approach to psychological treatment that falls within the broad category of CBT. It helps clients think about what really matters to them and then take action to enrich their lives based on their personal values. But ACT is different than traditional CBT in that it does not emphasize symptom reduction. Rather, it takes the perspective that people can learn to live fulfilling lives regardless of psychological symptoms (such unpleasant thoughts and feelings) by responding to such symptoms with mindfulness.

Theoretical Basis

Psychologist Steven Hayes developed ACT in the 1980s as a treatment based on learning theory that adds aspects of mindfulness and an explicit focus on the client's values.

ACT is grounded in **relational frame theory**—the idea that our ability to relate one concept to another is the foundation of human language (for a more detailed explanation of this theory and how it relates to ACT, see A CLOSER LOOK: *ACT and Relational Frame Theory*). The idea is that most clients seek treatment because they want to gain better control over their unpleasant thoughts and feelings. They want to get rid of anxiety, depression, guilt, anger, urges to use drugs and alcohol, traumatic memories, low self-esteem, fear of rejection, grief, and so on. This unwillingness to have difficult thoughts, feelings, and other internal events is termed **experiential avoidance** and it is characterized by attempts to control or minimize such experiences even when doing so takes up time and interferes with functioning (Hayes et al., 1996).

Epoxydude/Getty Images

To illustrate, there are times when we all choose to avoid distressing thoughts and feelings—we decide not to watch a horror movie or we skip a song on our playlist that reminds us of a sad event. This may be a perfectly good strategy for managing emotions every now and then, but when experiential avoidance becomes habitual, rigid, and automatic it tends to cause even more distress and impairment in peoples' lives. Imagine a client who goes through a difficult relationship break-up and then withdraws from all social interactions (so he doesn't have to face his friends and talk about what happened) to the point that his grades and personal relationships begin to suffer. Using alcohol or drugs as an escape from feelings of anxiety, guilt, or anger is another form of experiential avoidance. So too are Kiara's compulsive checking and washing rituals, which she performs to reduce obsessional anxiety despite the fact that these rituals interfere with her functioning. A large body of research suggests that experiential avoidance plays a role in a variety of clinical problems such as anxiety (e.g., Hayes-Skelton & Eustis (2020), depression (e.g., Moroz & Dunkley, 2019),

Experiential avoidance is a coping strategy that involves trying to push away unpleasant thoughts, emotions, cravings, and other private experiences. But it's a trap! The harder one tries *not* to think about having another drink, the more intense their craving becomes.

problems with alcohol and substance use (e.g., Shorey et al., 2017), and borderline personality disorder (Jacob et al., 2013). A good way to think about experiential avoidance is as a trap — the more a person doesn't want to have a particular experience, the more they'll have it and the more time and energy they'll spend fruitlessly trying to push it away.

A Closer Look   ACT and Relational Frame Theory

Have you ever thought about your ability to associate words — which are really just sounds — with objects or events? While your pet dog or cat might be able to connect the dots between hearing the word "treat" then getting food, the human brain goes well beyond such simple connections to much broader and more abstract associations, including those between words and their meanings. This is what allows us to learn a tremendous amount of information and communicate complicated ideas . . . *like relational frame theory!*

Relational frame theory, or RFT, is a theory of language that proposes that human cognition and communication are founded in our capacity for identifying and creating links between stimuli (Cullinan & Vitale, 2009). To illustrate, imagine you always said the word "soda" to a child before, during, and after giving her a cup filled with a cold, sweet, fizzy drink. Before long, she would connect the word "soda" with drinking this substance. If you then told the child that "pop" was another word for "soda," she would easily connect the new word to the event of drinking soda. From that point forward, the questions "Would you like some soda?" and "Would you like some pop?" would be answered with the same enthusiastic "Yes!" by the child.

This ability to form relationships between concepts is one of the unique features of the human brain and it is learned through a process of reinforcement. Importantly, it also lays the foundational bricks for language (verbal, written, and body). Researchers call these associations *relational frames*. For example, if our soda-loving child tries Coke, Sprite, Root Beer, and Dr. Pepper and is told that each is a kind of "soda," she will soon be able to label sodas she has never tried before as "soda" because she has developed a relational frame: drinks that are cold, sweet, and fizzy are all types of soda. But what does all of this have to do with ACT?

ACT helps clients modify maladaptive relational frames around unpleasant internal stimuli, such as negative thoughts and feelings. Clients often perceive these stimuli as "symptoms," which implies they are "bad," "harmful," or "abnormal," and therefore something to be gotten get rid of in order to be "healthy" and "normal." But this frame leads to experiential avoidance, which causes more problems and takes the person away from what is meaningful to them in life. Therefore, the goal of ACT is to develop new relational frames in which unwanted internal experiences are seen as merely unpleasant aspects of life that do not need to be "struggled with" or "gotten rid of."

Imagine there's a plant that you judge as "ugly," growing right in the middle of your garden. And suppose there's no way to get rid of it without destroying your entire garden. If you view this plant as a "weed," chances are you won't like it and you won't want it there. Maybe you'll get upset about it or waste time thinking about how much better your garden would be without it. You might even keep other people away from your garden for fear they'll think you're a poor gardener because of the "weed." In other words, this "weed" has now become an important *thing* in your life.

But what if you view this plant as just a fact of life — a natural part of the environment? It's the same plant in the same location, but your relationship with it has changed. You'll no longer feel the need to struggle with it, become upset or embarrassed over it, or waste time thinking about it. You can show your garden to others without hesitation. The plant has not changed, but it no longer takes up so much of your time and energy. This is similar to how ACT aims to help clients change relational frames involving unwanted thoughts and feelings. ■

Psychological flexibility is the ability to be in the moment and engage in meaningful activities even when difficult thoughts and feelings "show up" inside.

The goal of ACT, therefore, is not to reduce, change, avoid, or control the clients' unwanted thoughts and feelings, but rather to reduce the *impact* and *influence* of these feelings. Specifically, by addressing the six principles described in **Table 13.1**, clients learn to stop struggling with their difficult private experiences, and instead "make room" for them. In doing so, ACT helps clients develop **psychological flexibility**, which is the ability to be in the present moment, engage in activities that are personally important, and live a meaningful life despite the fact that difficult experiences will sometimes "show up." You can think of psychological flexibility as the opposite of experiential avoidance.

Table 13.1 The Six Core Principles of Acceptance and Commitment Therapy	
Principle	**Definition**
Acceptance	Making room for unpleasant private experiences; allowing them to come and go without struggling with them or giving them too much attention
Cognitive defusion	Learning to perceive private experiences as bits of language, words, and pictures, rather than taking them as facts
Contact with the present moment	Bringing full awareness to the here and now; focusing on, and engaging fully in, whatever one is doing
The observing self	Understanding that thoughts and feelings are not the essence of who we are; they are just aspects of us that change constantly
Values	Clarifying what is most important, significant, and meaningful in life
Committed action	Setting goals, guided by values, and taking action to achieve them

Consider anger, which is a normal human emotion. There are times when it is useful to act on anger, such as if you see a child being mistreated or someone violates your own personal boundaries. But there are also times when you're better off looking past angry feelings and carrying on with whatever you're doing, such as if someone cuts you off in heavy traffic or your boss turns down your request for an extra day off. ACT aims to alter the client's relationship with unpleasant inner experiences from one in which these experiences seem to *demand* action to one in which they are only *suggestions* for action. Indeed, research consistently finds that mindfulness, acceptance, and openness to unwanted thoughts and feelings are associated with reduced emotional problems and improved regulation of behavior (e.g., Creswell, 2017).

Implementing ACT

ACT promotes the principles presented in Table 13.1 to help clients develop acceptance of unwanted private experiences and commitment (and action) to living life based on what's important and meaningful to them. The first step is to help clients understand that experiential avoidance is the *problem* rather than the *solution*. Clients therefore identify the various strategies they have been using to try to avoid or get rid of unwanted private experiences, such as behavioral avoidance, compulsive rituals, stress eating, relaxation techniques, using drugs or alcohol, ruminating and overanalyzing situations, and so on. Next, the psychologist asks questions such as "How well does that work in the long term?" "What does this strategy cost you in terms of time and energy?" and "Does doing this bring you closer to the life you want?" The aim of these questions, and the discussion it generates, is to increase clients' awareness that these strategies don't work very well and so it's time to find a new approach for when unwanted thoughts and feelings show up.

Metaphors are used throughout ACT to help illustrate concepts and make the treatment more experiential. Here, a clinician might use the following analogy to quicksand:

> *Imagine you're caught in quicksand. What would you do? For most people, their first instinct is to vigorously struggle to stay afloat . . . only the more you struggle, the faster the quicksand sucks you under! In quicksand, struggling is the worst thing you can possibly do. Believe it or not, the way to survive is to lie back, spread out your arms, and float on the surface. That's right, you have to get <u>with</u> the quicksand to get out of it. It's tricky, because every instinct tells you to struggle; but if you do, you'll drown. The same principle applies to difficult thoughts and feelings: the more we obey our natural instinct to fight them, the more they overwhelm us. But if we lean into them, we can discover that they're not so overwhelming. Let's talk about how this relates to what brought you in to see me.*

Once the client accepts the futility of experiential avoidance, treatment turns to fostering psychological flexibility by working toward the six principles from Table 13.1. As we discuss next, each principle has its own set of techniques and metaphors, some of which may be more useful for some clients than for others.

Acceptance

An important early focus in ACT is giving clients an alternative to experiential avoidance. Because unwanted thoughts and feelings cannot be controlled in a meaningful way, and because attempting to control them tends to make the experiences more intense, *acceptance* is offered as an alternative. Acceptance techniques help clients make space for unpleasant thoughts, feelings, body sensations, urges, and other private experiences. They encourage willingness to have these universal experiences whenever and wherever they show up without struggling with them, running from them, or giving them too much attention.

One technique is to ask the client to imagine hosting a party for the entire neighborhood, but then realizing that there is one particular neighbor that no one seems to like. This neighbor represents the client's unwanted thoughts and feelings, and the client gets stuck guarding the door to keep this person from showing up and ruining the party. In doing so, however, the client is missing out on all the fun of the party. The therapist and client then discuss how

The Party metaphor is often used in ACT to facilitate acceptance. Clients imagine they are hosting a large party, and instead of spending the whole time trying to keep out uninvited guests, they decide they're going to enjoy the party no matter who shows up.

the client could welcome the neighbor to the party even though it would be preferable not to have this person there. In other words, clients could choose to "open up" to upsetting thoughts and feelings (instead of getting "stuck at the door") so they're not missing out on important things in their life.

Cognitive Defusion

When clients are in a state of cognitive *fusion*, their thoughts and feelings seem like literal truths—rules that must be obeyed, crucial events that require undivided attention, or threats that must be dealt with. Take Kiara, for example. Her obsessive doubts had enormous influence over her behavior, sometimes causing her to go into work in the middle of the night to check that she hadn't made any mistakes. **Cognitive defusion**, however, means stepping back and just *observing* thoughts and feelings without being "caught up" in them. If Kiara could see her obsessional thoughts merely as passing private events—an ever-changing stream of words, sounds, and pictures—they would have much less impact and influence. There are many techniques and metaphors to promote defusion. As illustrated in IN PRACTICE: *Kiara's Defusion Metaphor*, Kiara's psychologist used a metaphor called the "Passengers on the Bus" to help Kiara learn how to change her relationship with her obsessional thoughts.

In Practice   **Kiara's Defusion Metaphor**

The Passengers on the Bus metaphor (Hayes et al., 2016) helps clients find more useful ways to think about their unwanted private experiences. Although a part of ACT, this exercise is fully consistent with other treatment techniques, such as exposure therapy, which aim to also change how Kiara responds to obsessional thoughts and anxiety (e.g., Twohig et al., 2015). Therefore, Kiara's therapist used this exercise to help set the stage for exposure and response prevention:

Therapist: Imagine that you are a bus driver. The bus represents your life, and your bus route represents how you lead your life. The passengers on your bus are your own thoughts, feelings, and other private experiences — some seem pleasant, and others not so much. Passengers continually get on and off the bus. At one point, though, a bunch of mean-looking passengers have gotten on your bus and they represent your obsessional thoughts, anxiety, and uncertainty. They're sitting right up in front and trying to intimidate you by saying nasty things like "You've probably made a terrible mistake; you'd better check again," "You're going to get someone sick; you'd better wash your hands again," and so on. What are some other things these passengers are saying to you?

Kiara: They're saying things like "You're going to be responsible for a patient dying," "You weren't careful enough when you were dosing your patient's medicines," and "You won't be able to sleep until you've made sure you didn't kill any patients."

Therapist: Right! And sooner or later you get tired of being bullied by these passengers, so you decide to try to throw them off the bus. Except because these passengers are bigger and stronger than you, you realize that trying to scuffle with them isn't such a good idea. Does this sound familiar?

Kiara: Oh yeah. It's just like how I try to get rid of my obsessional thoughts. I try to push them away or do rituals to quiet them down, but that never works for very long.

Therapist: Exactly! But since you can't kick the passengers off the bus, you go back to driving . . . until you think of another idea. This time, you propose a deal to the passengers: if they promise to go to the back of the bus, duck behind their seats so you don't have to see them, and stop yelling nasty things, then you promise to drive the bus wherever *they* want to go — even if it's not where *you* want to go. Does that sound familiar? Have you made a similar deal with your obsessions?

Kiara: Yes. That's exactly what happens with the OCD. I've gotten into this routine of continually washing and checking so that the passengers — my obsessions — stay quiet and I don't have to worry too much. But I don't want to wash and check so much.

Therapist: So, it seems you're stuck with having to appease the passengers to keep them from coming back up front and yelling at you. And now, this has become a routine. They don't have to remind you where to turn and how fast to go anymore. You know exactly what they want you to do. But let's look at the big picture here: *you're* sitting in the driver's seat and *you* actually have control over where you drive the bus. Yet by trying to control the passengers, you've actually given up control. It's like you've become so consumed in quieting down the passengers — in keeping yourself from feeling anxious — that you've lost sight of the fact that *you* still get to determine where your bus is going; that is, where you truly want to go in life.

Kiara: That makes sense. In trying to get control, I've given it up.

Therapist: That's right. So, what if you just decided to start driving your bus where *you* want to go instead of letting the passengers make the decisions for you?

Kiara: But if I break my end of the deal, won't the passengers break theirs and come back up to the front of the bus and start yelling at me again?

Therapist: Yes, and that's just the point. They probably will. But the worst they'll do is try to get your attention by saying nasty things. Although it sure *seems* like they'll grab the wheel and crash the bus, they've never done anything like that before. Nor have you really tried driving your bus where you want to go and just letting the passengers yell all the way *without trying to shut them up*. What if you could see your obsessional thoughts and anxiety as passengers on your bus who are just *along for the ride*?

From here, Kiara and her therapist discussed using exposure and response prevention as opportunities to practice "driving the bus" and "just letting the passengers tag along." The idea here is to refuse to get caught up in the *content* of the obsessional thoughts, and instead see them for what they are — just mental noise or "passengers on the bus." ▬

Contact with the Present Moment

ACT interventions focus on helping clients become fully aware of the "here and now" and mindful of whatever they are doing. For example, a therapist might give clients a grape and ask them to eat it in "slow motion" while focusing intently on its taste and texture. If distracting thoughts and feelings arise, clients can notice them, but just let them come and go while they keep their attention focused on eating the grape. This experience, which often leads to noticing all sorts of tastes and other sensations that people usually overlook, can be used to draw an analogy with situations where clients become so caught up in their thoughts and feelings that they don't engage fully in what they are doing and end up missing out on the "richness" of the experience. Clients can be given homework to practice mindfully engaging (with all five senses) in daily routines such as brushing teeth, talking with others, and walking or driving.

The Chessboard metaphor is a commonly used ACT strategy to help clients see the distinction between themselves and their thoughts and feelings.

The Observing Self

Working on this principle helps clients see themselves as distinct from their unwanted thoughts and feelings — which are events that occur within us, but are not the essence of who we are. The **Chessboard metaphor**, in which clients think of their thoughts and feelings as chess pieces, is one widely used technique. The pieces of one team represent unpleasant, negative, self-critical, or anxiety-provoking thoughts, feelings, and memories; those of the opposing team represent positive thoughts and feelings of confidence, satisfaction, success, and belonging. Just like in a game of chess, clients often "choose sides" and then ride into battle to defeat the unpleasant thoughts and feelings. But the cost of this battle is the time, energy, and resources invested in trying to defeat the unwanted experiences, which turns out to be futile.

So, clients are helped instead to imagine themselves as the *chessboard* and to notice the distinction between themselves and the pieces. As the board, they are in contact with all of the pieces and can notice them moving around, but the board is not changed by the pieces or their movements. Similarly, clients can notice their thoughts and feelings while remaining who they are. The point is that we all have thoughts, emotions, and feelings; but they are not *who we are*.

Values

An important component of ACT is helping clients clarify what gives meaning to their life — that is, their personal **values**. Importantly, values are different from *goals* in that we never "accomplish" a value. Values are more like a compass that helps a client make choices based on the directions in which they want their lives to go. Examples of *goals* include (a) running a mile in under 8 minutes, (b) writing a novel, and (c) spending more time with family this year. The corresponding *values*, however, would be (a) athleticism, (b) creativity, and (c) family and interpersonal connections. When clients connect with their values, they are able to move their life in meaningful directions, even in the face of difficult or painful private experiences. ACT therefore aims to better align clients' behavior with how they would like to live. IN PRACTICE: *Shane's Values* describes an ACT technique — the **values bull's eye** — that Shane's psychologist used toward the beginning of treatment for this purpose. In particular, this exercise helped Shane see how treatment would help him move closer to the kinds of relationships and successes in school that were important to him.

In Practice   Shane's Values

The "bull's eye" is a values-clarification exercise developed by Swedish psychologist Tobias Lundgren and colleagues (2012) that Shane's therapist used to help Shane see how well his behavior reflects what's important to him. The dart board (shown on the next page) is divided into four domains of life: school, free time, relationships, and personal growth and health. Guided by his psychologist, Shane first identified his values within each of these domains.

Next, he marked with an "X" the location on the dart board that corresponded to how well his actual behavior was aligned with his values. As can be seen, when Shane began treatment, he felt that his behavior was inconsistent with his desire to do well in school and have trusting relationships with others. On the other hand, his behavior was more consistent with what he wanted out of free time and personal growth experiences. These insights were used to identify treatment goals, and after several weeks, the bull's eye exercise was repeated to measure Shane's progress toward living life in better harmony with his values.

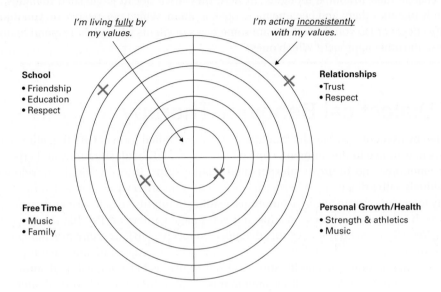

Committed Action

Once values are identified, ACT involves setting goals for taking steps toward these values. For example, Kiara might set a goal of cutting back on compulsive rituals despite having obsessional urges to check and wash; and Shane might set the goal of resisting impulses to act aggressively toward his classmates and parents, even when they act in ways he doesn't like. The aim of **committed action** is to help clients learn to engage in value-driven activities even when unwanted thoughts and feelings show up. Interestingly, many clients find that although reducing unwanted private experiences is not a stated goal of ACT, it is often a pleasant by-product.

Client–Practitioner Relationship

As in any psychological treatment, clinicians using ACT demonstrate compassion, empathy, respect, and the ability to stay psychologically present even when clients express strong emotions. A unique feature of ACT, however, is that clinicians are really "in the same boat" as their clients when it comes to experiencing unwanted thoughts, feelings, and other unpleasant private experiences, as these are universal human events. Therefore, clinicians don't play the role of an all-knowing expert. Rather, they might explain to clients, "I don't want you to think that I'm perfectly able to accept my unwanted thoughts and feelings, or act according to my values, either. It's more like you're climbing your mountain over there and I'm climbing my mountain over here; and it happens to be the case that from where I am on my mountain, I can see obstacles on your mountain that you can't see. So I can point those out to you, and maybe show you some alternative routes around them."

Think Like a Clinical Psychologist In traditional CBT, clients learn to challenge and change their irrational thoughts. In ACT, they learn not to judge such thoughts, but merely to notice them and become more open to them. Which perspective do you think is more effective? Do you think there are some types of clients who might respond better to one or the other approach? Which ones?

▌▌ Dialectical Behavior Therapy

Created by psychologist Marsha Linehan, DBT is a modified form of CBT that aims to teach clients how to live in the moment, cope effectively with difficult situations and crises, regulate emotions, and improve interpersonal relationships. It was originally developed for individuals with a diagnosis of borderline personality disorder which is characterized by difficulty managing strong negative emotions, leading to impulsive behavior and severe problems with interpersonal relationships and self-image (American Psychiatric Association, 2013). Yet, clients need not have this diagnosis to receive DBT, as many psychologists also apply this treatment with individuals presenting with a range of mental health problems including depression, suicidal ideation and self-injurious behavior, eating disorders, substance use, and PTSD. As we will see later in this chapter, DBT is a well-studied intervention that can be effective, although whether it is any more effective than other forms of treatment remains unclear.

Theoretical Basis

Psychologist Marsha Linehan developed and researched DBT in the 1980s as a treatment for clients with borderline personality disorder.

The foundation for DBT is the **biosocial theory of personality functioning**, which views difficulties with emotion regulation and the other problems described above as stemming from the interaction of biological and environmental factors (Lee et al., 2021; Linehan, 1993). Specifically, the main biological factor is a vulnerability to experiencing intense negative emotions, while the environmental factors refer to a chronic invalidating environment. An invalidating environment may consist of others telling the person that their experiences, thoughts, and feelings are wrong, which leads to attributing one's own emotional reactions as a sign of weakness. Such invalidation can be subtle, such as when

Peter Yates/The New York Times/Redux Pictures

others implicitly punish, disregard, or dismiss the person's feelings; or it can be overt, as in the case of sexual and physical abuse. Importantly, the chronicity and pervasiveness of invalidation, rather than occasional experiences, are what appear to predict borderline personality disorders traits (Fruzzetti et al., 2005). To manage the intense emotions, and feelings of invalidation, individuals might turn to substance use, self-injurious behavior, and other maladaptive coping strategies which interfere with relationships and lower one's self-concept.

DBT takes the position that even though clients are not at fault for causing their difficulties, they still must work to solve their problems. Therefore, instead of focusing on assigning blame, emphasis is placed on giving clients the skills to set goals for themselves so they can live the kind of life they want. The *dialectical* aspect of DBT captures the treatment's core philosophy that seemingly conflicting ideas can be true at the same time: clients can accept where they are *and* strive to grow. They can recognize that they are both doing their best *and* must continue working hard.

Implementing DBT

DBT is a multicomponent treatment package that combines standard CBT interventions for emotion regulation and reality-testing with concepts of distress tolerance, acceptance, and mindful awareness. Treatment is highly structured and may include weekly individual or group sessions over the course of about 6 months, and perhaps as long as a year (Linehan, 1993). As outlined in **Table 13.2** (and described in detail below), DBT progresses through four modules in which clients learn the following skills: mindfulness, distress tolerance, interpersonal effectiveness, and emotion regulation.

Table 13.2 The Four Modules in Dialectical Behavior Therapy		
Module	**Typical Number of Weeks**	**Description**
Mindfulness	2	Learning how to become aware of the present moment without judgment
Distress tolerance	6 or more	Accepting reality as it is and learning to effectively manage adversity
Emotion regulation	6 or more	Understanding and reducing vulnerability to strong emotions
Interpersonal effectiveness	6 or more	Developing skills for cultivating and maintaining interpersonal relationships

During the first few sessions the client and therapist begin developing a trusting relationship so the client gains comfort with the idea of treatment. The dialectic of acceptance and change is also introduced. One of the core ideas within DBT is that of the **wise mind**. As depicted in **Figure 13.1**, the notion is that everyone occasionally becomes emotional, moody, or reactive—what is called *emotion mind*. When ruled by emotion mind, moods, feelings, and behavioral urges (rather than reason and logic) determine our behaviors. On the other hand, *rational mind* is ruled by facts, reason, and pragmatics (rather than personal values or feelings). In this state, we approach people in the same systematic way that we might handle trying to solve a math problem. While both of these mental states have useful qualities, spending too

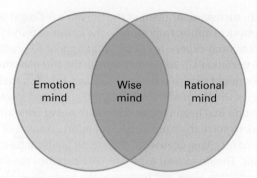

Figure 13.1 The Wise Mind An aim of DBT is to operate using wise mind, which represents the balance between emotion mind and reason mind.

much time in either causes frustration. In contrast, the overlap between emotion and rational mind — called *wise mind* — allows us to remain in control while also being emotionally sensitive. Finding this balance is therefore one of the primary goals of working through the four DBT modules as described next.

Mindfulness

Learning to focus on the present and live in the moment are often the first skills taught in DBT because they lay the groundwork for the other three modules. Sessions might focus on learning how to face situations, both positive and negative, without judgment and practicing how to pay attention to thoughts, feelings, body sensations, and impulses. Clients also learn how to use their senses to tune in to what's happening around them (e.g., what they see, hear, smell, and touch) without evaluating these experiences and observations as good or bad.

Consider Shane, who, following arguments with his mother, would experience negative automatic thoughts such as "I'm no good," "I can't do anything right," and "I'll never get over my problems." These thoughts lead to feeling depressed and ashamed, and to disqualifying positive behaviors and aspects of himself. Shane's psychologist might teach Shane how to simply observe his thoughts and feelings, label them, and then immerse himself in an activity that he enjoys, such as a video game or sports. This would help him learn to experience his negative thoughts as "just thoughts" rather than as "facts." It would also help him see his thoughts as separate from who he is as a person. The goal is for Shane to be able to think differently about his argument ("Arguments aren't the end of the world; mom loves me and just wants to help") and put him in a better state of mind to think through what he could do to the next time he feels himself becoming angry with his mother.

Distress Tolerance

Distress tolerance skills build on mindfulness and give clients coping strategies for managing emotional pain and avoiding destructive behavior when crisis situations arise (Linehan, 2014). These skills do not necessarily fix the crisis permanently, but help clients endure it as effectively as possible until the worst has passed. **Table 13.3** describes various **crisis survival skills** which might be learned and practiced as part of this module.

Table 13.3 Crisis Survival Skills in the Distress Tolerance Module of DBT

Skill	Description
Self-soothing	Alleviating distress through comforting and nurturing oneself when experiencing a crisis. Clients assemble a kit of self-soothing material for the five senses (e.g., favorite music, photos of loved ones, soft blanket, coffee, scented candle) that they access to mentally ground themselves when experiencing a crisis.
T.I.P.P. skills	Using **T**emperature (e.g., cold water), **I**ntense exercise, **P**aced breathing, or **P**rogressive muscle relaxation to reduce intense emotional arousal.
S.T.O.P. skills	Learning to respond to crises in the following way: **S**top and do nothing instead of the typical reaction, **T**ake a step back and a deep breath, **O**bserve what's happening in the situation, and **P**roceed using mindfulness and acceptance skills.
Pros and cons	Taking a moment to think logically (perhaps making a list of pros and cons) about the situation and next steps so that decisions are made thoughtfully and carefully, rather than impulsively and based on strong emotions.
Radical acceptance	Observing the situation as it is without judgment or trying to change it (i.e., "It is what it is"), and understanding that some things are simply out of our control.
Distraction	Temporarily doing something else until the client is able to more calmly approach the crisis situation. This might involve physically leaving a location, or engaging in an action such as calling a friend or playing with pets.
Improving the moment	Using other strategies to get through the crisis, such as trying to find a sense of purpose in the crisis, praying, using muscle relaxation, and breaking the crisis down into parts that can be addressed one at a time.

Emotion Regulation

Emotion regulation skills help clients understand the function of emotions and modify associated behavioral tendencies that might be inappropriate or cause them problems; for example, the tendency to scream at or insult someone when feeling angry, or to completely withdraw and isolate oneself when feeling depressed. Clients are first taught how to identify and label their emotions, and to understand that although emotions are worth listening to, it is sometimes best not to act on them immediately. For instance, it might be more useful to take some time to cool off, collect one's thoughts, and develop a plan for responding in a more effective way that won't lead to more problems.

An important method that clients learn to use within this module is **opposite action**, which, as its name suggests, involves behaving contrary to the urge provoked

TORWAISTUDIO/Shutterstock

Cold water provides a shock to the brain's limbic system. In DBT, clients having difficulty regulating their emotions may be taught to splash cold water on their face, take a cold shower, or hold ice cubes in their hands to calm themselves.

by the strong emotion. The first step is identifying the emotion the client wants to work on, along with the behavioral urges associated with it. Next, clients learn to consider whether the emotion in question fits the actual facts of the situation triggering it and, perhaps more importantly, whether it would be effective to act on the associated behavioral urges. Indeed, in some circumstances, an emotion fits the facts of a situation but acting on it is not in the client's best interest. For example, if someone in a position of power does something unfair it might *seem* appropriate to challenge that individual, yet doing so in that moment may not be a wise choice.

Once it is decided that the emotion (or its intensity) does not fit the facts of the situation, or that acting on the behavioral urge is unwise, clients engage in opposite action by (a) identifying what the emotional urge "wants" them to do, and (b) behaving in ways that are in contrast with the urge. For example, if Shane was feeling angry and had the urge to verbally or physically attack someone, he would avoid the person with whom he's frustrated, use distress tolerance exercises (e.g., self-soothing, S.T.O.P. skills) to calm himself, and try to find some small part of how the other person is acting that he can understand and feel empathy for. If he is feeling sad and wants to withdraw, he might try walking tall, maintaining eye contact, and getting out and doing activities to stay busy. Opposite action creates more choices for the client and helps them become more resilient to strong emotions.

Interpersonal Effectiveness

Once clients have learned mindfulness, distress tolerance, and emotion regulation skills, they are ready to work on cultivating healthy relationships. One way this is addressed in DBT is by focusing on conflict resolution, active listening, and assertiveness strategies. Emphasis is placed on teaching clients how to balance *priorities* versus *demands*, demonstrate self-respect in their relationships, and clarify what's important to them.

Although Shane did not undergo a full course of DBT, his psychologist introduced a commonly used set of DBT **interpersonal effectiveness skills** called G.I.V.E. Specifically, Shane learned and practiced the following tactics that he was encouraged to apply when he felt provoked by other children at school or when his mother became upset with him:

- **G**entle. Don't attack, threaten, or judge the other person.
- **I**nterest. Use good listening skills (e.g., don't interrupt) to show interest in what the other person is saying.
- **V**alidate. Acknowledge the other person's thoughts and feelings (even if you disagree with them).
- **E**asy. Try to have a leisurely attitude (smile often and be lighthearted).

Thomas Barwick/Getty Images

Good listening skills include using body language and facial expression to show interest in what the other person is saying.

Client–Practitioner Relationship

The therapeutic relationship is an essential element of DBT (Barnicot et al., 2012). It is common for clinicians using this modality, especially with clients prone to interpersonal crises and suicidal behavior, to end up learning a great deal about their clients' lives and relationships. They will sometimes find themselves having to juggle priorities during treatment and respond in session to address predicaments that arise for clients between appointments. Accordingly, flexibility is a much needed characteristic. Linehan (1993) also highlights the importance of recognizing that clients indeed wish to improve their condition, even if they (and the psychologist) occasionally experience frustration that strains the therapeutic relationship. Although it may sometimes appear that clients aren't making an effort to change, expressing such a viewpoint directly can be invalidating and further reinforce the client's self-criticism. Instead, the clinician is advised to recognize that anxiety, shame, the lack of experience in practicing new behaviors, and the occasional reinforcement of maladaptive behavior all play a role in clients' difficulties. Finally, it is common for psychologists using DBT to seek out supervision, consultation, and support from other professionals using this approach.

Think Like a Clinical Psychologist Do you agree that the four modules of DBT can be applied broadly to people of different races, ethnicities, cultures, religious backgrounds, sexual orientations, socioeconomic statuses, ages, and physical or intellectual abilities? Why or why not?

Multicultural Considerations

As we have seen in previous chapters, Western/dominant cultural values (e.g., individualism, assertiveness, and rationality) that may not be shared by all clients are inherent in many psychological treatments. The developers of ACT (and some other mindfulness-based interventions), however, have argued that because ACT helps clients clarify their own values and change how they relate to their thoughts and feelings, it is less value-laden and therefore overcomes the issues inherent in many other psychological treatments (e.g., Hayes, 2004). Let's explore this claim in greater detail.

True to its basis in relational frame theory, ACT takes the stance that clients' experience of distress is influenced by social and historical factors (Hayes et al., 2006). Perhaps this makes it culturally sensitive and relevant for people from both privileged and marginalized or underserved backgrounds. Emotional distress is also viewed as an inevitable and natural human experience to be understood in context, normalized, and validated before encouraging values-consistent behavioral change. This contextualized approach may resonate with clients from nondominant cultural and marginalized backgrounds who, due to understandable mistrust of the mental health system, may assume that they will be blamed in treatment for their current circumstances. On the other hand, as we noted at the beginning of this chapter, mindfulness and the idea that emotional distress is natural and inevitable are also culturally laden in and of themselves (i.e., they derive from Eastern philosophies).

Perhaps the metaphors used to illustrate principles of mindfulness and acceptance are helpful when working

Mindfulness is a culturally laden value that derives from Buddhist traditions.

with clients from cultural backgrounds in which emotional distress and other psychological processes are viewed as signs of weakness. Indeed, using metaphors to validate distress and illustrate more effective ways of responding to internal experience may serve to normalize psychological challenges. In addition, ACT metaphors can be personalized to best match the lived experiences of particular clients and cultural groups. As we have discussed throughout this book, these issues underscore the importance of multicultural competence when using ACT or any other clinical psychological intervention.

The dialectical stance in DBT, which involves empathically connecting with clients' distress, while also challenging them to take steps toward life-enriching behavioral change as well as emphasizing engaging in actions consistent with one's values, may resonate with clients who feel that they lack control over their environment due to systemic oppression and discrimination. Given that individuals from marginalized or nondominant backgrounds have relatively little control over systemic oppression and related opinions and beliefs sometimes held by others, validating this reality while also helping such clients identify the actions that are within their control and consistent with what matters most to them, may be helpful. This unique combination of validation and change also has the potential to diminish the power dynamic inherent in psychological treatment and enhance collaboration between client and practitioner. To this end, Johnson and Melton (2020) have developed a multicultural version of DBT that specifically addresses race-based stress; and Sloan, Berke, and Shipherd (2017) have described how to apply a DBT framework when working with transgender individuals. Finally, the exploration of client-specific values and valued actions allows for a consideration of the role of cultural and familial expectations that may or may not be consistent with a client's own values.

Think **Like a Clinical Psychologist** How value-laden are mindfulness-based CBT approaches? With regard to this issue, in what ways are third-wave approaches different from traditional CBT? In what ways are they different?

Evaluating Acceptance, Mindfulness, and Dialectical Approaches

Scientific Support

ACT is by far the most researched third-wave treatment, with hundreds of outcome studies and meta-analyses evaluating its efficacy and effectiveness (e.g., A-tjak et al., 2015). On the whole, however, the quality of this body of research is less rigorous than that which supports traditional behavioral and cognitive approaches. Still, the available studies suggest that ACT can be more effective than no treatment for many psychological problems, such as those associated with anxiety and depression, substance use, chronic pain, anger, and stress, as well as habit behaviors (e.g., hair pulling), some forms of psychosis, and certain eating disorders (e.g., Villanueva et al., 2019). Moreover, ACT can be effectively delivered with adults and children, (e.g., Fan & Ding, 2020) individually, in groups, over the Internet, and in outpatient and more intensive treatment settings (e.g., Morgan et al., 2021; Thompson et al., 2021). ACT, however, does not appear to be any more effective than other psychological treatments (Craske et al., 2014; Jiménez, 2012; Öst, 2014), nor does it appear to add to the effectiveness of other forms of CBT (e.g., Twohig et al., 2018). This raises questions about whether the processes of change in ACT are really that different from those operating in traditional CBT.

There is also a wealth of research on DBT, and this has provided optimism for the treatment of clients with severe emotion regulation difficulties — a problem that was once considered highly resistant to treatment. Yet, as with ACT, many studies of DBT have been criticized as lacking rigor (e.g., Öst, 2008; Reddy & Vijay, 2017). For example, few if any studies include long-term follow-up data and in many instances, the outcome assessors are not blind to clients' treatment condition. As a result, DBT does not meet the most stringent criteria for an empirically supported treatment (Tolin et al., 2015). The few well-conducted trials that are available largely indicate that DBT, while more effective than receiving no treatment (e.g., Stiglmayr et al., 2014), is only slightly more effective than other general therapeutic approaches when it comes to improving depression, suicidal behavior, anger, feelings of emptiness, general life satisfaction, and work or school performance (e.g., McMain et al., 2009).

Criticisms

As you probably noticed, many of the concepts and techniques in ACT are abstract and highly intellectual. This raises questions about its use with individuals who are more concrete (e.g., those with autism spectrum disorders) and those who have intellectual and learning disabilities or attention difficulties. It also raises concerns about its use with individuals from societies where education and abstract thinking are less valued. To date there is very little research testing the effectiveness of ACT for these populations (Byrne & O'Mahony, 2020; Patterson et al., 2019). It is, however, possible that reducing the duration of treatment sessions, increasing the structure of sessions, a greater reliance on visual materials, and the involvement of caregivers might help clinicians adapt ACT for some such individuals (Spain et al., 2015).

As alluded to earlier, some experts have also questioned whether third-wave treatments are really all that different from more traditional behavioral and cognitive interventions (e.g., Arch & Craske, 2008; Hofmann & Asmundson, 2008). For example, the developers of ACT (strongly) assert that this intervention works by fostering psychological flexibility — *not* by changing clients' dysfunctional thinking as traditional cognitive-behavioral treatments aim to do (e.g., Hayes et al., 2006). Yet, psychological flexibility entails a shift in perspective when it comes to thinking about one's own thoughts and feelings (e.g., Kashdan & Rottenberg, 2010), and the cognitive defusion and acceptance exercises described earlier in this chapter appear to foster such a change in thinking (albeit via a different method than in traditional CBT). Similarly, the committed action exercises for Kiara described earlier in this chapter would be a lot like the exposure and response prevention instructions a more traditional behavior therapist would prescribe (see Chapter 11, *Behavioral Interventions*); and opposite action strategies are very similar to behavioral activation (also discussed in Chapter 11). Indeed, research demonstrates that the mechanisms of change in ACT, DBT, and traditional forms of CBT do indeed overlap to a large extent (e.g., Niles et al., 2014; Twohig et al., 2018). Whether or not the ideas and techniques in third-wave interventions are entirely novel is probably not as important as the fact that these approaches have provided fresh ways to communicate with clients about their problems and what it takes to overcome them.

Finally, DBT is a demanding treatment in that clients have to attend weekly treatment sessions (sometimes multiple [group and individual] sessions) as well as complete regular homework assignments. Clinicians also require a great deal of training and ongoing supervision and support, and have to be available 24/7 to provide emergency coaching (although rules can be laid down to limit such "after hours" involvement). This presents problems with dissemination and resource usage, especially in nonacademic centers, in the community, and in populations with fewer resources (Reddy and Vijay, 2017).

Think Like a Clinical Psychologist What do you see as the similarities and differences between third-wave approaches and the more traditional behavioral and cognitive-behavioral treatments?

▓ Chapter Summary

The "third wave" of CBT developed during the later decades of the 20th century and includes treatments based on behavioral and cognitive principles, and also incorporates mindfulness, acceptance, and dialectical thinking. Thus, rather than focusing on the content of a client's thoughts and internal experiences, these interventions are more focused on the context, processes, and functions of how a person relates to internal experiences (i.e., thoughts, urges, sensations). The two most widely used and widely studied interventions from this group are ACT and DBT.

ACT is an experiential treatment that teaches clients mindfulness skills to help them live and behave in ways that are consistent with personal values while developing psychological flexibility. Psychological flexibility means being in contact with the present moment, fully aware of emotions, sensations, and thoughts; welcoming them; including the undesired ones; and moving in a pattern of behavior in the service of chosen values. The opposite of psychological flexibility is experiential avoidance, which is considered a maintaining factor in psychological distress and dysfunction and is defined as attempts to suppress unwanted internal experiences, such as emotions, thoughts, memories, and bodily sensations. Therapeutic exercises and metaphors in ACT target six core principles: acceptance, cognitive defusion, contact with the present moment, the observing self, values, and committed action.

DBT is a multicomponent treatment program that addresses problems such as borderline personality disorder, suicidality, and other difficulties with emotion regulation. This treatment is based largely on CBT principles and focuses on problem solving and acceptance strategies. It operates, however, within a framework of dialectical methods, which focus on the client's ability to view issues from multiple perspectives and arrive at a resolution of seemingly contradictory information and positions.

Third-wave treatments have had a large impact on the field of clinical psychology over the past 30 years. Yet, although these approaches are widely used by clinicians, and widely studied by treatment outcome researchers, questions remain regarding whether they are actually novel treatments, or a repackaging of existing behavioral and cognitive techniques. Although proponents argue that these approaches overcome issues of cultural bias and values-based treatment, whether this is true remains a matter of debate. Finally, there are questions about the methodological quality of many studies on third-wave treatments. Thus, while it is clear these interventions work better than receiving no treatment at all, their mechanisms of action and efficacy relative to traditional CBT remain understudied.

Applying What You've Learned

Exercise 1: Use the six core principles of ACT to plan a treatment for a 21-year-old college student with depression who is struggling at school. Specify how you might implement the various techniques and metaphors described in this chapter

Exercise 2: Now, provide three examples of using DBT Distress Tolerance Skills to help this student with depression.

Key Terms

Acceptance: The willingness to embrace internal experiences — such as thoughts, feelings, and physical sensations — even when they seem unpleasant.

Acceptance and commitment therapy: An experiential, contextual approach to psychological treatment that helps clients think about what really matters to them and then take action to enrich their lives based on their personal values; clients are instructed to use mindfulness to accept unpleasant thoughts and feelings.

Biosocial theory of personality functioning: Theoretical foundation of DBT; views difficulties with emotion regulation and the related problems as stemming from the interaction of biological and environmental factors. The main biological factor is a vulnerability to experiencing intense negative emotions, while the environmental factors refer to a chronic invalidating environment.

Chessboard metaphor: A technique in which clients think of their thoughts and feelings as chess pieces. The pieces of one team represent unpleasant, negative, self-critical, or anxiety-provoking thoughts, feelings and memories; those of the opposing team represent positive thoughts and feelings of confidence, satisfaction, success, and belonging. Clients imagine themselves as the chessboard to notice the distinction between themselves and the pieces.

Cognitive defusion: In ACT, learning to perceive private experiences as bits of language, words, and pictures, rather than taking them as facts.

Committed action: In ACT, setting goals, guided by values, and taking action to achieve them.

Crisis survival skills: In DBT, a set of strategies clients are taught to help promote distress tolerance when in a difficult situation.

Dialectical behavior therapy: A modified form of CBT that aims to teach clients how to live in the moment, cope effectively with difficult situations and crises, regulate emotions, and improve interpersonal relationships.

Dialectical thinking: Being able to view issues from multiple perspectives, bring together seemingly contradictory positions, and accept that two opposing ideas can be true at the same time.

Distress tolerance skill: DBT skill that builds on mindfulness and gives clients coping strategies for managing emotional pain and avoiding destructive behavior when crisis situations arise.

Emotion regulation skill: In DBT, this helps clients understand the function of emotions and modify associated behavioral tendencies that might be inappropriate or cause them problems.

Experiential avoidance: Attempts to control or minimize difficult thoughts, feelings, and other internal events.

Interpersonal effectiveness skill: In DBT, conflict resolution, active listening, and assertiveness strategy to balance *priorities* versus *demands*, demonstrate self-respect in relationships, and clarify what's important to oneself.

Mindfulness: Present moment awareness; paying attention to the present moment in a purposeful way and nonjudgmentally.

Opposite action: Involves behaving contrary to the urge provoked by a strong emotion.

Psychological flexibility: The ability to be in the present moment, engage in activities that are personally important, and live a meaningful life despite the fact that difficult experiences will occur.

Relational frame theory: The idea that our ability to relate one concept to another is the foundation of human language; the goal of ACT is to develop new relational frames in which unwanted internal experiences are seen as merely unpleasant aspects of life that do not need to be "struggled with" or "gotten rid of."

Value: In ACT, clarifying what is most important, significant, and meaningful in life.

Value bull's eye: A dart board is divided into quadrants that illustrate the client's values to help align behavior with the values.

Wise mind: Idea in DBT that the intersection of emotion and rational mind is the balance that allows us to remain in control while also being emotionally sensitive.

CONNECT ONLINE:

 Check out our videos and additional resources located at: www.macmillanlearning.com

Early Approaches to Psychotherapy: Psychodynamic and Client-Centered Perspectives

FOCUS QUESTIONS

1. What are the major assumptions of Freudian theory?
2. What techniques are used in psychoanalytic treatment?
3. How does contemporary psychodynamic psychotherapy differ from psychoanalytic treatment?
4. What are the major features that characterize client-centered therapists?
5. What occurs in client-centered therapy and what does *not* occur?

CHAPTER OUTLINE

For good reason, this book focuses on psychological interventions that have been repeatedly tested in empirical studies and consistently found to have efficacy and effectiveness. For the most part these interventions fall within the broad umbrella of behavioral and cognitive-behavioral treatments. Yet there are countless types of therapies — over 500 according to one report (Weisz & Kazdin, 2010). Some of these approaches *might* work, but because they have not been systematically studied; we simply don't know for sure. Others *have* been studied, with the evidence suggesting they are either not effective at all, or no more effective than placebo (e.g., expressive writing interventions for depression, energy therapies such as thought field therapy; Reinhold et al., 2018; Sharp et al., 2008). Still others have been studied, yet the data suggest they do more harm than good (e.g., critical incident stress debriefing for PTSD; Williams et al., 2021). As research on treatment outcomes continues, and additional treatments are developed, it has become increasingly challenging for psychologists to stay informed about which therapies do and don't work (although websites such as effectivechildtherapy.org and div12.org/psychological-treatments provide useful information about psychological treatments and their degree of research support).

Of course, we cannot (and should not) describe all these many alternative therapies; many of which have little or no research support to back them up. Yet, we would be remiss not to introduce two approaches that have great historical and foundational — as opposed to *scientific* — significance. Before CBT gained widespread acceptance in the field, it was the *psychoanalytic/psychodynamic* and *client-centered* approaches that dominated clinical psychology. Yet, while these approaches laid the foundations for modern clinical practice, training programs rarely teach these methods any longer; and the number of psychologists practicing these approaches dwindles with each passing decade (Norcross et al., 2011).

▥ Psychoanalysis and Psychodynamic Therapy

Psychotherapy arguably began with Sigmund Freud's **psychoanalytic theory**, which forms the basis of **psychoanalysis** and the **psychodynamic** approach to therapy which has evolved over the past century. Freud was a Viennese neurologist, whose fascination with understanding and treating psychological problems grew out of an interest in **hysteria**, a psychological condition (thought to affect mostly women) marked by paralysis, blindness, and deafness. Although these symptoms suggested a neurological basis, no organic cause could be found.

Freud was especially taken with how his colleague, Josef Breuer, was treating a young female client called "Anna O" using hypnosis. During one session, Breuer had Anna talk about her symptoms under hypnosis, and when she came out of her hypnotic trance, these symptoms had seemingly disappeared. Breuer successfully repeated the same procedures over and over until a complication arose: Anna developed a strong emotional attachment to Breuer. The intensity of this reaction, coupled with a session in which Anna began showing physically unexplained labor pains (apparently a symptom of hysteria), convinced Breuer to stop his work with Anna.

Still, these events helped prompt Freud's initial theories. He treated many of his own clients with hypnosis, although not all were good candidates for hypnotic procedures. Others were easily hypnotized but could not remember what had transpired during the trance, which undermined most of the advantages of hypnosis. An example was "Elisabeth," a client Freud saw in 1892. Freud asked Elisabeth, while she was fully awake, to concentrate on her ailment and to remember when it began. He asked her to lie on a couch as he pressed his hand against her forehead. Subsequently, Freud found that placing his hand on clients' foreheads and asking them to remember events surrounding the origin of the symptom was just as effective as hypnosis. He soon gave up placing his hand on clients' foreheads and simply asked them to talk about whatever came to their minds. This was the beginning of what came to be known as the method of *free association*, a process in psychoanalysis in which clients say anything and everything that comes to mind to shed light on unconscious thoughts and urges. Over time, Freud developed a number of theories regarding the underlying roots of psychological symptoms and the approaches to alleviate them, which we next discuss briefly. IN HISTORICAL PERSPECTIVE: *A Brief Biography of Sigmund Freud* provides a brief look at Freud's life.

Freudian Psychoanalytic Theory

Psychic Determinism and the Unconscious

A major assumption of Freudian theory, **psychic determinism**, held that everything we do has meaning and purpose, and is goal directed. Moreover, Freud believed that the meaning, purpose, and goals are **unconscious** — that is, not able to be understood by the conscious mind. Such a view enables the therapist (called an *analyst* in Freudian psychoanalysis) to utilize an exceptionally large amount of data in searching for the roots of the client's problems. The mundane behavior, the bizarre behavior, the dream, and the slip of the tongue all were assumed to be relevant to understanding unconscious motivation for psychological problems. Healthy behavior, in contrast, was believed to result when the person was aware of the motivation. Therefore, it follows that the goal of psychoanalytic/psychodynamic therapy is to make the unconscious conscious.

Instincts

Unconscious energy assumed to facilitate human functioning was thought to be provided by two sets of instincts: the **life instincts (Eros)** and the **death instincts (Thanatos)**. The life instincts were the basis for all the positive and constructive aspects of behavior; they include bodily urges such as sex, hunger, and thirst as well as the creative components of culture such as art, music, and literature. But all these activities can serve destructive ends as well. When this happens, the death instincts are responsible. In practice, modern psychoanalysts pay little attention to death instincts. However, Freud believed they explained the dark side of human behavior (e.g., self-destructive behavior). For Freud, the ultimate explanation for all behavior was an instinctual one, even though the instincts he posited were unobservable, could not be measured, and seemed better able to explain events *after* they occur (rather than before).

Personality Structures

In psychoanalysis, personality was viewed as composed of three basic structures: the *id, ego,* and *superego.* The **id** represented the deep, inaccessible portion of the personality. Freud believed we gain information about the id through the analysis of dreams. Within the id resides instinctual urges and a desire for immediate gratification. It is without values, ethics, or logic and thought to obey the **pleasure principle**, trying to get rid of any tension as quickly as possible. Freud believed its purpose was to attain gratification of urges and achieve a state free from all tension.

Freud believed the **ego** was the executive of the personality. It is an organized, rational system that uses perception, learning, memory, and so on in the service of need satisfaction. It arises out of the inadequacies of the id in serving and preserving the organism. It operates according to the **reality principle**, deferring the gratification of instinctual urges until a suitable object and mode are discovered. To do this, it employs processes such as learning, memory, planning, and judgment. The role of the ego is to mediate the demands of the id, the superego, and the real world to provides satisfaction while also preventing it from being destroyed by the real world.

The third component of the personality was the **superego**. It develops from the ego during childhood, upon resolution of the **Oedipus complex** (the child's sexual attraction to the parent of the opposite sex), and represents the ideals and values of society as they are conveyed to the child through rewards and punishments delivered by the parents. Punished behavior becomes incorporated into the individual's conscience, whereas rewarded behavior becomes a part of the ego. Thus, the superego can make the person feel guilty. In general, however, the role of the superego is to block unacceptable id impulses and generate strivings toward perfection. The interrelationship of the id, ego, and superego is illustrated in **Figure 14.1**.

● ● ● ● ● In Historical Perspective

A Brief Biography of Sigmund Freud

Sigmund Freud was born in Austria (in an area that later became part of the Czech Republic) on May 6, 1856. Most of his childhood was spent in Vienna. He was the oldest of seven children. After a classical education, he began medical studies at the University of Vienna and received an MD degree in 1881. After a short period in research, he began a private practice, even though such work did not greatly interest him. At least three things helped him make this decision. First, he knew that as a Jew he stood little chance of advancement in a research-academic environment rife with anti-Semitic feelings. Second, his research efforts did not seem likely to produce much income. Third, he had fallen in love with Martha Bernays. Just as it does today, marriage required money, and

Sigmund Freud (1856–1939) was a Viennese neurologist who developed the psychoanalytic model of the mind and its corresponding treatment approach, psychoanalysis.

Freud had very little. Consequently, he decided to open a practice as a neurologist. His marriage to Martha produced six children, one of whom, Anna, became a famous psychoanalyst herself.

Around this time, Freud began a brief but very productive collaboration with Josef Breuer, a renowned physician in Vienna. Together they sought an explanation for Breuer's discovery of the **talking cure**, a method by which a client's neuroses (what we would now call anxiety and depression) are alleviated just by talking about them. In 1895, Breuer and

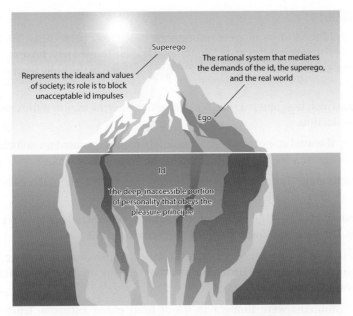

Superego

Represents the ideals and values of society; its role is to block unacceptable id impulses

The rational system that mediates the demands of the id, the superego, and the real world

Ego

Id

The deep, inaccessible portion of personality that obeys the pleasure principle

Figure 14.1 Freud's Structure of the Mind

Freud published *Studies on Hysteria*, a landmark psychiatric treatise. A bit later, the two men had a falling out for reasons that are not completely clear. Some suggest the problem was a disagreement over money, whereas others believed it had to do with Breuer's alarm over Freud's growing emphasis on sexual factors as a cause of hysteria.

Freud's most acclaimed work, *The Interpretation of Dreams*, appeared in 1900, capping a remarkably productive decade of work. As the 20th century dawned, his professional stature was growing, and his work had begun to attract a dedicated band of followers. Several of these devotees later left the Freudian camp to develop their own psychoanalytic theories. Notable among these were Alfred Adler, Carl Jung, and Otto Rank. Freud became a truly international figure when, in 1909, he was invited to lecture at Clark University in the United States.

Many books and papers followed. But so did Nazi harassment in the 1930s. They burned Freud's books and turned him into an anti-Semitic target. Finally, Freud was allowed to emigrate to England. In his declining years, he suffered from cancer of the jaw, experiencing great pain and undergoing about 32 operations. A heavy cigar smoker, he periodically gave them up, but never completely. Freud died in England in September 1939. ∎

Bettmann/Getty Images

Anna Freud (1895–1982) was the youngest daughter of Sigmund Freud and a prolific psychoanalytic writer. While her father's work was primarily with adults, Anna focused on children and how psychoanalytic theory and therapy could be applied to youth.

Psychosexual Stages

Freud considered childhood to be of great importance in shaping personality. He believed that each person goes through a series of developmental stages. Termed **psychosexual stages**, each is marked by the involvement of a particular erogenous zone of the body (especially during the first 5 years).

- The **oral stage**, which lasts about a year, is a period in which the mouth is the chief means of reaching satisfaction.

- It is followed by the **anal stage**, in which attention becomes centered on defecation and urination; this stage may span the period from 6 months to 3 years of age.

- Next is the **phallic stage** (from 3 to 7 years of age), during which the sexual organs become the prime source of gratification.

- Following these stages, the child enters **latency**, which is characterized by a lack of overt sexual activity. This stage may extend from about ages 5 until 12.

- Following the onset of adolescence, the **genital stage** begins. Ideally, this stage will culminate in a mature expression of sexuality, assuming that the sexual impulses have been handled successfully by the ego.

Psychological problems were thought to result from either excessive frustration or overindulgence at a particular psychosexual stage. Eating disorders and alcohol abuse, for example, suggest the influence of the oral stage. Kiara's obsessive-compulsive problems would be interpreted to signify that she failed to successfully negotiate the anal stage. Overly vain, exhibitionistic, and sexually aggressive behavior, according to Freud, has its roots in the phallic stage.

Defense Mechanisms

When one experiences the wrath of the superego or the unleashed lusts of the id, where does one turn? The answer lies in the *ego defenses* or, as they are sometimes called, **defense mechanisms**. These mechanisms are generally regarded as pathological because they divert psychic energy from more constructive activities and at the same time distort reality. All the defense mechanisms were thought to operate without the person's awareness.

The basic ego defense is **repression**. This can be described as the banishment from consciousness of highly threatening sexual or aggressive material. In some instances, the process operates by preventing the offending impulse from reaching consciousness in the first place. **Fixation** occurs when the frustration and anxiety of the next psychosexual stage are so great that the individual remains at their present level of psychosexual development. **Regression** involves a return to a stage that earlier provided a great deal of gratification; this may occur following extensive frustration. **Reaction formation** is said to

According to Freud, *regression* is an ego defense mechanism by which the person returns to an earlier stage of development to avoid distress and frustration.

occur when an unconscious impulse is consciously expressed by its behavioral opposite. Thus, "I hate you" is expressed as "I love you." **Projection** is revealed when one's unconscious feelings are attributed not to oneself but to another. Thus, the feeling "I hate you" is transformed into "You hate me."

The Process of Psychoanalysis

Freud believed that to truly recover from their problems, clients needed to achieve **insight** — a total understanding of the unconscious determinants of their irrational thoughts, feelings, and behaviors. Once these unconscious reasons are fully confronted and understood, the need for defense mechanisms will disappear. All of the techniques described next were designed to facilitate insight.

Free Association

During **free association**, the client lies on a couch with the analyst sitting out of sight in order to avoid any unintended influences on the client. The client is encouraged to say anything and everything that comes to mind while the analyst listens carefully, takes notes, and only speaks to encourage the client to continue talking. The assumption underlying this technique is that when clients are asked to free associate, their defense mechanisms are relaxed and unconscious material will emerge through verbalizations. Of course, clients are unaware of the latent meaning of their verbalizations, yet the analyst is trained to interpret what clients say to understand their unconscious motivations.

Freud's consulting room.

Dream Analysis

Freud believed that dreams were the "royal road to the unconscious" (Freud, 1955), and that during sleep, the ego's defense mechanisms are relaxed so that unconscious processes may operate freely and express themselves. **Dream analysis** is therefore used in psychoanalysis to help reveal the client's unconscious motivations. There are two levels of dream content:

- **Manifest content** is the actual description of the dream as recalled by the client (e.g., "I leaned back and all of my teeth fell into my mouth").

- **Latent content** is what the manifest content is thought to symbolize (e.g., teeth falling out in a woman's dream represent the desire to become pregnant). Psychoanalysts believe that the latent content of dreams is so unacceptable to the conscious mind that it has to be disguised as manifest content so that clients can remain asleep and remember their dreams when they awaken.

Interpretation

In psychoanalysis, **interpretation** refers to the analyst restating the client's behavior based on what's been uncovered during free association and dream analysis. In other words, the analyst provides a description of the unconscious meaning of what the client generates. Often, this material relates back to unresolved unconscious conflicts from childhood, or between the client and other people, that the ego has tried to keep from conscious awareness. To this end, the analyst must make sure that the client is ready to accept the interpretation since the ego has been working so hard to keep it out of conscious awareness.

Resistance

As we have discussed, ego defense mechanisms serve the purpose of suppressing unconscious needs, drives, and other material too disturbing for conscious awareness. It is thought, however, that during psychoanalysis, while the analyst is working to understand the unconscious, these defense mechanisms involuntarily turn up their **resistance**, which may manifest in the form of defiant behaviors such as disagreeing with the analyst, being late for therapy sessions, or missing them entirely. When clients have trouble speaking about difficult topics (e.g., when they "beat around the bush"), this is also interpreted as resistance.

Transference and Countertransference

The client–analyst relationship often becomes a focal point in psychoanalysis. This occurs when the client is thought to be projecting unconsciously held feelings onto the analyst — a process that occurs subconsciously as the client tries to manage disturbing feelings brought up during analysis. For example, a client might respond to the analyst as if the analyst were his rejecting parent, jealous lover, or childhood abuser. A classic example of such **transference** is falling in love with one's therapist. Transference, however, is thought to bring the client's unconscious needs and conflicts into consciousness, where they can be discussed in therapy, resolved, and used to promote change. In this way, working through transferred feelings is an important part of psychoanalysis, and the nature of the transference is thought to provide clues to the client's problems. Simultaneously, analysts must be aware that their own internal conflicts could be transferred into their client. This process, known as **countertransference** (e.g., developing feelings of attraction or anger toward the client) can muddy the therapeutic relationship and requires clinicians to work through their own thoughts and feelings.

Process Stages

Perhaps not surprisingly psychoanalysis was a slow, tedious, and often lengthy process that unfolded in four stages (as described in **Table 14.1**). Therapy sessions typically occurred several days per week over the course of several years.

Contemporary Psychodynamic Psychotherapy

Over the past 50 years, the number of psychologists practicing strict Freudian psychoanalysis has decreased substantially. Yet, many clinicians continue to practice **psychodynamic psychotherapy**, which is more or less based on psychoanalytic theory and contains only

Table 14.1 The Stages of Freud's Psychoanalysis	
Stage	**Content**
Arranging therapy	Agreeing on the frequency and length of therapy, as well as the fee, was viewed as an important part of the treatment process. Any cancellations or changes to appointments were taken seriously by the therapist and interpreted as being unconsciously motivated.
Free association	The client laid on a couch with the therapist out of sight and said whatever came to mind. This information was later analyzed and interpreted for the client.
Transference	Clients developed unconscious feelings about others in their life — including the therapist. These feelings were used to help foster insight into the unconscious determinants of their thoughts, feelings, and behaviors.
Ending therapy	Defense mechanisms might make a last stand in the form of "separation anxiety" that must be worked through.

remnants of psychoanalysis (Shedler, 2010). It is also important to note that there is great diversity in the techniques used within this approach, since there are few standardized psychodynamic treatment manuals (Gibbons et al., 2008). For example, contemporary psychodynamic psychotherapy may involve only a single session per week instead of multiple sessions, and the entire treatment process can be either short-term or open-ended (Shedler, 2010). The therapist is no longer seated behind the client's couch but now often sits at a desk. Perhaps the easiest way to characterize these and other modifications is to say that greater flexibility has been introduced. Although many traditional Freudian tenets are still observed, the overall context is not so rigid. For example, free association is no longer required, the importance of dreams may be downplayed, and hypnosis may or may not be used. **Table 14.2** lists key features of contemporary psychodynamic psychotherapy as outlined by Shedler (2010).

Research Support

Psychoanalytic theories are largely derived from Freud's anecdotal experiences with clients and his thoughtful self-reflection. They are not based on any degree of scientific study, and

Table 14.2 Key Features of Psychodynamic Psychotherapy
• Encourages clients to focus on affect and the expression of emotion
• Helps clients explore their attempts to avoid distressing thoughts and feelings
• Identifies and focuses on recurring themes and patterns in clients' thoughts, feelings, and behaviors
• Helps clients discuss how past experiences affect their current relationships, feelings, and behavior
• Focuses on interpersonal relationships and interpersonal experience
• Focuses on the therapeutic relationship between the therapist and client
• Encourages clients to explore fantasy life (e.g., uncensored thoughts, feelings, dreams).

Adapted from "The efficacy of psychodynamic psychotherapy." *American Psychologist*, 65, pp. 98–109. Copyright © 2010 by the American Psychological Association.

modern clinical psychology has produced virtually no data to support Freud's claims. For instance, there is no evidence that children progress through stages of psychosexual development; that little boys lust after their mothers; or that the id, ego, or superego exist. Even more modern iterations of psychodynamic concepts that use Freud's work as a reference point have no empirical support. As Crews (1996) put it, "There is literally nothing to be said, scientifically or therapeutically, to the advantage of the entire Freudian system or any of its component dogmas" (p. 63).

Still, a great deal of research has been conducted on psychodynamic psychotherapy. This work, however, suffers from important methodological limitations that constrain the conclusions that can be drawn about treatment efficacy (McKay, 2011). First, many studies group together individuals with various sorts of problems, so it is difficult to make assumptions about the efficacy of therapy for particular concerns or DSM disorders (e.g., OCD, conduct disorder). A second limitation is that the instruments used to assess outcome are often of questionable reliability and validity. Many studies, for example, rely on projective tests based on psychodynamic constructs that do not have scientific support (e.g., the Rorschach), raising questions about what is actually changing during therapy and whether it meaningfully relates to functioning outside of the clinical setting. Finally, because treatment goals and outcomes are defined somewhat vaguely (e.g., changes in emotional expression and interpersonal relatedness), it is difficult to tease apart whether any observed improvements are due to specific aspects of psychodynamic therapy (e.g., working with transference, exploring the client's fantasy life and relationships) or nonspecific factors common to all psychological interventions (e.g., communicating with a caring and attentive professional) as we discussed in Chapter 10, *Psychological Treatment: Science and Practice.*

Thus, while psychodynamically oriented therapy can still offer improvements for clients, perhaps due to nonspecific factors, there is little evidence to suggest that it is generally as efficacious as other treatments (e.g., behavioral and CBT approaches) for specific problems (e.g., McKay, 2011). One notable exception is **interpersonal psychotherapy (IPT**; Klerman et al., 1984; Weissman, 2020)—a brief psychodynamic treatment that has been successfully applied primarily for clients with depression. IPT exemplifies the radical shift from traditional psychoanalytic therapy to a more focused, time-limited treatment. It involves a thorough assessment of depressive thoughts, feelings, and behaviors, and targets major problem areas such as grief, role transitions, and communication or social skill deficits. Research shows that IPT is as effective as cognitive therapy in reducing depressive episodes and suicidal ideation (Lemmens et al., 2019, 2020; van Bentum et al., 2021). A CLOSER LOOK: *Features of Interpersonal Psychotherapy (IPT)* outlines the characteristics of IPT, which appears to be a worthy form of psychological treatment for depression.

A Closer Look **Features of Interpersonal Psychotherapy (IPT)**

IPT is a brief form of psychodynamic psychotherapy that has been studied extensively. It is cited as one of the examples of empirically supported treatments by the Division 12 Task Force of the American Psychological Association. Weissman and Markowitz (1998) describe IPT as follows:

Focus

IPT focuses on the connection between the onset of clinical problems and current interpersonal problems (with friends, partners, relatives). Treatment addresses clients' current social problems rather than their enduring personality traits or styles.

Length

Typically 12 to 16 weeks.

Role of the IPT Therapist

IPT therapists are active, non-neutral, and supportive. They use realism and optimism to counter clients' typically negative and pessimistic outlook. Therapists emphasize the possibility for change and highlight options that may affect positive change.

Phases of Treatment

1. *First phase* (up to three sessions): This includes an assessment of interpersonal functioning and education about the nature of depression. The therapist provides a clinical formulation of the client's difficulties by linking symptoms to current interpersonal problems, issues, and situations.

2. *Second phase*: Depending on which interpersonal problem area has been chosen (e.g., grief, role transitions, communication deficits), specific strategies and goals are pursued. For example, treatment focusing on problems with role transitions would help the client explore the problematic relationships, the nature of the problems, and the options for resolving them. If an impasse has been reached in a relationship, the therapist helps the client find ways to circumvent whatever is hindering progress or to end the relationship.

3. *Third phase* (last two to three sessions): The client's progress and mastery experiences are reinforced and consolidated. The IPT therapist reinforces the client's sense of confidence and autonomy. Methods of dealing with a recurrence of clinical problems are discussed. ▬

Think Like a Clinical Psychologist In what ways do you think psychoanalysis and other forms of psychodynamic therapy have influenced modern behavioral and cognitive-behavioral treatment approaches?

🔳 Client-Centered Therapy

Freud held a somewhat negative view of human nature. His theories were also deterministic, meaning that they afforded people very little free will. Psychoanalysis emphasized the need for clients to gain greater insight into the deep and dark unconscious processes that were believed to motivate conscious behavior. However, as described in IN HISTORICAL PERSPECTIVE: *Carl Rogers and Client-Centered Therapy*, the 1940s saw the emergence of an alternative view of human nature as fundamentally positive and autonomous. For Carl Rogers, psychotherapy was squarely focused on helping clients reach their full potential as human beings. Accordingly, he named his approach **client-centered therapy**.

◉ ◖ ◖ ◖ ◐ In Historical Perspective

Carl Rogers and Client-Centered Therapy

Born in Oak Park, Illinois on January 8, 1902, Carl Rogers was the fourth of six children and grew up in a financially secure and devoutly religious family. As a child, Rogers spent much of his time alone reading. He was an outstanding student, but not comfortable in social situations. After graduating from the University of Wisconsin in 1924 with a degree in history, he married Helen Elliott (with whom he had two children) and moved to New York City to attend Union Theological Seminary. However, a growing religious skepticism coupled with a desire to help others more directly led him to transfer to Columbia University and pursue training in clinical psychology. He was awarded a PhD in 1931 and moved to Rochester, New York, where he became a staff psychologist in a clinic focused on children.

Carl Rogers (1902–1987) was an American psychologist who developed the client-centered approach to psychotherapy.

Like most psychologists of his time, Rogers had been trained to think psychoanalytically. Yet while in Rochester, he was exposed to the ideas of Otto Rank (another Viennese psychoanalyst) and Jessie Taft, who believed that clients should have a larger role in therapy than was afforded to them in traditional psychoanalysis. Taft, in particular, regarded the client–therapist relationship as more important than any intellectual explanations of the client's problems. These ideas fit with Rogers's religious beliefs and democratic convictions regarding the nature of human relationships in society, and in 1940, he moved to Ohio State University and began developing his own "client-centered" approach to psychotherapy (Rogers, 1942) as a reaction to what Rogers considered the basic limitations of psychoanalysis: (a) the largely negative and deterministic view of Freud and the psychoanalysts, (b) the view the therapist could know clients better than clients know themselves, (c) the lack of a

Theoretical Basis

Rogers (1951) believed psychotherapy should be based on **phenomenological theory**, which states that the basic human urge is to preserve and enhance the **phenomenal self**. The phenomenal self is the part of our experience that we call the "I." From this perspective, psychological problems arise when the phenomenal self is threatened. Thus, people will experience threat whenever they perceive that the phenomenal self is in danger.

However, what is a threat for one person is not necessarily a threat for another. An example might help clarify this idea. Consider Ricardo and Giao—two students who perceive themselves as highly intelligent. Ricardo may become depressed or anxious if he fails an exam because this represents a threat to his self-concept (his "I"). Faced with such a threat, he may adopt a variety of defensive postures, such as rationalization (e.g., "The test was unfair"). Giao, on the other hand, is able to integrate positive and negative experiences into her phenomenal self. So, if she fails an exam, rather than claiming unfairness, she might psychologically "make room" for the poor exam performance by revising her self-concept. She might, for example,

Jessie Taft (1882–1960) and Otto Rank (1884–1939) were major influences on Carl Rodgers's development of client-centered therapy.

focus on the therapeutic relationship, and (d) the lack of emphasis on helping clients to develop their potential to help themselves.

In 1945, Rogers moved to the University of Chicago and developed a theoretical structure to buttress his therapeutic practices (Rogers, 1951). Then, in 1957, he accepted a position at the University of Wisconsin to extend his ideas about psychotherapy to more seriously impaired populations, such as individuals living in psychiatric institutions with schizophrenia (Rogers et al., 1967). From 1968 until his death in February 1987, Rogers trained and supervised clinicians at the Center for Studies of the Person in La Jolla, California. Along with Freud, he is often considered one of the founders of psychotherapy. ■

think to herself, "Maybe I am not as good at organic chemistry as I thought; but I do well in other classes, so this doesn't diminish me as a person," or "I failed the exam, but with more effort I think I can do better; and if not, I will look for other subjects where I can succeed." This will keep Giao from experiencing excessive anxiety or depression.

Rogers also proposed that individuals exist in a world of experience in which they are the center. This experience can only be known by the person. Therefore, the person is the best source of information about the phenomenal self. These views led the client-centered movement to rely on verbal self-report as a primary source of information, rather than on inferences from test data or behavioral observations. Because people react to the world as they themselves experience it, their own perception is reality. In other words, objective knowledge about stimuli is not enough to predict behavior. The clinician must know about the client's awareness of those stimuli. The client-centered approach therefore rejects objectivity in favor of the inner world of experience as reported by the client. If you're on your toes, you might recognize similarities between this idea and that of the cognitive approaches developed by Albert Ellis and Aaron Beck described in Chapter 12, *Cognitive-Behavioral Interventions*. It's different terminology but the same basic concept.

Another tenant of phenomenological theory is that the basic human tendency is toward **self-actualization**—the fulfillment of one's talents and potentials. Examples include being able to find satisfaction in what one is doing and achieve enjoyment or contentment out of the present moment (does that sound like mindfulness to you?). This, according to Rogers, is what produces the forward movement of life—a force upon which therapy relies heavily. But this forward movement can occur only when choices in life are clearly perceived and adequately symbolized. Behavior is fundamentally a set of goal-directed attempts by the client to satisfy experienced needs. All needs can ultimately be subsumed under the single urge of enhancement of the phenomenal self.

SDI Productions/E+/Getty Images

Conveying empathy and cultivating a strong therapeutic relationship are cornerstones of client-centered therapy.

Rogers (1959) also wrote that psychotherapy is the "releasing of an already existing capacity in a potentially competent individual, not the expert manipulation of a more or less passive personality" (p. 221). He referred to this as **growth potential**, and proposed that client-centered therapy permits the client's self-actualizing tendencies to gain ascendance over previously internalized factors that restricted acceptance of personal worth. The three therapist characteristics that precipitate self-actualization and growth potential are (a) *empathy*, (b) *unconditional positive regard*, and (c) genuineness or *congruence*.

Empathy

To convey **empathy** is to transmit to clients a sense of being understood—a sensitivity to their needs, feelings, and circumstances. When clients realize their therapist is making every effort to understand them, the foundation for a strong therapeutic relationship is in place. Rogers believed empathy was tremendously reassuring and therapeutic, more than words and other techniques a therapist might use. As Rogers (1946) himself put it:

> If we can provide understanding of the way the client seems to himself at this moment, he can do the rest. The therapist must lay aside his preoccupation with diagnosis and his diagnostic shrewdness, must discard his tendency to make professional evaluations, must cease his endeavors to formulate an accurate prognosis, must give up the temptation subtly to guide the individual, and must concentrate on one purpose only; that of providing deep understanding and acceptance of the attitudes consciously held at this moment by the client. (pp. 420–421)

Unconditional Positive Regard

In most relationships, approval and acceptance are conditional upon meeting certain stipulations. An employer is accepting if employees are prompt and efficient. An intimate partner requires reciprocal interest and love. Rogers believed that in therapy, however, there must be no conditions. Acceptance is given without hidden clauses or subtle disclaimers. **Unconditional positive regard** is a respect for clients as human beings, setting aside all preconceived notions and conveying trust in their ability to achieve their inner potential. This, coupled with a complete lack of evaluative judgments, creates an atmosphere in which the client is able to begin to grow as a person.

Congruence

Therapists express **congruence** when they genuinely communicate how they feel toward the client. For example, if a client makes upsetting remarks toward the therapist during the session, congruent therapists let the client know that they feel upset (Rogers, 1961). Although this might seem to contradict the need for unconditional positive regard, expressing how one *feels* (e.g., "I was hurt when you said that") is not the same as *judging* someone's worth (e.g., "You're no good for saying such a hurtful thing"). Think of it this way: you might become angry with a family member because of something she does or says, yet you still love her. The fact that you become upset might even be a sign of how much you love her. Rogers believed that clients respond favorably to honesty and congruence.

The Process of Client-Centered Therapy

Perhaps the most striking aspect of client-centered therapy is what does *not* occur. Client-centered therapists *do not*:

- Provide information or advice
- Use reassurance or persuasion
- Ask questions
- Teach skills
- Offer interpretations of client behavior
- Make any criticisms of how clients have handled situations

So what *does* happen? Clients are encouraged to express their thoughts and feelings with no consequences to outside relationships. To this end, therapists primarily use **reflection statements** to (a) show that they understand clients' thoughts and feelings and (b) give clients the space to further clarify their own thoughts and feelings. In one study, approximately 75% of all client-centered therapists' responses were reflections of what the client had said (Greenberg et al., 1994). Comments are also made that convey to the client the therapist's total and unconditional acceptance. What does a session actually look like? IN PRACTICE: *Therapist–Client Interactions in Client-Centered Therapy* provides a sample transcript of part of a client-centered therapy session with Maria, a woman with chronic depression and anxiety.

| In Practice | **Therapist–Client Interactions in Client-Centered Therapy** |

In this excerpt of a client-centered therapy session, the client, Maria, is talking about her relationship with her teenaged daughter. Notice how the therapist focuses on Maria's emotions and on making her feel understood. There is no advice-giving or skills training. In client-centered therapy, the unconditional positive regard and other aspects of the therapeutic relationship are assumed to result in the client's growth.

Maria: I'm so ashamed of the way I've been acting toward my daughter. I don't feel like I'm doing a good job of parenting. I feel like all I do is yell at her. It's no wonder she tells me she hates me all the time.

Therapist: Okay. I see. It seems like it's one thing after another, and you're questioning whether you're a competent parent. Or at least whether your daughter accepts you.

Maria: And I *need* her to accept me. So, I try not to get upset with her. I try to have a good time with her. But then she goes and misbehaves and I feel like I should discipline her. And that always sets her off. We start yelling at each other and I'm afraid she'll give up on me.

Therapist: And reject you as her mother.

Maria: Yeah. The guilt I feel about punishing her is unbearable. I just want her to be happy. To feel good about herself. To feel good about me. If I punish her — like taking away her phone or something — she'll just get upset with me. And she'll be upset with herself. And I don't want to make her feel that way.

Therapist: Mhm. Parenting can be tricky.

Maria: And yet, as her mom, I know I have to teach her how to behave properly. I mean, there must be rules, right?

Therapist: And so it seems you're really in a pickle. On the one hand, you see the need to use discipline, but on the other, doing so ends up making everyone feel worse.

Maria: Yeah. Why won't she just grow up and learn that you can't just do and get what you want all the time!? When is she going to realize that?

Therapist: I guess, judging from your tone of voice, you're very concerned about her well-being. And also frustrated with her inability to respect your rules and boundaries. ▬

Client-centered therapy sessions are usually scheduled once a week. More frequent sessions, extra sessions, and phone calls are discouraged because these can lead to a dependence that will stifle any sense of growth. The general sequence or process of therapy has been described by Rogers as involving a series of seven stages that the client undergoes (Meador & Rogers, 1984). **Table 14.3** provides an overview of these stages.

Table 14.3	Stages of Client-Centered Therapy
Stage	**Description**
One	Unwillingness to reveal self; own feelings not recognized; rigid constructs; close relationships perceived as dangerous
Two	Feelings sometimes described, but the client is still remote from their own personal experience; still externalizes heavily, but begins to show some recognition that problems and conflicts exist
Three	Description of past feelings as unacceptable; freer flow of expressions of self; begins to question validity of own constructs; recognition that problems are inside rather than outside the individual
Four	Free description of personal feelings as owned by the self; recognition that long-denied feelings may break into the present; loosening of personal constructs; some expression of self-responsibility; begins to risk relating to others on a feeling basis
Five	Free expression of feelings and acceptance of them; previously denied feelings, although fearsome, are clearly in awareness; recognition of conflicts between intellect and emotions; acceptance of personal responsibility for problems; a desire to be what one is
Six	Acceptance of feelings without the need for denial; a vivid, releasing sense of experience; willingness to risk being oneself in relationships with others; trusts others to be accepting
Seven	Client is now comfortable with experiencing the self; experiences new feelings; little incongruence; ability to check validity of experience

Research Support

Research providing empirical support for Rogers's theories is scarce, although there is support for an association between self-actualization and psychological well-being (Patterson & Joseph, 2007). On the other hand, the efficacy and effectiveness of client-centered therapy has been studied for decades and there is evidence that it is associated with decreases in distress and increases in well-being as compared to placebo controls or no treatment (Erekson & Lambert, 2015). Specific problems, depression, and relationship and interpersonal difficulties appear to respond to client-centered approaches, although such approaches appear to be less effective than cognitive-behavioral treatments for anxiety-related problems such as OCD, PTSD, phobias, and panic attacks. These results, as well as findings from meta-analyses (e.g., Ahn & Wampold, 2001) raise questions about the role that common versus specific factors play in efficacy. In fact, a meta-analysis suggests that common factors account for a much larger portion of change in client-centered therapy than do specific techniques (Cuijpers et al., 2012).

Think Like a Clinical Psychologist Which concepts and characteristics of client-centered therapy can be seen (in one form or another) in contemporary psychological treatments?

▥ Multicultural Considerations

Although some psychodynamic and client-centered therapists have argued that these interventions are "culture-free" (e.g., Tummala-Narra, 2013), as we have seen with other conceptual and treatment approaches, theories and therapies indeed reflect the philosophical underpinnings of the culture in which they originated. Freud, for example, grew up in an upper-middle-class home in 19th-century Vienna, Austria. Being Jewish, he was keenly aware of anti-Semitism directed toward his family and other Jews even though he never wrote about the effects of this oppression, nor incorporated it into his professional works (Moskowitz, 1995). He did, however, claim to be sensitive to matters of culture and social class, and wanted psychoanalysis to be widely accessible (Aron & Starr, 2013). In retrospect, however, his focus on intrapsychic phenomena largely overlooks how sociocultural contexts—such as race, gender, religion, socioeconomic status, and education—influence emotion and behavior.

Carl Rogers was raised in a middle-class family in the midwestern United States. His father was a civil engineer and his mother did not work outside the home. He was the fourth of six children in a devoutly Christian family and a high achiever in school from an early age. It was only after attending a Christian conference in China in 1922 that Rogers began to question his initial career choice of studying to become a minister. In later writings (Rogers, 1980), he indicated that Taoism was a major influence on his development of client-centered therapy.

As we have also discussed, clinicians reveal their own values and attitudes in how they engage clients in the therapeutic relationship; interpret clients' behavior (especially culturally specific behavior); and work through issues such as trauma, loss, stress, sexuality, and self-esteem. When working with clients from ethnic and cultural backgrounds different from one's own, therapists are at risk of misinterpreting norms and traditions based on their own background, which may bias psychodynamic interpretations, or interfere with the display of empathy and congruence in client-centered therapy. On a broader level, clients raised in societies that value collectivism over individualism may not identify with the Western traditions inherent in psychodynamic concepts and the emphasis on sharing thoughts and feelings in client-centered therapy, and thus not respond to these forms of treatment (e.g., Nel & Govender, 2020). Accordingly, as we have covered in other places in this book, it is important for clinicians to gain an understanding of their clients' heritage and make sure to maintain sensitivity to such individual and cultural differences.

Unfortunately, little attention has been paid to multicultural processes in psychodynamic and client-centered therapy (e.g., Shedler, 2010). A comprehensive review of 104 studies (including over 9000 clients) on psychodynamic treatment found that approximately 75% did not provide any information about the race or ethnicity of the participants (Watkins, 2012). Such exclusion is also evident in clinical case discussions, where the background of clients (and therapists) is either not mentioned at all or mentioned only briefly without connecting social identity factors with clinical presentation or the therapeutic process. This leaves room for culturally biased assumptions of what constitutes "healthy" and "unhealthy" behaviors and emotions.

Think Like a Clinical Psychologist In what ways might Freud and Rogers have been influenced by their unique cultural heritage? How might these influences have impacted the psychotherapies that they developed? What cultural adaptations (if any) might you make to broaden these therapies for clients who come from different backgrounds?

▥ Chapter Summary

The psychodynamic approach to therapy evolved from the work of Sigmund Freud. It focuses on the analysis of past experience and emphasizes unconscious motives and conflicts in the search for the roots of behavior. According to this viewpoint, psychological problems result from the conflicting demands of the id, ego, superego, and reality. Techniques of psychodynamic psychotherapy are aimed at uncovering unconscious conflicts and motivation. For example, dreams are analyzed, as are free associations and the nature of the transference. Psychoanalytic theory and therapy have been modified considerably over the years. Specifically, the length of treatment has become shorter and the focus is more on the here and now. Interpersonal psychotherapy is a form of brief psychodynamic therapy that has good empirical support for treating depression.

Client-centered therapy was developed from Carl Rogers's reaction to traditional psychoanalytic perspectives on psychopathology and on psychological health. Instead of adopting a deterministic and, to some degree, pessimistic perspective, Rogers emphasized the client's own phenomenological world and experience, and the inherent tendency toward self-actualization. Client-centered therapists seek to facilitate the client's growth potential by providing empathic understanding, unconditional positive regard, and genuineness. Diagnosis, formal assessment, and traditional therapeutic "techniques" (e.g., giving advice) are generally avoided. This form of treatment has made noteworthy contributions to the field of psychotherapy. Clients' internal experience, feelings, free will, and growth potential have been brought to the forefront. Demonstrating the importance of the therapeutic relationship and of rapport is another major contribution.

Applying What You've Learned

Exercise 1: Compare and contrast the treatment for a 21-year-old college student with depression who is struggling at school from a psychoanalytic and from a psychodynamic perspective.

Exercise 2: How might a client-centered therapist conceptualize the problems of a 40-year-old anxious sales manager for a software company? How would this therapist likely provide treatment for this individual?

Key Terms

Anal stage: The psychosexual stage that extends from about 6 months to 3 years of age, during which the child focuses on urination and defecation as means of satisfaction.

Client-centered therapy: A psychotherapy developed by Carl Rogers that emphasizes the importance of the client's perceptions of their experience and recognizes an inherent human tendency toward developing one's capacities. This therapy orientation seeks to facilitate the client's growth potential.

Congruence: One of the three therapist characteristics considered essential for client-centered work (also referred to as *genuineness*). Congruence refers to the honest expression by the therapist of the behaviors, feelings, and attitudes that have been stimulated by the client.

Countertransference: Analysts' own internal conflicts that could be transferred onto their client (e.g., developing feelings of attraction or anger toward the client).

Death instincts (Thanatos): The innate drives that are responsible for all of the negative or destructive aspects of behavior.

Defense mechanism: Strategy used by the ego to stave off threats originating internally, from one's id or superego. (Also referred to as *ego defense*.)

Dream analysis: A psychoanalytic technique that attempts to shed light on unconscious material. Because dreams are regarded as heavily laden with unconscious wishes in symbolic form, the analysis of dreams is believed to provide important clues to these wishes.

Ego: The organized, rational component of the personality. The ego uses perception, learning, planning, and so forth to satisfy the needs of the organism while at the same time preserving its place in the world.

Empathy: One of the three therapist characteristics considered essential for client-centered work. Empathy refers to sensitivity to the needs, feelings, and circumstances of clients so that they feel understood.

Fixation: The defense mechanism that occurs when the frustration and anxiety of the next psychosexual stage cause the individual to be arrested at their current level of psychosexual development.

Free association: A cardinal rule of psychoanalysis in which clients are required to say anything and everything that comes to mind. Over time, free association is believed to shed light on unconscious thoughts and urges.

Genital stage: The psychosexual stage that follows the onset of adolescence and ideally culminates in a mature expression of sexuality.

Growth potential: A capacity for competence that all individuals possess. The goal of client-centered therapy is to release this capacity.

Hysteria: A psychological condition (thought to affect mostly women) marked by paralysis, blindness, and deafness; no neurological basis can be found for these symptoms.

Id: The deep, inaccessible portion of the personality that contains the instinctual urges. The id is without order, logic, or morals and operates solely to gratify the instinctual urges.

Insight: In psychoanalytic psychotherapy, a complete understanding of the unconscious determinants of one's irrational and problematic thoughts, feelings, or behaviors.

Interpersonal psychotherapy (IPT): A brief, insight-oriented therapy that is psychodynamic in tone. IPT has been applied primarily to the treatment of depression and is considered a "well-established" empirically supported treatment for this problem.

Interpretation: A method in which the psychoanalyst reveals the unconscious meanings of the client's thoughts and behaviors, thus helping the client to achieve insight. Interpretation is the cornerstone of nearly every form of dynamic psychotherapy.

Latency stage: The psychosexual stage that extends from about 5 to 12 years of age, during which the child is characterized by a lack of overt sexual activity (and perhaps even a negative orientation toward anything sexual).

Latent content: The symbolic meaning of a dream's events.

Life instincts (Eros): The innate drives that are responsible for all of the positive or constructive aspects of behavior.

Manifest content: What actually happens during a dream.

Oedipus complex: The phase in which a child feels sexual attraction for the parent of the opposite sex and feelings of hostility toward the parent of the same sex. The superego emerges from the resolution of this complex.

Oral stage: The psychosexual stage spanning about the first year of life, during which the mouth is the chief source of pleasure and satisfaction.

Phallic stage: The psychosexual stage that extends from about 3 to 7 years of age, during which the sexual organs become the primary source of gratification.

Phenomenal self: The part of the phenomenal field that the person experiences as "I." According to phenomenological theory, humans have a basic urge to preserve and enhance the phenomenal self.

Phenomenological theory: A philosophical/theoretical approach asserting that an individual's behavior is completely determined by their phenomenal field, or everything that is experienced by the person at any given point in time.

Pleasure principle: The rule of conduct by which one seeks pleasure and avoids pain. The id operates according to the pleasure principle.

Projection: The defense mechanism that occurs when a person attributes their unconscious feelings to someone else.

Psychic determinism: A major assumption of Freudian theory that holds that everything one does has meaning and is goal directed.

Psychoanalysis: An approach to treatment developed by Freud.

Psychoanalytic theory: The basis of psychoanalysis and the psychodynamic approach to therapy which has evolved over the past century.

Psychodynamic: An approach that emphasizes early experiences in the development of human behavior, feelings, and emotions.

Psychodynamic psychotherapy: A technique based on psychoanalytic theory that contains only remnants of psychoanalysis.

Psychosexual stages: A series of developmental stages posited by Freud, each of which is marked by the involvement of a particular erogenous zone of the body.

Reaction formation: The defense mechanism that occurs when an unconscious impulse is consciously expressed by its behavioral opposite.

Reality principle: The rule of conduct by which one defers the gratification of instinctual urges until a suitable object and mode of satisfaction are discovered. The ego operates according to the reality principle.

Reflection statements: Used by client-centered therapists to (a) show that they understand clients' thoughts and feelings, and (b) give clients the space to further clarify their own thoughts and feelings.

Regression: The defense mechanism that occurs when extensive frustration causes a person to return to a stage that once provided a great deal of gratification.

Repression: The most basic defense mechanism. Repression serves to keep highly threatening sexual or aggressive material out of conscious awareness, often involuntarily.

Resistance: Any attempt by the client to ward off the therapist's efforts to dissolve their neurotic methods for resolving problems. Any client action or behavior that prevents insight or prevents bringing unconscious material into consciousness.

Self-actualization: The basic human tendency toward maintaining and enhancing the self.

Superego: The component of the personality that represents the ideals and values of society as they are conveyed to the child through the words and deeds of their parents. The role of the superego is to block unacceptable id impulses and to pressure the ego to serve the ends of morality rather than those of expediency.

Talking cure: Discovered by Breuer, the use of techniques that encourage client talking as a way of addressing and alleviating neurotic symptoms.

Transference: A key phenomenon in psychoanalytic therapy in which the client reacts to the therapist as if the therapist represented an important figure from the client's personal life.

Unconditional positive regard: One of the three therapist characteristics considered essential for client-centered work. Unconditional positive regard refers to complete acceptance of and respect for the client as a human being, without conditions or requirements.

Unconscious: The portion of the mind that is not accessible to awareness.

CONNECT ONLINE:

 | Check out our videos and additional resources located at: www.macmillanlearning.com

Group, Family, and Couple-Based Interventions

FOCUS QUESTIONS

1. Describe how psychologists go about forming groups for group therapy.
2. What are the major approaches to group therapy and what techniques distinguish them from each other?
3. What are the goals of family therapy and what are the techniques used in this intervention?
4. What are the most effective couple-based interventions? How are they similar to each other and how are they different?
5. What are multicultural issues that clinical psychologists must keep in mind when working with couples and families?

CHAPTER OUTLINE

The previous chapters in this section have, for the most part, focused on interventions for the *individual* client. Yet, most of the emotional and behavioral problems that bring child, adolescent, or adult clients to clinical psychologists are influenced, at least to some degree, by interactions with others. Problems with unassertiveness, for example, manifest in how we communicate with others. Relationship conflicts, by definition, involve two people. And children's disruptive behavior typically occurs in the context of the family. Therefore, it is important to consider psychological interventions that take place in groups or dyads and address such interpersonal factors.

For the psychologist, practically speaking, group and family therapies are more efficient and economical than individual treatment (Kazdin & Blase, 2011). More clients can be helped at one time and often at a lower cost per client. Many insurance providers demand more cost-effective mental health treatment, so making interventions that can effectively serve more people at a reduced cost is preferable from a business standpoint. Whatever the reasons, a variety of methods for working with multiple clients at one time, including group therapy, family therapy, and interventions for couples, have become increasingly popular. In this chapter, we discuss these approaches in detail.

Group Interventions

Group therapy, the idea of implementing psychological interventions in groups, has been around for over a century (see IN HISTORICAL PERSPECTIVE: *The Group Therapy Movement*). At first, this approach was practiced by only a handful of clinicians. Some used it because their caseload was so large that seeing clients in groups was the only way to manage the overload. Others considered groups only as supplemental to individual treatment. A psychologist, for example, might work individually with a client to increase assertiveness; then, during a group session, other members of the group might reinforce the importance of acting more assertively. Instead of being seen as an add-on form of treatment, however, group methods have now achieved considerably more visibility and respectability. They are used in different ways to facilitate improvements in mental and behavioral functioning based on a range of theoretical perspectives. In this section, we discuss the main approaches used in group therapy today.

Types of Groups

As with individual treatment, there are many different approaches to group therapy. For the most part, these can be subdivided into *directive groups*, generally based on behavioral and cognitive-behavioral interventions, and *nondirective groups*.

Directive Groups

Directive groups are usually time limited (e.g., 12 weekly sessions) and comprised of clients with similar problems. As the term "directive" might suggest, the therapist plays an active, almost didactic role, providing lessons, skills training, and homework assignments. In fact, these groups tend to be structured a lot like individual cognitive-behavioral treatment, except for the fact that the interventions are conducted with multiple clients in the room. But is it feasible to

● ● ● ● ● In Historical Perspective

The Group Therapy Movement

In parallel with individual therapy, group psychotherapy was first used by the psychoanalysts. Although obviously different from individual therapy in some respects (e.g., clients can be influenced by other members of the group), the focus was still on phenomena such as free association, transference, and dream interpretation. Another early use of group methods was Joseph H. Pratt's work with depressed tuberculosis patients in 1905 (Pinney, 1978). Pratt used lectures and group discussion to successfully help lift the spirits of individuals with this disease and promote their adherence to medical treatments.

Jacob Moreno was another major figure in the group therapy movement (as well as another Viennese physician) who introduced **psychodrama**, in which clients act out events from their past as if performing in a play. Moreno, and those who use contemporary versions of psychodrama, believed that the acting brings about emotional relief and spontaneity to heighten self-understanding. Clients may be asked to play themselves or another role, and at times even switch roles in the midst of a dramatization. The drama may involve the reenactment of an event from the client's past or an anticipated upcoming event.

But it was the aftermath of World War II that really brought group methods to center stage. The large number of war veterans with anxiety, depression, and posttraumatic stress symptoms sharply increased the demand for psychological services, and group methods were required to meet this need. Once mental health workers recognized the pragmatism of group methods, respectability was but a short distance away. As a result, nearly every school or approach to individual treatment now has a corresponding group counterpart. There are group interventions based on psychoanalysis, Gestalt therapy, cognitive-behavioral principles, and many other types as well.

The increased demand for mental health services as a result of stress, anxiety, and depression associated with the COVID-19 pandemic has once again brought group treatments to the forefront. To be able to meet the needs of more clients at once, many clinical psychologists are turning to the use of groups — at least as an initial intervention.

Wavebreakmedia/Deposit Photos

Psychodrama is a psychodynamic group therapy technique in which clients act out events from their past as if performing in a play.

implement behavioral and cognitive interventions within a group setting? It is. Teaching and practicing interpersonal skills, using cognitive restructuring, and conducting exposure therapy trials, for example, are all fairly straightforward to apply with several clients simultaneously. In addition, clients in groups often identify and build relationships with one another, which promotes the normalization of experiences and allows group members to receive feedback from one another—feedback which may even be viewed as more genuine and impartial (i.e., objective) than that which comes from the therapist. Finally, group treatment promotes skill mastery by giving clients built-in opportunities to apply treatment skills right there in the session with other clients. In other words, clients get to practice becoming their own therapist by helping other group members, thereby solidifying their own skills.

In group-based assertiveness training, for example, clients have opportunities to learn and practice expressing themselves with greater confidence (e.g., Lubis, 2020). Such groups typically involve direct teaching, with the therapist describing the group's goals and the problems that nonassertiveness can generate for people. Other therapeutic aspects include cooperative problem solving, honesty, and acceptance among group members; clients are provided with opportunities to comment and give constructive criticism regarding how other group members present themselves. New assertiveness skills are discussed, demonstrated, and practiced, and homework assignments are often given. As in most behavioral interventions, group members complete a number of assessment instruments before, during, and after treatment to monitor changes in target problems.

Another example is cognitive-behavioral group therapy for social anxiety (Heimberg & Becker, 2002; Neufeld et al., 2020). In this intervention, group members are first introduced to a conceptual model of social anxiety that incorporates cognitive, behavioral, and physiological components. Next, group members are taught cognitive therapy skills, receive social skills training (e.g., how to initiate, maintain, and discontinue conversations), and practice exposure to feared social situations. Simply being part of a group is often an exposure exercise for socially anxious clients. Doing treatment in groups also allows for opportunities to practice social skills (e.g., appropriate nonverbal behavior) and give constructive feedback to other group members—something that many people with social anxiety are afraid to do. Research demonstrates the efficacy of group cognitive-behavioral treatment for social phobia (e.g., Neufeld et al., 2020). In fact, due to the nature of social anxiety, group treatment is arguably the intervention of choice.

Group therapy also is popular in working with young children and adolescents. Because youth are often comfortable with a classroom-type setting, the use of a group approach can be a nice fit for interventions focused on social skill development, learning anxiety management techniques, and reducing aggressive behavior. In some cases, such as for youth with pervasive developmental disorders (e.g., high-functioning autism), the group setting allows for immediate practice of social and other daily life skills that may be otherwise difficult to obtain.

Group behavioral and cognitive-behavioral therapy sessions, like other time-limited approaches, typically take place on a weekly basis for a predetermined number of weeks (e.g., eight sessions for a group consisting of members dealing with a life crisis). When preparing to begin group therapy, the clinician carefully screens and considers each group member to ensure that all participants (a) have similar presenting problems and (b) possess the requisite skills to contribute constructively to the group.

Finally, it needs to be mentioned that there is an exception to directive groups being comprised most often of clients with similar problems. See A CLOSER LOOK: *The Unified Protocol.*

A Closer Look   The Unified Protocol

Psychologist David Barlow and his team at Boston University have developed a multicomponent cognitive-behavioral treatment package called the Unified Protocol for Transdiagnostic Treatment of Emotional Disorders (UP) for clients with various behavioral and psychological problems characterized by depression, anxiety, and related issues such as psychosomatic and dissociative symptoms (Barlow et al., 2020). What makes this program different from most of the behavioral and cognitive-behavioral interventions described in Chapters 11 and 12 of this book? The UP includes a set of core cognitive-behavioral interventions that have been demonstrated to be effective and that simultaneously target key cognitive and behavioral processes shared across different psychological problems. Therefore, the same general treatment protocol (individually tailored for each client) can be used for clients in groups with a wide range of common presenting complaints. The core interventions include:

- Mindfulness and emotional awareness
- Cognitive therapy
- Acceptance of strong emotions (similar to ACT)
- Awareness and tolerance of physical sensations
- Exposure therapy

The UP is efficient and cost-effective—clinicians only need to become proficient in one treatment manual to provide empirically supported therapy for a range of problems. But research also shows that implementing the UP in group settings (i.e., as a directive group) makes it even more powerful. Specifically, the following group-related factors are thought to facilitate the effectiveness of the UP (Bullis et al., 2018):

- Group members are able to share their experiences with strong emotions and learn from one another, which helps normalize psychological symptoms and enhance motivation to work hard throughout the program.
- Other group members observe and help with each client's exposure therapy practices, which helps instill confidence in one's own ability to complete personally relevant (and often challenging) exposure tasks.
- Clients practice specific treatment skills—such as cognitive therapy and mindfulness—in small groups, which gives them the opportunity to "try on" the role of therapist; for example, they lead each other through cognitive therapy (e.g., asking questions such as "Do you know for certain that other people would laugh at you if you got the answer wrong?"). This helps reinforce these skills and allows clients to more easily apply them to their own sources of emotional distress.

In their study, Bullis and colleagues (2018) found medium to large effect sizes for improvements in depression and anxiety, quality of life, functional impairment, and experiential avoidance. Client feedback also indicated that the UP was an acceptable treatment, which is particularly noteworthy because although many group-based therapies produce effects equivalent to individual therapy, the vast majority of clients prefer individual therapy (e.g., Semple et al., 2006). Thus, the UP may be an effective and acceptable intervention when delivered in a group format in a routine clinical setting. ▬▬

SDI Productions/E+/Getty Images

In some nondirective group therapies, clients are encouraged to give each other candid feedback.

Nondirective Groups

Nondirective groups are less structured or "classroom-like" than directive groups; and instead are oriented toward the experience of the individual client. They tend to be grounded in psychoanalytic, psychodynamic, interpersonal, client-centered, or gestalt principles (even though they may sometimes incorporate aspects of behavioral and cognitive interventions). Nondirective groups are also more likely than directive groups to include clients with different types of presenting complaints. Some nondirective groups are time-limited, while others do not have specific end points or are meant to be long-term treatments. **Interpersonal group psychotherapy** for personality disorders (Budman et al., 1996) provides an illustrative example. After a thorough screening process that involves observing potential group members in various interpersonal situations, a group of about 10 clients (including all genders) is formed and meets weekly for 90 minutes over the course of 72 weeks. The therapist's role is to emphasize the group environment and the idea that the group is a microcosm of outside-the-group issues. There is minimal application of structured exercises, no formal "teaching" by the therapist, and all group members are encouraged to engage in the process of learning from one another and their interactions within the group. For example, group members provide feedback regarding the adaptive and maladaptive aspects of other members' interpersonal behavior (e.g., "When you said that I don't know what I am talking about, I felt hurt and angry at you") and have the opportunity to modify their own interpersonal behavior. Peer pressure may also encourage individual group members to change their behavior—that is, to decrease problematic behaviors (e.g., verbally lashing out at others) and increase more adaptive responses (e.g., explaining how one feels to other members).

Gestalt group therapy, another type of nondirective group approach, uses notably different strategies, leading clients to an awareness of the "now" and an appreciation of "being in the world" (Perls, 1973). This is achieved by focusing on one group member at a time (while the other members serve as observers); sometimes called "being in the hot seat." Clients are asked to experience their feelings and behavior—to "lose their minds and find their senses." But other group members are not just passive observers; they may be called on to say how they regard the person in the hot seat. At times, there may be role playing, the reporting of dreams, and dialogue between clients. But regardless of whether a member is an observer or in the hot seat, there tends to be intense involvement in the group.

Group Composition

How large are treatment groups? Who are good (and poor) candidates for group therapy? Can clients join a group already in progress? Most psychotherapy groups consist of five to ten clients and one or two therapists who meet at least once a week for 90-minute to 2-hour sessions. Group members and therapists are often seated in a circle or around a table so that they can interact with each other. Groups can also take place using teleconference software, such as Zoom, so that all group members can see each other. In some instances, the therapist sees the clients only at group meetings; in others, the therapist sees all group members concurrently on an individual basis. Still other group interventions, such as group dialectical behavior therapy (DBT), necessitate that clients also engage in outside individual treatment with a DBT-trained clinician of their own choosing.

As alluded to earlier, the composition of the group may vary depending on (a) the particular mode of therapy and (b) practical considerations. Nondirective groups, for example, are often conducted with a diverse set of clients with regard to gender, cultural background, and presenting problems. Groups based on cognitive-behavioral interventions may be culturally diverse, but tend to

Group therapy sessions often take place in a circle (sometimes around a table) to facilitate verbal and nonverbal communication among the group members and therapist(s).

be homogeneous with regard to the presenting problem (e.g., composed exclusively of people with alcohol use problems). In settings with access to large numbers of potential clients, such as residential facilities, it may be easy to form groups in which all members have the same problem (e.g., individuals with depression or social skill deficits). In outpatient practice, however, this can be challenging because clinicians have to rely on the flow of clients into their clinic or office. Thus, they may be forced to either run smaller groups or be less flexible regarding the criteria for inclusion in the group.

Group treatments also vary with respect to when (and *if*) new members may join. **Open groups** admit new members at any point if someone wants to join or to replace someone who decides to leave the group. **Closed groups**, on the other hand, usually have starting and ending points, and admit no new members once the group has begun. Many (but not all) cognitive-behavioral group treatments are closed because they follow a treatment manual in which each session builds on what was learned in the previous sessions.

Finally, not all clients are appropriate for group therapy, and clinicians must "screen" for certain characteristics when considering individuals for participation. For example, most psychologists try to avoid including in heterogeneous groups clients with severe cognitive dysfunction, as such impairments can make it difficult for these clients to process and retain information during sessions (although groups exclusively for individuals with such difficulties might be quite helpful). Individuals prone to monopolizing discussions, or who are extremely pessimistic or antagonistic, or have difficulty with controlling themselves, are also generally to be avoided because such behavior is often disruptive to the group.

Confidentiality

Perhaps you're wondering how confidentiality works in group settings. Indeed, clients are more likely to be open and honest with others about their own problems (and thus optimally benefit from group therapy) when they can trust that "what happens in the group stays in the group." Moreover, there is the potential for group members to publicly reveal sensitive information about others in the group, which could cause damage to their personal or professional lives. Accordingly, when orienting clients to group therapy (either during an initial group session or during an individual appointment beforehand), psychologists explain important rules and regulations for how the group will function—including issues of confidentiality. Clients learn about the definition and importance of confidentiality, including the harmful effects that violations could have on fellow group members. The therapist will therefore insist that clients keep other group members' names (and other identifying information) and the content of group discussions strictly private. Still, clients are not ethically (or legally) bound by an enforceable ethics code the way that professional psychologists are, so therapists provide frequent reminders about the confidentiality rule and are extremely careful about their own behavior regarding this issue. Still, group members must be cautioned that despite the aforementioned insistence on privacy, it is simply not possible to *guarantee* confidentiality.

Efficacy and Effectiveness

It has long been understood that various forms of group psychotherapy are more effective than no treatment (Burlingame et al., 2004; Schwartze et al., 2017). This is particularly true for adults and youth with depression, panic attacks, social anxiety, insomnia, obsessive-compulsive disorder (OCD), and eating disorders, and for those treated with other forms of structured, time limited cognitive-behavioral group interventions (e.g., Schwartze et al., 2017; Janis et al., 2021). However, group treatments do not appear to be any *more* effective than similar treatments delivered individually to clients. Thus, the major advantage of group therapy is that it is more efficient and more economical, especially the time-limited group treatments.

In general, research on group therapy has not advanced much beyond answering the general question of overall effectiveness. However, evidence is mounting to show that some types of group treatments work better than others for different psychological problems and disorders (Burlingame et al., 2018). **Table 15.1** summarizes a set of "curative factors" that theorist Irving Yalom (2005) has proposed to be critical to the success of group treatment. These factors can be considered similar to the nonspecific (or *common*) factors in psychological treatments discussed in Chapter 10, *Psychological Treatment: Science and Practice*, because they are present in virtually all group interventions. Relatively few empirical studies, however, have examined the validity of these factors, or whether they account for improvement over and above any specific techniques used in the particular treatment approach (e.g., group exposure therapy or being in the hot seat). Moreover, the few studies that have been conducted are plagued with conceptual and methodological problems that make it difficult to draw strong conclusions. Clearly, more research investigating the process of group psychotherapy and the proposed mechanisms of change is needed to better understand how group therapy works (Bulingame et al., 2018).

The Future of Group Treatment

Although group treatments can save time and money, and reach more clients at once, they remain underutilized. One reason is that clients and psychologists alike still tend to view groups as a second-choice form of treatment—indeed, fewer clients are referred for group treatment

Table 15.1 Common Factors in Group Treatment	
Factor	**Description**
Imparting information	Group members can receive advice and guidance not just from the therapist but also from other group members.
Instilling hope	Observing others who have successfully grappled with problems helps to instill hope.
Universality	Group members discover that they are not alone and that others have similar problems, fears, and concerns.
Altruism	Helping others in the group leads to greater self-worth.
Interpersonal learning	Interacting with others in the group teaches clients about interpersonal relationships, social skills, sensitivity to others, resolution of conflicts, and so on.
Imitative behavior	Watching and listening to others leads to the modeling of more useful behaviors.
Corrective recapitulation of the primary family	The group context can help clients learn more adaptive methods for coping with family-related problems.
Catharsis	Learning how to express feelings about others in the group in an honest, open way builds a capacity for mutual trust and understanding.
Group cohesiveness	Group members develop relationships with one another that enhance self-esteem through acceptance.

as compared with other forms of treatment, and those who are referred are less likely to follow up and join a group (e.g., Rolnick, 2019). However, with managed behavioral health care companies providing incentives for more efficient treatments, the demand for group therapy will likely increase. To take advantage of these opportunities, psychologists can better educate the public and health care professionals about this mode of treatment, aggressively lobby governments and managed behavioral health care companies to financially support evidence-based group treatments, and better educate themselves about managed care and the health care needs that remain unfulfilled.

Think Like a Clinical Psychologist In what ways do you think the group setting makes a difference over and above the treatment techniques themselves?

📚 Family-Based Interventions

When one member of a family develops a psychological or behavioral problem, others in the family are often affected in some way. Inversely, sometimes dysfunctions within a family can lead one individual member to express psychological symptoms. As we have seen, for example, Shane's parents were constantly disciplining their son for his aggressive behavior; and despite their intent, the increased attention this gave Shane ended up reinforcing the very behavior they were trying to curb. **Family therapy** is a treatment approach in which behavioral

In family therapy, all family members are present for therapy sessions, and problems are thought to develop from dysfunctional interactions among family members.

and psychological problems are conceptualized as arising from (and as maintained by) interactions among family members. In family therapy, these interaction patterns are known as the **family system**. But family therapy differs from simply involving family members in a client's individual treatment. While it is common for parents to play a substantial role in the treatment of youth (as we have seen with Shane in previous chapters), and while a partner, spouse, sibling, or other relative may be asked to attend one or more treatment sessions for an adult client (e.g., Wittenborn et al., 2020), family therapy, as we will see in this section, is characterized by its own philosophical approach and methods. Most crucially, all family members are present for all therapy sessions. IN HISTORICAL PERSPECTIVE: *The Inauspicious Beginnings of Family Therapy* (on p. 343) provides an overview of the development of this form of treatment.

Emphasis on Communication

Family therapy is rooted in **general systems theory**, which views behavioral and psychological problems and disorders as stemming from failures in communication among family members. A good way to think about general systems theory is to conceptualize the family as constantly striving to maintain a homeostasis. That is, one person's behaviors (e.g., a child's difficulties in school) may shift attention away from conflict between the parents. Sometimes the family successfully adapts to their particular pattern of interaction within this system. However, when the system changes (e.g., the child is no longer experiencing difficulties in school), the family has to adjust to a new homeostasis. General systems theory suggests that this "unbalanced" state is the focus for family therapy. The therapist achieves change by using feedback that alters the way the system functions and reestablishes a new, healthy homeostasis (Bowen, M., 1966).

The Process of Family Therapy

What sorts of professionals are best suited to conduct family therapy? Family therapists may receive training through different degree programs, including clinical psychology, counseling psychology, psychiatry, social work, family and child development, and education. Some clinicians use family therapy as one of several techniques; others consider themselves exclusively "family therapists." There are also different theoretical approaches to family therapy, including systemic, psychodynamic, cognitive-behavioral, and others that purport to integrate various theoretical practices. Finally, there are numerous "forms" of family therapy with distinctive titles — behavioral family therapy, conjoint family therapy, concurrent family therapy, collaborative family therapy, network family therapy, and structural family therapy, among others.

◐ ◔ ◖ ◗ ◕ In Historical Perspective

The Inauspicious Beginnings of Family Therapy

Family therapy has its roots in the 19th-century social work movement, although it was not until the mid-20th century that it became a popular form of psychological treatment. Some of the delay had to do with the long-standing dominance of psychoanalysis. When behavioral and client-centered approaches offered alternatives to psychoanalysis, this paved the way for other interventions, such as family therapy, to become a viable option for clinicians. For the first time, the problems of individuals were conceptualized in systemic terms—as a manifestation of family dysfunction.

This new perspective on clinical problems was famously applied to severe psychiatric disorders such as schizophrenia. In trying to understand schizophrenia, Jackson and Weakland (1961) proposed a family systems approach focused on the communication among family members. Specifically, they called attention to a phenomenon known as the **double bind** (e.g., Bateson et al., 1956) in which parents repeatedly place their child in a "no-win" situation. For example, the child might be told by their father, "Always stand up for your rights, no matter who, no matter what!" But the same father also might tell the same child, "Never question my authority. I am your father, and what I say goes!" The contradiction inherent in these two messages ensures that no matter what the child does in relation to the father, it will be wrong. According to Bateson and colleagues, this contradiction, the father's failure to admit that there is a contradiction, and the lack of support from other family members, can set the stage for the child to develop schizophrenia. As it turns out, empirical research neither supports the double bind theory of schizophrenia nor establishes the double bind as a reliable or valid communication phenomenon (Schuham, 1967). Nevertheless, this hypothesis largely nourished the development of family therapy.

Theodore Lidz and his research team also emphasized the family in the etiology of schizophrenia (Lidz et al., 1957). When committed partners (e.g., marital spouses) fail to meet each other's psychological and emotional needs, one partner may form a pathological alliance with the child, ultimately precipitating the child's schizophrenia. Bowen's (1960) and Ackerman's (1966) observations of clients with schizophrenia who lived together with their parents in a psychiatric hospital for sustained periods led to the conclusion that the entire family unit was pathogenic, not just the client. This work is important not because it explained the development of schizophrenia (it did not) but because it gave impetus and direction to the family therapy movement—a movement rich in technique, theory, and history. ■

The double bind theory of schizophrenia, which has been refuted by scientific research, holds that children can develop this disorder when they are repeatedly put in no-win situations by their parents.

tomaz/E+/Getty Images

In many ways, however, the similarities among these approaches are greater than the differences. Specifically, most family therapies share the goals of (a) improving communication within the family and (b) deemphasizing individual family members' problems in favor of addressing the problems of the family as a whole.

What brings families to family therapy? There are no hard-and-fast rules as to when family therapy is appropriate and when it is not. Sometimes it is relational difficulties between parents and children, such as problems with setting limits and boundaries, and implementing appropriate discipline. Perhaps the whole family has become entangled in one child's problem, such as an eating disorder, so that family therapy is the only sensible course of action. Maybe there has been a family crisis, such as an extramarital affair or the death of a family member, which propels the entire family unit into despair almost as one. In other families, there may be conflicts over values, such as if one family member rejects the family's religious traditions or comes out as gay or lesbian. Perhaps the family is having difficulty adjusting to a son or daughter who begins to take drugs, becomes sexually promiscuous, or joins a cult. Some theoretical orientations even propose that individual diagnoses are actually a symptom of a family dysfunction. In other words, an adolescent's symptoms of anorexia may be a marker for a family that is too enmeshed or has not adapted well to a change in the family's homeostasis (e.g., a parents' new job, or the birth of a new sibling).

Still other approaches suggest that child or adolescent symptoms reflect generational conflicts in families. For instance, psychologist Dr. Jose Szapocznik and colleagues (1986) theorized that conduct disorder among Latinx youth in south Florida reflects acculturation stress among first-generation immigrant families. Values consistent with a family's country of origin may conflict with "Americanized" values, and adolescents may be especially likely to feel "stuck in the middle" as a form of acculturative stress. Symptoms of conduct disorder

A family might enter family therapy to help them adjust when there are conflicts over values and traditions.

displayed by the teen thus are not seen as an indicator of an individual-level concern, but rather a manifestation of the family unit experiencing dysfunction. This is an important perspective, because it shifts an understanding of psychopathology from reflecting deficiencies within an individual, or within a specific group of people, to an understanding of symptoms as a marker of normative shifts that may occur due to the stress involved in immigration, which is less stigmatizing.

As with most other interventions, family therapy begins with an assessment of the family's history and, of course, the presenting problem that brought the family to seek help. Family members also have a shared frame of reference, a common history, and a shared language that may be foreign to the therapist. Accordingly, upon beginning to work with a family, it is important for the therapist to learn about their unique subculture. This information may then be used to enhance communication or, on occasion, to confront family members. At the same time, where disagreements arise within the family, the therapist must be careful not to become aligned with one family member at the expense of another. This can be a delicate task because family members will often attempt to use the therapist in their power struggles or in their defenses against open communication.

It is also important to assess how each family member views the presenting problem. Indeed, different individuals are likely to have differing (or even conflicting) perspectives. When the family problem is placed in the larger context of information about the family's history, this can sometimes be used to improve communication and understanding. Laying out the entire panorama of family history—its extended members and their goals, aspirations, fears, and frailties—can lead to deeper understanding, empathy, and tolerance. This larger context can promote a shared frame of reference that was not possible earlier. A child can begin to learn what it meant for her mother to relinquish her own aspirations in favor of the family or what it meant for the father to experience abuse from his own father. In the controlled setting of family therapy, a parent may, at the same time, remember (via the current experience of the children) what it was like to encounter peer pressure.

Types of Family Therapy

Conjoint Family Therapy

In **conjoint family therapy**, the entire family is seen at the same time by one therapist. In some varieties of this approach, the therapist plays a passive, nondirective role. In other varieties, the therapist is an active force, directing the conversation, assigning tasks to various family members, imparting direct instruction regarding communication strategies, and so on. In general, the family therapist is a resource person who observes the family process in action and then illustrates to family members how they can communicate better and thereby bring about more satisfying relationships. The dialogue in A CLOSER LOOK: *Conjoint Family Therapy* illustrates this process for one family consisting of a husband (Ayman), his wife (Leyla), and their 16-year-old son (Elias). **Table 15.2** describes five common communication patterns that family therapists might help families recognize in conjoint family therapy (as well as other forms of family therapy; Banmen, 2020). These modes are thought to cover the essence of communication and feelings.

A Closer Look	Conjoint Family Therapy

Therapist: (to Ayman) I noticed your facial expression, Ayman. Your brow is wrinkled. Does that mean you're angry?

Ayman: Is it that obvious?

Therapist: Sometimes our body language lets others know how we're feeling even when we're trying to hide our feelings from them. As far as you can tell, what were you thinking and feeling just now?

Ayman: I was just thinking about something Leyla said a minute ago.

Therapist: What was it specifically?

Ayman: She said that she wishes I would let her know when she starts talking so loud.

Therapist: Okay, and what were you thinking about that?

Ayman: I never thought about telling her because I figured she would get mad.

Therapist: Ah, then maybe your expression meant you were puzzled because your wife was hoping you would do something that you did not know she wanted you to do. Do you think that by wrinkling your brow you were signaling that you were puzzled?

Ayman: Yeah, I guess so.

Therapist: As far as you know, have you ever been in that same spot before; that is, have you felt puzzled by something Leyla said or did in the past?

Ayman: Yes, lots of times.

Therapist: Have you ever told Leyla when you were surprised about these kinds of things?

Leyla: (interrupting) He never says *anything*!

Therapist: (smiling, to Leyla) OK, just a minute Leyla, let me hear what Ayman thinks. Ayman, how do you let Leyla know when you are surprised in this way?

Ayman: I just assume that she knows.

Therapist: Well, let's see. Suppose you ask Leyla if she knows.

Ayman: Ask her? Now? Right here? This is silly.

Therapist: (smiling) I guess it seems silly in this situation, because Leyla is right here and she already knows what you're going to ask her. I wonder, though, whether you and Leyla are sometimes not on the same page about what the other is thinking. Maybe it would be beneficial to work on skills to help you two to be on the same page. Leyla, let's go back to when I commented on Ayman's facial expression. Did you notice it, too?

Leyla: (complaining) Yes, he always looks like that.

Therapist: What kind of message did you get from his expression—his wrinkled brow?

Leyla: That he doesn't want to be here. He doesn't care. He never talks. He just looks at the television or he isn't home.

Therapist: I'm curious. Do you mean that when Ayman has a wrinkled brow you take this as his way of saying, "I don't care about you, Leyla"?

Leyla: (tearfully) I don't know.

Therapist: Well, maybe the two of you have not yet worked out clear ways of conveying your love to each other. People need ways to send clear messages. (to Elias) What do you know, Elias, about how you send messages to your parents?

Elias: What do you mean?

Therapist: Do you love your mother?

Elias: Of course.

Therapist: So, how do you let her know that you love her? Everyone feels different ways at different times. When you are feeling glad to have your mother around, how do you let her know?

Elias: I do what she tells me to do. Schoolwork and stuff.

Therapist: Okay, and what do you do to let your father know that you love him?

Elias: (after a pause) I can't think of anything.

Therapist: Okay, let me put it another way. What do you know that you could do that would put a smile on your father's face?

Elias: I could get better grades in school.

Therapist: Okay, let's check this out. Do you, Leyla, get a message of love from Elias when he does his homework?

Leyla: I suppose—though he doesn't do very much!

Therapist: So for you, Leyla, you don't get many signs of love from Elias. But are there any other ways that he might show that he loves you without realizing he's sending that message?

Leyla: (softly) The other day he told me I looked nice.

Therapist: What about you, Ayman, does Elias perceive correctly that if he got better grades you would smile?

Ayman: I don't imagine I will be smiling for some time.

Therapist: I hear that you don't think he is getting good grades, but would you smile if he did?

Ayman: Sure, I would be very happy!

Therapist: Good Ayman, and how do you think you would show it? How would he know?

Leyla: (interrupting) You never know when Ayman is pleased.

Therapist: So, Layla and Ayman, we have discovered that you don't always have clear ways of showing your feelings toward one another. Maybe you, Layla, are now observing this between Elias and Ayman. What do you think, Ayman? Do you suppose it would be hard for Elias to find out when he has pleased you? ▬

Table 15.2 Common Communication Patterns among Families

Mode	Description
Placating	Always agreeing, no matter the situation
Blaming	Finding fault with others
Super-reasonable	Using logic even if the person feels differently from what they are saying
Irrelevant	When one's words are unrelated to the situation
Congruent	When one's words do relate to the situation

Other Common Types

As already alluded to, there are numerous types of family therapy. In **concurrent family therapy**, the overall goals are the same as those of conjoint therapy, yet the therapist works with each family member individually rather than as a group. In **collaborative family therapy**, each family member sees a different therapist. The therapists then get together to discuss their clients and the family as a whole. In a variation of this approach, co-therapists are sometimes assigned to work with the same family. That is, two or more therapists meet with the family unit. Some clinicians (e.g., Hutcheson, 2019) take a behavioral approach and view family relations in terms of reinforcement contingencies and skills training. Thus, in **behavioral family therapy**, the therapist first conducts a functional (behavioral) analysis to identify (a) behaviors to increase or decrease and (b) the factors (e.g., rewards) that serve to maintain undesirable behaviors or that will enhance desired behaviors. Next, a treatment plan is developed in which family members provide the appropriate reinforcements to one another for the desired behaviors. Finally, **cognitive-behavioral family therapy** involves teaching family members to self-monitor problematic behaviors and patterns of thinking, to develop new skills (communication, problem resolution, negotiation, conflict management), and to challenge interpretations of family events and reframe these interpretations if necessary (Hutcheson, 2019).

A more recently developed mode of family therapy, **multisystemic therapy** (MST) (Henggeler, 2017), is an intervention primarily for juvenile offenders and their families. The model behind MST assumes that clinical problems are determined by multiple factors, including the individual, the family, the school environment, and the neighborhood. These influences are viewed as "systems" of influence within which each person operates. MST sees the family as the most important link in changing problematic behavior, and this approach is characterized by several key components: (a) treatment is delivered in the person's home, school, or other community locations; (b) MST therapists are available for consultation 24 hours a day, 7 days a week; (c) the caseloads of MST therapists are kept intentionally low (4 to 6 families) in order to provide intensive services to each family; and (d) MST therapists serve on a team in order to provide continuity of services and to be available for backup should the need arise (Henggeler, 2017). MST uses several evidence-based techniques (e.g., cognitive-behavioral), and both individual and family outcomes are tracked. MST has been shown to be both efficacious (compared to no treatment) as well as effective (Henggeler, 2017). Finally, MST has been modified to address various clinical problems in youth, including substance use disorders, family abuse and neglect, and child/youth health problems (Henggeler, 2017).

Multisystemic family therapy was developed specifically to help families of juvenile offenders.

Despite the wide variety of approaches available, family therapy is not always appropriate. Sometimes a family's functioning is so disrupted that helping family members learn healthier modes of communication is simply not possible. Sometimes one or more family members refuse to cooperate. In other instances, one or more family members might be suffering with an extremely severe mental health condition (e.g., substance use, depression) to the point that it gets in the way of working with the family as a unit. Accordingly, one must sometimes weigh the costs and benefits when considering family interventions. Although family therapy might benefit some members of the family, it could have negative consequences for others. Some individuals and families may not cope effectively with upsetting discussions that may take place during family therapy sessions. Deciding when to use this approach often requires careful assessment and a great deal of clinical sensitivity.

Ethical and Multicultural Considerations

Confidentiality

As we saw with group therapy, confidentiality issues and dilemmas can also arise in family therapy. Imagine working with a family in which the 15-year-old daughter mentions in a brief one-to-one conversation with you before a session that she has become pregnant and doesn't want her parents to know. Do you keep this information from her parents, or tell them since the daughter is only 15? Keep in mind that either way, you would be betraying someone's trust! More broadly, family therapists have to consider whether *any* information they learn from a single family member should be shared with all family members. Perhaps whether to share depends on how serious or critical this information is to the rest of the family. But then who decides what's serious or critical enough to share—where should the limits be set? Such dilemmas do not have straightforward solutions (Turliuc & Candel, 2019). Accordingly, family therapists are advised to set ground rules for privacy and confidentiality at the very beginning of treatment (e.g., when obtaining informed consent) so that all family members know how private conversations will be handled. Some family therapists avoid all conversations with individual family members (e.g., "If you have something to say to me, you'll need to tell me in front of your family") so that situations like the one described above can be avoided. This helps keep the therapist from having to remember—in the heat of a therapy session—not only what sensitive information they might have been told but also how they learned it and whether they have permission to share the information with the rest of the family.

Culture and Family Therapy

It goes without saying that each family comes to therapy with their own lived experience and cultural background (e.g., Tadros et al., 2021). Thus, multicultural competence and sensitivity are particularly pertinent to family therapy. It is important for clinicians to have a full appreciation of the values and sociocultural background of the families with whom they work, including characteristics such as religion, socioeconomic status, and ethnicity. In some families, different family members have grown up in different cultural worlds. The parents or caregivers, for example, might have been raised in separate countries or with different religious backgrounds. Multigenerational families living in the same home may include members with different degrees of acculturation. For example, the children might be quite assimilated, their parents somewhat less so, and their grandparents—perhaps having emigrated from another country—much more traditional. Some families are comprised of same-gender parents, and others include adopted children of a different race or ethnicity from that of their parents. In all of these cases (and others not mentioned here), family therapists must consider culture as a potentially important aspect of the target problem itself.

Because family therapy (and the theories it is based on) was predominantly developed by, and tested with, families comprised of white, cis-gender, heterosexual, upper-middle-class people from Western nations, it is reasonable to ask whether this approach is applicable for everyone else. Data suggest that family therapy can be adapted for families with different types of identities and cultural experiences that may be confronted with unique circumstances (McDowell et al., 2017), for example, with same-gender-parented families that face discrimination. It is also important for psychologists to recognize that the emphasis on communication about thoughts and feelings (a major focus in traditional family therapy) is a Western value that might not be pertinent for families comprised of clients from other cultural backgrounds. Thus, multicultural considerations may impact various aspects of the family therapy process, including assessment, goal-setting, and interventions themselves (McDowell et al., 2017). Fortunately, today there are many cultural adaptations of family therapy that can provide a safe, nonjudgmental, and understanding therapeutic environment for families of diverse backgrounds and structures (e.g., Zamani & Kim, 2021).

Efficacy and Effectiveness

Although not as plentiful as research on individual treatment, numerous studies have examined the effects of family therapy. Overall, the evidence suggests that family therapy works and that the various approaches to family therapy are similarly effective (e.g., Bernal & Gomez-Arroyo, 2017). Specific problems for which family therapy has been shown to be effective include schizophrenia, anorexia nervosa in youth, nonsuicidal self-injury among adolescents, child delinquency, conduct disorder, and other disruptive disorders in children (e.g., Jewell et al., 2016). As in individual and group therapy, there is strong evidence that nonspecific (common) factors, such as the therapeutic relationship and the expectation of improvement, play an important role in the success of family therapy (e.g., Friedlander et al., 2018).

There are, however, some interesting methodological caveats that researchers must consider when studying the effects of family therapy. For one thing, different members of the same family might have very different views about the results of treatment. If, for instance, therapy results in very traditional parents reluctantly coming to terms with the fact that their son or daughter no longer practices their family's traditional religion, the son or daughter might view treatment as a success, whereas the parents may not.

Think **Like a Clinical Psychologist** Imagine you are a psychologist who is about to work with a family that comes from a cultural background (or has a family structure) that you know very little about. What (if anything) would you do differently to prepare for working with this family compared to a family with the same cultural background (or structure) as your own?

▓ Couple-Based Interventions

As with families, various types of problems may come between two adults in a committed relationship, including recurring arguments; feelings of disconnection; an affair; issues related to sex; and problems related to external stressors such as finances, extended family, child care, and health. In addition, when one partner in a relationship is affected by a behavioral or emotional problem, the other partner is likely to be impacted. Consider Ashwin, who has panic attacks and agoraphobia, and his partner Sezmin. While it is Ashwin who experiences the debilitating anxiety episodes and does not leave their home, Sezmin has given up her social life and changed jobs so she can stay at home to comfort Ashwin, or drive him to the emergency department when he insists he's having a heart attack. Sezmin loves Ashwin and feels it is important to take care of her partner. But at the same time, she often feels frustrated and stuck in what seems like a dysfunctional relationship.

Couples therapy is a form of psychological treatment in which the partners in a relationship work together with a psychologist to improve the aspects of their relationship that are contributing to distress or dissatisfaction. We use the term "couples therapy" in this book, yet this approach is not limited to married couples and can be provided to unmarried partners, same- and other-gender couples, and other types of intimate or nonintimate partnerships (e.g., Pentel & Baucom, in press). IN HISTORICAL PERSPECTIVE: *The Transformation of Couples Therapy* provides a brief (and surprising) history of this form of treatment.

Types of Couples Therapy

As with family therapy, there are numerous approaches to couple-based therapy—yet not all are equally effective. To illustrate the process and techniques used in *effective* couple-based interventions, we describe *cognitive-behavioral couples therapy* (CBCT) and *emotion-focused couples therapy* (EFCT) in this section. As we will see, these two approaches stand out in terms of their strong and consistent research support (Bodenmann et al., 2020).

A couple might seek couples therapy for any number of reasons, including frequent disagreements over finances, extended family, or childcare.

Couples therapy can be provided to married or unmarried partners, same- and other-gender couples, as well as other types of intimate or nonintimate committed partnerships.

> ● ● ● ● ● **In Historical Perspective**
>
> ## The Transformation of Couples Therapy
>
> Disconcertingly, couples therapy originated in Germany in the 1920s as part of the eugenics movement that sought to promote marital and family stability in order to "purify" the German race (Kline, 2001). Also regrettably, the first couples counseling centers in the United States, which began in the 1930s, were started by American eugenicists, such as Paul Popenoe, who fervently promoted racial segregation and the sterilizing of individuals with severe mental illness and developmental disabilities. Once the Nazi Holocaust came to light, however, the field of couples counseling distanced itself from eugenics and racism, and focused solely on improving couples' relationships. By the 1950s, relationship counseling had become a formal, professional service and psychologists, psychiatrists, counselors, and social workers replaced religious leaders and local elders as interventionists. Over the past 70 years, couples-based treatments have been developed within the various schools of psychological theories and intervention. Today, the most popular approaches are cognitive-behavioral, emotion-focused, sex therapy, and insight-oriented (psychodynamic) couples therapy. Although many clinical psychology doctoral programs provide comprehensive training in couples therapy, one can also earn a degree and certification to practice as a *licensed marriage and family therapist* (LMFT) through a briefer and less-rigorous training program focused exclusively on general systems theory as described earlier in this chapter. ■

Cognitive-Behavioral Couples Therapy

Cognitive-behavioral couples therapy (CBCT) relies on principles from social learning theories and focuses on partners' cognitions, behaviors, and emotional responses to help them improve how they communicate and solve problems (Baucom et al., 2019). Specifically, psychologists working from a CBCT perspective strive to (a) improve how partners share thoughts and feelings with one another, (b) build a teamwork approach to making decisions and solving problems, and (c) identify and modify partners' unrealistic expectations (e.g., "She *should* want to have sex every night") and other dysfunctional beliefs and assumptions (e.g., "If he doesn't listen to me, it means he doesn't love me") that contribute to relationship distress (Bradbery & Bodenmann, 2020). The overall goals are to improve relationship quality and decrease emotions such as anger, sadness, and disgust (e.g., Baucom et al., 2019).

As with other cognitive-behavioral interventions, a central premise in CBCT is that cognitions cause emotions and subsequent behaviors. For example, the thought "You don't care about me" may lead to emotions such as anger and sadness that motivate coercive behavior to get more attention. Thus, the assumption is that negative mood (e.g., dissatisfaction) and emotions (e.g., anger, disappointment), mirrored in detrimental relationship-based behaviors (e.g., criticism, defensiveness, contempt, aggression), are a major reason that couples seek help (Bradbury & Bodenmann, 2020). Accordingly, CBCT includes cognitive restructuring in which the psychologist helps partners to identify and challenge partner- and relationship-related cognitions much the same as in individual cognitive therapy as described in Chapter 12, *Cognitive-Behavioral Interventions*.

Communication skills are also emphasized in CBCT in order to allow partners to disclose their needs and emotions without the risk of negative reactions. Instead of blaming their partner, the couple learns to express their thoughts and feelings to one another using techniques such as those described in A CLOSER LOOK: *Emotional Expressiveness Training*. If, for example, Andrew is upset that his partner, Stephen, hasn't helped with household chores in several days, he might approach Stephen and explain that he feels frustrated that duties like making the bed, taking out the trash, and cleaning the bathrooms have all fallen to him recently. Rather than defending himself (even if there is a good reason for his reduced involvement), Stephen would carefully listen to Andrew and let him know that he understands his partner's concerns. Next, Stephen would nondefensively explain his position and Andrew would similarly listen and acknowledge his partner's position. Couples then learn how to

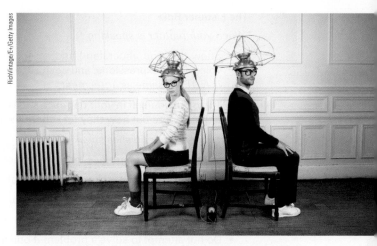

No need to concoct a science experiment with raingear and cookware! In CBCT, partners are taught how to appropriately share their thoughts and feelings so they don't have to read each others' minds.

work together to make decisions and solve problems as a team. Thus, once they understand each other's thoughts and feelings, Andrew and Stephen would learn how to compromise on a solution to their problem. From the point of view of CBCT, confusion over when to share thoughts and feelings versus problem solve contributes to relational distress and therefore such skills are considered a critical piece of treatment (e.g., Baucom et al., 2019).

A Closer Look   Emotional Expressiveness Training

From the point of view of CBCT, communication skills play an important role in relationship satisfaction—and *dissatisfaction*. Thus, CBCT teaches distressed couples effective ways to share difficult thoughts and emotions with, and listen effectively to, one another. One particular skill-building module is called **emotional expressiveness training** (EET), in which partners learn ways to (a) convey how they feel and (b) listen attentively to their partner. The general idea is to avoid putting one's partner on the defensive, and to show you understand what the other person is saying. The psychologist reviews the guidelines below, and then the couple takes turns role playing the "speaker" and "listener" parts until the skills have been acquired.

The Speaker Role

- Talk about your opinions subjectively, as your own feelings and thoughts, not as absolute truths.
- Include your emotions or feelings (e.g., "I feel angry that you spent the money without telling me").
- When you share negative emotions or concerns, try to include positive feelings as well.
- Be as specific as possible, both in terms of emotions and thoughts.
- Speak in "paragraphs" to give your partner a chance to respond to one main idea.
- Use tact and timing so that your partner can listen to what you are saying without becoming defensive.

The Listener Role

When your partner is speaking . . .

- Show that you understand and accept what your partner has to say. Use your tone of voice, facial expressions, and posture to show understanding. *Remember that acceptance is NOT the same as agreement.*
- Try to put yourself in your partner's shoes. Think about the situation from their perspective to help figure out how they feel about the issue.

When your partner finishes speaking . . .

- Summarize your partner's most important feelings, desires, conflicts, and thoughts.
- Do not ask questions, except for clarification.
- Do not express your own viewpoint or opinion.
- Do not change the meaning of your partner's statements.
- Do not attempt to solve a problem if one exists.
- Do not judge what your partner has said. ▬▬

Emotion-Focused Couples Therapy

Emotion-focused couples therapy (EFCT) is a short-term intervention used to improve attachment and bonding among couples. It was developed by psychologists Sue Johnson and Les Greenberg (Greenberg & Goldman, 2019) and is focused on helping couples build new emotional experiences to foster attachment security based on the idea that relationship distress results from an insecure attachment bond where partners signal distress to one another in ways that paradoxically keep their partner at a distance (Greenman et al., 2019). In EFCT, couples express and process their emotions (e.g., feelings of hurt, as well as inadequacy and deprivation of love, respect, and appreciation) to develop more functional interaction patterns that match their specific attachment needs (Johnson, 2019).

There are three stages in EFCT (Greenman et al., 2019).

- The first, **de-escalation**, is focused on recognizing problematic interaction patterns that lead to conflict, identifying negative emotions related to attachment problems, and then helping couples better see how fears and insecurities hinder their relationship. Partners learn to view undesirable behaviors (e.g., shutting down or becoming angry) as "protests of disconnection" and learn to be more emotionally available, empathic, and engaged with each other, strengthening their attachment bond.

- In the second stage, **restructuring**, the partners share their emotions and show acceptance and compassion for each other. This helps the couple become more responsive to each other's needs, reducing conflict and strengthening their emotional bond. Couples learn to express deep, underlying emotions from a place of vulnerability and ask for their needs to be met.

- Finally, the **consolidation** stage involves learning and practicing new communication strategies. This helps couples see how they have been able to change and how new interaction patterns can prevent conflict.

A common technique used in EFCT is **enactment**, in which the therapist guides the couple through conversations about emotion and encourages each partner to engage in a release of that emotion to increase self-awareness (Gladding, 2015). Reminiscent of Gestalt therapy described earlier in this chapter, enactment sessions help partners explore and express deeper emotions and become more aware of each other's feelings, thus increasing empathy.

Multicultural Considerations

As with other forms of psychological treatment, working with couples requires sensitivity in approaching issues of cultural diversity. Like individuals and families, couples enter treatment with culturally influenced beliefs about relationships and help-seeking that may differ from those of the psychologist. What a clinician from one cultural heritage might view as dysfunctional may be a culturally appropriate style of interaction for the couple that is in therapy. Couples from some cultures, for example, have a higher tolerance for arguments than is customary from an American/Western perspective. Similarly, different cultures view seeking help for relationship or marital problems with a greater or lesser degree of discomfort. Couple therapists, therefore, must become aware of their own cultural influences and biases, and how these impact current beliefs, values, and behaviors regarding norms for intimate relationships (e.g., Knudson-Marti et al., 2020; Poulsen, 2020).

When assessing a couple's presenting problem, it is important to understand how each partner views the issue from their unique cultural perspective. This entails asking each partner about their cultural norms and family of origin, and how these impact their roles within the home and within their family or relationship. Other areas of assessment with culturally diverse couples include norms for marriage (if applicable), such as culturally influenced expectations for each partner (e.g., a husband or wife), basis for mate selection, responsibilities of each spouse, beliefs about sex, and expectations for interaction with outsiders (Bhugra & De Silva, 2000). It is important for the therapist to learn about the couple's views of treatment and how the need for outside help is viewed within their culture. Does the couple feel that they must hide the fact that they are in treatment from friends and family members? Do they trust help from an outsider who may not understand the nuances of their heritage, religious background, or sexual orientation? These factors can impact the couple's willingness to engage in and benefit from couple-based interventions.

What one culture views as overly harsh words between couples might fall within the usual limits of communication in a different culture.

Efficacy and Effectiveness

CBCT is the most widely studied couple-based intervention—since the 1980s, several dozen randomized controlled trials (RCTs) have been conducted that support its efficacy and effectiveness (Bradbury & Bodenmann, 2020). These studies tend to use strong methodology, so it is possible to draw strong conclusions from their results. On average, 70% of couples improve immediately after CBCT (Baucom et al., 1998), and 50% maintain their improvement over a period of up to five years (Christensen et al., 2010). The efficacy of EFCT has also been examined in 10 RCTs, yet the methodology is typically not as sound as that used for evaluating CBCT. Nonetheless, studies on EFCT generally support its efficacy and reveal improvements in relationship quality in up to 50% of couples at post-test, with 70% showing improvement at two-year follow-up (e.g., Wiebe et al., 2017).

A number of studies have tried to compare CBCT to EFCT with the aim of evaluating which intervention is most effective. One meta-analysis, for example, included 21 studies on CBCT and 12 on EFCT, with a combined total of 2730 couples (Rathgeber et al., 2019). Results revealed a medium overall effect size at post-test (0.60), with no significant differences at either post-treatment or follow-up. Together, meta-analyses of existing studies support both CBCT and EFCT, with 60% to 72% of couples experiencing reliable pre–post improvements in relationship satisfaction (Bradbury & Bodenmann, 2020).

Finally, research also indicates that the effects of couples therapy extend beyond improvements in relationship satisfaction. Consider, for example, couples in which one partner has a problem such as depression, anxiety, an eating disorder, obsessive-compulsive disorder (OCD), sexual dysfunction, or a problem with their physical health (e.g., migraines or chronic pain). In addition to causing distress for the individual, these clinical problems often get in the way of relationship functioning. CBCT includes teaching partners to practice cognitive and behavioral interventions as a team that can be used not only to reduce clinical problems but also increase relationship functioning for *both* partners. For example, Abramowitz and colleagues (2013) used a CBCT approach in the treatment of couples in which one partner had OCD. The treatment program involved training the couple to practice exposure and response prevention together to help the partner with OCD overcome this problem. In a follow-up study, Belus and colleagues (2014) found that this program increased relationship functioning (as rated by *both* partners) in addition to reducing OCD symptoms.

Think Like a Clinical Psychologist Generally, the aim of couples therapy is to bring partners closer together emotionally and behaviorally. But do you think there are times when separation would be a desired outcome? If so, under what circumstances might this be the case?

▊ Chapter Summary

Over the years, group, family, and couple therapies have become more viable treatment options. Group therapy developed primarily out of the necessity of managing heavy caseloads. However, some clinicians came to view it as a treatment of choice. Unlike its predecessors, contemporary group therapy is typically focused and time limited (meeting for a predetermined number of sessions). These groups are efficient and economical for clinicians, managed behavioral health care organizations, and clients. Unfortunately, from a research perspective, we know relatively little about group therapy other than it is more effective than no treatment, but no more effective than other forms of therapy. Family interventions conceptualize problems in systemic terms, as manifestations of relational problems. As with group therapy, many forms of family therapy exist. They are distinguished by their methods and techniques as well as by their underlying theoretical orientation. There are also numerous types of couples therapy, yet two have consistent research support: CBCT and EFCT. Although these two approaches involve distinct techniques, both generally focus on improving how partners communicate with each other, including sharing their thoughts and emotions. Short- and long-term outcomes of CBCT and EFCT indicate that these interventions can improve relationship functioning with lasting results.

Applying What You've Learned

Exercise 1: Describe how you might develop and implement a cognitive-behavioral group treatment for depressed young adults. What decisions would you need to make about the structure and length of the group? Pick three common factors for group therapy in general and explain how your group would instill or address these.

Exercise 2: How does couples therapy differ from family therapy? Which type of couples therapy would you use to treat a couple that has a partner that tends to overuse alcohol when experiencing stress? How might EFCT and CBCT differ in their approaches to this treatment situation?

Key Terms

Behavioral family therapy: An approach to family therapy that views family relations in terms of reinforcement contingencies. Here, the therapist's role is to generate a behavioral analysis of family problems and induce family members to reinforce each other so as to increase the frequency of desired behaviors. A more cognitively focused therapist might teach individual family members to self-monitor problematic behaviors and patterns of thinking and challenge their interpretations of family events.

Closed group: Usually has starting and ending points, and admits no new members once the group has begun.

Cognitive-behavioral couples therapy: Relies on principles from social learning theories and focuses on partners' cognitions, behaviors, and emotional responses to help them improve how they communicate and solve problems.

Cognitive-behavioral family therapy: Involves teaching family members to self-monitor problematic behaviors and patterns of thinking, to develop new skills (communication, problem resolution, negotiation, conflict management), and to challenge interpretations of family events and reframe these interpretations.

Collaborative family therapy: Family therapy in which each family member sees a different therapist. The

therapists then get together to discuss their clients and the family as a whole.

Concurrent family therapy: A form of family therapy in which one therapist sees all family members in individual sessions. In some cases, the therapist may not only conduct traditional psychotherapy with the principal client but also occasionally see other members of the family.

Conjoint family therapy: A form of family therapy in which one therapist meets with the entire family at the same time.

Consolidation: Stage in emotion-focused couples therapy that involves learning and practicing new communication strategies. This helps couples see how they have been able to change and how new interaction patterns can prevent conflict.

Couples therapy: A form of psychotherapy in which a couple (married, unmarried, or same or other gender) meets with one or more therapists to work on any number of issues.

De-escalation: Stage in emotion-focused couples therapy focused on recognizing problematic interaction patterns that lead to conflict, identifying negative emotions related to attachment problems, and then helping couples better see how fears and insecurities hinder their relationship.

Directive group: Usually time limited (e.g., 12 weekly sessions) and comprised of clients with similar problems; the therapist plays an active—almost didactic—role, providing lessons, skills training, and homework assignments.

Double bind: The case in which individuals are told two contradictory messages by an important figure in their life such that every response they make with regard to that figure is wrong. At one time, double-bind situations were erroneously believed to contribute to the development of schizophrenia.

Emotional expressiveness training: Module of cognitive-behavioral couples therapy in which partners learn ways to (a) convey how they feel and (b) listen attentively to their partner.

Emotion-focused couples therapy: A short-term intervention used to improve attachment and bonding among couples. The interventions of EFT attempt to change partners' problematic interactional styles and emotional responses so that a stronger and more secure emotional bond can be established.

Enactment: A common technique used in emotion-focused couples therapy in which the therapist guides the couple through conversations about emotion and encourages each partner to engage in a release of that emotion to increase self-awareness.

Family system: Interaction patterns among family members.

Family therapy: A form of psychotherapy in which several members of a family, in addition to the identified client, are seen by the therapist. This therapy modality is based on the idea that everyone in a family is affected when one member develops a problem and that the home environment may have contributed to the development of the problem in the first place. Although there are a variety of theoretical family approaches, most share the primary goal of improving communication within the family.

General systems theory: An important concept in family therapy that conceives of the family as a system and believes that "pathology" is best reduced by altering the way that the system functions.

Gestalt group therapy: A group approach in which the therapist focuses on one client at a time and asks that person to experience feelings and behaviors while the other group members are asked to observe or provide feedback to the person in the "hot seat."

Group therapy: A form of psychotherapy in which one or more therapists treat a number of clients at the same time. Generally speaking, most groups consist of five to ten clients who meet with the therapist at least once a week for 90-minute to 2-hour sessions. However, groups may differ greatly in their theoretical orientations, their rules and exclusions, and whether they are viewed as primary or supplemental modes of treatment.

Interpersonal group psychotherapy: A nondirective group therapy for individuals with personality disorders in which group members learn from their interactions within the group and modify their behavior based on feedback they receive from other group members.

Multisystemic therapy: A form of family therapy originally developed to treat juvenile offenders and their families. It is unique in that it is administered in the home, school, or neighborhood and focuses on the family's role in the problems.

Nondirective group: Approach to group therapy that is less structured and classroom-like; instead, it is oriented toward the experience of the individual client. Nondirective interventions tend to be grounded in psychoanalytic, psychodynamic, interpersonal, client-centered, or gestalt principles.

Open groups: Admit new members at any point if someone wants to join or to replace someone who decides to leave the group.

Psychodrama: A form of role playing developed by Moreno in which one client in a group acts out events from the past as if performing in a play.

Restructuring: Stage in emotion-focused couples therapy in which the partners share their emotions and show acceptance and compassion for each other. This helps the couple become more responsive to each other's needs, reducing conflict and strengthening their emotional bond. Couples learn to express deep, underlying emotions from a place of vulnerability and ask for their needs to be met.

CONNECT ONLINE:

 | Check out our videos and additional resources located at: www.macmillanlearning.com

Clinical Psychology and Medical Health

FOCUS QUESTIONS

1. What are the major psychosocial factors that influence medical health and illness?
2. What are the primary intervention methods used by health psychologists?
3. How are prevention techniques used to address behavioral factors in medical illness?
4. What kinds of services can clinical psychologists provide to medical patients?
5. What professional, ethical, and multicultural considerations are unique to health and pediatric psychologists?

CHAPTER OUTLINE

S o far, we have focused on clinical psychology's role in understanding and intervening in the realm of *mental health*. But what about *physical health*? Is there a place for clinical psychology in the medical field? Certainly, our emotions and behaviors affect our physical health — many chronic diseases (e.g., heart disease, cancer, and stroke) are associated with emotional (e.g., chronic stress) and behavioral (e.g., smoking, overeating) factors (Sanderson, 2018). Accordingly, clinical psychology has a great deal to contribute to the field of medical health, and *health psychology* (also known as *behavioral medicine*) has become a fast-growing area of practice and research. Many clinical psychology doctoral programs provide training in health psychology, as well as in *pediatric psychology* (also known as *child health psychology*). Several scientific journals (e.g., *Health Psychology*, *Journal of Behavioral Medicine*, and *Journal of Pediatric Psychology*) also publish research in these fields. In this chapter, we will explore the interface between clinical psychology and medical health through the lenses of health psychology and pediatric psychology.

▥ The Mind–Body Link

The link between mind and body has been recognized since at least early Greek civilization, yet as described in IN HISTORICAL PERSPECTIVE: *The Evolution of Health Psychology*, it was not until the late 1970s that the field of **health psychology** began to crystallize. Encompassing the integration of psychological and behavioral sciences with the practice of medicine, health psychology is defined as "the contributions of psychology to the promotion and maintenance of health, the prevention and treatment of illness, and the identification of etiologic and diagnostic correlates of health, illness and related dysfunction" (Matarazzo, 1980, p. 815).

The COVID-19 pandemic provides a dramatic example of the mind–body connection. Stress and worry associated with COVID have negatively affected many people's mental health and created new barriers for those already suffering from psychological problems. For example, during the pandemic, about 4 in 10 adults in the United States have reported symptoms of an anxiety or depressive disorder, which is up from 1 in 10 adults in June 2019 (Kaiser Family Foundation, 2021). In addition, many adults report greater problems with sleeping (36%) and eating (32%), and increases in alcohol consumption and substance use (12%). As we will see in this section, it is not at all surprising that these psychological and behavioral effects, which are the direct result of worry and stress over the coronavirus, are also associated with exacerbations of chronic medical conditions. Since behavior, lifestyle, and social factors are all linked to health and illness, we begin by focusing on the role of these psychosocial factors on medical conditions.

Stress

We all know **stress** when it shows up in our lives, but *what is stress*? Health psychologists view it as a process that involves interactions between people and their environment. Specifically, the components of stress include (a) an event (the **stressor**); (b) its appraisal by the individual (is it challenging or threatening?) and (c) the person's physiological, emotional, cognitive, and behavioral responses (Ben-Zur et al., 2019). This **transactional model of stress** is depicted

The Evolution of Health Psychology

One way to understand health and illness is from the **biomedical perspective** of Hippocrates. This Western point of view focuses exclusively on biological factors (i.e., anatomy and physiology) and has led to advances such as germ theory and the study of genetics to help us understand illness and disease. Yet for centuries, the medical field has also recognized that psychological and social processes likewise play a role in illness and disease. By the 1940s, this **psychosocial perspective** had coalesced into the field of **psychosomatic medicine**, which assumed that certain physical conditions — for example, stomach ulcers, high blood pressure, and bronchial asthma — were caused in part by psychological factors (e.g., Alexander, 1950). Some adopted a psychodynamic view that these psychosomatic illnesses were influenced by unconscious conflicts. Yet these ideas were not supported by empirical research.

In parallel with the behavioral movement of the mid-20th century, behavioral psychologists focused on medical conditions such as obesity and headaches and targeted behaviors whose reduction or elimination might reduce individuals' vulnerability to these problems. By the 1960s, attention turned to cardiovascular diseases, respiratory diseases, and cancer — the three top causes of death worldwide. Behaviors such as overeating, smoking, and drinking were identified as important correlates of these diseases (e.g., Inoue-Choi et al., 2017).

Research also indicated that daily hassles, stressful life events, and certain personality styles were risk factors for illness (e.g., Holmes & Rahe, 1967; Lazarus, 1984). For example, a set of traits and behaviors — the so-called **Type A personality pattern** — appeared to be shared by many people with coronary heart disease (CHD; Friedman & Rosenman, 1974). This pattern is characterized by being extremely hardworking, driven to succeed, competitive, and easily irritated (to the point of hostility) when confronted with barriers to success. Although research ultimately failed to support a direct link between Type A personality and heart disease (Sanderson, 2018), this hypothesis stimulated much research and focused attention on other behavioral risk factors for CHD (e.g., smoking and lack of exercise) as well as on prevention efforts.

In the 1970s, recognition that biological (e.g., genetic predisposition, nutritional deficiencies), psychosocial (e.g., cognition, emotion), and social (e.g., social support, stressful events) factors influence illness and health gave rise to the **biopsychosocial model** (Engel, 1977). This model represents how health psychologists conceptualize problems and plan interventions today. Behavioral medicine was formally recognized as a field in 1977; and in 1979, the Society of Behavioral Medicine (SBM) was established as an organization for researchers and practitioners to share ideas and research findings. Today, the SBM holds an annual professional conference and publishes a scientific journal called the *Annals of Behavioral Medicine* to help disseminate research findings. The range of topics addressed by health psychologists is very wide and includes aging, anxiety, cardiovascular disease, chronic pain, depression, diabetes, eating disorders, environmental health, headaches, HIV/AIDS, insomnia, quality of life, sexually transmitted diseases, social support, and substance abuse. In addition, there is growing recognition in the field of health and pediatric psychology that psychological factors are not only relevant for physical disease onset but also may be related to the maintenance of health promotion behaviors, medical management, and recovery. ■

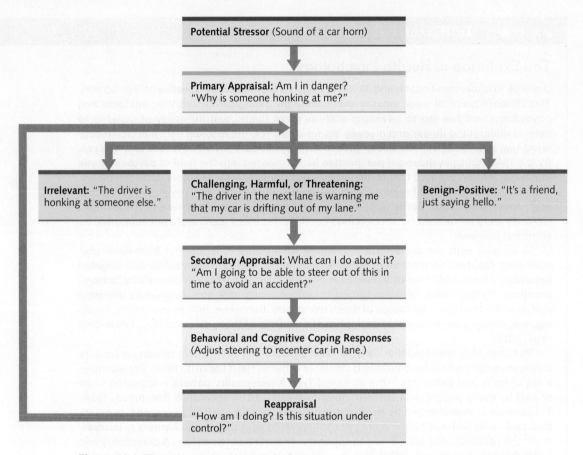

Figure 16.1 The transactional model of stress.

From Health Psychology 6e by Richard Straub. Copyright 2019 by Worth Publishers. All rights reserved. Used by permission of the publisher Macmillan Learning.

in **Figure 16.1**. Stress is important because it affects the hormonal, autonomic, and immune systems, which control the body's ability to stay healthy when it encounters inevitable injury and infection. Let's explore this in more detail.

The physiological effect of stress on the body involves a complex chain of events (Slavich, 2020). Specifically, stress causes the **sympathetic nervous system**, which is responsible for mobilizing body resources in urgent situations, to stimulate the production and release of epinephrine (adrenaline), norepinephrine, and cortisol into the bloodstream. These chemicals automatically increase heart rate, respiration, blood flow, and muscle strength to increase energy levels. Although this response is adaptive for survival—indeed it is life-saving in urgent situations—prolonged activation of these systems can have adverse effects on body organs, mental functions, and the immune system.

For example, just as with physical illness or injury, sustained periods of stress can overtax the immune system. When the immune system is activated, it stimulates the production of **cytokines**, which regulate the body's inflammatory response to help fight disease or injury.

But chronic stress over long periods of time causes an overproduction of cytokines, which leads to chronic inflammation and increases the risk of autoimmune diseases, diabetes, heart disease, osteoporosis, and allergies (Slavich, 2020). **Psychoneuroimmunology** (PNI) is the field of study that examines how stress interacts with these body systems and shapes human behavior. Using a variety of research methods with both humans and animals, PNI has helped clarify how stress and the immune system affect cognition, emotion, brain functioning, and behavior, and how these increase the risk of a variety of mental and physical health problems, including anxiety; depression; posttraumatic stress disorder (PTSD); cardiovascular disease; chronic pain; certain cancers; and neurodegenerative diseases such as multiple sclerosis, Alzheimer's disease, and Parkinson's disease.

Have you ever become sick when under lots of stress? A survey conducted by the American Psychological Association (2018) examined factors that cause stress among people in "generation Z" (those born from 1997 onward). Events such as rising rates of sexual harassment and assault, gun violence, and political debates about topics such as immigration were reported as significantly more stressful among this group relative to older adults. Among Black and Hispanic adults, 46% and 36%, respectively, reported that experiencing discrimination was an important source of stress. Indeed, **race-related stress** (RRS) refers to "race-related transactions between individuals or groups and their environment that emerge from the dynamics of racism, and that are perceived to tax or exceed existing individual and collective resources or threaten well-being" (Harrell, 2000, p. 44). RRS can take the following forms:

- Racism-related life events (personal experiences with discrimination)
- Vicarious racism (observing or hearing about others' experiences)
- Daily racism microstressors (subtle slights and exclusions)
- Chronic-contextual stress (social systemic and institutional racism)
- Collective experiences (cultural-symbolic and sociopolitical manifestations of racism)

Research in PNI shows that RRS affects health outcomes over time and plays a role in the overall poorer health of Black Americans as compared to other ethnic groups (e.g., Arriola et al., 2021; Hudson, 2019; Thorpe et al., 2019). It increases the frequency of stress, intensifies the experience of other stressors, and exaggerates the lack of sufficient resources to manage such stressors. In one study (Arriola et al., 2021), for example, Black individuals with varying levels of chronic kidney disease (CKD) were randomly assigned to recall either a general or race-related stressful experience. Before, during, and after the recall, participants' blood pressure and inflammatory response were monitored. Results indicated that recalling an RRS event was associated with greater autonomic arousal and inflammatory response, highlighting the uniqueness of this type of stressor and its association with disease-promoting physiological factors among Black individuals. A CLOSER LOOK: *COVID-19's Disproportional Impact on Black Americans* provides a vivid example of the effects of RRS on physical health.

A Closer Look   COVID-19's Disproportional Impact on Black Americans

It's a fact: Black Americans have been disproportionately affected by the COVID-19 pandemic. Psychologist Enrique Neblett and his team at the University of Michigan have been studying how and why this has happened (e.g., Yu et al., 2021) and how society can work to end this disparity.

We've been aware, since early in the pandemic, that Black Americans had unexpectedly high rates of infection, hospitalization, and death relative to their percentage of the population. Take Milwaukee and Chicago as examples: Black Americans in these cities are about a third of the population, but represented over 70% of the earliest COVID-related deaths. Similarly, in Georgia, Black Americans make up only a third of the population but represented 80% of hospitalizations at the beginning of the pandemic. One nationwide survey even indicated that Black Americans are nearly three times as likely to personally know someone who has died from the virus than white Americans do (Stafford & Fingerhut, 2020).

But why? Dr. Neblett's work suggests there's a complex set of factors, not the least of which is systemic racism and the increased stress it places on Black Americans relative to other groups. For example, there are inequities in access to critical resources necessary to maintain good health that leave Black Americans more likely to have higher rates of illnesses, including COVID-19, relative to whites. Availability and access to COVID-19 testing is another important factor. In many Black communities, testing is limited or unavailable, or there are delays in processing test results — both of which interfere with getting urgent and needed medical care.

Another factor is occupational vulnerability. Black Americans are more likely than whites to hold jobs that are essential to the function of critical infrastructure. These are jobs that require continuous in-person interaction with the public (increasing the risk of exposure to the virus) and, in some cases, don't offer benefits such as paid vacation or the option to work from home.

Poverty is another determinant of health, influenced by structural racism, that has played a role in COVID-19 disparities. Lack of access to medical care to seek treatment, quality health insurance, healthy food, standard housing, and clean water are all factors that can indirectly contribute to heightened vulnerability to exposure and infection and lead to more harmful COVID-19 outcomes.

Psychologist Enrique Neblett

Photo by Austin Thomason, Michigan Photography, University of Michigan

How are clinical psychologists working to end these disparities? Dr. Neblett and his team are developing and studying several strategies that can be mobilized to work against systemic racism and, in turn, the impact of COVID-19 on Black Americans. For one thing, reading and self-educating about systemic racism and how it operates are important. When we raise awareness and seek concrete actions for eradicating racism, it catches the eye of lawmakers who can create legislation to level the playing field. Community groups and organizations also possess valuable knowledge and expertise, represent critical assets, and are well positioned to write letters and make calls to lawmakers. Other strategies include helping Black communities build their infrastructure to be able to respond better to disasters like COVID-19. You can read more about Dr. Neblett's work as part of the Detroit, Michigan, Urban Research Center at https://detroiturc.org/. ▄▄

Behavior and Cognition

Cognitive-behavioral factors also affect health and disease. You are no doubt aware of the negative effects of behaviors such as smoking and vaping, excessive alcohol and drug use, poor eating habits, a sedentary lifestyle, and deficient hygiene. Cognitive variables influence our decisions to engage in healthy or unhealthy behaviors (Bandura, 2001). **Protection motivation theory** (PMT; Maddux et al., 1995), for example, posits that behavior is a function of **threat appraisal**, an evaluation of the perceived risks, and **coping appraisal**, an evaluation of one's ability to avoid or cope with negative outcomes. Coping appraisal is further influenced by **self-efficacy**, which is one's confidence in their ability to control their own behavior and the social environment.

As an example, consider Janey, an adolescent girl facing a decision about whether to start smoking marijuana because her friends are doing it. Janey's *threat appraisal* might involve evaluating the potential health and legal risks. To the extent that she perceives these as severe or immediate, or not, she'll be less or more likely to partake. Janey's *coping appraisal* might involve an evaluation of the social consequences of abstaining, for example, how well she could handle being mocked by her peers for abstaining. Thus, *self-efficacy* can play a prominent role in behavior and lifestyle choices that ultimately influence health.

Cognitive factors, including appraisals of threat and coping ability, contribute to the decision to engage in risky behavior patterns such as smoking.

Psychologist Hope Landrine conducted numerous studies to understand why Black Americans engage in smoking behavior at significantly higher rates than white Americans (e.g., Landrine & Corral, 2016). Her work revealed that smoking is particularly more prevalent among Black American adults who live in poverty, have low acculturation (i.e., are immersed in Black American culture), and report frequent experiences with racial discrimination. This is likely due to the stress of discrimination and its negative effects on self-efficacy, with smoking often used as a strategy for coping with such stress.

Personality

Perhaps the most widely studied association between a personality trait and illness is the relation between the Type A personality pattern and CHD. Although research has ultimately failed to support a direct link between

Psychologist Hope Landrine

Type A personality and heart disease (Sanderson, 2018), as mentioned in the history box on page 361, it appears that the anger-hostility component is the most important risk factor for CHD (e.g., Smith & MacKenzie, 2006). Research has focused on the relationship between anger-hostility and stress. One explanation posits that hostile individuals experience larger increases in heart rate, blood pressure, and stress-related hormones in response to stressors, which promote the development of CHD (Smith, 1992). Another explanation proposes that hostile individuals experience a more stressful psychosocial environment because they are mistrusting and suspicious (e.g., Smith, 1992). The transactional model of stress described earlier proposes that people high in hostility create more stress in their lives through their mistrust of others and hostile behavior, which provokes hostile behavior from others in return. Finally, there is a relationship between Type A personality and behavior. Hostile individuals are more susceptible to CHD because they tend to engage in poor health habits (e.g., smoking, excessive alcohol use, poor exercise habits).

Social Support

Social support refers to the quantity and quality of relationships one has with others (e.g., can you confide in your friends, parents, and family members?), and health psychologists have been interested in the role it plays as a "buffer" against adverse health outcomes (Cohen & McKay, 2020). The idea is that the tangible and emotional support associated with interpersonal ties protects against illness and disease by (a) shielding people from the prolonged effects of stress (and therefore also from cortisol) and (b) increasing the probability that they will engage in healthy behavior patterns. Williams and colleagues (1992), for example, followed approximately 1400 people with CHD for about 9 years and found that those who reported greater social support showed lower rates of mortality during this period. This relation held even after controlling for demographic variables and medical risk factors.

More recent research, however, suggests that receiving social support can involve both benefits and risks (Zee et al., 2020). For example, "helpers" may give "too much" advice or

become upset when their advice is not followed, leading the recipient to feel worse (Lee et al., 2020). Research also shows that the buffering effect of social support differs by gender, culture, and race. In a 25-year longitudinal study that followed 3361 adults (Assari, 2017), more social contacts predicted longer life expectancy in the overall sample; yet, the protective effect of social support was smaller for Blacks than for whites. In another study, women (on average) benefitted more from social support than did men, perhaps because women tend to have more emotionally intimate relationships (Brannon et al., 2018). In some groups, social relations may be more strongly associated with conflicts for men than for women, and some social gatherings may involve unhealthy behaviors (e.g., drug or alcohol use), particularly for men (e.g., Henderson, 2015).

Social and emotional support can reduce the negative effects of stress on health, yet research shows that the protective effects of such support are smaller for Black individuals than for those who are white.

Think Like a Clinical Psychologist What are your own sources of stress? How do you think they compare to those of others your own age (consider your cultural context)? Do sources of stress change over time? How might your sources of stress differ from those of your parents or grandparents?

Intervention Methods

Medical interventions typically consist of drug therapy, surgery, or the use of a device (e.g., pacemaker or artificial joint). In prescribing or applying these treatments, however, physicians often pay little attention to variations in the psychosocial factors discussed in the previous section. Interventions in health psychology are designed to use what we know about human behavior to affect the actions that individuals take regarding their health. Health behavior encompasses many facets, and so health psychology interventions are similarly broad. A CLOSER LOOK: *Health Psychology and Cardiovascular Disease* illustrates how health psychologists apply psychological theory and interventions to this particular medical condition. We then describe some of the more widely employed intervention strategies used by health and pediatric psychologists. These interventions generally derive from the behavioral, cognitive-behavioral, and mindfulness/acceptance approaches described in earlier chapters.

A Closer Look   Health Psychology and Cardiovascular Disease

The process of cardiovascular disease begins with **risk factors** — characteristics of individuals that increase the likelihood of a serious illness. Whereas some risk factors are beyond one's control, such as a family history of heart disease, others, such as high cholesterol, smoking, and obesity, are (at least partly) under behavioral control. People with these risk factors are more likely than those at lower risk to suffer medical emergencies such as heart attacks and strokes. There are a range of effective therapies that can be used in the aftermath of such emergencies, including medications, balloon angioplasty, and coronary artery bypass surgery. Similarly, clinical trials have examined which medications are most effective in managing hypertension, high cholesterol, and diabetes.

Health psychology, however, targets *behavioral* risk factors to reduce the risk of medical emergencies, such as helping people stop smoking, lowering consumption of fatty foods, exercising regularly, and visiting physicians for regular check-ups. The idea is to preemptively change peoples' behavior, rather than waiting to intervene until after an emergency.

An important aspect of health psychology is recognizing how multicultural factors impact the risks for poor health outcomes. **Health disparities** refer to differences in the rates of illnesses among different groups and communities. For example, although the overall rate of death from cardiovascular disease has declined among adults in the United States by more than 50% since 1950, studies still show higher death rates among Black as compared with white adults (Tajeu et al., 2020). Reasons for health disparities include poorer access to high-quality care, fewer (or lower-quality) resources for mitigating behavioral risk factors (e.g., lack of access to fitness centers or healthy food), longer wait times for treatment, and stress due to discrimination and racism. Health psychologists therefore never assume that everyone has equal access to resources, and they collect information from clients to understand factors that might influence prevention or treatment.

Finally, health psychology interventions can be implemented at three levels. *Individual interventions* help people at high risk for a particular disease make changes to their behavior, such as quitting smoking, adhering to medication instructions, eating healthier and exercising more, and attending medical check-ups. *Community interventions* are designed to modify the environment to support healthy behaviors, such as free screening for high blood pressure at the local mall. *National interventions*, such as changes in public policy, have also been used to affect health-related behaviors. For example, when the government taxes cigarettes and restricts where smoking is allowed, cigarette use drops. In at least some cases, national interventions have a long-term record of success. Most notably, the campaign launched by the U.S. government in 1964 to warn people about tobacco has played a significant role in the reduction in smoking over the past half century. Similarly, information campaigns about the danger of high cholesterol have led to sustained reductions in consumption of red meat, eggs, and high-fat dairy products. ▬▬

Biofeedback and Relaxation

Under certain conditions, people can learn to bring physiological processes, such as heart rate, blood pressure, and perhaps even brain waves, under conscious control. **Biofeedback** refers to procedures in which some aspect of physiological functioning (e.g., heart rate, blood pressure, skin temperature) is monitored by an apparatus that allows the person to observe the physiological response in real time (e.g., in the form of an auditory or visual signal) and modify that signal by changing the physiological function. Thus, a client experiencing severe chronic headaches might have electrodes placed on their forehead that pick up tiny muscle contractions in that region of the head and transform them into colors on a screen; for example, red means tense muscles, blue means relaxed muscles. The colors change on a continuum (e.g., shades of red, purple, and blue) as the muscular activity changes, and the client's task is to make the screen appear blue, thus signaling a reduction in muscle tension and a corresponding reduction in the headache. With repeated practice, clients can learn how to consciously regulate (at least to some degree) the physiological process.

Health psychologists have developed and are testing methods of providing biofeedback remotely via telehealth (e.g., Chung et al., 2021). Such methods provide real-time video and audio interactivity and allow the clinician to monitor and control biofeedback equipment located at a remote site. This has improved access to biofeedback during the COVID-19 pandemic and is especially useful for individuals located in rural areas at considerable distance from their providers.

Research demonstrates the efficacy of biofeedback (in comparison to placebo treatment) for several different problems (Brannon et al., 2018). For example, it has been used successfully in the reduction of both migraine and tension headaches, hypertension, and low back pain. That said, the effects of biofeedback are not necessarily superior to those of progressive muscle relaxation (PMR; as we described in Chapter 11, *Behavioral Interventions*), which is also widely used by health psychologists. This is important because biofeedback requires expensive equipment and trained personnel. Thus, it is more costly than PMR. And because biofeedback and relaxation are often included in the same treatment package, it is sometimes hard to separate the effects of one from the other. However, in studies that have done so, biofeedback does indeed provide unique positive effects, especially for those who do not respond to PMR (Lehrer et al., 1994).

Still, there remain many critics of biofeedback. Some of the skepticism is a response to the impassioned claims of biofeedback's effectiveness based in large part on anecdotal evidence (Frank et al., 2010). Another reason for concern is that some studies suggest biofeedback operates largely as a placebo (Hunyor et al., 1997). When effective, it tends to be part of a multicomponent treatment package that also includes PMR or cognitive-behavioral strategies; if removed from such a package, it loses its effectiveness. That said, biofeedback may be a useful technique for (a) teaching people to become more aware of their bodily signals and (b) reinforcing the (important) view that self-regulation in life is possible.

Stevica Mrdja/EyeEm/Alamy

Biofeedback allows clients to observe their own physiological processes, such as muscle tension and blood pressure, and learn how to bring them under conscious control.

Behavioral Techniques

Health psychologists use the principles of operant conditioning to increase healthy behaviors and decrease those that contribute to health problems. The treatment of pain provides an excellent example. **Chronic pain** is pain that persists longer than 3 months in the absence of identifiable tissue damage (or beyond the expected time of healing). It interferes with a person's ability to work, engage in daily activities, enjoy recreation, and function in interpersonal relationships; it is also associated with depression, anxiety, irritability, and trouble with attention and concentration (e.g., Tankha et al., 2020). Some responses to chronic pain, such as searching for cures on the Internet, complaining, and inactivity (e.g., remaining in bed, using a wheelchair), actually *worsen* the subjective experience of pain and keep the person from learning to better manage their pain (e.g., Demerouti & Cropanzano, 2017). But such unhealthy and maladaptive behaviors may be positively reinforced by the sympathy, time off from work, and reduced expectations that they often engender. To help the person become more adaptive to pain, pain management programs typically include helping family members and medical staff to (a) reinforce healthy coping behaviors such as physical activity and (b) ignore maladaptive behaviors such as talking (or complaining) about the pain (Murphy et al., 2014).

Contingency management, as described in Chapter 11, may also be used wherein the psychologist and client draw up a contract that specifies healthy and unhealthy behaviors, as well as the consequences for engaging in each. Positive reinforcement, for example, might be given for participating in physical therapy and exercise, reducing the number of pain-related complaints, and engaging in pleasant "coping" activities (e.g., going for a drive, engaging in a hobby). Reinforcement may take the form of tokens that can be exchanged for something of value to the client.

Cognitive-Behavioral Methods

Health psychologists also use a variety of cognitive-behavioral techniques, which may be implemented alone or in concert with other strategies such as PMR. As you might imagine from reading Chapter 12, *Cognitive-Behavioral Interventions*, these methods emphasize the role of thinking in the development and maintenance of health-related problems and aim to modify maladaptive and dysfunctional cognitions and perceptions. To illustrate, we'll return to the example of chronic pain, since cognitive-behavioral techniques play a prominent role in its treatment as well (Murphy et al., 2014). Treatment begins with a psychoeducational component in which the client learns about the relationship between thoughts, pain, mood, and behaviors. Specifically, as pain gets worse, thoughts become more negative, and negative thoughts increase pain. Negative thoughts also lead to avoiding activities and people, which makes it more difficult to use healthy methods for coping with pain (e.g., engaging in pleasant activities). The chain reaction of negative thinking, feeling upset, avoiding others, and not using active coping skills is the cycle that treatment aims to break. Clients are then taught to self-monitor their thinking processes (using a form such as that shown in **Figure 16.2**) whenever pain occurs.

The clinician then uses the self-monitoring data to tailor specific interventions. First, attempts are made to connect situations, thoughts, and the emotional and behavioral responses. The psychologist emphasizes that thoughts are a crucial link in the process that maintains chronic pain and that these thought patterns can be modified. The client's

Figure 16.2 Example of a Self-Monitoring Record for Chronic Pain

Time	Situation	Thoughts	Feeling (0–100)	Behavior
8:00 a.m. Friday	Plain flares up when I try to get out of bed	I'm going to have a terrible day.	Anxiety (75) Depressed (50)	Complain to my partner. Stay in bed until 10:00.
3:30 p.m. Friday	Standing up from my desk and my lower back hurts	This pain is killing me. I can't take it anymore.	Anxiety (50) Frustration (80)	Look up information about pain on the Internet.
11:30 a.m. Saturday	Cleaning the garage and the pain flares up	This is terrible. I can't do anything.	Anxiety (80) Frustration (70)	Go rest on the couch instead. Talk to my partner about how bad I'm feeling.
2:00 p.m. Saturday	Helping my son with a school project and I notice the pain in my stomach and back	I'm useless.	Anger (90) Anxiety (60)	Have to go lie down for a while.
1:30 a.m. Saturday	Can't find a comfortable position to sleep; it hurts to move around in bed	I'll never get a good night's sleep again. This nightmare is never going to end.	Depression (80) Anger (80)	Crying. Walk around the house. Stay on the couch where it's more comfortable.

maladaptive thoughts and beliefs associated with pain are examined closely and their validity challenged using methods similar to Ellis's rational emotive therapy and Beck's cognitive therapy as described in Chapter 12. For example, thoughts such as "I can't do *anything*" and "This pain will *never* go away" keep the person focused on their pain and lead to anxiety and frustration, all of which intensify the feelings of discomfort. A therapist might challenge these thoughts ("Is it really true that you can't do *anything*?") and train the client to disrupt the situation → thought → pain process by using alternative thinking strategies (such as asking oneself, "How would someone I admire cope with this?" or "How can I set an example for my kids about coping with life's challenges?").

Acceptance

Interventions from acceptance and commitment therapy (ACT) (as discussed in Chapter 13, *Acceptance and Dialectical Interventions*) can also be effectively applied in the context of health psychology (e.g., Li et al., 2021; Zhang et al., 2018). For example, someone experiencing anxiety that leads to chronic muscle tension, headaches, and other sorts of pain could work toward acknowledging the thoughts and feelings of anxiety with a sense of curiosity and allow themselves to experience these emotions and sensations where and when they occur. Defusion techniques can be used to help change clients' relationship to thoughts such as "I can't stand this pain" and "These headaches will never go away," so that they are not viewed as literal truths, and instead accepted as unwanted but normal private experiences. Clients can also be helped to use values-based and mindfulness exercises to foster contact with the present moment so that they can be present in their lives even though they might be faced with health-related concerns. Finally, committed action interventions can help clients set behavioral goals toward valued health-related activities, such as reducing the number of cigarettes or alcoholic beverages they consume per day, or following through on physical therapy exercises.

Think Like a Clinical Psychologist What are the similarities and differences between psychological interventions used in the context of physical health and those used in the context of mental health?

▥ Prevention Strategies

Nearly everyone agrees that a few simple behaviors — stopping smoking, increasing exercise, healthy eating — if widely practiced, would dramatically reduce the risk of illness. But simply giving people advice is very different from helping them make lasting behavioral change. Health psychologists, often in collaboration with medical professionals, have developed programs to help with the latter. In this section, we discuss these efforts as they relate to cigarette smoking, alcohol abuse, and weight control.

Reducing Cigarette Smoking

Cigarette smoking is linked to an increased risk of cardiovascular disease and cancer, the two leading causes of death in the United States. Still, people continue to smoke. Why? Research shows that the reasons include short-term stress relief, social pressure, rebelliousness, and the addictive nature of nicotine (Sanderson, 2018). A variety of techniques have been used to help people stop smoking, including educational programs, aversion therapy (e.g., rapid smoking), behavioral contracts, acupuncture, pharmacological interventions, cognitive-behavioral treatment, and group support (Sanderson, 2018). Relapse rates are high (70% to 80%), however, and research findings on which smoking cessation approach is best are conflicting. The fact is that most smokers who quit do so on their own.

Therefore, the best approach seems to be preventing the habit from starting in the first place. Unfortunately, education alone (e.g., warning messages on packages) does not appear to deter young people from smoking (Sanderson, 2018). What seems more effective is focusing on immediate rather than delayed negative consequences, providing information on social/peer influences, teaching skills for how to refuse in the face of peer pressure, and increasing feelings of self-efficacy (Cocchiara et al., 2020). The first effective smoking prevention program for children and teenagers was based on social learning principles and used peer role models (Evans, 1976). It included videotaped presentations, discussion groups, role-playing, and self-monitoring of smoking. This program was superior to those previously used that focused on the long-term negative effects of smoking, suggesting that emphasizing immediate negative consequences (e.g., from peers) rather than delayed ones (e.g., cancer) makes a difference. The smoking prevention programs in use today remain very similar to these early intervention approaches (e.g., Cocchiara et al., 2020).

Decreasing Problem Drinking

Over 70% of adolescents have tried alcohol by the time they graduate high school, and about half of adults in the United States consume alcoholic beverages regularly (Pleis et al., 2010). The highest rates of alcohol use are among adults with a bachelor's degree or higher (64%), those with a family income of $100,000 or more (67%), and white males (66%). Although light to moderate alcohol use does not pose general health risks for most people, excessive drinking increases the risk of numerous serious outcomes, including liver damage, neurological impairment, certain forms of cancer, cardiovascular problems, fetal alcohol syndrome, physical aggression, suicide, motor vehicle accidents, and violence (Brannon et al., 2018). This extensive list makes the treatment of problem drinking a high-priority preventative measure.

There are many approaches to the treatment of problem drinking, most of which view excessive alcohol use as a disease (e.g., alcoholism, addiction) and preach *abstinence*—which means quitting drinking entirely—as the only solution. Interventions from this perspective include medications such as disulfiram (Antabuse) and naltrexone, traditional psychotherapy, and group treatments such as Alcoholics Anonymous. However, problem drinking is difficult to treat. Only 36% of people maintain abstinence at post-treatment, and even fewer at follow-up (e.g., Frimpong et al., 2016).

For many people, making the commitment to change is an important obstacle. The idea of giving up drinking can seem so intimidating that it reduces the drive to get help despite the health risks, financial costs, and social and/or legal consequences of excessive alcohol use. Denial that one even needs help can also keep clients from initiating treatment. **Motivational interviewing** (MI; Frey et al., 2021; Miller & Rollnick, 2012) is a technique for strengthening one's commitment to a particular goal that they are hesitant to pursue, such as reducing alcohol use. Rather than being confronted about the need to make changes, MI is a collaborative approach in which the psychologist and client explore problems and solutions, and the client is given autonomy in making decisions. It begins with developing a trusting and respectful relationship, after which the client is helped to identify their own problems, as well as their own reasons for both making and not making changes. The heart of MI involves promoting and reinforcing **change talk**, which is the client's own arguments for wanting things to be different (and better). Here, the psychologist must recognize even subtle instances where the client brings up their desire to change and bring attention to this internal motivation without pushing too hard. Change talk fosters confidence and empowerment and promotes the client's internal voices of motivation (Miller & Rollnick, 2012). Once the client has resolved their ambivalence in the direction of wanting to decrease their alcohol use, treatment can begin; although it is often necessary to revisit MI throughout the process of reducing problem drinking.

In the 1970s, Linda and Mark Sobell developed a behavioral treatment for alcohol use problems called **controlled drinking** (Sobell & Sobell, 1978; von Greiff & Skogens, 2020). As the name implies, the goal of this intervention is light to moderate (and disciplined) drinking (as opposed to complete abstinence). Treatment incorporates the various components listed in **Table 16.1** and is tailored to individual clients based on factors such as their goals, baseline level of alcohol use, and high-risk situations for problem drinking (Sobell & Sobell, 1978). Clients are helped to self-monitor their alcohol intake, recognize high-risk situations, and implement skills to effectively navigate them without having to resort to drinking. Treatment can range from 6 to 12 sessions (or more).

The field is divided as to the merits of abstinence versus controlled drinking, but research does suggest that controlled drinking is a viable treatment option for *some* people with alcohol

Table 16.1   Components of Controlled Drinking Treatment
Self-monitoring of alcohol use
Set goals for how many days per week, and how much, alcohol can be consumed
Implement slow, or paced, drinking when deciding to drink
Eat before or while drinking
Avoid high-risk situations when possible
Have a plan in place to deal with urges or high-risk situations that can't be avoided
Learn and use coping strategies other than alcohol
Learn, and feel comfortable with, skills for refusing alcohol

use disorders (von Greiff & Skogens, 2021). Many alcohol treatment programs also incorporate **relapse prevention** training (Marlatt & Gordon, 1985) since most clients treated for alcohol problems have a relapse episode soon after treatment is terminated. Rather than view this as a failure, clients are taught coping skills and behaviors they can use in high-risk situations to make total relapse less likely (Senn et al., 2020).

Addressing Obesity

Not only is obesity a risk factor for diseases such as diabetes, hypertension, cardiovascular disease, and certain cancers, but weight bias stigmatizes individuals and can increase depression and inhibit functioning in various life domains. Over 60% of adults in the United States are overweight (and between 25% and 30% meet criteria for obesity — a body mass index of 30 or greater; Pleis et al., 2010). Although obesity has a genetic component

SPECIAL FOR KITCHENER-WATERLOO RECORD ATT'N CLIFFORD CUNNINGHAM TORONTO OUT (CPT18-Mar. 4)—These recent, undated file photos show researchers Mark and transmitted in response to a member request. (CP LASERPHOTO) 1983 (

Mark Sobell (left) and Linda Sobell (right) pioneered the behavioral treatment of problem drinking in the 1970s and 1980s.

(Bouchard, 2020), its causes involve complex interactions among biological, social, and behavioral factors, and the exact mechanisms are difficult to pin down. That said, the rising rate of obesity appears to be more a function of changes in our eating habits and activity levels than in our gene pool (De Lorenzo et al., 2020; Wadden et al., 2002). Traditional medical and dietary treatments have not been very effective; individuals may lose weight but then quickly regain it. Furthermore, the dropout rate is high in traditional weight-control programs. Pharmacologic and surgical treatments for obesity are on the increase (Wadden et al., 2002), although surgeries are expensive and people using medications experience only modest long-term weight loss of between 3% and 7% on average (Tak & Lee, 2021). Behavioral and cognitive-behavioral treatments (e.g., Brownell, 2004), which can be offered in person or via telehealth, have somewhat better long-term success because they incorporate the following:

- Setting realistic (as opposed to impractical or uncontrollable) behavioral goals
- A focus on making gradual changes so that new behavior patterns can be maintained in the long term

- Attention to environmental and social factors that influence food choices and intake
- Self-monitoring
- Flexibility rather than rigidity

Again, however, early prevention appears to be the best (and healthiest) road to weight control. A classic example is the Stanford Adolescent Obesity Project (Coates & Thoresen, 1981), which included self-monitoring, elimination of eating cues, and family support. A 10-year outcome study found that early intervention in childhood had lasting changes in weight control (Epstein et al., 1994). Meta-analyses of school-based obesity prevention programs suggest that the following components are most beneficial: (a) modifying the home environment to limit food access, increase physical activity, and model healthy eating; (b) reducing screen time; (c) modifying school policies to support improved dietary practices (e.g., removing vending machines) and encourage physical activity; and (d) providing classroom instruction on healthy dietary practices (e.g., Kropski et al., 2008).

Think Like a Clinical Psychologist Abstinence or controlled drinking? What are your thoughts on these different approaches to reducing the risks associated with excessive alcohol use?

Health and Pediatric Psychology in Medical Settings

It is common for hospital patients, and those under the long-term care of physicians, to feel anxious, angry, depressed, and/or frustrated by their medical condition. The stress of being seriously ill or severely injured can put strain on relationships; make it harder to accomplish career and life goals; and as we have mentioned, further complicate the medical problem itself. Health and pediatric psychologists working in hospitals and outpatient medical clinics — an area of the field sometimes referred to as **consultation/liaison psychology** — collaborate with medical staff to deliver mental health care to medical patients (Rutledge et al., 2020). This may include any of the following:

- Conducting individual assessment, consultation, and treatment at bedside for anxiety or depression related to a serious or life-threatening illness (e.g., cancer) or an upcoming procedure (e.g., an organ transplant)
- Holding support groups for hospitalized patients facing similar problems
- Providing psychological treatment as part of a multidisciplinary pain rehabilitation program
- Providing behavioral interventions for weight management for patients undergoing weight-loss surgery
- Facilitating productive communication between patients and their loved ones or caretakers

Such psychologists often find themselves working within interdisciplinary teams of physicians (e.g., oncologists), pharmacists, psychiatrists, and physical and occupational therapists (and trainees these various disciplines). Unfortunately, many people undergoing medical care fail to comply with instructions from their providers. The prospect of facing surgery, a visit to the dentist, and a variety of medical examinations can all be extremely stressful. Faced with such procedures, many people delay their visits or even forgo them entirely. Health and pediatric psychologists have developed interventions to help individuals deal with the stress surrounding such procedures, so to illustrate how psychologists work in medical settings, let's begin there.

Health and pediatric psychologists working in hospitals collaborate with medical staff and function as part of the treatment team for patients with acute and chronic medical illnesses.

Coping with Medical Procedures

Some people find certain medical examinations or procedures especially daunting. Without them, however, they may not be properly diagnosed and miss out on health-saving interventions. A good example is the colonoscopy, an exam used to detect abnormalities in the large intestine (colon) and rectum. During a colonoscopy, a flexible tube (colonoscope) is inserted into the rectum, and a tiny camera at the tip of the tube allows the doctor to view the inside of the colon. While colonoscopy aids in the early detection and prevention of colon cancer — and is not as painful as it sounds — it does involve several days of preparation (changes in diet and use of medication to clear the bowel), and the procedure itself seems alarming to many people. Accordingly, psychological interventions have been developed that help patients cope with the anxiety associated with undergoing such procedures.

What is most likely to help? In many situations (such as colonoscopy), simply providing information is extremely effective in reducing anxiety. Evidence also supports the use of behavioral interventions. For example, venipunctures (e.g., to get a blood sample or deliver medication) are common in medical settings yet feared by many children and adults. Manne and colleagues (1990) developed a program to reduce such fear among children that includes distraction (using a party blower during the procedure), positive reinforcement (e.g., receiving stickers for cooperation), and parent coaching. This program markedly reduced children's distress and parents' anxiety.

Research has also addressed the anticipatory anxiety that commonly accompanies the prospect of surgery. For most surgical patients, learning PMR strategies, receiving education about the medical procedure and what it will feel like, and cognitive therapy help alleviate such anxiety — at least to the point that they are able to effectively prepare for and undergo their procedure (Sanderson, 2018). In one controlled study of 700 patients undergoing abdominal surgery, learning and practicing PMR improved self-reported anxiety and medical outcomes associated with recovery (Wilson, 1981). As we have seen with other interventions, these strategies can be delivered face-to-face or via various telehealth platforms.

Diabetes is a chronic illness that affects how the body uses blood sugar (glucose). To remain healthy, people with this disease must routinely monitor their blood sugar levels and often need to administer medication intravenously. Poor compliance with these procedures could result in serious health complications and even death.

Increasing Compliance with Medical Instructions

Sometimes noncompliance with medical instructions occurs due to a miscommunication or misunderstanding, whereas at other times it results from fear and anxiety. Examples of non-compliance include using the incorrect dose of prescription medication, poor self-care following surgery, and failure to self-monitor blood sugar levels or self-administer medication in the case of diabetes. But the consequences of poor compliance can be quite serious, including long-term ill health and even pre-mature death. What factors predict compliance with medical regimens? As summarized in **Table 16.2**, research shows there are four categories of predictors: (a) characteristics of the disease itself, (b) characteristics of the patient, (c) environmental factors, and (d) characteristics of the practitioner–patient relationship (Brannon & Feist, 2010).

Table 16.2	Summary of Research Findings on Predictors of Compliance with Medical Instructions
Factor	**Research Findings**
Disease characteristics	Increased compliance is associated with: • The patient's perception that the illness is severe • The illness interfering with the patient's physical appearance • The illness being associated with pain Decreased compliance is associated with: • Unpleasant drug side effects • Needing increased medication doses
Personality factors	Increased compliance is associated with conscientiousness, optimism that treatment will work, and greater self-efficacy. Decreased compliance is associated with older age, the presence of stressful life events, depression, and less confidence in the treatment's effectiveness. In addition, women are more compliant than men when it comes to maintaining a healthy diet.
Environmental factors	Increased compliance is associated with support for engaging in healthy behaviors, as well as acculturation to Western culture and to cultures that place trust in physicians. Decreased compliance is associated with lower income, less social support, lack of insurance coverage, living alone, and belief in alternative/traditional healing methods.
Patient–practitioner relationship	Increased compliance is associated with confidence in the provider, agreement on treatment approaches, and the provider's friendliness. Decreased compliance is associated with poor verbal communication and feeling like the provider is disrespectful.

From: Brannon, L., & Feist, J. (2010). *Health psychology: An introduction to behavior and health* (7th ed.), pp. 84–86. Wadsworth, Cengage.

Behavioral interventions appear to be more helpful than educational methods in improving compliance. For example, DiMatteo and DiNicola (1982) found that the following strategies work well: (a) using prompts as reminders (e.g., taking medicine before each meal, telephone calls from providers), (b) tailoring the treatment regimen to the patient's schedule and lifestyle, and (c) using written contracts that promise a reward to the patient for complying with treatment guidelines. As illustrated in IN PRACTICE: *Consultation/Liaison Psychology*, clinical psychologists can play an especially important role in cases where medical patients refuse psychiatric medications.

In Practice   Consultation/Liaison Psychology

Dylana was a 37-year-old divorced woman with a history of Crohn's disease and a diagnosis of bipolar disorder. Although she was initially admitted to the hospital because of stomach pain and the suspicion of a Crohn's flare-up, a full medical examination (including colonoscopy and functional MRI [fMRI] scans) turned out to be negative. Because of the extensiveness of the medical testing and obstacles to discharge (e.g., use of a gastrostomy tube to increase her nutrition), however, Dylana remained in the hospital for longer than is usual for someone with a negative medical workup. As time went by, she began to display sharp mood swings when her physicians and family members suggested that it was time for her to be discharged and return home. Her caregivers responded to these dramatic behavioral displays by backing down. After 6 weeks of refusing to leave the hospital, Dylana's medical team requested a consultation from Dr. Edwards, a consultation/liaison psychologist in the Internal Medicine/Gastroenterology Department.

Dr. Edwards completed an initial bedside assessment with Dylana, which included a clinical interview and the administration of several reliable and valid interview and self-report measures. This assessment suggested DSM-5-TR diagnoses of somatic symptom disorder, with predominant pain, and borderline personality disorder. When Dr. Edwards presented these findings to Dylana's medical team, they suggested prescribing Dylana a cocktail of psychiatric medications to help calm her anxiety and stabilize her mood. Dylana, however, was unwilling to consider psychiatric medications. Accordingly, Dr. Edwards worked closely with Dylana, the medical team, and Dylana's family to establish a psychological treatment plan with the goal of discharge from the hospital. With Dylana, Dr. Edwards implemented evidence-based interventions to assist her with emotional management (e.g., dialectical behavior therapy techniques) and pain management (e.g., relaxation and biofeedback). She also worked with the medical team and Dylana's family to help them decrease their reinforcement of sick role behaviors (e.g., not responding to mood swings) and increase reinforcement of functional behaviors (e.g., with attention, praise, and other rewards). Within a few weeks, these interventions helped Dylana achieve her nutritional goals and discharge successfully. ▬▬

Think Like a Clinical Psychologist What are some of the challenges clinical psychologists might face when working as part of an interdisciplinary medical team?

▥ Multicultural Competence

As we have already discussed in this chapter, disparities exist between different cultural and ethnic groups in terms of health and health care. For example, on average, the general health and quality of health care in the United States is significantly better among white and Asian American populations than among Black and Indigenous American populations

(La Veist, 2005). There are also, on average, diverging attitudes toward hospitals, doctors, and the medical establishment. As we have discussed in previous chapters, there is an historical context for the mistrust of the medical establishment among some Black people and other historically marginalized groups, including studies like the Tuskegee syphilis study in which hundreds of Black men with this disease were deceived and refused treatment for decades. Health psychologists must be cognizant of these factors and how they sometimes affect interactions between members of different racial/cultural groups and the health care system. At the same time, they must not assume that everyone of a particular heritage thinks and feels the same way. Indeed, there is diversity within each cultural group as well.

Multicultural factors may also shape how individuals think about the causes of their medical illnesses. Individuals from Western cultures, for example, are socialized to attribute illness to internal biomedical causes. In many non-Western cultures, however, illness is often attributed to external factors such as natural or supernatural forces (e.g., witchcraft, angry gods; Huff & Kline, 1999). Accordingly, health psychologists must keep in mind that for some groups, the locus of control regarding health may be different than that implied in Western medicine. Appreciating this difference and adjusting one's practice are necessary to enhance client health; and guidelines have been developed for successfully doing so (Sangraula et al., 2021). Research also indicates that adapting health psychology interventions for specific cultural groups increases their effectiveness for members of those particular groups (Castro et al., 2010).

As an example, Latinas living in the United States have a prevalence of adult-onset (type 2) diabetes (which is associated with weight gain) that is almost twice that found for non-Latina white women. Latinas also tend to have more disease complications. To address these health disparities, Osuna and colleagues (2011) modified the Mediterranean Lifestyle Program, which was developed with non-Latina white women in mind, by making it more appealing to Latinas. This included adding Spanish translation to the educational materials, modifying recipes, giving women a choice of various forms of exercise (and offering exercise classes in Spanish), and adding more problem-solving and social support elements. The resulting cultural adaption was renamed "Viva Bien!" (which means "Live Well!") and was shown to be effective in improving psychosocial, behavioral, and quality of life outcomes for Latinas with type 2 diabetes (Toobert et al., 2011).

Think Like a Clinical Psychologist What might be the benefits and drawbacks of a health or pediatric psychologist who shares the same identity (e.g., racial, ethnic, sexual, gender identity) as their patient?

▥ Professional and Ethical Issues

Working in multidisciplinary teams with medically ill individuals raises unique professional and ethical issues and challenges for health and pediatric psychologists. We explore the most common issues in this section.

Professional Issues

Verbal and Written Communication

Psychologists working in health care settings must be able to communicate well with those working in other health care fields. They often find themselves seeing patients alongside members of other disciplines and collaborating on treatment plans and case presentations. They therefore receive specialized training in how to communicate effectively with colleagues who might not fully understand (or even acknowledge) the role of psychological factors and interventions in medicine. Assertiveness skills can be especially important in this subfield due to the frequent need to initiate conversations with busy medical providers (e.g., Rutledge et al., 2020). Health and pediatric psychologists must be comfortable providing education and recommendations directly to the consulting medical team.

Charting and record keeping in health and pediatric psychology are also unique from most other areas of clinical psychology practice. For example, psychologists in medical settings are expected to write notes directed primarily to the medical team; succinctly address specific consult questions; minimize psychological jargon; and integrate information about medical conditions, medications, and psychosocial factors. Despite their complexity, such reports need to be concise and completed promptly (usually the same day) due to the rapid pace of medical care.

Medical and Pharmacological Knowledge

Because treatment recommendations frequently include referrals for psychiatric medications, health and pediatric psychologists receive training in psychopharmacology. Although most psychologists do not prescribe medicine themselves, they routinely consult as part of the decision-making process about prescriptions. For example, in discussions involving the risk–benefit ratio of antipsychotic medications, a clinical psychologist might need to integrate information from the patient's electrocardiogram to monitor concerns for cardiac issues. Psychopharmacological training is not available in most clinical psychology training programs, yet medical and psychopharmacological education can be obtained through continuing education courses.

Ethics

Informed Consent

Along with the ethical issues covered earlier in this book, health psychologists sometimes encounter additional unique ethical dilemmas. Obtaining informed consent and discussing confidentiality, for example, present special challenges for psychologists working in hospital settings. Patients and clients are often referred from medical professionals and are not actively seeking mental health services; they may even view the referral as disparaging or indicating that the doctor thinks "It's all in my head." It is therefore crucial for health psychologists to clarify the nature and purpose of the referral, and the role of mental health intervention. Providing this information as part of the informed consent process (both in writing and verbally) helps build trust through transparency. Medical settings can be fast-paced and pressured, and psychologists need to be particularly mindful not to gloss over these issues in the interest of being "efficient."

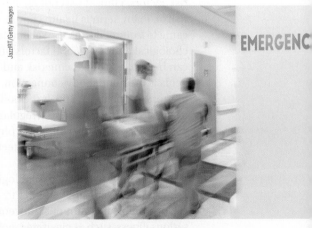

Psychologists working in hospitals must be attentive to their professional ethical principles even if the pace and pressure of hospital settings calls for efficiency.

Another important part of informed consent is making sure the patient is clear about how records will be kept in the medical environment and who will have access to mental health information. The use of electronic health records allows information about patients to be easily accessible to the medical team, yet psychologists are still obligated to protect private and confidential information. While it is important for mental health information to be accessible to the treatment team, health psychologists are careful to write their notes as if the patient were reading the chart, using behavioral terms (e.g., "The patient strongly disagreed that psychological treatment would help her") and avoiding vague, subjective, or judgmental comments (e.g., "The patient was resistant and difficult").

Confidentiality

There are additional concerns about confidentiality that arise when working within a multidisciplinary treatment team. As part of informed consent, health psychologists must explain to their patients that the team will likely discuss any psychological evaluation and treatment. Yet at the same time, the psychologist has the responsibility to keep such discussions relevant to the question at hand. Finally, health psychologists in hospital settings often find themselves having to perform assessments and interventions at bedside and in hospital rooms or suites where there might be staff or other patients within earshot. This has obvious implications for confidentiality, and it is optimal to find a time when the patient is alone, or able to move to a more private setting such as an unoccupied room or the corner of a quiet sitting area or lounge.

Think Like a Clinical Psychologist Should information about hospital patients' mental health be included in their medical record and accessible to everyone on their treatment team? Why or why not?

▌▌▌ Chapter Summary

Because many medical illnesses and diseases are associated with behavioral and psychological risk factors, clinical psychology has applications for helping those with, and minimizing the risk of, many serious health conditions. The fields of health and pediatric psychology — which came to fruition during the second half of the 20th century — focus on understanding how psychological and behavioral factors affect medical conditions and how psychological principles can be applied to reducing risk and helping those affected by ill health. A foundation of these fields is the mind–body connection, which has been recognized for centuries. The experience of stress, for example, affects the body's immune system in ways that reduce its ability to defend itself against infection and irregular cells that can lead to cancer. Cognitive, behavioral, and personality factors also influence physical health, and social support can act as a buffer against illness, although the extent of protection offered by social support is also related to factors such as race and gender.

Health and pediatric psychologists use empirically supported cognitive, behavioral, and acceptance-based interventions to help individuals manage the symptoms associated with chronic medical conditions. Prevention programs are also used to reduce behavioral risks of serious illness, such as cigarette smoking, problem drinking, and obesity. Whereas some health and pediatric psychologists work in clinics and private practices, others work in hospitals where they are part of multidisciplinary treatment teams. Such practitioners may provide assessment and treatment at bedside and consult with physicians when patients have difficulties following their instructions for self-care.

There are important multicultural issues that clinical psychologists must consider when working with medical patients, including the fact that health and health care disparities exist between privileged and less privileged cultural communities and racial groups. In addition, because of certain historical examples of mistreatment by the medical community, members of some groups may be less trusting of the health care system. Culturally adapted health psychology interventions are also available for members of diverse cultural groups. Finally, a number of unique professional and ethical considerations exist for health and pediatric psychologists involving collaborations with professionals from other disciplines, obtaining informed consent, and maintaining confidentiality.

Applying What You've Learned

Exercise 1: Using the framework of the transactional model of stress, describe the potential precursors, appraisals, and consequences of a 22-year-old student getting a bad grade on a psychology exam.

Exercise 2: Explain how the following interventions might be used to treat chronic pain in a 50-year-old construction worker: (a) biofeedback, (b) cognitive-behavioral therapy, and (c) acceptance therapy.

Key Terms

Biofeedback: A wide array of procedures through which a patient learns to modify or control certain physiological processes. Usually, the physiological process of interest is monitored by an apparatus, and the information is fed back to the patient in the form of an auditory, tactile, or visual signal. The patient then attempts to modify the signal (and thus change the physiological response) using a variety of techniques.

Biomedical perspective: A Western point of view that focuses exclusively on the biological factors of illness.

Biopsychosocial model: A theoretical model that holds that health and illness are a function of biological (e.g., genetic predispositions, nutritional deficiencies), psychological (e.g., the individual's cognitions and emotions), and social (e.g., friends and family, life events) influences.

Change talk: The client's own arguments for wanting things to be different (and better).

Chronic pain: Pain that persists longer than 3 months and in the absence of identifiable tissue damage (or

beyond the expected time of healing). It interferes with a person's ability to work, engage in daily activities, enjoy recreation, and function in interpersonal relationships, and is associated with depression, anxiety, irritability, and trouble with attention and concentration.

Consultation/liaison psychology: An area of the health care field where health and pediatric psychologists work in hospitals and outpatient medical clinics and collaborate with medical staff to deliver mental health care to medical patients.

Controlled drinking: A controversial approach to the treatment of alcohol problems that has as its goal light to moderate drinking. Clients are taught to monitor their alcohol intake closely and to develop coping responses that do not involve drinking.

Coping appraisal: In protection motivation theory, the evaluation of one's ability to successfully avoid or cope with negative outcomes. If one concludes that one is unlikely to cope effectively (by refraining from an undesired behavior), one will be more likely to engage in the behavior.

Cytokine: Regulates the body's inflammatory response to help fight disease or injury; overproduction of cytokines can lead to chronic inflammation.

Health disparity: Difference in the rates of illnesses among different groups and communities.

Health psychology: A specialty area within psychology (also known as *behavioral medicine*) that applies the tools of the discipline to the prevention of illness, the enhancement and maintenance of health, the identification of the correlates of illness and health, and the treatment of individuals in the health care system.

Motivational interviewing (MI): A technique for strengthening one's commitment to a particular goal that they are hesitant to pursue. MI is a collaborative approach in which the psychologist and client explore problems and solutions, and the client is given autonomy in making decisions.

Protection motivation theory: A model of health behavior positing that behavior is a function of both threat appraisal and coping appraisal.

Psychoneuroimmunology: The field of study that examines how stress interacts with body systems and shapes human behavior.

Psychosocial perspective: A recognition that psychological and social factors play a role in illness and disease.

Psychosomatic medicine: A field originating from the 1940s that was based on the assumption that certain illnesses and disease states were caused in part by psychological factors. Some adherents believed that each psychosomatic illness corresponded to a specific unconscious conflict that predisposed the patient to that illness.

Race-related stress: Race-related transactions that tax or exceed existing individual and collective resources or threaten well-being.

Relapse prevention: A range of strategies for preventing relapse, usually in the context of treating the addictive behaviors. Patients are directed to anticipate problem situations and are taught coping skills to navigate their way through these situations without engaging in the undesired behavior. Or in the event of a lapse, patients are taught how to respond so as to prevent a total relapse.

Risk factor: Characteristic of individuals that increases the likelihood of a serious illness.

Self-efficacy: People's beliefs about their capacity to control or gain mastery over the events that affect them. This construct plays a prominent role in most social-cognitive models of health behavior.

Social support: The number and quality of one's social relationships. Several studies have shown that social support is positively associated with better health outcomes.

Stress: A process that involves interactions between people and their environment.

Stressor: A situation, event, or other stimulus that a person appraises as challenging or threatening, leading to the stress response.

Sympathetic nervous system: The portion of the nervous system that is responsible for mobilizing body resources in urgent situations. Prolonged sympathetic activation can have adverse effects on body organs, mental functions, and the immune system.

Threat appraisal: In protection motivation theory, the evaluation of negative factors (e.g., the potential for harm) that affect the likelihood of engaging in a particular behavior. If one concludes that there is little immediate threat to oneself, one will be more likely to engage in the behavior.

Transactional model of stress: A model that views stress as a process that involves: (a) an environmental event; (b) the individual's appraisal of the event (as threatening or benign); and (c) the individual's physiological, emotional, cognitive, and behavioral responses to the event.

Type A personality pattern: A personality pattern that has been associated with anger and hostility, and which indicates increased risk for coronary heart disease.

CONNECT ONLINE:

 Check out our videos and additional resources located at: www.macmillanlearning.com

CHAPTER
17

Clinical Psychology and the Law

FOCUS QUESTIONS

1. What historical events influenced the development of the forensic psychology specialty?
2. What are the major roles of forensic psychologists?
3. What are the similarities and differences among the three major legal standards of insanity?
4. How might a forensic psychologist contribute to the following processes: jury selection, preparing a witness, and aiding an attorney who will cross-examine an eyewitness?
5. What multicultural and ethical considerations are specific to forensic psychology?

CHAPTER OUTLINE

D o you enjoy watching true crime shows? Are you interested in psychology, the law, or both? Because clinical psychologists are experts on human behavior, it is not surprising that their knowledge and skills are often sought out by those involved in the legal system — attorneys, judges, law enforcement officials, accusers, and defendants. Indeed, over the years, clinical psychologists have played a role in many famous legal cases. Consider the case of Jared Lee Loughner, who shot 13 people — killing 9 and injuring U.S. representative Gabby Giffords — on January 8, 2011, in Tucson, Arizona. After his arrest, a psychological evaluation revealed a diagnosis of schizophrenia and determined that Loughner was not able to understand the legal case against him (i.e., he was *incompetent to stand trial*). As a result, his trial was suspended. In August 2012, after months of treatment, another evaluation showed that Loughner *was* competent to stand trial. At that point, he pled guilty to murder and was sentenced to life plus 140 years in prison. Another example is the case of John Wayne Gacy, a serial killer who murdered more than 30 young men. When he was caught, he tried to use an insanity plea, claiming he was not in control of his actions. Yet, after extensive interviews, psychologists were able to prove that Gacy knew exactly what he was doing. In this chapter, you will learn about the interface between clinical psychology and the law, including how psychologists can be involved in various aspects of the legal system and legal proceedings.

▓ What Is Forensic Psychology?

Forensic psychology is the application of clinical psychological science and practice to questions and issues relating to law and the legal system. The term evolved from the Latin word "forensis," meaning "of the forum," where the law courts of ancient Rome were held. **Table 17.1**

Table 17.1 The Scope of Forensic Psychology: Areas of Research, Practice, and Expertise
Commitment to (and release from) psychiatric hospitals
Child custody issues
Determination of the need for a guardian due to incapacity
Criminal responsibility and competency to stand trial (insanity defense)
Predicting violence
Criminal profiling
Psychological damages suffered as the result of another's negligence
Law enforcement psychology
Determination of disability for Social Security claims
Workers' compensation claims
Eyewitness testimony and identification
Jury selection
Interviewing youth to understand incidents of maltreatment
Advice to attorneys regarding factors that may affect jurors' behavior
Offender treatment programs

illustrates just how broad these applications are. Forensic psychologists may be involved in helping to determine whether an individual is mentally competent to stand trial, sufficiently mentally ill or dangerous enough to warrant forced hospitalization, or was sane at the time they committed a crime. They might also be called upon to answer questions relating to child custody, guardianship, and the execution of wills. Another common activity is serving as expert witnesses in legal proceedings. Other pursuits include providing assessment and treatment for law enforcement agencies; for example, administering personality or intelligence tests to candidates for police work to screen out individuals who are not psychologically fit for such work (e.g., Weiss, 2010). Some forensic psychologists assist detectives in developing criminal psychological profiles, or ensure that witnesses are questioned in ways that lead to valid indictments. Others study jury decision making (perhaps collaborating with cognitive psychologists) and provide guidance to attorneys about jury selection and how best to question witnesses or present opening and closing arguments to win over jury members.

As described in IN HISTORICAL PERSPECTIVE: *The Origins and Growth of Forensic Psychology*, although clinical psychologists have been offering expertise to the courts since the early 1900s, it is only within the past 50 years that forensic psychology has become a recognized branch of the field with its own scientific journals, training programs, and credentialing system. As we will see in the next section, this branch of clinical psychology has taken off in many directions — it's not all about spouting expert analysis from the witness stand or convincing criminals to admit their guilt!

T**hink Like a Clinical Psychologist** Many people are drawn to the field of forensic psychology because of an interest in watching, listening to, or reading crime-related material. How do you feel about studying and working with attorneys, law enforcement professionals, or people who have committed (or been accused of committing) crimes?

▥ Activities of Forensic Psychologists

The growth of forensic psychology has placed clinical psychologists into many different roles. In some of these positions, they assume an impartial position, whereas in others, they may use their expertise to help one side of the case. Here, we will focus on six such roles, beginning with the forensic psychologist as an expert witness.

Providing Expert Testimony

Consider the following scenario:

> Mr. Costanza, an employee of Vandelay Industries, was working at his desk on April 28, 2020, when his supervisor, Ms. Benes, stopped by. Ms. Benes had a history of telling dirty jokes to Mr. Costanza, commenting on his physical attributes, and asking personal questions about his sex life. This day, however, she made it clear that if he wanted to keep his job at Vandelay, he would have to agree to have sex with her. Mr. Costanza refused, and two weeks later he was fired. Subsequently, he hired an

●⊂ ℓ ⊄ 🖩 In Historical Perspective

The Origins and Growth of Forensic Psychology

In 1908, Hugo von Münsterberg, a German psychologist (and later a professor at Harvard University) and pioneer in applying psychological principles to everyday life, published a controversial book called *On the Witness Stand* in which he accused the legal profession of relying too heavily on their intuition rather than on the emerging science of psychology. Among other things, he argued that eyewitness testimony was unreliable and that judges and jurors could easily be consciously and unconsciously swayed during legal proceedings. Although many consider Münsterberg the founder of forensic psychology (indeed, psychological studies have supported many of his assertions), psychology had relatively little influence on the law until 1962, when Judge David Bazelon, writing for the majority on the U.S. Court of Appeals for the District of Columbia Circuit (*Jenkins v. United States*, 1962), established clinical psychologists' legal status by ruling that they were appropriately qualified to testify in court as experts on mental disorders (psychiatrists had already enjoyed the privilege of providing expert testimony for many years).

Hugo von Münsterberg's (1863–1916) controversial book *On the Witness Stand* is considered the catalyst of modern-day forensic psychology.

This decision, and the respectability that clinical psychology had gained because of its contributions to the U.S. military during and after both world wars, helped pave the way for the field of forensic psychology to develop. The American Psychology-Law Society (AP-LS) was created in 1969 and became Division 41 of the American Psychological Association (APA) in 1980. As the field expanded, more organizations devoted to the study and application of psychology to the law began to appear. In 1976 the American Board of Forensic Psychology was chartered and eventually became part of the American Board of Professional Psychology in 1985. This merger signified the development of the first certification for forensic psychologists. Later organizations and conferences helped solidify the field, and forensic psychology was finally officially recognized as a professional specialty under the APA in 2001.

Today, psychologists regularly testify as experts in virtually every area of criminal, civil, family, and administrative law. In addition, they serve as consultants to agencies and individuals throughout the legal system. Several journals in this area publish research and practical articles, including *Law and Human Behavior; Criminal Justice Journal; Law and Psychology Review; Criminal Justice and Behavior; Behavioral Sciences and the Law; American Journal of Forensic Psychology;* and *Psychology, Public Policy, and Law*. Numerous clinical psychology PhD/PsyD and postdoctoral training programs also offer training in forensic psychology, which involves gaining expertise in research methodology and statistics, legal knowledge, integrative law psychology, ethics and professional issues, and clinical forensics. Each year, the number (and scope) of such programs continues to grow. In addition, academic psychology departments are increasingly offering forensic courses for undergraduate students. ∎

attorney, filed sexual harassment charges against Ms. Benes, and sought damages for psychological suffering.

Dr. Kramer, a clinical psychologist, was hired by Mr. Costanza's attorney. He conducted extensive interviews with Mr. Costanza along with several of his co-workers at Vandelay. Dr. Kramer also administered several tests. Mr. Newman, a co-worker, had overheard the April 28, 2020, conversation between Mr. Costanza and his supervisor and had also previously observed some of the alleged sexual harassment.

During the trial, Mr. Newman served as a **lay witness**, testifying to the facts with reference to his own observations. As a psychologist, however, Dr. Kramer served as an **expert witness**, giving his opinions and inferences about psychological damage to Mr. Costanza. This illustrates the basic difference between a lay witness, who may testify only to events observed, and an expert witness, who may offer judgements to help the court understand and evaluate evidence or determine a fact at issue (Pozzulo et al., 2021). The opinions, judgments, and inferences of an expert witness are called **expert testimony**. Depending on their qualifications and particular area of expertise, psychologists may provide expert testimony on any of the topics listed in Table 17.1, as well as other topics deemed necessary by the court.

Irrespective of the topic, testifying in a court of law can be a challenging experience for psychologists who assume the expert witness role. The expert may be asked to testify by the judge or by counsel (attorneys) for either the defendant (the accused) or the plaintiff (the accuser). Regardless, behavioral experts are needed only when complicated or thorny matters need to be settled; and being grilled (sometimes aggressively) by attorneys on both sides of the issue can be anxiety-provoking for even the most knowledgeable psychologist. Therefore, pretrial preparation is a must. This may involve hours of studying, interviewing, testing, and conferences, depending on the case. Even still, in addition to providing actual expert testimony, psychologists may be asked provocative questions during cross-examination to challenge their credibility. Examples include the following:

- "Isn't it true that most of your experiments are done with rats and college students?"
- "You're a *PhD*, not an *MD*, right?"
- "You can't tell what's going on up *here*, can you?" (attorney points to her own head)

How should psychologists behave in the courtroom under such circumstances? Much has been written on courtroom strategies and how to respond when being cross-examined — even to the point of how to dress (e.g., Brodsky, 2013; Gutheil, 2004). Most important, however, is to be prepared, be honest, stick to the scientific data, listen carefully to the wording of questions, take time to think before giving answers, admit weaknesses, and speak in personally meaningful terms.

Testifying in Criminal Cases

For generations, society has grappled with how best to deal with people who have committed criminal acts but were so mentally ill at the time that it is debatable whether they were personally responsible for their actions. Also difficult are instances when it is unclear as to whether people accused of crimes can understand the trial proceedings and thus cooperate in their own defense.

The Insanity Plea

If someone accused of a crime is judged to have been **sane** — that is, of sound mind and mentally healthy — at the time of the alleged crime, then conviction will bring probation, fines, imprisonment, or perhaps the death penalty. However (in all but four states: Montana, Idaho, Kansas, and Utah), someone judged to be **insane** — that is, unable to think clearly or sensibly — at the time of the crime will, if convicted, be regarded as not responsible and thus held for treatment rather than punishment. For example, say a woman who suffers from hallucinations and paranoia kills a person she believes was out to harm her. If, at her murder trial, a psychologist demonstrates that schizophrenia made her incapable of differentiating between right and wrong, she might be found **not guilty by reason of insanity (NGRI)**. Importantly, in most jurisdictions, being under the influence of drugs or alcohol (or having an addiction problem) at the time of a crime cannot be used as the basis for an NGRI plea.

Despite many popular conceptions to the contrary, however, the NGRI plea is only rarely used in court; and when used, it is rarely successful (Greenberg et al., 2020). One reason for this is that (in most jurisdictions) an insanity plea places the **burden of proof** on the accused. That is, defendants must prove that they were insane at the time of the criminal offense. Indeed, defendants are typically assumed to be responsible for their alleged criminal behavior. It should be noted that "insanity" is a legal term, not a medical, psychiatric, or psychological term. The legal system assumes that people make premeditated and rational choices. Therefore, to behave irrationally is evidence of insanity. But most psychologists would not agree that all normal behavior is rationally chosen. The deterministic view of science creates problems for such a simple notion.

Andrea Yates (left) admitted to drowning her five young children (their ages ranged from six months to seven years) in a bathtub in 2001 and was convicted of murder in 2002. Her conviction was later overturned, and in 2006 she was retried and found NGRI. Psychologists successfully demonstrated that Yates's postpartum depression and psychosis led to the drownings. She currently resides in a Texas psychiatric hospital.

So, how is it decided that someone was insane at the time of a crime? Although standards vary from state to state, one of three standards typically prevails. The oldest test for criminal insanity is the **M'Naghten rule**. In 1843, Daniel M'Naughten, a Scottish woodcutter, killed the secretary to the prime minister of England, Sir Robert Peel, in a botched attempt to assassinate the prime minister himself. During the trial, witnesses testified that M'Naughten believed the prime minister was to blame for his personal and financial misfortunes. When the jury found M'Naughten not guilty on account of these delusions, Queen Victoria, upset by the decision, asked the House of Lords to tighten the standard. Indeed, the judges ruled that defendants should not be held responsible for their actions if they could not tell that their actions were wrong at the time they were committed. This rule governed legal responsibility in cases of insanity in England and was used by American courts for over 100 years.

A second standard is the **Durham standard**, which was adopted by Judge David Bazelon of the U.S. Court of Appeals in 1954 in response to concerns that the M'Naghten rule was outdated. The Durham standard (named for the defendant in the case, Monte Durham) holds that people accused of a crime are not criminally responsible if their unlawful act was the product of mental illness. A version of this rule had previously been in place since the 1890s in New Hampshire, where it remains law to this day. However, many judges and lawyers (including Judge Bazelon himself) later expressed dissatisfaction with this standard because, in their view, the expert testimony of mental health professionals weighed too heavily in the decision.

Accordingly, a third standard was developed in 1972 by the American Law Institute (ALI), and states that defendants cannot be held criminally responsible if at the time of the behavior in question, as a result of a mental disease or defect, they lack substantial capacity either to appreciate the criminality of their conduct or to conform their conduct to the requirements of the law (Dressler & Garvey, 2019). This **ALI standard** is viewed as the most liberal or expansive in that criminal responsibility can be excused if mental illness causes a lack of substantial capacity to understand what one is doing (*a cognitive deficit*) or an inability to control one's behavior (*a volitional deficit*).

On March 30, 1981, John Hinckley Jr. tried to assassinate President Ronald Reagan. Reagan survived, and Hinckley was charged with attempted murder of the president. Hinckley raised the defense of legal insanity, and the case was tried in a federal court which had adopted the ALI standard, requiring the prosecution to prove beyond a reasonable doubt that the defendant was not legally insane. In the end, the jury found Hinckley NGRI — a very unpopular verdict that unleashed widespread criticism of (and vigorous debate over) the insanity defense and led to the Insanity Defense Reform Act (IDRA) that was passed by the U.S. Congress in 1984. Perhaps the most important part of the IDRA was that instead of narrowing the standard for legal insanity, it shifted the burden of proof to the defendant, which makes it more difficult for the defendant to succeed. The IDRA also prohibits expert witnesses (for either side) from testifying directly as to whether the defendant was sane or insane. They are allowed only to testify as to the person's mental health and capacities, with the question of sanity to be decided by the judge or jury. Although the IDRA has been criticized as unfair because it creates too much risk that a defendant who is genuinely insane will be convicted, it has been deemed constitutional and remains in use in federal courts.

In several states today, an additional verdict of **guilty but mentally ill** is available to jurors (Greenberg et al., 2020). Depending on the jurisdiction, under this verdict, convicted individuals may initially be sent to a psychiatric facility for treatment. If eventually judged to be sane, they are then sent to prison to serve what is left of their sentence. Others may begin serving their prison time immediately after sentencing and receive psychological services there.

To conduct an evaluation for criminal insanity, the psychologist must address whether the person has a mental disorder and what the person's mental status was at the time of the alleged crime. In the process, the psychologist will assess many factors, including the defendant's history (and family history), intellectual status, neuropsychological factors, competency to stand trial, reading skills, personality, and measures of response style or the tendency to exaggerate (Blau, 1998).

Competency to Stand Trial

What about a defendant's state of mind *during their trial*? Should someone such as Jared Lee Loughner (discussed at the beginning of this chapter) be required to stand trial and take part in their own legal defense if they are presently cognitively impaired by symptoms of schizophrenia such as hallucinations or delusions? The issue of **competency to stand trial** refers to the defendant's mental status at the time of the trial, rather than when the crime was allegedly committed.

In 1960, Milton Dusky, a 33-year-old man, was charged with assisting in the kidnapping and rape of an underage female. Even though he had a diagnosis of schizophrenia, he was determined competent to stand trial and received a sentence of 45 years in prison. His lawyers, however, petitioned the Supreme Court, which took up the case and ruled that to be competent to stand trial, a defendant must have both (a) the ability to consult with a lawyer with a reasonable degree of rational understanding and (b) a rational as well as factual understanding of the legal proceedings. The court also made clear that a brief mental status exam was insufficient to determine competency. When Dusky went to trial again, his sentence was reduced to 20 years.

Testifying in Civil Cases

Whereas *criminal* cases are filed by the government and led by a prosecuting attorney, *civil* cases are filed by an individual or corporation against another individual or corporation. As described in this section, two areas that are especially important for clinical psychologists are (a) commitment to and release from mental institutions and (b) domestic issues such as child custody disputes.

Commitment to Mental Institutions

Picture this scenario: Not too long ago, a disheveled man in his late 30s entered a restaurant and began haranguing customers as they approached the cashier to pay their checks. He was incoherent, but it was possible to pick out the offensive comments that peppered his remarks. He did this for about five minutes, whereupon the manager appeared and escorted him to the door. Outside, he continued his tirade while pacing back and forth in front of the door. He repeatedly accosted customers and tried to make them listen to him. The manager finally called the police. After a brief interrogation, they "helped" the man into a patrol car and subsequently dropped him off at the local psychiatric hospital.

Hospitalization that occurs against the will of the individual is referred to as an **involuntary commitment**. Some authors (e.g., Rosenhan, 1973) have argued that involuntary hospitalization is a dangerous and often misused power that has been repeatedly used to maintain control over those who will not conform to certain social dictates. The permissible length of involuntary commitment typically varies from one day to three weeks or so depending on the jurisdiction. After that, a hearing must be held to decide whether detention should continue. In a **voluntary commitment**, the individual agrees to admission and is allowed to leave at any time. Some hospitals require that such individuals indicate their intent to leave several days in advance, which allows the hospital to initiate commitment proceedings if the individual is believed to be seriously mentally ill or dangerous. Thus, "voluntary" admission is often not as voluntary as it appears at first glance. There may also be strong pressure from relatives, friends, police, court authorities, or mental health professionals.

Anyone can petition the court for an examination of someone they believe requires commitment. Usually, it is family or friends, or sometimes the police or welfare officials, who act as petitioners. If the court agrees, an order is issued and the person is required to undergo psychological assessment. For the court to commit someone, it must be determined that the person is (a) dangerous to self or others or (b) psychologically disabled that they are incapable of making responsible decisions about self-care and hospitalization. Once these conditions are no longer met, the person must be released.

Domestic Issues

Domestic issues that require intervention by the courts include child custody decisions, parental fitness, visitation rights, child abuse, juvenile misbehavior, and adoption (among others). Because divorce has become prevalent in our society, child custody disputes have proliferated as well. Family roles and norms have likewise changed; for example, fathers have increasingly assumed childcare responsibilities and mothers are now commonly employed outside the home. These and other factors have made custodial questions more complex than in the past. However, the doctrine of the "best interests of the child" takes precedence in custody disputes. **Table 17.2** lists the factors that courts typically consider when ruling on what is in a child's best interests when it comes to their custody.

Table 17.2 Factors Considered by Courts when Making Child Custody Rulings
The love, affection, and other emotional ties existing between the competing parties and the child
The capacity and disposition of competing parties to give the child love, affection, and guidance, and continuation of educating and raising the child in a religion or creed, if any
The capacity and disposition of competing parties to provide the child with food, clothing, medical care, or other remedial care recognized and permitted under the laws of the specific state in lieu of medical care or other material needs
The length of time the child has lived in a stable satisfactory environment and desirability of maintaining continuity
The permanence, as a family unit, of the existing or proposed custodial home
The moral fitness of the competing parties
The home, school, and community records of the child
The mental and physical health of the competing parties
The reasonable preference of the child (if the court deems the child to be of sufficient age to express preference)
Any other factor considered by the court to be relevant to a particular child custody dispute

SOURCE: Michigan Custody Act of 1970.

Although 150 years ago children of divorce were automatically awarded to the father, and 50 years ago almost always to the mother, such reflexive decisions no longer hold today. The present norm is **joint custody** in which the child's living arrangements (i.e., *physical* custody) and the ability to make legal decisions on matters impacting the child (i.e., *legal* custody) are shared by both parents. This rests on the belief that children should maintain ties with both parents whenever possible. In fact, many divorces culminate in informal joint custody decisions by the divorced couple; thus, a formal ruling by the court is never needed. But is joint custody always in the best interests of the child? No. For example, it may be contraindicated when the parents have an emotionally charged, conflictual relationship. In these instances, physical custody may be granted to one parent, while the other parent is granted **visitation rights** — the court-given right of the noncustodial parent to see and visit the child, absent extraordinary circumstances.

When a custody dispute needs to be settled legally, a forensic psychologist might be hired by the court, or by one or both parents, to perform an evaluation of the child and one or both parents, as well as conduct interviews with other relatives, teachers, and anyone else who might be able to provide useful information to aid in a recommendation to the court regarding custody and visitation. According to the American Psychological Association (2010), such a **child custody evaluation** must address three major issues: (a) the child's development and psychological welfare, (b) each parent's strengths and limitations, and (c) the way each member of the family interacts with the others.

Predicting Dangerousness and Psychological Criminal Profiling

Predicting Dangerousness

As we saw in Chapter 3, *Ethics in Clinical Psychology*, the Tarasoff case resulted in a California court decision that psychologists have a duty to warn potential victims of their clients' violent behavior. But how accurately can psychologists predict dangerous behavior? Although a history of violence is more common among those with mental disorder diagnoses (especially substance use disorders) as compared to those without, the vast majority of people with such diagnoses have no history of violence (Varshney et al., 2016). This is true even for people with *severe* mental illness: a meta-analysis indicated that to prevent one stranger homicide, 35,000 individuals with schizophrenia judged to be at "high risk of violence" would need to be detained (Large et al., 2011). This clearly contradicts the widespread belief that individuals with severe mental illness are a threat. The fact is that violent acts are highly overpredicted. Even when using reliable and valid (i.e., empirically supported) methods, a large percentage of people predicted to become violent do not do so (e.g., Rossdale et al., 2020).

The discussion of clinical judgment versus actuarial (statistical) prediction in Chapter 4, *The Science of*

tillsonburg/E+/Getty Images

POLICE LINE DO NOT CROSS POLICE LINE DO NO

POLICE

Despite what many people think, it is extremely difficult to predict who will commit acts of violence. Even people diagnosed with severe mental disorders are highly unlikely to be dangerous.

Assessment, also applies to the issue of how best to predict dangerousness. Whereas there is considerable evidence that actuarial methods, including newer machine learning and artificial intelligence methods, should be used in place of clinical judgment, others have pointed out that there is not enough empirical evidence that such tools are superior to clinical (i.e., human) impression (e.g., McKay, 2020; Viljoen et al., 2021). Some have even raised ethical concerns over newer artificial intelligence (AI) tools as proprietary products with in-built statistical bias (McKay, 2020). This is not to say that research efforts to develop and improve methods for the prediction of dangerousness should cease. Rather, because of the tremendous implications for public policy, to say nothing of human values, much more research is needed in this area.

Psychological Criminal Profiling

If the goal of predicting dangerousness is to answer the question "Who *will* do it?" **psychological criminal profiling** addresses the question "Who *did* it?" Specifically, it is a method of identifying criminal suspects using emotional and behavioral clues from the crime scene. One major assumption of this type of profiling is **behavioral consistency**, the idea that an offender's crimes tend to be similar to one another. Another assumption is **homology**, the notion that similar crimes are committed by similar offenders. As described in A CLOSER LOOK: *Profiling the "Unabomber,"* one of the most famous cases of psychological criminal profiling came in 1996, with the arrest of Ted Kaczynski. Kaczynski was a mathematics prodigy who became a recluse and engaged in a nationwide mail bombing campaign from 1978 to 1995 during which he sent exploding packages to people he believed were contributing to the advancement of modern technology and the destruction of the environment. He was responsible for killing 3 people and injuring 23 more. The extensive FBI investigation that resulted in his arrest and imprisonment involved psychological analyses of Kaczynski's writings and other behavioral patterns.

A Closer Look   Profiling the "Unabomber"

Despite being active for nearly 20 years, the Unabomber was careful to leave no evidence that could be traced to him. He was also cautious to avoid being seen. But in 1993 when he began communicating, first in letters to some of his victims and then with the media, he was, unbeknownst to him, also communicating with the FBI. Investigators, including Kathleen Puckett, were analyzing his every word to understand his ideas, his interests, and books that were meaningful to him. To Puckett, who was also a clinical psychology PhD student at the time, these communications revealed aspects of his education, age, and personality.

After lethal bombings in 1994 and 1995, the Unabomber wrote to several publications (including the *New York Times*) and asked them to publish an essay he believed would memorialize his philosophy and his deeds. He promised to end his bombings if this manifesto was published, and the FBI urged the media to publish it in hopes that someone would recognize the unique and very passionate writing style and identify him. Indeed, he had probably held these beliefs for a long time. Puckett also pointed to particular spellings and phrases — such as the British spelling of the word "analyse" — as identifiers in the text that she hoped would catch someone's eye.

Sure enough, a few months after the essay was published, a lawyer representing David Kaczynski called the FBI. He provided them with a 23-page essay his client's brother, Theodore (Ted) Kaczynski, wrote in 1971. Agents who read it instantly spotted similarities. For example, the phrase

"sphere of human freedom" in Kaczynski's essay also appeared in the Unabomber's manifesto. The similarities in the texts along with other evidence that came to light as Puckett and other agents investigated more of Kaczynski's past and records made them more and more certain that they had their man. That was enough to get a search warrant for the rustic cabin in Montana where Ted Kaczynski lived. Among the evidence found in the cabin were thousands of pages of handwritten notes, including confessions to all 16 bombings. ▬

Psychologist Kathleen Puckett (left) helped lead the FBI criminal profiling team that identified Ted Kaczynski (right) as the Unabomber, eventually leading to his arrest in 1996.

How effective is psychological criminal profiling? Although there is some evidence that certain offender characteristics are associated with certain kinds of crimes (e.g., Homant & Kennedy, 1998), there are also reasons for caution. For one thing, profilers tend to rely more on their personal hunches and intuitions than on research findings. As a result, inaccurate profiles are quite common. Even in the Unabomber case there were several failed profiling attempts before the FBI finally identified Kaczynski. In addition, there is little evidence that professional criminal profilers possess special expertise. In fact, studies have shown that profiles created by experts are only minimally better (if at all) than those generated by college students with no training in understanding criminal behavior (e.g., Snook et al., 2008). Perhaps a reason for this is that the methodology and terminology used by profilers are often not operationally defined (Bartol & Bartol, 2016). These concerns raise doubts about whether human criminal profilers are essential for identifying criminal suspects. That is, would we be better off from a validity (not to mention a financial and efficiency) standpoint relying on computer-driven actuarial formulas generated from the large quantities of data on the characteristics of various kinds of crimes and criminals?

Conducting Psychological Autopsies

From time to time, deaths occur under uncertain (or even suspicious) circumstances, and the mental state of the deceased person needs to be understood. For example, if there is any question as to how someone with a life insurance policy has died, the insurance company will want to determine the precise cause of death since benefits may be denied in the case of a suicide. A **psychological autopsy** is an evaluation that aims to reconstruct a person's psychological state — their thoughts, mood, and behavioral tendencies — at the time of their death to shed light on contextual factors preceding their death, including any involvement they might have had in their own passing (Conner et al., 2021). Psychological autopsies might also be desired in the following circumstances:

- A criminal defendant who claims that the person they are accused of killing actually died by suicide

- A workers' compensation case in which the employee's family alleges that improper working conditions led to their relative's death by accident or suicide

- A dispute over whether a deceased loved one had the mental capacity necessary to competently execute or change their will

There is no standardized format for conducting psychological autopsies. Most psychologists rely on interviews with those who knew the deceased and can speak to matters such as changes in the person's mood and behavior in the time leading up to their death, interactions with family and peers, and performance at school or at work. Documents and other life records that the person has left behind may also be examined for additional circumstantial information (Mérelle et al., 2020).

The most important limitation of psychological autopsies, of course, is that because the individual about whom inferences are being made cannot be assessed directly, this information must come from secondhand sources. Accordingly, it is impossible to establish their validity — that is, whether they accurately portray the person's state of mind at the time of death. Moreover, as

Psychological autopsies involve interviews with family and friends of the deceased to try to determine the person's state of mind at the time of their death.

we discuss later in this chapter, information obtained through interviews may be distorted by intentional or unintentional biases, such as memory bias and other attempts to cast a person in an especially virtuous or shady light. As a result, the courts have mixed reactions to psychological autopsies when they are presented as evidence. In cases concerning workers' compensation claims and questions over whether insurance benefits should be paid, judges may accept them as evidence. On the other hand, in criminal cases and in cases involving questions of whether a person had the mental capacity to draft a will, they are less likely to be considered (Canter, 2017).

Consulting with Lawyers about Their Cases

Many of the activities already discussed involve some manner of consultation with members of the legal profession. Here, we focus on how clinical psychologists (along with developmental, cognitive, and social psychologists) may consult with, and lend their expertise to, lawyers as part of the prosecution or defense team.

Jury Selection

A forensic psychologist may work with attorneys in the process of jury selection (Pozzulo et al., 2021). The legal term **voir dire** refers to that part of a trial during which attorneys conduct a preliminary examination of potential jurors. Attorneys on both sides are given the opportunity to question potential jurors to discover their biases, gain hints as to which side of the case they are likely to identify with, and determine whether they will be receptive to the attorney's arguments and strategies. All of this is designed to give an attorney an edge when they ultimately select who they want to serve on the jury. Forensic psychologists may work with attorneys to help them in different ways to select jurors likely to give them a favorable verdict. **Table 17.3** summarizes the contributions forensic psychologists can make at various stages of the *voir dire* process.

Table 17.3 Contributions of Forensic Psychologists to Jury Selection	
Stage of Jury Selection	**Contributions**
Preparation for *voir dire*	Interview the client and key informants, and learn about the legal strategy to be used in the case. Use this information to develop a jury selection strategy and develop questions to help identify appropriate (and inappropriate) jurors.
During *voir dire*	Observe the process and help the attorney identify favorable jurors. If applicable, provide expert testimony on whether to sequester the jury, rules for jury selection, and other issues related to jury composition.
Selecting jurors	Develop a rating system to identify jurors as favorable/unfavorable based on (for example) experience, intelligence, attitudes/opinions, and influenceability.

Jury Shadowing

Another form of consultation is **jury shadowing**. Here, the psychologist hires individuals similar to those serving on the actual jury and assesses their reactions to the attorney's and witnesses' planned testimony and arguments. Like focus groups used by marketing strategists, shadow juries can be used to identify and explore how the actual jury might think and behave in response to the tactics being planned for the courtroom and help the psychologist and attorneys prepare an optimally informed case strategy.

Witness Preparation

Of course, it would be unethical for a forensic psychologist to in any way encourage a witness to alter the facts during testimony. The line, however, is a thin one and the goal of **witness preparation** is to help witnesses present their testimony in ways that (a) remain loyal to the truth, but (b) optimize the likelihood of a favorable verdict. Strategies used in witness preparation may include the following:

- Instructing witnesses in how to talk about the facts of the case when they're on the witness stand
- Coaching witnesses in how to display emotions when in front of the judge and jury
- Preparing witnesses for the sheer experience of being in a courtroom
- Preparing the witness for being cross-examined by the opposing side
- Making suggestions for the witnesses' dress and physical appearance
- Role-playing how to respond to threats or other pressure tactics by the opposing attorney

There is definitely some gray area between *coaching* witnesses in how to behave on the stand and encouraging them to *alter* what would otherwise be their testimony (see **Think Like a Clinical Psychologist** at the end of this section). Accordingly, some psychologists choose to work only with witnesses in *civil* proceedings — not in *criminal* cases.

Helping Attorneys Present Their Arguments

Finally, psychologists can often help attorneys in the way they present their cases and evidence (within the allowable constraints of the judicial system) to jurors. For example, using the results of psychological research, they can assist attorneys in predicting how jurors will respond to certain kinds of evidence or methods of presentation, especially in opening and closing arguments. In effect, the beliefs, feelings, and behavior of jurors are the targets here. The forensic psychologist then helps attorneys find the best way to present their cases.

Think Like a Clinical Psychologist Some psychologists are uncomfortable with the idea of using their knowledge of human behavior and emotion to influence the legal process. Discuss where you would draw the line, for example, between coaching a witness to present their honest testimony and encouraging them to alter their verbal or nonverbal behavior in ways that are likely to persuade a judge or jury (i.e., witness tampering).

Research in Forensic Psychology

Virtually any type of psychological research could become relevant to some forensic issue. For example, studies on the differences between postpartum OCD (in which a new mother has benign unwanted thoughts of harm) and psychosis (in which delusions can, in extremely rare circumstances, lead to violence) may be critical in a mental competency hearing; and research on the nature of prejudice may be important to determining whether a hate crime has been committed. That said, there are a few areas of research that are unique to forensic psychology, and we will examine two such topics here: eyewitness testimony and jury behavior.

Eyewitness Identification and Testimony

Nothing can be as dramatic, or as crucial to a court case, as an eyewitness who identifies the person accused of a crime. Such **eyewitness testimony** has been a powerful factor in the conviction of countless individuals over the years. But it has also led to many convictions of innocent people (Green & Heilbrun, 2011; Pozzulo et al., 2021). In fact, mistaken eyewitness identifications contribute to 69% of wrongful convictions in the United States that are later overturned by DNA evidence (Innocence Project, 2017). Why? Because eyewitness testimony is often unreliable and inaccurate. In addition, societal biases and media depictions of criminal activity often suggest a stereotype of the accused (e.g., gender, race/ethnicity, physical appearance, occupation) that can bias perceptions of who may be assumed to be engaged in criminal activity. A case in point occurred in 1979 in Wilmington, Delaware, where a Catholic priest was put on trial because a citizen told authorities that the priest looked very much like a police artist's sketch of a man accused of robbery. Later, seven eyewitnesses to the robbery positively identified the priest as the robber. The trial was halted, however, when another man came forward and confessed to the crime! What had happened with these eyewitnesses? Apparently, before showing pictures of suspects to the witnesses, the police had quietly revealed that the robber might be a priest. And the priest's picture was the only one in which the subject was wearing a clerical collar.

Psychologist Elizabeth Loftus and her colleagues performed a number of studies showing that eyewitnesses' memory can easily be distorted by cognitive biases and subsequent information. For example, Loftus, Miller, and Burns (1978) had research participants view color images of an automobile accident. For half of the participants, there was a *stop sign* present; the other half saw a *yield sign*. Afterward, participants answered questions about the images. The critical question asked whether a particular sign (either *stop* or *yield*) was present; but the question was worded such that half the participants were asked about the sign they had seen earlier while the other half were asked about the sign they had not seen. Still later, the

Elizabeth Loftus is well-known for her pioneering research on cognitive processes, such as memory, and their applications to forensic settings.

participants were shown 15 images and asked to pick out the one they had seen before. Interestingly, participants asked about the sign they had actually seen chose the correct sign 75% of the time, whereas those asked about the opposite sign made the correct choice only 41% of the time. This demonstrates (a) how fallible our memory can be, and (b) that the way questions are worded can influence how eyewitnesses "remember" what they observed.

Since Loftus's pioneering work, additional laboratory research has continued to improve our understanding of eyewitness identification and help identify the conditions in a specific case that might produce distortions in testimony. In general, these studies involve exposing participants ("witnesses") to a simulated crime — sometimes live, sometimes a video — for which the researchers know the true identity of the "culprit" or "suspect." Participants then take part in an identification procedure, typically a photo lineup, in which the culprit's photo is embedded among filler photos (or in some cases absent from the array and replaced with the photo of an innocent person). Using this basic paradigm, researchers then systematically manipulate variables, such as the witness's view of the culprit, similarity of the filler photos to the culprit's, instructions given to the eyewitness prior to viewing, or suggestive behaviors of the lineup administrator, to see how these kinds of variables affect the responses of the eyewitnesses. Such studies have revealed that factors such as stress, the amount of information present, the procedures for identification, personal biases and stereotypes, whether a weapon was present, and the age of the eyewitness all influence eyewitness identification (e.g., Wells et al., 2020).

The main strengths of these types of studies are that (a) the researchers know which person is the actual "culprit" and (b) they randomly assign participants to conditions, which permits inferences about the cause of any effects observed in the responses. On the other hand, a limitation of lab experiments is that the consequences of a mistaken identification are trivial since the "accident" or "crime" is not real (Mecklenburg, 2008). The argument is that actual witnesses to serious crimes would be more thoughtful when identifying who they thought was the culprit. Therefore, perhaps laboratory studies overestimate the eyewitness misidentification problem.

To address these concerns, researchers have examined the results of police lineups conducted as part of actual criminal investigations (e.g., Mecklenburg et al., 2008). Such "field studies" report how often eyewitnesses identify the actual suspect, identify an innocent "filler person" (usually someone who was in prison at the time of the crime and therefore is known to be innocent), or make no identification. If the eyewitness identifies the suspect, it might or might not be an accurate identification because the truth is not known with absolute certainty in actual cases. But when an eyewitness identifies a filler, it is clearly a mistaken identification. Although field studies are limited by their lack of random assignment, they do help counter the criticism that laboratory experiments overestimate misidentification. Specifically, they can be used to estimate how often actual eyewitnesses to serious crimes mistakenly identify a filler from a lineup.

So, how do the results of laboratory experiments compare with those from field studies? Fairly well. A meta-analysis showed that the average filler identification rate was 27.9% across

94 laboratory studies and 23.7% across 11 field studies (Wells et al., 2020). These results suggest that experimental studies are not producing highly inflated rates of mistaken identification compared with what happens with actual eyewitnesses to serious crimes. Accordingly, lab studies are valuable for isolating cause–effect relations among variables, which field studies are unable to do (Horry et al., 2014). Alarmingly, these data also suggest that about one in every four witnesses who are shown a lineup select an innocent filler! Fortunately, forensic psychology research has also led to the empirically based recommendations described in **Table 17.4** that law enforcement and judicial personnel often use to reduce the frequency of such misidentifications during procedures such as police lineups (Wells et al., 2020).

Table 17.4   Research-Supported Recommendations for Minimizing Eyewitness Misidentifications
Perform a Prelineup Interview. As soon as possible after the crime has occurred, and before the lineup, witnesses should be interviewed to document (a) their descriptions of the culprit, (b) the conditions under which they witnessed the crime, and (c) any prior familiarity with the culprit. The interview should be videorecorded.
Double-Blind Lineups. Neither the administrator nor the witness should know who the suspect is in the lineup.
Lineup Fillers. There should be only one suspect and at least five fillers per lineup. Fillers should not make the suspect stand out in terms of physical appearance.
Prelineup Instructions. When inviting an eyewitness to attend a lineup, police should *not* (a) give any information that the witness has not already provided, (b) tell the witness whether the culprit will be in the lineup, nor (c) tell the witness whether any arrests have been made. The eyewitness should be instructed that (a) the lineup administrator does not know which person in the lineup is the actual suspect; (b) the culprit might not be in the lineup at all, so the correct answer might be "none of these"; (c) if they can't make a decision, they may respond, "I don't know"; (d) after making a decision, they will be asked how confident they are in that decision; and (e) the investigation will continue even if no identification is made.
Immediate Confidence Statement. A confidence statement should be taken from witnesses as soon as an identification decision (either positive or negative) is made.
Video-Recording. The entire lineup procedure, including prelineup instructions and confidence statement, should be videorecorded.
Avoid Repeated Identifications. Repeating a lineup with the same suspect and same eyewitness should be avoided.

From: Wells, G. L., Kovera, M. B., Douglass, A. B., Brewer, N., Meissner, C. A., & Wixted, J. T. (2020). Policy and procedure recommendations for the collection and preservation of eyewitness identification evidence. *Law and Human Behavior*, *44*(1), 3–36.

Jury Behavior

Juries have an enormous amount of responsibility. They affect the outcomes of trials, including whether a defendant is found guilty or not guilty and, in many cases, what the penalty will be. With the capacity to strip people of their liberty (and sometimes their lives), a fair trial requires that juries function without bias. But do they? Are jurors capable of interpreting evidence and testimony fairly? Can they really disregard inadmissible evidence? Can they understand instructions given by the judge? And if not, what changes would help? For example, an individual may be charged with several instances of a crime. Sometimes these instances are joined into one indictment; in other cases, the defendant is tried separately for each instance. Greene and Loftus (1981) found that when charges are joined into one indictment, the jury is more likely to hand down harsher verdicts than when the charges are tried separately.

Research has also focused on how juries respond to instructions given to them in the courtroom. It has long been known that jurors are easily confused by jury instructions, perhaps influencing the verdicts they reach. In a seminal study, Severance and Loftus (1982) modified the pattern of instructions given to mock juries. Specifically, they wrote instructions in the *active* rather than *passive* voice and made the messages short and concise. In addition, they gave mock juries concrete explanations of abstract concepts such as *reasonable doubt*. The result was a more accurate application of the law by jurors than is usually the case. Even the order in which the judge's instructions are presented can have an effect on jurors. For example, Kassin and Wrightsman (1979) instructed mock jurors to watch a videotaped trial and found that informing jurors as to the requirements of proof *before* presenting the evidence (rather than *after*) had an effect: jurors in the former condition were more likely to presume innocence than were those in the latter condition.

More recently, research on jury instructions has been applied in the courtroom to improve comprehension and jury decision making. Overall, this work shows that overly complex language and excessive jargon lead to poor comprehension (Alvarez et al., 2016). In addition, some types of jury instructions backfire, and can threaten the defendant's right to a fair trial. For instance, instructions meant to protect a defendant from bias are often ineffective and can even have the opposite effect. Research, however, has informed the development of better instructions which reduce bias in jurors' decision making. An example is the use of plain English instructions, written copies of instructions, the use of audiovisual aids, and encouraging judges to provide clarification when requested (e.g., Smith & Haney, 2011). Still, additional research is needed to make such instructions even more effective at helping jurors correctly apply the law.

Think Like a Clinical Psychologist Discuss how the following psychological research studies might be applied in forensic settings (you might read more about these famous studies before your discussion): (a) Solomon Ash's studies on conformity, (b) Albert Bandura's bobo doll studies, and (c) Stanley Milgram's infamous experiment on obedience.

▌▌▌ Multicultural Considerations

Psychologists working in forensic settings encounter some of the most diverse populations, thus making cultural competence a critical attribute. They must recognize the impact that individual and group differences have in legal situations and understand the effects of their own biases on their professional work. Accordingly, as we have seen in all other areas of the field, forensic psychologists are sensitive to, and skilled in, working with individuals, groups, and communities representative of all aspects of individual and cultural diversity. Self-awareness, open-mindedness, and continuing education all minimize the likelihood that personal bias will contaminate their work. Another important role of the forensic psychologist is to work toward protecting members of diverse, underrepresented, and marginalized groups from being disadvantaged by the legal system (e.g., Perlin & McClain, 2009).

An excellent example is the work of psychologist Jennifer Eberhardt, a leading researcher studying the association between race and criminal justice. Eberhardt and her colleagues have shown, for example, how racial stereotypes can impact perceptions of Black people and influence how white people might misremember or neglect evidence that isn't accurate for a Black defendant (Hetey & Eberhardt, 2018). She has also found evidence that physical traits related to race, such as skin color and the shape of facial features, can influence sentencing decisions, including who might be sentenced to death (Eberhardt et al., 2006). In 2015, Eberhardt worked with the Oakland, California, Police Department using computational linguistics to analyze verbal interactions between officers and members of the Oakland community. Although they found no explicit racial bias, they did find that when speaking to white drivers, officers were reassuring, used positive words, and expressed concern for safety. In contrast, when speaking to Black drivers, they more often used negative terms, stuttered, used informal language, and used less explanatory terms (Voigt et al., 2017). Following this research, Eberhardt and her team have worked closely with the Oakland Police Department to implement evidence-based recommendations for reducing such racial disparities.

Psychologist Jennifer Eberhardt is a leading expert in the association between race and criminal justice.

Multicultural competence is also important when interviewing people accused of crimes. The likelihood that interview data will yield material which could potentially vindicate a defendant largely depends on the psychologist's ability to assess the context of criminal behavior. Thus, the examiner's sensitivity to the attitudes, beliefs, and values unique to the worldview of such defendants, as well as cultural norms in social interactions, is vital. Suspiciousness and paranoia are common in forensic interviews; thus, psychologists must first build trust. This can be done by engaging initial discussions regarding personal and familial boundaries and the limits of confidentiality. Identifying the defendant's preferences regarding the time and location of the assessment, along with other variables that might make the individual feel more at ease, also enhances information-gathering. Enlisting the help of family to provide information regarding sociocultural norms can lend weight to court testimony concerning motives, ultimately influencing the legal outcome (e.g., Lee, 2017).

Think Like a Clinical Psychologist How might forensic psychologists impact the way law enforcement professionals interact and work with diverse populations.

Ethical Considerations

As you might imagine, all the ethical principles and guidelines we have explored in previous chapters also apply to practice and research in forensic psychology. Yet because forensic psychology differs in important ways from more traditional practice areas, the American Psychological Association (APA) has developed Specialty Guidelines for Forensic Psychologists that expand on APA's overall ethics code. For example, recall from Chapter 3, *Ethics in Clinical Psychology*, that psychologists are required to avoid dual relationships in which they have affiliations with clients outside the therapeutic context. This principle is also important within the area of forensic psychology, as it is considered unethical for a treating clinical psychologist to become involved in their clients' court cases as an expert. Most recently revised in 2013 (APA, 2013), these specialty guidelines cover the various topics listed and described in **Table 17.5** and are meant to be aspirational, rather than a basis for disciplinary action if violated.

Table 17.5 Overview of Specialty Guidelines for Forensic Psychologists	
Topic	**Summary of the Guidelines**
Responsibilities	Forensic psychologists strive for accuracy, honesty, and truthfulness in science and practice; they try to resist partisan pressures to provide services in any way that might tend to be misleading or inaccurate.
Competence	Forensic psychologists continually develop and maintain their knowledge and skills, keeping up with developments in the fields of psychology and the law.
Diligence	Forensic psychologists are clear about the scope, time frame, and compensation regarding their work, and they provide their services promptly. They exercise discretion in determining the extent and means by which their services are provided.
Relationships	Forensic psychologists recognize that their obligations and duties vary as a function of the nature of their relationships with those retaining their services. They strive to avoid conflicts of interest and dual relationships.
Fees	Forensic psychologists consider their experience, time, and labor when setting fees. They seek to avoid being influenced by compensation and avoid situations in which fees are contingent on the outcome of a case. They also contribute a portion of their services for no fee (e.g., to clients in low-income brackets).
Informed consent, notification, and assent	Because rights, liberties, and properties may be at risk in forensic matters, forensic psychologists fully inform their clients about the nature and parameters of the services they provide.
Conflicts in practice	When conflicts occur, forensic psychologists make the conflict known to the relevant parties and consider the rights and interests of these parties when resolving conflicts.
Privacy, confidentiality, and privilege	Forensic psychologists maintain the confidentiality of information relating to a client or retaining party, except insofar as disclosure is consented to by the client or retaining party, or required or permitted by law.
Methods and procedures	Forensic psychologists use appropriate methods and procedures when performing examinations, consultations, educational activities, and research.
Assessment	Forensic psychologists use assessment methods in ways that are consistent with the evidence for their usefulness and application.
Professional and other public communications	Forensic psychologists make reasonable efforts to ensure that the products of their services, as well as their own public statements and professional reports and testimony, are communicated in ways that promote understanding and avoid deception.

From: www.apa.org/practice/guidelines/forensic-psychology

▌▌▌ Chapter Summary

Forensic psychology is concerned with the application of psychological methods, theories, and concepts to the legal system. Although Hugo von Münsterberg's 1908 book proclaimed that psychology had much to offer to the legal system, little influence was observed until the 1950s. Today, the influence and popularity of forensic psychology are apparent; many journals, books, and specialty training programs exist. In this chapter, we have discussed the activities of forensic psychologists. Forensic psychologists may serve as expert witnesses or as consultants for both criminal and civil cases. They may also be called on to predict whether someone is likely to be a danger to self or to others, or to profile characteristics of the likely perpetrator after harm has been committed. They sometimes are asked to provide judgments about a person's psychological state when they died. Forensic psychologists also serve as consultants regarding jury selection and witness preparation. Finally, forensic psychologists may conduct research on topics such as eyewitness testimony and jury behavior, the results of which have direct implications for the legal system. As with other areas of clinical psychology, there are consequential multicultural and ethical considerations within the practice of, and research in, forensic psychology.

Applying What You've Learned

Exercise 1: Consider Ted Kaczynski, the so-called Unabomber. Discuss how the M'Naghten rule, the Durham standard, and the ALI standard might be applied to his case to judge whether he is competent to stand trial. What types of evidence would be of greatest importance to determine of his competency?

Exercise 2: As mentioned in this chapter, a child custody evaluation must address three major issues: (a) the child's development and psychological needs, (b) each parent's strengths and limitations, and (c) the way each member of the family interacts with the others. Given what you have learned in this course, as a clinical psychologist, what types of assessments would you use in your evaluation to address these issues?

Key Terms

ALI standard: The most liberal standard for determining the insanity of a defendant. This standard attests that the defendant is not responsible for an unlawful act if it resulted from a mental disease or defect such that the defendant lacked substantial capacity either to appreciate the criminality of the act (a cognitive deficit) or to conform to the law (a volitional deficit).

Behavioral consistency: The assumption that an offender's crimes tend to be similar to one another.

Burden of proof: The obligation to establish the truth of an assertion in a court of law. In the case of the insanity plea, the burden of proof is usually on the defense.

Child custody evaluation: When a custody dispute needs to be settled legally, a forensic psychologist might be hired by the court, or by one or both parents, to perform an evaluation of the child and one or both parents, as well as conduct interviews with other relatives, teachers, and anyone else who might be able to provide useful information to aid in a recommendation to the court regarding custody and visitation.

Competency to stand trial: The defendant's state of mind at the time of trial. To be deemed competent, it must be shown that the defendant is capable of cooperating with an attorney with a reasonable degree of rational understanding as well as maintaining an understanding of the criminal proceeding and charges being faced.

Durham standard: Developed in response to concerns that the M'Naghten rule was outdated; holds that people accused of a crime are not criminally responsible if their unlawful act was the product of mental illness.

Expert testimony: Testimony of a trained individual, such as a psychologist, giving opinions and inferences about psychological damage.

Expert witness: An individual who has unique training, or experience, and is called upon to help the court understand and evaluate evidence or offer opinions and inferences on an issue.

Eyewitness testimony: Testimony given by an individual who has witnessed part or all of an event (e.g., a crime, an accident). Eyewitness testimony is often inaccurate, unreliable, and distorted by subsequent information. One role of forensic psychologists is to help identify the conditions in a specific case that might produce distortions in testimony.

Forensic psychology: A psychology subspecialty that focuses on applying psychological concepts and methods to questions/problems arising within the context of the legal system. Forensic psychologists may be called upon to provide expertise on matters of child custody, jury selection, the prediction of dangerousness, and so on.

Guilty but mentally ill: Under this verdict, convicted individuals are sent to a psychiatric facility for treatment. If eventually judged to be sane, they are sent to prison to serve what is left of their sentence.

Homology: The assumption that similar crimes are committed by similar offenders.

Insane: The state of being unable to think clearly or sensibly at the time that one commits a crime.

Involuntary commitment: Hospitalization that occurs against the will of the individual.

Joint custody: An arrangement in which both parents share in the custody of a child following divorce. Many "joint custody" arrangements are determined informally by the parents; formal court orders tend to be issued only in cases where the parties could arrive at no satisfactory agreement on their own.

Jury shadowing: The process of hiring individuals similar to those who are serving on a given jury and monitoring their reactions to the testimony as it is presented at the trial. The reactions of the shadow jurors are used to anticipate the reactions of the actual jurors and may serve as the basis for a shift in courtroom strategy.

Lay witness: A witness who may testify only to events observed.

M'Naghten rule: The oldest standard for determining the insanity of a defendant. This rule requires the defense to prove that at the time of the unlawful act, the defendant's reasoning was so impaired by "a disease of the mind" that they either did not appreciate what they were doing or did not comprehend that it was wrong.

Not guilty by reason of insanity (NGRI): A legal determination that a mental illness makes one incapable of differentiating between right and wrong; rarely used or successful.

Psychological autopsy: An evaluation that aims to reconstruct a person's psychological state — their thoughts, mood, and behavioral tendencies — at the time of their death to shed light on contextual factors preceding their death, including any involvement they might have had in their own passing.

Psychological criminal profiling: A method of identifying criminal suspects using emotional and behavioral clues from the crime scene.

Sane: A legal determination that an individual was of sound mind and mentally healthy at the time of the alleged crime.

Visitation rights: Court-given right of the noncustodial parent to see and visit the child, absent extraordinary circumstances.

Voir dire: A legal term that refers to that part of the trial during which attorneys conduct a preliminary examination of potential jurors to determine with which side of the case they are likely to identify.

Voluntary commitment: The circumstance in which an individual agrees to be admitted to a psychiatric hospital and is permitted to leave at any time, though some hospitals require that such individuals indicate their intent to leave several days in advance. This allows time to initiate commitment proceedings if it is determined the individual is seriously mentally ill or dangerous.

Witness preparation: Helping witnesses present their testimony more effectively without changing the facts to which their testimony is directed. Forensic psychologists may be consulted to assist with many aspects of witness preparation (e.g., preparing them for the sheer experience of being a witness in the courtroom or making recommendations as to their appearance, the manner in which they present facts).

CONNECT ONLINE:

 | Check out our videos and additional resources located at: www.macmillanlearning.com

Examining Psychology's Contributions to the Belief in Racial Hierarchy and Perpetuation of Inequality for People of Color in U.S.

A Historical Chronology from the American Psychological Association (October 2021)

The American Psychological Association commissioned and compiled this chronology as part of its development of the *Apology to People of Color for APA's Role in Promoting, Perpetuating, and Failing to Challenge Racism, Racial Discrimination, and Human Hierarchy in U.S.* and the *Role of Psychology and APA in Dismantling Systemic Racism Against People of Color in U.S.* Based on this chronology, APA issued a public apology and an action plan to address systemic racism with psychological science, education, practice, and all of its work advocating for psychology in the public interest.

Project Background

Since the early months of 2020, COVID-19 has resulted in more than 4.6 million deaths worldwide (World Health Organization, 2021). People of color have been disproportionately affected by this pandemic, with some of these groups being twice as likely as White, non-Hispanic groups to become infected, three times as likely to be hospitalized, and twice as likely to die from COVID-19 (Centers for Disease Control, 2021). It is an understatement to say that this pandemic has laid bare serious racial health inequities in the United States, a situation that results not from simple variables such as health care access, but rather from a long history of structural racism (Khazanchi, Evans, & Marcelin, 2020).

During this devastating global health crisis, the country also witnessed the murder of George Floyd by Minneapolis police officers in May of 2020. Floyd's death was historically one of many, but it sparked protests across the country and internationally. COVID-19 also highlighted and reinforced existing systemic racism, xenophobia, blaming, and othering of Asian Americans throughout the pandemic (Starks, 2021). Racist ideologies, the glaring inequities highlighted by COVID-19, and a polarized political climate led many to describe the United States as simultaneously battling a "pandemic of racism" (American Psychological Association, 2020, May 29).

In 2020, APA launched a series of efforts aimed at dismantling racism in psychology, in APA, and in society more generally. As part of this effort, the Association sought a historical review of how psychology and APA have harmed people of color since the formal institutionalization of U.S. psychology in the late 1800s. The goal of the review was to document the long history of harm to these communities, and to provide a resource that could inform APA's work on an apology.

The Cummings Center for the History of Psychology (CCHP) at The University of Akron conducted the historical review. The CCHP is a research and humanities center that collects, preserves, and shares the history of psychology with a variety of audiences through the National Museum of Psychology and the Archives of the History of American Psychology. It is home to more than 3,000 linear feet of unpublished papers, artifacts, and media documenting psychology's history from the 1800s to the present.

Overview and Approach

The review was conducted by a writing group and a working group with psychologists from across the country. The writing group is comprised of Cummings Center staff and faculty, including three historians of psychology and an archives assistant with a background in American history and archival theory and practice. We have relied on primary and secondary sources in the history of psychology and related human sciences.

The writing group has relied on feedback from and discussion with a working group comprised of seven academics, including historians of psychology and psychologists with long and valuable experience with the field and its historical and present relationship with people of color. This working group represents many communities of color and has lived and studied psychology's history in relation to race, culture, ethnicity, class, and social and political issues. They have worked to create, preserve, and advance psychologies that emanate from, attend to, and serve communities of color.

The following review begins with a summary of our findings, followed by a chronology representing the historical data used to inform those findings. It is important to note that silences — moments when the field could have spoken or acted on behalf of communities of color but failed to do so — were difficult to demonstrate with historical actions, particularly in a timeline format. We fully acknowledge that silences, omissions, and failures to act are underrepresented in this account.

It is also important to note that the data in the chronology are necessarily incomplete. It is nearly impossible to document every instance of harm in one chronology. The historical data are comprised of examples of harm that we and other historians have deemed most salient and impactful based on our assessment of the extent to which they serve as exemplars of repeated and prominent trends in the field's history and their degree of direct connection with organized psychology. We stress, however, that these specific harms are part of a larger problematic culture in psychology, rooted in oppressive and exclusionary psychological science and practice.

In addition, it is important to note that this review does not constitute a complete history of psychology or of APA. We specifically focused on moments of harm and did not attend to actions that have promoted equity, advanced people of color within the field, and addressed the concerns of communities of color. This focus was necessary for the purpose of informing an apology. Psychology's history contains examples of both harm and help. Nonetheless, our review of the literatures suggests that moments of harm have been the dominant theme in psychology's history.

This review focuses broadly on harms done to racial and ethnic groups and does not fully attend to the unique experiences of each group or to the specific historical harms central for mixed-race, biracial, and multiethnic persons. Many individuals with intersectional identities have been harmed by psychologists through some of these same patterns of exclusion, othering, and pathologizing and some that are more unique to each group.

A Note on Language

In many places in this review, we have chosen to retain phrasing as it appears in the historical literature to demonstrate the ways in which people of color were in fact dehumanized through language used by psychology and other fields of inquiry. When using this language, we do so in quotations.

In all other cases, we use contemporary language, following APA's guidelines for writing about racial and ethnic identity (American Psychological Association, 2020).

Throughout this document, we use common socially referenced racial categories such as White, Black, Asian, and First Peoples. We acknowledge that this kind of categorization is artificial and does not account for the great diversity of history, experience, and ways of being within each category. In the context of this review, "White" refers to people of European ancestry, though we note that Southern and Eastern Europeans have been discriminated against and harmed by mainstream, Western-oriented psychology.

Executive Summary

Psychologists have contributed directly and indirectly to the belief in human hierarchies through scientific racism, defined as "the use of scientific concepts and data to create and justify ideas of an enduring, biologically based hierarchy" (Winston, 2020, p. 2). Results from a century's worth of psychological studies of individual difference were interpreted as evidence of innate, hereditary difference in ability between racial and ethnic groups, an interpretation that runs counter to current findings from genetic research demonstrating significant variability within traditional racial groupings and considerable variability between different traditional racial groups (Baker, 2021). Historically, groups found to score differently on assessments designed by White psychologists and normalized on White populations were deemed inferior based on those results. These interpretations have created and upheld existing racial stereotypes and prejudices against people of color and reinforced the belief in White supremacy. Such beliefs found strong support in the early 20th century among psychologists and other social scientists, particularly those involved in the eugenics movement.

Psychological data have been used by psychologists and others to justify social policies that harmed people of color, including racial segregation, diminished educational opportunities, restrictions on immigration, institutionalization, forced sterilization, and antimiscegenation laws. In the face of ongoing critiques of methods and practices that discriminate against people of color, psychologists have often failed to listen, speak up, or create change. This is difficult to document in a historical study, but psychology's history includes many critical moments of silence and inaction at times when proactive acts or speaking out were warranted. Psychology has sustained and failed to challenge research, practice, and policy frameworks rooted in White normativity that support the continued belief in White superiority.

Finally, people of color have been marginalized and excluded in the field of psychology in a multitude of ways, from educational and employment opportunities to gatekeeping (e.g., journal editorships, student supervision) and governance roles. In addition, issues of central concern to these communities have not been adequately addressed. Throughout our work, we were repeatedly confronted by the fact that the entire narrative of psychology — from textbooks to histories to journal articles — often excludes people of color and their voices. This chronology fails in this same manner: in an attempt to document the harms done to people of color, we often gave too much voice to White psychologists.

Our analysis of the historical record suggests that one of the central issues for U.S. psychology, both past and present, is its strong ties to hegemonic science and practice. Such an approach privileges certain ways of knowing, being, and doing as natural, normative, and progressive (Adams, Kurtiş, Gómez, Molina, & Dobles, 2018). Historically, psychology has accepted Whiteness as a standard or norm and presented other modes of being as marginal, unnatural, or in some way straying from the norm. Recently, this has appeared in the psychological literature as a WEIRD (Western, educated, industrial, rich, democratic) approach (Henrich, Heine, & Norenzayan, 2010), but people of color have noted versions of it in the literature since at least the beginning of the 20th century (Du Bois, 1903).

It is important to distinguish between our historical review and the legacies resulting from that history as reflected in contemporary policies and practices. History is dynamic and there are often prospective consequences of history. We were charged with conducting a retrospective review of the history of harm to people of color and have therefore not included the many ways in which this history has left a legacy in our present. We acknowledge that history is not simply a thing of the past: it is the very foundation for our current cultural mindset and our present modes of thinking, being, and doing as psychologists. There is a common notion that we should learn history so that we can avoid repeating past mistakes. We would argue, with historian Avner Segall (1999), that "it is not the repetitive past we ought to fear . . . but rather, the legacy of the past in our present" (p. 366). The harms identified in this review are part of our past, but they continue to provide the platform for contemporary psychology.

This chronology demonstrates ways in which research and practice have focused on White culture and used it as a global standard. This culture, evident from the very beginnings of the field, is inseparable from the social and political landscape of the United States at the end of the 19th century. Organized psychology grew up in these conditions, helped to create and sustain them, and continues to bear their indelible imprint.

In sum, our historical review of psychology's harms to people of color indicates that psychologists have, in both the past and present:

- Established and participated in scientific models and approaches rooted in scientific racism;
- Created, sustained, and promulgated ideas of human hierarchy through the construction, study, and interpretation of racial difference;

- Promoted the idea that racial difference is biologically based and fixed;
- Used psychological science and practice to support segregated and subpar education for people of color;
- Created and promoted widespread use of psychological tests and instruments that discriminated against people of color;
- Failed to take concerted action in response to calls for an end to testing and psychometric racism;
- Supported the widespread use of educational assessments and interventions that were lucrative for the field of psychology, but harmed people of color;
- Provided ideological support for and failed to speak out against the colonial framework of the boarding and day school systems for First Peoples of the Americas;
- Created, sustained, and promoted a view of people of color as deficient or damaged;
- Applied psychological science and practice to oppose "race-mixing" and to support segregation, sterilization, and antimarriage laws, using the ideas of early 20th century eugenics;
- Failed to represent the approaches, practices, voices, and concerns of people of color within the field of psychology and within society;
- Failed to respond or responded too slowly in the face of clear social harms to people of color

Psychology and the Belief in Racial Hierarchy: A Chronology

1850–1900

The formal institutionalization of U.S. psychology (as indicated by the creation of programs, departments, degrees, societies, and schools) occurred in the years surrounding the Civil War, centered on national debates about slavery; the passing of the Indian Appropriations Act, which removed First Peoples from their tribal lands to government reservations; the Chinese Exclusion Act, which suspended Chinese immigration; and the Supreme Court's *Plessy v. Ferguson* decision, which held that segregation laws did not violate the equal protection clause of the Fourteenth Amendment. The formalized psychology established at this time was led primarily by White men and leaned heavily on evolutionary theory, with its emphasis on survival and adaptation of the species. The field almost immediately lent its support to the notion of White superiority, with its focus on demonstrating individual differences among different racial groups.

1869: Francis Galton, who was recognized as an early leader in psychology (among other professions) publishes *Hereditary Genius*, a central early event in the study of individual differences and psychometrics in European and U.S. psychology. In this work, he ranked the "comparative worth of different races" and concluded that "the average intellectual standard of the negro race is some two grades below our own" (Galton, 1869, pp. 336–338). In 1883, Galton would introduce the word "eugenics," described as a science of improving "racial stock." This work was heavily cited and used by the first generation of psychologists who established APA, the first recognized psychology journals, and the most influential research programs.

1892: The American Psychological Association is founded, with G. Stanley Hall as president and 31 White males elected to membership.

1895: One of the earliest examples of scientific racism — defined as the use of scientific concepts and data to create and justify ideas of an enduring biologically based hierarchy (Winston, 2020) — is published in *Psychological Review*, one year after the journal is first established (Bache, 1895). First Peoples and Black participants were reported to have faster reaction times than White participants. The author argued that reaction time was a primitive reflex and that the superior, more evolved intelligence of White participants resulted in more contemplative thought and slower reaction times.

1897: In a study of Black and White children, Stetson (1897) found that Black children outperformed White children on a memory task. The author attributed this to the greater mnemonic ability of their "primitive brains." He further described Black children as being deficient in reasoning.

1897: APA funds a Committee on Physical and Mental Tests, its first financial commitment to an activity other than its own administration (Baldwin, Cattell, & Jastrow, 1898).

1900–1925

As U.S. psychology established itself in the early 1900s, the U.S. experienced the First World War, massive growth, and unprecedented immigration. More than 15 million new immigrants, the majority of whom arrived from southern and eastern Europe, came to the U.S. in the first quarter of the century. Antiimmigration sentiment increased, fueling the eugenics movement, which sought to "improve the human race" using principles of heredity. Scholars and lawmakers debated the "Negro Question," which often focused on schooling and curriculum for people of color. Education was also a question at the forefront with First Peoples of the Americas, as more than 6,000 students were enrolled in federal boarding schools that attempted to replace First Peoples culture with an education that fit Anglo-American standards. Many psychologists continued to focus on individual differences among races and became actively involved in the eugenics movement, using their science to support eugenical aims.

1904: APA forms an ad hoc committee on testing standards, forming the Association's first committee on standards for apparatus, procedures, and results of group and individual tests. The resulting Committee on Measurement consists of early psychologists who frequently supported ideas of racial hierarchy and/or eugenics, including James R. Angell, Charles H. Judd, Walter B. Pillsbury, and Carl E. Seashore.

1904: G. Stanley Hall, founding president of APA, publishes the highly influential text, *Adolescence*. In it, he described First Peoples as childlike, with adults from this group being more similar to White children or adolescents in their development. Hall supported the development of "civilizing programs" tailored to what he deemed to be the needs of First Peoples (Hall, 1904; 1905; Richards, 1997). These programs, once enacted, were attempted to eradicate First Peoples' culture, language, and spiritual life. Hall's views were echoed by other psychologists during this period (e.g., Chamberlain, 1909).

1910: The Eugenics Record Office is established as a department of the Carnegie Institution of Washington's Station for Experimental Evolution. It became the center for eugenics advocacy, research, and publication in the U.S. Leaders of organized psychology, including Edward Thorndike, Robert Yerkes, Arthur Estabrook, Paul Achilles, and Lewis Terman were founders and active members of this office. They also led and contributed to other eugenics-based organizations in this period, including the Cold Spring Harbor Laboratory, the Galton Society, and the American Eugenics Society (Zenderland, 2001). Through these groups, they promoted sterilization initiatives for "unfit and inferior races" and supported race-based immigration policies and negative heredity laws (Brigham, 1923; Engs, 2005). Psychological tests were regularly used in the work of these organizations. Between 1892 and 1947, 31 presidents of APA acted in leadership positions in eugenics organizations, during their time as president, but also in the years surrounding their presidencies (Yakushko, 2019).

1913: A 70-page psychological monograph reports inferiority of school performance among Black children in integrated schools in New York, a finding the author attributes to "race heredity" (Mayo, 1913). Early papers like this set the tone and pattern for later work on difference and were used to argue against improved schooling opportunities for Black children (Richards, 1997).

1914: Psychologist William McDougall, writing in the *Eugenical Review,* lays out a plan for how experimental psychology can serve the goals of eugenics, focusing on the study of the hereditary basis of mental qualities (McDougall, 1914). McDougall, chair of psychology at Harvard, argued in favor of restrictions on interracial marriage, claiming that mixed race individuals are mentally defective and that such mixing would produce a "race of submen" (McDougall, 1921, p. 132). He further argued for the creation of a separate territory for Black Americans to prevent "race amalgamation" (McDougall, 1925, p. 162).

1914: Psychological research, tests, and instruments are used at some boarding schools with First Peoples during this period. For example, a teacher at the Phoenix Indian School described psychological testing and research in education in the *Indian School Journal,* noting use of the early Binet scales and citing the work of psychologists J. Wallace Wallin and Stuart Appleton Courtis (Scott, 1914).

1914: Psychologist Henry Goddard, a pioneer of the U.S. testing movement, serves as the psychology representative on the *Committee to Study and Report on the Best Practical Means of Cutting Off the Defective Germ-Plasm in the American Population.* The Committee, established by the Research Committees of the Eugenics Section of the American Breeders Association, recommended segregation, and sterilization as the best methods of preserving "the blood of the American people" (Laughlin, 1914, p. 6). The Committee called on psychology to help determine standards and tests for identifying "mental degenerates and defectives proposed for sterilization" (p. 7). By 1930, 35,000 people in the U.S. had been sterilized, mostly individuals who had been deemed "feebleminded" or socially or mentally unfit (Greenwood, 2017). Many of these individuals were immigrants, Black people, First Peoples of the Americas, poor White people, and people with disabilities (Kevles, 1998).

1915: Psychologists leading the California Bureau of Juvenile Research at Whittier State School oversee some of the earliest eugenics fieldwork projects, examining the family trees and conducting psychological testing of boys confined at the institution. Psychologist J. Harold Williams, a student of Lewis Terman, directed the project and presented results on "White, Mexican, and Colored children." Historians have documented the biased procedures and results of this project that harmed hundreds or perhaps thousands of youths incarcerated in California by increasing the incarceration rate of these youth and promoting sterilization (Chávez-García, 2015).

1916: Lewis Terman creates the Stanford-Binet Scale. He used differences on this scale as a justification for a segregated system of education geared toward building Black, Mexican, and First Peoples children into "efficient workers" (Terman, 1916), a proposal supported by other psychologists in the early 20th century (Young, 1922). This model was adopted in predominantly Mexican American schools throughout the American Southwest (Gonzalez, 2013, p. 82).

1916: G. O. Ferguson (1916) publishes "The psychology of the Negro," considered to be a classic example in the history of scientific racism (Guthrie, 1998). Ferguson linked performance (including reasoning, association, memory, and intelligence) with skin color and argued that Black people are more emotionally volatile, unstable, and less capable of abstract thought. Ferguson also espoused the prominent "mulatto hypothesis," the idea that the mental characteristics of Black people were greater among those who had a higher proportion of "White blood."

1917: APA president Robert Yerkes launches the Committee on the Psychological Examination of Recruits during the First World War. The Committee was created under the auspices of the National Research Council and headed by Yerkes, reporting to the Office of the Surgeon General. Yerkes and a team of psychologists recommended mental examination of every soldier, and by the end of the War, they had administered psychological tests to nearly 2 million men. Culturally biased test questions and examination procedures, along with an assumption of White, American normativity, led to results that established a clear racial hierarchy of performance with White, American-born recruits scoring highest on IQ tests and Black recruits, particularly those from the American south, scoring the lowest. 89% of Black recruits were labelled by the Committee as "morons" (Kevles, 1968; Rury, 1988; Yerkes, 1921). These tests are the forerunners of the National Intelligence Test and the Scholastic Aptitude Test (SAT). Concerns about large racial gaps in SAT scores continue in the present (see Brookings Institution, 2017).

1917: During this time, APA president Robert Yerkes served as chairman of the Committee on the Inheritance of Mental Traits at Cold Spring Harbor. He also served on the Committee on Eugenics of the National Commission on Prisons and the Board of Directors for the Human Betterment Foundation under eugenicist Paul Popenoe (Engs, 2005; Paul, 1965). In the years after the War, APA's work in supporting the war effort and in "segregating the incompetent" was praised (Riley, 1919, p. 2).

1921: Many psychologists continue to examine racial difference and a formal definition of "racial psychology" appears in the *Journal of Applied Psychology*. Work contrasting "mixed" and "full blood" First Peoples on a battery of psychological tests concluded that those with "White blood" outperform those without (Garth, 1921). Though Garth would later become a critic of scientific racism, his early work contributed significantly to its prevalence.

1921: At the Second International Congress of Eugenics in New York City, APA president-elect Knight Dunlap hosts an exhibit on using psychology to better the human race both physically and mentally. The exhibit presented racial differences between White, Black, and First Peoples. Psychology journals like the *Journal of Applied Psychology* are exhibited alongside eugenics publications (Doyle, 2014).

1922: Many psychologists continue to support the idea of White superiority in both public and academic outlets. Psychologist James Rowland Angell, president of Yale University, delivered a series of addresses describing the hierarchy of the races, espousing White superiority, and discussing the low intelligence of "savages lowest in the human scale" (Angell, 1922, p. 115). This same year, the *Journal of Comparative Psychology* published research linking the degree of "White blood" in First Peoples to higher intelligence test scores (Hunter & Sommermeier, 1922). Five years later, an additional study on intelligence and "White blood" among First Peoples was published in the same journal (Fitzgerald & Ludeman, 1927). In 1933, further research was published arguing that First Peoples children demonstrate more dishonesty than White children and describing the entire Navajo Nation as "notoriously dishonest" (Pressey & Pressey, 1933, p. 129).

1923: Lewis Terman, widely known for his promotion of eugenics and his belief in racial hierarchy, becomes president of APA.

1924: The Johnson-Reed Act passes, limiting immigration from Southern and Eastern Europe and favoring immigrants from Northern and Western Europe. The goal of the Act, as stated, was to preserve American homogeneity. Italians, Greeks, and Eastern European Jews were heavily impacted and Syrian immigration was limited to 100 people per year. It further extended a ban on Asian immigration. Psychological research was cited by eugenics leaders in congressional testimony leading up to passage of the Act. It was argued that immigrants from Southern and Eastern Europe were endowed with inherently poor genetic material and that restriction was needed to preserve American racial stock (Doyle, 2014; Laughlin, 1923; Tucker, 1994; Gelb, Allen, Futterman, & Mehler, 1986).

1925–1950

The U.S. exited one war, contended with the Great Depression, and then entered another global conflict. Under Executive Order 9066, more than 120,000 Americans of Japanese ancestry were forced from their homes into internment camps around the United States. During this time, communities of color around the United States began challenging the racist and exclusionary structure of the country. There were several challenges to segregated schooling, with cases arising regarding schooling for Black and Latinx children. First Peoples of the Americas continued to organize and dispute government control of lands and education, forming the National Congress of American Indians in 1944. Similarly, the Congress of Spanish Speaking People formed in 1939. The second World War resulted in massive growth in psychology across a wide variety of areas, including assessment and treatment of war-related trauma, as well as occupational classification, leading to close ties between psychology and the military. More people of color begin receiving PhDs in psychology, and psychologists of color begin challenging the findings and practices of predominantly White mainstream psychology (Guthrie, 1998). Psychology grew and changed in unprecedented ways during this time and many psychologists began a public retreat from their explicitly stated views of White supremacy in the years following World War II. The Society for the Psychological Study of Social Issues was established in 1936, with the intention of directly addressing social issues and issuing public statements, including statements on racism. Nonetheless, leaders of psychological science and practice continued to support the idea of a natural human hierarchy to a greater extent than other social and behavioral sciences.

1926: Psychologists Stanley Porteus and Marjorie Babcock publish *Temperament and Race*, reporting on studies of Chinese, Hawaiian, Portuguese, Filipino, and Puerto Rican people in

Hawaii. While some of these individuals were born in Hawaii, some were immigrants. The results reinforced stereotypes of these groups, and the authors argued that racial hierarchy and racial differences are rooted in genetics. Porteus continued to publish on this topic, and his work inspired further research in this area. In 1929, for example, Pratt compared the school achievement of Japanese, Chinese, Hawaiian, and Part-Hawaiian school children using achievement tests and reports that Hawaiians have lower achievement scores. The author concludes that Hawaiians are "by native abilities and interests, completely unfitted" to education (Pratt, 1929, p. 667).

1927: Research on racial differences continues. An article in the *Journal of Experimental Psychology*, a journal then edited by eugenicist psychologist Madison Bentley, compared First Peoples to White people and describes them as slower at decision making, less confident, and having poorer coordination of impulses (Downey, 1927). This is one of many examples of this kind of research during this time (see Garth & Barnard, 1927; Jamieson & Sandiford, 1928).

1927: The College Entrance Examination Board's Scholastic Aptitude Test (SAT) is first administered. The test was developed by Carl Brigham, rooted in the work of military psychologists in the World War I testing program.

1932: George I. Sanchez, known as the founder of Chicano psychology, challenges biased research literature on the intelligence of Mexican American children in a *Journal of Applied Psychology* article, "Group differences in Spanish-speaking children: A critical review."

1933: Inez Beverly Prosser completes her doctorate in psychology from the College of Education at the University of Cincinnati, becoming the first African American women to earn the degree.

1933: Psychologist Raymond Cattell argues against the "mixture of blood between racial groups" (Cattell, 1933, p. 155). A few years later, he declared that Black individuals have "contributed practically nothing to social progress and culture" and argued against their full citizenship (Cattell, 1937, p. 56). Cattell argued that these individuals should "be brought to euthanasia" for this inferiority. In 1972, he again argued that such "race mixing" would result in "the intelligent maintainers of the culture being completely replaced by lower intelligences" (Cattell, 1972, p. 154). He continued to maintain the dangers of race-mixing through the early 1990s.

1933: Black psychologists publish a number of studies countering the findings of White psychologists. Albert Beckham published a study of 1,100 schoolchildren, presenting results that suggest environment plays a central role in shaping intelligence scores (Beckham, 1933). Similar research was published by Howard Hale Long in 1935. In 1936, Herman Canady outlined the impact White examiners have on the test scores of Black test takers. Studies like these, conducted by leading Black psychologists, were often dismissed, and testing continued to be used to support ideas regarding innate racial hierarchy (see Guthrie, 1998; Richards, 1997).

1934: A survey indicates that 25% of psychologists believe that data supports the inherent mental inferiority of Black people (Thompson, 1934). This is compared to 24% of those working in education and 5% of sociologists and anthropologists.

1939: Mamie Phipps Clark and Kenneth Clark conduct experiments on children's perception of race, finding that children become aware of race at a very young age and are attuned to positive and negative attributes associated with racial categories (Clark & Clark, 1939).

1943: A chapter on "The Hopi Child" describes delayed age of walking among the Hopi children compared to White children. This study is just one of many examples of social and behavioral scientists comparing people of color to White populations and using Whiteness as a cultural, racial, and normative standard (Dennis, 1943).

1945: Alexander H. Leighton publishes *The Governing of Men: General Principles and Recommendations Based on Experience at a Japanese Relocation Camp.* Navy psychiatrist Alexander H. Leighton applied the tools of social psychological theory and human management to the administration of the Poston Relocation Center for Japanese Americans. Psychological science strengthened eugenic ideologies of mental inferiority which contributed to the internment of Japanese Americans during World War II. (Herman, 2020, Tyner, 1998).

1950: Despite continuous concerns regarding cultural and racial bias in psychological testing (Canady, 1943), APA establishes the Committee on Test Standards, which issues technical recommendations for test administration and design that some believed did not adequately address race, ethnicity, and culture (Holliday & Holmes, 2003; Jackson, 1975; Simpkins & Raphael, 1970). The same year, the Graduate Record Examination (GRE) was published (Holliday & Holmes, 2003). One year later, anthropologist Allison Davis examined the effects of race and social class on test performance and reiterated ongoing critiques centered on the cultural bias inherent in common psychological tests. Davis noted few differences between groups when controlling for social class (Eels et al., 1951).

1950: From the 1950s on, psychologists received money from the Pioneer Fund, created in the 1930s to promote racial homogeneity, "repatriation" of Black Americans to Africa, and segregation. Money was funneled to White Citizens Councils for "massive resistance" to the *Brown* decision, and later funded nearly all major scientific racist projects (Tucker, 2002). From the 1960s on, psychologists gave explicit assistance to and participated in racial extremist, White nationalist, and neo-Nazi groups, including organizations promoting Holocaust denial (Jackson, 2005; Jackson & Winston 2021; Tucker, 1994, 2002, 2009).

1951–1975

The Civil Rights movement, played out against the backdrop of the Vietnam War, gained traction in the U.S., culminating in legislation such as the McCarran-Walter Act of 1952, the Civil Rights Act of 1964, and the Voting Rights Act of 1965. The famous 1954 *Brown v. Board of Education* Supreme Court decision rendered segregated schooling unconstitutional. Despite these gains, people of color continued to experience direct harm. The U.S. Congress continued to abolish tribal lands and relocate First Peoples of the Americas. However, continued organization and resistance among First Peoples during the Civil Rights era resulted in the McCarran-Walter Act that reinstituted basic rights and returned some power to tribes. Asian Americans, though given citizenship through the 1952 Act, experienced hostility and xenophobia and came under suspicion during the McCarthy era. In the 1960s, the myth of Asian Americans as a "model minority" in comparison to other communities of color publicly emerges in popular print. The Watts Uprising occurred in 1965, when 14,000 members of the National Guard were deployed to a primarily Black and impoverished neighborhood in Los Angeles to respond to the largest urban rebellion of the Civil Rights era. The 1960s also saw the development and expansion of nationwide community mental health programs, many of which were beginning to seek out ways of serving diverse communities. Throughout this period, some leading psychologists continue to support eugenics and explore racial inferiority in their work. Research, including cross-cultural research, done in this period sometimes fails to acknowledge culture, context, and tradition in different communities, positing instead universal human traits and universal patterns of development. APA begins to grapple with the lack of diversity in the field, which continued to be dominated by White men. Many psychologists of color begin forming associations and societies of their own, expressing dissatisfaction with APA's attention to the concerns of communities of color.

1951: Efrain Sanchez-Hidalgo is the first Puerto Rican to be awarded a PhD in psychology, by Columbia University. In 1954, he becomes the founding president of the Puerto Rican Psychological Association.

1952: Carolyn Lewis Attneave becomes the first American Indian to earn a doctorate in psychology, from Stanford University.

1952: Former APA president Henry E. Garrett provides judicial testimony in support of segregation in *Davis v. County School Board*, a precursor to *Brown v. Board of Education* (Winston, 1998). He argued that segregation would not harm Black or White students if school facilities were equal. This idea was later echoed by the three judges who ruled in favor of continued segregation. Garrett's own writings promoted the idea of an innate racial hierarchy until his death in 1973 (Garrett, 1973; Tucker, 1994). During this period, Garrett worked with racial extremist and neo-Nazi groups (Tucker, 2002; Winston, 1998).

1954: *Brown v. Board of Education* is decided, ending legal segregation in the United States. The work and testimony of psychologists Mamie Phipps Clark and Kenneth Clark, along with other social science research, was used to support desegregation and cited in the final decision (Kluger, 1975, Jackson, 2001). Some psychologists opposed desegregation. In 1963, psychologists testified in support of segregation in *Stell v. Savannah Board of Education*, a case brought to challenge the 1954 *Brown* decision (Jackson, 2005).

1958: Psychologist Audrey Shuey, former student of Henry Garrett, publishes *The Testing of Negro Intelligence*, summarizing existing work on racial differences and concluding that White people are innately superior to other races (Shuey, 1958).

1958: The Indian Adoption Project begins, allowing U.S. government officials and others to remove First Peoples children from their parents and communities to be adopted by White families. Transracial adoption practices also impacted children of all racial backgrounds and continue to the present day. Lee (2003) demonstrates that psychological research on transracial adoption has failed to directly attend to the well-being of adoptees. Peters et al. (2015) argue that all such cases must take cultural considerations into account to protect a child's best interests. Further, the Society of Indian Psychologists has outlined the need for any expert testifying in such cases to be an expert in a tribe's culture and customs.

1959: The International Association for the Advancement of Ethnology and Eugenics is founded. The group promoted race science, lobbied to overturn the *Brown* decision, and fought to preserve segregation. The Board and editors include noted academics and neo-Nazi activists. The group actively assisted White Citizens Councils during Southern "massive resistance" to integration (Winston, 1998; Tucker, 2002). Throughout its history, several psychologists (including Henry Garrett, Stanley Porteus, Frank McGurk, Audrey Shuey, and Raymond Cattell) were involved in its leadership and led and contributed to its journal, *Mankind Quarterly* (Winston, 2020).

1962: Martha Bernal is the first Mexican American woman awarded a PhD in psychology, from Indiana University. In 1979, she helped to establish the National Hispanic Psychological Association. In 1979, she examined how APA-accredited clinical psychology programs prepare for treating multicultural populations and she finds the curricula inadequate.

1963: The APA Ad Hoc Committee on Equality of Opportunity in Psychology is established to review challenges in training and employment in psychology in relation to race. They found that there are few opportunities for training Black students, few opportunities for employment for Black psychologists, and little representation within APA governance and Central Office (Pickren & Tomes, 2002; Wispe et al., 1969).

1966: Psychologist Kenneth Clark becomes the first Black president of APA, 74 years after the organization was established.

1966: APA's Standards for Educational and Psychological Tests and Manuals are published. The standards addressed test bias primarily through a focus on test validity. These standards were used by the Equal Employment Opportunity Commission in establishing guidelines for test use, centered primarily on test validity. However, concerns regarding discriminatory use of tests that nonetheless met these validity guidelines continued to be voiced (Plotkin, 1972).

1966: Arthur McDonald becomes the first American Indian man to earn a doctorate in psychology, from the University of South Dakota.

1967: Psychological research continues to be used to justify "acculturation" in residential, boarding, and day school systems in hearings before the U.S. Senate's Special Subcommittee on Indian Education of the Committee on Labor and Public and Public Welfare (Indian Education, 1967). Psychologists were also employed at the schools into the 1970s ("Presentation of Navajo," 1975).

1967: Cross-cultural research, rooted in tests and hypotheses that are developed with urban U.S. samples and then transferred to other cultural contexts, concludes that key aspects of development are transcultural. This work continued into the early 2000s and was extended from race and ethnicity to gender (see Gutmann, 1964, 1967).

1967: Psychologist Henry E. Garrett testifies in opposition to the passage of the Civil Rights Act. Garrett argued that Black people cannot reach the intelligence levels or abilities of White people. He further argues that equal rights will only confuse and frustrate the Black community. Garrett, listed in the Congressional Senate hearing record as "past President, American Psychological Association," had served as APA president in 1946 and was the only psychologist on record to testify (U.S. Government Printing Office, 1967).

1967: Head Start is launched by an interdisciplinary team and included psychologist Edward Zigler among its architects and early leaders. Some psychologists voiced opposition to the program, using SAT scores and other standardized test results to argue that compensatory education programs make no difference for people of color (Jensen, 1985).

1967: The Society for the Psychological Study of Social Issues, along with Kenneth Clark, invites Martin Luther King Jr. to give an invited address at the annual APA convention (Pickren & Tomes, 2002).

1967: Psychologist Arthur Jensen delivers an address, "Social class, race and genetics: Implications for education," to the American Educational Research Association's annual meeting. The address, and much of Jensen's ensuing work, emphasized the genetic roots of group differences in the educability in children of color. The address, delivered in the social context of the Coleman Report exploring educational equality, fueled considerable debate regarding group differences in IQ and ability (Jensen, 1967).

1968: The Association of Black Psychologists (ABPsi) is formed when 75 Black psychologists leave APA, charging that APA had failed to address poverty, racism, and social concerns (Holliday, 2009; Nelson, 1968). The group asks that APA help increase representation of Black psychologists in the field. ABPsi also called for a moratorium on testing, charging that such tests were culturally biased, racist, and unfair (Williams & Mitchell, 1978). In response, APA formed the *APA Ad Hoc Committee on Educational Uses of Tests with Disadvantaged Students*. The Committee issued a report acknowledging the problems with testing but claimed that the central problem was the misuse and misinterpretation of tests, not the tests themselves.

1969: Psychologist Arthur Jensen revives arguments of hereditary influence on racial differences in IQ scores in the *Harvard Educational Review*, claiming that compensatory education programs have failed (Jensen, 1969). His work is widely used by racist and neo-Nazi groups.

1969: The Black Student Psychology Association (BSPA) raises a series of demands from APA, emphasizing the need for recruitment, retention, and training of Black students and Black faculty (Holliday & Holmes, 2003; Simpkins & Raphael, 1970). A resolution was submitted to the APA Council of Representatives calling for proportional representation of "minority" groups at all job levels in firms working with APA. A substitute resolution passed, specifying that APA would adopt a strategy of supplier diversity, aiming to work with firms that are actively trying to increase representation of minority groups in their organizations (Sawyer & Senn, 1973).

1970: The Association of Psychologists Por La Raza is founded at the annual APA convention.

1971: APA members Jack Sawyer and David J. Senn (1971) accuse APA of institutional racism, stating that APA had ignored systemic racism in the organizations with which it affiliates. They note that APA's largest printer, Lancaster Press, employed only a single Black employee, a man who served as the washup man in the pressroom (see also Pickren & Tomes, 2002).

1971: Psychologist Anderson J. Franklin publishes an article in *The Counseling Psychologist*, arguing that counseling research and training, along with psychology education more generally, fails to prepare students for understanding and working with Black clients (Franklin, 1971).

1972: The Asian American Psychological Association is founded, inspired by the civil rights movement and the founding of ABPsi (Alvarez, Singh, & Wu, 2012).

1973: A national survey finds only 15 Chicano psychology faculty in a total of 1,335 psychology faculty. The survey also found only 51 Latino graduate students enrolled in master's programs in psychology and 37 in PhD programs (Ramirez, 2004).

1974: APA sponsors the Vail Conference, leading to recommendations that any psychologist counseling persons of culturally diverse backgrounds must be trained and competent to work with such groups. This led to the establishment of several boards and committees, along with guidelines and further recommendations. However, few institutions offered training in this skill, and in 1977, fewer than 1% of psychologist counselor educators required students to study diverse cultures. Practitioners representing these groups called for specific ethical requirements and reflection of those requirements in accreditation and licensing (Casas, Ponterotto, & Gutierrez, 1986).

1974: APA announces a Minority Fellowship Program, funded with a $1 million grant from the National Institute of Mental Health Center for Minority Group Mental Health Programs.

1975: Psychological testing continues to be the subject of legal arguments. In *Albemarle Paper Co v. Moody* (1975), the Supreme Court ruled that intelligence tests used in employment testing discriminated against Black employees, and those tests must be proven to be reasonable measures of job performance (see also Holliday & Holmes, 2003).

1975: The Society of Indian Psychologists (SIP) is formed independently of APA, merging the American Indian Interest Group and the Network of Indian Psychologists. The group was concerned with the lack of representation of First Peoples within APA (Gray, 2012).

1975–2020

Over the past 50 years, critics contend that U.S. psychology has failed to fully represent people of color and the concerns of communities of color. Furthermore, it has failed to address ongoing concerns about White normativity in psychology and the use of instruments and practices that discriminate against people of color. Between 1975 and the present, several guidelines and recommendations were issued, which do not have the force of professional ethics codes, and compliance remains voluntary. Separate associations and societies continued to be formed during this time to create space for psychologists of color and the issues that are central for communities of color.

1978: The first report from the President's Commission on Mental Health is issued, documenting overrepresentation of people of color in mental health statistics and the lack of effective services for these communities. Subpanels attending to individual ethnic and racial groups stressed the presence of discriminatory barriers for people of color seeking services and the need for policies that accounted for the needs and experiences of each group (Grob, 2005).

1978: Thirty representatives of the Ethnic Minority Psychology Associations (EMPAs) convene with APA leadership to urge APA to provide a strong presence for ethnic minority concerns in the organization (Jones, 1999; Smith & Pickren, 2018; Sue, 1983). They recommended the formation of a Board of Ethnic Minority Affairs (BEMA). Council rejected this proposal, and APA formed the Office of Ethnic Minority Affairs. The following year, the APA Board proposed creating a standing bylaws committee instead of BEMA, but Council rejected this and put the issue to the membership (Conger, 1980). It passed, and APA established the Board of Ethnic Minority Affairs in 1980. In 1990, BEMA was sunset, and the Committee on Ethnic Minority Affairs took its place.

1979: Several organizations coalesce to form the National Hispanic Psychological Association, which later became the National Latinx Psychological Association.

1979: Congressional hearings for the Truth in Testing Act are held. White psychologists testified regarding the utility of ability-based scoring and the generalizability of testing. Black psychologists reiterated that standardized testing is problematic and discriminatory (US Government Printing Office, 1980). This same year, the Federal District Court of Northern California rules in favor of five Black students who had been placed in special education classes due to their performance on psychological tests. The case centered on the use of psychological tests and their role in blocking educational and economic opportunities for Black youth in California (*Larry P. v. Riles*, 1979).

1980: Chicano Studies professors James Vásquez and Clotilde Gold publish *Counseling and Minorities: A Bibliography*. They noted that limited amount of work had been done on counseling with communities of color and that the work that did exist often went unnoticed by practitioners, professors, and students. Less than 4% of the articles in the bibliography were from psychology journals and only three were from either the flagship or mainstream journals of APA.

1983: Rogler (1983) provides data demonstrating Puerto Rican and Black people are more frequently diagnosed with mental illness and more frequently admitted to community mental health centers.

1985: APA, along with the American Educational Research Association and the National Council on Measurement in Education, issues a new set of *Standards for Educational and Psychological Testing*. This is the fifth set of standards spanning a 30-year period. The new edition highlights rights and privileges of test takers and includes attention to nonnative English speakers, along with race, ethnicity, and culture (Wagner, 1987).

1985: In *Personality and Individual Differences*, psychologist J. Philippe Rushton publishes the first of more than 150 articles claiming that compared to Whites, Africans evolved to have lower intelligence, have more children and care for them poorly, and have a greater tendency to commit crime.

1986: Logan Wright becomes the first American Indian to serve as president of APA, 93 years after the Association's founding (Gray, 2012).

1986: Division 45, the Society for the Psychological Study of Ethnic Minority Issues, was established to draw attention to issues related to ethnic minority psychology (Holliday & Holmes, 2003; Morales, Lau, & Ballesteros, 2012).

1988: Ponteretto (1988) reviews articles published in the *Journal of Counseling Psychology* between 1976 and 1986 and finds that 5.7% of the articles focus on people of color. Furthermore, people of color made up only 6.5 to 11.1% of regular editorial board reviewers.

1990: Psychologist Arthur Jensen is invited as keynote speaker for the Society for General Psychology at the annual APA convention. At this time, Jensen was continuing to assert the importance of heredity in explaining the social position of Black Americans and continued to speak publicly of the dangers of compensatory social programs until his death in 2012.

1990: Throughout the 1990s and 2000s, people of color are grossly underrepresented in APA and in the field more generally due to historical marginalization and exclusion (Bernal & Castro, 1994). They represented only 17% of members of boards and committees (primarily serving on public interest boards and committees) and only 6% of the Council of Representatives (Hall, 1997). During this time, people of color represented 26.3% of the U.S. population. In 2000, racial/ethnic minority psychologists represented 5.8% of APA's total membership. This includes .3% American Indian, 1.7% Asian, 2.1% Hispanic, 1.7% Black, and <.1% Multiracial/Multiethnic. Numbers in the U.S. workforce were similar in 2000: 90% White, 2% Asian, 5% Hispanic, and 2% Black (American Psychological Association, 2020b). In a 2007 report, Division 45 summarized the number of awards given to people of color, demonstrating that members of these groups have been historically marginalized and excluded within APA. They also note disparities in governance and Council participation, Fellow status, and distribution of NIH funding (Division 45 Science Committee, 2007).

1990: Sue and Sue report that 50% of people identified as minority group members terminate counseling after the first session. This is compared to 30% of White people. Further research suggested this was related to negative experiences and lack of cultural sensitivity on the part of therapists (Fukuyama, 1990).

1992: Reviews of APA's Ethical Principles of Psychologists and Code of Conduct find little mention of race and ethnicity (Hall, 1997). The following year, APA issues Guidelines for Providers of Psychological Services to Ethnic, Linguistic, and Culturally Diverse Populations (American Psychological Association, 1993).

1992: Graham (1992) reviews literature in six top APA journals and finds that, between 1970 and 1989, 3.6% of published articles are focused on African Americans, a number that showed a steady decrease. She further finds that most of the published work is focused on complexities of using standardized instruments with Black people and notes that while it is important to attend to these complexities, it means that little to no work is published addressing healthy personality development and competent intellectual functioning.

1994: Alice Chang becomes the first person of color to serve on APA's Board of Directors.

1997: Raymond Cattell is selected the winner of the APA Gold Medal Award for Life Achievement in Psychological Science. A small group of psychologists protested the award, charging that Cattell's work was racist, promoted White supremacy, and supported eugenics and neo-Nazi activists. APA delayed the award in order to form a committee to investigate the charges. A larger group of APA members protested its postponement. The following year, Cattell withdrew his name from consideration. Cattell died in 1998 but remains one of the few psychologists (along with Arthur Jensen, Linda Gottfredson, and Richard Lynn) listed on the Southern Poverty Law Center's Extremist Files (Southern Poverty, n.d.; Tucker, 2009).

1998: Psychologist Glayde Whitney writes the foreword to *My Awakening*, the autobiography of racial extremist and former Klansman David Duke. Whitney blames "organized Jewry" for suppressing the "truth" about racial differences.

1999: Psychologist Richard Suinn is elected the first Asian American president of APA, more than a century after the Association's founding.

2001: The U.S. Surgeon General report on Mental health: Culture, race, and ethnicity — A supplement to mental health showed evidence and reported concerns that the gap between research and practice is particularly wide for racial and ethnic minorities (Sue & Zane, 2006).

2003: The President's New Freedom Commission on Mental Health finds racial and ethnic differences in rates of psychopathology and points to continued inaccessibility and ineffectiveness of treatment options. Echoing previous reports, the Commission found that clients of color often saw psychotherapists or received treatments that did not consider the clients' experiences, cultural and linguistic backgrounds, and race-based life circumstances (Sue & Zane, 2006).

2003: APA files an amicus brief in support of the University of Michigan's right to consider race in admissions procedures in order to achieve a diverse student body. The Supreme Court ruled in favor of the University.

2005: Representatives of the EMPAs begin attending APA Council of Representatives meetings as observers. Council requests that APA Boards and Committees begin exploring bylaw changes to provide voting seats for EMPA representatives on Council. The issue went in front of Council, Boards and Committees, and the membership three times over 15 years, failing to pass. The bylaw change was finally approved by the membership in 2020 (American Psychological Association, 2012; 2020a).

2005: Jessica Henderson Daniels becomes the first Black woman elected to the APA Board of Directors.

2006–2015: Psychologist Richard Lynn's books on racial differences are published by Washington Summit Publishers, designated a hate group by the SPLC.

2007: Research shows that Black clients' experiences of microaggressions from White therapists have a significant impact on therapeutic alliances and their ratings of satisfaction with both the counselor and counseling in general. Constantine notes that "in the face of perceived racial microaggressions in counseling, African American clients, in fact, might feel much worse after their counseling experiences than before" (Constantine, 2007, p. 13; see also Helms & Cook, 1999).

2011: Melba J. T. Vasquez is elected the first Latina president of APA.

2013: Members of racial/ethnic minority groups account for 16.4% of the psychology workforce, compared to 39.6% of the overall workforce and 25.8% of the doctoral/professional workforce (American Psychological Association, 2015).

2014: APA, along with the American Educational Research Association and the National Council on Measurement in Education, issues a new set of Standards for Educational and Psychological Testing. This is the sixth set of standards spanning a 30-year period. The new edition elevates considerations of fairness alongside considerations of reliability and validity in educational and psychological testing (Worrell & Roberson, 2016).

2017: APA membership data provides the following demographics of APA members in 2017: American Indian, .2%; Hispanic, 1.7%; Black, 2.0%; White, 60.1%; Pacific Islander, 0%; Multiracial/multi-ethnic, 0.7%; Other, 0.2%; Not specified, 32.6% (American Psychological Association, 2017).

2017: The American Arab, Middle Eastern, and North African Psychological Association (AMENAPsy) is established.

2018: Jessica Henderson Daniel elected first Black woman president of APA.

2018: Examining the editorship of six top-tier psychology journals from 1974 to 2018, researchers find that only 5% of editors were people of color (Roberts et al., 2020). The authors chose these journals based on their strong reputation as top journals in social, cognitive, and developmental psychology.

2019: The APA Center for Workforce Studies reports the following demographic statistics for the field of psychology: Asian, 4% (4,887); Black/AA, 3% (3,733); Hispanic, 7% (8,203); Other, 2% (2,145); White 83% (91,302). According to the report, "Other includes American Indian, Alaska Native, Native Hawaiian and other Pacific Islander, other race and those with two or more." Population data in the United States from this same period provides the following demographics: Asian, 5.9%; Black/AA, 13.4%; Hispanic, 18.5%; Other, 4.3%; and White, 60.1%. While all groups (other than non-Hispanic Whites) represented approximately 42% of the general population, they represented only 16% of psychologists (American Psychological Association, 2020b; U.S. Census Bureau, 2021).

2021: The APA Council of Representatives votes to adopt the APA Resolution on Racism: *Harnessing Psychology to Combat Racism: Adopting a Uniform Definition and Understanding.*

Glossary

ABC model   A way to conceptualize psychological problems. "A" stands for *activating event, activity, or adversity* and represents a situation that actually happens; "B" stands for *beliefs* and signifies automatic thoughts, appraisals, perceptions, and interpretations of the situation at "A"; and "C" stands for the emotional and behavioral *consequences* that occur as a result of "B" that primarily lead to "C" (consequences).

Academy of Psychological Clinical Science   An organization of clinical psychology programs and clinical psychology internship sites committed to the clinical scientist model of training. The academy is affiliated with the Association for Psychological Science (APS).

Acceptance   The willingness to embrace internal experiences — such as thoughts, feelings, and physical sensations — even when they seem unpleasant.

Acceptance and commitment therapy   An experiential, contextual approach to psychological treatment that helps clients think about what really matters to them and then take action to enrich their lives based on their personal values; clients are instructed to use mindfulness to accept unpleasant thoughts and feelings.

Active listening   Not only hearing what the client is saying but also understanding what has been said; the therapist will often use reflection to demonstrate understanding.

Actuarial prediction   Judgments and decisions based on statistically determined probabilities.

ALI standard   The most liberal standard for determining the insanity of a defendant. This standard attests that the defendant is not responsible for an unlawful act if it resulted from a mental disease or defect such that the defendant lacked substantial capacity either to appreciate the criminality of the act (a cognitive deficit) or to conform to the law (a volitional deficit).

American Board of Professional Psychology (ABPP)   An organization that offers certification of professional competence in many psychology specialties. ABPP certification may be sought after five years of postdoctoral experience and is granted on the basis of an oral examination, the observed handling of a case, and records from past cases.

Anal stage   The psychosexual stage that extends from about 6 months to 3 years of age, during which the child focuses on urination and defecation as means of satisfaction.

Antecedent   Stimulus condition, or condition that leads up to the behavior of interest.

Appraisal   Judgment we make; type of automatic thought.

Assertiveness training   Using behavioral rehearsal and other techniques to train people to express their needs effectively without infringing on the rights of others.

Assessment report   Contains test results, interpretations, and conclusions. It includes the reason for referral along with background information and history to set the context for the assessment, a discussion of test scores and conclusions, and recommendations for how to address the questions and concerns raised in the referral.

Associated feature   Aspect of a psychiatric disorder such as its prevalence, course, prognostic factors, or common co-occurring diagnoses.

Association for Psychological Science (APS)   The professional psychological organization formed in 1988 when an academic-scientific contingent broke off from the American Psychological Association. Goals of the APS include advancing the discipline of psychology, preserving its scientific base, and promoting public understanding of the field and its applications.

Attribution   Explanation we come up with in our mind to explain why something happened; type of automatic thought.

Automatic thought   Maladaptive pattern of self-talk that may become habitual.

Aversive conditioning   A treatment in which an undesired behavior is followed consistently by an unpleasant consequence (e.g., nausea, disgust), thus decreasing the strength of the behavior over time.

Awareness training   First stage of habit reversal training in which clients keep a running log of each incident of the target behavior throughout the day.

Baker Act   Bill granting the authority to judges, law enforcement officials, physicians, and mental health professionals to involuntarily admit suicidal individuals for an emergency psychiatric evaluation.

Behavioral activation (BA)   Behavioral treatment in which clients are helped to (a) more routinely engage in pleasurable and rewarding activities that provide consistent positive reinforcement to improve their mood and (b) decrease engagement in activities that increase the risk of feeling depressed.

Behavioral approach task (BAT)   An assessment technique used to measure levels of fear and avoidance in which an individual approaches a feared situation until unable to proceed further.

Behavioral assessment   An assessment approach that focuses on the interactions between situations and behaviors for the purpose of effecting behavioral change; based on learning theory.

Behavioral consistency The assumption that an offender's crimes tend to be similar to one another.

Behavioral experiment Method for clients to "put their beliefs to the test."

Behavioral family therapy An approach to family therapy that views family relations in terms of reinforcement contingencies. Here, the therapist's role is to generate a behavioral analysis of family problems and induce family members to reinforce each other so as to increase the frequency of desired behaviors. A more cognitively focused therapist might teach individual family members to self-monitor problematic behaviors and patterns of thinking and challenge their interpretations of family events.

Behavioral genetics A research specialty that evaluates both genetic and environmental influences on the development of behavior.

Behavioral interview Interview conducted for the purpose of identifying a problem behavior, the situational factors that maintain the behavior, and the consequences that result from the behavior.

Behavioral observation A primary technique of behavioral assessment that typically involves a clinician or researcher directly monitoring (e.g., seeing, hearing) and then systematically documenting an individual's (or group's) behavior as it occurs in a natural setting, such as at home, in the classroom, within the peer group, on the playground, or under contrived conditions in a laboratory or clinic. Observation is often used to gain a better understanding of the frequency, strength, and pervasiveness of the problem behavior as well as the factors that are maintaining it.

Behavioral treatment A framework for treating disorders that is based on the principles of conditioning or learning. The behavioral approach is scientific in nature and deemphasizes the role of inferred (i.e., unobservable) variables on behavior.

Beneficence and nonmaleficence One of five general ethical principles stating that psychologists strive to benefit those they serve and to do no harm.

Biofeedback A wide array of procedures through which a patient learns to modify or control certain physiological processes. Usually, the physiological process of interest is monitored by an apparatus, and the information is fed back to the patient in the form of an auditory, tactile, or visual signal. The patient then attempts to modify the signal (and thus change the physiological response) using a variety of techniques.

Biomedical perspective A Western point of view that focuses exclusively on the biological factors of illness.

Biopsychosocial model A theoretical model that holds that health and illness are a function of biological (e.g., genetic predispositions, nutritional deficiencies), psychological (e.g., the individual's cognitions and emotions), and social (e.g., friends and family, life events) influences.

Biosocial theory of personality functioning Theoretical foundation of DBT; views difficulties with emotion regulation and the related problems as stemming from the interaction of biological and environmental factors. The main biological factor is a vulnerability to experiencing intense negative emotions, while the environmental factors refer to a chronic invalidating environment.

Board certification Awarded by the American Board of Professional Psychology to document expertise within a specific specialty area in psychology.

Boulder Conference A professional conference (held in Boulder, Colorado) that spelled out the scientist-practitioner model (also known as the Boulder model) of doctoral training in clinical psychology.

Burden of proof The obligation to establish the truth of an assertion in a court of law. In the case of the insanity plea, the burden of proof is usually on the defense.

Case formulation A hypothesis about the particular psychological mechanisms, grounded in research-based theories, that give rise to and maintain an individual's psychological distress and dysfunction.

Change talk The client's own arguments for wanting things to be different (and better).

Chessboard metaphor A technique in which clients think of their thoughts and feelings as chess pieces. The pieces of one team represent unpleasant, negative, self-critical, or anxiety-provoking thoughts, feelings and memories; those of the opposing team represent positive thoughts and feelings of confidence, satisfaction, success, and belonging. Clients imagine themselves as the chessboard to notice the distinction between themselves and the pieces.

Child custody evaluation When a custody dispute needs to be settled legally, a forensic psychologist might be hired by the court, or by one or both parents, to perform an evaluation of the child and one or both parents, as well as conduct interviews with other relatives, teachers, and anyone else who might be able to provide useful information to aid in a recommendation to the court regarding custody and visitation.

Chronic pain Pain that persists longer than 3 months and in the absence of identifiable tissue damage (or beyond the expected time of healing). It interferes with a person's ability to work, engage in daily activities, enjoy recreation, and function in interpersonal relationships, and is associated with depression, anxiety, irritability, and trouble with attention and concentration.

Chronological age   What we commonly refer to as age; years of life.

Clarifying questions   Questions used by therapists to make sure they understand what the client is expressing.

Client-centered therapy   A psychotherapy developed by Carl Rogers that emphasizes the importance of the client's perceptions of their experience and recognizes an inherent human tendency toward developing one's capacities. This therapy orientation seeks to facilitate the client's growth potential.

Clinical adult psychology   Specialty focusing on psychological problems and psychiatric disorders among those 18 years of age and older.

Clinical child/adolescent psychology   Specialty focusing on psychological problems and psychiatric disorders among children and youth.

Clinical health psychology   A psychological specialty that focuses on the prevention of illness, the promotion and maintenance of good health, and the psychological treatment of individuals with diagnosed medical conditions.

Clinical interview   One of the most basic techniques employed by the clinical psychologist for the purpose of answering a referral question. If administered skilfully, the assessment interview can provide insight into the problem and inform clinical decision making.

Clinical judgment   An approach to clinical interpretation that is largely intuitive and experiential. Subjective or clinical interpretation requires that the clinician be sensitive to information from a wide range of sources and make a series of inductive or deductive generalizations to link the observations and predict the outcome.

Clinical psychologist   A mental health professional devoted to understanding and treating individuals affected by a variety of emotional, behavioral, and/or cognitive difficulties. Clinical psychologists may be involved in numerous activities, including psychotherapy, assessment and diagnosis, teaching, supervision, research, consultation, and administration.

Clinical psychology   Field of psychology devoted to research, teaching, and services relevant to the applications of principles, methods, and procedures for understanding, predicting, and alleviating intellectual, emotional, medical, psychological, social, and behavioral maladjustment, disability, and discomfort applied to a wide range of client populations.

Clinical scientist model   A training model that encourages rigorous training in empirical research methods and the integration of scientific principles into clinical practice.

Closed group   Usually has starting and ending points, and admits no new members once the group has begun.

Code of ethics   As pertains to psychologists, enforceable rules of professional conduct identified by the American Psychological Association (APA).

Cognition   The way we think about events and situations in our environment.

Cognitive-behavioral assessment   An assessment approach recognizing that the person's thoughts or cognitions play an important role in behavior.

Cognitive-behavioral couples therapy   Relies on principles from social learning theories and focuses on partners' cognitions, behaviors, and emotional responses to help them improve how they communicate and solve problems.

Cognitive-behavioral family therapy   Involves teaching family members to self-monitor problematic behaviors and patterns of thinking, to develop new skills (communication, problem resolution, negotiation, conflict management), and to challenge interpretations of family events and reframe these interpretations.

Cognitive-behavioral treatment (CBT)   A psychological treatment modality that focuses on correcting maladaptive patterns of thinking and behaving.

Cognitive bias modification (CBM)   An experimental intervention in which clients complete game-like screen-based tasks to change biased thinking processes such as the tendency to preferentially attend to negative aspects of situations and jump to negative conclusions.

Cognitive defusion   In ACT, learning to perceive private experiences as bits of language, words, and pictures, rather than taking them as facts.

Cognitive perspective   Emphasizes how our thinking — that is, our beliefs, interpretations, judgments, attributions, expectations, and other forms of "self-talk" — influence our emotions and behaviors.

Cognitive revolution   A paradigm shift during which psychological scientists began to recognize that operant and classical conditioning, even with their precision and objectivity, could not completely explain the entirety of human experience.

Cognitive specificity   The phenomena that the same event can be associated with different emotional and behavioral reactions depending on what the person is thinking.

Collaborative empiricism   Practitioners and clients discover together how the client's maladaptive thinking contributes to distress and how adopting healthier thinking patterns can reduce this distress.

Collaborative family therapy   Family therapy in which each family member sees a different therapist. The therapists then get together to discuss their clients and the family as a whole.

Committed action   In ACT, setting goals, guided by values, and taking action to achieve them.

Common factors   A set of features that characterize many therapy orientations and that may be the source of the positive changes effected by psychological treatment.

Competence   An ethical principle that calls upon psychologists to recognize the boundaries of their professional expertise and to keep up-to-date on information relevant to the services they provide.

Competency to stand trial   The defendant's state of mind at the time of trial. To be deemed competent, it must be shown that the defendant is capable of cooperating with an attorney with a reasonable degree of rational understanding as well as maintaining an understanding of the criminal proceeding and charges being faced.

Competing response practice   Responding to the urge to perform the target behavior by instead engaging in a behavior that is incompatible with the target.

Concordance rate (or similarity index)   An index of similarity between individuals. The simplest form of concordance rate is the percentage of instances in which two individuals exhibit similar behaviors or characteristics.

Concurrent family therapy   A form of family therapy in which one therapist sees all family members in individual sessions. In some cases, the therapist may not only conduct traditional psychotherapy with the principal client but also occasionally see other members of the family.

Confidentiality   An ethical principle that calls upon psychologists to respect and protect the information shared with them by clients, disclosing this information only when they have obtained the client's consent (except in extraordinary cases in which failing to disclose the information would place the client or others at clear risk for harm).

Confronting questions   Questions used by therapists to challenge inconsistencies or contradictions.

Congruence   One of the three therapist characteristics considered essential for client-centered work (also referred to as *genuineness*). Congruence refers to the honest expression by the therapist of the behaviors, feelings, and attitudes that have been stimulated by the client.

Conjoint family therapy   A form of family therapy in which one therapist meets with the entire family at the same time.

Consequence   Outcome, or event that follows from the behavior of interest.

Consolidation   Stage in emotion-focused couples therapy that involves learning and practicing new communication strategies. This helps couples see how they have been able to change and how new interaction patterns can prevent conflict.

Constructive negative emotion   Universal experience that may be an appropriate response in certain circumstances.

Construct validity   The extent to which interview scores predict the characteristic being evaluated and correlate with other measures or behaviors in a logical and theoretically consistent way. To be construct valid, an interview must demonstrate both convergent and discriminate validity.

Construct validity approach   An approach to test construction in which scales are developed based on a specific theory, refined using factor analysis and other procedures, and validated by showing (through empirical study) that individuals who achieve certain scores behave in ways that could be predicted by their scores.

Consultation/liaison psychology   An area of the health care field where health and pediatric psychologists work in hospitals and outpatient medical clinics and collaborate with medical staff to deliver mental health care to medical patients.

Content validation   The process by which one ensures that a test will adequately measure all aspects of the construct of interest. Methods of content validation include carefully defining all relevant aspects of the construct, consulting experts, having judges assess the relevance of each potential item, and evaluating the psychometric properties of each potential item.

Contingency management   Any one of a variety of operant conditioning techniques that attempts to control a behavior by manipulating its consequences.

Contracting   A contingency management technique in which the therapist and client draw up a contract that specifies the behaviors that are desired and undesired as well as the consequences of engaging or failing to engage in these behaviors.

Control group   In psychotherapy research, the group that does not receive the treatment under investigation.

Controlled drinking   A controversial approach to the treatment of alcohol problems that has as its goal light to moderate drinking. Clients are taught to monitor their alcohol intake closely and to develop coping responses that do not involve drinking.

Controlled observation   An observational method in which the clinician exerts a certain amount of purposeful control over the events being observed; also known as *analogue behavioral observation*. Controlled observation may be preferred in situations where a behavior does not occur very often on its own or where normal events are likely to draw the patient outside the observer's range.

Convergent validity   The extent to which scores correlate with scores on other relevant measures administered at the same time.

Coping appraisal   In protection motivation theory, the evaluation of one's ability to successfully avoid or cope with negative outcomes. If one concludes that one is unlikely to cope effectively (by refraining from an undesired behavior), one will be more likely to engage in the behavior.

Correlation   A statistic (usually symbolized by r) that describes the relationship between two variables. r ranges between –1.0 and +1.0; its sign indicates the direction of the association, and its absolute value indicates the strength.

Correlational research   Research methods that allow us to determine whether one variable is related to another. In general, correlational methods do not allow us to draw inferences about cause and effect.

Counseling psychologists   Psychologists whose interests and activities overlap significantly with those of clinical psychologists. Traditionally, counseling psychologists have provided individual and group psychotherapy for normal or moderately maladjusted individuals and have offered educational and occupational counseling.

Countertransference   Analysts' own internal conflicts that could be transferred onto their client (e.g., developing feelings of attraction or anger toward the client).

Couples therapy   A form of psychotherapy in which a couple (married, unmarried, or same or other gender) meets with one or more therapists to work on any number of issues.

Covert sensitization   A form of aversion therapy in which clients are directed to imagine themselves engaging in an undesired behavior and then are instructed to imagine extremely aversive events occurring once they have the undesired behavior clearly in mind.

Crisis survival skills   In DBT, a set of strategies clients are taught to help promote distress tolerance when in a difficult situation.

Cross-sectional design   A research design that compares different individuals or groups of individuals at one point in time.

Crystallized ability   One of two higher-order factors of intelligence conceived by Cattell. Crystallized ability refers to the intellectual capacities obtained through culture-based learning.

Cue exposure   Repeated exposure to conditioned stimuli while resisting the usual behavioral response (e.g., drinking, gambling, and pornography use).

Culturally responsive modification   The notion that CBT methods can pivot in order to incorporate experiences of oppression and other stressors related to being a member of a historically underrepresented group in order to make the intervention more appropriate to the client.

Cultural syndromes   Signs and symptoms of psychopathology that are restricted to a limited number of cultures.

Cytokine   Regulates the body's inflammatory response to help fight disease or injury; overproduction of cytokines can lead to chronic inflammation.

Danger-based expectations   Prediction about what the client assumes will happen when exposed to the feared situation.

Death instincts (Thanatos)   The innate drives that are responsible for all of the negative or destructive aspects of behavior.

Debriefing   The legal requirement that researchers explain to participants the purpose, importance, and results of the research following their participation.

Deception   Instances when the purpose of the research or the meaning of a participant's responses is withheld so as to not influence the participant's response.

De-escalation   Stage in emotion-focused couples therapy focused on recognizing problematic interaction patterns that lead to conflict, identifying negative emotions related to attachment problems, and then helping couples better see how fears and insecurities hinder their relationship.

Defense mechanism   Strategy used by the ego to stave off threats originating internally, from one's id or superego. (Also referred to as *ego defense.*)

Dependent variable   The variable in an experimental design that is measured by the investigator (i.e., the outcome of interest).

Descriptive diagnosis   The use of signs and symptoms to identify psychiatric disorders because there are no definitive causes or objective tests for these disorders.

Deviation IQ   A concept introduced by Wechsler to address problems observed when applying the ratio IQ to older individuals. Individual performances on an IQ test are compared to those of their age peers.

Diagnostic and Statistical Manual of Mental Disorders (DSM)   The diagnostic catalogue of mental disorders containing descriptions and diagnostic criteria that clinicians use when determining which disorder best characterizes a client, published by the American Psychiatric Association.

Diagnostic interview   An interview conducted for the purpose of arriving at a DSM-5 diagnostic formulation.

Dialectical behavior therapy   A modified form of CBT that aims to teach clients how to live in the moment, cope effectively with difficult situations and crises, regulate emotions, and improve interpersonal relationships.

Dialectical thinking   Being able to view issues from multiple perspectives, bring together seemingly contradictory positions, and accept that two opposing ideas can be true at the same time.

Directive group   Usually time limited (e.g., 12 weekly sessions) and comprised of clients with similar problems; the therapist plays an active — almost didactic — role, providing lessons, skills training, and homework assignments.

Direct questions   Questions used by therapists to gather information; best used once rapport has been established and the client is taking responsibility.

Discriminant validity   The extent to which interview scores do not correlate with measures other than those related to the construct being measured.

Dismantling study   Investigates treatment that has multiple components with the goal of identifying those techniques that are most strongly associated with treatment benefit.

Disputation strategy   Challenge to irrational thinking.

Distress tolerance skill   DBT skill that builds on mindfulness and gives clients coping strategies for managing emotional pain and avoiding destructive behavior when crisis situations arise.

Dizygotic (DZ) twins   Fraternal twins, or twins that share about 50% of their genetic material.

Doctor of philosophy (PhD) degree   An advanced degree in psychology which involves an original research contribution to the field in the form of a doctoral dissertation.

Doctor of psychology (PsyD) degree   An advanced degree in psychology with a relative emphasis on clinical and assessment skills, and less emphasis on research competence.

Double bind   The case in which individuals are told two contradictory messages by an important figure in their life such that every response they make with regard to that figure is wrong. At one time, double-bind situations were erroneously believed to contribute to the development of schizophrenia.

Downward arrow technique   Involves (1) identifying a particular activating event, (2) asking the client what this situation means, and (3) continuing to ask the same question until one or more dysfunctional beliefs are revealed.

Dream analysis   A psychoanalytic technique that attempts to shed light on unconscious material. Because dreams are regarded as heavily laden with unconscious wishes in symbolic form, the analysis of dreams is believed to provide important clues to these wishes.

DSM-5-TR   Official diagnostic and classification system for mental disorders.

Dual relationships   Instances when a psychologist has any type of affiliation with the client outside the therapeutic context. A second relationship or role with a client inherently introduces motives, knowledge, or social goals that are inconsistent with the foundation of an adaptive psychologist–client relationship, and thus must be avoided.

Durham standard   Developed in response to concerns that the M'Naghten rule was outdated; holds that people accused of a crime are not criminally responsible if their unlawful act was the product of mental illness.

Dysfunctional belief   Inaccurate, logically flawed, exaggerated, inflexible, way of thinking that is incongruent with goal attainment.

Ecological momentary assessment (EMA)   A method of behavioral assessment in which participants record their thoughts, feelings, or behaviors as they occur in the natural environment; also known as experience sampling. This is typically accomplished through the use of electronic diaries or smartphones.

Ecological validity   In the context of behavioral assessment, the extent to which the behaviors analyzed or observed are representative of a person's typical behavior.

Effectiveness   Refers to how well an intervention performs outside of the research setting. A treatment is considered effective to the extent that clients report clinically significant benefit from the treatment.

Efficacy   Refers to how well a treatment performs in research studies. A treatment is considered efficacious to the extent that the average person receiving the treatment in clinical trials is demonstrated to be significantly less dysfunctional than the average person not receiving any treatment (e.g., those on a waiting list for treatment).

Ego   The organized, rational component of the personality. The ego uses perception, learning, planning, and so forth to satisfy the needs of the organism while at the same time preserving its place in the world.

Emotional expressiveness training   Module of cognitive-behavioral couples therapy in which partners learn ways to (a) convey how they feel and (b) listen attentively to their partner.

Emotion-focused couples therapy   A short-term intervention used to improve attachment and bonding among couples. The interventions of EFT attempt to change partners' problematic interactional styles and emotional responses so that a stronger and more secure emotional bond can be established.

Emotion regulation skill   In DBT, this helps clients understand the function of emotions and modify associated behavioral tendencies that might be inappropriate or cause them problems.

Empathy   One of the three therapist characteristics considered essential for client-centered work. Empathy refers to sensitivity to the needs, feelings, and circumstances of clients so that they feel understood.

Empirical criterion keying An approach to test development that emphasizes the selection of items by members of different diagnostic groups, regardless of whether the items appear theoretically relevant to the diagnoses of interest.

Empirical dispute A disputation strategy that uses objective, verifiable data and evidence (such as observations and research results) to challenge irrational thinking.

Empirically supported treatment (EST) Treatment for various psychological conditions that has been shown through careful empirical study to be either "well established" or "probably efficacious." A list of ESTs is updated and published periodically by the APA's Division of Clinical Psychology.

Enactment A common technique used in emotion-focused couples therapy in which the therapist guides the couple through conversations about emotion and encourages each partner to engage in a release of that emotion to increase self-awareness.

Epidemiology The study of the incidence, prevalence, and distribution of illness or disease in a given population.

Essentialism The view that those with psychiatric disorders are intrinsically different from everyone else.

Event recording A procedure in which the observer records each discreet occurrence of the target behavior during the entire observation period.

Evidence-based assessment When psychologists choose assessment instruments on the basis of demonstrated reliability, validity, and standardization.

Evidence-based practice (EBP) Treatments informed by a number of sources, including scientific evidence about the intervention, clinical expertise, and client needs and preferences.

Evidence-based treatment (EBT) An intervention or technique that has produced significant change in clients in controlled trials.

Examination for Professional Practice in Psychology (EPPP) Exam required for licensure. Part 1 is designed to assess knowledge in broad bases of human behavior, and Part 2 is designed to assess competencies needed to ethically and appropriately work with clients.

Experiential avoidance Attempts to control or minimize difficult thoughts, feelings, and other internal events.

Experimental study Research study that allows the researcher to determine cause-and-effect relationships between variables or events.

Expert testimony Testimony of a trained individual, such as a psychologist, giving opinions and inferences about psychological damage.

Expert witness An individual who has unique training, or experience, and is called upon to help the court understand and evaluate evidence or offer opinions and inferences on an issue.

Exposure and response prevention (ERP) A behavioral technique often used for the treatment of OCD. In this technique, clients are exposed to the situation that spurs their obsession (e.g., touching a doorknob) and are prevented from engaging in the compulsive behavior that relieves the obsession (e.g., repeated handwashing). Ultimately, clients will habituate to their obsession, and the compulsive behavior will be extinguished.

Exposure hierarchy A list or "menu" of the feared situations, thoughts, body sensations, and other stimuli that will be confronted during exposure trials.

Exposure therapy A behavioral technique for reducing anxiety in which clients expose themselves (in real life or in fantasy) to stimuli or situations that are feared or avoided. To be effective, the exposure must provoke anxiety, must be of sufficient duration, and must be repeated until all anxiety is eliminated.

External validity The ability to generalize study findings to people and settings outside the study; stronger in effectiveness studies.

Extinction The elimination of an undesired response (e.g., behavioral, emotional).

Eyewitness testimony Testimony given by an individual who has witnessed part or all of an event (e.g., a crime, an accident). Eyewitness testimony is often inaccurate, unreliable, and distorted by subsequent information. One role of forensic psychologists is to help identify the conditions in a specific case that might produce distortions in testimony.

Facilitative questions Questions used by therapists to encourage clients' flow of conversation.

Factor analytic approach A statistical method often used in test construction to determine whether potential items are or are not highly related to each other.

Family system Interaction patterns among family members.

Family therapy A form of psychotherapy in which several members of a family, in addition to the identified client, are seen by the therapist. This therapy modality is based on the idea that everyone in a family is affected when one member develops a problem and that the home environment may have contributed to the development of the problem in the first place. Although there are a variety of theoretical family approaches, most share the primary goal of improving communication within the family.

Fidelity and responsibility One of five general ethical principles stating that psychologists have professional and scientific responsibilities to society and to establish relationships characterized by trust.

Five-Factor Model (FFM) A comprehensive model of personality that comprises the dimensions of

Neuroticism, Extraversion, Openness, Agreeableness, and Conscientiousness as well as six facets belonging to each dimension.

Fixation The defense mechanism that occurs when the frustration and anxiety of the next psychosexual stage cause the individual to be arrested at their current level of psychosexual development.

Fluid ability One of two higher-order factors of intelligence conceived by Cattell. Fluid ability refers to a person's genetically based intellectual capacity, culture-free mental skills.

Forensic psychology A psychology subspecialty that focuses on applying psychological concepts and methods to questions/problems arising within the context of the legal system. Forensic psychologists may be called upon to provide expertise on matters of child custody, jury selection, the prediction of dangerousness, and so on.

Free association A cardinal rule of psychoanalysis in which clients are required to say anything and everything that comes to mind. Over time, free association is believed to shed light on unconscious thoughts and urges.

Functional analysis A central feature of behavioral assessment. In a functional analysis, careful analyses are made of the stimuli preceding a target behavior and the consequences following from it to gain a precise understanding of the relationship between the target behavior and the situational factors that, according to learning theory, exert control over that behavior.

General intelligence factor (*g*) The term introduced by Charles Spearman to describe his concept of a general intelligence.

General systems theory An important concept in family therapy that conceives of the family as a system and believes that "pathology" is best reduced by altering the way that the system functions.

Genital stage The psychosexual stage that follows the onset of adolescence and ideally culminates in a mature expression of sexuality.

Geropsychology Specialty of psychologists interested in working with the elderly.

Gestalt group therapy A group approach in which the therapist focuses on one client at a time and asks that person to experience feelings and behaviors while the other group members are asked to observe or provide feedback to the person in the "hot seat."

Group therapy A form of psychotherapy in which one or more therapists treat a number of clients at the same time. Generally speaking, most groups consist of five to ten clients who meet with the therapist at least once a week for 90-minute to 2-hour sessions. However, groups

may differ greatly in their theoretical orientations, their rules and exclusions, and whether they are viewed as primary or supplemental modes of treatment.

Growth potential A capacity for competence that all individuals possess. The goal of client-centered therapy is to release this capacity.

Guided discovery Used in cognitive therapy where clients are helped to notice and challenge their own thinking mistakes.

Guilty but mentally ill Under this verdict, convicted individuals are sent to a psychiatric facility for treatment. If eventually judged to be sane, they are sent to prison to serve what is left of their sentence.

Habit reversal training Behavior change technique that involves a series of steps including awareness training, stimulus control, and competing response practice.

Habituation The elimination of a response that comes about from the repeated and/or prolonged presentation of the provoking stimulus.

Health disparity Difference in the rates of illnesses among different groups and communities.

Health psychology A specialty area within psychology (also known as *behavioral medicine*) that applies the tools of the discipline to the prevention of illness, the enhancement and maintenance of health, the identification of the correlates of illness and health, and the treatment of individuals in the health care system.

Homology The assumption that similar crimes are committed by similar offenders.

Hysteria A psychological condition (thought to affect mostly women) marked by paralysis, blindness, and deafness; no neurological basis can be found for these symptoms.

Id The deep, inaccessible portion of the personality that contains the instinctual urges. The id is without order, logic, or morals and operates solely to gratify the instinctual urges.

Idiographic Consistent with behavioral assessment, this approach emphasizes target behaviors and influences that are specific to the individual person.

Illusory correlation In the context of projective testing, the phenomenon by which certain test responses become associated with specific personality characteristics. These responses come to be viewed as signs of the trait in question and may be given undue weight when interpreting the test.

Imaginal exposure Confronting oneself with unwanted thoughts, doubts, and memories that provoke elevated fear (such as by writing or talking about them).

Incidence The rate of new cases of a disease or disorder that develop within a given period of time. Incidence figures allow us to determine whether the rate of new cases is stable or changing from one time period to the next.

Incremental validity   The extent to which a scale score provides information about a person's behavior, personality features, or psychopathology features that is not provided by other measures.

Independent variable   The variable in an experimental design that is manipulated by the investigator.

Index score   Score that corresponds to one of the major ability factors that underlie the WAIS-IV subtest scores (i.e., Verbal Comprehension, Perceptual Reasoning, Working Memory, and Processing Speed).

Informed consent   In clinical practice, the legal requirement that researchers sufficiently inform clients about the proposed course of treatment such that the clients can make an informed decision about whether to enter treatment. In research, the requirement to inform potential participants about the general purpose of the study; the procedures that will be used; any risks, discomforts, or limitations on confidentiality; any compensation for participation; and their freedom to withdraw from the study at any point.

Insane   The state of being unable to think clearly or sensibly at the time that one commits a crime.

Insight   In psychoanalytic psychotherapy, a complete understanding of the unconscious determinants of one's irrational and problematic thoughts, feelings, or behaviors.

Intake-admission interview   An interview conducted for the purposes of (a) determining why the client has come to an agency (e.g., clinic, hospital), (b) determining whether the agency can meet the client's needs and expectations, and (c) informing the client about the agency's policies and procedures.

Integrity   One of five general ethical principles stating that, in all their activities, psychologists strive to be accurate, honest, and truthful.

Intelligence   There is no universally accepted definition of intelligence. However, many definitions of intelligence emphasize the ability to think abstractly, the ability to learn, and the ability to adapt to the environment.

Intelligence quotient   A term developed by Stern in 1938 to address problems with using the difference between chronological age and mental age to represent deviance. Typically, a deviation IQ score is used.

Internal consistency   The degree to which the items in a test all measure the same characteristic.

Internal validity   In the context of psychotherapy research, the ability to draw strong cause and effect conclusions about the relationship between treatment and outcome; stronger in efficacy studies (RCTs).

Interoceptive exposure   Self-generating bodily sensations that trigger inappropriate fear, such as a racing heart, breathlessness, and feeling lightheaded. Such sensations are activated using exercises such as hyperventilation, breathing through a straw, and spinning in a swivel chair.

Interpersonal effectiveness skill   In DBT, conflict resolution, active listening, and assertiveness strategy to balance *priorities* versus *demands*, demonstrate self-respect in relationships, and clarify what's important to oneself.

Interpersonal group psychotherapy   A nondirective group therapy for individuals with personality disorders in which group members learn from their interactions within the group and modify their behavior based on feedback they receive from other group members.

Interpersonal psychotherapy (IPT)   A brief, insight-oriented therapy that is psychodynamic in tone. IPT has been applied primarily to the treatment of depression and is considered a "well-established" empirically supported treatment for this problem.

Interpretation (in psychoanalysis)   A method in which the psychoanalyst reveals the unconscious meanings of the client's thoughts and behaviors, thus helping the client to achieve insight. Interpretation is the cornerstone of nearly every form of dynamic psychotherapy.

Interpretation (in cognitive-behavioral therapy)   Meaning that we assign when there is uncertainty in a particular situation; type of automatic thought.

Interrater reliability   The level of agreement between at least two interviewers who have evaluated the same client independently. Agreement can refer to consensus on symptoms assigned, diagnoses assigned, and so on.

Interval coding   Procedure in which the observer records whether the target behavior occurs within a specific period of time (i.e., the interval). This procedure is preferred when the target behavior is lengthy or occurs less frequently, or the starting or ending point of the behavior is less apparent.

***In vivo* exposure**   Direct confrontation with actual situations and objects, such as animals (e.g., spiders, dogs), social or evaluative situations (e.g., speaking up in class), and environments (e.g., shopping malls, elevators).

Involuntary commitment   Hospitalization that occurs against the will of the individual.

Irrational belief   Dysfunctional thinking pattern.

Item analysis   A process for examining responses to an individual test item to determine whether the item might be unclear or misleading.

Joint custody An arrangement in which both parents share in the custody of a child following divorce. Many "joint custody" arrangements are determined informally by the parents; formal court orders tend to be issued only in cases where the parties could arrive at no satisfactory agreement on their own.

Jury shadowing The process of hiring individuals similar to those who are serving on a given jury and monitoring their reactions to the testimony as it is presented at the trial. The reactions of the shadow jurors are used to anticipate the reactions of the actual jurors and may serve as the basis for a shift in courtroom strategy.

Justice One of five general ethical principles stating that all persons are entitled to access to and benefit from the profession of psychology; psychologists should recognize their biases and boundaries of competence.

Latency stage The psychosexual stage that extends from about 5 to 12 years of age, during which the child is characterized by a lack of overt sexual activity (and perhaps even a negative orientation toward anything sexual).

Latent content The symbolic meaning of a dream's events.

Lay witness A witness who may testify only to events observed.

Licensed professional counselors (LPCs) Mental health providers who are trained to work with individuals, families, and groups in treating mental, behavioral, and emotional problems and disorders, including substance use disorders. These professionals work in a wide variety of settings, and the approach of LPCs may vary but typically involves psychoeducational techniques with individuals, families, and groups, along with consultations with individuals, couples, families, groups, and larger organizations.

Life instincts (Eros) The innate drives that are responsible for all of the positive or constructive aspects of behavior.

Logical dispute A disputation strategy where rules of reason and logic are used to challenge and modify the client's irrational beliefs.

Longitudinal design A research design that compares the same group of individuals at two or more points in time.

M'Naghten rule The oldest standard for determining the insanity of a defendant. This rule requires the defense to prove that at the time of the unlawful act, the defendant's reasoning was so impaired by "a disease of the mind" that they either did not appreciate what they were doing or did not comprehend that it was wrong.

Manifest content What actually happens during a dream.

Manifesto for a Science of Clinical Psychology Richard McFall's "call to action" for scientifically oriented clinical psychologist in which he spelled out the goals of clinical psychology and objectives of graduate training from the clinical scientist perspective.

Manualized treatment Psychotherapeutic treatment that is presented and described in a standardized, manual format (i.e., outlining the rationales, goals, and techniques that correspond to each phase of the treatment).

Marriage and family therapists (MFTs) Mental health professionals trained in psychotherapy and family systems. They are licensed to diagnose and treat mental, behavioral, and emotional problems within the context of marriage, relationships, and family systems. MFTs focus on the individual's behavior in relationship to a couple or a family as a whole. Licensed MFTs have graduate training (a masters or doctoral degree) in marriage and family therapy that includes at least two years of specialized training and supervised clinical experience.

Mechanism Empirically supported factor that maintains the problematic behavior, cognitions, and emotions of a client.

Mental age A term introduced by Binet as an index of mental performance. This idea was based on the notion that individuals of a certain age should have mastered certain abilities.

Mental disorder According to the DSM, a syndrome characterized by clinically significant disturbance in an individual's cognition, emotion regulation, or behavior that reflects a dysfunction in the psychological, biological, or developmental processes underlying mental functioning. Usually associated with significant distress or disability in social, occupational, or other important activities.

Mental illness A pattern of behavior, thinking, or feeling that causes significant personal distress or interference in daily functioning.

Mental status examination An interview conducted to evaluate the client for the presence of cognitive, emotional, or behavioral problems. In the MSE interview, the clinician assesses the client in a number of areas, including (but not limited to) general presentation, quality of speech, thought content, memory, and judgment.

Meta-analysis A method of research in which one compiles all studies relevant to a topic or question and combines the results statistically.

Mindfulness Present moment awareness; paying attention to the present moment in a purposeful way and nonjudgmentally.

Minnesota Multiphasic Personality Inventory (MMPI) A measure of psychopathology that was originally developed using the empirical criterion keying approach. The current version (MMPI-3) contains 335 true/false items and includes 52 scales addressing virtually all domains of individual and interpersonal psychopathology. Most clinicians ask respondents to complete the test using computer software which scores the test and provides a report for the clinician. This report includes a thorough interpretation of each individual's responses corresponding to the 52 clinical and validity scales. This MMPI-3 profile may then be used by the clinician as a piece of data along with other assessment information.

Monozygotic (MZ) twins Identical twins, or twins that share 100% of their genetic material.

Motivational interviewing (MI) A technique for strengthening one's commitment to a particular goal that they are hesitant to pursue. MI is a collaborative approach in which the psychologist and client explore problems and solutions, and the client is given autonomy in making decisions.

Multicultural assessment research The study of the extent to which psychological tests are valid for different populations.

Multicultural humility Awareness, knowledge, and skills in addressing what psychologists don't know about their clients due to the unique life experiences that may shape psychologists' own perceptions and assumptions.

Multimethod assessment The use of more than a single method when evaluating an individual.

Multisystemic therapy A form of family therapy originally developed to treat juvenile offenders and their families. It is unique in that it is administered in the home, school, or neighborhood and focuses on the family's role in the problems.

Naturalistic observation Carrying out observations in the person's own environment, such as in their home, at school, or in the hospital. No attempt is made to intervene or manipulate the situation — the goal is merely to observe and document behavior as it naturally occurs. The environment chosen for observation is usually one in which the person spends a great deal of time, or in which the target behavior is likely to occur.

Neuroimaging studies Studies in which brain scanning techniques are used to examine the brain's structure or function.

Nomothetic In contrast to behavioral assessment, this diagnostic approach emphasizes target behaviors and influences that apply to the general population, not to a specific individual.

Nondirective group Approach to group therapy that is less structured and classroom-like; instead, it is oriented toward the experience of the individual client. Nondirective interventions tend to be grounded in psychoanalytic, psychodynamic, interpersonal, client-centered, or gestalt principles.

Norms Data about the average scores that can be expected in a certain population. Norms are established by administering the test to a large sample of the type of individuals for whom it is designed.

Not guilty by reason of insanity (NGRI) A legal determination that a mental illness makes one incapable of differentiating between right and wrong; rarely used or successful.

Objective personality test Personality assessment tool in which the examinee responds to a standard set of questions or statements using a fixed set of options (e.g., true or false, dimensional ratings).

Oedipus complex The phase in which a child feels sexual attraction for the parent of the opposite sex and feelings of hostility toward the parent of the same sex. The superego emerges from the resolution of this complex.

Open-ended questions Questions used by therapists to give clients responsibility and latitude for responding; these questions require more than a yes or no answer.

Open groups Admit new members at any point if someone wants to join or to replace someone who decides to leave the group.

Opposite action Involves behaving contrary to the urge provoked by a strong emotion.

Oral stage The psychosexual stage spanning about the first year of life, during which the mouth is the chief source of pleasure and satisfaction.

Outcome measure In psychotherapy research, indicator of client functioning following treatment; used to gauge the treatment effectiveness.

Paraprofessional Individual without advanced education in psychology who has been trained to assist professional mental health workers.

Pediatric psychologist Clinical health psychologist interested in working with youth. Pediatric psychologists tend to work in general hospital settings more often than other clinical psychologists do.

Personality The continuity in a person's behavior and emotional style over time.

Personality trait A stable and consistent way of perceiving the world and of behaving. Traits may be influenced by the environment, biology, or a combination of these factors.

Phallic stage The psychosexual stage that extends from about 3 to 7 years of age, during which the sexual organs become the primary source of gratification.

Phenomenal self The part of the phenomenal field that the person experiences as "I." According to phenomenological theory, humans have a basic urge to preserve and enhance the phenomenal self.

Phenomenological theory A philosophical/theoretical approach asserting that an individual's behavior is completely determined by their phenomenal field, or everything that is experienced by the person at any given point in time.

Pie graph technique A behavioral experiment cognitive therapists can use to help clients gain perspective on their own role in causing negative events.

Pleasure principle The rule of conduct by which one seeks pleasure and avoids pain. The id operates according to the pleasure principle.

Postdoctoral fellowship Time after graduation during which additional supervised clinical experience (usually an additional 2000 hours) can be obtained to apply for licensure.

Practitioner-scholar model (also called the Vail model) Training model developed to place a primary emphasis on practice and less emphasis on science.

Precipitant Factor that triggers or worsens the client's problems.

Predictive validity The extent to which a test can be used to forecast future behavior.

Predisposing factor Factor that makes the client more susceptible to developing problems.

Predoctoral internship A full-time year-long training required to complete doctoral training in clinical psychology. Internships are offered at a variety of training sites all over the country (e.g., Veterans Affairs hospitals and clinics, medical schools, private psychiatric facilities, community mental health centers, campus mental health centers).

Premack principle Also known as "**Grandma's rule**," the contingency management technique in which a behavior is reinforced by allowing the individual to engage in a more attractive activity once the target behavior is completed.

Presenting problem The concerns and problems that lead a client to treatment.

Prevalence The overall rate of cases (new or old) within a given period of time. Prevalence figures allow us to estimate what percentage of the target population is affected by the illness or disorder.

Primary mental abilities Seven factors of intelligence derived by Thurstone on the basis of his factor analytic work: numerical facility, word fluency, verbal comprehension, perceptual speed, special visualization, reasoning, and memory.

Problem list First step in a case formulation. The psychologist and client develop a list of presenting problems; the list is usually kept to five to eight items and is often developed using data from a clinical interview.

Process research Research that investigates the specific events that occur in the course of the interaction between therapist and client. Some therapy processes have been shown to relate to treatment outcome.

Professional schools of psychology Schools offering advanced training in psychology that differs from training offered by traditional doctoral programs. In general, professional schools offer relatively little training in research, emphasizing instead training in assessment and psychotherapy.

Progressive muscle relaxation (PMR) A series of actions to produce a state of lowered anxiety, stress, and physiological arousal. Relaxation may be induced by tensing and then relaxing various muscle groups or via breathing exercises, imagery exercises, or hypnosis.

Projection The defense mechanism that occurs when a person attributes their unconscious feelings to someone else.

Projective hypothesis Proposes that people unconsciously reveal critical aspects of their personality when trying to make sense of ambiguous material.

Projective personality test Psychological testing technique that uses people's responses to ambiguous test stimuli to make judgments about their adjustment–maladjustment. Proponents believe that examinees "project" themselves onto the stimuli, thus revealing unconscious aspects of themselves.

Protection motivation theory A model of health behavior positing that behavior is a function of both threat appraisal and coping appraisal.

Psychiatric nurses Registered nurses who work with individuals, families, groups, and communities assessing their mental health needs. A psychiatric nurse might make diagnoses, create and implement treatment plans, and then evaluate the treatment's effectiveness. Psychiatric nurses have a masters or doctoral degree in psychiatric–mental health nursing, and certified nurse practitioners now have prescription privileges in all but a few U.S. states.

Psychiatrists Physicians with intensive training in the diagnosis and treatment of a variety of mental disorders. Because of their medical backgrounds, psychiatrists may prescribe medications for the alleviation of problematic behavior or psychological distress.

Psychic determinism   A major assumption of Freudian theory that holds that everything one does has meaning and is goal directed.

Psychoanalysis   An approach to treatment developed by Freud.

Psychoanalytic theory   The basis of psychoanalysis and the psychodynamic approach to therapy which has evolved over the past century.

Psychodrama   A form of role playing developed by Moreno in which one client in a group acts out events from the past as if performing in a play.

Psychodynamic   An approach that emphasizes early experiences in the development of human behavior, feelings, and emotions.

Psychodynamic psychotherapy   A technique based on psychoanalytic theory that contains only remnants of psychoanalysis.

Psychological assessment   The process of collecting and synthesizing information for the purposes of understanding a client's patterns of thinking and behavior, classifying the problems they have, developing a plan for intervention, measuring the effects of interventions, and conducting research to better understand psychological phenomena.

Psychological autopsy   An evaluation that aims to reconstruct a person's psychological state — their thoughts, mood, and behavioral tendencies — at the time of their death to shed light on contextual factors preceding their death, including any involvement they might have had in their own passing.

Psychological criminal profiling   A method of identifying criminal suspects using emotional and behavioral clues from the crime scene.

Psychological flexibility   The ability to be in the present moment, engage in activities that are personally important, and live a meaningful life despite the fact that difficult experiences will occur.

Psychological treatment   Specific research-supported techniques and procedures that are grounded in psychological theory and derived from models of psychopathology to target particular causal or maintenance mechanisms and improve specific aspects of psychological, emotional, behavioral, or physical health and related functioning.

Psychology Interjurisdictional Compact (PSYPACT)   An interstate agreement developed during the COVID-19 pandemic to facilitate the practice of telepsychology and the temporary in-person, face-to-face practice of psychology across state lines.

Psychometric evaluation   A process in which the developer subjects assessment instruments to rigorous statistical analyses to determine whether they meet certain standards.

Psychoneuroimmunology   The field of study that examines how stress interacts with body systems and shapes human behavior.

Psychosexual stages   A series of developmental stages posited by Freud, each of which is marked by the involvement of a particular erogenous zone of the body.

Psychosocial perspective   A recognition that psychological and social factors play a role in illness and disease.

Psychosomatic medicine   A field originating from the 1940s that was based on the assumption that certain illnesses and disease states were caused in part by psychological factors. Some adherents believed that each psychosomatic illness corresponded to a specific unconscious conflict that predisposed the patient to that illness.

Psychotherapy   In the context of a professional relationship, refers to methods of inducing changes in a person's behavior, thoughts, or feelings with the aim of improving their mental or physical health and related functioning.

Punishment   The notion that when a behavior is followed by an unpleasant consequence, it will diminish.

Race-related stress   Race-related transactions that tax or exceed existing individual and collective resources or threaten well-being.

Random assignment   The random placement of participants into experimental or control groups to help ensure that any differences between and within the participant groups are not systematic at the outset of the experiment.

Randomized controlled trial (RCT)   RCTs are studies in which one or more groups of clients (all with the same problem) receive a particular treatment (the experimental condition) and another group receives a control condition.

Rapport   A word often used to characterize the relationship between client and clinician. In the context of the clinical interview, building good rapport involves establishing a comfortable atmosphere and sharing an understanding of the purpose of the interview.

Rating scale   In behavioral assessment, the use of checklists or inventories to identify and assess the severity of behaviors, emotional responses, and perceptions of the environment. This method involves the patient's, or the patient's caregivers', completion of one or more standardized questionnaires either online or using paper and pencil forms.

Rational emotive behavior therapy (REBT)   A form of CBT developed by Albert Ellis that expanded the ABC model to place more emphasis on emotions and to recognize the integration of behavioral and cognitive therapy.

Rational thinking The ability to objectively consider facts, opinions, judgments, and data to arrive at a sound conclusion; can include both positive and negative ideas.

Reaction formation The defense mechanism that occurs when an unconscious impulse is consciously expressed by its behavioral opposite.

Reactivity In the context of observation, the phenomenon in which individuals respond to the fact that they are being observed by changing their behavior.

Reality principle The rule of conduct by which one defers the gratification of instinctual urges until a suitable object and mode of satisfaction are discovered. The ego operates according to the reality principle.

Reason for referral A description in the psychological assessment of why the psychologist's services are being sought (e.g., Why is a particular child earning poor grades?).

Reflection statements Used by client-centered therapists to (a) show that they understand clients' thoughts and feelings, and (b) give clients the space to further clarify their own thoughts and feelings.

Regression The defense mechanism that occurs when extensive frustration causes a person to return to a stage that once provided a great deal of gratification.

Relapse prevention A range of strategies for preventing relapse, usually in the context of treating the addictive behaviors. Patients are directed to anticipate problem situations and are taught coping skills to navigate their way through these situations without engaging in the undesired behavior. Or in the event of a lapse, patients are taught how to respond so as to prevent a total relapse.

Relational frame theory The idea that our ability to relate one concept to another is the foundation of human language; the goal of ACT is to develop new relational frames in which unwanted internal experiences are seen as merely unpleasant aspects of life that do not need to be "struggled with" or "gotten rid of."

Reliability The consistency with which the test measures a particular variable, such as anxiety, intelligence, or extraversion.

Repression The most basic defense mechanism. Repression serves to keep highly threatening sexual or aggressive material out of conscious awareness, often involuntarily.

Research Domain Criteria (RDoC) System designed to promote research integrating genetics, neuroscience, and behavioral science leading eventually to an objective diagnostic system of "biotypes" that align with effective (mainly biologically based) treatments.

Resistance Any attempt by the client to ward off the therapist's efforts to dissolve their neurotic methods for resolving problems. Any client action or behavior that prevents insight or prevents bringing unconscious material into consciousness.

Respect for people's rights and dignity One of five general ethical principles stating that psychologists respect the rights and dignity of all people and enact safeguards to ensure protection of these rights.

Response prevention A behavioral intervention in which clients are helped to refrain from performing compulsive rituals.

Restructuring Stage in emotion-focused couples therapy in which the partners share their emotions and show acceptance and compassion for each other. This helps the couple become more responsive to each other's needs, reducing conflict and strengthening their emotional bond. Couples learn to express deep, underlying emotions from a place of vulnerability and ask for their needs to be met.

Revised NEO-Personality Inventory (NEO-PI-R) A self-report measure of the FFM that consists of 240 statements, each of which is rated on a 5-point scale. This test yields scores on all five domains of the FFM (Neuroticism, Extraversion, Openness, Agreeableness, and Conscientiousness) as well as the six facets corresponding to each domain.

Risk factor Characteristic of individuals that increases the likelihood of a serious illness.

Rorschach A projective technique that interprets people's responses to a series of 10 inkblots.

Sample Behavioral assessment uses a "sample" orientation to assessment — that is, the goal is to gather examples that are representative of the situations and behaviors of interest.

Sane A legal determination that an individual was of sound mind and mentally healthy at the time of the alleged crime.

Schema The way we make sense of the world, driven by frameworks of knowledge and associations; exist in our long-term memory.

School psychologists Psychologists who work with educators to promote the intellectual, social, and emotional growth of school-age children. Activities of school psychologists may include evaluating children with special needs, developing interventions or programs to address these needs, and consulting with teachers and administrators about issues of school policy.

Scientist-practitioner model The predominant training model for clinical psychologists (also known as the Boulder model). This model strives to produce professionals who integrate the roles of scientist and practitioner (i.e., who practice psychotherapy with skill and sensitivity, and conduct research on the hypotheses they have generated from their clinical observations).

Self-actualization   The basic human tendency toward maintaining and enhancing the self.

Self-efficacy   People's beliefs about their capacity to control or gain mastery over the events that affect them. This construct plays a prominent role in most social-cognitive models of health behavior.

Self-monitoring   An observational technique in which individuals observe and record their own behaviors, thoughts, or emotions (including information on timing, frequency, intensity, and duration).

Semistructured interview   Interview that includes standardized questions or "prompts," but also leaves room for the psychologist to follow up with questions of their own.

Sensate focus   Involves a series of structured touching and discovery exercises that a couple performs together to extinguish performance-related anxiety, enhance communication, and learn about one's own and their partner's sexual response.

Shaping   A contingency management technique in which a behavior is developed by first rewarding any behavior that approximates it and then by selectively reinforcing behaviors that more and more resemble the target behavior.

Sign   Outwardly observable phenomenon.

Silence   Effective in communicating safety to a client by conveying that the psychologist is present exclusively for their client's needs, will not rush the client, and is comfortable with anything that is said or needs to be contemplated by their client. Silence also often prompts the client to continue talking, and in doing so, to further elaborate on their own thoughts.

Situational perspective   The perspective that people's behavior is entirely a product of the environment and factors such as operant and classical conditioning.

Social history interview   An interview conducted for the purpose of gaining a thorough understanding of the client's background and the historical-developmental context in which a problem emerged.

Social skills training   Behavioral intervention to improve social skills necessary for healthy interpersonal relationships and successful employment (e.g., communicate effectively, display appropriate manners, use good hygiene, show empathy and consideration for others, and tactfully express one's own needs and opinions).

Social support   The number and quality of one's social relationships. Several studies have shown that social support is positively associated with better health outcomes.

Social workers   Mental health professionals trained in psychiatric diagnosis and in individual and group psychotherapy. Compared to psychologists and psychiatrists, social workers' training is relatively brief, limited to a two-year masters degree. Social workers are intensely involved in the day-to-day lives of their patients and focus more on the social and environmental factors contributing to their patients' difficulties.

Socratic dialogue   A method in which the therapist asks the client pointed, open-ended questions that encourage reflection and promote new and more logical perspectives.

Specific factors perspective   Holds that theories and procedures particular to a given approach to treatment *are* necessary for psychological or behavioral change; specific interventions are necessary to prompt the client to take some sort of action, which results in (a) changes to the psychological processes that cause or maintain the target problem and (b) reductions in psychological distress and dysfunction.

Split-half reliability   The extent to which an individual's scores on one half of a test (e.g., the even-numbered items) are similar to scores on the other half (e.g., the odd-numbered items).

Standardization   The precise directions for administering, scoring, and interpreting an assessment instrument. It ensures that anyone being assessed has the same experience and scoring criteria, which allows psychologists to compare scores (such as IQ scores) across different people.

Stanford-Binet Fifth Edition (SB-5)   An intelligence test that measures five general cognitive factors (fluid reasoning, quantitative reasoning, visual-spatial processing, working memory, and knowledge), each of which includes both verbal and nonverbal subtest activities.

State or provincial board of psychology   Board for each state or province that determines the requirements for licensure in that jurisdiction and approves each individual license.

Stimulus control   Stage in habit reversal training in which the client and therapist use the data from awareness training logs to design strategies for reducing the influence of conditioned stimuli that trigger the target behavior.

Stimulus value   The way the therapist appears and behaves; may affect individual clients in different ways.

Stress   A process that involves interactions between people and their environment.

Stressor   A situation, event, or other stimulus that a person appraises as challenging or threatening, leading to the stress response.

Structured diagnostic interview   A diagnostic interview that consists of a standard set of questions asked in a specified sequence. The questions may be keyed to the diagnostic criteria for a number of disorders.

Structured interview   An interview that requires the clinician to ask, verbatim, a set of pre-determined, standardized questions in a specified sequence.

Superego   The component of the personality that represents the ideals and values of society as they are conveyed to the child through the words and deeds of their parents. The role of the superego is to block unacceptable id impulses and to pressure the ego to serve the ends of morality rather than those of expediency.

Sympathetic nervous system   The portion of the nervous system that is responsible for mobilizing body resources in urgent situations. Prolonged sympathetic activation can have adverse effects on body organs, mental functions, and the immune system.

Symptom   Subjective experience reported by the client.

Systematic desensitization   A behavioral technique for reducing anxiety in which clients practice relaxation while visualizing anxiety-provoking situations of increasing intensity. In this way, the client becomes "desensitized" to the feared stimulus.

Talking cure   Discovered by Breuer, the use of techniques that encourage client talking as a way of addressing and alleviating neurotic symptoms.

Tarasoff case   A landmark 1976 case in which the California Supreme Court ruled that a therapist was legally remiss for not informing all appropriate parties of a client's intention to harm. This case legally established a therapist's "duty to protect."

Target behavior   Initial focus of behavioral assessment in which the problematic behavior is defined and characterized by how often it occurs (its *frequency*), its severity (or *intensity*), and how long each instance lasts (its *duration*). In functional analysis, the target behavior is understood in terms of its relationship to the situational factors that (according to learning theory) exert control over that behavior.

Test bias   The situation in which different decisions or predictions are made for members of two groups, even when they obtain the same score on an instrument.

Test–retest reliability   The consistency of assessment test scores over time. Generally, we expect individuals to receive similar diagnoses from one administration to the next if the interval between administrations is short.

Thematic Apperception Test (TAT)   A projective technique that purports to reveal clients' personality characteristics by interpreting the stories they produce in response to a series of pictures.

Theory of multiple intelligences   A theory forwarded by Gardner that posits the existence of eight intelligences: linguistic, musical, logical-mathematical, spatial, bodily-kinesthetic, naturalistic, interpersonal, and intrapersonal.

Threat appraisal   In protection motivation theory, the evaluation of negative factors (e.g., the potential for harm) that affect the likelihood of engaging in a particular behavior. If one concludes that there is little immediate threat to oneself, one will be more likely to engage in the behavior.

Time-out   A contingency management technique in which a person is removed temporarily from the situation that is reinforcing the undesired behavior.

Token economy   A system in which desired behaviors are promoted through the strict control of reinforcements. Establishing such a system requires specifying the immediate reinforcers for each behavior as well as the backup reinforcers for which clients can exchange their immediate reinforcers.

Transactional model of stress   A model that views stress as a process that involves: (a) an environmental event; (b) the individual's appraisal of the event (as threatening or benign); and (c) the individual's physiological, emotional, cognitive, and behavioral responses to the event.

Transference   A key phenomenon in psychoanalytic therapy in which the client reacts to the therapist as if the therapist represented an important figure from the client's personal life.

Treatment group   In psychotherapy research, the group that receives the treatment under investigation. Despite the term "group," clients in treatment studies do not necessarily all receive treatment at once.

Treatment planning   Process of using a case formulation to guide the selection of an intervention.

Type A personality pattern   A personality pattern that has been associated with anger and hostility, and which indicates increased risk for coronary heart disease.

Unconditional positive regard   One of the three therapist characteristics considered essential for client-centered work. Unconditional positive regard refers to complete acceptance of and respect for the client as a human being, without conditions or requirements.

Unconditional self-acceptance   Becoming comfortable viewing oneself as fallible and seeing one's own self-worth as separate from one's behaviors and circumstances.

Unconscious   The portion of the mind that is not accessible to awareness.

Unstructured interview   An interview in which the clinician asks any questions that come to mind in any order.

Validity   The extent to which a test measures what it intends to measure.

Validity scale   Test scale that attempts to shed light on the respondent's test-taking attitudes and motivations (e.g., to present themselves in an overly favorable light, to exaggerate their problems or symptoms, to engage in random responding).

Value   In ACT, clarifying what is most important, significant, and meaningful in life.

Value bull's eye   A dart board is divided into quadrants that illustrate the client's values to help align behavior with the values.

Visitation rights   Court-given right of the noncustodial parent to see and visit the child, absent extraordinary circumstances.

Voir dire   A legal term that refers to that part of the trial during which attorneys conduct a preliminary examination of potential jurors to determine with which side of the case they are likely to identify.

Voluntary commitment   The circumstance in which an individual agrees to be admitted to a psychiatric hospital and is permitted to leave at any time, though some hospitals require that such individuals indicate their intent to leave several days in advance. This allows time to initiate commitment proceedings if it is determined the individual is seriously mentally ill or dangerous.

Waiting list   A control group whose members receive treatment only after the study is completed.

Wechsler Adult Intelligence Scale (WAIS)   An adult intelligence test that is now in its fourth edition. The WAIS-IV is comprised of 15 subtests and yields a Full Scale IQ score, in addition to Index scores for Verbal Comprehension, Perceptual Reasoning, Working Memory, and Processing Speed.

Wechsler Intelligence Scale for Children Fifth Edition (WISC-V)   An intelligence test designed for children between the ages of 6 and 17 years.

Wechsler Preschool and Primary Scale of Intelligence   An intelligence test divided into two age groups: 2 years, 6 months to 3 years, 11 months; 4 years to 7 years, 7 months. The test is currently in its fourth edition.

Wise mind   Idea in DBT that the intersection of emotion and rational mind is the balance that allows us to remain in control while also being emotionally sensitive.

Witness preparation   Helping witnesses present their testimony more effectively without changing the facts to which their testimony is directed. Forensic psychologists may be consulted to assist with many aspects of witness preparation (e.g., preparing them for the sheer experience of being a witness in the courtroom or making recommendations as to their appearance, the manner in which they present facts).

Word-sentence association training   A technique used to teach users to make benign, rather than negative, interpretations of uncertain or ambiguous situations.

References

Abramovitch, A., Abramowitz, J. S., & McKay, D. (2021). The OCI-12: A syndromally valid modification of the obsessive-compulsive inventory-revised. *Psychiatry Research, 298*, 113808.

Abramowitz, J. S. (2006). The psychological treatment of obsessive–compulsive disorder. *The Canadian Journal of Psychiatry, 51*(7), 407–416.

Abramowitz, J. S., & Blakey, S. M. (2020). *Clinical handbook of fear and anxiety: Maintenance processes and treatment mechanisms.* American Psychological Association.

Abramowitz, J. S., & Buchholz, J. L. (2020). Psychological treatment for OCD. In N. Simon, E. Hollander, B. O. Rothbaum, & D. J. Stein (Eds.), *The American Psychiatric Association Publishing textbook of anxiety, trauma, and OCD-related disorders* (3rd ed., pp. 315–339). American Psychiatric Association Publishing.

Abramowitz, J. S., & Jacoby, R. J. (2014). *Obsessive-compulsive disorder in adults.* Hogrefe.

Abramowitz, J. S., Baucom, D. H., Wheaton, M. G., Boeding, S., Fabricant, L. E., Paprocki, C., & Fischer, M. S. (2013). Enhancing exposure and response prevention for OCD: A couple-based approach. *Behavior Modification, 37*(2), 189–210.

Abramowitz, J. S., Deacon, B. J., & Whiteside, S. P. (2019). *Exposure therapy for anxiety: Principles and practice.* Guilford.

Abramowitz, J. S., Deacon, B. J., & Whiteside, S. P. W. (2019). *Exposure therapy for anxiety: Principles and practice* (2nd ed.). Guilford.

Abramowitz, J. S., Fabricant, L. E., Taylor, S., Deacon, B. J., McKay, D., & Storch, E. A. (2014). The relevance of analogue studies for understanding obsessions and compulsions. *Clinical Psychology Review, 34*(3), 206–217. https://doi.org/10.1016/j.cpr.2014.01.004

Abramowitz, J. S., Whiteside, S. P., & Deacon, B. J. (2005). The effectiveness of treatment for pediatric obsessive-compulsive disorder: A meta-analysis. *Behavior Therapy, 36*(1), 55–63.

Achenbach, T. M. (2009). *The Achenbach System of Empirically Based Assessment (ASEBA): Development, findings, theory, and applications.* University of Vermont Research Center for Children, Youth, & Families.

Ackerman, N. W. (1966). Family psychotherapy: Theory and practice. *American Journal of Psychotherapy, 20*(3), 405–414.

Adams, G., Kurtis, T., Gómez, L, Molina, L. E., & Dobles, I. (2018). Decolonizing knowledge in hegemonic psychological science. In N. N. Wane & K. L. Todd (Eds.), *Decolonial pedagogy: Examining sites of resistance, resurgence, and renewal* (pp. 35–53). Springer, Cham.

Afshar, M., Mohammad-Alizadeh-Charandabi, S., Merghti-Khoei, E. S., & Yavarikia, P. (2012). The effect of sex education on the sexual function of women in the first half of pregnancy: A randomized controlled trial. *Journal of Caring Sciences, 1*(4), 173.

Ahn, H. N., & Wampold, B. E. (2001). Where oh where are the specific ingredients? A meta-analysis of component studies in counseling and psychotherapy. *Journal of Counseling Psychology, 48*(3), 251.

Alexander, F. (1950). *Psychosomatic medicine.* Norton.

Alvarez, A. N., Sing, A. A., & Wu, J. (2012). The Asian American Psychological Association: Parallels and intersections with counseling psychology. *The Counseling Psychologist, 40*, 646–655. doi: 10.1177/0011000012450416

Alvarez, M. J., Miller, M. K., & Bornstein, B. H. (2016). "It will be your duty . . .:" The psychology of criminal jury instructions. In M. Miller and B. Bornstein (Eds.), *Advances in psychology and law* (pp. 119–158). Springer.

American Psychiatric Association. (2013). *Diagnostic and statistical manual of mental disorders* (5th ed.). American Psychiatric Association.

American Psychiatric Association (2022). *Diagnostic and statistical manual of mental disorders* (5th edition, text revision). Washington DC: Author.

American Psychological Association. (1953). *Ethical standards of psychologists.* American Psychological Association.

American Psychological Association. (2002). Ethical principles of psychologists and code of conduct. *American Psychologist, 57*, 1060–1073.

American Psychological Association. (2010). *2007 Doctorate Employment Survey.* Compiled by American Psychological Association Center for Workforce Studies.

American Psychological Association. (2010). Guidelines for child custody evaluations in divorce proceedings. *American Psychologist, 49*(7), 677–680.

American Psychological Association. (2012). *Council of Representatives agenda book, August 1 to August 3.* American Psychological Association.

American Psychological Association. (2013). Specialty guidelines for forensic psychology. *The American Psychologist, 68*(1), 7–19.

American Psychological Association. (2015). 2005–13: Demographics of the U.S. psychology workforce. www.apa.org/workforce/publications/13-demographics

American Psychological Association. (2017). 2017: APA member profiles. www.apa.org/workforce/publications/17-member-profiles

American Psychological Association. (2018). *Stress in America.* www.apa.org/images/state-nation/tcm7-225609.pdf

American Psychological Association. (2020, May 29). "We are living in a racism pandemic," says APA president. [Press release]. www.apa.org/news/press/releases/2020/05/racism-pandemic

American Psychological Association. (2020a). *Council of Representatives agenda book, August 5 to August 6.* American Psychological Association.

American Psychological Association. (2020b). *Demographics of the U.S. psychology workforce.* [Interactive data tool]. www.apa.org/workforce/data-tools/demographics

American Psychological Association. (2020c). *Publication manual of the American Psychological Association* (7th ed.). American Psychological Association.

American Psychological Association Guideline Development Panel for the Treatment of PTSD in Adults. (2017). Clinical practice guideline for the treatment of posttraumatic stress disorder (PTSD) in adults. www.apa.org/ptsd-guideline/ptsd.pdf

Angell, J. R. (1922). *The evolution of intelligence: Lectures delivered before the Yale Chapter of Sigma Xi, 1921–1922.* Yale University Press.

Arch, J. J., & Craske, M. G. (2008). Acceptance and commitment therapy and cognitive behavioral therapy for anxiety disorders: Different treatments, similar mechanisms? *Clinical Psychology: Science and Practice, 15*(4), 263.

Aron, L., & Starr, K. (2013). *A psychotherapy for the people: Toward a progressive psychoanalysis.* Routledge.

Arriola, K. J., Lewis, T. T., Pearce, B., Cobb, J., Weldon, B., Valentin, M. I. Z., Lea, J., & Vaccarino, V. (2021). A randomized trial of race-related stress among African Americans with chronic kidney disease. *Psychoneuroendocrinology, 131,* 105339.

Arvey, R. D., et al. (1994, December 13). Mainstream science on intelligence. *Wall Street Journal,* p. A18.

Assari, S. (2017). Whites but not Blacks gain life expectancy from social contacts. *Behavioral Sciences, 7*(4), 68–77.

Association of Psychology Postdoctoral and Internship Centers. (2019, October). *Match rates by doctoral program.* https://www.appic.org/Portals/0/downloads/APPIC_Match_Rates_2011-2019_by_UniversityV2.pdf

Association of State and Provincial Psychology Boards. (2016). *Psychology licensing exam scores by doctoral program.* https://cdn.ymaws.com/www.asppb.net/resource/resmgr/EPPP_/2016_Scores_by_Doctoral_Prog.pdf

A-tjak, J. G., Davis, M. L., Morina, N., Powers, M. B., Smits, J. A., & Emmelkamp, P. M. (2015). A meta-analysis of the efficacy of acceptance and commitment therapy for clinically relevant mental and physical health problems. *Psychotherapy and Psychosomatics, 84*(1), 30–36.

Avery-Clark, C., Weiner, L., & Adams-Clark, A. A. (2019). Sensate focus for sexual concerns: An updated, critical literature review. *Current Sexual Health Reports, 11*(2), 84–94.

Axelsson, E., Hesser, H., Andersson, E., Ljótsson, B., & Hedman-Lagerlöf, E. (2020). Mediators of treatment effect in minimal-contact cognitive behaviour therapy for severe health anxiety: A theory-driven analysis based on a randomised controlled trial. *Journal of Anxiety Disorders, 69,* 102172.

Azriel, O., & Bar-Haim, Y. (2020). Attention bias. In J. S. Abramowitz & S. M. Blakey (Eds.), *Clinical handbook of fear and anxiety: Maintenance processes and treatment mechanisms* (pp. 203–218). American Psychological Association.

Bache, R. M. (1895). Reaction time with reference to race. *Psychological Review, 2*(5), 475–486. doi: 10.1037/h0070013

Baker, B. (2021). Race and biology. *BioScience, 71*(2), 119–126. doi.org/10.1093/biosci/biaa157

Baker, T., McFall, R., & Shoham, V. (2009, November 15). Is your therapist a little behind the times? *Washington Post.*

Balderrama-Durbin, C. M., Snyder, D. K., Heyman, R. E., & Haynes, S. N. (2020). Systematic and culturally sensitive assessment of couple distress. *The Handbook of Systemic Family Therapy, 3,* 27–48.

Baldwin, J. M., Cattell, J. M., & Jastrow, J. (1898). Physical and mental tests. *Psychological Review, 5,* 172–179.

Bandura, A. (1969). *Principles of behavior modification.* Holt, Rinehart & Winston.

Bandura, A. (1977a). Self-efficacy: Toward a unifying theory of behavioral change. *Psychological Review, 84,* 191–215.

Bandura, A. (1977b). *Social learning theory.* Prentice Hall.

Bandura, A. (1982). Self-efficacy mechanism in human agency. *American Psychologist, 37*(2), 122–147.

Bandura, A. (2001). Social cognitive theory: An agentic perspective. *Annual Review of Psychology, 52,* 1–26.

Banmen, J. (2020). The Satir model: Yesterday and today. *Contemporary Family Therapy, 24*(1), 7–22.

Barbian-Shimberg, A. L. (2020). Minnesota Multiphasic Personality Inventory (MMPI). *The Wiley encyclopedia of personality and individual differences: Measurement and assessment* (pp. 293–308). Wiley.

Barkham, M., Lutz, W., & Castonguay, L. (Eds.) (2021). *Bergin and Garfield's handbook of psychotherapy and behavior change* (7th ed.). John Wiley & Sons.

Barlow, D. H. (2004). Psychological treatments. *American Psychologist, 59*(9), 869–878.

Barlow, D. H. (2010). The dodo bird—again—and again. *The Behavior Therapist, 33,* 15–16.

Barlow, D. H. (2021) (Ed.). *Clinical handbook of psychological disorders* (6th ed.). Guilford.

Barlow, D. H., & Farchione, T. J. (Eds.). (2017). *Applications of the unified protocol for transdiagnostic treatment of emotional disorders.* Oxford University Press.

Barlow, D. H., Farchione, T. J., Bullis, J. R., Gallagher, M. W., Murray-Latin, H., Sauer-Zavala, S., Bently, K., Thompson-Hollands, J., Conklin, L., Boswell, J., Ametaj, A., Carl, J., Boettcher, H., & Cassiello-Robbins, C. (2017). The unified protocol for transdiagnostic treatment of emotional disorders compared with diagnosis-specific protocols for anxiety disorders: A randomized clinical trial. *JAMA Psychiatry, 74*(9), 875–884.

Barlow, D. H., Harris, B. A., Eustis, E. H., & Farchione, T. J. (2020). The unified protocol for transdiagnostic treatment of emotional disorders. *World Psychiatry, 19*(2), 245–246.

Barnicot, K., Katsakou, C., Bhatti, N., Savill, M., Fearns, N., & Priebe, S. (2012). Factors predicting the outcome of psychotherapy for borderline personality disorder: A systematic review. *Clinical Psychology Review, 32,* 400–412.

Bartol, C., & Bartol, A. (2016). *Criminal behavior: A psychological approach* (11th ed). Pearson.

Bate, K. S., Malouff, J. M., Thorsteinsson, E. T., & Bhullar, N. (2011). The efficacy of habit reversal therapy for tics, habit disorders, and stuttering: A meta-analytic review. *Clinical Psychology Review, 31*(5), 865–871.

Bateson, G., Jackson, D. D., Haley, J., & Weakland, J. (1956). Toward a theory of schizophrenia. *Behavioral Science, 1*(4), 251–264.

Baucom, D. H., Fischer, M. S., Hahlweg, K., & Epstein, N. B. (2019). Cognitive behavioral couple therapy. In B. H. Fiese, M. Celano, K. Deater-Deckard, E. N. Jouriles, & M. A. Whisman (Eds.), *APA handbook of contemporary family psychology: Family therapy and training* (pp. 257–273). American Psychological Association.

Baucom, D. H., Shoham, V., Mueser, K. T., Daiuto, A. D., & Stickle, T. R. (1998). Empirically supported couple and family interventions for marital distress and adult mental health problems. *Journal of Consulting and Clinical Psychology, 66*(1), 53–58.

Beard, C., & Peckham, A. D. (2020). Interpretation bias modification. In J. S. Abramowitz & S. M. Blakey (Eds.), *Clinical handbook of fear and anxiety: Maintenance processes and treatment mechanisms* (pp. 359–377). American Psychological Association.

Beck, A. T. (1979). *Cognitive therapy and the emotional disorders.* Penguin.

Beck, A. T., & Dozois, D. J. (2011). Cognitive therapy: Current status and future directions. *Annual Review of Medicine, 62,* 397–409.

Beck, A. T., Emery, G. & Greenberg, R. (1985). *Anxiety disorders and phobias: A cognitive perspective.* Basic Books.

Beck, A. T., Ward, C. H., Mendelson, M., Mock, J. E., & Erbaugh, J. K. (1962). Reliability of psychiatric diagnoses: 2. A study of consistency of clinical judgments and ratings. *American Journal of Psychiatry, 119,* 351–357.

Beckham, A. S. (1933). A study of the intelligence of colored adolescents of differing social-economic status in typical metropolitan areas. *Journal of Social Psychology, 4,* 70–91. doi: 10.1080/00224545.1933.9921558

Bedoya, C. A., Dale, S. K., & Ehlinger, P. P. (2017). Cultural competence within behavioral medicine: Culturally competent CBT with diverse medical populations. In A. Vranceanu, J. A. Greer, & S. Safren (Eds.), *The Massachusetts General Hospital handbook of behavioral medicine* (pp. 321–334). Elsevier.

Behenck, A. D. S., Wesner, A. C., Guimaraes, L. S. P., Manfro, G. G., Dreher, C. B., & Heldt, E. (2021). Anxiety sensitivity and panic disorder: Evaluation of the impact of cognitive-behavioral group therapy. *Issues in Mental Health Nursing, 42*(2), 112–118.

Belus, J. M., Baucom, D. H., & Abramowitz, J. S. (2014). The effect of a couple-based treatment for OCD on intimate partners. *Journal of Behavior Therapy and Experimental Psychiatry, 45*(4), 484–488.

Bender, S. (2020). The Rorschach Test. *The Wiley encyclopedia of personality and individual differences: Measurement and assessment* (pp. 367–376). Wiley.

Benjamin Jr., L. T., & Baker, D. B. (2000). Boulder at 50: Introduction to the section. *American Psychologist, 55*(2), 233–236.

Bennett, C. M., & Miller, M. B. (2010). How reliable are the results from functional magnetic resonance imaging? *Annals of the New York Academy of Sciences, 1191*(1), 133–155.

Bennett, C., Baird, A., Miller, M., & Wolford, G. (2010). Neural correlates of interspecies perspective taking in the post-mortem Atlantic salmon: An argument for proper multiple comparisons correction. *Journal of Serendipitous and Unexpected Results, 1*(1), 1–5.

Ben-Porath, Y. S., & Tellegen, A. (2020). *MMPI-3 Manual for administration, scoring, and interpretation.* University of Minnesota Press.

Bentum, J. S., Bronswijk, S. C., Sijbrandij, M., Lemmens, L. H. J. M., Peeters, F. F. P. M. L., Drukker, M., & Huibers, M. J. H. (2021). Cognitive therapy and interpersonal psychotherapy reduce suicidal ideation independent from their effect on depression. *Depression and Anxiety, 38,* 940–949.

Benuto, L. T., Casas, J. B., Bennett, N. M., & Leany, B. D. (2020). The MMPI-2-RF: A pilot study of Latinx vs. non-Latinx whites profiles. *Professional Psychology: Research and Practice, 51*(5), 496.

Ben-Zur, H., Zeigler-Hill, V., & Shackelford, T. K. (2019). Transactional model of stress and coping. *Encyclopedia of Personality and Individual Differences*, pp. 1–4. Springer.

Berenbaum, H., Washburn, J. J., Sbarra, D., Reardon, K. W., Schuler, T., Teachman, B. A., Hollon, S. D., Atkins, M. S., Hamilton, J. L., Hetrick, W. P., Tackett, J. L., Cody, M. W., Klepac, R. K., & Lee, S. S. (2021). Accelerating the rate of progress in reducing mental health burdens: Recommendations for training the next generation of clinical psychologists. *Clinical Psychology: Science and Practice, 28*(2), 107–123.

Bernal, G., & Gómez-Arroyo, K. (2017). Family therapy: Theory and practice. In *Comprehensive textbook of psychotherapy: Theory and practice* (pp. 239–253). Oxford University Press.

Bernal, M. E., & Castro, F. G. (1994). Are clinical psychologists prepared for service and research with ethnic minorities? Report of a decade of progress. *American Psychologist, 49*(9), 797–805. doi:10.1037/0003-066X.49.9.797

Bersoff, D. N. (1976). Therapists as protectors and policemen: New roles as a result of Tarasoff? *Professional Psychology, 7*, 267.

Beutler, L. E., (1995). Integrating and communicating findings. In L. E. Beutler & M. R. Berren (Eds.), *Integrative assessment of adult personality* (pp. 25–64). Guilford.

Bhugra, D., & De Silva, P. (2000). Couple therapy across cultures. *Sexual and relationship therapy, 15*(2), 183–192.

Bieling, P. J., & Kuyken, W. (2003). Is cognitive case formulation science or science fiction? *Clinical Psychology: Science and Practice, 10*(1), 52–69.

Blakey, S. M., Abramowitz, J. S., Buchholz, J. L., Jessup, S. C., Jacoby, R. J., Reuman, L., & Pentel, K. Z. (2019). A randomized controlled trial of the judicious use of safety behaviors during exposure therapy. *Behaviour Research and Therapy, 112*, 28–35.

Blakey, S. M., Abramowitz, J. S., Leonard, R. C., & Riemann, B. C. (2019). Does exposure and response prevention behaviorally activate clients with obsessive-compulsive disorder? A Preliminary Test. *Behavior Therapy, 50*(1), 214–224.

Blakey, S. M., Jennifer, Y. Y., Calhoun, P. S., Beckham, J. C., & Elbogen, E. B. (2019). Why do trauma survivors become depressed? Testing the behavioral model of depression in a nationally representative sample. *Psychiatry Research, 272*, 587–594.

Blashfield, R. K., & Draguns, J. G. (1976). Evaluative criteria for psychiatric classification. *Journal of Abnormal Psychology, 85*(2), 140–150.

Blau, T. H. (1998). *The psychologist as expert witness* (2nd ed.). Wiley.

Bodenmann, G., Kessler, M., Kuhn, R., Hocker, L., & Randall, A. K. (2020). Cognitive-behavioral and emotion-focused couple therapy: Similarities and differences. *Clinical Psychology in Europe, 2*(3), 1–12.

Bordin, E. S. (1979). The generalizability of the psychoanalytic concept of working alliance. *Psychotherapy, 16*, 252–260.

Bouchard, C. (2020). *The genetics of obesity*. CRC Press.

Bowen, M. (1960). A family concept of schizophrenia. In D. D. Jackson (Ed.), *The etiology of schizophrenia* (pp. 346–372). Basic Books.

Bowen, M. (1966). The use of family theory in clinical practice. *Comprehensive Psychiatry, 7*(5), 345–374.

Braakmann, D. (2015). Historical paths in psychotherapy research. In O. Gelo, A. Pritz, & B. Rieken (Eds.), *Psychotherapy research* (pp. 39–65). Springer.

Bradbury, T. N., & Bodenmann, G. (2020). Interventions for couples. *Annual Review of Clinical Psychology, 16*(7), 99–123.

Brannon, L., & Feist, J. (2010). *Health psychology: An introduction to behavior and health. Australia* (7th ed.). Wadsworth, Cengage.

Brannon, L., Updegraff, J., & Feist, J. (2018). *Health psychology: An introduction to behavior and health* (8th ed.). Cengage Learning.

Breuer, J., & Freud, S. (1895/1955). *The standard edition of the complete psychological works of Sigmund Freud: Vol. II. Studies on hysteria*. Hogarth.

Brewin, C. R. (1989). Cognitive change processes in psychotherapy. *Psychological review, 96*(3), 379–394.

Brigham, C.C. (1923). *A study of American intelligence*. Princeton University Press.

Brodsky, S. (2013). *Testifying in court: Guidelines and maxims for the expert witness*. American Psychological Association.

Brosan, L., Hoppitt, L., Shelfer, L., Sillence, A., & Mackintosh, B. (2011). Cognitive bias modification for attention and interpretation reduces trait and state anxiety in anxious patients referred to an out-patient service: Results from a pilot study. *Journal of Behavior Therapy and Experimental Psychiatry, 42*(3), 258–264.

Brownell, K. (2004). *The LEARN program for weight management*. American Health Publishing.

Bruchmüller, K., Margraf, J., Suppiger, A., & Schneider, S. (2011). Popular or unpopular? Therapists' use of structured interviews and their estimation of patient acceptance. *Behavior Therapy, 42*(4), 634–643.

Buchholz, J. L., & Abramowitz, J. S. (2020). The therapeutic alliance in exposure therapy for anxiety-related disorders: a critical review. *Journal of Anxiety Disorders, 70*, 102194.

Buchholz, J. L., Abramowitz, J. S., Blakey, S. M., Reuman, L., & Twohig, M. P. (2019). Sudden gains: How important are they during exposure and response prevention for obsessive-compulsive disorder? *Behavior Therapy, 50*(3), 672–681.

Buckhout, R. (1975). Nearly 2000 witnesses can be wrong. *Social Action and the Law, 2,* 7.

Budman, S. H., Demby, A., Soldz, S., & Merry, J. (1996). Time-limited group psychotherapy for patients with personality disorders: Outcomes and dropouts. *International Journal of Group Psychotherapy, 46*(3), 357–377.

Bullis, J. R., Bentley, K. H., & Kennedy, K. A. (2018). Group treatment applications of the Unified Protocol. In D. H. Barlow & T. J. Farchione (Eds.), *Applications of the Unified Protocol for transdiagnostic treatment of emotional disorder* (pp. 252–267). Oxford University Press.

Burgoyne, N., & Cohn, A. S. (2020). Lessons from the transition to relational teletherapy during COVID-19. *Family Process, 59*(3), 974–988.

Burlingame, G. M., Fuhriman, A., & Johnson, J. E. (2004). Process and outcome in group counseling and psychotherapy. In *Handbook of group counseling and psychotherapy* (pp. 49–61). Sage.

Burlingame, G. M., McClendon, D. T., & Yang, C. (2018). Cohesion in group therapy: A meta-analysis. *Psychotherapy, 55*(4), 384.

Butcher, J. N. (2010). Personality assessment from the nineteenth to the early twenty-first century: Past achievements and contemporary challenges. *Annual Review of Clinical Psychology, 6,* 1–20.

Byrne, G., & O'Mahony, T. (2020). Acceptance and commitment therapy (ACT) for adults with intellectual disabilities and/or autism spectrum conditions (ASC): A systematic review. *Journal of Contextual Behavioral Science, 18,* 247–255.

Canady, H. G. (1943). The problem of equating the environment of Negro-white groups for intelligence testing in comparative studies. *Journal of Social Psychology, 17,* 3–15. doi.org/10.1080/00224545.1943.9712259

Canter, D. (2017). *Criminal psychology.* Routledge.

Carlbring, P., Andersson, G., Cuijpers, P., Riper, H., & Hedman-Lagerlöf, E. (2018). Internet-based vs. face-to-face cognitive behavior therapy for psychiatric and somatic disorders: An updated systematic review and meta-analysis. *Cognitive Behaviour Therapy, 47*(1), 1–18.

Carpenter, J. K., Andrews, L. A., Witcraft, S. M., Powers, M. B., Smits, J. A., & Hofmann, S. G. (2018). Cognitive behavioral therapy for anxiety and related disorders: A meta-analysis of randomized placebo-controlled trials. *Depression and Anxiety, 35*(6), 502–514.

Carvalho, J. P., & Hopko, D. R. (2011). Behavioral theory of depression: Reinforcement as a mediating variable between avoidance and depression. *Journal of Behavior Therapy and Experimental Psychiatry, 42*(2), 154–162.

Casas, J. M., Ponterotto, J. G., & Gutierrez, J. M. (1986). Counseling research and training: The crosscultural perspective. *Journal of Counseling and Development, 64,* 347–348.

Castro, F. G., Barrera Jr., M., & Holleran Steiker, L. K. (2010). Issues and challenges in the design of culturally adapted evidence-based interventions. *Annual Review of Clinical Psychology, 6,* 213–239.

Cattell, R. B. (1933). *Psychology and social progress: Mankind and destiny from the standpoint of a scientist.* C. W. Daniel.

Cattell, R. B. (1937). *The fight for our national intelligence.* P. S. King.

Cattell, R. B. (1965). *The scientific analysis of personality.* Penguin.

Cattell, R. B. (1972). *A new morality from science: Beyondism.* Pergamon.

Cautela, J. R. (1967). Covert sensitization. *Psychological Reports, 20*(2), 459–468.

Centers for Disease Control and Prevention. (2021, May 26). *Risk for COVID-19 infection, hospitalization, and death by race/ethnicity.* www.cdc.gov/coronavirus/2019-ncov/covid-data/investigations-discovery/hospitalization-death-by-race-ethnicity.html

Chamberlain, A. F. (1909). Note on some difference between "savages" and children. *Psychological Bulletin, 6*(6), 212–214. doi: 10.1037/h0069629

Chambless, D. L., & Ollendick, T. H. (2001). Empirically supported psychological interventions: Controversies and evidence. *Annual Review of Psychology, 52*(1), 685–716.

Chambless, D. L., Baker, M., Baucom, D. H., Beutler, L. E., Calhoun, K. S., Crits-Christoph, P., Daiuto, A., DeRubeis, R., Detweiler, J., Haaga, D., Johnson, S., McCurry, S., Mueser, K., Pope, K., Sanderson, W., Shoham, V., Stickle, T., Williams D., & Woody, S. (1998). Update on empirically validated therapies: II. *Clinical Psychologist, 51*(1), 3–16.

Chapman, L. J., & Chapman, J. P. (1969). Illusory correlation as an obstacle to the use of valid psychodiagnostic signs. *Journal of Abnormal Psychology, 74*(3), 271.

Chávez-García, M. (2012). Mildred S. Covert: Eugenics fieldworker, racial pathologist. In *States of Delinquency* (pp. 79–111). University of California Press.

Chen, J., & Gardner, H. (2005). Assessment based on multiple-intelligences theory. In D. P. Flanagan & P. L. Harrison (Eds.), *Contemporary intellectual assessment: Theories, tests, and issues* (2nd ed., pp. 77–102). Guilford.

Chorpita, B. F., Daleiden, E. L., Ebesutani, C., Young, J., Becker, K. D., Nakamura, B. J., & Starace, N. (2011). Evidence-based treatments for children and adolescents: An updated review of indicators of efficacy and effectiveness. *Clinical Psychology: Science and Practice, 18* (2), 154–172.

Christensen, A., Atkins, D. C., Baucom, B., & Yi, J. (2010). Marital status and satisfaction five years following a randomized clinical trial comparing traditional versus integrative behavioral couple therapy. *Journal of Consulting and Clinical Psychology, 78*(2), 225–232.

Chung, A. H., Gevirtz, R. N., Gharbo, R. S., Thiam, M. A., & Ginsberg, J. P. (2021). Pilot study on reducing symptoms of anxiety with a heart rate variability biofeedback wearable and remote stress management coach. *Applied Psychophysiology and Biofeedback, 46*(4), 347–358.

Clark, D. M. (2018). Realizing the mass public benefit of evidence-based psychological therapies: The IAPT program. *Annual Review of Clinical Psychology, 14*, 159–183.

Clark, D. M., Salkovskis, P. M., Hackmann, A., Middleton, H., Anastasiades, P., & Gelder, M. (1994). A comparison of cognitive therapy, applied relaxation and imipramine in the treatment of panic disorder. *The British Journal of Psychiatry, 164*(6), 759–769.

Clark, K. B., & Clark, M. P. (1939). The development of consciousness of self and the emergence of racial identification in Negro preschool children. *Journal of Social Psychology, 10*, 591–599. doi.org/10.1080/00224545.1939.9713394

Claro, S., Paunesku, D., & Dweck, C. S. (2016). Growth mindset tempers the effects of poverty on academic achievement. *Proceedings of the National Academy of Sciences, 113*(31), 8664–8668.

Coates, T. J., & Thoresen, C. E. (1981). Treating obesity in children and adolescents: Is there any hope? In J. M. Ferguson & C. B. Taylor (Eds.), *The comprehensive handbook of behavioral medicine* (Vol. 2). Spectrum.

Cocchiara, R. A., Sestili, C., Di Bella, O., Backhaus, I., Sinopoli, A., D'Egidio, V., Lia, L., Saulle, R., Mannocci, A., & La Torre, G. (2020). "GiochiAMO": A gaming intervention to prevent smoking and alcohol habits among children. A single-arm field trial. *Games for Health Journal, 9*(2), 113–120.

Cohen, S., & McKay, G. (2020). Social support, stress and the buffering hypothesis: A theoretical analysis. In *Handbook of Psychology and Health* (Vol. IV, pp. 253–267). Routledge.

Colella, A., Hebl, M., & King, E. (2017). One hundred years of discrimination research in the *Journal of Applied Psychology*: A sobering synopsis. *Journal of Applied Psychology, 102*(3), 500.

Conger, J. J. (1980). Proceedings of the American Psychological Association, Incorporated, for the year 1979: Minutes of the Annual Meeting of the Council of Representatives. *American Psychologist, 35*(6), 501–536. doi.org/10.1037/h0078342

Conner, K. R., Chapman, B. P., Beautrais, A. L., Brent, D. A., Bridge, J. A., Conwell, Y., Falter, T., Holbrook, A., & Schneider, B. (2021). Introducing the psychological autopsy methodology checklist. *Suicide and Life-Threatening Behavior, 51*, 673–683.

Constantine, M. G. (2007). Racial microaggressions against African American clients in cross-racial counseling relationships. *Journal of Counseling Psychology, 54*(1), 1–16.

Constantino, M. J., Vîslă, A., Coyne, A. E., & Boswell, J. F. (2018). A meta-analysis of the association between patients' early treatment outcome expectation and their posttreatment outcomes. *Psychotherapy, 55*(4), 473–485.

Costa, P. T., & McCrae, R. R. (1992). Normal personality assessment in clinical practice: The NEO Personality Inventory. *Psychological Assessment, 4*(1), 5.

Craske, M. G., Meadows, E. A., & Barlow, D. H. (2000). *Mastery of your anxiety and panic: MAP-3. Therapist guide for anxiety, panic, and agoraphobia.* Graywind.

Craske, M. G., Niles, A. N., Burklund, L. J., Wolitzky-Taylor, K. B., Vilardaga, J. C. P., Arch, J. J., Saxbe, D., & Lieberman, M. D. (2014). Randomized controlled trial of cognitive behavioral therapy and acceptance and commitment therapy for social phobia: Outcomes and moderators. *Journal of Consulting and Clinical Psychology, 82*(6), 1034.

Craske, M. G., Treanor, M., Conway, C. C., Zbozinek, T., & Vervliet, B. (2014). Maximizing exposure therapy: An inhibitory learning approach. *Behaviour Research and Therapy, 58*, 10–23.

Creswell, J. D. (2017). Mindfulness interventions. *Annual Review of Psychology, 68*, 491–516.

Crews, F. (1996). The verdict on Freud. *Psychological Science, 7*(2), 63–68.

Cristea, I. A., Gentili, C., Cotet, C. D., Palomba, D., Barbui, C., & Cuijpers, P. (2017). Efficacy of psychotherapies for borderline personality disorder: A systematic review and meta-analysis. *JAMA Psychiatry, 74*(4), 319–328.

Cuijpers, P., Driessen, E., Hollon, S. D., van Oppen, P., Barth, J., & Andersson, G. (2012). The efficacy of non-directive supportive therapy for adult depression: A meta-analysis. *Clinical Psychology Review, 32*(4), 280–291.

Cuijpers, P., Reijnders, M., & Huibers, M. J. (2019). The role of common factors in psychotherapy outcomes. *Annual Review of Clinical Psychology, 15*, 207–231.

Cuijpers, P., Van Straten, A., & Warmerdam, L. (2007). Behavioral activation treatments of depression: A meta-analysis. *Clinical Psychology Review, 27*(3), 318–326.

Cullinan, V., & Vitale, A. (2009). The contribution of Relational Frame Theory to the development of interventions for impairments of language and cognition. *The Journal of Speech and Language Pathology: Applied Behavior Analysis, 4*(1), 132–145.

Custody Act, 91 Michigan. (1970). www.legislature.mi.gov/documents/mcl/pdf/mcl-act-91-of-1970.pdf

Cuthbert, B. N. (2020). The role of RDoC in future classification of mental disorders. *Dialogues in Clinical Neuroscience, 22*(1), 81–85.

Danaher, J. (2018). Moral enhancement and moral freedom: A critique of the little Alex problem. *Royal Institute of Philosophy Supplements, 83,* 233–250.

David, D., Cotet, C., Matu, S., Mogoase, C., & Stefan, S. (2018). 50 years of rational-emotive and cognitive-behavioral therapy: A systematic review and meta-analysis. *Journal of Clinical Psychology, 74*(3), 304–318.

Dawes, R. M. (1994). *House of cards: Psychology and psychotherapy built on myth.* Free Press.

Dawes, R. M., Faust, D., & Meehl, P. E. (1989). Clinical versus actuarial judgment. *Science, 243*(4899), 1668–1674.

de Felice, G., Giuliani, A., Halfon, S., Andreassi, S., Paoloni, G., & Orsucci, F. F. (2019). The misleading Dodo bird verdict. How much of the outcome variance is explained by common and specific factors? *New Ideas in Psychology, 54,* 50–55.

De Lorenzo, A., Romano, L., Di Renzo, L., Di Lorenzo, N., Cenname, G., & Gualtieri, P. (2020). Obesity: A preventable, treatable, but relapsing disease. *Nutrition, 71,* 110615.

Deacon, B. J. (2013). The biomedical model of mental disorder: A critical analysis of its validity, utility, and effects on psychotherapy research. *Clinical Psychology Review, 33*(7), 846–861.

Deary, I. J., Penke, L., & Johnson, W. (2010). The neuroscience of human intelligence differences. *Nature Reviews Neuroscience, 11,* 201–211.

Demerouti, E., & Cropanzano, R. (2017). The buffering role of sportsmanship on the effects of daily negative events. *European Journal of Work and Organizational Psychology, 26*(2), 263–274.

Dennis (1943). Dennis, W. (1942). The performance of Hopi children on the Goodenough Draw-a-man Test. *Journal of Comparative Psychology, 34*(3), 341–348. doi: 10.1037/h0055172

DeRubeis, R. J., Siegle, G. J., & Hollon, S. D. (2008). Cognitive therapy versus medication for depression: Treatment outcomes and neural mechanisms. *Nature Reviews Neuroscience, 9*(10), 788–796.

Dickstein, S., Hayden, L. C., Schiller, M., Seifer, R., & San Antonio, W. (1994). Providence Family Study mealtime family interaction coding system. Adapted from the McMaster Clinical Rating Scale. EP Bradley Hospital.

Digiuseppe, R., & Bernard, M. E. (2006). REBT assessment and treatment with children. In A. Ellis & M. Bernard (Eds.), *Rational emotive behavioral approaches to childhood disorders* (pp. 85–114). Springer.

DiLillo, D., DeGue, S., Cohen, L. M., & Morgan, R. D. (2006). The path to licensure for academic psychologists: How tough is the road? *Professional Psychology: Research and Practice, 37*(5), 567–586.

DiMatteo, M. R., & DiNicola, D. D. (1982). *Achieving patient compliance: The psychology of the medical practitioner's role.* Pergamon.

Dinne, D. L., Forgays, D. K., Hayes, S. A., & Lonner, W. J. (Eds.). (2020). *Merging past, present, and future in cross-cultural psychology.* Garland Science.

Division 45 Science Committee. (2007, Winter). Division 45 Science Committee report: Representation of racial/ethnic minority scientists (scientists-practitioners) within the American Psychological Association. *Focus,* 11–14.

Dobson, K. S., Poole, J. C., & Beck, J. S. (2018). The fundamental cognitive model. *Science and Practice in Cognitive Therapy: Foundations, Mechanisms, and Applications,* 29–47.

Downey, J. E. (1927). Types of dextrality among Native American Indians. *Journal of Experimental Psychology, 10*(6), 478–488. doi: 10.1037/h0069041

Doyle, J. (2014). Measuring "problems of human behavior": The eugenic origins of Yale's Institute of Psychology, 1921–1929. *MSSA Kaplan Prize for Use of MSSA Collections, 15.* https://elischolar.library.yale.edu/cgi/viewcontent.cgi?article=1065&context=mssa_collections

Dressler, J., & Garvey, S. (2019). *Criminal law: Cases and materials.* West Academic Publishing.

Du Bois, W. E. B. (1903). *The souls of black folks: Essays and sketches.* A. C. McClurg.

Duckworth, A. L., Quinn, P. D., & Tsukayama, E. (2012). What No Child Left Behind leaves behind: The roles of IQ and self-control in predicting standardized achievement test scores and report card grades. *Journal of Educational Psychology, 104*(2), 439.

Eberhardt, J. L., Davies, P. G., Purdie-Vaughns, V. J., & Johnson, S. L. (2006). Looking deathworthy: Perceived stereotypicality of Black defendants predicts capital-sentencing outcomes. *Psychological Science, 17*(5), 383–386.

Elliott, M. L., Knodt, A. R., Ireland, D., Morris, M. L., Poulton, R., Ramrakha, S., Sison, M. L., Moffitt, T., Caspi, A., & Hariri, A. R. (2020). What is the test-retest reliability of common task-functional MRI measures? New empirical evidence and a meta-analysis. *Psychological Science, 31*(7), 792–806.

Ellis, A. (1957). Rational psychotherapy and individual psychology. *Journal of Individual Psychology, 13*(1), 38–44.

Ellis, A. (1962). *Reason and emotion in psychotherapy.* Lyle Stuart.

Engel, G. L. (1977). The need for a new medical model: A challenge for biomedicine. *Science, 196,* 129–136.

Engs, R. (2005). *The eugenics movement: An encyclopedia.* Greenwood Press.

Epstein, L. H., Valoski, A., Wing, R. R., & McCurley, J. (1994). Ten-year outcomes of behavioral family-based treatment for childhood obesity. *Health Psychology, 13*, 373–383.

Erekson, D. M., & Lambert, M. J. (2015). Client-centered therapy. *The Encyclopedia of Clinical Psychology, 1–5.* Wiley.

Evans, R. I. (1976). Smoking in children: Developing a social psychological strategy of deterrence. *Preventive Medicine, 5*, 122–127.

Everitt, B. J., & Robbins, T. W. (2016). Drug addiction: Updating actions to habits to compulsions ten years on. *Annual Review of Psychology, 67*, 23–50.

Exner Jr., J. E. (1993). *The Rorschach: A comprehensive system. Basic foundations, Vol. 1.* John Wiley & Sons.

Exner Jr., J. E., & Exner, D. E. (1972). How clinicians use the Rorschach. *Journal of Personality Assessment, 36*(5), 403–408.

Eysenck, H. J. (1952). The effects of psychotherapy: An evaluation. *Journal of Consulting and Clinical Psychology, 16*, 319–324.

Fan, S., & Ding, D. (2020). A meta-analysis of the efficacy of acceptance and commitment therapy for children. *Journal of Contextual Behavioral Science, 15*, 225–234.

Feldman, J. S., Tung, I., & Lee, S. S. (2017). Social skills mediate the association of ADHD and depression in pre-adolescents. *Journal of Psychopathology and Behavioral Assessment, 39*(1), 79–91.

Ferguson, G. O. (1916). The psychology of the Negro: An experimental study. *Archives of Psychology, 36*, 1–138.

Field, S. (1992). The effect of temperature on crime. *The British Journal of Criminology, 32*(3), 340–351.

Fiese, B. H. (2021). Family mealtimes: Promoting health and well-being. *Families, Food, and Parenting: Integrating Research, Practice and Policy*, 77–94.

Finch Jr., A. J., Simon, N. P., & Nezu, C. M. (2006). The future of clinical psychology: Board certification. *Clinical Psychology: Science and Practice, 13*(3), 254–257.

First, M. B., Williams, J. B. W., Karg, R. S., & Spitzer, R. L. (2016). *Structured Clinical Interview for DSM-5 Disorders, Clinician Version (SCID-5-CV).* American Psychiatric Association.

Fitzgerald, J. A., & Ludeman, W. W. (1927). The intelligence of Indian children. *Journal of Comparative Psychology, 64*(4), 319–328. doi: 10.1037/h0071550

Flaskas, C., Mason, B., & Perlesz, A. (Eds.). (2018). *The space between: Experience, context, and process in the therapeutic relationship.* Routledge.

Foa, E. B., Liebowitz, M. R., Kozak, M. J., Davies, S., Campeas, R., Franklin, M. E., Huppert, J. D., Kjernisted, K.,

Rowan, V., Schmidt, A. B., Smpson, H. B., & Tu, X. (2005). Randomized, placebo-controlled trial of exposure and ritual prevention, clomipramine, and their combination in the treatment of obsessive-compulsive disorder. *American Journal of Psychiatry, 162*(1), 151–161.

Fodor, L. A., Georgescu, R., Cuijpers, P., Szamoskozi, Ş., David, D., Furukawa, T. A., & Cristea, I. A. (2020). Efficacy of cognitive bias modification interventions in anxiety and depressive disorders: A systematic review and network meta-analysis. *The Lancet Psychiatry, 7*(6), 506–514.

Fortney, J. C., Unützer, J., Wrenn, G., Pyne, J. M., Smith, G. R., Schoenbaum, M., & Harbin, H. T. (2017). A tipping point for measurement-based care. *Psychiatric Services, 68*(2), 179–188.

Frank, D. L., Khorshid, L., Kiffer, J. F., Moravec, C. S., & McKee, M. G. (2010). Biofeedback in medicine: Who, when, why and how? *Mental Health in Family Medicine, 7*(2), 85–91.

Frank, J. D. (1982). *Therapeutic components shared by all psychotherapies.* In J. H. Harvey & M. M. Parks (Eds.), *Master lecture series: Vol. 1. Psychotherapy research and behavior change* (pp. 9–37). American Psychological Association.

Franklin, A. (1971). To be young, gifted and black with inappropriate professional training: A critique of counseling programs. *The Counseling Psychologist, 2*(4), 107–112. doi.org/10.1177/001100007100200411

Freud, S. (1955). *The interpretation of dreams.* Basic Books.

Frey, A. J., Lee, J., Small, J. W., Sibley, M., Owens, J. S., Skidmore, B., Johnson, L., Bradshaw, C., & Moyers, T. B. (2021). Mechanisms of motivational interviewing: A conceptual framework to guide practice and research. *Prevention Science, 22*(6), 689–700.

Frey, M. C. (2019). What we know, are still getting wrong, and have yet to learn about the relationships among the SAT, intelligence and achievement. *Journal of Intelligence, 7*(4), 26.

Friedlander, M. L., Escudero, V., Welmers-van de Poll, M. J., & Heatherington, L. (2018). Meta-analysis of the alliance–outcome relation in couple and family therapy. *Psychotherapy, 55*(4), 356.

Friedman, M., & Rosenman, R. H. (1974). *Type A behavior and your heart.* Knopf.

Frimpong, J. A., Guerrero, E. G., Kong, Y., & Kim, T. (2016). Abstinence at successful discharge in publicly funded addiction health services. *The Journal of Behavioral Health Services & Research, 43*(4), 661–675.

Frost, R. O., Steketee, G., & Grisham, J. (2004). Measurement of compulsive hoarding: Saving Inventory–Revised. *Behaviour Research and Therapy, 42*(10), 1163–1182.

Fruzzetti, A. E., Shenk, C., & Hoffman, P. D. (2005). Family interaction and the development of borderline personality disorder: A transactional model. *Development and Psychopathology, 17,* 1007–1030.

Fukuyama, M. A. (1990). Taking a universal approach to multicultural counseling. *Counselor Education and Supervision, 30*(1), 6–17. doi.org/10.1002/j.1556-6978.1990.tb01174.x

Gallagher, T., Petersen, J., & Foa, E. B. (2020). Prolonged exposure for PTSD. In L. F. Bufka, C. V. Wright, & R. W. Halfond (Eds.), *Casebook to the APA Clinical Practice Guideline for the treatment of PTSD* (pp. 123–137). American Psychological Association.

Galton, F. (1869). *Hereditary genius: An inquiry into its laws and consequences.* Macmillan and Co.

Garb, H. N., Florio, C. M., & Grove, W. M. (1998). The validity of the Rorschach and the Minnesota Multiphasic Personality Inventory: Results from meta-analyses. *Psychological Science, 9*(5), 402–404.

Gardner, H. (1999). *Intelligence reframed: Multiple intelligences for the 21st century.* Basic Books.

Garrett, H. E. (1973). *IQ and racial differences.* Noontide Press.

Garth, T. R. (1921). The results of some tests on full and mixed blood Indians. *Journal of Applied Psychology, 5,* 359–372. doi: 10.1037/h0071643

Garth, T. R., & Barnard, M. A. (1927). The will-temperament of Indians. *Journal of Applied Psychology, 11*(6), 512–518. doi: 10.1037/H0071493

Gelb, S. S., Allen, G. E., Futterman, A., & Mehler, B. (1986). Rewriting mental testing history: The view from the *American Psychologist. Sage Race Relations Abstracts, 11,* 18–31.

Gibbons, M. B. C., Crits-Christoph, P., & Hearon, B. (2008). The empirical status of psychodynamic therapies. *Annual Review of Clinical Psychology, 4,* 93–108.

Gladding, S. T. (2015). *The creative arts in counseling.* American Counseling Association.

Goldberg, L. R. (1993). The structure of phenotypic personality traits. *American Psychologist, 48*(1), 26.

Goldfried, M. R., & Davison, G. C. (1994). *Wiley series in clinical psychology and personality: Clinical behavior therapy.* John Wiley & Sons.

Gonzalez, G. G. (2013). *Chicano education in the era of segregation.* University of North Texas Press.

Gonzalez, J. E., Nelson, J. R., Gutkin, T. B., Saunders, A., Galloway, A., & Shwery, C. S. (2004). Rational emotive therapy with children and adolescents: A meta-analysis. *Journal of Emotional and Behavioral Disorders, 12*(4), 222–235.

Goodenough, F. (1926). *Measurement of intelligence by drawings.* World Book.

Gould, S. J., & Gold, S. J. (1996). *The mismeasure of man.* WW Norton & Company.

Graham, J. R., Sorenson, S., & Hayes-Skelton, S. A. (2013). Enhancing the cultural sensitivity of cognitive behavioral interventions for anxiety in diverse populations. *Behavior Therapist, 36*(5), 101–108.

Graham, S. (1992). "Most of the subjects were white and middle class": Trends in published research on African Americans in selected APA journals, 1970–1989. *American Psychologist, 47*(5), 629–639. doi: 10.1037/0003-066X.47.5.629

Gray, J. (2012). Society of Indian Psychologists: Honoring the ancestors, strengthening the future. *Communique.* www.apa.org/pi/oema/resources/communique/2012/11/american-indian-psychologists

Graziano, P. A., Ros-Demarize, R., & Hare, M. M. (2020). Condensing parent training: A randomized trial comparing the efficacy of a briefer, more intensive version of Parent-Child Interaction Therapy (I-PCIT). *Journal of Consulting and Clinical Psychology, 88*(7), 669.

Green, E., & Heilbrun, K. (2011). *Wrightsman's psychology and the legal system* (7th ed.). Wadsworth/Cengage.

Greenberg, D., Eagle, K., & Felthous, A. R. (2020). The insanity defense and psychopathic disorders in the United States and Australia. *The Wiley International Handbook on Psychopathic Disorders and the Law,* 385–412.

Greenberg, L. S., & Goldman, R. N. (2019). *Clinical handbook of emotion-focused therapy.* American Psychological Association.

Greenberg, L., Elliott, R., & Lietaer, G. (1994). Research on experiential psychotherapies. In A. E. Bergin & S. L. Garfield (Eds.), *Handbook of psychotherapy and behavior change* (4th ed., pp. 509–539). Wiley.

Greene, E., & Loftus, E. (1981). The person perceiver as information processor. *Psyccritiques, 26*(5), 343–345.

Greenman, P. S., Johnson, S. M., & Wiebe, S. (2019). Emotionally focused therapy for couples: At the heart of science and practice. In B. H. Fiese, M. Celano, K. Deater-Deckard, E. N. Jouriles, & M. A. Whisman (Eds.), *APA handbook of contemporary family psychology: Family therapy and training* (pp. 291–305). American Psychological Association.

Greenwood, J. (2017). Psychologists go to war. *Behavioral Scientist.* https://behavioralscientist.org/psychologists-go-war/

Griner, D., & Smith, T. B. (2006). Culturally adapted mental health intervention: A meta-analytic review. *Psychotherapy: Theory, Research, Practice, Training, 43,* 531–548.

Grob, G. N. (2005). Public policy and mental illnesses: Jimmy Carter's Presidential Commission on Mental Health. *The Milbank Quarterly, 83*(3), 425–456. doi: 10.1111/j.1468-0009.2005.00408

Gutheil, T. G. (2004). The expert witness. In R. I. Simon & L. H. Gold (Eds.), *The American Psychiatric Publishing textbook of forensic psychiatry* (pp. 75-89). American Psychiatric Publishing.

Guthrie, R. V. (1998). *Even the rat was white: A historical view of psychology.* Allyn and Bacon.

Gutmann, D. (1964). An exploration of ego configurations in middle and later life. In B. Neugarten (Ed.), *Personality in middle and later life* (pp. 114-148). Atherton.

Gutmann, D. (1967). Aging among the Highland Maya: A comparative study. *Journal of Personality and Social Psychology, 7*(28), 28-35.

Hall, G. C. N., & Ibaraki, A. Y. (2016). Multicultural issues in cognitive-behavioral therapy: Cultural adaptations and goodness of fit. In C. M. Nezu & A. M. Nezu (Eds.), *The Oxford handbook of cognitive and behavioral therapies* (pp. 465-481). Oxford University Press.

Hall, G. C. N., Berkman, E. T., Zane, N. W., Leong, F. T., Hwang, W. C., Nezu, A. M., Nezu, C. M., Hong, J. J., Chu, J. P., & Huang, E. R. (2021). Reducing mental health disparities by increasing the personal relevance of interventions. *American Psychologist, 76*(1), 91-103.

Hall, G. C. N., Ibaraki, A. Y., Huang, E. R., Marti, C. N., & Stice, E. (2016). A meta-analysis of cultural adaptations of psychological interventions. *Behavior Therapy, 47*(6), 993-1014.

Hall, G. S. (1904). *Adolescence: Its psychology and its relation to physiology, anthropology, sociology, sex, crime, religion, and education, Vol. 1.* D. Appleton and Company. doi: 10.1037/10616-000

Hall, G. S. (1905). *Adolescence: Its psychology and its relation to physiology, anthropology, sociology, sex, crime, religion, and education, Vol. 2.* D. Appleton and Company. doi: 10.1037/14677-000

Handelsman, M. M. (1990). Do written consent forms influence clients' first impressions of therapists? *Professional Psychology: Research and Practice, 21*(6), 451.

Haney, C., Banks, W. C., & Zimbardo, P. G. (1973). A study of prisoners and guards in a simulated prison. *Naval Research Review, 30,* 4-17.

Hans, E., & Hiller, W. (2013a). Effectiveness of and dropout from outpatient cognitive behavioral therapy for adult unipolar depression: A meta-analysis of nonrandomized effectiveness studies. *Journal of Consulting and Clinical Psychology, 81*(1), 75.

Hans, E., & Hiller, W. (2013b). A meta-analysis of nonrandomized effectiveness studies on outpatient cognitive behavioral therapy for adult anxiety disorders. *Clinical Psychology Review, 33*(8), 954-964.

Harden, K. P. (2021). "Reports of my death were greatly exaggerated": Behavior genetics in the postgenomic era. *Annual Review of Psychology, 72,* 37-60.

Harkness, A. R., & Lilienfeld, S. O. (1997). Individual differences science for treatment planning: Personality traits. *Psychological Assessment, 9*(4), 349-360.

Harrell, S. P. (2000). A multidimensional conceptualization of racism-related stress: Implications for the well-being of people of color. *American Journal of Orthopsychiatry, 70,* 42-57.

Harris, D. B. (1963). *Children's drawings as measures of intellectual maturity.* Harcourt, Brace & World.

Harris, G. (2011). Talk doesn't pay, so psychiatry turns instead to drug therapy. *New York Times,* p. 6.

Hartmann, A. S., & Lyons, N. (2017). Body dysmorphic disorder. In J. Abramowitz, E. Storch, & D. McKay (Eds.), *The Wiley handbook of obsessive compulsive disorders* (pp. 774-789). John Wiley & Sons. doi.org/10.1002/9781118890233.ch43

Hathaway, S. R., & McKinley, J. C. (1943). *The Minnesota multiphasic personality inventory* (Rev. ed., 2nd printing). University of Minnesota Press.

Hayes, S. C. (2004). Acceptance and commitment therapy, relational frame theory, and the third wave of behavioral and cognitive therapies. *Behavior Therapy, 35*(4), 639-665.

Hayes, S. C., Luoma, J. B., Bond, F. W., Masuda, A., & Lillis, J. (2006). Acceptance and commitment therapy: Model, processes and outcomes. *Behaviour Research and Therapy, 44*(1), 1-25.

Hayes, S. C., Strosahl, K. D., & Wilson, K. G. (2016). *Acceptance and commitment therapy: The process and practice of mindful change* (2nd ed.). Guilford.

Hayes, S. C., Wilson, K. G., Gifford, E. V., Follette, V. M., & Strosahl, K. (1996). Experiential avoidance and behavioral disorders: A functional dimensional approach to diagnosis and treatment. *Journal of Consulting and Clinical Psychology, 64*(6), 1152.

Hayes-Skelton, S. A., & Eustis, E. H. (2020). Experiential avoidance. In J. S. Abramowitz & S. M. Blakey (Eds.), *Clinical handbook of fear and anxiety: Maintenance processes and treatment mechanisms* (pp. 115-131). American Psychological Association.

Hazlett-Stevens, H., & Bernstein, D. (2021). *Progressive relaxation training: A guide for professionals, students, and researchers.* Praeger/ABC-CLIO.

He, X., Wang, H., Chang, F., Dill, S. E., Liu, H., Tang, B., & Shi, Y. (2021). IQ, grit, and academic achievement: Evidence from rural China. *International Journal of Educational Development, 80,* 102306.

Heilbrun, K. (1997). Prediction versus management models relevant to risk assessment: The importance of legal decision-making context. *Law and Human Behavior, 21*(4), 347-259.

Heimberg, R. G., & Becker, R. E. (2002). *Cognitive-behavioral group therapy for social phobia: Basic mechanisms and clinical strategies*. Guilford.

Helms, J. E., & Cook, D. A. (1999). *Using race and culture in counseling and psychotherapy: Therapy and process*. Allyn & Bacon.

Henderson, L. (2015). Racial isolation and chlamydia rates in US counties. *Race and Social Problems, 7*(2), 111–122.

Henggeler, S. W. (2017). Multisystemic therapy. In *The encyclopedia of juvenile delinquency and justice* (pp. 1–5). Wiley.

Henrich, J., Heine, S., & Norenzayan, A. (2010). The weirdest people in the world? *Behavioral and Brain Sciences, 33*, 61–83. doi: 10.1017/S0140525X0999152X

Herman, E. (2020). *The romance of American psychology* (pp. 25–29). University of California Press.

Herrnstein, R. J., & Murray, C. (1994). *The bell curve: Intelligence and class structure in American life*. Simon and Schuster.

Hetey, R. C., & Eberhardt, J. L. (2019). The numbers don't speak for themselves: Racial disparities and the persistence of inequality in the criminal justice system. *Current Directions in Psychological Science, 27*(3), 183–187.

Hobbs, N. (1948). The development of a code of ethical standards for psychology. *American Psychologist, 3*, 80–84.

Hofmann, S. G. (2020). Imagine there are no therapy brands, it isn't hard to do. *Psychotherapy Research, 30*(3), 297–299.

Hofmann, S. G., & Asmundson, G. J. (2008). Acceptance and mindfulness-based therapy: New wave or old hat? *Clinical Psychology Review, 28*(1), 1–16.

Hofmann, S. G., Asnaani, A., Vonk, I. J., Sawyer, A. T., & Fang, A. (2012). The efficacy of cognitive behavioral therapy: A review of meta-analyses. *Cognitive Therapy and Research, 36*(5), 427–440.

Holliday, B. G. (2009). The history and visions of African American psychology: Multiple pathways to place, space, and authority. *Cultural Diversity and Ethnic Minority Psychology, 15*(4), 317–337. doi: 10.1037/a0016971

Holliday, B. G., & Holmes, A. L. (2003). A tale of challenge and change: A history and chronology of ethnic minorities in psychology in the United States. In G. Bernal, J. E. Trimble, A. K. Burlew, & F. T. L. Leong (Eds.), *Handbook of racial and ethnic minority psychology* (pp. 15–64). Sage.

Hollingshead, A. B., & Redlich, F. C. (1958). *Social class and mental illness: Community study*. John Wiley & Sons.

Hollon, S. D., DeRubeis, R. J., Fawcett, J., Amsterdam, J. D., Shelton, R. C., Zajecka, J., Young, P., & Gallop, R. (2014). Effect of cognitive therapy with antidepressant medications vs antidepressants alone on the rate of recovery in major depressive disorder: A randomized clinical trial. *JAMA Psychiatry, 71*(10), 1157–1164.

Hollon, S. D., Jarrett, R. B., Nierenberg, A. A., Thase, M. E., Trivedi, M., & Rush, A. J. (2005). Psychotherapy and medication in the treatment of adult and geriatric depression: Which monotherapy or combined treatment? *The Journal of Clinical Psychiatry, 66*, 455–468.

Holmes, T. H., & Rahe, R. H. (1967). The Social Readjustment Scale. *Journal of Psychosomatic Research, 11*, 213–218.

Homant, R. J., & Kennedy, D. B. (1998). Psychological aspects of crime scene profiling: Validity research. *Criminal Justice and Behavior, 25*(3), 319–343.

Hopwood, C. J., & Bornstein, R. F. (Eds.). (2014). *Multimethod clinical assessment*. Guilford.

Horry, R., Halford, P., Brewer, N., Milne, R., & Bull, R. (2014). Archival analyses of eyewitness identification test outcomes: What can they tell us about eyewitness memory? *Law and Human Behavior, 38*(1), 94–108.

Hudson, D. L. (2019). How racism has shaped the health of African Americans and what to do about it. In C. L. Ford, D. M. Griffith, M. A. Bruce, & K. L. Gilbert (Eds.), *Racism: Science & tools for the public health professional* (pp. 429–444). American Public Health Association.

Huff, R. M., & Kline, M. V. (1999). *Promoting health in multicultural populations: A handbook for practitioners*. Sage.

Hughes, M. C., Gorman, J. M., Ren, Y., Khalid, S., & Clayton, C. (2019). Increasing access to rural mental health care using hybrid care that includes telepsychiatry. *Journal of Rural Mental Health, 43*(1), 30–37.

Hunsley, J., & Mash, E. J. (2007). Evidence-based assessment. *Annual Review of Clinical Psychology, 3*, 29–51.

Hunsley, J., & Mash, E. J. (2020). The role of assessment in evidence-based practice. In M. M. Antony & D. H. Barlow (Eds.), *Handbook of assessment and treatment planning for psychological disorders* (pp. 3–23). Guilford.

Hunt, E. (2011). *Human intelligence*. Cambridge University Press.

Hunter, W. S., & Sommermeier, E. (1922). The relation of degree of Indian blood to score on the Otis Intelligence Test. *Journal of Comparative Psychology, 2*, 257–277.

Hunyor, S. N., Henderson, R. J., Lal, S. K., Carter, N. L., Kobler, H., Jones, M., Bartrop, R., Craig, A., & Mihailidou, A. S. (1997). Placebo-controlled biofeedback blood pressure effect in hypertensive humans. *Hypertension, 29*(6), 1225–1231.

Hutcheson, C. L. (2019). Cognitive behavioral family therapy. In L. Metcalf (Ed.), *Marriage and family therapy: A practice-oriented approach* (pp. 95–118). Springer.

Indian Education: The Study of Indian Children. Hearings before the Senate Committee on Labor and Public Welfare, 90th Congress. (1967). (Testimony of John F. Byrde).

Innocence Project. (2017). Eyewitness misidentification. www.innocenceproject.org/causes/eyewitness-misidentification

Inoue-Choi, M., Liao, L. M., Reyes-Guzman, C., Hartge, P., Caporaso, N., & Freedman, N. D. (2017). Association of long-term, low-intensity smoking with all-cause and cause-specific mortality in the National Institutes of Health–AARP Diet and Health Study. *JAMA Internal Medicine, 177*(1), 87–95.

Insel, T., Cuthbert, B., Garvey, M., Heinssen, R., Pine, D. S., Quinn, K., Sanislow, C., & Wang, P. (2010). Research Domain Criteria (RDoC): Toward a new classification framework for research on mental disorders. *American Journal of Psychiatry, 167*, 748–751.

Ivy, J. W., Meindl, J. N., Overley, E., & Robson, K. M. (2017). Token economy: A systematic review of procedural descriptions. *Behavior Modification, 41*(5), 708–737.

Jackson Jr., J. P. (2001). *Social scientists for social justice: Making the case against segregation.* NYU Press.

Jackson Jr., J. P. (2005). *Science for segregation: Race, law, and the case against Brown v. Board of Education.* NYU Press.

Jackson, D. D., & Weakland, J. H. (1961). Conjoint family therapy: Some considerations on theory, technique, and results. *Psychiatry, 24*(Sup. 2), 30–45.

Jackson, G. D. (1975). On the report of the Ad Hoc Committee on Educational Uses of Tests with Disadvantaged Students: Another psychological view from the Association of Black Psychologists. *American Psychologist, 30*, 88–93. doi.org/10.1037/0003-066X.30.1.88

Jackson, J. P., & Winston, A. S. (2021). The mythical taboo on race and intelligence. *Review of General Psychology, 25*(1), 3–26. doi.org/10.1177/1089268020953622

Jackson, L. C., Schmutzer, P. A., Wenzel, A., & Tyler, J. D. (2006). Applicability of cognitive-behavior therapy with American Indian individuals. *Psychotherapy: Theory, Research, Practice, Training, 43*(4), 506–517.

Jacob, G. A., Ower, N., & Buchholz, A. (2013). The role of experiential avoidance, psychopathology, and borderline personality features in experiencing positive emotions: A path analysis. *Journal of Behavior Therapy and Experimental Psychiatry, 44*, 61–68.

Jacobson, E. (1938). Progressive muscle relaxation. *Journal of Abnormal Psychology, 75*(1), 18.

Jacoby, R. J., Abramowitz, J. S., Buchholz, J., Reuman, L., & Blakey, S. M. (2018). Experiential avoidance in the context of obsessions: Development and validation of the Acceptance and Action Questionnaire for Obsessions and Compulsions. *Journal of Obsessive-Compulsive and Related Disorders, 19*, 34–43.

Jalili, A., Hejazi, M., Entesar Fomani, G., & Morovvati, Z. (2018). The correlation between IQ with educational performance and problem solving mediation. *Journal of Health Promotion Management, 7*(1), 1–8.

Jamieson, E., & Sandiford, P. (1928). The mental capacity of Southern Ontario Indians. *Journal of Educational Psychology, 19*(8), 536–551. doi: 10.1037/h0073482

Janis, R. A., Burlingame, G. M., Svien, H., Jensen, J., & Lundgreen, R. (2021). Group therapy for mood disorders: A meta-analysis. *Psychotherapy Research, 31*(3), 342–358.

Jauhar, S., McKenna, P. J., Radua, J., Fung, E., Salvador, R., & Laws, K. R. (2014). Cognitive-behavioural therapy for the symptoms of schizophrenia: Systematic review and meta-analysis with examination of potential bias. *British Journal of Psychiatry, 204*(1), 20–29.

Jensen, A. R. (1969). How much can we boost IQ and scholastic achievement? *The Harvard Educational Review, 39*(1), 1–123. doi: 10.17763/haer.39.1.l3u15956662742k7

Jensen, A. R. (1985). The nature of the Black–white difference on various psychometric tests: Spearman's hypothesis. *Behavioral and Brain Sciences, 8*(2), 193–263. doi: 10.1017/S0140525X00020392

Jewell, T., Blessitt, E., Stewart, C., Simic, M., & Eisler, I. (2016). Family therapy for child and adolescent eating disorders: A critical review. *Family Process, 55*(3), 577–594.

Jiménez, F. J. R. (2012). Acceptance and commitment therapy versus traditional cognitive behavioral therapy: A systematic review and meta-analysis of current empirical evidence. *International Journal of Psychology and Psychological Therapy, 12*(3), 333–358.

Johnson, M. M., & Melton, M. L. (2020). *Addressing race-based stress in therapy with black clients: Using multicultural and dialectical behavior therapy techniques.* Routledge.

Johnson, S. M. (2019). *Attachment theory in practice: Emotionally focused therapy (EFT) with individuals, couples, and families.* Guilford.

Jones, A. C., Robinson, W. D., & Seedall, R. B. (2018). The role of sexual communication in couples' sexual outcomes: A dyadic path analysis. *Journal of Marital and Family Therapy, 44*(4), 606–623.

Jones, D. J., Loiselle, R., Zachary, C., Georgeson, A. R., Highlander, A., Turner, P., Youngstrom, J., Khavjou, O., Anton, M., Gonzalez, M., Bresland, N. L., & Forehand, R. (2021). Optimizing engagement in behavioral parent training: Progress toward a technology-enhanced treatment model. *Behavior Therapy, 52*(2), 508–521.

Jones, E. B., & Sharpe, L. (2017). Cognitive bias modification: A review of meta-analyses. *Journal of Affective Disorders, 223*, 175–183.

Jones, M. C. (1924). The elimination of children's fears. *Journal of Experimental Psychology, 7*, 383–390.

Kabat-Zinn, J. (1994). *Wherever you go, there you are: Mindfulness meditation in everyday life.* Hyperion.

Kahneman, D. (2011). *Thinking, fast and slow.* Macmillan.

Kaiser Family Foundation. (2021). Adults reporting symptoms of anxiety or depressive disorder during COVID-19 pandemic. www.kff.org/other/state-indicator/adults-reporting-symptoms-of-anxiety-or-depressive-disorder-during-covid-19-pandemic/?currentTimeframe

Kamphaus, R. W. (2019). *Clinical assessment of child and adolescent intelligence.* Springer.

Kane, L., Dawson, S. J., Shaughnessy, K., Reissing, E. D., Ouimet, A. J., & Ashbaugh, A. R. (2019). A review of experimental research on anxiety and sexual arousal: Implications for the treatment of sexual dysfunction using cognitive behavioral therapy. *Journal of Experimental Psychopathology, 10*(2), 1–24.

Kapse, P. P., & Nirmala, B. P. (2017). Efficacy of social skills training among persons with schizophrenia. *International Journal of Psychosocial Rehabilitation 20th Edition, 20*, 45–50.

Kashdan, T., & Rottenberg, J. (2010). Psychological flexibility as a fundamental aspect of health. *Clinical Psychology Review, 30* (7), 865–878.

Kassin, S. M., & Wrightsman, L. S. (1979). On the requirements of proof: The timing of judicial instruction and mock juror verdicts. *Journal of Personality and Social Psychology, 37*(10), 1877–1887.

Kaufman, J., Birmaher, B., Axelson, D., Perepletchikova, F., Brent, D., & Ryan, N. (2016). *K-SADS-PL DSM-5.* Western Psychiatric Institute and Clinic.

Kazantzis, N., & Ronan, K. R. (2006). Can between-session (homework) activities be considered a common factor in psychotherapy? *Journal of Psychotherapy Integration, 16*(2), 115–127.

Kazantzis, N., Whittington, C., Zelencich, L., Kyrios, M., Norton, P. J., & Hofmann, S. G. (2016). Quantity and quality of homework compliance: A meta-analysis of relations with outcome in cognitive behavior therapy. *Behavior Therapy, 47*(5), 755–772.

Kazdin, A. E. (2008). Evidence-based treatment and practice: New opportunities to bridge clinical research and practice, enhance the knowledge base, and improve patient care. *American Psychologist, 63*(3), 146–159.

Kazdin, A. E. (2009). Understanding how and why psychotherapy leads to change. *Psychotherapy Research, 19*(4–5), 418–428.

Kazdin, A. E. (2018). *Innovations in psychosocial interventions and their delivery: Leveraging cutting-edge science to improve the world's mental health.* Oxford University Press.

Kazdin, A. E., & Blase, S. L. (2011). Rebooting psychotherapy research and practice to reduce the burden of mental illness. *Perspectives on Psychological Science, 6*(1), 21–37.

Kellman-McFarlane, K., Stewart, B., Woody, S., Ayers, C., Dozier, M., Frost, R. O., Grisham, J., Isemann, S., Steketee,

G., Tolin, D., & Welsted, A. (2019). Saving Inventory–Revised: Psychometric performance across the lifespan. *Journal of Affective Disorders, 252*, 358–364.

Kessler, R. C., Berglund, P., Demler, O., Jin, R., Merikangas, K. R., & Walters, E. E. (2005). Lifetime prevalence and age-of-onset distributions of DSM-IV disorders in the National Comorbidity Survey Replication. *Archives of General Psychiatry, 62*(6), 593–602.

Kessler, R. C., Berglund, P., Demler, O., Jin, R., Merikangas, K. R., & Walters, E. E. (2005). Lifetime prevalence and age-of-onset distributions of DSM-IV disorders in the National Comorbidity Survey Replication. *Archives of General Psychiatry, 62*, 593–602.

Kevles, D. J. (1968). Testing the Army's intelligence: Psychologists and the military in World War I. *The Journal of American History, 55*(3), 565–581. doi: 10.2307/1891014

Kevles, D. J. (1998). *In the name of eugenics: Genetics and the uses of human heredity.* Harvard University Press.

Khazanchi, R., Evans, C. T., & Marcelin, J. R. (2020). Racism, not race, drives inequity across the COVID-19 continuum. *JAMA Network Open, 3*(9), e2019933. doi: 10.1001/jamanetworkopen.2020.19933

Klerman, G. L., Weissman, M. M., Rounsaville, B. J., & Chevron, E. S. (1984). *Interpersonal psychotherapy of depression.* Basic Books.

Kline, W. (2001). *Building a better race: Gender, sexuality, and eugenics from the turn of the century to the baby boom.* University of California Press.

Kluger, R. (2004) *Simple justice: The history of Brown v. Board of Education and Black america's struggle for equality.* Vintage Books.

Knudson-Martin, C., McDowell, T., & Bermudez, J. M. (2020). Sociocultural attunement in systemic family therapy. *The Handbook of Systemic Family Therapy, 1*, 619–637.

Koran, L. M., & Simpson, H. B. (2013). *Guideline watch: Practice guideline for the treatment of patients with obsessive-compulsive disorder.* American Psychiatric Association.

Krasner, L. (1971). Behavior therapy. *Annual Review of Psychology, 22*(1), 483–532.

Krompinger, J. W., Van Kirk, N. P., Garner, L. E., Potluri, S. I., & Elias, J. A. (2019). Hope for the worst: Occasional reinforced extinction and expectancy violation in the treatment of OCD. *Cognitive and Behavioral Practice, 26*(1), 143–153.

Kropski, J. A., Keckley, P. H., & Jensen, G. L. (2008). School-based obesity prevention programs: An evidence-based review. *Obesity, 16*, 1009–1018.

La Veist, T. A. (2005). *Minority populations and health.* Jossey-Bass.

Laajaj, R., Macours, K., Hernandez, D. A. P., Arias, O., Gosling, S. D., Potter, J., Rubio-Codina, M., & Vakis, R. (2019).

Challenges to capture the big five personality traits in non-WEIRD populations. *Science Advances, 5*(7), eaaw5226.

Lambert, M. J., & Bergin, A. E. (1994). The effectiveness of psychotherapy. In A. E. Bergin & S. L. Garfield (Eds.), *Handbook of psychotherapy and behavior change* (4th ed., pp. 143–189). Wiley.

Lambert, M. J., & Ogles, B. M. (2004). The efficacy and effectiveness of psychotherapy. In M. J. Lambert (Ed.), *Bergin and Garfield's handbook of psychotherapy and behavior change* (5th ed., pp. 139–193). Wiley.

Landrine, H., & Corral, I. (2016). Sociocultural correlates of cigarette smoking among African-American men versus women: Implications for culturally specific cessation interventions. *Journal of Health Psychology, 21*(6), 954–961.

Large, M., Ryan, C., & Singh, P. (2011). The predictive value of risk categorization in schizophrenia. *Harvard Law Review, 19*, 25–33.

Larry P. v. Riles, 495 F. Supp. 926. (1979). https://law.justia.com/cases/federal/district-courts/FSupp/495/926/2007878/

Laska, K. M., Gurman, A. S., & Wampold, B. E. (2014). Expanding the lens of evidence-based practice in psychotherapy: A common factors perspective. *Psychotherapy, 51*(4), 467.

Laughlin, H. (1914). *Report of the committee to study and to report on the best practical means of cutting off the defective germ-plasm in the American population*. Bulletin No. 10A; 64. Eugenics Record Office.

Laughlin, H. (1923). Analysis of America's modern melting pot: Hearings before the Committee on Immigration and Naturalisation, House of Representatives, Sixty-seventh Congress, Third Session, November 21, 1922. Statement by Harry H. Laughlin. (Serial 7-C.) Pp. 723–831. U.S. Government Printing Office.

Lawes-Wickwar, S., McBain, H., & Mulligan, K. (2018). Application and effectiveness of telehealth to support severe mental illness management: Systematic review. *JMIR Mental Health, 5*(4), e62.

Lazarus, R. S. (1984). Puzzles in the study of daily hassles. *Journal of Behavioral Medicine, 7*, 375–389.

Lebowitz, M. S., & Appelbaum, P. S. (2019). Biomedical explanations of psychopathology and their implications for attitudes and beliefs about mental disorders. *Annual Review of Clinical Psychology, 15*, 555–577.

Lee, C. (2017). Cultural convergence: Interest convergence theory meets the cultural defense. *Arizona Law Review, 49*, 911–959.

Lee, D. S., Orvell, A., Briskin, J., Shrapnell, T., Gelman, S. A., Ayduk, O., Yibarra, O., & Kross, E. (2020). When chatting about negative experiences helps—and when it hurts: Distinguishing adaptive versus maladaptive social support in computer-mediated communication. *Emotion, 20*(3), 368–375.

Lee, R. M. (2003). The transracial adoption paradox: History, research, and counseling implications of cultural socialization. *The Counseling Psychologist, 31*(6), 711–744. doi: 10.1177/0011000003258087

Lee, S. S., Keng, S. L., & Hong, R. Y. (2021). Examining the intergenerational transmission of parental invalidation: Extension of the biosocial model. *Development and Psychopathology*, 1–11.

Lehrer, P. M., Carr, R., Sargunaraj, D., & Woolfolk, R. L. (1994). Stress management techniques: Are they all equivalent, or do they have specific effects? *Biofeedback and Self-Regulation, 19*, 353–401.

Lejuez, C. W., Hopko, D. R., & Hopko, S. D. (2001). A brief behavioral activation treatment for depression: Treatment manual. *Behavior Modification, 25*(2), 255–286.

Lemmens, L. H., van Bronswijk, S. C., Peeters, F. P., Arntz, A., Roefs, A., Hollon, S. D., DeRubeis, R. J., & Huibers, M. J. (2020). Interpersonal psychotherapy versus cognitive therapy for depression: How they work, how long, and for whom. Key findings from an RCT. *American Journal of Psychotherapy, 73*(1), 8–14.

Lemmens, L. H., Van Bronswijk, S. C., Peeters, F., Arntz, A., Hollon, S. D., & Huibers, M. J. (2019). Long-term outcomes of acute treatment with cognitive therapy v. interpersonal psychotherapy for adult depression: Follow-up of a randomized controlled trial. *Psychological Medicine, 49*(3), 465–473.

Lewin, A. B. (2019). Evidence-based assessment of child obsessive-compulsive disorder (OCD): Recommendations for clinical practice and treatment research. In L. J. Farrell, T. H. Ollendick, & P. Muris (Eds.), *Innovations in CBT for childhood anxiety, OCD, and PTSD: Improving access and outcomes* (pp. 313–331). Cambridge University Press.

Lewinsohn, P. M., Shaffer, M. (1971). Use of home observations as an integral part of treatment of depression: Preliminary report and case studies. *Journal of Consulting and Clinical Psychology, 37*(1), 87–94.

Lewis, C. C., Boyd, M., Puspitasari, A., Navarro, E., Howard, J., Kassab, H., Hoffman, M., Scott, K., Lyon, A., Douglas, S., Simon, G., & Kroenke, K. (2019). Implementing measurement-based care in behavioral health: A review. *JAMA Psychiatry, 76*(3), 324–335.

Li, H., Wong, C. L., Jin, X., Chen, J., Chong, Y. Y., & Bai, Y. (2021). Effects of acceptance and commitment therapy on health-related outcomes for patients with advanced cancer: A systematic review. *International Journal of Nursing Studies, 115*, 103876.

Lidz, T., Cornelison, A. R., Fleck, S., & Terry, D. (1957). The intrafamilial environment of the schizophrenic patient. *Psychiatry, 20*(4), 329–350.

Lilienfeld, S. O. (2007). Psychological treatments that cause harm. *Perspectives on Psychological Science, 2*(1), 53–70.

Lilienfeld, S. O. (2014). The Research Domain Criteria (RDoC): An analysis of methodological and conceptual challenges. *Behaviour Research and Therapy, 62*, 129–139.

Lilienfeld, S. O., Lynn, S., & Lohr, J. (2014). *Science and pseudoscience in clinical psychology*. Guilford.

Lilienfeld, S. O., Ritschel, L. A., Lynn, S. J., Cautin, R. L., & Latzman, R. D. (2013). Why many clinical psychologists are resistant to evidence-based practice: Root causes and constructive remedies. *Clinical Psychology Review, 33*(7), 883–900.

Lilienfeld, S. O., Wood, J. M., & Garb, H. N. (2000). The scientific status of projective techniques. *Psychological Science in the Public Interest, 1*(2), 27–66.

Lindsley, O. R., & Skinner, B. F. (1954). A method for the experimental analysis of the behavior of psychotic patients. *American Psychologist, 9*, 419–420.

Lindzey, G., & Silverman, M. (1959). Thematic Apperception Test: Techniques of group administration, sex differences, and the role of verbal productivity. *Journal of Personality, 27*, 311–323.

Linehan, M. (1993). *Cognitive-behavioral treatment of borderline personality disorder*. Guilford.

Linehan, M. M. (2014). *DBT training manual*. Guilford.

Linehan, M. M., Armstrong, H. E., Suarez, A., Allmon, D., & Heard, H. L. (1991). Cognitive-behavioral treatment of chronically parasuicidal borderline patients. *Archives of General Psychiatry, 48*(12), 1060–1064.

Litt, M. D., Kadden, R. M., & Kabela-Cormier, E. (2019). Individualized assessment and treatment program for alcohol dependence: Results of an initial study to train coping skills. *Addiction, 104*(11), 1837–1838.

Lo, C. F. (2017). Is there a relationship between high IQ scores and positive life outcomes? A critical review. *Psychology, 8*(4), 627.

Loftus, E. F. (1979). *Eyewitness testimony*. Harvard University Press.

Loftus, E. F., Miller, D. G., & Burns, H. J. (1978). Semantic integration of verbal information into a visual memory. *Journal of Experimental Psychology: Human Learning and Memory, 4*(1), 19–31

Lovibond, P. F., & Lovibond, S. H. (1995). The structure of negative emotional states: Comparison of the Depression Anxiety Stress Scales (DASS) with the Beck Depression and Anxiety Inventories. *Behaviour Research and Therapy, 33*(3), 335–343.

Lubis, K. (2020). The effectiveness of assertiveness training group format to improve students' interpersonal relationship skills. *Bisma: The Journal of Counseling, 4*(3), 273–283.

Luborsky, L., Singer, B., & Luborsky, L. (1975). Is it true that everyone has won and all must have prizes? *Archives of General Psychiatry, 32*, 995–1008.

Luiggi-Hernández, J. G., & Rivera-Amador, A. I. (2020). Reconceptualizing social distancing: Teletherapy and social inequality during the COVID-19 and loneliness pandemics. *Journal of Humanistic Psychology, 60*(5), 626–638.

Lundgren, T., Luoma, J. B., Dahl, J., Strosahl, K., & Melin, L. (2012). The bull's-eye values survey: A psychometric evaluation. *Cognitive and Behavioral Practice, 19*(4), 518–526.

MacDonald, A. W., Goodman, S. H., & Watson, D. (2021). The *Journal of Psychopathology and Clinical Science* is the future of the *Journal of Abnormal Psychology*: An editorial. *Journal of Abnormal Psychology, 130*(1), 1–2.

Maddux, J. E., Brawley, L., & Boykin, A. (1995). Self-efficacy and healthy behavior: Prevention, promotion, and detection. In J. E. Maddux (Ed.), *Self-efficacy, adaptation, and adjustment: Theory, research, and application* (pp. 173–202). Plenum.

Maloney, M. P., & Ward, M. P. (1976). *Psychological assessment: A conceptual approach*. Oxford University Press.

Manne, S. L., Redd, W. H., Jacobsen, P. B., Gorfinkle, K., Schorr, O., & Rapkin, B. (1990). Behavioral intervention to reduce child and parent distress during venipuncture. *Journal of Consulting and Clinical Psychology, 58*(5), 565–572.

Marchand, E. (2020). Psychological and behavioral treatment of female orgasmic disorder. *Sexual Medicine Reviews, 9*, 194–211.

Marks, D. F. (2010). IQ variations across time, race, and nationality: An artifact of differences in literacy skills. *Psychological Reports, 106*(3), 643–664.

Marlatt, G. A., & Gordon, J. R. (1985). *Relapse prevention: Maintenance strategies in the treatment of addictive behaviors*. Guilford.

Masters, W., & Johnson, V. E. (1970). *Human sexual inadequacy*. Little, Brown and Company.

Matarazzo, J. D. (1980). Behavioral health and behavioral medicine: Frontiers for a new health psychology. *American Psychologist, 35*(9), 807–817.

Mayne, T. J., Norcross, J. C., & Sayette, M. A. (1994). Admission requirements, acceptance rates, and financial assistance in clinical psychology programs: Diversity across the practice-research continuum. *American Psychologist, 49*(9), 806–811.

Mayo, M. J. (1913). The mental capacity of the American Negro. *Archives of Psychology, 4*(28), 70.

McAleavey, A. A., & Castonguay, L. G. (2015). The process of change in psychotherapy: Common and unique factors. In *Psychotherapy research* (pp. 293–310). Springer.

McAleavey, A. A., Youn, S. J., Xiao, H., Castonguay, L. G., Hayes, J. A., & Locke, B. D. (2019). Effectiveness of routine psychotherapy: Method matters. *Psychotherapy Research, 29*(2), 139–156.

McCabe, D. P., & Castel, A. D. (2008). Seeing is believing: The effect of brain images on judgments of scientific reasoning. *Cognition, 107*(1), 343–352.

McConaughy, S. H., & Achenbach, T. M. (2009). *Guide for the ASEBA Direct Observation Form.* University of Vermont, Research Center for Children, Youth, & Families.

McDougall, W. (1914). Psychology in the service of eugenics. *The Eugenics Review, 5*(4), 295–308.

McDougall, W. (1921). *Is America safe for democracy?* Charles Scribner's Sons.

McDougall, W. (1925). *The indestructible union.* Little, Brown and Company.

McDowell, T., Knudson-Martin, C., & Bermudez, J. M. (2017). *Socioculturally attuned family therapy: Guidelines for equitable theory and practice.* Routledge.

McFall, R. M. (1991). Manifesto for a science of clinical psychology. *The Clinical Psychologist, 44*(6), 75–88.

McFall, R. M. (2006). Doctoral training in clinical psychology. *Annual Review of Clinical Psychology, 2,* 21–49.

McGuire, J. F., Piacentini, J., Lewin, A. B., Brennan, E. A., Murphy, T. K., & Storch, E. A. (2015). A meta-analysis of cognitive behavior therapy and medication for child obsessive–compulsive disorder: Moderators of treatment efficacy, response, and remission. *Depression and Anxiety, 32*(8), 580–593.

McHugh, R. K., Hearon, B. A., & Otto, M. W. (2010). Cognitive behavioral therapy for substance use disorders. *Psychiatric Clinics, 33*(3), 511–525.

McKay, C. (2020). Predicting risk in criminal procedure: Actuarial tools, algorithms, AI and judicial decision-making. *Current Issues in Criminal Justice, 32*(1), 22–39.

McKay, D. (2011). Methods and mechanisms in the efficacy of psychodynamic psychotherapy. *American Psychologist, 66,* 147–148.

McKay, D., & Jensen-Doss, A. (2021). Harmful treatments in psychotherapy. *Clinical Psychology: Science and Practice, 28,* 2–4.

McMain, S. F., Links, P. S., Gnam, W. H., Guimond, T., Cardish, R. J., Korman, L., & Streiner, D. L. (2009). A randomized trial of dialectical behavior therapy versus general psychiatric management for borderline personality disorder. *American Journal of Psychiatry, 166*(12), 1365–1374.

Meador, B. D., & Rogers, C. R. (1984). Client-centered therapy. In R. J. Corsini (Ed.), *Current psychotherapies* (2nd ed.). F. E. Peacock.

Mecklenburg, S. H., Bailey, P. J., & Larson, M. R. (2008). The Illinois field study: A significant contribution to understanding real world eyewitness identification issues. *Law and Human Behavior, 32*(1), 22–27.

Melbye, S., Kessing, L. V., Bardram, J. E., & Faurholt-Jepsen, M. (2020). Smartphone-based self-monitoring, treatment, and automatically generated data in children, adolescents, and young adults with psychiatric disorders: Systematic review. *JMIR Mental Health, 7*(10), e17453.

Mellentin, A. I., Skøt, L., Nielsen, B., Schippers, G. M., Nielsen, A. S., Stenager, E., & Juhl, C. (2017). Cue exposure therapy for the treatment of alcohol use disorders: A meta-analytic review. *Clinical Psychology Review, 57,* 195–207.

Mérelle, S., Van Bergen, D., Looijmans, M., Balt, E., Rasing, S., van Domburgh, L., Nauta, M., Sijperda, O., Mulder, W., Gilissen, R., Franx, G., & Popma, A. (2020). A multi-method psychological autopsy study on youth suicides in the Netherlands in 2017: Feasibility, main outcomes, and recommendations. *PLoS One, 15*(8), e0238031.

Michel, W. (1968). *Personality and assessment.* Wiley.

Miller, C. B., Gu, J., Henry, A. L., Davis, M. L., Espie, C. A., Stott, R., Heinz, A., Bentley, K., Goodwin, G., Gorman, B., Craske, M., & Carl, J. R. (2021). Feasibility and efficacy of a digital CBT intervention for symptoms of generalized anxiety disorder: A randomized multiple-baseline study. *Journal of Behavior Therapy and Experimental Psychiatry, 70,* 101609.

Miller, W. R., & Rollnick, S. (2012). *Motivational interviewing: Helping people change.* Guilford.

Mischel, W. (1973). Toward a cognitive social learning reconceptualization of personality. *Psychological Review, 80*(4), 252.

Mischel, W. (2013). *Personality and assessment.* Psychology Press.

Miu, A. S., Vo, H. T., Palka, J. M., Glowacki, C. R., & Robinson, R. J. (2020). Teletherapy with serious mental illness populations during COVID-19: Telehealth conversion and engagement. *Counselling Psychology Quarterly,* 1–18.

Montero-Marin, J., Garcia-Campayo, J., López-Montoyo, A., Zabaleta-del-Olmo, E., & Cuijpers, P. (2018). Is cognitive-behavioural therapy more effective than relaxation therapy in the treatment of anxiety disorders? A meta-analysis. *Psychological Medicine, 48*(9), 1427–1436.

Morales, E., Lau, M. Y., & Ballesteros, A. (2012). Division 45: The Society for the Psychological Study of Ethnic Minority Issues. *The Counseling Psychologist, 40*(5), 699–709. doi: 10.1177/0011000012450425

Morgan, C. D., & Murray, H. A. (1935). A method for investigating fantasies: The Thematic Apperception Test. *Archives of Neurology & Psychiatry, 34*(2), 289–306.

Morgan, T. A., Dalrymple, K., D'Avanzato, C., Zimage, S., Balling, C., Ward, M., & Zimmerman, M. (2021). Conducting outcomes research in a clinical practice setting: The effectiveness and acceptability of acceptance and commitment therapy (ACT) in a partial hospital program. *Behavior Therapy, 52*(2), 272–285.

Moroz, M., & Dunkley, D. M. (2019). Self-critical perfectionism, experiential avoidance, and depressive and anxious symptoms over two years: A three-wave longitudinal study. *Behaviour Research and Therapy, 112*, 18–27.

Morris, S. H., Zickgraf, H. F., Dingfelder, H. E., & Franklin, M. E. (2013). Habit reversal training in trichotillomania: Guide for the clinician. *Expert Review of Neurotherapeutics, 13*, 1069–1077.

Moskowitz, M. (1995). Ethnicity and the fantasy of ethnicity. *Psychoanalytic Psychology, 12*, 547–555.

Mueller, A. E., & Segal, D. L. (2014). Structured versus semistructured versus unstructured interviews. In *The Encyclopedia of Clinical Psychology* (pp. 1–7). Wiley.

Munder, T., Flückiger, C., Leichsenring, F., Abbass, A. A., Hilsenroth, M. J., Luyten, P., Raberg, S., Steinert, C., & Wampold, B. E. (2019). Is psychotherapy effective? A re-analysis of treatments for depression. *Epidemiology and Psychiatric Sciences, 28*(3), 268–274.

Münsterberg, H. (1908). *On the witness stand.* McClure.

Murphy, J. L, McKellar, J. D., Raffa, S. D., Clark, M. E., Kerns, R. D., & Karlin, B. E. (2014). *Cognitive behavioral therapy for chronic pain among veterans: Therapist manual.* U.S. Department of Veterans Affairs.

Murtza, M. H., Gill, S. A., Aslam, H. D., & Noor, A. (2020). Intelligence quotient, job satisfaction, and job performance: The moderating role of personality type. *Journal of Public Affairs*, e2318.

Naeem, F. (2019). Cultural adaptations of CBT: A summary and discussion of the special issue on cultural adaptation of CBT. *The Cognitive Behaviour Therapist, 12*, E40.

Namaky, N., Glenn, J. J., Eberle, J. W., & Teachman, B. A. (2021). Adapting cognitive bias modification to train healthy prospection. *Behaviour Research and Therapy*, 103923.

Neisser, U., Boodoo, G., Bouchard Jr., T. J., Boykin, A. W., Brody, N., Ceci, S. J., Halpern, D., Loehlin, J. C., Perloff, R., Sternberg, R. J., & Urbina, S. (1996). Intelligence: Knowns and unknowns. *American Psychologist, 51*, 77–101.

Nel, K. A., & Govender, S. (2020). Psychodynamic therapy: A cross-cultural and generational failure. In E. Vanderheiden & C-H. Meyer (Eds.), *Mistakes, errors and failures across cultures* (pp. 401–415). Springer.

Nelson, B. (1968). Black psychologists' association makes proposals to APA. *Science, 162*(3850), 243–243.

Nenadić, I., Lorenz, C., & Gaser, C. (2021). Narcissistic personality traits and prefrontal brain structure. *Scientific Reports, 11*(1), 1–9.

Neufeld, C. B., Palma, P. C., Caetano, K. A., Brust-Renck, P. G., Curtiss, J., & Hofmann, S. G. (2020). A randomized clinical trial of group and individual cognitive-behavioral therapy approaches for social anxiety disorder. *International Journal of Clinical and Health Psychology, 20*(1), 29–37.

Niles, A. N., Burklund, L. J., Arch, J. J., Lieberman, M. D., Saxbe, D., & Craske, M. G. (2014). Cognitive mediators of treatment for social anxiety disorder: Comparing

acceptance and commitment therapy and cognitive-behavioral therapy. *Behavior Therapy, 45*(5), 664–677.

Norcross, J. C., & Lambert, M. J. (2018). Psychotherapy relationships that work: III. *Psychotherapy, 55*(4), 303–315.

Norcross, J. C., Ellis, J. L., & Sayette, M. A. (2010). Getting in and getting money: A comparative analysis of admission standards, acceptance rates, and financial assistance across the research–practice continuum in clinical psychology programs. *Training and Education in Professional Psychology, 4*(2), 99–106.

Norcross, J. C., Sayette, M. A., & Mayne, T. J. (2008). *Insider's guide to graduate programs in clinical and counseling psychology* (2008/2009 ed.). Guilford.

Norcross, J. C., Sayette, M. A., Mayne, T. J., Karg, R. S., & Turkson, M. A. (1998). Selecting a doctoral program in professional psychology: Some comparisons among Ph.D. counseling, Ph.D. clinical, and Psy.D. clinical psychology programs. *Professional Psychology: Research and Practice, 29*(6), 609–616.

Norcross, J. C., VandenBos, G. R., & Freedheim, D. K. (2011). *History of psychotherapy: Continuity and change.* American Psychological Association.

Nunnally, J. C., & Bernstein, I. H. (1994). *Psychometric Theory.* McGraw-Hill.

Öst, L. G. (2008). Efficacy of the third wave of behavioral therapies: A systematic review and meta-analysis. *Behaviour Research and Therapy, 46*(3), 296–321.

Öst, L. G. (2014). The efficacy of acceptance and commitment therapy: An updated systematic review and meta-analysis. *Behaviour Research and Therapy, 61*, 105–121.

Osuna, D., Barrera Jr., M., Strycker, L. A., Toobert, D. J., Glasgow, R. E., Geno, C. R., Almeida, F., Perdomo, M., King, D., & Tinley Doty, A. (2011). Methods for the cultural adaptation of a diabetes lifestyle intervention for Latinas: An illustrative project. *Health Promotion Practice, 12*(3), 341–348.

Pachankis, J. E., Hatzenbuehler, M. L., Rendina, H. J., Safren, S. A., & Parsons, J. T. (2015). LGB-affirmative cognitive-behavioral therapy for young adult gay and bisexual men: A randomized controlled trial of a transdiagnostic minority stress approach. *Journal of Consulting and Clinical Psychology, 83*(5), 875–889.

Pan, M. R., Huang, F., Zhao, M. J., Wang, Y. F., Wang, Y. F., & Qian, Q. J. (2019). A comparison of efficacy between cognitive behavioral therapy (CBT) and CBT combined with medication in adults with attention-deficit/hyperactivity disorder (ADHD). *Psychiatry Research, 279*, 23–33.

Paniagua, F. A. (2013). *Assessing and treating culturally diverse clients: A practical guide.* Sage.

Parker, K. C., Hanson, R. K., & Hunsley, J. (1988). MMPI, Rorschach, and WAIS: A metaanalytic comparison of reliability, stability, and validity. *Psychological Bulletin, 103*(3), 367–373.

Patterson, C. W., Williams, J., & Jones, R. (2019). Third-wave therapies and adults with intellectual disabilities: A systematic review. *Journal of Applied Research in Intellectual Disabilities, 32*(6), 1295–1309.

Patterson, T. G., & Joseph, S. (2007). Person-centered personality theory: Support from self-determination theory and positive psychology. *Journal of Humanistic Psychology, 47*(1), 117–139.

Paul, J. (1965). *Three generations of imbeciles are enough: State eugenic sterilization laws in American thought and practice.* Walter Reed Army Institute of Research.

Pentel, K. Z., & Baucom, D. H. (in press). A clinical framework for sexual minority couple therapy. *Couple and Family Psychology: Research and Practice.*

Perlin, M. L., & McClain, V. (2009). "Where souls are forgotten": Cultural competencies, forensic evaluations, and international human rights. *Psychology, Public Policy, and Law, 15*(4), 257–277.

Perls, F. (1973). *The gestalt approach & eye witness to therapy.* Science & Behavior Books.

Persons, J. B. (2012). *The case formulation approach to cognitive-behavior therapy.* Guilford.

Persons, J. B., & Silberschatz, G. (1998). Are results of randomized controlled trials useful to psychotherapists? *Journal of Consulting and Clinical Psychology, 66*(1), 126.

Peters, W., Morse, G., Tehee, M., Foster, D., & Blume, A. (2015) *Position statement regarding the updated guidelines to the Indian Child Welfare Act.* The Society of Indian Psychologists. www.nativepsychs.org/position-statements

Peterson, D. R. (1968). The doctor of psychology program at the University of Illinois. *American Psychologist, 23*(7), 511–516.

Peterson, D. R. (1971). Status of the doctor of psychology program, 1970. *Professional Psychology, 2*(3), 271–275.

Pickren, W. E., & Tomes, H. (2002). The legacy of Kenneth B. Clark to the APA: The Board of Social and Ethical Responsibility for Psychology. *American Psychologist, 57*(1), 51–59. doi: 10.1037/0003-066X.57.1.51

Pinney, E. L. (1978). The beginning of group psychotherapy: Joseph Henry Pratt, MD, and the reverend Dr. Elwood Worcester. *International Journal of Group Psychotherapy, 28*(1), 109–114.

Pleis, J. R., Ward, B. W., & Lucas, J. W. (2010). Summary health statistics for U.S. adults: National Health Interview Survey, 2009. National Center for Health Statistics. *Vital Health Stat, 10*(249).

Plomin, R., DeFries, J. C., McClearn, G. E., & McGuffin, P. (2008). *Behavioral genetics* (5th ed.). Worth.

Plotkin, L. (1972). Coal handling, steamfitting, psychology, and law. *American Psychologist, 27*, 202–204.

Polo, A. J., Makol, B. A., Castro, A. S., Colón-Quintana, N., Wagstaff, A. E., & Guo, S. (2019). Diversity in randomized clinical trials of depression: A 36-year review. *Clinical Psychology Review, 67*, 22–35.

Pompoli, A., Furukawa, T. A., Efthimiou, O., Imai, H., Tajika, A., & Salanti, G. (2018). Dismantling cognitive-behaviour therapy for panic disorder: A systematic review and component network meta-analysis. *Psychological Medicine, 48*(12), 1945–1953.

Ponterotto, J. G. (1988). Racial/ethnic minority research in the *Journal of Counseling Psychology*: A content analysis and methodological critique. *Journal of Counseling Psychology, 35*(4), 410–418.

Poulsen, S. S. (2020). Improving couple interventions for underserved populations. *The Handbook of Systemic Family Therapy, 3*, 511–531.

Power, C. T. (1979). The Time-Sample Behavioral Checklist: observational assessment of patient functioning. *Journal of Behavioral Assessment, 1*(3), 199–210.

Pozzulo, J., Bennell, C., & Forth, A. (2021). *Forensic psychology.* Psychology Press.

Pratt, H. G. (1929). Some conclusions from a comparison of school achievement of certain racial groups. *The Journal of Educational Psychology, 20*, 661–668. doi: 10.1037/h0070412

Premack, D. (1959). Toward empirical behavior laws: I. Positive reinforcement. *Psychological Review, 66*, 219–233.

"Presentation of Navajo." (1975, February 7). Presentation of Navajo Rug to Mrs. Ford, Background Information. Ford Committee on Mental Retardation. Records of Betty Ford White House Papers 1973–77, Record Group 309. National Archives at College Park, College Park, MD, United States.

Pressey, S. L., & Pressey, L. C. (1933). Results of certain honesty tests given to a group of rural white children and to two groups of Indian children. *Journal of Applied Psychology, 17*(2), 120–129. doi: 10.1037/h0067621

Racine, N., Hartwick, C., Collin-Vézina, D., & Madigan, S. (2020). Telemental health for child trauma treatment during and post-COVID-19: Limitations and considerations. *Child Abuse & Neglect, 110*, 104698.

Ramirez III, M. (2004). Mestiza/o and Chicana/o psychology: Theory, research, and application. In R. Velazquez, L. Arellano, & B. McNeill (Eds.), *The Handbook of Chicana/o Psychology and Mental Health* (pp. 3–17). Lawrence Erlbaum Associates.

Rathgeber, M., Bürkner, P. C., Schiller, E. M., & Holling, H. (2019). The efficacy of emotionally focused couples therapy and behavioral couples therapy: A meta-analysis. *Journal of Marital and Family Therapy, 45*(3), 447–463.

Ratliff-Black, M., & Therrien, W. (2020). Parent-mediated interventions for school-age children with ASD: A meta-analysis. *Focus on Autism and Other Developmental Disabilities*, doi: 1088357620956904

Reddy, M. S., & Vijay, M. S. (2017). Empirical reality of dialectical behavioral therapy in borderline personality. *Indian Journal of Psychological Medicine*, 39(2), 105–108.

Redelmeier, D. A., Ferris, L. E., Tu, J. V., Hux, J. E., & Schull, M. J. (2001). Problems for clinical judgement: Introducing cognitive psychology as one more basic science. *CMAJ: Canadian Medical Association Journal*, 164(3), 358.

Regier, D. A., Narrow, W. E., Clarke, D. E., Kraemer, H. C., Kuramoto, S. J., Kuhl, E. A., & Kupfer, D. J. (2013). DSM-5 field trials in the United States and Canada: Part II. Test-retest reliability of selected categorical diagnoses. *American Journal of Psychiatry*, 170(1), 59–70.

Reinhold, M., Bürkner, P. C., & Holling, H. (2018). Effects of expressive writing on depressive symptoms: A meta-analysis. *Clinical Psychology: Science and Practice*, 25(1), e12224.

Reynolds, C. R., & Suzuki, L. A. (2013). Bias in psychological assessment: An empirical review and recommendations. In J. R. Graham, J. A. Naglieri, & I. B. Weiner (Eds.), *Handbook of psychology: Assessment psychology* (pp. 82–113). John Wiley & Sons.

Richards, G. (1997). *"Race," racism and psychology: Towards a reflexive history*. Routledge.

Riley, W. (1919). General reviews and summaries: Historical contributions. *Psychological Bulletin*, 16(1), 1–3.

Rimfeld, K., Kovas, Y., Dale, P. S., & Plomin, R. (2016). True grit and genetics: Predicting academic achievement from personality. *Journal of Personality and Social Psychology*, 111(5), 780.

Roberts, S. O., Bareket-Shavit, C., Dollins, F. A., Goldie, P. D., & Mortenson, E. (2020). Racial inequality in psychological research: Trends of the past and recommendations for the future. *Perspectives on Psychological Science*, 15(6), 1295–1309. doi.org/10.1177/1745691620927709

Robinson, H. B., & Robinson, N. M. (1965). *The mentally retarded child*. McGraw-Hill.

Rogers, C. R. (1942). *Counseling and psychotherapy*. Houghton Mifflin.

Rogers, C. R. (1946). Significant aspects of client-centered therapy. *American Psychologist*, 1, 415–422.

Rogers, C. R. (1951). *Client-centered therapy*. Houghton Mifflin.

Rogers, C. R. (1959). A theory of therapy, personality, and interpersonal relationships, as developed in the client-centered framework. In S. Koch (Ed.), *Psychology: A study of a science* (Vol. 3). McGraw-Hill.

Rogers, C. R. (1961). *On becoming a person*. Houghton Mifflin.

Rogers, C. R. (1980). *A way of being*. Houghton Mifflin.

Rogers, C. R., Gendlin, E. T., Kiesler, D. J., & Truax, C. B. (1967). *The therapeutic relationship and its impact*. University of Wisconsin Press.

Rogler, L. H. (1983). *A conceptual framework for mental health research on Hispanic populations* (No. 10). Hispanic Research Center, Fordham University.

Roid, G. H. (2003). *Stanford-Binet Intelligence Scales, Fifth Edition*. Riverside.

Roid, G. H., & Pomplun, M. (2005). Interpreting the Stanford-Binet Intelligence Scales, Fifth Edition. In D. P. Flanagan & P. L. Harrison (Eds.), *Contemporary intellectual assessment: Theories, tests, and issues* (2nd ed., pp. 325–343.). Guilford.

Rolnick, A. (2019). *Theory and practice of online therapy: Internet-delivered interventions for individuals, groups, families, and organizations*. Routledge.

Rosellini, A. J., & Brown, T. A. (2021). Developing and validating clinical questionnaires. *Annual Review of Clinical Psychology*, 17, 55–81.

Rosenhan, D. L. (1973). On being sane in insane places. *Science*, 179(4070), 250–258.

Rosenzweig, S. (1954). A transvaluation of psychotherapy: A reply to Eysenck. *Journal of Abnormal Psychology*, 49, 298–304.

Roskies, A. L. (2007). Are neuroimages like photographs of the brain? *Philosophy of Science*, 74(5), 860–872.

Rosmarin, D. H. (2018). *Spirituality, religion, and cognitive-behavioral therapy: A guide for clinicians*. Guilford.

Rossdale, S. V., Tully, R. J., & Egan, V. (2020). The HCR-20 for predicting violence in adult females: A meta-analysis. *Journal of Forensic Psychology Research and Practice*, 20(1), 15–52.

Rotter, J. B. (1970). Some implications of a social learning theory for the practice of psychotherapy. In D. J. Levis (Ed.), *Learning approaches to therapeutic behavior change* (pp. 208–241). Aldine.

Rousseau, A., Bőthe, B., & Štulhofer, A. (2020). Theoretical antecedents of male adolescents' problematic pornography use: A longitudinal assessment. *The Journal of Sex Research*, 58, 331–341.

Rury, J. L. (1988). Race, region, and education: An analysis of Black and White scores on the 1917 Army Alpha Intelligence Text. *Journal of Negro Education*, 57(1), 51–65.

Rutledge, T., Gould, H., Hsu, A., & Beizai, K. (2020). Consultation-liaison psychology: Training and research recommendations for this emerging interprofessional practice. *Professional Psychology: Research and Practice*, 51(4), 383–389.

Sackett, P. R., Borneman, M. J., & Connelly, B. S. (2008). High stakes testing in higher education and employment: Appraising the evidence for validity and fairness. *American Psychologist*, 63(4), 215.

Saha, S., Chant, D., Welham, J., & McGrath, J. (2005). A systematic review of the prevalence of schizophrenia. *PLoS Med, 2*(5), e141.

Samaan, M., Diefenbacher, A., Schade, C., Dambacher, C., Pontow, I. M., Pakenham, K., & Fydrich, T. (2021). A clinical effectiveness trial comparing ACT and CBT for inpatients with depressive and mixed mental disorders. *Psychotherapy Research, 31*(3), 372–385.

Sanderson, C. A. (2018). *Health psychology: Understanding the mind-body connection.* SAGE.

Sangraula, M., Kohrt, B. A., Ghimire, R., Shrestha, P., Luitel, N. P., van't Hof, E., Dawson, K., & Jordans, M. J. (2021). Development of the mental health cultural adaptation and contextualization for implementation (mhCACI) procedure: A systematic framework to prepare evidence-based psychological interventions for scaling. *Global Mental Health, 8*, 1–13.

Saslow, G., & Matarazzo, J. D. (1962). A psychiatric service in a general hospital: A setting for social learning. *Psychiatric Services, 13*(4), 217–226.

Satcher, D. (2000). Mental health: A report of the Surgeon General. Executive summary. *Professional Psychology: Research and Practice, 31*(1), 5.

Satel, S., & Lilienfeld, S. O. (2013). *Brainwashed: The seductive appeal of mindless neuroscience.* Basic Civitas Books.

Sauce, B., & Matzel, L. D. (2018). The paradox of intelligence: Heritability and malleability coexist in hidden gene-environment interplay. *Psychological Bulletin, 144*(1), 26–47.

Sawyer, J., & Senn, D. J. (1973). Institutional racism and the American Psychological Association. *Journal of Social Issues, 29*(1), 67–79. doi: 10.111/j.1540-4560.1973.tb00061.x

Schatzberg, A. F., & Nemeroff, C. B. (2009). *The American Psychiatric Publishing textbook of psychopharmacology.* American Psychiatric Publishing.

Schmidt, N. B., Lerew, D. R., & Jackson, R. J. (1997). The role of anxiety sensitivity in the pathogenesis of panic: Prospective evaluation of spontaneous panic attacks during acute stress. *Journal of Abnormal Psychology, 106*(3), 355–364.

Schomerus, G., Schwahn, C., Holzinger, A., Corrigan, P. W., Grabe, H. J., Carta, M. G., & Angermeyer, M. C. (2012). Evolution of public attitudes about mental illness: A systematic review and meta-analysis. *Acta Psychiatrica Scandinavica, 125*(6), 440–452.

Schuham, A. I. (1967). The double-bind hypothesis a decade later. *Psychological Bulletin, 68*(6), 409–410.

Schwartze, D., Barkowski, S., Strauss, B., Burlingame, G. M., Barth, J., & Rosendahl, J. (2017). Efficacy of group psychotherapy for panic disorder: Meta-analysis of randomized, controlled trials. *Group Dynamics: Theory, Research, and Practice, 21*(2), 77.

Scott, C. L. (1914). Experimentation in education. *The Indian School Journal, 14*(5), 1888–1889.

Segall, A. (1999). Critical history: Implications for history/social studies education. *Theory and Research in Social Education, 27*, 358–374. doi: 10.1080/00933104.1999.10505885

Seligman, M. E. P. (1995). The effectiveness of psychotherapy: The *Consumer Reports* study. *American Psychologist, 50*, 965–974.

Semple, C. J., Dunwoody, L., Sullivan, K., & Kernohan, W. G. (2006). Patients with head and neck cancer prefer individualized cognitive behavioural therapy. *European Journal of Cancer Care (English Language Edition), 15*, 220–227.

Senn, S., Odenwald, M., Sehrig, S., Haffke, P., Rockstroh, B., Pereyra Kröll, D., Menning, H., Wieber, F., Volken, T., & Rösner, S. (2020). Therapeutic success in relapse prevention in alcohol use disorder: The role of treatment motivation and drinking-related treatment goals. *Journal of Addictive Diseases, 39*(1), 88–95.

Severance, L. J., & Loftus, E. F. (1982). Improving the ability of jurors to comprehend and apply criminal jury instructions. *Law and Society Review, 17*, 153–165.

Sewart, A. R., & Craske, M. G. (2020). Inhibitory learning. In J. S. Abramowitz & S. M. Blakey (Eds.), *Clinical handbook of fear and anxiety: Maintenance processes and treatment mechanisms* (pp. 265–285). American Psychological Association.

Sharf, R. S. (2012). *Theories of psychotherapy and counseling: Concepts and cases* (5th ed.). Brooks/Cole, Cengage Learning, Belmont.

Sharp, I. R., Herbert, J. D., & Redding, R. E. (2008). The role of critical thinking skills in practicing clinical psychologists' choice of intervention techniques. *The Scientific Review of Mental Health Practice, 6*, 21–30.

Shaw, B. F. (1977). Comparison of cognitive therapy and behavior therapy in the treatment of depression. *Journal of Consulting and Clinical Psychology, 45*(4), 543–551.

Shedler, J. (2010). The efficacy of psychodynamic psychotherapy. *American Psychologist, 65*(2), 98–109.

Sheehan, D. (2016). *The MINI International Neuropsychiatric Interview* (Version 7.0. 2) *for DSM-5.* Harm Research Institute.

Sheehan, D. V. (1983). Sheehan disability scale. *Handbook of Psychiatric Measures, 2*, 100–102.

Sheldon, K. M. (1994). Emotionality differences between artists and scientists. *Journal of Research in Personality, 28*(4), 481–491.

Shorey, R. C., Gawrysiak, M. J., Elmquist, J., Brem, M., Anderson, S., & Stuart, G. L. (2017). Experiential avoidance, distress tolerance, and substance use cravings among adults in residential treatment for substance use disorders. *Journal of Addictive Diseases, 36*, 151–157.

Shuey, A. M. (1958). *The testing of Negro intelligence.* J. P. Bell.

Simonazzi, N., Salotti, J. M., Dubois, C., & Seminel, D. (2020, August). Emotion detection based on smartphone using user memory tasks and videos. In *International Conference on Human Interaction and Emerging Technologies* (pp. 244–249). Springer, Cham.

Simpkins, G., & Raphael, P. (1970). Black students, APA, and the challenge of change. *American Psychologist, 25*(5), xxi–xxvi. doi.org/10.1037/h0037752

Skinner, B. F. (1953). *Science and human behavior.* Macmillan.

Slavich, G. M. (2020). Psychoneuroimmunology of stress and mental health. In K. Harkness & E. Hayden (Eds.), *The Oxford handbook of stress and mental health* (pp. 519–546). Oxford University Press.

Sloan, C. A., Berke, D. S., & Shipherd, J. C. (2017). Utilizing a dialectical framework to inform conceptualization and treatment of clinical distress in transgender individuals. *Professional Psychology: Research and Practice, 48*(5), 301–307.

Smith, A. E., & Haney, C. (2011). Getting to the point: Attempting to improve juror comprehension of capital penalty phase instructions. *Law and Human Behavior, 35*, 339–350.

Smith, D. J., Langan, J., McLean, G., Guthrie, B., & Mercer, S. W. (2013). Schizophrenia is associated with excess multiple physical-health comorbidities but low levels of recorded cardiovascular disease in primary care: Cross-sectional study. *BMJ Open, 3*(4), e002808.

Smith, M. B., & Pickren, W. E. (2018). The American Psychological Association in relation to social responsibility and social justice. In W. E. Pickren & A. Rutherford (Eds.), *125 years of the American Psychological Association* (pp. 359–391). American Psychological Association. doi: 10.1037/0000050-012

Smith, M. L., Glass, G. V., & Miller, T. I. (1980). *The benefits of psychotherapy.* Johns Hopkins University Press.

Smith, T. W. (1992). Hostility and health: Current status of a psychosomatic hypothesis. *Health Psychology, 11*, 139–150.

Smith, T. W., & MacKenzie, J. (2006). Personality and risk of physical illness. *Annual Review of Clinical Psychology, 2*, 435–467.

Snagowski, J., Laier, C., Duka, T., & Brand, M. (2016). Subjective craving for pornography and associative learning predict tendencies towards cybersex addiction in a sample of regular cybersex users. *Sexual Addiction & Compulsivity, 23*(4), 342–360.

Snook, B., Cullen, R. M., Bennell, C., Taylor, P. J., & Gendreau, P. (2008). The criminal profiling illusion: What's behind the smoke and mirrors? *Criminal Justice and Behavior, 35*(10), 1257–1276.

Snyder, W. U. (1945). An investigation of the nature of nondirective psychotherapy. *Journal of General Psychology, 33*, 193–223.

Soares, E. E., Bausback, K., Beard, C. L., Higinbotham, M., Bunge, E. L., & Gengoux, G. W. (2021). Social skills training for autism spectrum disorder: A meta-analysis of in-person and technological interventions. *Journal of Technology in Behavioral Science, 6*(1), 166–180.

Sobell, M. B., & Sobell, L. C. (1978). *Behavioral treatment of alcohol problems: Individualized therapy and controlled drinking.* Plenum.

Southern Poverty Law Center. (n.d.). Extremist files individual profiles. www.splcenter.org/fighting-hate/extremist-files/individual/raymond-cattell

Spain, D., Sin, J., Chalder, T., Murphy, D., & Happe, F. (2015). Cognitive behaviour therapy for adults with autism spectrum disorders and psychiatric co-morbidity: A review. *Research in Autism Spectrum Disorders, 9*, 151–162.

Spearman, C. (1927). *The abilities of man.* Macmillan.

Speed, B. C., Goldstein, B. L., & Goldfried, M. R. (2018). Assertiveness training: A forgotten evidence-based treatment. *Clinical Psychology: Science and Practice, 25*(1), e12216.

Spiegler, M. D., & Guevremont, D. C. (2010). *Contemporary behavior therapy* (5th ed.). Wadsworth/Cengage Learning.

Stafford, K., & Fingerhut, H. (2020, June 15). Poll: Black Americans most likely to know a COVID-19 victim. *Associated Press.* https://apnews.com/article/virus-outbreak-mi-state-wire-il-state-wire-race-and-ethnicity-ny-state-wire-52ed0842bd17102560e5d896be79d38c

Starks, B. (2021). The double pandemic: COVID-19 and white supremacy. *Qualitative Social Work, 20*(1–2), 222–224. doi:10.1177/1473325020986011

Steketee, G., Frost, R. O., & Kyrios, M. (2003). Cognitive aspects of compulsive hoarding. *Cognitive Therapy and Research, 27*(4), 463–479.

Stern, W. (1938). *General psychology from the personalistic point of view.* Macmillan.

Sternberg, R. J. (2003). A broad view of intelligence: The theory of successful intelligence. *Consulting Psychology Journal: Practice and Research, 55*, 139–154.

Sternberg, R. J. (2005). The triarchic theory of successful intelligence. In D. P. Flanagan & P. L. Harrison (Eds.), *Contemporary intellectual assessment: Theories, tests, and issues* (2nd ed., pp. 103–119.). Guilford.

Sternberg, R. J. (2018). Theories of intelligence. In S. I. Pfeiffer, E. Shaunessy-Dedrick, & M. Foley-Nicpon (Eds.), *APA handbooks in psychology®: APA handbook of giftedness and talent* (pp. 145–161). American Psychological Association.

Stetson, G. R. (1897). Some memory tests of whites and blacks. *Psychological Review, 4*(3), 285–289. doi: 10.1037/h0069814

Stewart, R. E., & Chambless, D. L. (2009). Cognitive-behavioral therapy for adult anxiety disorders in clinical practice: A meta-analysis of effectiveness studies. *Journal of Consulting and Clinical Psychology, 77*(4), 595–606.

Stiglmayr, C., Stecher-Mohr, J., Wagner, T., Meißner, J., Spretz, D., Steffens, C., Fydrich, T., Salbach-Andrae, H., Schulze, J., & Renneberg, B. (2014). Effectiveness of dialectic behavioral therapy in routine outpatient care: The Berlin Borderline Study. *Borderline Personality Disorder and Emotion Dysregulation, 1*(1), 1–11.

Stip, E., & Letourneau, G. (2009). Psychotic symptoms as a continuum between normality and pathology. *The Canadian Journal of Psychiatry, 54*(3), 140–151.

Stone, A. A., Shiffman, S., Schwartz, J. E., Broderick, J. E., & Hufford, M. R. (2002). Patient non-compliance with paper diaries. *BMJ, 324*(7347), 1193–1194.

Strauss, M. E., & Smith, G. T. (2009). Construct validity: Advances in theory and methodology. *Annual Review of Clinical Psychology, 5*, 1–25.

Strenze, T. (2007). Intelligence and socioeconomic success: A meta-analytic review of longitudinal research. *Intelligence, 35*, 401–426.

Strunk, D. R., & DeRubeis, R. J. (2001). Cognitive therapy for depression: A review of its efficacy. *Journal of Cognitive Psychotherapy, 15*(4), 289–297.

Strupp, H. H., & Hadley, S. W. (1977). A tripartite model of mental health and therapeutic outcomes: With special reference to negative effects in psychotherapy. *American Psychologist, 32*(3), 187–196.

Sturmey, P. (Ed.). (2020). *Functional analysis in clinical treatment*. Academic Press.

Sue, S., & Zane, N. (2006). Ethnic minority populations have been neglected by evidence-based practices. In J. C. Norcross, L. E. Beutler, and R. F. Levant (Eds) *Evidence-based practices in mental health: Debate and dialogue on the fundamental questions* (pp. 329–337). American Psychological Association. doi.org/10.1037/11265-008

Sue, S., Zane, N., Nagayama Hall, G. C., & Berger, L. K. (2009). The case for cultural competency in psychotherapeutic interventions. *Annual Review of Psychology, 60*, 525–548.

Sundberg, N. D. (1977). *Assessment of persons*. Pearson Education.

Suppiger, A., In-Albon, T., Hendriksen, S., Hermann, E., Margraf, J., & Schneider, S. (2009). Acceptance of structured diagnostic interviews for mental disorders in clinical practice and research settings. *Behavior Therapy, 40*, 272–279.

Syeda, M. M., & Climie, E. A. (2014). Test review: Wechsler Preschool and Primary Scale of Intelligence–Fourth Edition. *Journal of Psychoeducational Assessment, 32*(3), 265–272.

Szapocznik, J., Rio, A., Perez-Vidal, A., Kurtines, W., Hervis, O., & Santisteban, D. (1986). Bicultural Effectiveness Training (BET): An experimental test of an intervention modality for families experiencing intergenerational/intercultural conflict. *Hispanic Journal of Behavioral Sciences, 8*(4), 303–330.

Szasz, T. S. (1960). The myth of mental illness. *American Psychologist, 15*(2), 113–118.

Tadros, E., Owens, D., & Middleton, T. (2021). Systemic racism and family therapy. *The American Journal of Family Therapy, 49*(1), 1–11.

Tajeu, G. S., Safford, M. M., Howard, G., Howard, V. J., Chen, L., Long, L., Tanner, R. M., & Muntner, P. (2020). Black–white differences in cardiovascular disease mortality: A prospective US study, 2003–2017. *American Journal of Public Health, 110*(5), 696–703.

Tak, Y. J., & Lee, S. Y. (2021). Long-term efficacy and safety of anti-obesity treatment: Where do we stand? *Current Obesity Reports, 10*(1), 1–17.

Tankha, H., Caño, A., & Dillaway, H. (2020). "Now I have hope": Rebuilding relationships affected by chronic pain. *Families, Systems, & Health, 38*(1), 51–56.

Thomas Tobin, C. S., Erving, C. L., Hargrove, T. W., & Satcher, L. A. (2020). Is the Black-white mental health paradox consistent across age, gender, and psychiatric disorders? *Aging & Mental Health*, 1–9.

Thompson, C. H. (Ed.). (1934). *The Journal of Negro Education, 3*(1). www.jstor.org/stable/2292134

Thompson, E. M., Destree, L., Albertella, L., & Fontenelle, L. F. (2021). Internet-based acceptance and commitment therapy: A transdiagnostic systematic review and meta-analysis for mental health outcomes. *Behavior Therapy, 52*(2), 492–507.

Thongseiratch, T., Leijten, P., & Melendez-Torres, G. J. (2020). Online parent programs for children's behavioral problems: A meta-analytic review. *European Child & Adolescent Psychiatry, 29*, 1555–1568.

Thorndike, R. M. (1997). *The early history of intelligence testing*. In D. P. Flanagan, J. L. Genshaft, & P. L. Harrison (Eds.), *Contemporary intellectual assessment: Theories, tests, and issues* (pp. 3–16). Guilford.

Thorpe, R. J., Norris, K. C., Beech, B. M., & Bruce, M. A. (2019). Racism across the life course. In C. L. Ford, D. M. Griffith, M. A. Bruce, & K. L. Gilbert (Eds.), *Racism: Science & tools for the public health professional* (pp. 209–219). American Public Health Association.

Thurstone, L. L. (1938). Primary mental abilities. *Psychometric Monographs, 1*, ix–121.

Tolin, D. F. (2010). Is cognitive–behavioral therapy more effective than other therapies? A meta-analytic review. *Clinical Psychology Review, 30*(6), 710–720.

Tolin, D. F. (2010). Is cognitive–behavioral therapy more effective than other therapies? A meta-analytic review. *Clinical Psychology Review, 30*(6), 710–720.

Tolin, D. F., McKay, D., Forman, E. M., Klonsky, E. D., & Thombs, B. D. (2015). Empirically supported treatment: Recommendations for a new model. *Clinical Psychology: Science and Practice, 22*(4), 317.

Toobert, D. J., Strycker, L. A., Barrera Jr., M., Osuna, D., King, D. K., & Glasgow, R. E. (2011). Outcomes from a multiple risk factor diabetes self-management trial for Latinas: ¡Viva bien! *Annals of Behavioral Medicine, 41*(3), 310–323.

Trauer, J. M., Qian, M. Y., Doyle, J. S., Rajaratnam, S. M., & Cunnington, D. (2015). Cognitive behavioral therapy for chronic insomnia: A systematic review and meta-analysis. *Annals of Internal Medicine, 163*(3), 191–204.

Truijens, F., Zühlke-van Hulzen, L., & Vanheule, S. (2019). To manualize, or not to manualize: Is that still the question? A systematic review of empirical evidence for manual superiority in psychological treatment. *Journal of Clinical Psychology, 75*(3), 329–343.

Trull, T. J., & Sher, K. J. (1994). Relationship between the five-factor model of personality and Axis I disorders in a nonclinical sample. *Journal of Abnormal Psychology, 103*(2), 350.

Tucker, W. H. (1994). *The science and politics of racial research*. University of Illinois Press.

Tucker, W. H. (2002). *The funding of scientific racism: Wickliffe Draper and the Pioneer Fund*. University of Illinois Press.

Tummala-Narra, P. (2013). Psychoanalytic applications in a diverse society. *Psychoanalytic Psychology, 30*(3), 471.

Turliuc, M. N., & Candel, O. S. (2019). Ethical issues in couple and family research and therapy. In *Ethics in research practice and innovation* (pp. 226–242). IGI Global.

Twohig, M. P., Abramowitz, J. S., Bluett, E. J., Fabricant, L. E., Jacoby, R. J., Morrison, K. L., Reuman, L., & Smith, B. M. (2015). Exposure therapy for OCD from an acceptance and commitment therapy (ACT) framework. *Journal of Obsessive-Compulsive and Related Disorders, 6*, 167–173.

Twohig, M. P., Abramowitz, J. S., Smith, B. M., Fabricant, L. E., Jacoby, R. J., Morrison, K. L., Bluett, E. J., Reuman, L., Blakey, S. M., & Ledermann, T. (2018). Adding acceptance and commitment therapy to exposure and response prevention for obsessive-compulsive disorder: A randomized controlled trial. *Behaviour Research and Therapy, 108*, 1–9.

Tyner, J. A. (1998). The geopolitics of eugenics and the incarceration of Japanese Americans. *Antipode, 30*(3), 251–269.

U.S. Census Bureau. (2021). Quick facts: Race and Hispanic origin. www.census.gov/quickfacts/fact/table/US/PST045219

U.S. Government Printing Office. (1967). Civil Rights Act of 1967: Hearings before the Subcommittee on Constitutional Rights of the Committee on the Judiciary, United States Senate, on S. 1026, S. 1318, S.1359, S. 1362, S. 1462, H.R. 2516 and H.R. 10805, proposed Civil Rights Act of 1967. (Washington, D.C., August 1, 8, 9, and 14; September 19, 20, 21, 26, and 27, 1967.)

U.S. Government Printing Office. (1980). Truth in Testing Act of 1979. The Education Testing Act of 1979. Hearings before the Subcommittee on Elementary, Secondary and Vocational Education of the Committee on Education and Labor, House of Representatives, Ninety-Sixth Congress, First Session on H.R. 3564 and H.R. 4949 (Washington, D.C., July 31, August 1, September 10, September 24, and October 10-11, 1979).

van Bentum, J. S., van Bronswijk, S. C., Sijbrandij, M., Lemmens, L. H., Peeters, F. F., Drukker, M., & Huibers, M. J. (2021). Cognitive therapy and interpersonal psychotherapy reduce suicidal ideation independent from their effect on depression. *Depression and Anxiety, 38*, 940–949.

van Dis, E. A. M., van Veen, S. C., Hagenaars, A., Batelaan, N. M., Bockting, C. L. H., van den Heuvel, R. M. Cuijpers, P., & Engelhard, I. M. (2020). Long-term outcomes of cognitive behavioral therapy for anxiety disorders: A systematic review and meta-analysis. *JAMA Psychiatry, 77*, 265–273.

Varshney, M., Mahapatra, A., Krishnan, V., Gupta, R., & Deb, K. S. (2016). Violence and mental illness: What is the true story? *Journal of Epidemiology and Community Health, 70*(3), 223–225.

Verhaak, P. F. M, Prins, M. A., Spreeuwenberg, P., Draisma, S., van Balkom, T. J., Bensing, J. M., Laurant, M., van Marwijk, H. W. J., van der Meer, K., & Penninx, B. W. J. H. (2009). Receiving treatment for common mental disorders. *General Hospital Psychiatry, 31*(1), 46–55.

Viljoen, J. L., Vargen, L. M., Cochrane, D. M., Jonnson, M. R., Goossens, I., & Monjazeb, S. (2021). Do structured risk assessments predict violent, any, and sexual offending better than unstructured judgment? An umbrella review. *Psychology, Public Policy, and Law, 27*(1), 79–97.

Villanueva, J., Meyer, A. H., Rinner, M. T., Firsching, V. J., Benoy, C., Brogli, S., Walker, M., Bader, K., & Gloster, A. T. (2019). "Choose change": Design and methods of an acceptance and commitment therapy effectiveness trial for transdiagnostic treatment-resistant patients. *BMC Psychiatry, 19*(1), 1–12.

Voigt, R., Camp, N. P., Prabhakaran, V., Hamilton, W. L., Hetey, R. C., Griffiths, C. M., Jurgens, D., Jurafsky, D., & Eberhardt, J. L. (2017). Language from police body camera footage shows racial disparities in officer respect. *Proceedings of the National Academy of Sciences, 114*(25), 6521–6526.

von Greiff, N., & Skogens, L. (2020). Abstinence or controlled drinking: A five-year follow-up on Swedish clients reporting positive change after treatment for substance use disorders. *Drugs and Alcohol Today, 20*, 147–158.

Wadden, T. A., Brownell, K. D., & Foster, G. D. (2002). Obesity: Responding to the global epidemic. *Journal of Consulting and Clinical Psychology, 70*, 510–525.

Wakefield, S., Kellett, S., Simmonds-Buckley, M., Stockton, D., Bradbury, A., & Delgadillo, J. (2021). Improving Access to Psychological Therapies (IAPT) in the United Kingdom: A systematic review and meta-analysis of 10-years of practice-based evidence. *British Journal of Clinical Psychology, 60*(1), 1–37.

Wampold, B. (1997). Methodological problems in identifying efficacious psychotherapies. *Psychotherapy Research, 7*(1), 21–43.

Wampold, B. E. (2015). How important are the common factors in psychotherapy? An update. *World Psychiatry, 14*(3), 270–277.

Wampold, B. E., & Imel, Z. E. (2015). *The great psychotherapy debate: The evidence for what makes psychotherapy work*. Routledge.

Wang, Y., Fridberg, D. J., Shortell, D. D., Leeman, R. F., Barnett, N. P., Cook, R. L., & Porges, E. C. (2021). Wrist-worn alcohol biosensors: Applications and usability in behavioral research. *Alcohol, 92*, 25–34.

Waskow, I. E., & Parloff, M. B. (1975). *Psychotherapy change measures: Report of the clinical research branch outcome measures project*. National Institute of Mental Health.

Wasserman, J. D. (2018). *A history of intelligence assessment: The unfinished tapestry*. In D. P. Flanagan & E. M. McDonough (Eds.), *Contemporary intellectual assessment: Theories, tests, and issues* (pp. 3–55). Guilford.

Watkins, C. E. (2012). Race/ethnicity in short-term and long-term psychodynamic psychotherapy treatment research: How "White" are the data? *Psychoanalytic Psychology, 29*, 292–307.

Watson, J. B., & Rayner, R. (1920). Conditioned emotional reactions. *Journal of Experimental Psychology, 3*, 114.

Wechsler, D. (1939). *The measurement of adult intelligence*. Williams & Wilkins.

Wechsler, D. (2014). *WISC-V: Technical and interpretive manual*. Pearson.

Wegner, E. E. (1987). A review of the 1985 *Standards for Educational and Psychological Testing*: User responsibility and social justice. *Journal of Counseling and Development, 66*, 202–203. doi.org/10.1002/j.1556-6676.1987.tb00849.x

Weiner, L., & Avery-Clark, C. (2017). *Sensate focus in sex therapy: The illustrated manual*. Taylor & Francis.

Weisberg, R. B., Gonsalves, M. A., Ramadurai, R., Braham, H., Fuchs, C., & Beard, C. (2021). Development of a cognitive bias modification intervention for anxiety disorders in primary care. *British Journal of Clinical Psychology, 61*, 73–92.

Weiss, L. G., & Saklofske, D. H. (2020). Mediators of IQ test score differences across racial and ethnic groups: The case for environmental and social justice. *Personality and Individual Differences, 161*, 109962.

Weiss, P. A. (Ed.). (2010). *Personality assessment in police psychology: A 21st century perspective*. Charles C Thomas.

Weissman, M. M. (2020). Interpersonal psychotherapy: History and future. *American Journal of Psychotherapy, 73*(1), 3–7.

Weissman, M. M., & Markowitz, J. C. (1998). An overview of interpersonal psychotherapy. In J. C. Markowitz (Ed.), *Interpersonal psychotherapy* (pp. 1–33). American Psychiatric Press.

Weisz, J. R., & Kazdin, A. E. (Eds.). (2010). *Evidence-based psychotherapies for children and adolescents*. Guilford.

Weisz, J. R., Jensen-Doss, A., & Hawley, K. M. (2006). Evidence-based youth psychotherapies versus usual clinical care: A meta-analysis of direct comparisons. *American Psychologist, 61*(7), 671.

Wells, G. L., Kovera, M. B., Douglass, A. B., Brewer, N., Meissner, C. A., & Wixted, J. T. (2020). Policy and procedure recommendations for the collection and preservation of eyewitness identification evidence. *Law and Human Behavior, 44*(1), 3–36.

Westmacott, R., & Hunsley, J. (2007). Weighing the evidence for psychotherapy equivalence: Implications for research and practice. *The Behavior Analyst Today, 8*(2), 210.

Wetterneck, C. T., Burgess, A. J., Short, M. B., Smith, A. H., & Cervantes, M. E. (2012). The role of sexual compulsivity, impulsivity, and experiential avoidance in internet pornography use. *The Psychological Record, 62*(1), 3–18.

Whitman, M. R., Tylicki, J. L., Mascioli, R., Pickle, J., & Ben-Porath, Y. S. (2020). Psychometric properties of the Minnesota Multiphasic Personality Inventory-3 (MMPI-3) in a clinical neuropsychology setting. *Psychological Assessment, 33*, 142–155.

Whitney, D. G., & Peterson, M. D. (2019). Disparities in prevalence and treatment of mental health disorders in children: Reply. *JAMA Pediatrics, 173*(8), 800–801.

Wiebe, S. A., Johnson, S. M., Lafontaine, M. F., Burgess Moser, M., Dalgleish, T. L., & Tasca, G. A. (2017). Two-year follow-up outcomes in emotionally focused couple therapy:

An investigation of relationship satisfaction and attachment trajectories. *Journal of Marital and Family Therapy, 43*(2), 227–244.

Williams, A. D., Blackwell, S. E., Mackenzie, A., Holmes, E. A., & Andrews, G. (2013). Combining imagination and reason in the treatment of depression: A randomized controlled trial of Internet-based cognitive-bias modification and Internet-CBT for depression. *Journal of Consulting and Clinical Psychology, 81*(5), 793.

Williams, A. J., Botanov, Y., Kilshaw, R. E., Wong, R. E., & Sakaluk, J. K. (2021). Potentially harmful therapies: A meta-scientific review of evidential value. *Clinical Psychology: Science and Practice, 28*(1), 5.

Williams, A. J., Botanov, Y., Kilshaw, R. E., Wong, R. E., & Sakaluk, J. K. (2020). Potentially harmful therapies: A meta-scientific review of evidential value. *Clinical Psychology: Science and Practice*, e12331.

Williams, R. B., Barefoot, J. C., Califf, R. M., Haney, T. L., Saunders, W. B., Pryor, D. B., Hlatky, M., Siegler, I. C., & Daniel, M. (1992). Prognostic importance of social and economic resources among medically treated patients with angiographically documented coronary artery disease. *Journal of the American Medical Association, 267*, 520–524.

Williams, R. L., & Mitchell, H. (1978). What happened to ABPsi's moratorium on testing: A 1968 to 1977 reminder. *Journal of Black Psychology, 4*(1–2), 25–42. doi: 10.1177/009579847800400104

Wilson, G. T. (1981). Behavior therapy as a short-term therapeutic approach. In S. H. Budman (Ed.), *Forms of brief therapy* (pp. 131–166). Guilford.

Wilson, G. T. (2007). Manual-based treatment: Evolution and evaluation. In T. A. Treat, R. R. Bootzin, & T. B. Baker (Eds.), *Psychological clinical science: Papers in honor of Richard M. McFall* (pp. 105–132). Psychology Press.

Winston, A. S. (1998). Science in the service of the far right: Henry E. Garrett, the IAAEE, and the Liberty Lobby. *Journal of Social Issues, 54*(1), 179–210. doi: 10.1111/00220-4537.00059

Winston, A. S. (2020). Scientific racism and North American psychology. In O. Braddick (Ed.), *The Oxford research encyclopedia of psychology*. Oxford University Press. doi: 10.1093/acrefore/9780190236557.013.516

Wispe, L., Awkard, J., Hoffman, M., Ash, P., Hicks, L. H., & Porter, J. (1969). The Negro psychologist in America. *American Psychologist, 24*(2), 142–150. doi: 10.1037/h0027107

Wittenborn, A. K., Baucom, B. R., Leifker, F. R., & Lachmar, E. M. (2020). Couple-based interventions for the treatment of depressive and anxiety disorders. *The Handbook of Systemic Family Therapy, 3*, 207–226.

Wolpe, J. (1973). *The practice of behavior therapy* (2nd ed.). Pergamon.

World Health Organization. (2021, September 19). WHO coronavirus (COVID) dashboard. https://covid19.who.int/

Worrell, F. C., & Roberson, C. C. B. (2016). 2014 Standards for Educational and Psychological Testing: Implications for ethnic minority youth. In S. L. Graves Jr. & J. J. Blake (Eds.), *Psychoeducational assessment and intervention for ethnic minority youth: Evidence-based approaches* (pp. 41–57). American Psychological Association. doi: 10.1037/14855-004

Yakushko, O. (2019). Eugenics and its evolution in the history of Western psychology: A critical archival review. *Psychotherapy and Politics International, 17*(2), e1495. doi: 10.1002/ppi.1495

Yalom, I. D. (2005). *The Schopenhauer cure*. HarperCollins.

Yerkes, R. M. (1921). *Psychological examining in the U. S. Army. Memoirs of the National Academy of Sciences, No. 15.* National Academy of Sciences.

Yim, S. J., Lui, L. M., Lee, Y., Rosenblat, J. D., Ragguett, R. M., Park, C., Subramanipillai, M., Cao, B., Zhou, A., Rong, C., Lin, K., Ho, R., Coles, A. S., Majeed, A., Wong, E., Phan, L., Nasri, F., & McIntyre, R. S. (2020). The utility of smartphone-based, ecological momentary assessment for depressive symptoms. *Journal of Affective Disorders, 274*, 602–609.

Young, K. (1922). *Mental differences in certain immigrant groups: Psychological tests of south Europeans in typical California schools with bearing on the educational policy and on the problems of racial contacts in this country* (Vol. 1, No. 11). University of California.

Yu, Q., Salvador, C. E., Melani, I., Berg, M. K., Neblett, E. W., & Kitayama, S. (in press). Racial residential segregation and economic disparity jointly exacerbate COVID-19 fatality in large American cities. *Annals of the New York Academy of Sciences*.

Yuan, S., Zhou, X., Zhang, Y., Zhang, H., Pu, J., Yang, L., Liu, X., Jiang, X., & Xie, P. (2018). Comparative efficacy and acceptability of bibliotherapy for depression and anxiety disorders in children and adolescents: A meta-analysis of randomized clinical trials. *Neuropsychiatric Disease and Treatment, 14*, 353–365.

Zamani, N., & Kim, C. D. H. (Eds.). (2021). *Bilingualism, culture, and social justice in family therapy*. Springer.

Zayfert, C., & Becker, C. B. (2020). *Cognitive-behavioral therapy for PTSD: A case formulation approach*. Guilford.

Zee, K. S., Bolger, N., & Higgins, E. T. (2020). Regulatory effectiveness of social support. *Journal of Personality and Social Psychology, 119*(6), 1316–1358.

Zenderland, L. (1998). *Measuring minds: Henry Herbert Goddard and the origins of American intelligence testing*. Cambridge University Press.

Zettle, R. D. (2005). The evolution of a contextual approach to therapy: From comprehensive distancing to ACT. *International Journal of Behavioral Consultation and Therapy, 1*(2), 77.

Zhang, C. Q., Leeming, E., Smith, P., Chung, P. K., Hagger, M. S., & Hayes, S. C. (2018). Acceptance and commitment therapy for health behavior change: A contextually-driven approach. *Frontiers in Psychology, 8*, 2350.

Zuckerman, M. (1994). *Behavioral expressions and biosocial bases of sensation seeking.* Cambridge University Press.

Name Index

Subject Index